SPC METHODS FOR QUALITY IMPROVEMENT

SPC METHODS FOR QUALITY IMPROVEMENT

Charles P. Quesenberry

JOHN WILEY & SONS, INC.

New York · Chichester · Weinheim · Brisbane · Singapore · Toronto

Library of Congress Cataloging in Publication Data:
Quesenberry, C. P.
    SPC methods for quality improvement / Charles P. Quesenberry.
       p.   cm.
    Includes bibliographical references (p.).
    ISBN 0-471-13087-7 (cloth : alk. paper)
    1. Process control—Statistical methods.   2. Quality control.
  I. Title.
  TS156.8.Q47   1997
  658.5′62—dc20
                                                   96-44726

Printed in the United States of America

10 9 8 7 6 5 4 3 2 1

■■■■■ CONTENTS

3.2	Graphs of Data Sets: Dot Plots, Histograms, Pareto Diagrams, Stem-and-Leaf Diagrams	96
3.3	Cause-and-Effect or Ishikawa Diagrams	103
3.4	Studying Samples, Descriptive Statistics	104
3.5	Properties of Sampling Distributions of Sample Means, Variances, and Ranges	117
3.6	Concepts of Statistical Inference: Estimation, Prediction	125
	Problems	127

4. Classical Shewhart Control Charts for Variables — **135**

4.1	Work Process Control and Quality Variables	135
4.2	Observed and Expected Mean Squares	141
4.3	Shewhart Control Charts for Variables—General Description	142
4.4	The $\bar{X}$-, R-, and S-Charts for both σ and μ "Known"	147
4.5	Runs Tests for 3-Sigma $\bar{X}$ Control Chart Patterns, μ and σ Known	158
4.6	Assessing $\bar{X}$-Chart Performance: OC and Power Functions, Run Length Distributions, μ and σ both Known	163
4.7	The OC, Power, and ARL Functions for an S-Chart, σ Known	173
4.8	Estimating μ, σ, and the Control Limits	177
4.9	Examples of $\bar{X}$-, S-, and R-Charts; Stratification and Rational Subgroups	185
4.10	Charts for Individual Measurements	196
4.11	Estimating Shewhart Charts Control Limits from Past Data, Sample Size Considerations	203
4.12	Summary	220
	Problems	220

5. Classical Shewhart Control Charts for Attributes — **227**

5.1	Introduction	227
5.2	The Classical 3-Sigma p-Chart for Fraction Nonconforming	228
5.3	c-Charts for Numbers of Nonconformities	241
5.4	u-Charts for the Average Number of Defects per Standard Inspection Unit	250
5.5	c- and u-Charts when Sample Sizes Vary—Standardized Charts	258

CHAPTER 1

Introduction to Quality Control Concepts

In this chapter we discuss briefly the history of quality control concepts and practices, the Japanese quality movement, quality assurance, some elements of quality control, some concepts of leadership, and Deming's 14 points on quality management. In the last section we give a brief description of what we call the Q statistics paradigm that will be used for a number of models in this book.

1.1 INTRODUCTION—HISTORICAL SKETCH

In general usage the word *quality* can convey a number of different meanings. It may, for example, refer to the *nature* of an object, or to a *property* or *characteristic*. However, it is often used in the quality profession in a narrow sense to refer to the ability of a product or service to meet reasonable performance expectations or requirements of the purchaser or user. Man undoubtedly has long been concerned about the ability of a product to function properly for the purpose for which it was intended. In the Stone Ages, a hunter must have been concerned that the spear point produced by the local flint knapper was sharp enough to serve its intended purpose when thrust against a mammoth or saber-toothed tiger. In the Middle Ages in Europe, the powerful merchant and craft guilds were concerned with guarding the skills of artisans who produced high-quality products. Apprentice systems were used to train skilled craftsmen and control and guard the pool of craftsmen, and the quality of the products, which depended largely upon the skills of individual craftsmen such as blacksmiths, cobblers, coopers, and wainwrights. Production was by individual craftsmen, perhaps working with a small number of apprentices and journeymen. According to Ferguson and Bruun (1952, p. 285), "[T]he guild regulated prices, the quality of goods, wages, and the hours of labor."

In the eighteenth and nineteenth centuries the advance of the Industrial Revolution changed the systems by which products were made. During the Industrial Revolution, machines were invented to perform the work that had previously been done by craftsmen. Manufacturing then took place in factories that produced large quantities of products; however, these were often of poor quality. By the early twentieth century, due to the many technical advances of the industrial age, and especially with the mass production technology developed by Henry Ford, Alfred Sloan (General Motors), and others, final products were generally assembled using modules produced by many different people and processes. Mass production involves manufacturing the many modules (engine, transmission, body, etc.) of a larger assembly (car) in separate operations, and then integrating these subunits into the whole unit. For this method of production to be successful, the parts must be interchangeable. That is, we must be able to make parts that are identical, or at least sufficiently alike to permit any one to function properly in the car. If a piston wrist pin is chosen randomly from supply, then it must fit and function properly in the particular piston it happens to be mated with. As final assemblies have become more and more complex, the need for uniformity of parts and subassemblies has become more pronounced.

Another development of the late nineteenth and early twentieth centuries was crucial to the development of the modern field of quality control. Led by Pearson, Fisher, et al., the field of statistics was developing in Britain and later also in India (Mahalanobis et al.) and the United States (Neyman et al.). Statistics is especially concerned with the study of variability represented in sets of numbers and was to provide many ideas and techniques that would be crucial to the production of products of high uniformity and quality. The application of concepts and techniques of statistics to quality problems was initiated at Western Electric's Bell Telephone Laboratories beginning in about 1924. This pioneering work by a group of statisticians and engineers was led, *inter alios,* by Walter A. Shewhart and Harold F. Dodge. Many of the concepts and techniques important in quality control today were introduced by this group. These include "Shewhart Charts" which is the principle method of statistical process control, and these charts will be studied in detail later in this work.

The quality field was expanded steadily during the 1930s. World War II inspired much activity in the development of the field of quality control and a tremendous growth in the use of quality control methods in manufacturing in the United States, due to the adoption of these new methods by the Department of Defense (DoD). The military required large quantities of high-quality materials and machines and was in a position to require suppliers to adopt these new methods. Unfortunately, after World War II, during the 1950s and 1960s, use of the concepts and methods of quality control in the United States declined.

1.2 THE JAPANESE QUALITY MOVEMENT AFTER WORLD WAR II

Immediately after World War II, the Japanese economy was shattered and the country was in severe economic straits. As Japanese industry was struggling to recover in 1950, during the American occupation of Japan, the American statistician Dr. W. Edwards Deming gave an eight-day seminar on quality control in Japan sponsored by the Union of Japanese Scientists and Engineers (JUSE). In his lectures, Dr. Deming discussed the Plan, Do, Check, Act paradigm (PDCA, the *Deming cycle* that will be discussed in section 1.4); the importance of recognizing dispersion in statistics; and the use of SPC charts. In 1954, another American quality expert, Dr. J. M. Juran, gave lectures to upper- and middle-level managers from many major companies in Japan that emphasized the necessity of leadership from management for effective quality systems. The Japanese accepted the challenge to convert their industries, which before and during the war had produced largely for the military, to produce high-quality products at low cost for their domestic and world consumer markets. It should be noted that Japanese industry was at that time already advanced technologically. Indeed, the Japanese military equipment used during World War II was some of the best in the world. For example, the Zero was the best fighter plane in the world during much of the war, at least until the United States Navy and Marines introduced the Vaught F4U Corsair in 1943. They also had excellent guns, ships, and trucks.

Since Japanese accepted the challenge of the American experts in the early 1950s, many of the Japanese companies have become remarkably successful at producing high-quality products at low cost. As a result, they are now major competitors in world consumer markets. We consider briefly some of the elements that have contributed to their competitive thrust.

1.2.1 Education

The Japanese mounted a major effort in quality education. An important aspect of this effort was that it was led at the national level by scientists and engineers of the Union of Japanese Scientists and Engineers (JUSE), which did much to assure the *quality* of the quality movement in Japan. JUSE played a central role by organizing training courses for personnel at all levels from top management to floor workers, by serving as certified consultants to companies, and working collaboratively with company personnel to solve quality problems, and doing research to find improved approaches to both technical and managerial issues of quality control. As a result of this emphasis on quality education, today many believe that the Japanese have the best-trained personnel in the quality field in the world, at least at the shop floor level. In these efforts, the country had the advantage of a homogeneous population that speaks one language and has a generally high literacy rate. The culture is education oriented and a strong work ethic is ingrained. There is no organization in the United States comparable to JUSE, and there are serious problems with the quality of the so-called quality movement.

An interesting and important outgrowth of the quality education initiative in Japan has been the quality circles movement. According to Ishikawa (1985), when the journal *Quality Control for Foremen* was begun in 1962, it recommended that quality control activities be conducted under the name of the QC circle. The initial QC circles were formed as volunteer study groups of foremen. The reasons for this were to encourage the foremen to actually study the journal, that studying in groups would provide more continuity, and that it would stimulate the circle members to work together more effectively to implement the ideas in the workplace. The techniques taught were largely simple statistical methods for gathering and interpreting data.

1.2.2 Work Organization and Management Policies

The so-called scientific management movement in America was largely due to the engineer and manager Frederick W. Taylor. The Taylor management method consists of having products and production processes designed by engineers and managers, and having the actual work carried out by a class of workers. The work processes are designed so that workers perform simple repetitive tasks that require little thinking or decision making. Workers are expected to function pretty much as machines or automatons. The system was successful in improving productivity in the early twentieth century; however, there are problems in implementing such a management system. This type of highly repetitive work tends to be boring, degrading, and demoralizing for workers. Moreover, the work standards and specifications set by often remote engineers and managers may be unrealistic and may fail to take advantage of the abilities and detailed technical knowledge of the processes of the operators. The Japanese recognized that this system of management was designed essentially to utilize workers with low levels of training and whose abilities were largely undeveloped. They have organized management systems that at once require major emphasis on training the work force and utilizing the abilities of the work force to constantly improve quality. These systems involve a significant degree of worker empowerment. The basic idea is to use the intelligence and knowledge of the entire work force at all levels to improve the quality of processes and products. The QC circles mentioned earlier have been a significant factor in these management systems, and there are now many different types of QC circles in addition to those of foremen. The circles provide a practical approach to solving many types of problems; however, it should be remembered that the first Japanese quality circles were formed as study groups.

The Taylor method assumes a class structure of elite managers and engineers of one class and of unthinking workers of another class. The Japanese quality system moves away from this type of elitism. Education for all workers to develop continuously is the key to moving away from such elitism and making efficient use of the talents of all personnel. Operators are trained to qualify to perform different jobs, and the number of jobs they are certified for is often a factor in their pay scales. This worker flexibility and the resultant efficiency would apparently be difficult to achieve for a company with a strong craft union contract, like those of many companies in the West. In addition to basing pay on seniority and job qualifications, there are other motivations such as the satisfaction and pleasure people naturally feel when they know they are doing high-quality, important work. Recognition by management and peers is gratifying—aside from pay itself.

Turnover for personnel tends to be very low by Western standards, and many employees spend their entire careers working for one company. An important consequence of this stable employment is that companies can afford to invest in the training of employees, since there will be a long-term return on the investment.

1.2.3 Japanese QC, TQC, and CWQC

According to Ishikawa (1985), the Japanese Industrial Standards define quality control as follows: "A system of production methods which economically produces quality goods or services meeting the requirements of consumers. Modern quality control utilizes statistical methods and is often called statistical quality control."

We will use either QC or SQC to refer to this notion. The Japanese use the expressions *total quality control* (TQC) or, sometimes, *company-wide quality control* (CWQC) to refer to a broader system. TQC or CWQC as practiced by the Japanese generally involves having all divisions (meaning also subcontractors, distribution systems, and affiliated companies) and all employees of a company studying and promoting quality control in all operations of the company. This is not the same as the TQC concept of Dr. Armand V. Feigenbaum in his book *Total Quality Control: Engineering and Management* (1961). Feigenbaum recommended having the quality control functions performed by a management division of QC specialists. Japanese TQC places responsibility for quality on all company personnel. This does not exclude having employees who are specialists in quality control who work cooperatively and collaboratively with management, engineering, and workers.

1.2.4 Total Quality Management—TQM

In the United States today, there is a broadly based movement with some of the basic elements of Japanese TQC that is called *total quality management* (TQM). TQM may mean something somewhat different in some institutions, but appears to this writer to, in general, be basically Japanese TQC, with one important difference. That difference is in the emphasis placed on analytical statistical methods. The Japanese TQC places more emphasis on the use of statistical methods than does American TQM. The statistical methods used are for the most part simple first principle methods.

1.2.5 Further Readings and Elements

It is not our purpose, nor possible in the space that we can devote to the topic here, to give more than this brief summary of such a vast movement as the quality revolution in Japan since World War II. For more detailed expert accounts, see Ishikawa (1985, 1990), Mizuno (1988), Imai (1986), Suzaki (1987), and Juran (1994).

1.3 QUALITY ASSURANCE

Recall that we previously defined quality as the ability of a product or service to meet reasonable requirements of the customer. Actually, we sometimes consider quality more generally and speak of the quality of a process, an organization, an individual. Quality assurance (QA) is all of the elements concerned with the quality of products; it is the objective of TQM. There are three areas of activity or modes directly involved in quality assurance:

- Product and process development
- Process control
- Inspection of products

1.3.1 Inspection and Quality Assurance

Inspection can be carried out in the following situation. Suppose that for each unit of product there are specific standards or specifications that must be met. Units of product that do not meet the given conditions are generally called *defectives*. Suppose another specification requires that the mean proportion of products not meeting specifications (the *fallout*) must not exceed a value p_a (the *acceptable quality limit*, AQL). Unless a given process has fallout that is much less than an acceptable quality limit p_a, some form of inspection will be necessary to assure that individual batches of shipped product have less than p_a proportion defectives, at least with high probability.

   Inspection, and especially sampling inspection, was the first approach to quality assurance for many companies. However, there are problems in trying to assure quality by inspection methods, such as the following:

- Due to human errors and other difficulties in operating an inspection plan, there will always be some defectives that are not recognized by an inspection scheme.
- When there is inspection, the production people may consider their objective as simply to have products pass inspection. This is a mistake because production should be concerned with meeting consumers' requirements.

- Some things simply cannot be guaranteed by any form of inspection: items requiring destructive testing and reliability tests; complex assemblies and components.
- Inspection data are not sufficiently stratified, timely, or generally useful for process improvement. Thus inspection is not very helpful for improving a process and thereby reducing the percentage of defectives. Defectives result in scrap or expensive rework. Reworked items are often still of poor quality, and cost *more* than items not requiring rework.
- All inspection costs reduce productivity since inspection produces nothing.

In spite of these problems with inspection schemes, we repeat the assertion that unless a process produces an average percentage of defectives that is much below an acceptable quality limit, it will be necessary to use some form of inspection to avoid delivering unacceptably large percentages of defectives in individual lots. In some cases the manufacturing technology is simply not available to lower fallout to acceptable levels. For example, in some parts of the electronics industry, the percentage of fallout is as high as 20%. Parts must therefore be sorted, probably using 100% inspection schemes.

1.3.2 Process Control and Quality Assurance

Statistical process control has as its objective to bring a process into a state of statistical control such that the average proportion of out-of-spec units is below some specified level. When this can be achieved it will not be necessary to operate inspection schemes, and there will be savings from this, as well as overall improved quality. Often the target value for the proportion of out-of-spec units is zero, which is in theory impossible to actually achieve. It may be observed that setting a target of zero defectives is logically the equivalent of adopting a principle of commitment to continuously improve a process. Statistical process control is the principal topic of this book, and will be studied extensively in later chapters.

1.3.3 Product Development and Quality Assurance

Quality is not necessarily assured, even if production processes are stable and produce few or no defectives. The product may still not meet the consumers' requirements unless these requirements are kept in mind during product development and are reflected in controlled quality variables. The suitability of the product to meet the users' needs must be carefully analyzed and incorporated into product planning and design. There must also be feedback channels from consumers after the product is marketed to permit design modifications to correct any weaknesses due to design (or production) found by customers.

Finally, even a good design requires both production process control and, possibly, inspection to find defectives to assure quality.

1.4 SOME ASPECTS OF QUALITY AND QUALITY CONTROL

In section 1.1 we remarked that the word quality is often used in the QC field to refer to the ability of a product or service to meet the user's requirements. However, we note that we cannot, in general, define the word *quality,* simply because it already has meaning in the English language and we do not have authority to change that meaning. Quality is not used only in reference to salable products and services, but in many expressions such as "quality person," "quality time," "a high-quality process," "quality management," and so on.

1.4.1 The QCDS Paradigm

There are four aspects of quality to be considered in order to meet customers' needs. The product must be usable for its intended purpose, it must be sold at a price the customer can pay, it must be delivered at the time it is needed, and service after sales must be provided. This is sometimes referred to as the QCDS paradigm (Quality, Cost, Delivery, Service).

Quality refers to characteristics of quality in its narrow sense. These are characteristics such as dimensions, weights, purity, tolerances, reliability, fallout, rework ratio, etc.

Cost refers to characteristics related to cost and price such as unit cost, losses, productivity, cycle time, raw materials costs, equipment costs, yield, profit, unit price, etc.

Delivery characteristics include production volume, cycle times, yield, changeover times, shipping time, loading time, inventory, consumption rates, etc.

Service requires consideration of safety and environmental characteristics, product liability, warranties, recalls, before and after sales

service, parts replacement, repairability, training service technicians, user manuals, service manuals, etc.

Each part of this QCDS paradigm must be considered if customer
requirements are to be satisfied. Not only must each of these aspects
be considered separately, but they must be considered simultaneously.
The separate aspects are often to some degree in opposition or competition for emphasis. For example, by using the most advanced (and
expensive) methods and materials it is often possible to produce units
of very high quality; however, this may force a price that is so high
that the product cannot be sold at a profit. Emphasis should be upon
production of high-quality products at the lowest possible costs. Even
if a high-quality product can be produced and sold at a competitive
price, it will likely have limited commercial success if it cannot be
delivered to the customers in a timely manner. Service is an important
contributor to customer satisfaction, and, therefore, to the ability to
keep customers for long-term and repeat sales—the foundation of any
business.

1.4.2   The Supplier-Customer Chain

Implementation of control of a process should recognize that every
process, simple or complex, can be broken down and represented as a
chain of successive stages or subprocesses. Each stage, or link

$$\rightarrow \text{Stage 1} \rightarrow \text{State 2} \rightarrow \text{Stage 3} \rightarrow \cdots$$

in the chain is a customer for a previous stage and a supplier to a
subsequent stage. Material enters a stage and is worked or altered in
some manner and is passed on to the next stage. Process control of the
entire manufacturing process entails designing the layout and use of
machines, the successive stages, the operations at the stages or cells,
and the coordination and communication among cells.

Improvement of the process generally requires improvement of two
types: (1) improvement in the operations of individual stages, and (2)
improvement of the process by improvement of communication and
coordination among stages. People at each stage should know what is
going on and required both upstream and downstream. Management is
responsible to assure that everyone understands the customers' needs.
Suzaki (1987) describes a "product-oriented" production layout that
was developed by the engineer Taiichi Ohno at Toyota Motor Co. that
has been highly successful in eliminating waste and permitting flexible

manufacturing of different products on the same production line. This layout is organized around material flow and emphasizes just-in-time (JIT) delivery of units of product to succeeding stages. One major advantage to this is that it results in a large reduction of in-process inventory and the cost of that inventory. In order for such JIT processes to operate successfully, it is crucial that individual stages operate in control.

1.4.3   The Deming (Shewhart) Cycle (PDCA)

We mentioned in section 1.2 that in 1950 Dr. Deming advocated the Plan, Do, Check or Study Act (PDCA) paradigm to Japanese manufacturers (see Fig. 1.1). This cycle is a useful scheme in many QC activities such as product design and process improvement. It is a strategy for improving a stage or a process. The cycle can be likened to a computer algorithm that calls four subroutines in sequence and is stuck in a loop. The code looks like this:

Step 1. PLAN: Study the process to see what can be done for improvements. What changes will help? What are the important quality variables? Are they in control? Are charts in use? Properly? Can they be improved? What are process capabilities? Would experimentation to test ideas be helpful? Plan a change or test. Use design of experiments (DOE), if needed.

Step 2. DO: Carry out the change or experimental test.

Step 3. CHECK or STUDY: Analyze the results to determine the effects of the change or experiment.

Step 4. ACT: What has been learned? Can we now better predict output values from this test or stage? If so, are these values improved? Take

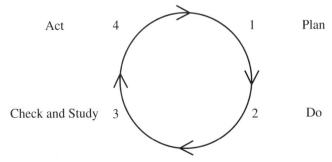

Figure 1.1   The Deming or Shewhart Cycle (Deming 1986, p. 88)

such action as the new information indicates to modify standards to make improvements permanent.

GO TO Step 1. and begin the cycle anew.

In product design the Plan phase refers to product planning and initial design; the Do phase can be considered the manufacturing step; the Check phase can be considered actually checking the usefulness to customers by selling the product and collecting after-sales service and market survey data; and finally, the Act phase uses the information to make any needed redesign of either the product or production process.

1.4.4 True and Substitute or Surrogate Quality Characteristics

Since the purpose of quality control is to assure that products meet consumers' requirements, we must be able to identify and interpret consumers' needs. Consumers' requirements are generally expressed as *true quality characteristics.* For example, if we ask potential car buyers what features they consider important and will affect their purchasing decision, there is a long list of possibilities, such as: handles well, is peppy, is quiet, good fuel economy, looks nice, good buy, is reliable, reputation of manufacturer, reputation of dealer, service and parts availability, etc. Note that in order to consider these true quality characteristics in the design, production, and marketing of automobiles, we must carefully study these characteristics and in most cases find *substitute* or *surrogate characteristics* that we can more readily utilize. For example, "handles well" is very important but is also quite complex because it involves the steering system, suspension, motor, transmission, etc. In turn, the transmission will contribute positively to good overall handling if it shifts smoothly and positively. So we must manufacture a transmission that shifts efficiently and smoothly. In order to do this, we set specification target values and tolerances for the dimensions of many components, taking into consideration the process capabilities of the production processes. These dimensions are called surrogate or substitute quality variables.

Designing and manufacturing products requires that we determine the true quality characteristics defined by the customers' requirements, and then design and produce units of product to satisfy these requirements. However, true quality characteristics are often not quantitative variables that have values found by measurement or counting procedures, and therefore are frequently difficult or impossible to use directly as criteria in designing and manufacturing products. Thus it is necessary to find *surrogate quality variables* that can be used in the design and manufacture of products. This requires careful study of the relationships among the true quality characteristics and surrogate quality variables. This process of relating true quality characteristics and surrogate quality variables is called "quality analysis" or "quality function deployment,"—QFD. Cause-and-effect diagrams (to be considered in Chapter 3) and QFD tables can be used to study these relationships; however, in many cases more powerful statistical methods including design of experiments and regression analysis will be helpful. This type of work in quality analysis generally entails product research with prototype and pilot products.

1.4.5 Determining Values of Quality Variables

Quality variables are quality characteristics (either true or surrogate) that have numerical values. In order for quality variables to be useful in designing and making quality products they must be carefully specified. This requires that the unit of product they measure be carefully defined. The method of determining a numerical value for the quality variable must be completely and unambiguously specified. When products are in discrete units, such as batteries, cameras, or automobiles, then we must assure the quality, or value of the quality variable, for each unit. However, for "continuous" products such as liquids, gases, carpets, electrical wire or cable, etc., the unit of product, called the *assurance unit,* and the sampling method to be used must be understood and agreed upon by all parties including suppliers and purchasers. Defining the methods and standards for evaluating quality is a major management responsibility.

   In some cases the nature of true quality characteristics as expressed by consumers may be such that the only reasonable way to assign numerical values is by sensory or organoleptic tests. For example, we can have randomly selected customers in a supermarket rank three brands or blends of coffee according to their taste preferences. Drivers may assign a score of 1 to 10 to the "drivability" of cars, etc. Such schemes for assigning numerical values must be carefully planned and executed to assure the numbers truly represent the quality requirements in question. The data may require analysis using nonparametric statistical methods.

1.4.6 Classifying Quality Characteristics

Products generally have many quality characteristics, and Ishikawa recommends that some of these, such as defects and flaws, can be considered as "backward-looking" quality characteristics. They can also be called *negative* quality characteristics. Quality attributes that make a product more desirable or add value, such as "drives good" for a car, are called "forward-looking" or *positive* quality attributes. In designing and manufacturing products we need to be aware of, and concerned with, all of the associated quality attributes, both positive and negative. Of course, not all attributes are equally important. For this reason it will sometimes be useful to sort defects into classes. A useful scheme in some cases is to categorize defects into three or four classes. Possibly: critical defects such as those that affect safety or destroy function (a steering mechanism that locks up, brakes that fail, major engine or transmission defects); major defects that affect the functioning of the product such as an automobile engine that is hard to start or stalls; less important defects such as a noisy engine or minor flaws in fit and finish. We will consider statistical methods for assigning weights to types of defects and constructing a control chart for such a weighted sum in Chapter 8. Generally, we should aim for products without defects; however, some minor defects may sometimes be acceptable.

Positive quality attributes may also be classified into categories and they can be used to distinguish or differentiate a product from its competition and enhance its sales appeal. For example, General Motors runs ads asserting that its automatic transmissions are exceptionally trouble-free and long-lasting and that its brakes are also especially long-lasting. In designing a product and its manufacturing process, a company may give special emphasis to selected positive quality characteristics to achieve a marketing advantage. Such positive attributes are "selling points" that can be honestly emphasized in advertising and by sales personnel.

1.4.7 Defectives and Nonconformities

The determination of whether a unit of product has or does not have a particular defect is made by an inspection procedure that involves using either the five senses or a gauge or measuring device. The exact details of this procedure must be set out in standards with operational definitions agreed upon by all parties including design, engineering, manufacturing, suppliers, customers, management, etc. In some cases it may be difficult to obtain agreement as to whether a product is or is not a defective. For example, different inspectors may not agree upon whether a minor paint flaw is a defect.

Blueprints generally set target values and tolerances for dimensional measurements. Parts that are gauged to be out of tolerance are often designated as defectives. This can cause problems due to the fact that blueprint tolerances may not be carefully designed by realistically taking into account manufacturing capabilities and functional necessities of the parts.

In a large automobile engine plant, the supervisor of manufacturing reported the following problem to this author. Two mounting holes for starters were drilled within blueprint tolerances, and the corresponding holes on the starters were also within tolerance. Yet there was a problem because some of these starters would not mount, that is, the holes did not properly align. The real problem was not in manufacturing but due to a design mistake in two-dimensional tolerancing. The real defect was in the blueprint.

The percentage of defective units produced is an important quality variable; however, exactly what units are to be counted must be clear. The true defectives percentage or fallout of a process includes not only those that fail inspection but also those units that require either adjustment or rework and those units that fail in service. When fallout is high it may be desirable to reconsider inspection standards. Tolerances may be set tighter than necessary to assure satisfactory performance.

A common practice when inspection consists of comparing one or more measurements with tolerance ranges is to accept units when measurements are near specification limits. The reasoning behind this practice is that the tolerance limits approach to setting standards of acceptability of products is a poor one because it essentially assigns a loss of zero to values in the tolerance interval and considers the loss on parts outside tolerance unacceptably large. As we will later consider in some detail, a far better approach will be to work to improve process capability so as to eliminate the need for inspection by producing a high percentage of product within tolerance and thereby obviating inspection.

There are two types of quality as described by J. M. Juran. *Quality of design* is the quality level that is decided upon in the planning and design stages of product development. In setting this quality level, it is necessary that manufacturing participate to assure that the quality level conforms with manufacturing capabilities. *Quality of conformance* is the actual level of quality achieved in production. According to Juran, Deming, Ishikawa, and other gurus, we can expect unit costs to decrease, cycle times to decrease, productivity to increase, and general improvement as quality of conformance is improved. An informed discussion of quality developments in the United States and Japan is given by Juran (1994).

1.4.8 Operational Definitions

Throughout this book we shall refer to numbers that are measurements or counts of some sort, to processes, procedures, and various other concepts. A major cause of problems in the use of words or phrases is that they may be interpreted differently by different people. Terms must be carefully stated in *operational definitions,* agreed upon by all affected parties. According to Deming (1986), an operational definition puts communicable meaning into a concept. We illustrate with some simple examples.

Suppose a specification simply says that the diameter of a certain round rod is to be in an interval: 0.5 ± 0.003 in. Is this meaningful? First, what do we mean by "round" rod? Does it mean all possible diameter measurements are the same? How could one possibly verify that a rod is round? The point is that roundness is a geometry concept. As a practical matter, if we are to decide whether a rod is indeed round, we would have to take some measurements in a very carefully specified manner and subject them to a specified analysis to make the decision. Next, what does it mean to have a diameter be in the interval 0.5 ± 0.003 in.? Is it good enough to find one place that measures in this interval? How do we take a measurement at a specified location? Do we take one measurement there or ten? If we take ten, do we use the largest? The smallest? The mean? The median? What measurement system should we use? There are many types of gauges. They won't all agree. And so on.

To assure that specifications are interpreted by different parties in the same way, they must be carefully stated, taking into account the details of the performance of the measurement system.

1.5 LEADERSHIP: RESPONSIBILITY, AUTHORITY, AND KNOWLEDGE

In organizing human activities for any purpose, and, in particular, in organizing the employees of a company to produce quality goods or services, the following general principal should be recognized and followed. Every position, from top management to floor workers, must have well-understood responsibilities and sufficient authority and knowledge to meet those responsibilities. For individuals or organized groups, such as committees or teams, there must be a balance of responsibility and authority. We are inviting failure if responsibility is assigned without sufficient authority or knowledge available to meet the responsibility. One person or group cannot have responsibility while appropriate authority rests with others.

Those with broad authority, such as company CEOs, ships' captains, etc., also must be held broadly responsible for the success of the enterprise. The classic example is that of a captain of a Navy ship. Especially at sea, the captain of a ship has virtually absolute authority. Also, the captain is responsible for anything that happens to the ship. If the ship runs aground, it is the captain's responsibility, and it does not matter if he was asleep in quarters at the time. He is still responsible.

An operator can be held responsible for defective units only if the units were clearly due to some failure on the operator's part to take actions that were within his or her authority. According to many authorities, the majority of defective units manufactured, perhaps 80 percent or so, are due to the systems for designing and producing the units, which are the responsibility of management, and operators have little or no authority to affect them. Management has both the responsibility and the authority to plan, design, and maintain the system so as to assure quality products. Managers who attempt to promote quality products solely by pressuring or even by encouraging operators to improve quality are likely to have limited success.

The third factor required for a company to produce high-quality products is *knowledge.* An individual or group with responsibilities and a balance of authority must have the required knowledge to meet the responsibilities. Presumably a company will fill all positions with the best-qualified people available; however, in many cases people with sufficient knowledge may not be available. Then further education and training are necessary. For example, developing sufficient knowledge of statistical process control and other relevant statistical methodology is a major challenge for all companies today.

Another source of problems in American business is the widespread belief in the exchangeability of managers. This idea is based on the assumption that training or experience in a specialized area such as accounting, finance, engineering, and so on, constitutes qualification for virtually any management position. To be effective, managers require a thorough knowledge of the particular operations and activities to be managed, and this includes a basic understanding of variability and its ramifications on the enterprise.

As an example of people in management positions for which they are unqualified, we cite the following. Most companies have a position with a title such as Quality Assurance Manager or Manager of Quality Control. I have met many of these officials and have sometimes been appalled at their lack of knowledge in the quality field, especially of variability and basic statistical methods. This seems to be a common place to park a weak executive. It also says something about the competence of the authorities who appoint them. It would seem that in today's competitive world, companies would see fit to seek well-qualified managers of quality assurance. In many cases the best way to obtain well-qualified quality assurance managers, or other personnel trained in the quality area, is to develop them in-house. This, of course, requires long-range planning and commitment, as do most functions of QC and TQM.

There is a need today for people with training in quality control and TQM at all levels from CEOs to operators. Knowledge of variability as it manifests itself in quality variables is critical. Statistics is the discipline that is most concerned with variability in data, and important techniques such as Shewhart charting methods have been contributed to the quality profession by statistics. Today, there is a need for more development of statistical methods to help solve remaining problems in the quality field, and for training to treat problems caused by variability in all areas including management, engineering, and floor operations. The objective of this book is to present statistical methods that are helpful for these areas, especially for bringing processes into control and reducing variability of in-control processes.

1.5.1 Leadership for Quality

We stated earlier that the CEO must be held responsible for the success of the company and this certainly includes responsibility for the quality program. The company chief executive must set the company policies and goals with regard to quality and provide direct leadership in functions to achieve those goals. Authorities such as Deming, Juran, Ishikawa, et al. are in agreement that leadership from top management is crucial for a successful QC program. The responsibility for quality cannot be delegated.

A critical element of a quality program is a policy of commitment to continuously improve products and services. A policy of continuous improvement is essentially a policy of continuous learning, which requires a commitment to education and training of personnel. However, and very importantly, continuous learning entails far more than the learning achieved in formal education and training programs. Learning involves the constant study of work processes and finding ways to improve them. Education and training programs will enhance the ability to improve work processes by giving personnel the tools needed to study and improve work processes.

There are two distinct approaches to making improvements. These are improvements through breakthroughs in science or technology, and improvements by working continuously on products and processes and in this way making many small improvements. Breakthroughs in science and technology are generally major innovations such as those on which major new products, or even new industries, can be based. The Japanese call the approach by many small improvements *kaizen,* and Imai (1986) feels that this approach is responsible for much of Japan's competitive success in world markets. This approach requires constant and continuous efforts by every element of a company to improve efficiency by improving in every operation and process. Small improvements can be by improving quality, reducing cost to produce the same quality, reducing cycle times, or improving scheduling precision. Apparently, the quality circles in some Japanese companies have played important roles in these kaizen activities.

1.6 QUALITY MANAGEMENT PRINCIPLES: DEMING'S 14 POINTS

Dr. W. Edwards Deming has summarized much of his personal philosophy of quality management in 14 points for the transformation of Western management (1986, p. 23). Many of these points address specific classes of problems caused by variation. In the following, we quote Deming in boldface. The elaboration of his points also generally follows his extended discussion, but differs in some cases, and he is not quoted exactly.

Deming's 14 Points for Transformation of Western Industry

The 14 points apply anywhere, to small organizations as well as to large ones, to the service industry as well as to manufacturing. They apply to a division within a company.

1. Create constancy of purpose toward improvement of product and service, with the aim to become competitive and to stay in business, and to provide jobs. Managers have two classes of concerns and responsibilities. First, the company must be run from hour to hour and day to day, and this short-term management activity inevitably absorbs much time and attention. Second, plans for the future of the business must be made and implemented. It is the problems of the future that are most often neglected, but require constancy of purpose if the business is to thrive. Stable maintenance and expansion of market share are more important than quick profits to shore up the next quarterly report in order to make the managers look good. Top management must take time and have the imagination to innovate to plan new and improved products to meet future expectations of the market. Work constantly to improve the product or service. Research should develop new and innovative products and contribute to improved methods for conducting all company operations. Education should compliment and support both short-term production and research. In summary, management should be dominated by the long-term perspective.

2. Adopt the new philosophy. We are in a new economic age. Western management must awaken to the challenge, must learn their responsibilities, and take on leadership for change. The *new philosophy* recognizes that the efficiency of most institutions in the United States today as seen in the level of errors and the quality of products is poor. For example, there has been a large decline in the quality of education at all levels from elementary school to graduate school in the last 20 to 30 years. Production facilities produce far too much scrap. The responsibility for poor systems rests with top management; therefore, effective action for improvement must be taken by management. Defective units of product are not free. It costs as much to make a bad bearing as a good one and then an additional amount to dispose of it as scrap. A poorly educated graduate will cost society an enormous sum in the long run. In the past there has often been an implicit assumption that some percentage of scrap is natural and unavoidable. This assumption is no longer acceptable.

3. Cease dependence on inspection to achieve quality. Eliminate the need for inspection on a mass basis by building quality into the product in the first place. According to many experienced quality practitioners, even 100% inspection plans identify only 60–80% of units correctly for many reasons. Inspection of products is essentially only a way of sorting units and cannot improve quality. That is, it does not reduce the number or percentage of defectives made, and, in the end, the customer must pay for all of the units made, both good and bad. Routine 100% inspection amounts to planning for defects and acknowledging that the production process is not capable of meeting the specifications. Time and money spent on sampling inspection systems would be better spent improving the ability of the production process to meet specifications. Most of this book will be concerned with methods for accomplishing this, that is, methods for bringing a process into a state of control so that it produces products that meet specifications. Specifications themselves should be examined to determine if they can be met by the production process. If a production process is stable and is still producing defective units of product, then the specifications themselves should be carefully examined to determine if the specifications are realistic.

There are exceptions where acceptance sampling inspection may be necessary because the technology may not be available to improve the process sufficiently, at acceptable cost, to avoid using acceptance sampling schemes. For example, in some work in the electronics industry the fallout is often as much as 20% of product, and there does not exist practical, affordable technology to further improve this figure. In this case, acceptance sampling inspection schemes are necessary to reduce the amount of defective product shipped.

4. End the practice of awarding business on the basis of price tag. Instead, minimize total cost. Move toward a single supplier for any one item, on a long-term relationship of loyalty and trust. Purchasing decisions must not be based on price alone without consideration of the quality of the purchased units. Obtaining objective evidence of uniformity and reliability must form part of the purchasing process. Without evidence of the quality of purchased units, the lowest quality producer will underbid the competition. Today much of American industry, the U.S. government, state governments, and both public and private universities often award contracts to the lowest bidder and in return receive low-quality, shoddy products.

The aim in the purchase of tools and equipment should be to minimize the total cost per hour, or unit of product, over the life of the equipment. In fact, to be even more realistic, the costs should also include those directly related to the production units such as warranty costs and market losses due to shoddy products, etc. Assessing these costs requires more knowledge and work on the part of management and purchasing agents. Statistical training will be essential here. Some of the most important costs, such as the loss of reputation from marketing shoddy products, are by their nature unknown and unknowable in any precise way, but are nevertheless important and of major concern.

A major source of variation in products and the resultant reduction in quality is due to variation inherited from incoming purchased parts and materials. Supplier qualification manuals must receive careful attention. Supplier contracts for parts should require evidence that processes are in control. Since there is always variation among suppliers, this variation can be reduced by a policy of purchasing from as few different suppliers as possible. Establishing stable long-term relations with one or a small number of suppliers permits and encourages these suppliers to devote time and capital to improving their processes. It also permits and encourages interaction and cooperative efforts to assure that the supplier's products integrate to produce continuous improvement of the final product. Stable long-term relations with suppliers based on loyalty and trust are the ideal.

5. Improve constantly and forever the system of production and service, to improve quality and productivity, and thus constantly decrease costs. This is Deming's famous "continuous improvement" principle. One place that a company should continually strive for improvement is in the system for designing new products. The highest priority in product design is to meet the customer's needs and expectations. This means input at the design stage from departments such as marketing and advertising. All departments and activities that will eventually be involved in making and marketing a product should be represented in designing a new product. Manufacturability must be given careful attention at the design stage. Specifications that cannot be met in everyday production without fallout are a major problem. Redesign at later stages when unanticipated problems arise is costly and often less effective than getting it right the first time. Designing and continually improving the system for designing products is the responsibility of top management. This is necessarily so because top-level authority is necessary to coordinate the many contending interests that product design entails. The intent to design and make high-quality products must be clearly fixed by top-level management and communicated to all members of the company.

The continuous improvement principle is to be applied to all aspects of manufacturing and marketing a product. In order to improve each particular process, the process must first be brought into a state of statistical control, as will be explained in detail in later chapters on statistical process control. Once a process is in control it will produce predictable results, and only then can we seek to actually improve the process by finding ways to identify and remove or reduce effects from common causes of variation.

Continuous improvement is to be pressed in all downstream activities involved in any way in making and marketing the product. Note that the classical system of setting out specification limits for a parameter and making parts with the goal of making them within these specification limits is in direct conflict with this principle of striving for continuous improvement. Continuous improvement entails continually reducing the variation of the parameter of interest. It will often be necessary to utilize methods of experimental design to reduce variability of important process parameters.

Process improvement includes better allocation of human effort. It includes hiring practices, placement, training, and retraining in order to give everyone the opportunity to improve their professional level and make a greater contribution to the company's success, and, at the same time, to advance their own careers.

6. Institute training on the job. In addition to the general management principles learned in business schools, managers need a thorough knowledge of the company operations from incoming materials to the consumers of the products, the particular functions to be managed, and an appreciation of variation and how it affects activities, so that informed decisions can be made in its presence. In particular, managers should have detailed knowledge of the stability and levels of in-control variation of processes under their responsibility, so they can make informed decisions about operations of these processes. Supervisors need a thorough understanding of the work they oversee in order to assist the workers to improve their work skills. Japanese managers and supervisors have an advantage over their American counterparts in that they usually have spent time in beginning level jobs on the factory floor and in other departments in the same company. American supervisors often have not had this experience. Workers must be trained for each specific job. On-the-job training should continue by a skilled supervisor until a worker's performance is stable. Control charts can be used to determine when this point has been reached, and to give an indication of proficiency not beclouded by inherent variation. A confident worker who knows how to perform his or her job well is likely to be a happy worker who takes pride in his or her performance and makes quality products. Inadequate training wastes a company's greatest resource—the natural abilities of its people.

A major problem is failure to maintain constant work standards for what is acceptable work and what is not. When the crunch is on to fill an order by a deadline, it is easy to permit standards to slip in favor of turning out enough units of product. Varying standards frustrate workers. If standards vary, how is anyone to know what is required at the moment?

7. Institute leadership (see point 12). The aim of supervision should be to help people and machines and gadgets to do a better job. Supervision of management is in need of overhaul, as well as

supervision of production workers. Managers at all levels must be leaders, and this requires knowledge of two types. Sound management requires knowledge of the activities to be managed, and an understanding of variation in order to make management decisions in its presence and avoid the many pitfalls that arise because of it.

The vision required for leadership in long-term planning and implementation for continuous improvement must be based on a thorough understanding of activities supervised. Without knowledge of the activities under one's supervision, it is not possible to give leadership by planning improvements and leading the effort in constantly improving processes and products. High turnover rates due to job hopping by management results in managers with insufficient knowledge to give leadership to the activities supervised. Some management concepts and methods focus on outcomes (management by objective—MBO, work standards, making it to spec, zero defects, performance appraisals), when attention should be given to improving systems. The mistake in this type of managerial focus on outcomes is in kind the same as that from relying on sampling inspection schemes for quality control systems rather than methods directed at improving processes.

Failure to understand the nature of randomness and variation is a major shortcoming of many managers and supervisors at all levels from the executive suite to the shop floor. Most numbers used for management decisions entail a random component. Decisions based on these numbers must therefore carefully consider this randomness. For example:

> A company rates its plant managers each year according to the profits for the year. All managers that are below average receive no bonus for the year. Managers who are in the lowest ten percent are assigned to other duties. What is wrong with this from the point of view of random variation? Suppose that the managers are of about equal ability, all are working hard at their jobs, and there are no further factors—beyond their control—that affect profits. About half of them will still be below average and some will from randomness alone be in the lowest ten percent. So bonuses are being given based purely on randomness that is entirely or largely beyond their control, and some that may well be just as competent as the others are being transferred. This is bad for morale for all concerned.

Many examples can be given of situations where management decisions are based on numbers that contain an increment due to random variation and, perhaps even worse, to factors other than the one supposedly being measured. See Deming (1986, p. 64 on).

Managerial integrity can be a problem. Decisions are sometimes made for the wrong reasons. For example, the real reason for a decision may be to make the next quarterly report look good, and therefore enhance a manager's career prospects, even if the decision is not in the long-run best interests of the company. Hiring and promotion decisions may be based on irrelevant factors, such as race, ethnicity, or sex. A manager may hire the prettiest applicant, even if she is less well qualified professionally. A department head may give larger raises for "politically correct" reasons, but will, of course, claim that the recommendation is based on merit. When decisions are made for the wrong reasons, they are likely to be explained with dishonest statements. This is demoralizing for people trying to advance their careers with hard work and performance.

8. Drive out fear, so that everyone may work effectively for the company. Secure means without fear. Managers and workers need security to give their best performances. Fear comes from many sources. The shop worker is afraid to suggest a way to improve the process because of uncertainty about the supervisor's reaction. A worker is unsure if he is doing the job correctly, but does not tell the supervisor for fear he will be judged incompetent. Many are afraid that the new quality improvement program will make them look bad. Top management invests little in research and education for fear it will not produce tangible results that can be used immediately. A foreman is afraid to stop a production line for repairs although quality would be improved, and a later breakdown might be avoided. Salaried workers are terrified of annual rating systems. As well they should be.

An excellent example of the effect of fear can be observed in colleges. A common practice of college managers for the last 20 years is the so-called "teacher evaluation." A form is passed out and each student—or at least those who bother to participate—"grades" the professor on a scale of 1 to 10. No attempt is made to assess the amount of knowledge that has been imparted, and there are of course a large number of assignable causes that contribute an enormous amount of variation to the numbers obtained. Yet academic administrators consider these numbers to be valuable, precise measures of teaching quality. Causes of variation include such things as class level (freshman, sophomore, graduate), class size (anything from three or four to several hundred), discipline (mathematics, statistics, engineering, physics, liberal arts, social sciences, education), professor's personality, etc. Undoubtedly, the most important factor of all is the professor's own grading policy. Of course, generally speaking, professors are not stupid, so they know this and the effect has been a huge inflation in grade point averages. Professors, and especially young untenured ones, are terrified at the prospect of getting a low "evaluation" to the point that this fear has a profound effect, but the effect is not to improve the quality of the course. The effect is to water down course content and give much higher grades. The final result has been a general lowering of the quality of higher education in the United States. The cost of course has been enormous.

9. Break down barriers between departments. People in research, design, sales, and production must work as a team, to foresee problems of production and in use that may be encountered with the product or service. Management must see that various departments work cooperatively to minimize problems in producing and marketing quality products. Research personnel, design engineers, and materials purchasing agents need to communicate with production people in order to increase their awareness of problems that may arise in production and assembly. Production personnel will be more alert to potential problems in manufacturability and this may result in fewer instances requiring redesign at later stages. Sales and service people can contribute feedback information about the strengths and weaknesses of the product with customers. There is often much unused potential information from customers. Failure to collect and act on this information can result in customer dissatisfaction that can be disastrous for the long run.

Cooperation among all departments to optimize the performance of the entire company is crucial. Teamwork within departments is necessary, but some management policies inadvertently discourage teamwork. When relative annual ratings systems are used, an individual is likely to feel that helping a co-worker will work to his or her own disadvantage.

10. Eliminate slogans, exhortations, and targets for the work force asking for zero defects and new levels of productivity. Such exhortations only create adversarial relationships, as the bulk of the causes of low quality and low productivity belong to the system and thus lie beyond the power of the work force. Since most causes of low quality are due to the system, and the system is the responsibility of management, these methods of flogging the work force are doomed to failure. Even worse, due to the negative effect on morale, they are likely to be counterproductive. Rather than engage in poster sloganeering campaigns, management must set about studying processes in order to remove special causes and bring them into control. Once processes are stable, the real work of improving the process by reducing or eliminating common causes can begin.

The Communist production system of the former Soviet Union relied heavily on slogans, exhortations of workers, posters, and so on. Yet, the poor quality of consumer products made in that system was a principal cause of its total collapse.

11. a. Eliminate work standards (quotas) on the factory floor. Substitute leadership. b. Eliminate management by objective. Eliminate management by numbers, numerical goals. Substitute leadership. a. Work standards are numerical quotas for hourly workers. A textiles worker may have a quota of 20 dozen units per 8-hour shift. What is wrong with this? It ignores natural variation. If the work standard is set at the average for the work force, then about half the work force will be able to meet the standard without difficulty, while about half will be unable to meet it. For everyone to meet the standard, it must be determined by the slowest worker on the entire force. Someone is always the slowest worker. All but the slowest worker on the entire work force will stand idle for part of the day, having finished their quotas. If the work rate is set too high for a particular worker, then the result will be an increase in the rate of defectives made. The natural emphasis on numbers made ignores quality and quality suffers.

Piecework involves paying workers for the numbers of units made but does not include a quality requirement. So the hourly worker on piece work gets paid just as well for making defectives and scrap as for good units. Defectives and scrap can be made more quickly and easily. Thus, lots of defectives and scrap are made and the cost of production per good unit soars. Incentive pay is similar to piecework since it too is based on the numbers of units made.

Management systems based on work standards, piecework and incentive pay for hourly workers must be replaced by intelligently planned systems that emphasize careful training for jobs and provide motivation to produce quality units rather than emphasizing the total numbers of units produced.

b. Management by objective—MBO—is an attempt by management to accomplish an objective essentially by declaring it to be desirable, and without a detailed, specific, and realistic plan to accomplish the desired end. Examples: (1) Make zero defects, (2) Increase productivity by 10% this year, (3) Decrease defectives by 5% this year. All of these are, indeed, desirable goals, but if one of them is to be realized, the statement of the goal must be accompanied by a detailed plan of attack. To decrease defectives by *any* percentage—and it will be impossible to realistically give a specific number—the plan or road map for reaching the destination must include budgeting for implementing process control on the production processes involved, and this will surely entail plans for training personnel in modern SPC methods. If SPC methods show that the system is unstable, then the only goal possible must entail first bringing the system into control. After a system is brought into a state of control, there is no point in stating numerical goals, because you will get whatever the system is capable of delivering. Real improvement for a stable system must come about from finding and implementing ways to reduce or eliminate common causes in the processes, but it will not be possible to state numerical goals in advance. This last step may require investment in new equipment, improved maintenance, and so on. Attempts at management by numerical goals means that the manager does not have sufficient knowledge of the activities managed and statistical methods to know what to do, and is based on the premise that intimidation of the work force can somehow accomplish the desired objective. This is, of course, management by fear, and the goals will prove to be illusory.

12. a. Remove barriers that rob the hourly worker of his right to pride of workmanship. The responsibility of supervisors must be changed from sheer numbers to quality. b. Remove barriers that rob people in management and in engineering of their right to pride of workmanship. This means, *inter alia,* **abolishment of annual or merit rating and of management by objective.** a. Barriers to pride of workmanship for hourly workers are mainly built into the system, which is the responsibility of management, and not to failures of workers themselves. Management must provide leadership to assure that workers have good training, materials, and tools in order to do their jobs well. In this context, "management" should be construed to include labor unions also, since unions play a role in the design of the overall system. Workers must clearly understand exactly what is expected of them. That is, they must know exactly what is acceptable work and what is not. Most workers are diligent and even eager to work hard to produce quality work. Given proper direction by leaders and the tools and materials required, they will produce products in which they can take pride.

b. Managers and engineers face numerous barriers which make it difficult to meet responsibilities in a manner in which they can take pride. Lack of constancy of a proper purpose is one barrier. Emphasis on short-term goals such as making the next quarterly dividend look good reflects this inconstancy of purpose. The need to show short-term profits may be the result of pressure from sources outside a company itself, such as bankers and stockholders. Merit ratings and other forms of annual review may be implemented without awareness of natural variation and can result in demoralized and fearful management. Fear of costs from legal liability, both institutionally and personally, is a real handicap for many managers and engineers. Medical costs are an enormous burden for companies. Costs associated with excessive government regulation and the associated red tape are a constant problem. The national trend toward socialism, as reflected in the ever-increasing costs of "entitlement" programs and the taxes they entail, is a major handicap for American management.

13. Institute a vigorous program of education and self-improvement. In order for a company to implement point 5 and improve continuously, it is necessary that its people improve. People improve largely through learning, which is accomplished in many ways. Formal education and training programs, while important, are but one way. Managers, supervisors, and associates must continuously study all processes in their realms of responsibility in order to thoroughly understand them. A primary leadership responsibility is to create a learning atmosphere by coaching and encouragement. Knowledge is power for individuals and, collectively, for institutions. There is always a need for people on the higher rungs of the ladder of relevant knowledge.

Improvement in knowledge is needed in all fields. However, the material treated in this book is a field that is especially needed if companies are to be competitive. Many of the methods used in quality control are applications of ideas and techniques of probability and statistics. The professional field of statistics in the United States today, especially in the industrial statistics subfield, is undoubtedly the strongest in the world. Yet, it is a fact that many graduates from colleges in management and engineering have little or no training in statistics. A large majority of all B.S. graduates in engineering from U.S. universities have had no courses in statistics. Companies hiring engineers and management majors with undergraduate or graduate degrees would be well advised to inquire about their training in statistics. An education plan should be a component of any plan for quality improvement for a company.

14. Put everybody in the company to work to accomplish the transformation. The transformation is everybody's job. Management must accept the need for transformation to a quality-oriented operation and provide leadership in accomplishing it by convincing a critical mass of people that it is necessary for economic survival. Implementation of a quality improvement program will recognize that every process, large and small, can be broken down and represented as successive stages on a flow diagram. Improvement of a process proceeds by improving the operations within individual stages, and by improvement of interactions among stages.

$$\rightarrow \text{Stage } 1 \rightarrow \text{Stage } 2 \rightarrow \text{Stage } 3 \rightarrow$$

Each stage is a customer for a previous stage (or stages) and a supplier to a subsequent stage. Material enters a stage and is altered (worked on) in some manner and is passed along to the next stage. Improvement of the process generally requires improvement of two types: (1) improvement in the operations of individual stages, and (2) improvement of the process by improvement of communication and coordination among stages. People at each stage should know what is going on and required both upstream and downstream. Management is responsible to see that every person understands his (her) customers' needs.

The Shewhart cycle is a useful strategy for improving a stage. Statistical methods are needed in the stages of the cycle to extract meaningful information from data and to guard against invalid conclusions arising from natural variation. This does not mean that sophisticated methods are necessarily required. Sometimes rather simple techniques and so-called common sense are sufficient.

1.7   THE Q-STATISTICS PARADIGM IN SPC

In section 1.1 the pioneering work of a group of statisticians and engineers at the Bell Telephone Laboratories was mentioned. Perhaps the most important single document ever written in the quality field, which may be regarded as essentially defining the beginning of modern quality control, was a memorandum by Walter Shewhart in 1924 in which he set out the first Shewhart control chart (see Olmstead 1967). This first Shewhart chart was essentially what is today called a binomial p-chart.

The basic purpose of these statistical process control (SPC) charts was to use measurements or count data analytically to determine if a process is stable in the sense that the variable's values could be predicted. Shewhart defined a process to be stable or in control with respect to a quality variable if the variable's values could be predicted in advance. Most implementations of this concept, by Shewhart and others, have involved the following approach. The variable, possibly a vector, is assumed to have a distribution that is a member of a particular parametric class of distributions: normal, binomial, Poisson, etc. Formulas for control limits, actually prediction limits, are then set out as functions of the distribution's parameters. These limits are estimated by replacing the unknown parameters in the formulas for the control limits by estimates—the "plug-in" method of estimation. The limits and charts are then used as though they are the correct limits. Now, this procedure works well if the parameter estimates are based on large data sets taken when the process was stable. Such large data sets can often be obtained in classical high-value manufacturing, and these charting methods have proved very valuable in this context.

However, in many areas of modern manufacturing, and for many other types of work processes where the basic Shewhart concept of predictable stable processes is clearly relevant, we simply have no way to obtain large, prior data sets, and methods are needed for treating work processes when such data sets are not available. Also, values of some important quality variables cannot be satisfactorily modeled by assuming that observations are identically and independently distributed (i.i.d.), but can be predicted by using models that violate either the assumption of identical distributions or independence, such as regression or time series models. For many types of parametric models that are useful for quality variables, including i.i.d. models, regression models, time series, and the like, issues of model validity and stability can be analyzed by studying residuals from estimated versions of the models. In many cases these residuals can be so defined that they will have known distributions, either exactly or approximately, and deviations from these distributions reflect instability in the underlying model. In particular, we will give formulas for many models that are transformations to sequences of values that we call Q statistics, which are i.i.d. normal statistics with mean zero and variance one, either exactly or approximately, when a specific parametric model is correct. We refer to this general procedure as the *Q statistics paradigm.*

1.8 SUMMARY

This chapter has given a brief discussion of the history and some of the basic concepts of the quality management field. The central purpose of this discussion is to establish the intellectual framework that is the context for statistical process control, the central topic to be considered in this book. For further discussion of many of these issues, see Deming (1986) and Juran (1994).

PROBLEMS

1.1 **(a)** Describe the Taylor management method, and its historical significance.

   (b) Describe management factors of Japanese quality control, and, especially, Total Quality Control—TQC.

   (c) Compare the systems described in parts (a) and (b).

1.2 What are three areas of activity of quality assurance? Describe each briefly.

1.3 Describe the Shewhart (Deming) cycle.

1.4 What are the advantages of organizing a production layout by material flow utilizing just-in-time (JIT) coordination?

1.5 What is a substitute or surrogate quality characteristic?

1.6 Describe a particular position that you have observed, or at least know of, that has large responsibility and small authority?

1.7 What is kaizen? What is its role in TQC?

1.8 Give reasons why kaizen is desirable to move from inspection systems to process control systems.

1.9 At what stages of design, manufacturing, and marketing should the continuous improvement principle be applied?

1.10 Explain why quality improvement efforts that depend on exhorting workers to greater efforts to raise quality are doomed to failure?

1.11 A clothing manufacturer requires that sewing operators meet a work standard of 40 units per shift. If more units are produced, the operator is rewarded on a pro rata basis per unit. If fewer units are produced, the operator is docked on a pro rata basis. Discuss this plan from the view of the effect on quality and productivity.

1.12 What is quality of design? What is quality of conformance? Are the concepts important? Why?

1.13   The 12 operators on second shift are producing an overall average of about 5% out-of-spec units. Management is unhappy with this, and plans to implement the following scheme to improve this number. Each month operators who produce fewer than 3% out-of-spec units will receive a 10% bonus on their hourly wage, while operators who produce more than 5% out-of-spec units will have their hourly pay reduced by 10%. Management feels that this is a financially sound plan because the 2% improvement from those receiving bonuses should be of enough value to cover the cost of the bonuses, and the reduction of wages for the others will be a pure saving for the company. Do you think this is a good plan? If you do not, discuss your reasons, and suggest an alternative possible general approach to the problem.

CHAPTER 2

Probability Distributions to Describe Variability in Data Sets

In this chapter we discuss using probability distributions to model the natural variability in measurements or counts, and study briefly the distributions that are used most often in quality improvement. The material in this chapter is not intended to be a comprehensive discussion for those who have not been introduced to probability and statistics. It is assumed that the reader has studied at least beginning level material in probability and statistics. The purpose of this presentation is to review ideas and define terminology and notation before we begin the presentation of the material on quality improvement.

2.1 THE VARIABILITY INHERENT IN MEASUREMENTS, REFERENCE DISTRIBUTIONS FOR CONTINUOUS VARIABLES

In quality improvement we usually work with sets of numbers or *observations*. These may be on continuous variables or discrete variables. *Continuous* variables can be measurements of dimensions of parts such as the lengths of steel rods, the angles of gear teeth; the resistance of transistors, the percentage of a component of a chemical compound, the percentage of defectives in lots of purchased items, and so on. A variable is continuous if it can take any value in an interval of values. *Discrete* variables can be the number of typographical errors on a page, the number of defective items in a batch of items, or the number of warranty claims on an automobile in its first 12 months of service. Such *quality variables,* both continuous and discrete, are important in the control and improvement of quality for both manufactured products and services.

The data in Table 2.1 are breaking strengths of 80 pieces of polyester viscose yarn. Table 2.2 shows a *frequency distribution* of this data, and Fig. 2.1 shows a relative frequency *histogram* of this data. The histo-

TABLE 2.1 Breaking Strength in Pounds of Polyester Viscose Yarn

16.7	14.6	12.8	16.8	19.9	18.7	14.3	18.8	16.5	17.4
16.9	13.6	18.3	15.8	15.4	15.5	15.8	13.4	12.9	13.0
15.0	17.1	17.0	17.1	18.3	17.3	18.5	16.2	15.1	17.8
14.6	17.1	18.9	14.6	18.4	13.4	16.2	14.4	16.1	17.6
13.7	13.6	16.3	18.2	15.6	16.2	13.0	15.6	19.7	17.3
15.4	16.5	17.1	15.7	14.0	15.3	16.6	19.0	12.9	11.1
15.2	17.4	18.4	19.1	14.9	16.3	17.9	13.6	16.2	17.9
16.0	15.9	14.5	16.8	18.0	21.1	18.1	13.8	15.4	17.0

gram is essentially a picture of the data that is made by considering the range of values in the data set and dividing that range into a number of intervals, as shown in Table 2.2. Rectangles are drawn over the intervals with areas equal to the proportion of the data that are in the intervals. The midpoint of the ith interval is the class mark, M_i. A histogram is essentially a picture of a set of numbers that shows how the mass of the numbers (assigning each number a unit mass) is distributed on the real line. The construction and use of histograms will be discussed in more detail and illustrated in section 3.2 of Chapter 3.

Note that these breaking strengths vary from about 11 to 22 lb. Using the information from these 80 observations and the way that they are distributed on the real number line as displayed in the histogram, we can deduce useful information. Suppose that we decide to take one more piece of polyester viscose yarn of the same type to test. Then, before observing the additional value, by considering the *reference distribution* of Figure 2.1, we can *predict* the value that we will obtain

TABLE 2.2 Frequency Distribution for Breaking Strength Data of Polyester Yarn

Class	Class Interval $L_i < x \leq U_i$	Class Mark (M_i)	Tally	Frequency (n_i)	Relative Frequency (f_i)
1	$11 < x \leq 12$	11.5	|	1	0.0125
2	$12 < x \leq 13$	12.5	|||	3	0.0375
3	$13 < x \leq 14$	13.5	||||| ||||	9	0.1125
4	$14 < x \leq 15$	14.5	||||| |||	8	0.1000
5	$15 < x \leq 16$	15.5	||||| ||||| ||||	14	0.1750
6	$16 < x \leq 17$	16.5	||||| ||||| |||||	15	0.1875
7	$17 < x \leq 18$	17.5	||||| ||||| ||||	14	0.1750
8	$18 < x \leq 19$	18.5	||||| |||| |	11	0.1375
9	$19 < x \leq 20$	19.5	||||	4	0.0500
10	$20 < x \leq 21$	20.5		0	0.0000
11	$21 < x \leq 22$	21.5	|	1	0.0125

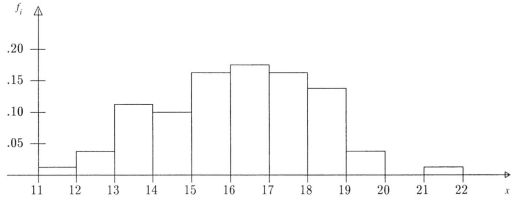

Figure 2.1 Relative Frequency Histogram for Yarn Breaking Strength Data

for this new piece, before the new piece is obtained. We would feel quite sure that the new value will be between 11 and 22, and that it is reasonably likely to be between, say, 13 and 19.

The histogram plotted from the 80 values of breaking strengths is an empirical distribution, and if we were to take 80 new values on exactly the same type of yarn and draw a histogram, it would not be exactly the same; however, the general shape should be similar. If we took even larger samples, say of size 8000, repeatedly, and made histograms, then we would expect that the shapes would be very similar. Indeed, if we let the number of observations become large enough, we would expect that the histogram would settle down or "converge" to a limiting shape. We cannot actually prove that such a convergence occurs, but we will assume that it does and use this limiting distribution as a basic concept in our work in this book. We will often call this limiting shape a *probability distribution* and one value of the variable obtained under the conditions that give this distribution a *random variable* from this distribution. If each member of a set of values X_1, X_2, $\cdots$, X_n is obtained under the conditions that produced the distribution, then this set of values is called a *sample* from this distribution.

In the following sections we consider a number of probability distributions that will be used in our work in quality improvement.

2.2 REFERENCE DISTRIBUTIONS FOR DISCRETE VARIABLES

In section 2.1 we considered sets of measurements on continuous variables, that is, on variables that can take values in intervals. We now

TABLE 2.3   Defectives Data

Day	No. Defectives	Day	No. Defectives	Day	No. Defectives	Day	No. Defectives
1	2	6	6	11	4	16	6
2	3	7	4	12	3	17	4
3	3	8	5	13	2	18	1
4	2	9	4	14	6	19	0
5	1	10	5	15	3	20	4

consider observed values on *discrete* variables. A variable is discrete if it can only take values in a specified set of values of the form $\{x_1, x_2, \cdots, x_i, \cdots\}$. In most cases considered in this book the numbers will be a subset of $\{0, 1, 2, \cdots\}$, since they are usually counts of some kind.

The number of defective items produced by an operator on 20 consecutive days is given in Table 2.3, and a bar chart of the relative frequency of the numbers of defects produced on a day is shown in Figure 2.2. The frequency distribution of these data is given in Table 2.4.

Now, if we consider the relative frequency bar graph in Figure 2.2, we can consider it an approximate or empirical reference distribution for defects produced by this particular operator. If we were to obtain data for another period of several days and plot a bar chart, it would likely look very much like this chart. Indeed, if the number of days was large, the chart should settle down to a limiting form that would tell us what we can reasonably expect in terms of a distribution of defects from this operator. In other words, it tells us the approximate

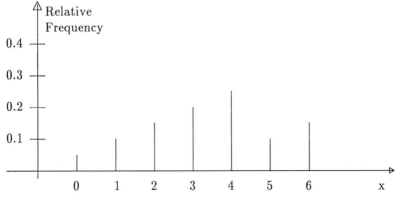

Figure 2.2   Bar Chart of Relative Frequency of Defectives

TABLE 2.4   Frequency Distribution of Numbers of Defectives

Value:	0	1	2	3	4	5	6
Frequency:	1	2	3	4	5	2	3
Relative Frequency:	.05	.10	.15	.20	.25	.10	.15

proportion of days that we can expect to get 0 defects, the approximate proportion of days with 1 defect, and so on. Note carefully the nature of the information that this distribution carries about this operator. It does not tell just how many defects he will have on a particular day, but it does tell quite a lot about his performance over the long run of many days.

2.3   SOME PROPERTIES OF THEORETICAL REFERENCE DISTRIBUTIONS

The theoretical limiting shape of a reference distribution of continuous variables is described by a *probability density function f(x)*. A function $f(x)$ can be a probability density function if it satisfies the two conditions of (2.3.1).

$$
\begin{array}{l}
\text{Conditions for a function } f(x) \text{ to be a proba-} \\
\text{bility density function:} \\[1em]
\text{(1) } f(x) \geq 0 \text{ for all } x \\[1em]
\text{(2) } \int_{-\infty}^{\infty} f(x)\, dx = 1
\end{array}
\qquad (2.3.1)
$$

Let X denote a variable that takes values according to a probability density function $f(x)$ as follows.

$$
P(a \leq X \leq b) = \int_{a}^{b} f(x)\, dx
\qquad (2.3.2)
$$

Then X is called a continuous *random variable* with (probability) density function $f(x)$. In this chapter we use a notation convention common in statistics of denoting random variables by uppercase letters.

When values are observed on discrete variables, as in the example for counts of defectives in the last section, it is often possible to find a formula that will give the probability of obtaining particular values. Such a function is a *probability function* and we consider some of the most important probability functions in this chapter. Let X denote a variable that takes values in a set $\{x_1, x_2, \cdots\}$ with some set of positive probabilities. Then X is is said to be a *discrete* random variable with probability function $p(x)$ on the set of *possible* values $S_x = \{x_1, x_2, \cdots\}$ when the following conditions are satisfied.

$$
\begin{array}{l}
(1)\ p(x_i) > 0 \text{ for every } i = 1, 2, \cdots \\[2mm]
(2)\ \sum_{i=1}^{\infty} p(x_i) = 1 \\[2mm]
(3)\ P(X = x_i) = p(x_i) \text{ for every } i = 1, 2, \cdots
\end{array}
\tag{2.3.3}
$$

A probability function can be drawn as a bar graph, as shown in Figure 2.3.

If X is a random variable, either continuous or discrete, then another function that will be important for the work in this book is the *probability distribution function,* which we will simply call the *distribution function.* The distribution function of a random variable X is

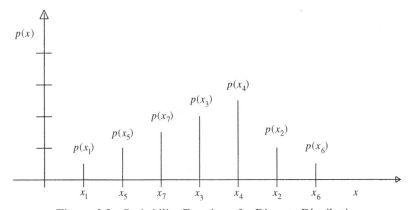

Figure 2.3 Probability Function of a Discrete Distribution

$$F(x) = P(X \leq x)$$

$$= \int_{-\infty}^{x} f(x) \, dx, \text{ if } X \text{ is continuous}$$

with density function $f(x)$

$$= \sum_{A} p(x), \text{ if } X \text{ is discrete with}$$

probability function $p(x)$, and A is the set of all possible points that are less than or equal to x.

(2.3.4)

For $g(x)$ a function of x, the *expected value* of this function is denoted $E[g(X)]$ and defined as follows.

$$E[g(X)] = \int_{-\infty}^{\infty} g(x)f(x) \, dx,$$

if X is continuous with density function $f(x)$, and

$$E[g(X)] = \sum_{S_x} g(x)p(x),$$

if X is discrete with probability function $p(x)$.

(2.3.5)

The mean, variance, and standard deviation of a random variable X are defined as follows:

$$\text{Mean}(X) = E(X)$$
$$\text{Var}(X) = E[X - E(X)]^2$$
$$\text{S.D.}(X) = \sqrt{\text{Var}(X)}$$

(2.3.6)

A mean will often be denoted by the Greek letter μ (mu) and a standard deviation by σ (sigma). For $0 \leq p \leq 1$ the pth *fractile,* or the

$100p^{th}$ *percentile,* of the distribution of a random variable X is that value x_p that satisfies

$$P(X \leq x_p) = p \tag{2.3.7}$$

The value x_p is sometimes said to cut off the amount p of probability below it.

2.4 THE HYPERGEOMETRIC DISTRIBUTION

Consider a set of N items. For definiteness, suppose that these are N items in a batch to be inspected. Let N_1 denote the number of defective items in the batch and let N_2 be the number of nondefectives, so that $N_1 + N_2 = N$. A sample is drawn *without replacement,* WOR, if an item is drawn randomly and not replaced before the next item is drawn.

Suppose that n items are drawn from the population of $N = N_1 + N_2$ items without replacement, and let X denote the number of defectives obtained in this sample. Then it can be shown that the probability function of X is given by the formula in display 2.4.1.

The Hypergeometric Probability Function:

$$h(x; n, N_1, N_2) = P(X = x) = \frac{\binom{N_1}{x}\binom{N_2}{n-x}}{\binom{N}{n}}$$

$$= \frac{\binom{Np}{x}\binom{Nq}{n-x}}{\binom{N}{n}} \tag{2.4.1}$$

for $\max\{0, n - N_2\} \leq x \leq \min\{n, N_1\}$, $N = N_1 + N_2$, $p = \dfrac{N_1}{N}$, $q = 1 - p$

Mean and Variance of Hypergeometric Probability Distribution:

$$E(X) = \frac{nN_1}{N} = np, \text{ and} \tag{2.4.2}$$

$$\text{Var}(X) = \left(\frac{N - n}{N - 1}\right) npq.$$

If X has the hypergeometric probability function of (2.4.1), then the hypergeometric distribution function is by definition $P(X \le x)$ and is given in detail in (2.4.3).

The *hypergeometric distribution function* at an integer x is

$$H(x; n, N_1, N_2) = P(X \le x)$$

$$= 0, \, x < x_0$$

$$= \sum_{J=x_0}^{x} \frac{\binom{N_1}{J}\binom{N_2}{n - J}}{\binom{N_1 + N_2}{n}}, \tag{2.4.3}$$

$$x_0 \le x \le x_1$$

$$= 1, \, x \ge x_1$$

For $x_0 = \max\{0, n - N_2\}$ and $x_1 = \min\{n, N_1\}$.

The probability and distribution functions $h(x; n, N_1, N_2)$ and $H(x; n, N_1, N_2)$ can be conveniently evaluated using a computer algorithm such as the one given on the Q-Charts disk.

Example 2.1: A lot of ten manufactured items contains four defectives. If five randomly selected items are sold to a customer, let X denote the number of defectives the customer will receive.

(a) Find the probability function $h(x)$ of X.

(b) Evaluate $h(x)$ in decimals for easy comparison of the probabilities and make a bar graph of $h(x)$.

(c) Evaluate the mean and standard deviation of X.

Solution

(a) The hypergeometric probability distribution obtains with $N = 10$, $N_1 = 4$, $N_2 = 6$, $n = 5$, $\max\{0, n - N_2\} = 0$, and $\min\{n, N_1\} = N_1 = 4$. Thus

$$h(x) = \binom{4}{x}\binom{6}{5-x}\Big/\binom{10}{5}; \; x = 0, 1, 2, 3, 4.$$

(b) $h(0) = \binom{4}{0}\binom{6}{5}\Big/\binom{10}{5} \doteq 0.023$

$h(1) = \binom{4}{1}\binom{6}{4}\Big/\binom{10}{5} = 0.238$

$h(2) = \binom{4}{2}\binom{6}{3}\Big/\binom{10}{5} \doteq 0.476, h(3) = 0.238, h(4) = 0.023$

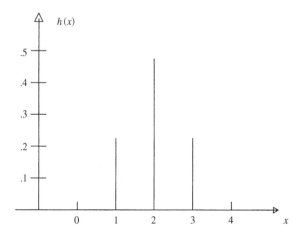

(c) $E(X) = np = 5(4/10) = 2,$

$$\text{Var}(X) = \left\{\frac{N - n}{n - 1}\right\} npq = \left\{\frac{10 - 5}{10 - 1}\right\} 5(4/10)(6/10) = 2/3,$$

Standard Deviation $(X) = \sqrt{2/3} \doteq 0.816.$ ∎

Example 2.2: A lot of 117 items contains 21 defectives. What is the probability that a sample of 31 items will contain at least five but fewer than 15 defectives?

Solution: Let X denote the number of defectives in the sample. From the distribution function on the Q-Charts disk with $n = 31$, $N_1 = 21$, and $N_2 = 96$, we obtain

$$\text{Answer} = P\{5 \le X < 15\} = P(4 < X \le 14)$$
$$= P(X \le 14) - P(X \le 4)$$
$$= H(14; 31, 21, 96) - H(14; 31, 21, 96)$$
$$= 1.00000 - 0.28775 = 0.71225$$ ∎

2.5 THE BINOMIAL DISTRIBUTION

In this section we study the class of distributions which is generally considered to be the most useful and important family of discrete distributions. It is crucially important for applications in quality control. The statistical process control (SPC) p-charts for attributes are based on it, and it is also the distribution on which much work in acceptance sampling is based.

Consider again the setting of the last section where a sample of size n is drawn from a population of N items of which a proportion p are "defectives"; however, now let the sampling be performed *with replacement*. A sample is drawn with replacement, WR, if it is obtained by first drawing one item randomly and inspecting it and then replacing it in the population being sampled before the next item is selected randomly. Again, we require the probability function $p(x)$ of the number X of defectives contained in the sample. When each item is selected, p is the probability of a defective, D, and $q = 1 - p$ is the probability of a nondefective, D^c, and the outcomes on different draws are independent. Consider a particular sample of n outcomes, of which x are defectives, D, and $(n - x)$ are nondefectives, D^c:

$$x \text{ defectives}$$

↓		↓	↓		↓	↓
D	D^c	D	D	$\cdots$	D^c	D

$$n \text{ trials}$$

The probability of this outcome is $p^x q^{n-x}$, since the probability of each of the x defectives is p, each of the $(n - x)$ nondefectives is q, and all trials are independent. Also, every sequence of trials having exactly x defectives and $(n - x)$ nondefectives will have this same probability. We require the number of different sequences possible having exactly x defectives and $(n - x)$ nondefectives, but this is just the number of ways to arrange a set of n objects on a line when x are indistinguishable of one type (D) and $(n - x)$ are indistinguishable of a second type (D^c). This is given by the formula

$$\frac{n!}{x!(n - x)!} = \binom{n}{x}$$

Thus, the probability function for X, the number of defectives, is

---

Binomial Probability Function:

$$b(x; n, p) = \binom{n}{x} p^x q^{n-x}$$ (2.5.1)

$$\text{for } x \in \{0, 1, 2, \cdots, n\}$$

This probability function is called a *binomial* probability function, due to the fact that this function is the summand in the binomial theorem. We now use the binomial theorem to verify that the binomial probability function sums to one. Consider

$$\sum_{x=0}^{n} b(x; n, p) = \sum_{x=0}^{n} \binom{n}{x} p^x q^{n-x} = (p + q)^n = 1^n = 1$$

The essential points in the above derivation of the binomial probability function are often satisfied in problems other than sampling from a finite population with replacement. These essential points involve the observation of outcomes of a sequence of trials when each trial has two possible outcomes, such as a defective or nondefective, a head or a tail, success or failure, etc.

> **Definition:** A sequence of trials that result in either event A or A^c on each trial is called a sequence of *Bernoulli trials* if
> (i) the probability $p = P(A)$ is the same on every trial; and
> (ii) the events A and A^c on separate trials are independent events.

(2.5.2)

These two defining properties of Bernoulli trials were used to derive the binomial probability function above; and thus, whenever these properties are satisfied, the number X of occurrences of event A in a particular number n of trials will be a binomial random variable. Some settings where binomial random variables can sometimes arise in contexts other than sampling with replacement are listed next.

(a) Let X be the number of tails observed in n tosses of a coin.
(b) Let n identical bulbs be turned on and X denote the number still burning at the end of 1,000 hours.
(c) A student answers 20 questions on a true-false test by flipping a coin. Let X be the number of questions answered correctly.
(d) Let X be the number of defective items in a sample of n taken from a production line. Here p is the proportion of defectives, the *fallout,* produced on the line (assuming a stable process).

Example 2.3: Twenty percent of the penlight batteries produced by a certain process are defective. Let X be the number of defective batteries contained in a sample of 15 of these batteries. Evaluate the probability of (a) no defectives, (b) at least two defectives.

Solution: Here $n = 5$ and $p = 1/5$.

(a) $b(x; p, n) = b\left(0; 15, \dfrac{1}{5}\right) = \dbinom{15}{0}(1/5)^0 \, (4/5)^{15} = \underline{0.035}.$

(b) $P(X \geq 2) = 1 - P(X < 2) = 1 - b\left(0; \ 15, \ \frac{1}{5}\right)$

$- b\left(1; \ 15, \frac{1}{5}\right) = 1 - 0.035 - 0.132 = \underline{0.833}.$ ■

Formulas for the mean and variance of the binomial distribution can be derived by straightforward algebraic methods and are as follows.

> If X is a binomial random variable with probability function $b(x; \ n, \ p)$, then $\qquad$ (2.5.3)
> $$E(X) = np, \text{ and } \mathrm{Var}(X) = npq$$

The reader should compare these formulas with those for the hypergeometric distribution given in (2.4.2). It will be observed that the means of the hypergeometric and binomial distributions are the same, and that the variance of the hypergeometric distribution differs from that of the binomial distribution by a factor of $[(N - n)/(N - 1)]$. This factor is called the *finite population correction, fpc,* factor. We now consider how the hypergeometric and binomial distributions are related.

Recall that the hypergeometric probability function $h(x)$ of (2.4.1) was derived as the probability of the number of defectives drawn in a sample of size n from a population of Np defectives and Nq nondefectives, when the sampling is without replacement. The binomial probability function $b(x; \ n, \ p)$ is obtained when the sampling is with replacement. Now, the probability of a defective on the first draw is p if sampling is either with or without replacement. If sampling is with replacement, then the probability of a defective on the second draw is still p; however, if sampling is without replacement, then the probability of a defective on the second draw is $(Np - 1)/(N - 1)$ if a defective was obtained on the first draw, and is $Np/(N - 1)$ if a nondefective was obtained on the first draw. In either case, if the total number of items in the population, N, is large, then the probability of a defective on the second draw is approximately the same as on the first draw, and the same is true for later draws. This means that when N is large, the sequence of drawings is almost a sequence of Bernoulli trials and the probabilities given by the hypergeometric and binomial probability functions are almost the same. In fact, it can be shown that with increasing N the hypergeometric probability function converges to the binomial probability function. We summarize this result in the following.

> For $h(x)$ the hypergeometric probability func-
> tion of (2.4.1), and $b(x; n, p)$ the binomial
> probability function of (2.5.1),
> $$\lim_{N \to \infty} h(x) = b(x; n, p).$$

(2.5.4)

The practical importance of this is that when population size N is large, it makes little difference if sampling is done with or without replacement, since the probabilities given by hypergeometric and binomial probability functions are nearly the same.

Example 2.4: A box of 24 diodes contains 6 defectives. If X is the number of defectives in a sample of 5, find the probability function of X, the probability of at least 2 defectives, and the mean, variance, and standard deviation of X when sampling is: (a) with replacement and (b) without replacement.

Solution: Here $N = 24$, $p = 6/24 = 1/4$, and $n = 5$. Thus

(a) $p(x) = b(x; n, p) = \binom{5}{x} (1/4)^x (3/4)^{5-x}$; $x = 0, 1, 2, 3, 4, 5$.

$P(X \geq 2) = 1 - P(X < 2) = 1 - P(X = 0) - P(X = 1)$,

$= 1 - \binom{5}{0} (1/4)^0 (3/4)^5 - \binom{5}{1} (1/4) (3/4)^4$

$= 1 - 0.237 - 0.396 = \underline{0.367}.$

$\mu = E(X) = np = 5(1/4) = \underline{1.25},$

$\sigma^2 = \text{Var}(X) = npq = 5(1/4)(3/4) = 0.9375, \sigma \doteq \underline{0.968}.$

(b) When sampling is without replacement

$p(x) = \binom{6}{x}\binom{18}{5-x} \Big/ \binom{24}{5}$; $x = 0, 1, 2, 3, 4, 5$.

$P(X \geq 2) = 1 - \binom{6}{0}\binom{18}{5} \Big/ \binom{24}{5} - \binom{6}{1}\binom{18}{4} \Big/ \binom{24}{5}$

$\doteq 1 - 0.202 - 0.432 = \underline{0.366}.$

$\mu = E(X) = np = 5(1/4) = \underline{1.25},$

$$\sigma^2 = \frac{N - n}{N - 1} npq = [(24\ 6)/23]5(1/4)(3/4) \doteq \underline{0.7337},$$

$$\sigma = \underline{0.857}. \qquad\qquad \blacksquare$$

> **The binomial distribution function** at a value x is
>
> $$B(x;\ n,\ p) = 0,\ x < 0$$
>
> $$= \sum_{J=0}^{[x]} b(J;\ n,\ p) \text{ for } 0 \le x < n \qquad (2.5.5)$$
>
> $$= 1,\ x \ge n, \text{ and } [x] \text{ the greatest integer function.}$$

The binomial probability and distribution functions $b(x;\ n,\ p)$ and $B(x;\ n,\ p)$ can be evaluated using the Q-Charts disk.

Example 2.5: Evaluate the probability that a $b(x;\ 100,\ 0.61)$ random variable X takes values below 58 and above 70.

Solution: From the Q-Charts disk

$$P(X < 58) = P(X \le 57) = B(57;\ 100,\ 0.61) = 0.235$$
$$P(X > 70) = 1 - P(X \le 70) = 1 - B(70;\ 100,\ 0.61)$$
$$= 1 - 0.976 = 0.024 \qquad\qquad \blacksquare$$

2.6 THE POISSON DISTRIBUTION

In this section we consider a class of discrete distributions which give convenient approximations to binomial distributions when p is small and n is large and, also, have many important applications in a class of problems that satisfy the conditions of *Poisson processes,* which we also study in this section. The c-charts and u-charts that we will consider in SPC charting for attributes are based on this Poisson distribution, and it is also the distribution used in some important acceptance sampling work. We first define Poisson probability and distribution functions.

Poisson Probability Function:

$$p(x; \lambda) = \frac{\lambda^x e^{-\lambda}}{x!}, \text{ for } x = 0, 1, 2, \cdots; \lambda > 0$$

Poisson Distribution Function:

$$F(x; \lambda) = P(X \le x) = 0, \, x < 0$$

$$= \sum_{J=0}^{[x]} \frac{\lambda^J e^{-\lambda}}{J!}, \text{ for } x \ge 0$$

(2.6.1)

Algorithms to evaluate both of these functions are given on the Q-Charts disk.

If X is a Poisson random variable with probability function $p(x; \lambda)$ of (2.6.1), then

$$E(X) = \lambda \text{ and } \text{Var}(X) = \lambda.$$

(2.6.2)

Next we consider some properties of the Poisson distribution which provide guidance in using this distribution in applied problems. First, we note that under certain conditions the Poisson distribution is approximately a binomial distribution.

If n becomes large and p becomes small while $\lambda = np$ remains constant, then the limiting form of the binomial probability function is a Poisson probability function, that is if $n \to \infty$, $p \to 0$, and $\lambda = np$ is constant, then

$$b(x; n, p) = \binom{n}{x} p^x (1 - p)^{n-x}$$

$$\to \frac{\lambda^x e^{-\lambda}}{x!} \text{ for } x \in \{0, 1, 2, \cdots\}.$$

(2.6.3)

This is important because it shows that for large n and small p the binomial probability function can be approximated by the Poisson probability function.

Example 2.6: The proportion of items made on a production line that do not pass inspection—the "fallout"—is $p = 0.01$. Use both the binomial and Poisson probability functions to evaluate the probabilities that a sample of 50 items will contain (a) exactly one defective item and (b) at least two defectives.

Solution: (a) Binomial: $b(1; 50, 0.01) = \binom{50}{1} (0.01) (0.99)^{49}$
$$\doteq 0.3056.$$
Poisson: $p(1; 0.5) = [(0.5) \, e^{-0.5}/1!] \doteq 0.3033.$
Note the close agreement.
(b) Binomial: Ans. $= 1 - b(0; 50, 0.01) - b(1; 50, 0.01)$
$$= 1 - 0.6050 - 0.3056 = 0.0894.$$
Poisson: Ans. $= 1 - (0.5)^0 e^{-0.05}/(0!) - (0.5)^1 e^{-0.5}/(1!)$
$$= 0.0902.$$
Again, note the closeness of these values. ∎

2.6.1 The Poisson Process

We now consider a setting in which Poisson random variables often occur and that is the basis for many useful applications in engineering and management science. Suppose a process is in operation which gives rise to occurrences of an event at points in time. For example, we can consider the ringing of a telephone or the arrivals of customers at a service counter. Denote by X_t the number of occurrences of the event of interest in the time interval $(0, t)$, and let the interval $(0, t)$ be partitioned into n small subintervals, each of length Δt, as shown in Fig. 2.4.

The random variable X_t is said to be generated by a Poisson process if the following three conditions are satisfied:

(a) The occurrence of the event in any subinterval of the partition of the interval $(0, t)$ is independent of its occurrence in any other nonoverlapping subinterval.
(b) The probability of occurrence of the event in any subinterval (of any length) of $(0, t)$ is proportional to the subinterval length, and this probability is αh for an interval of length h, $0 < h < t$.

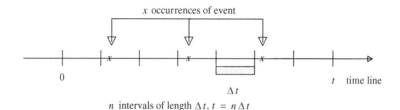

Figure 2.4   Events Occurring in Time

(c) The probability of more than one occurrence of the event in a subinterval of length Δt is negligible—that is, essentially zero.

> If an event that occurs in time satisfies the Poisson process conditions (a), (b), and (c) above, then the total number X_t of occurrences of the event in a time interval of length t is a Poisson random variable with Poisson probability function $p(x; \lambda)$, where $\lambda = \alpha t$, and α is the rate at which the event occurs per unit of time.
>
> (2.6.4)

Example 2.7: A manufacturing station has had an unscheduled work stoppage an average of once every 73 days for several years. This is a phenomenon for which the three conditions for a Poisson process appear to be satisfied, and we will assume that they hold. Let X denote the number of stoppages in a 219-day work year. We evaluate the probability of 0, 1, 2, 3, 4, 5, or 6 stoppages in such a work year, as well as the mean, variance, and standard deviation of X.

Solution: Here we have $\alpha = 1/73$, $t = 219$, and $\lambda = \alpha t = 3$. Then, $p(x; 3) = \dfrac{3^x e^{-3}}{x!}$, and evaluating this function for particular values of x gives the table:

x:	0	1	2	3	4	5	6	>6
$p(x; 3)$:	0.050	0.149	0.224	0.224	0.168	0.101	0.050	0.034

The mean of this distribution is $E(X) = \lambda = 3$, and the variance is $\text{Var}(X) = \lambda = 3$, also. The standard deviation is $S.D.(X) = \sqrt{\lambda} = \sqrt{3} = 1.732$. ■

In the above introduction to the Poisson process, events were considered which occur at points in time. While this is, perhaps, the most important setting, we also consider Poisson processes that occur in relation to variables other than time. Some examples where Poisson processes have been observed include the number of accidents that occur in a t-mile stretch of an interstate highway, and the number of flaws that occur in the insulation of a t-ft. roll of heavy electrical wiring.

Poisson processes can also occur with two- or three-dimensional concomitant variables. For these cases, we consider events that occur at points in an area or in space (three dimensions). Let t denote the total area or volume, and let this area or volume be partitioned into n subareas (volumes) with area (volume) Δt each. The Poisson process conditions (a), (b), and (c) are then imposed on this partition of an area or space.

Example 2.8: A medical supplies manufacturing company is studying retardant properties of a new sterilizing agent applied to surgical gauze. A 10-in. by 20-in. piece of gauze is sterilized by this agent and inspected at the end of one week. If it is known from preliminary research that the mean rate at which spore colonies develop in one week after this treatment is 0.02 per square inch of gauze, find the probability function, mean, and variance of the number X of spore colonies that are observed at the end of one week on this piece of gauze. Evaluate the probability that there will appear at least 8 colonies in a week.

Solution: Here we assume a Poisson process with $\alpha = 0.02$, and t is the total area of 200 square inches. Thus, the Poisson parameter λ is the rate at which colonies appear on the whole piece of gauze, and is $\lambda = (0.02)(200) = 4$. The probability function is

$$p(x; 4) = \frac{4^x e^{-4}}{x!}; x = 0, 1, 2, \cdots;$$

$$= 0, \text{ elsewhere;}$$

and $E(X) = \text{Var}(X) = \lambda = 4$. The probability of at least 8 colonies is, from the Q-Charts disk,

$$P(X \geq 8) = 1 - P(X \leq 7) = 1 - 0.949 = 0.051. \qquad \blacksquare$$

One class of problems with members which sometimes satisfy the Poisson process conditions, and therefore involve Poisson random variables, is known as *queuing* problems. These problems have arrivals as the events of interest, and some examples are the arrivals of customers at the service counter of a department store, or at the check-out counter of a grocery store; the arrivals of planes to land at an airport, or on an aircraft carrier; students arriving during a professor's office hours for help with statistics homework problems, and so on. In each of these cases, if the rate of arrivals exceeds the service rate, then a waiting line or queue will form; hence, the term queuing problems.

Example 2.9: Customers arrive at an automated bank service window at the rate of one every five minutes. What is the probability that between five and twenty, inclusive, customers will arrive in a one-hour period? Assume arrivals constitute a Poisson process.

Solution: Here $\alpha = \dfrac{1}{5}$ and $t = 60$, so that $\lambda = \dfrac{1}{5}(60) = 12$. Thus

$$P(5 \leq X \leq 20) = F(20) - F(4) = 0.988 - 0.008 = 0.980$$

Example 2.10: A machine breaks down, on the average, once in every 1000 hours of operation. This is a phenomenon for which the Poisson process conditions appear to be reasonably well satisfied, and we assume that they hold. Let c denote the number of times the machine will break down in the next month, during 340 hours of scheduled operation. Evaluate the probability of 0, 1, 2, and 3 breakdowns.

Solution: $\lambda = 340/1000 = 0.34$
   The probability function is

$$p(c) = \frac{\lambda^c e^{-\lambda}}{c!} = \frac{(0.34)^c\, e^{-0.34}}{c!}$$

Evaluating this for $c = 0, 1, 2,$ and 3 gives

c:	0	1	2	3
$p(c)$:	0.712	0.242	0.041	0.005

Thus the probability of at least one breakdown in a month of work is approximately

$$1 - p(0) = 0.29 \qquad \blacksquare$$

The Poisson distribution has an important additivity property that is summarized in the following.

2.6.2 Additivity Property of the Poisson Distribution

If X_1, X_2, $\cdots$, X_n are independent Poisson random variables with parameters λ_1, λ_2, $\cdots$, λ_n, respectively, then the sum

$$y = X_1 + X_2 + \cdots + X_n$$

is also a Poisson random variable and has parameter $\lambda = \lambda_1 + \lambda_2 + \cdots + \lambda_n$.

Example 2.11: Suppose that electric meter main boards are inspected for five types of defects that occur at a mean rate per 100 boards as follows: autoinsertion (9.25), solder mask (1.50), manual insertion (6.06), wave solder (2.74), and cleaning (0.46). If y denotes the total number of defects of all five types per 100 boards, then it is reasonable to consider y a Poisson random variable with mean rate (parameter) $\lambda = 9.25 + 1.50 + 6.06 + 2.74 + 0.46 = 20.01$. $\qquad \blacksquare$

2.7 THE NEGATIVE BINOMIAL OR WAITING TIME DISTRIBUTION

Suppose a lot of items contains a proportion p of defectives, and let X denote the total number of items drawn if we sample from the lot with replacement until we have drawn exactly k defectives. Similarly, we might let X denote the number of flips of an honest coin required to obtain exactly $k = 5$ tails; or X could denote the number of calls a salesman makes in order to make $k = 10$ sales. When we consider control charts in later chapters, we can let X denote the number of points plotted on a chart until a signal is observed by having a point fall outside the control limits, provided the events for different points are independent events and the process is stable.

In general, let X denote the number of Bernoulli trials required for an event A to occur exactly k times. Let $P(A) = p$, $P(A^c) = 1 - p =$

q, and we require the probability function $p(x) = P(X = x)$. It is apparent that the possible values are $x = k, k + 1, \cdots$. The probability function can be obtained as follows (see Fig. 2.5).

In order for the kth occurrence of A to be on the xth trial, we must have $(k - 1)$ occurrences of A in the first $(x - 1)$ trials, and then A must occur on trial x. The probability of $(k - 1)$ A's in $(x - 1)$ trials is $\binom{x - 1}{k - 1} p^{k-1} q^{x-k}$, and the probability of an A on trial x is p. Thus, since these two events are independent, the probability of the kth occurrence of A on the xth trial is the product of these probabilities, and is called the *negative binomial* or *Pascal* probability function.

Negative Binomial or Pascal Probability Function:

$$p(x) = \binom{x - 1}{k - 1} p^k q^{x-k}, \qquad (2.7.1)$$

for $x = k, k + 1, \cdots$

Example 2.12: If 20% of the items produced on a production line are defective, find the probability function for the number of items that must be inspected to find two defectives.

Solution: For X = number of trials

$$p(x) = P(X = x) = \binom{x - 1}{k - 1} p^k (1 - p)^{x-k}$$

$$= \binom{x - 1}{1} (0.2)^2 (0.8)^{x-2},$$

$$\Rightarrow p(x) = \binom{x - 1}{1} (0.04) (0.8)^{x-2} = (x - 1)(0.8)^x / 16 \text{ for}$$

$$x = 2, 3, \cdots. \qquad \blacksquare$$

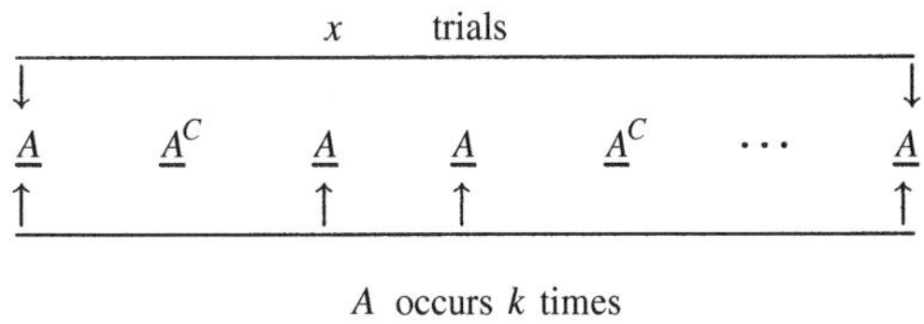

Figure 2.5 Bernoulli Trials for a Negative Binomial Random Variable

---

If X is a random variable with the negative binomial probability function $p(x)$ of (2.7.1), then

$$E(X) = \frac{k}{p}, \quad \text{Var}(X) = \frac{kq}{p^2},$$

$$SD(X) = \frac{\sqrt{k(1-p)}}{p}$$

(2.7.2)

We call attention to the behavior of the mean and the variance of a negative binomial random variable as the probability p varies over its range, $0 < p < 1$. The mean $\mu = k/p$ and variance $\sigma^2 = kq/p^2$ have derivatives

$$\frac{d\mu}{dp} = \frac{-k}{p^2} \text{ and } \frac{d(\sigma^2)}{dp} = \frac{k}{p^2}\left(1 - \frac{2}{p}\right)$$

and both derivatives are negative for $0 < p < 1$. The mean and variance of a negative binomial are both therefore decreasing functions of p. Consider this point for the mean, and we see that is indeed what we should expect, since if the probability p of event A on each trial increases, then the mean number of trials required to obtain k occurrences of event A should decrease.

Example 2.13: Find the mean and standard deviation of the number X of items inspected to find two defectives in Example 2.12.

Solution: Here $k = 2$ and $p = 1/5$, so

$$E(X) = \frac{k}{p} = \frac{2}{1/5} = 10, \ S.D.(X) = \sqrt{\frac{kq}{p^2}} = \sqrt{40} \doteq 2.62. \quad \blacksquare$$

The **negative binomial distribution function** is given by

$$NB(x; k, p) = P(X \leq x)$$
$$= 0, \quad x < k,$$
$$= \sum_{J=k}^{[x]} \binom{J-1}{k-1} p^k (1-p)^{J-k}$$
$$\text{for } x \geq k,$$

(2.7.3)

where $[x]$ is the greatest integer in x.

An algorithm for this distribution function is given on the Q-Charts disk.

Example 2.14: A company gives a standard test to all employment applicants, and 80% of the applicants pass this test. If four new employees are to be hired, let X denote the number of applicants that must be tested. Find the probability function $p(x)$, distribution function $F(x)$, mean, and s.d. of X. Make a bar graph of $p(x)$, a graph of $F(x)$, and discuss this selection problem.

Solution: Here X is a negative binomial random variable with $k = 4$, and $p = 0.8$. Then

$$p(x) = P(X = x) = \binom{x-1}{k-1} p^k (1-p)^{x-k}$$
$$= \binom{x-1}{3} (0.8)^4 (0.2)^{x-4}; \quad x = 4, 5, \cdots .$$

We evaluate a few terms in order to make a bar graph of $p(x)$.

x:	4	5	6	7	8	>8
$p(x)$:	0.41	0.33	0.16	0.07	0.02	0.01
$F(x)$:	0.41	0.74	0.90	0.97	0.99	—

The mean and s.d. are

$$E(X) = (k/p) = (4/0.8) = 5, \quad S.D.(X) = \sqrt{k(1 - p)/p^2}$$
$$= \sqrt{4(0.2)/(0.8)^2} \doteq 1.12$$

We observe that it will probably be necessary to test from four to eight applicants. Note that here the distribution function is particularly meaningful since it tells us the probability that the required four passes are obtained at least by the xth trial. For example, the probability that no more than six people will have to be tested is 0.90. The graphs of the probability and distribution functions are as follows:

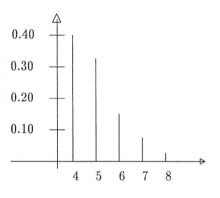

Probability Function

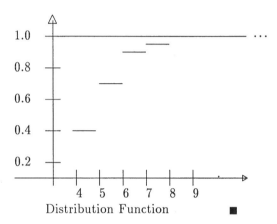

Distribution Function ∎

Example 2.15: A production process produces 1% defective units. Once each day, consecutively produced units are inspected until five defectives are found. Evaluate the probability that no more than x units will be inspected on a given day for $x = 100(100)1000$. (Read the notation $100(100)1000$ as "x equals 100 to 1000 in steps of 100.")

Solution: From the Q-Charts disk read $P(X \le 100) = NB(100; 5, 0.01) = 0.0034$, and so on.

x:	100	200	300	400	500	600	700	800	900	1000
$P(X \le x)$:	0.003	0.052	0.186	0.371	0.562	0.717	0.827	0.899	0.943	0.969

∎

2.7.1   The Geometric Distribution

Consider again the general setting above for a negative binomial random variable for the special case when $k = 1$. Then the random variable

X is the number of trials required to observe the *first* occurrence of the event A of interest. This special case of a negative binomial distribution is called a *geometric* distribution; and X is a *geometric* random variable. Geometric random variables occur frequently in quality control, and we will consider some of their special features here. By putting $k = 1$ in (2.7.1) and (2.7.2), we obtain the following.

Geometric Probability Function:

$$g(x;p) = pq^{x-1}; x = 1, 2, \cdots$$

Mean and Variance: (2.7.4)

$$\mu = E(X) = 1/p, \text{Var}(X) = q/p^2,$$
$$\sigma = SD(X) = \sqrt{1 - p}/p = \sqrt{\mu(\mu - 1)}$$

Note that this is a one-parameter family and that the standard deviation σ is a function of the mean μ. The distribution function for the geometric random variable X of (2.7.4) has a particularly convenient form, which we now consider. We first evaluate the distribution function of X at any positive integer x. That is, for $x = 1, 2, \cdots$,

$$G(x) = P(X \le x) = \sum_{J=1}^{x} pq^{J-1} = p\{1 + q + q^2 + \cdots + q^{x-1}\}$$

$$= p(1 - q^x)/(1 - q) = 1 - q^x$$

Notice, particularly, that we have summed a *geometric series* in this development, and this is why the distribution is called a geometric distribution. Note also that $x \to \infty$ implies $G(x) \to 1$. We summarize this result in the following.

The geometric probability function of (2.7.4) has corresponding distribution function

$$G(x;p) = P(X \le x) = 0, \text{ for } x < 1$$ (2.7.5)

$$= 1 - q^{[x]} \text{ for } x \ge 1$$

Example 2.16: If a production line produces 10% defectives, and if X denotes the number of items inspected until the first defective is found, then evaluate:

(a) $P(X \leq 10)$
(b) $P(X < 20)$
(c) $P(4 \leq X \leq 15)$

Solution:

(a) $P(X \leq 10) = G(10) = 1 - (1 - p)^{10} = 1 - (0.9)^{10} \doteq 0.65$
(b) $P(X < 20) = P(X \leq 19) = F(19) = 1 - (0.9)^{19} \doteq 0.865$
(c) $P(4 \leq X \leq 15) = G(15) - G(3) = 1 - (0.9)^{15} - [1 - (0.9)^3]$
    $= (0.9)^3 - (0.9)^{15} \doteq 0.523.$ ∎

2.8 THE NORMAL DISTRIBUTION

When observations are made on a continuous variable, such as the diameter of ball bearings or the percentage of a component in a chemical compound, then the theoretical reference distribution is a continuous distribution that is defined by a probability density function. An especially important continuous reference distribution is the normal distribution with probability density function given by (2.8.1). A graph of a normal density function is shown in Fig. 2.6.

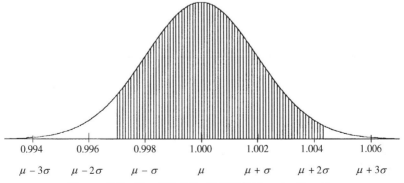

Figure 2.6 The $N(1.000, [0.002]^2)$ Density Function

A random variable X has a **normal distribution,** write $N(\mu, \sigma^2)$, if it has density function

$$f(x; \mu, \sigma^2) = \frac{1}{\sigma\sqrt{2\pi}} e^{-\frac{1}{2}[(x-\mu)/\sigma]^2},$$ (2.8.1)

$$-\infty < x < \infty$$

and $-\infty < \mu < \infty$, $\sigma^2 > 0$.

This normal density function has two parameters: μ and σ. The distribution mean is μ and σ is the distribution standard deviation. We often use the notation $N(\mu, \sigma^2)$ to refer to a normal random variable or distribution. In particular, suppose we know that the diameter X (measured in units of cm) of a randomly chosen ball bearing is a $N(1.000, [0.002]^2)$ random variable. The density function of this $N(1.000, [0.002]^2)$ distribution is shown in Fig. 2.6. The graph of the normal density function given by equation (2.8.1) is the famous bell-shaped curve. The probability that a random variable with this density function will fall between two points is given by the area under this curve between the two points. For example, the probability that a randomly chosen ball bearing will have a diameter between 0.9970 and 1.0044 is shown by the shaded area under the curve in Figure 2.6.

We now review some important properties of normal distributions. First, note that linear functions of normal random variables are also normal random variables, as stated in the following.

If $X_1, \cdots, X_n$ are normal random variables, independent or dependent, then any linear function of these random variables, say

$$Y = a_0 + a_1 X_1 + \cdots + a_n X_n$$ (2.8.2)

is itself a normal random variable.

In particular, the distribution of any linear function of *independent* normal random variables is completely determined, as given in the following display.

> If $X_1, \cdots, X_n$ are independent random variables with X_i a $N(\mu_i, \sigma_i^2)$ random variable for $i = 1, \cdots, n$; then $Y = a_0 + a_1X_1 + \cdots + a_nX_n$ is a $N(a_0 + a_1\mu_1 + \cdots + a_n\mu_n, a_1^2\sigma_1^2 + \cdots + a_n^2\sigma_n^2)$ random variable.   (2.8.3)

Data taken for use in quality control will frequently satisfy the conditions for the central limit theorem. This means that, *even if the process distribution is not itself a normal distribution,* the mean of a sample from it will still be approximately normal. This result is at the heart of much of the work in classical SPC charting, as we shall see in later chapters.

The normal distribution with mean $\mu = 0$ and variance $\sigma^2 = 1$, that is, the $N(0, 1)$ distribution, plays an especially important role in applications of normal distributions. This $N(0, 1)$ distribution is called the *standard normal* distribution. If X is a $N(\mu, \sigma^2)$ random variable, then consider

$$Z = \frac{X - \mu}{\sigma}$$

Since $E(Z) = 0$ and $Var(Z) = 1$, we see that Z is itself a standard normal random variable. Now, suppose we wish to evaluate the probability that a $N(\mu, \sigma^2)$ random variable X is between a and b. Then

$$P(a \leq X \leq b) = P\{(a - \mu)/\sigma \leq (X - \mu)/\sigma \leq (b - \mu)/\sigma\}$$
$$= P\{(a - \mu)/\sigma \leq Z \leq (b - \mu)/\sigma\}$$

> If X is a $N(\mu, \sigma^2)$ random variable, then
>
> $$P(a \leq X \leq b) = P[(a - \mu)/\sigma < Z$$
> $$< (b - \mu)/\sigma]$$
>
> where Z is a $N(0, 1)$ random variable.   (2.8.4)

Due to (2.8.4), the $N(0, 1)$ distribution plays an important role in evaluating probabilities of events for all normal distributions. Thus, it is especially important to be able to evaluate the probability that a $N(0, 1)$ random variable is in a particular interval. The $N(0, 1)$ distribution is of such importance that we reserve the letter Z to denote a $N(0, 1)$ random variable throughout this book. The distribution function of Z is denoted by

$$\Phi(z) \equiv P(Z \le z) = \frac{1}{\sqrt{2\pi}} \int_{-\infty}^{z} e^{-z^2/2} \, dz \qquad (2.8.5)$$

and the symbol Φ (uppercase Greek phi) will be used to denote only this distribution function in this book. To evaluate the probability of any interval (a, b) under the standard normal density, we have

$$P(a \le Z \le b) = \frac{1}{\sqrt{2\pi}} \int_{a}^{b} e^{-z^2/2} \, dz = \Phi(b) - \Phi(a) \qquad (2.8.6)$$

A graph of the standard normal distribution function is shown in Fig. 2.7. Note that this function maps every point z on the horizontal axis to a point $u = \Phi(z)$ with $0 < u < 1$. For example, as shown on the graph, the point $z = 1.288$ is taken to the point $u = 0.9$. The distribution function $\Phi(z)$ cannot be expressed in a simple form, and either a table, electronic calculator, or computer algorithm is needed to evaluate it. Table A.1 in the Appendix gives values of $\Phi(z)$ for z taking values between -3.99 and 3.99 in steps of 0.01. An algorithm to eval-

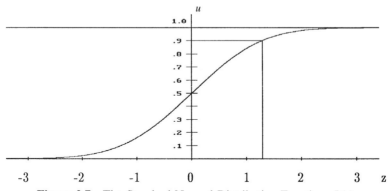

Figure 2.7   The Standard Normal Distribution Function, $\Phi(z)$

uate $\Phi(z)$ is given on the Q-Charts disk. From the symmetry of the density of Z about zero, it is apparent that $\Phi(-z) = 1 - \Phi(z)$.

If we consider a point u in the interval $0 < u < 1$ on the vertical axis, then the curve of Fig. 2.7 can also be used to map this point to a point on the horizontal axis. The curve used this way is called the *inverse normal* distribution function and denoted by $z = \Phi^{-1}(u)$. The Q-Charts disk has an algorithm to evaluate the inverse normal distribution function. For $0 < u < 1$, this inverse normal distribution function is the value that has probability u below it. The following examples illustrate some types of computations related to normal distributions.

Example 2.17: We use the relations in (2.8.4) and (2.8.6) to evaluate the probability between 0.9970 and 1.0044 under a $N(1.000, [0.002]^2)$ curve. This is the shaded area of Fig. 2.6. We have

$$P(0.9970 \leq X \leq 1.0044)$$
$$= P\left(\frac{0.9970 - 1.000}{0.002} \leq Z \leq \frac{1.0044 - 1.000}{.002}\right)$$
$$= P(-1.5 \leq Z \leq 2.2) = \Phi(2.2) - \Phi(-1.5)$$
$$= 0.98610 - 0.06681 = 0.91929 \qquad \blacksquare$$

Example 2.18: The percentage of a pollutant in the liquid discharged from an industrial plant into a river is a normal random variable with mean $\mu = 1.5$ and variance $\sigma^2 = 0.04$. What is the probability that one specimen will show more than 2% of this pollutant?

Solution: Let X denote the amount in one specimen, and we have

$$P(X > 2) = P[(X - 1.5)/0.2 > (2 - 1.5)/0.2]$$
$$= P(Z > 2.5) = 1 - \Phi(2.5)$$
$$= 1 - 0.9938 = \underline{0.0062} \qquad \blacksquare$$

In our work in later chapters, we shall frequently use percentage points of the $N(0, 1)$ distribution. If Z is a $N(0, 1)$ random variable, then the value z_α $(0 < \alpha < 1)$ that satisfies the equation

$$P(Z > z_\alpha) = \alpha \qquad (2.8.7)$$

is called either the $(1 - \alpha)^{\text{th}}$ fractile, the $100(1 - \alpha)^{\text{th}}$ percentile, or the upper $100\alpha^{th}$ percentage point of the standard normal distribution. Values of z_α can be evaluated approximately by interpolation in Table A.1 of the standard normal distribution function. Also, the normal inverse distribution function on the Q-Charts disk can be used to evaluate z_α, since

$$z_\alpha = \Phi^{-1}(1 - \alpha) \tag{2.8.7}'$$

Figure 2.8 shows the point z_α that cuts off α of the area under the density above it.

Example 2.19: Use the normal table or the inverse normal distribution function to evaluate: $z_{.025}$, $z_{.01}$, $z_{.05}$, and $z_{.95}$.

Solution: From the table we read $z_{0.025} = 1.96$. From the inverse normal algorithm we obtain

$$z_{0.01} = 2.326,\ z_{0.05} = 1.645,\ z_{0.95} = -1.645 \qquad \blacksquare$$

2.9 NORMAL SAMPLING DISTRIBUTIONS: CHI-SQUARED, STUDENT-t, AND F DISTRIBUTIONS

In Chapter 3 we will consider samples from normal distributions and define a number of sample statistics that will be used in later work in quality improvement. The distributions of statistics computed from samples are called *sampling distributions*. Next we present three important sampling distributions of statistics computed from samples from normal distributions. We first define and study briefly an impor-

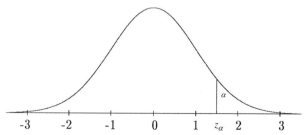

Figure 2.8 The z_α Point of a $N(0, 1)$ Density Function

tant mathematical function which is used to define the distributions of this section. The *gamma function*, $\Gamma(p)$, is defined for all $p > 0$ by

$$\Gamma(p) = \int_0^\infty x^{p-1} e^{-x} \, dx$$

It follows that $\Gamma(1) = 1$, and integrating the last integral once by parts shows that $\Gamma(p + 1) = p\Gamma(p)$. In particular, for n a positive integer

$$\Gamma(n + 1) = n\Gamma(n) = n(n - 1)\Gamma(n - 1)$$
$$= \cdots = n(n - 1) \cdots (2)(1) = n!$$

Thus, we see that the gamma function is essentially a generalization of the factorial function to the domain of all positive numbers. These results are summarized in display (2.9.1).

For $p > 0$, the *gamma function* is defined by

(i) $\Gamma(p) = \int_0^\infty x^{p-1} e^{-x} \, dx$, and satisfies

(ii) $(p + 1)\,p\Gamma(p)$,

(iii) $\Gamma(n + 1) = n!$, when n is a positive integer.

(2.9.1)

It can also be shown that $\Gamma\left(\dfrac{1}{2}\right) = \sqrt{\pi}$.

2.9.1 The Chi-Squared Distribution

We consider first the distribution of a random variable that is often denoted by the symbol χ_ν^2, read: "chi-squared with nu degrees of freedom." We summarize in (2.9.2) the basic properties of the chi-squared distribution.

A χ^2_ν random variable Y has

Density Function:

$$g_\nu(y) = \frac{y^{\nu/2-1}e^{-y/2}}{2^{\nu/2}\Gamma(\nu/2)}, \, y > 0,$$

$$= 0, \, y \le 0.$$

Distribution Function:

$$P(Y \le y) = G_\nu(y) = \int_0^y g_\nu(x) \, dx$$

$$\text{for } y \ge 0$$

Mean and Variance: $E(Y) = \nu$, $\text{Var}(Y) = 2\nu$

(2.9.2)

Note that a chi-squared random variable takes only positive values. The density function of a χ^2_5 random variable is shown in Fig. 2.9. Note especially that this density function is not symmetric. This asymmetry of chi-squared distributions will have important implications in our work in control charting to control process variances. The distribution function of a chi-squared random variable can be evaluated us-

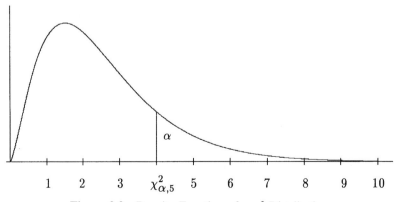

Figure 2.9 Density Function of a χ^2_5 Distribution

ing the distribution function on the Q-Charts disk. The $100(1 - \alpha)^{\underline{th}}$ percentile or $(1 - \alpha)^{\underline{th}}$ fractile is denoted by $\chi^2_{\alpha,\nu}$ and is defined by

$$P\{\chi^2_\nu > \chi^2_{\alpha,\nu}\} = \alpha \qquad\qquad (2.9.3)$$

This is the value that cuts off probability α above it under the chi-squared density function—see Fig. 2.9. Table A.2 gives values of $\chi^2_{\alpha,\nu}$ for selected values of α and $\nu = 1(1)30$. The inverse chi-squared distribution function can also be used to evaluate $\chi^2_{\nu,\alpha}$. An algorithm for the inverse chi-squared distribution function is also given on the Q-Charts disk.

Example 2.20: Use Table A.2 or the Q-Charts disk to evaluate each of the following quantities: $\chi^2_{0.05,10}$, $\chi^2_{0.90,30}$, $P\{\chi^2_{10} > 23.21\}$, $P\{\chi^2_{20} \le 8.26\}$.

Solution: $\chi^2_{0.05,10} = 18.31$, $\chi^2_{0.90,30} = 20.60$, $P\{\chi^2_{10} > 23.21\} = 0.01$,

$$P\{\chi^2_{20} \le 8.26\} = 1 - 0.99 = 0.01 \qquad\blacksquare$$

If the degrees of freedom ν are large, we can make use of the following approximation to obtain significance points of the chi-squared distribution. If Y is a χ^2_ν random variable, and ν is reasonably large ($\nu \ge 30$ is large enough for most purposes, and even smaller values will suffice in many cases), then $\sqrt{2Y} - \sqrt{2\nu - 1}$ is approximately a $N(0, 1)$ random variable (Fisher 1922), and, moreover

$$P(Y \le \chi^2_{\alpha,\nu}) = P(\sqrt{2Y} - \sqrt{2\nu - 1} \le \sqrt{2\,\chi^2_{\alpha,\nu}} - \sqrt{2\nu - 1}) = 1 - \alpha$$
$$\doteq P(Z \le \sqrt{2\,\chi^2_{\alpha,\nu}} - \sqrt{2\nu - 1})$$

which implies

$$z_\alpha \doteq \sqrt{2\,\chi^2_{\alpha,\nu}} - \sqrt{2\nu - 1}$$

and
$$\chi^2_{\alpha,\nu} \doteq \tfrac{1}{2}(z_\alpha + \sqrt{2\nu - 1})^2$$

Here z_α is the $(1 - \alpha)^{\text{th}}$ fractile of the $N(0, 1)$ distribution defined in (2.8.7) or (2.8.7)'.

$$\boxed{\begin{array}{c} \text{For } \nu \text{ large (say} \geq 30) \\ \chi^2_{\alpha,\nu} \doteq \tfrac{1}{2}(z_\alpha + \sqrt{2\nu - 1})^2 \end{array}} \qquad (2.9.4)$$

Example 2.21: Evaluate $\chi^2_{0.025,55}$.

Solution: $\chi^2_{0.025,55} = \tfrac{1}{2}(z_{0.025} + \sqrt{109})^2 = \tfrac{1}{2}(1.96 + \sqrt{109})^2 = \underline{76.88}$

From the Q-Charts disk we get $\chi^2_{0.025,55} = G_{55}^{-1}(0.975) = \underline{77.38}$

While these two values differ by 0.5, we note that the actual probability above 76.88 is 0.027, so that the value from the normal approximation may be considered adequate for many purposes.   ∎

We now state some properties of chi-squared random variables, which will be useful for reference in later applications of statistics to quality problems.

$$\boxed{\begin{array}{l} \text{1. If } Z \text{ is a } N(0, 1) \text{ random variable, then } Z^2 \\ \quad \text{is a } \chi^2(1) \text{ random variable.} \\ \text{2. If } \chi^2_{\nu_1} \text{ and } \chi^2_{\nu_2} \text{ are independent chi-squared} \\ \quad \text{random variables, then the sum } \chi^2_{\nu_1} + \\ \quad \chi^2_{\nu_2} \text{ is itself a } \chi^2_{\nu_1+\nu_2} \text{ random variable.} \\ \quad \text{By combining these two results, we have} \\ \quad \text{the following:} \\ \text{3. If } Z_1, \cdots, Z_n \text{ are independent } N(0, 1) \text{ ran-} \\ \quad \text{dom variables, then } Q = Z_1^2 + \cdots + Z_n^2 \\ \quad \text{is a } \chi^2_n \text{ random variable.} \end{array}} \qquad (2.9.5)$$

2.9.2 The Student-*t* Distribution

Definition:

If Y is a χ^2_ν random variable and Z is an independent $N(0, 1)$ random variable, then

$$T = \frac{Z}{\sqrt{\dfrac{Y}{\nu}}}$$

is a *Student-t* random variable with ν *degrees of freedom,* and has

(2.9.6)

Density Function:

$$h_\nu(t) = \frac{\Gamma[(\nu + 1)/2]}{\Gamma(\nu/2)\sqrt{\nu\pi}} \left(1 + \frac{t^2}{\nu}\right)^{-(\nu+1)/2},$$

Distribution Function:

$$P(T \le t) = H_\nu(t) = \int_{-\infty}^{t} h_\nu(x)\, dx$$

for $-\infty < t < \infty$.

We sometimes denote a Student-*t* random variable by T_ν if we wish to specifically note the value of the degrees of freedom parameter. It is readily seen that the density function satisfies $h(-t) = h(t)$ and is therefore a symmetric function about zero. Figure 2.10 shows the densities of two Student-*t* distributions and a $N(0, 1)$ density. The density of a Student-*t* random variable is similar in shape to that of a $N(0, 1)$ density; however, it is lower at zero and has thicker tails. As ν increases, the density function of a T_ν random variable tends to a $N(0, 1)$ density.

We have previously defined α significance points z_α and $\chi^2_{\alpha,\nu}$ of normal and chi-squared distributions. The $100(1 - \alpha)^{\text{th}}$ percentile, or

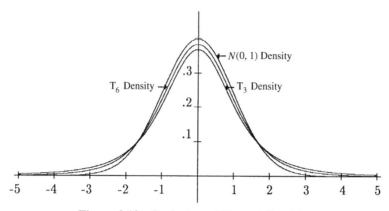

Figure 2.10   Student-t and Normal Densities

$(1 - \alpha)^{\text{th}}$ fractile of the distribution of a Student-t random variable, T_ν say, is denoted by $t_{\alpha,\nu}$ and satisfies

$$P\{T_\nu > t_{\alpha,\nu}\} = 1 - P\{T_\nu \leq t_{\alpha,\nu}\} = 1 - H(t_{\alpha,\nu}) = \alpha \quad (2.9.7)$$

The significance point $t_{\alpha,\nu}$ is shown in the graph of Fig. 2.11. As for normal distributions, the symmetry of the density function implies a relationship between upper and lower fractiles. The point that cuts off probability α *below* it is $t_{1-\alpha,\nu} = -t_{\alpha,\nu}$. The Q-Charts disk has algo-

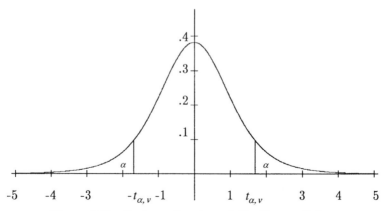

Figure 2.11   Student-t Density and Significance Points

rithms to evaluate the distribution function and inverse distribution function of the Student-t distribution. The inverse distribution function can be used to evaluate the fractiles of the distribution. The relationship is

$$t_{\alpha,\nu} = H_\nu^{-1}(1 - \alpha) \tag{2.9.8}$$

Values of $t_{\alpha,\nu}$ are given in Table A.3 for selected values of α and ν. The use of Table A.3 and the Q-Charts disk algorithms is illustrated in the following example.

Example 2.22: The Student-t Distribution

(a) From Table A.3 we read: $t_{0.10,10} = 1.372$, $t_{0.25,5} = 0.727$, $t_{0.01,20} = 2.528$, and $t_{0.99,20} = -t_{0.01,20} = -2.528$

(b) By using the Q-Charts disk algorithm for the Student-t distribution function we evaluate:

$$P(T_8 \leq 2.1) = 0.966, \; P(T_{12} \leq -1.5) = 0.080, \; P(T_9 > 1)$$
$$= 1 - P(T_9 \leq 1) = 1 - 0.828 = 0.172$$

(c) By using the Q-Charts disk algorithm for the inverse Student-t distribution function we evaluate:

$$t_{.03,5} = H_5^{-1}(.97) = 2.951,$$
$$t_{.94,10} = H_{10}^{-1}(.06) = -1.700,$$
$$t_{.32,20} = H_{20}^{-1}(.32) = -0.475 \qquad \blacksquare$$

2.9.3   The Snedecor-*F* Distribution

If Y and W are independent $\chi^2_{\nu_1}$ and $\chi^2_{\nu_2}$ random variables, respectively, then

$$F = \frac{Y/\nu_1}{W/\nu_2},$$

is a *Snedecor-F* random variable with ν_1 and ν_2 *degrees of freedom*, and has

Density Function:

$$h(f) = \frac{\Gamma\left(\dfrac{\nu_1 + \nu_2}{2}\right)\left(\dfrac{\nu_1}{\nu_2}\right)^{\nu_1/2} f^{\nu_1/2-1}}{\Gamma\left(\dfrac{\nu_1}{2}\right)\Gamma\left(\dfrac{\nu_2}{2}\right)\left[\dfrac{\nu_1}{\nu_2}f + 1\right]^{(\nu_1+\nu_2)/2}},$$

(2.9.9)

Distribution Function:

$$H_{\nu_1,\nu_2}(f) = \int_{-\infty}^{f} h(x)\, dx, \text{ both for } 0 < f < \infty.$$

The Snedecor-*F* distribution depends on the values of the parameters ν_1 and ν_2, and to note this dependence we frequently denote a random variable with this distribution by F_{ν_1,ν_2}. The density function $h(f)$ of this random variable is a nonsymmetric density on the positive numbers. Its shape is similar to that of the chi-squared density function shown in Fig. 2.9. The $100(1 - \alpha)^{th}$ percentile, or the $(1 - \alpha)^{th}$ fractile, is denoted by $F_{\alpha;\nu_1,\nu_2}$ and satisfies

$$P(F_{\nu_1,\nu_2} > F_{\alpha;\nu_1,\nu_2}) = \alpha, \ 0 < \alpha < 1 \qquad (2.9.10)$$

Table A.4 gives significance points $F_{\alpha;\nu_1,\nu_2}$ for $\alpha = 0.005, 0.025, 0.05,$ and 0.10 and selected values of ν_1 and ν_2. These are the values that are most often used. We can also obtain the lower $0.005, 0.025, 0.05,$ and 0.10 significance points from Table A.4 and the following relationship. If Y is an F_{ν_1,ν_2} random variable, then from (2.9.9) it is apparent that $(1/Y)$ is itself an F_{ν_2,ν_1} random variable. Thus for this reciprocal of Y we have

$$P(Y^{-1} < F^{-1}_{\alpha;\nu_1,\nu_2}) = P(Y > F_{\alpha;\nu_1,\nu_2}) = \alpha$$

or $P(Y^{-1} > F^{-1}_{\alpha;\nu_1,\nu_2}) = 1 - \alpha$. But the value $F_{1-\alpha;\nu_1,\nu_2}$ is a unique value of b that satisfies the equation: $P(Y^{-1} > b) = 1 - \alpha$, and so we have the important relation

$$F_{1-\alpha;\nu_2,\nu_1} = \frac{1}{F_{\alpha;\nu_1,\nu_2}}, \text{ for } 0 < \alpha < 1 \qquad (2.9.11)$$

that we use to find lower percentage points from upper ones.

The Q-Charts disk has algorithms to evaluate both the distribution function and the inverse distribution function for an F distribution. We illustrate using these algorithms in the following example.

Example 2.23: The Snedecor-F Distribution

(a) From Table A.4 we read:

$$F_{0.10;5,15} = 2.27, \quad F_{0.05;10,6} = 3.22,$$
$$F_{0.90;15,5} = 1/F_{0.10;5,15} = 1/2.27 = 0.441$$

(b) From the Q-Charts disk F distribution function algorithm we obtain:

$$P(F_{7,11} \leq 1.95) = 0.845, \quad P(F_{2,3} \leq 2.30) = 0.753$$
$$P(F_{4,6} > 2.64) = 1 - P(F_{4,6} \leq 2.64) = 1 - 0.861 = 0.139$$

(c) From the Q-Charts disk inverse F distribution function algorithm we obtain:

$$F_{.12;4,6} = H^{-1}_{4,6}(.88) = 2.872,$$
$$F_{.93;8,9} = H^{-1}_{8,9}(.07) = 0.337,$$
$$F_{.40;4,7} = H^{-1}_{4,7}(.60) = 1.171 \qquad \blacksquare$$

2.10 THE EXPONENTIAL DISTRIBUTION

In this section we consider a family of continuous distributions that is probably second only to the normal family in general importance in applied statistics.

A random variable with density function

$$f(x) = \alpha e^{-\alpha x}, \, x > 0, \, \alpha > 0$$
$$= 0, \, x \le 0 \qquad (2.10.1)$$

is an *exponential* random variable, write $EX(\alpha)$.

The distribution function for an $EX(\alpha)$ random variable is

$$F(x; \alpha) = \alpha \int_0^x e^{-\alpha y} \, dy = -e^{-\alpha y}\big|_{y=0}^{y=x} = 1 - e^{-\alpha x} \text{ if } x > 0,$$

and $F(x) = 0$ if $x \le 0$. The mean and variance of an $EX(\alpha)$ distribution can be obtained readily by integration. The results are summarized in display (2.10.2).

An $EX(\alpha)$ random variable X has
(i) **Distribution function:**

$$F(x) = 0, \, x \le 0$$
$$= 1 - e^{-\alpha x}, \, x > 0 \qquad (2.10.2)$$

(ii) **Mean and variance:**

$$E(X) = \frac{1}{\alpha}, \, \text{Var}(X) = \frac{1}{\alpha^2}$$

Graphs of the density and distribution functions of an $EX(\alpha)$ random variable are given in Fig. 2.12.

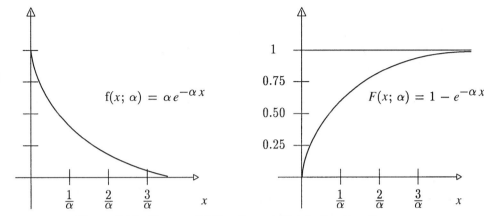

Figure 2.12 Exponential Density and Distribution Functions

One important setting where the exponential distribution appears, and will be basic to some of our work in SPC, is in connection with Poisson processes (see section 2.6). Consider a Poisson process operating in time t with average rate of occurrence α of the event of interest per unit of time. Then the probability of no occurrences of the event from time zero ($t = 0$) for a period of t time units is given by a Poisson probability function evaluated at zero, that is, it is given by

$$\frac{(\alpha t)^0 e^{-\alpha t}}{0!} = e^{-\alpha t}$$

Next, let the continuous random variable T denote the time elapsed until the first occurrence of the event. Then T will exceed a particular value t if and only if there are no occurrences of the event before t. Thus we have it that

$$P(T > t) = e^{-\alpha t}$$

and the distribution function of the continuous random variable T is

$$F(t) = P(T \le t) = 1 - e^{-\alpha t}, \, \alpha > 0, \, t > 0$$

The density function of T is

$$f(t) = \frac{dF(t)}{dt} = \alpha e^{-\alpha t}, \, \alpha > 0, \, t > 0$$

This is the density function $f(x)$ of (2.10.1). This result will be particularly useful for establishing charting methods for some processes that can be modeled as Poisson processes in time. In Chapter 7 we will consider using the exponential distribution associated with Poisson processes to establish control charting procedures such as outbreaks of nosocomial infections in hospitals, machine breakdowns, and other processes where Poisson process assumptions appear reasonable but the Poisson rate α is small.

Example 2.24: A certain type of light bulb has an exponential failure distribution with mean life of $\theta = 3{,}000$ hours. Suppose that 100 of these bulbs are installed in a building and left burning continuously.

(a) What is the probability that a particular one of these bulbs will be burning at the end of 3,000 hours?

(b) What is the expected number of bulbs that will be burning at the end of n hours? Evaluate this mean for $n = 1000$; 3000; 6000; 8000.

(c) What is the probability that at least 40 bulbs will be burning at the end of 3000 hours?

Solution:

(a) Let X denote the life length of the bulb in question. Then

$$P(X > 3000) = 1 - P(X \leq 3000) = 1 - (1 - e^{-3000/3000})$$
$$= e^{-1} \doteq 0.3679$$

(b) Let W denote the number of bulbs burning at the end of n hours. Then W is a binomial random variable with a $b(w;\ 100,\ e^{-n/3000})$ probability function. Thus

$$E(W) = (100)e^{-n/3000}$$

n:	1,000	3,000	6,000	8,000
$E(W)$:	72	37	14	7

(c) Let W be as in part (b) with $n = 3000$.

$$E(W) = 36.79, \ \text{Var}(W) = (100)e^{-1}(1 - e^{-1}) = 23.35,$$
$$S.D.(W) = 4.82.$$

$$P(W \geq 40) = P\left(\frac{W - 36.79}{4.82} \leq \frac{39.5 - 36.79}{4.82}\right) = P(Z \geq 0.56)$$
$$= 1 - P(Z \leq 0.56) = 1 - 0.7123 = 0.2877$$

By using the binomial df on the Q-Charts disk we obtain

$$P(W \geq 40) = 1 - P(W \leq 39) = 1 - 0.71496 = 0.2850 \quad \blacksquare$$

Example 2.25: The *reliability function R_t* of a system or a component is the probability that the system or component lasts to time t. Suppose component A has exponential life with mean life 1000 hours and component B has exponential life with mean life 1500 hours, and that components A and B fail independently. Find the reliability function for the systems in (a) and (b).

(a) S_1:

(b) S_2:

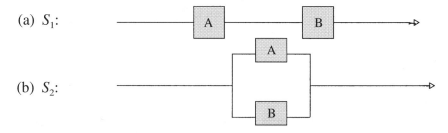

(c) Evaluate these system reliabilities for $t = 500, \ 1000, \ 1500$.

Solution: We will denote by T_A, T_B, T_1, and T_2 the times to failure of these components and systems, respectively.

(a) Then, $R_{S_1}(t) = P(T_1 > t) = P(T_A > t) \, P(T_B > t)$

$$= e^{-t/1000}e^{-t/1500} = \underline{e^{-t/600}}$$

(b) $R_{S_2}(t) = P(T_2 > t) = P(T_A > t \text{ or } T_B > t)$

$$= P(T_A > t) + P(T_B > t) - P(T_A > t) \, P(T_B > t)$$

$$= \underline{e^{-t/1000} + e^{-t/1500} - e^{-t/600}}$$

(c)

t:	500	1000	1500
$R_{S_1}(t)$:	0.434	0.189	0.082
$R_{S_2}(t)$:	0.888	0.692	0.509

■

2.11 SUMMARY

In this chapter we have discussed briefly the concept of probability distributions as limiting forms for the shapes of histograms or bar graphs of data sets taken under stable conditions. The remainder of the chapter discussed some of the basic properties of discrete and continuous distributions from the point of view of the way these distributions will be used in later chapters in SPC. Emphasis is on recognizing the settings where the discrete distributions are appropriate and the use of these distributions to compute probabilities. The normal distribution, its related sampling distributions, and the exponential distribution were discussed. This chapter is not intended as a detailed introduction to these concepts for readers who have not been introduced to them before. Rather, it is intended mainly as a review and to define terminology and notation that will be used extensively in later chapters.

PROBLEMS

2.1 Show that when n items are drawn without replacement from a population containing N_1 defectives and N_2 nondefectives that the number of defectives obtained is at least $\max\{0, n - N_2\}$.

2.2 A lot of 20 light bulbs contains five defectives. If five randomly selected bulbs are sold to a customer, evaluate:
(a) the probability that the customer receives
  (i) all good bulbs,
  (ii) more than three good bulbs
(b) the mean and standard deviation of the number of good bulbs the customer receives.

2.3 A statistics class contains 60 boys and 20 girls. If ten students are selected randomly to form a committee, evaluate:
(a) the probability that the committee will include
  (i) no girls

(ii) exactly two girls

(iii) at least five boys

(b) the mean and standard deviation of the number of girls on the committee.

2.4 An urn contains 12 white and 8 red balls. A random sample of six balls is drawn without replacement. Evaluate:

(a) the probability of at least five white balls,

(b) the mean and standard deviation of the number of white balls drawn.

2.5 If 20 of the 30 registered voters in a certain precinct are Democrats, and a random sample of ten voters is selected to participate in a poll, evaluate the mean and variance of the number of Democrats in the sample.

2.6 A magazine of artillery ammunition contains 1000 rounds of 105 mm howitzer ammunition, of which 20% are duds and will not fire. If 50 rounds are selected randomly, evaluate each of the following using the hypergeometric and the binomial distributions:

(a) the probability that at least 42 of these rounds will fire,

(b) the mean and standard deviation of the number of these 50 rounds that fire.

2.7 A box of 100 fuses contains 11 defectives. If 20 fuses are selected randomly without replacement, find the mean and standard deviation of the number of defectives selected.

2.8 Twelve-volt automobile batteries are shipped from the manufacturer in lots of 60. A random sample of n batteries is taken from each lot and inspected for defects. Suppose a particular lot contains 12 defectives.

(a) If $n = 10$, what is the probability that at least three defectives will be in the sample from this lot?

(b) What is the smallest sample size n that can be used in this procedure if the probability of drawing at least one defective from this lot is to be at least 0.95?

2.9 A manufacturer of lawn mowers purchases 3-HP gasoline motors from a supplier in lots of 50 motors. He uses the following sampling inspection plan. A random sample of n motors is taken from each lot; and if the sample contains no defective motors, the entire lot is accepted and is otherwise rejected. What is the smallest sample size n that he can take if he wishes the probability to be at least 0.90 that a lot containing ten defectives will be rejected?

2.10   A lot of 400 batteries contains 61 that are charged at a level below specifications. If 100 of these batteries are selected randomly and sold to a customer, what is the probability that the customer will get at least ten batteries with a charge that is below specifications?

2.11   The probability that a salesman will make a sale on one call is 0.3. Each day, this salesman makes 10 calls. Let X denote the number of sales made in one day.

(a) Find the probability function $f(x)$ of X and make a bar graph of $f(x)$.

(b) What is the probability that at least one but no more than five sales will be made on a given day, that is, find $P(1 \le X \le 5)$.

(c) Find the mean μ and variance σ^2 of the number of sales made in one day.

2.12   The probability that a salesman will make a sale on one call is 0.3. In planning his work for a day, what is the smallest number of calls he should plan to make if he wishes the probability to be at least 0.7 that he will make at least one sale?

2.13   The probability that a certain mother will have a son on each pregnancy is 0.52. If she plans to have seven children, find

(a) the probability she will have all boys

(b) the probability she will have no boys

(c) the probability of four sons

(d) the mean and standard deviation of the number of sons she will have.

2.14   What is the probability of throwing exactly two tails four times in five tosses of three honest coins?

2.15   What is the probability of throwing exactly three tails twice in six tosses of four honest coins?

2.16   What is the probability of rolling exactly two sixes in five rolls of two honest dice?

2.17 The probability that a basketball player will make a free throw is 0.7. What is the probability that he will make at least five out of seven free throws in a game, if his attempts are assumed to be Bernoulli trials? Comment upon the reasonableness of this assumption of Bernoulli trials.

2.18 A large bin of 3/16-in. taps contains 10% that are defectives. If 100 taps are selected randomly for use, what is the probability that at least eight defectives are drawn?

2.19 The percentage of the voters of a certain large population who voted for candidate C is 55. If a sample of 1000 voters from this population is drawn, find the mean and standard deviation of the percentage of the voters in the sample who voted for candidate C.

2.20 A production process has 1% fallout (percentage out of speci-fications). If 20,000 units are made in a day, what is the prob-ability that at least 200 units are out of spec? 250 units? Discuss the assumptions you are making to obtain your answers.

2.21 For X a Poisson random variable with probability function $p(x; \lambda)$, use the Q-Charts disk to evaluate each of the following:
(a) For $\lambda = 0.50$, $P(X \leq 1)$ and $P(X > 2)$.
(b) For $\lambda = 1.00$, $P(X \leq 3)$.
(c) For $\lambda = 1.50$, $P(X > 2)$.
(d) For $\lambda = 4.0$, $P(3 < X \leq 6)$.
(e) For $\lambda = 8.5$, $P(4 < X < 13)$.
(f) For $\lambda = 20$, $P(13 \leq X < 30)$.

2.22 If the proportion of defective items produced on a certain pro-duction line is 10^{-3}, find the probability function for the number X of defectives produced on a day when a total of 3000 items were produced. Draw a bar graph of this probability function and find the mean and variance of X.

2.23 For $b(x; n, p)$ and $p(x; \lambda)$, $\lambda = np$, the binomial and Poisson probability functions, respectively,
(a) show that $p(1; 1) = e^{-1}$ and $b\left(1; n, \dfrac{1}{n}\right) = ((n - 1)/n)^{n-1}$.

(b) For $p = p(1; 1)$ and $b = b\left(1; n, \dfrac{1}{n}\right)$, evaluate p, b, and $p - b$ to four places after the decimal in the table:

n		2	5	20	50	100	1000
p							
b							
$b - p$							

2.24 The telephone in an office rings on the average once per hour. Find the probability function, mean, and variance for the number of calls in an eight-hour work day.

2.25 Accidents occur at a certain intersection at the rate of one every three weeks. What is the probability of 16, 17, or 18 accidents at this intersection next year? Find the mean and *s.d.* of the number of accidents at this intersection per year.

2.26 On the average, one spore colony will develop per five square inches of area of a certain sterilized material when exposed to air for 24 hours. What is the probability that at least two spore colonies will develop on a 5-inch diameter disc of this material that is exposed for 24 hours?

2.27 The probability of finding a certain spring flower blooming in a 1/4-acre area of a certain 100-acre field is 0.001. What is the probability of finding at least one flower in the entire field?

2.28 The average number of flaws per running yard of a certain type of cotton fabric is 0.01.
   (a) What is the probability of no more than two flaws in a 100-yard roll of this fabric?
   (b) Find the mean and variance of the number of flaws in a 100-yard roll of this material.
   (c) Find the mean and variance of the number of flaws in ten 100-yard rolls of this fabric.

2.29 One patient appears for treatment per hour, on the average, at the emergency room of a certain hospital. Find the mean and *s.d.* of the number of patients treated during an eight-hour shift. What is the probability that no patients will be treated on one shift? Fewer than 15?

2.30 Three people are killed by black widow bites, on the average, per year in North Carolina. What is the probability that no one in North Carolina will die from black widow bites in the next two years?

2.31   A radioactive source emits particles at the mean rate of one every 40 minutes. Find the probability function, mean, and *s.d.* of the number of particles that will be emitted in one day.

2.32   When the speed limit on a certain 50-mile section of interstate highway was 65 mph, there was on this highway, on the average, one accident every 32 days. The first year after the speed limit was reduced to 55 mph, there were five accidents on this stretch of highway. Evaluate the probability of five or fewer accidents in one year if the accident rate is assumed to be unchanged. Do you believe it has changed?

2.33   Customers who require carburetor service arrive at a garage at the rate of two per day. Find the probability function, mean, and variance of the number of customers who will require carburetor service in a five-day work week. What is the probability that the number of customers in such a week will exceed 12?

2.34   For $k = 2$, compute the means and standard deviations for negative binomial random variables for $p = 0.1, 0.3, 0.7, 0.9$.

2.35   If 90% of the items produced on a production line are nondefective, let X denote the number of items that must be inspected in order to find three defectives. Find the mean and *s.d.* of X. Make a bar graph of the probability function of X and a graph of the distribution function of X. What is the probability that more than 40 items will be inspected?

2.36   A telephone salesperson averages one sale for every five calls. Let X be the number of calls required to meet a daily quota of two sales. Find the mean μ and variance σ^2 of X. Evaluate the probability that the number of calls required is within three *s.d.*'s of the mean, that is, evaluate

$$P(\mu - 3\sigma \le X \le \mu + 3\sigma).$$

2.37   Three men toss coins, and the odd man pays for coffee. If the coins all turn up the same, they are tossed again until someone loses.

(a) What is the probability that fewer than four tosses are required?

(b) Find the mean, variance, and *s.d.* of the number of tosses required.

2.38 Two honest coins are tossed until two tails are obtained. If X is the number of tosses required, evaluate:

(a) $P(X = 1)$, $P(X = 4)$,

(b) $E(X)$, $\text{Var}(X)$, $S.D.(X)$.

2.39 A fly fisherman averages one strike for 20 casts, and averages catching one legal-size fish for ten strikes. Find the mean μ and *s.d.* σ of the number of casts required to catch a daily limit of five legal-size fish. For X the number of casts required for a limit, evaluate $P(\mu - 3\sigma \le X \le \mu + 3\sigma)$. What is the probability of catching at least two fish in the first 200 casts?

2.40 A boy asks girls for a date until one accepts. If the probability that a girl will accept is (1/5) and "trials" are independent, find the mean μ and *s.d.* σ for the number of girls he asks in order to get a date. Evaluate the probability that he will ask (a) fewer than ten girls, (b) at least five girls.

2.41 Derive the geometric probability function of (2.7.4) by using the fact that the event that A occurs in the first x-1 trials is the complement of the event that A^c occurs on every one of the first x-1 trials.

2.42 In a certain machining process the "tool" is changed periodically after 1200 units of production. It has been determined experimentally that the probability that a tool will fail before producing 1200 units is 0.015.

(a) Find the mean and standard deviation of the total number of tools used before the first tool failure.

(b) Find the mean and standard deviation of the total number of units produced before the first tool failure.

(c) Evaluate the probability that the process will produce more than a units before the first tool failure, say P_a, for $a = $ 12,000; 60,000; 120,000; 240,000; 300,000. Plot these probabilities against a.

2.43 A manufacturing process produces a fallout of $100p = 2\%$ of nonconforming product. If units of production are inspected continuously once per week until two nonconforming units are found, evaluate the probability that more than x units will be inspected for $x \in \{50, 100, 150, 200, 250\}$.

2.44 For Z a $N(0, 1)$ random variable, evaluate
   (a) $P(Z \le 1.11)$ (g) $P\{((Z - 1)/2) \le 1)\}$
   (b) $P(Z > 1.11)$ (h) $P\{(|Z - 1|/2) \le 1\}$
   (c) $P(Z > -2.01)$ (i) $P(Z^2 + Z - 2 > 0)$
   (d) $P(Z < -1.05)$ (j) $P(Z \le 1.875)$
   (e) $P(|Z| > 1.96)$ (k) $P\{Z \ge -2.016\}$
   (f) $P(Z \le 1.96)$ (m) $P(-1.144 \le Z \le 1.435)$

2.45 For Z a $N(0, 1)$ random variable, evaluate
   (a) $P(Z \le 1.86)$ (g) $P(2Z + 1 \le 0)$
   (b) $P(Z > 1.86)$ (h) $P(|2Z + 1| \le 0)$
   (c) $P(Z > -1.67)$ (i) $P(Z^2 - Z - 2 > 1)$
   (d) $P(Z < -2.23)$ (j) $P(Z \le 2.405)$
   (e) $P(|Z| > 2.33)$ (k) $P(Z \ge -1.933)$
   (f) $P(|Z| \le 2.33)$ (m) $P(-1.223 \le Z \le 2.223)$

2.46 For X a $N(1, 4)$ random variable, evaluate
   (a) $P(X \le 5)$ (d) $P(|X| > 1.5)$
   (b) $P(X > 5)$ (e) $P(|X - 2| > 1)$
   (c) $P(X \le 0)$ (f) $P(X^2 - 3X - 4 > 0)$

2.47 For X a $N(6, 9)$ random variable, evaluate
   (a) $P(X \le 7)$ (d) $P(X > 3)$
   (b) $P(X > 7)$ (e) $P(|X - 3| < 2)$
   (c) $P(X \le 4)$ (f) $P(X^2 + 18 > 11x)$

2.48 For X a $N(\mu, \sigma^2)$ random variable, evaluate
   (a) $P(\mu - \sigma \le X \le \mu + \sigma)$
   (b) $P(\mu - 2\sigma \le X \le \mu + 2\sigma)$
   (c) $P(\mu - 3\sigma \le X \le \mu + 3\sigma)$

2.49 The diameter of a ball bearing produced by a machine is a normal random variable with mean 2.2 cm and s.d. 0.02 cm. If specifications require that the diameter be within 0.05 cm of 2.2 cm, what is the probability that one ball bearing will meet these specifications?

2.50 The weights of male students on a campus are normally distributed with mean $\mu = 175$ lb and s.d. $\sigma = 40$ lb. What is the probability that the weight of a randomly selected male student will exceed 210 lb?

2.51   Soft drink bottles are filled by a machine, and the quantity put in a bottle is a normal random variable with mean $\mu = 12$ oz and *s.d.* $= 0.2$ oz. What is the probability that one bottle will contain at least 11.5 oz? If a consumer purchases ten six-packs of these bottles, what is the probability that they will get at least one bottle with less than 11.5 oz of soft drink?

2.52   The length of time required for an auto mechanic to align the front wheels of an automobile is a normal random variable with mean $\mu = 22$ min. and *s.d.* $= 5$ min. What is the probability that he will complete the job on one auto in less than 15 min.?

2.53   The amount of time required to train a new employee to perform a certain task satisfactorily is a normal random variable with mean $\mu = 2$ hr and *s.d.* $\sigma = 30$ min. What is the probability that it will require more than three hours to train the next new employee?

2.54   Evaluate z_α for $\alpha = 0.2, 0.1, 0.005$, by
  (a) reading z_α as the closest value given in Table A.1.
  (b) using the inverse normal distribution function on the Q-Charts disk.

2.55   Evaluate z_α for $\alpha = 0.16, 0.08, 0.002$, by
  (a) reading z_α as the closest value given in Table A.1,
  (b) using the inverse normal distribution function on the Q-Charts disk.

2.56   Evaluate using Table A.2 in the Appendix:

$$\chi^2_{0.5,9}, \quad \chi^2_{0.05,20}, \quad \chi^2_{0.99,25}, \quad \chi^2_{0.025,60}, \quad \chi^2_{0.1,100}$$

2.57   Evaluate using the Q-Charts disk:

$$\chi^2_{0.95,28}, \quad \chi^2_{0.25,17}, \quad \chi^2_{0.12,9}, \quad \chi^2_{0.8,4}, \quad \chi^2_{0.002,100}, \quad \chi^2_{0.8,75}, \quad \chi^2_{0.001,115}$$

2.58   Fill in the values of $\chi^2_{\alpha,\nu}$ in a table like the following where "Exact" means values obtained from Table A.2 or the Q-Charts disk algorithm, and "Approx." means the values are obtained from equation (2.9.4). Use linear interpolation in the normal table or the inverse normal distribution function on the Q-Charts disk to evaluate z_α.

	$\chi^2_{0.95,30}$	$\chi^2_{0.05,30}$	$\chi^2_{0.95,100}$	$\chi^2_{0.05,100}$	$\chi^2_{0.05,150}$
Exact:					
Approx.:					

2.59 For T_ν a Student-t random variable,
(a) Evaluate each of the following:

$$P(T_5 \le 1.5),\ P(T_{10} > 2.0),\ P(T_{20} < -1),\ t_{.001,12},\ t_{.93,15}$$

(b) Find a in each of the following:

$$P(T_5 \le a) = 0.975,\ P(T_5 \le -a) = 0.025,$$
$$P(T_{10} \le a) = 0.10,\ P(T_{10} > a) = 0.80$$

2.60 For F_{ν_1,ν_2} an F random variable, evaluate each of the following:

$$P(F_{5,7} \le 1.5),\quad P(F_{5,7} > 2.5),$$
$$F_{0.05;5,7},\quad F_{0.95;7,5},\ F_{0.5;15,20},\quad F_{0.97;7,15},\quad F_{0.045;11,20}$$

2.61 An insurance company averages one claim per 1000 policy holders per year for a particular type of catastrophic insurance. If the company has 10,000 policy holders in a certain year, what is the probability that it will have ten or more claims? Fifteen or more? Twenty or more?

2.62 An ammunition manufacturer claims that 90% of his rifle shells contain between 47.8 g and 48.2 g of powder. A sample of 20 shells is selected randomly. If X is the number of shells that contain amounts of powder outside the specified limits, find $P(X \le 2)$, $E(X)$, $S.D.(X)$, assuming the claim is correct.

2.63 A girl asks randomly selected boys for a date. Let X denote the number of boys she asks to get an acceptance. If the probability that a boy will accept is $1/4$, find $E(X)$, $S.D.(X)$, and $P(X \le 2)$.

2.64 A statistics class of 75 students contains 15 girls and 60 boys. If five students are selected randomly for a special assignment, let X denote the number of boys chosen. Evaluate $P(X \geq 4)$, $E(X)$, $S.D.(X)$.

2.65 A machine making screws makes 0.5% defectives. If these screws are packaged 101 to a box, what is the probability that a box will contain at least 100 nondefective screws?

2.66 In problem 2.65, suppose ten of the boxes of screws are sold to a customer. What is the probability that at least nine of these boxes will contain at least 100 nondefective screws?

2.67 Do problems 2.65 and 2.66 if the screws are packaged 102 to a box.

2.68 The probability that someone will be killed by lightning in Wake County on a day in August is 0.001. What is the probability that no one will be killed by lightning in Wake County in August next year? Find the mean and variance of the number that will be killed by lightning in Wake County in August next year.

2.69 A lot of items contains N_1 defectives and N_2 nondefectives. If items are drawn without replacement until exactly $k(\leq N_1)$ defectives are obtained, let X denote the number of trials required. Verify that

$$P(X = x) = \frac{\binom{N_1}{k-1}\binom{N_2}{x-k}}{\binom{N_1+N_2}{x-1}}\left(\frac{N_1-k+1}{N_1+N_2-x+1}\right)$$

$$\text{for } x \in \{k, k+1, \cdots, k+N_2\}$$

2.70 (Discrete Uniform Distribution) A box contains N balls with numbers $1, 2, \cdots, N$ stamped on the individual balls, that is, 1 is on one ball, 2 is on one ball, etc. If one ball is drawn randomly, let X denote the number obtained.
(a) Find the probability function $p(x)$ of X.
(b) Evaluate the mean and standard deviation of X.

2.71 A manufacturer of hypodermic needles claims that the probability that one needle is not sterile is 0.000,001. This manufacturer sells 5,000,000 needles in one year. If his statement is correct, and X denotes the number of contaminated needles sold, find $E(X)$, $S.D.(X)$, $p(x) = P(X = x)$, and fill in the table:

$$x: 0\ 1\ 2\ 3\ 4\ 5\ 6\ 7\ 8\ 9\ 10$$
$$p(x):$$

2.72 The probability that a college senior will receive a job offer after an interview is $p = 1/4$. This senior continues interviews until he receives an offer. Give the probability function, the mean, and standard deviation for the number of interviews he will have. What is the probability that he will have more than five interviews? More than ten interviews? More than 20 interviews?

2.73 The fallout (proportion defectives) for a manufacturing process is $p = 0.1$. If 100 units are produced on a work shift, find the mean μ and variance σ^2 of the number of defectives produced. Compute the probability that the number of defectives produced on the shift is fewer than $\mu - 3\sigma$, and the probability that more than $\mu + 3\sigma$ are produced. Compare these probabilities with the corresponding probabilities under a normal distribution. Discuss these results.

2.74 A certain type of vacuum tube has a lifetime that is exponentially distributed with a mean life of 100 hours. Suppose 100 of these tubes are used continuously until they have all failed.

(a) What is the probability that a particular tube will last at least 50 hours?

(b) What is the probability that at least 10 tubes will not have failed in 200 hours?

(c) What is the mean and variance of the number of tubes that will be in operation at the end of 100 hours? 200 hours? x hours?

2.75 Accidents occur along a certain stretch of highway according to a Poisson process, and at the rate of two/month. What is the probability that there will be no accidents on this road in one week?

2.76 Suppose that all components fail independently and that the life of an A component is an $EX(800\ hr)$ random variable and that of a B component is an $EX(1100 \text{ hr})$ random variable. Find the reliability functions $R_1(t)$, $R_2(t)$, $R_3(t)$ of the systems S_1, S_2, and S_3.

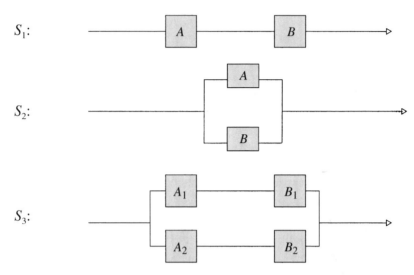

S_1:

S_2:

S_3:

Evaluate $R_1(t)$, $R_2(t)$, and $R_3(t)$ for $t = 800$ and 1200.

2.77   Show that the mean and variance formulas in (2.10.2) are correct by integrating to evaluate $E(X)$ and $E(X^2)$.

2.78   The *two-parameter* exponential distribution has density function

$$f(x) = \alpha e^{-\alpha(x-\mu)}, \; x \geq \mu$$
$$= 0, \; x < \mu$$

for $-\infty < \mu < \infty$, $\alpha > 0$.
(a) Sketch a graph of this density function.
(b) Find the distribution function and sketch its graph.
(c) Find the mean and variance of this distribution.

CHAPTER 3

Collecting and Studying Data Sets: Descriptive Statistics and Sampling Distributions

In this chapter we consider some methods for collecting data sets, some graphical methods for studying data sets, and statistics that summarize the information in data sets. When data sets are collected under conditions such that random sampling assumptions are reasonable, then the data are valuable in our work in quality improvement. On the other hand, when random sampling assumptions are not reasonable, the data may have little value. We consider random samples from finite and infinite populations, some graphical methods for studying samples, and statistics that summarize the information and estimate the parameters of the distribution from which the sample was drawn.

3.1 POPULATIONS AND SAMPLES

A *population* is simply a set, and usually one which we are interested in studying for some purpose. Some examples of *finite* populations are the black bears in Yellowstone Park today, the workers on the 7:00–3:00 shift, and the items in a lot purchased from a supplier. In other cases, such as the population of all ball bearings that may be produced by a certain manufacturing process, the population may be considered to be *infinite*. There is often a numerical variable associated with each element of the population that is of prime interest, and the set of these numbers may itself be considered to be the population. We might consider the set of hourly wages of shift workers or the diameters of individual ball bearings in the above examples.

A *sample* is a finite subset of a population. We are usually interested in populations and samples with elements that are numbers; and we consider selecting a sample from a population and using it to make inferences about the population. In order for a sample to be useful in making inferences about a population, it is important that the sample numbers be collected according to a controlled plan. We are especially interested in samples of numbers that are observed according to some probability distribution. That is, in samples with numbers that are random variables such as $X_1, \cdots, X_n$; say. These are *random samples,* and there are two types of random samples that are classified according to the size of the population from which they were drawn.

> Consider a finite population of numbers, $a_1, \cdots, a_N$, and let $n(\leq N)$ of these numbers be drawn randomly without replacement. Then the set of values obtained, say $X_1, \cdots, X_n$, is said to constitute a *random sample from a finite population.*   (3.1.1)

The sampling without replacement in (3.1.1) assures that every one of the $\binom{N}{n}$ samples of size n that can be drawn from the N numbers in the population has the same chance of being drawn. Note that it is not assumed that all of the numbers a_i $(i = 1, \cdots, N)$ are different, as will be illustrated in the following example.

Example 3.1 (a) Fifteen students in a statistics class made the following scores on a homework assignment: 7, 9, 5, 8, 7, 10, 8, 4, 0, 10, 8, 1, 6, 0, 9. If three students are selected randomly without replacement, then their scores of X_1, X_2, and X_3 constitute a random sample from the population of 15 scores. Note that there are a total of $\binom{15}{3} = 455$ different samples!
(b) A box contains $N = 1000$ ball bearings (bb's). A sample of ten bb's is drawn without replacement to give a random sample X_1, $X_2, \cdots, X_{10}$ of bb diameters.
(c) A voting precinct has 50 registered voters. A sample of ten voters is drawn randomly and if a voter favors candidate A she is assigned the number one, if she does not favor candidate A, she is assigned the number zero. Then the numbers assigned to the ten voters selected, $X_1, \cdots, X_{10}$, is a random sample of the 50 code numbers 1 and 0 that mean "favors A" and "does not favor A." ∎

We consider next the second type of sample alluded to above.

> If the random variables $X_1, \cdots, X_n$ are independent and every one has the same distribution as a random variable X, then $X_1, \cdots, X_n$ is called a *random sample* on the (parent or reference) random variable X, or a *sample from an infinite population.*   (3.1.2)

A random sample from an infinite population is obtained when a fiite population of numbers is sampled *with replacement.* In other cases, the population sampled may itself be considered infinite.

Example 3.2: (a) In Example 3.1(a) above, let the three students be randomly drawn with replacement and denote their scores by X_1, X_2, and X_3. Then each of these random variables takes each of the numbers listed with the same probability, and they are independent. This is a sample of size $n = 3$ on a parent random variable X with probability function $p(x)$ given by

x:	0	1	4	5	6	7	8	9	10
$p(x)$:	2/15	1/15	1/15	1/15	1/15	2/15	3/15	2/15	2/15

(b) Suppose that it is known from previous experience that the diameter of a randomly selected ball bearing (bb) produced by a certain manufacturing process has a $N(\mu, \sigma^2)$ distribution. If a sample of n bb's are selected, then their measured diameters $X_1, \cdots, X_n$ is a random sample on a $N(\mu, \sigma^2)$ parent distribution, or random variable. ∎

3.1.1 Random Sampling

In a sampling from either a finite or an infinite population, care must be exercised to ensure that the sampling is random. The statistical procedures that will be studied in the remainder of this book will depend on the random sampling assumption for validity. In some problems, such as in sampling ball bearings in a box, it may be possible to physically mix the population items so as to obtain a random sample. In many other cases it may be necessary to assign an index number from 1 to N to the population items, and then to select numbers randomly. In this selection tables of random numbers can be used, or, as is common today, a computer program can be used to select a sample of index numbers. The Q-Charts disk has an algorithm for selecting a random subset of size k from the set $\{1, 2, \cdots, N\}$. One run of this algorithm to select 5 numbers from $\{1, 2, \cdots, 20\}$ gave the values 5, 8, 9, 12, 16.

In sampling from an infinite population, we cannot assign index numbers to the population members, but must nevertheless take precautions to assure a random sample. If we are to select a sample of ball bearings produced by a machine, we might take one sample member and then take every 100th bb produced thereafter, or, take one bb at one-hour intervals until the required sample size is obtained. If we are generating numbers by some mechanical device such as tossing dice, or coins, or spinning a roulette wheel, then care should be exercised to avoid unintentionally favoring some outcomes. As will be seen later, we can in many cases investigate the values in a data set to decide if they can reasonably be considered a random sample from a particular parent distribution.

3.2 GRAPHS OF DATA SETS: DOT PLOTS, HISTOGRAMS, PARETO DIAGRAMS, STEM-AND-LEAF DIAGRAMS

Let $X_1, \cdots, X_n$ denote a random sample from either a finite or an infinite population. After the values of the sample have been observed, we denote these particular observed values by the lower case letters $x_1, \cdots, x_n$. These observed numbers contain information about the population of numbers from which they were drawn, in the case of sampling from a finite population, or about the parent probability distribution, when the sample is from an infinite population. In either case it will be necessary to study these observed values carefully in order to evaluate the information in the sample. We study the sample by making graphs that display important features of the data, and by computing certain numbers, called *statistics,* that summarize particular types of information about the set of sample values. We first consider three types of graphs that are pictures of the sample values in the set.

3.2.1 The Dot Plot or Diagram

The dot diagram is a simple but useful way to display a small sample. Suppose that the numbers of defective items produced on 10 consec-

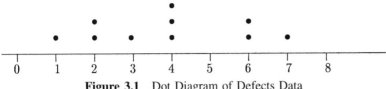

Figure 3.1   Dot Diagram of Defects Data

utive days were as follows: 4, 2, 6, 3, 4, 7, 1, 6, 4, 2. We plot these values on a dot diagram in Fig. 3.1. The numbers of defectives are given on the line and we see at a glance, for example, that there were three days with four defectives. The dot plot is a simple but useful picture of the data set that makes the information in the numbers easily grasped. The dot diagram reveals the structure of the data set much more clearly that a display of the data in a table. Dot diagrams are used mostly for small data sets with no more than, perhaps, 20 or 30 values. For these small data sets it is easy to make dot diagrams on graph paper manually and there is little need to use computer graphics methods. For larger data sets we prefer other "pictures" of the data such as stem-and-leaf diagrams or histograms, which will be presented next.

3.2.2   The Histogram

We consider now the polyester viscose breaking strength data of Table 2.1, the *relative frequency distribution* of Table 2.2, and the histogram of Fig. 2.1. The relative frequency distribution is constructed by first partitioning the real number axis into a set of *class intervals* so that each observation falls into exactly one interval. It is not necessary that all of the class intervals be of equal length, however, it is good practice to make them all of equal length since unequal lengths of intervals is likely to create confusion for some viewers, and equal length intervals are probably more easily understood by everyone. The first decision we make is to decide the number k of class intervals that we will use. This is a subjective decision but there are useful guidelines we can follow in choosing k. Basically, we want to get a good picture of the data set. If k is too small, that is, if there are too few classes, then the graph may not reveal important features of the data due to too much grouping and loss of information about the distributions of the values within the classes. On the other hand, if k is large and there are too many classes we can again get a poor image of the distribution of the data due to many cells containing a small number or no data values. A rough rule that often works pretty well is to take k approximately equal to the square root of the number of sample observations n. Ishikawa (1982) has given Table 3.1 of recommended values of k for different sample sizes. It will often be worthwhile to try plotting several different histograms for a particular data set to select the best one, especially when the plotting procedure is done by using a computer algorithm such as the one on the Q-Charts disk.

The *class mark* m_i is the midpoint of the ith class interval. The *frequency* f_i of the ith class is the number of observations in class i, and the ratio $r_i = f_i/n$ is the *relative frequency* of class i. Note that $n = f_1 + f_2 + \cdots + f_k$, so that $r_1 + r_2 + \cdots + r_k = 1$ and the relative frequencies sum to 1. By examining the data in Table 2.1 we can determine that all of the values are between 11 and 22 and we decide to try using the 11 class intervals as set out in Table 2.2. Note that we use the notation $(L_i, U_i]$ to denote the ith class interval, and the ith class interval does not include the value L_i, but it does include the value U_i. This is so that every number in the data set will fall into exactly one class interval. If the frequency distribution is being constructed by hand, rather than by computer, the tally column of Table 2.2 is a convenient way to obtain the class frequencies, f_i. Note also that when Table 2.2 is turned sideways, the tally marks themselves give a picture of the data that is very similar to the histogram of Fig. 2.1.

A histogram made from data that can be assumed to be a sample from a probability distribution is essentially a graphical estimate of the parent distribution density function, in the case of a continuous parent distribution, or of the parent probability function, in the case of a discrete parent distribution. It can be shown to have desirable theoretical properties as an estimator of these functions. Histograms are especially useful for large data sets and have many uses in process control and

TABLE 3.1   Ishikawa's Number of Classes Table

Sample Size	Number of Classes, k
Under 50	5–7
50–100	6–10
100–250	7–12
Over 250	10–20

other areas of quality control. For large data sets with large numbers of frequency classes, the histogram will give a good approximation to the actual parent density function for measurements. For this reason, histograms are often used in on-line process control systems, as we shall see later.

3.2.3 Histograms in Goodness-of-Fit Problems

One important use of histograms is to decide if a sample can be safely assumed to have a parent distribution from a particular class of parametric distributions. The most common application is to decide if a sample is from a normal distribution. We will consider other more efficient ways to study this question in Chapter 10. However, when the sample size is large, the approach given here utilizing histograms serves the purpose well. The approach is simply to draw a relative frequency histogram, that is, a histogram with the area of the rectangle of cell i equal to the relative frequency r_i, and then to draw an estimated density function on the same graph. If the class intervals are all of constant width w, say, then in order to make the area of rectangle i equal to r_i, the height, h_i, of rectangle i must be $h_i = r_i/w$. The estimated density is usually obtained by substituting estimates for the parameters into the density function itself. This is not the best way to estimate a normal density, but if the sample size is large enough to make a good histogram it is quite adequate. We illustrate this approach in the following example.

Example 3.3: To illustrate the use of a histogram with an overlaid normal density function to check the feasibility of the assumption of a normal distribution, we have plotted in Figure 3.2 a histogram with $k = 10$ classes and drawn a fitted normal density function for the 100

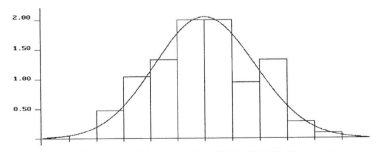

Figure 3.2   Histogram with Overlaid N(5.00, [0.19]^2) Density Function

values in Table 3.2. The smallest value in the data set is 4.58 and the largest is 5.42. The sample mean is 5.00 and the sample standard deviation is 0.19. We have omitted numbers on the horizontal axis since we are here interested in comparing the shapes of the two representations of the data sets and the horizontal scale is not important for this purpose. The normal density fits this data set quite well.   ∎

3.2.4   Histograms and Process Performance

A histogram can often be used to give a valuable summary of data from a high-volume manufacturing process, even when the data are also plotted on the control charts that will be considered in the following chapters of this book. Suppose that the measurements made on the parts made in a high-volume manufacturing process are accumulated and used to plot a histogram of the process distribution. Then with many data available a large number of narrow cells can be used, and the histogram gives an accurate picture of the proces distribution *that does not depend on assumptions about the form of the process distribution.* In particular, the specification limits (specification limits will be discussed in Chapter 10) can be drawn on the histogram. This gives a good picture of the performance of the process in meeting specifications, *over a long run of parts.*

3.2.5   Pareto Diagrams

Histograms are essentially a type of bar chart used to display a data set. There are many other types of bar charts that can be used to display and convey information. The bar chart is essentially a picure of a set of pairs such as (D_i, C_i), where D_i is a count, percent, or fraction associated with the value of a classification variable C_i. The classification variable C can be either a quantitative or qualitative variable.

TABLE 3.2   Data for Example 3.3

4.97	5.10	4.94	5.19	5.20	5.00	5.23	5.31	4.89	4.97
5.23	4.78	4.94	5.31	5.04	5.10	5.14	4.87	4.86	5.23
4.72	4.94	4.97	4.87	4.86	5.41	4.84	5.23	5.07	5.09
4.86	4.83	4.69	5.15	5.17	5.14	5.11	5.14	5.07	5.01
4.87	5.39	5.00	4.67	4.94	4.97	4.69	5.06	5.08	4.76
4.92	4.88	5.09	5.04	5.22	4.95	5.28	4.68	4.70	4.96
5.31	4.96	4.66	4.86	5.28	4.99	5.00	5.10	4.96	4.69
5.32	4.85	5.22	4.71	4.98	4.99	5.15	4.94	4.75	5.08
5.14	4.58	4.81	5.02	4.75	4.94	5.00	4.94	4.84	5.42
4.64	5.25	5.01	5.06	4.70	4.90	5.28	4.90	5.30	5.06

TABLE 3.3   Causes of Meter Main Board Defects

Operation	Number of Defects	Percent of Defects	Percent Distribution of Defects
Autoinsertion	142	9.3	46.3
Solder Mask	23	1.5	7.5
Manual Insertion	93	6.1	30.3
Wave Solder	42	2.7	13.7
Cleaning	7	0.5	2.3
Total	307	20.0	100.1

The classification variable C might take values that are the different types of defects or nonconformities that a unit of product can have. Defects or nonconformities can be grouped into categories in many other ways that can be useful for saving, storing, and studying the data. For example, it can be useful to classify a large number of automobile warranty defect claims according to the subsystem in which they occur: the fuel system, ignition system, internal motor block, power train, suspension and steering, electrical other than ignition, and so on.

As a concrete example, Table 3.3 gives a classification of 307 defects found on 1535 electric meter main boards. These defects are classified according to the manufacturing operation that caused the defect. A glance at Table 3.3 shows that the vast majority of the defects were due to the auto-insertion and manual insertion operations. Any attempt to reduce the defects created in the manufacturing process must pay careful attention to these two operations. Frequency data of the type given in Table 3.3 can be shown in graphical form in a histogram or bar graph. If the cells of the histogram are taken in decreasing order of magnitude of the frequencies, the graph is called a *Pareto diagram*. The Pareto diagram for the frequency Table 3.3 is shown in Fig. 3.3.

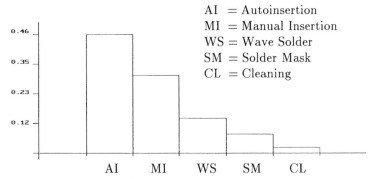

Figure 3.3   Pareto Diagram of Meter Boards Defects Data

```
3 │ 3
4 │ 4   7   8
5 │ 0   3   6   8   9   9
6 │ 1   1   1
7 │ 2   9
8 │ 1   3   5
9 │ 1   9
```

Figure 3.4 Stem-and-Leaf Plot of Table 3.4 Data

These simple charts are especially convenient for conveying information about the relative importance of the causes. Anyone can readily grasp the significance of the information in the diagrams.

In addition to total counts of defects or nonconformities, there are many other quantities that are sums or frequencies from different sources and that can be broken down or partitioned into ordered constituent contributing categories in a Pareto chart. The total amount of time to manufacture a unit of product can be partitioned into the time required for each processing operation or task. The funds in a budget must be allocated to different departments, or processes, or individuals, and so on. A frequency table and pareto diagram can be helpful in resource allocation.

3.2.6 The Stem-and-Leaf Diagram

The stem-and-leaf diagram is an easily used method for plotting small- to medium-size data sets by manual plotting. It is very similar to a histogram, but is particularly convenient when the plotting in done by hand. This technique was developed by Tukey (1977), who also gives many other techniques for what he calls *exploratory data analysis*—EDA. These diagrams can be used to good effect to display many types of data sets. The diagram consists of grouping the data first into a set of "stems," which are essentially class intervals, by the first one or more digits, and then listing the "leaves" for each stem as shown in Fig. 3.4 for the data of Table 3.4. One point that may sometimes be an advantage of this display, as compared to a histogram, is that the original data values can all be read directly from the stem-and-leaf diagram. In a histogram, or in a frequency table on which the

TABLE 3.4   Data for Stem-and-Leaf Plot

6.1	4.8	7.9	4.4	6.1	4.7	3.3	8.1	8.5	6.1
5.3	5.9	5.8	9.9	5.9	8.3	5.0	9.1	5.6	7.2

histogram is based, the individual values within frequency classes are not retained, so there is some loss of information from grouping.

3.3 CAUSE-AND-EFFECT OR ISHIKAWA DIAGRAMS

The cause-and-effect (C&E) diagram is also called a fishbone or an Ishikawa diagram after the Japanese engineer Kaoru Ishikawa who developed it in work with the Kawasaki Steel Works in 1943 during World War II.

The C&E diagram is a convenient, simple graphical technique for studying a system of causes that contribute to a particular resulting effect. C&E diagrams are often used in "brainstorming" sessions to study a process or system of causes, and to communicate this type of information. They are particularly convenient for consolidating ideas from the members of a group of individuals who have experience and knowledge of different aspects of a process. Such sessions should include all personnel who have knowledge of the system of causes under study. For a manufacturing process this would include floor operators as well as supervisors, engineers, managers, and the like.

Figure 3.5 shows a C&E diagram of factors affecting final part accuracy from an article by Elshennawy et al. (1988). This study assumed that parts dimensions were made by a coordinate measuring machine,

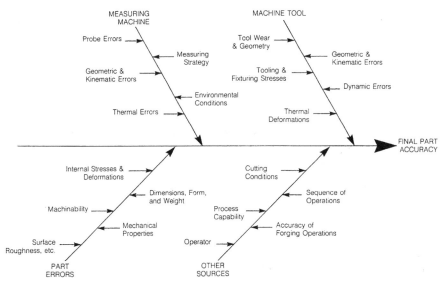

Figure 3.5 Factors Affecting Final Part Accuracy (© 1988 reproduced with permission from the American Society for Quality Control)

and devotes one whole branch to note possible areas of problems from the coordinate measuring machine. This is a *cause enumeration* type C&E diagram.

C&E diagrams provide an effective approach to studying and communicating information about a system of causes that influence a quality variable by permitting a simple step-by-step breakdown into a branching process that leads to identification of root causes. Ishikawa (1982) discusses three types of C&E diagrams classified according to purpose. These three types are for the analysis of dispersion, production process classification type, and the cause enumeration type.

The dispersion analysis C&E diagram is used to identify in detail all known causes of variability in a quality variable. Note that the term "known" necessarily refers to the group of people preparing the diagram. In order to have this representation of the system of causes be as complete as possible, advice should be sought from a broad group of people familiar with the process under study.

The production process classification C&E diagram reflects the flow of the production process by its main line, and branches are added to show parts of the process that may introduce variability.

3.4   STUDYING SAMPLES, DESCRIPTIVE STATISTICS

Let $X_{(1)}$ denote the smallest value in the sample $\{X_1, \cdots, X_n\}$, $X_{(2)}$ the second smallest value, $\cdots$, $X_{(n)}$ the largest value. Then the values $X_{(1)} \le X_{(2)} \le \cdots \le X_{(n)}$ are called the *order statistics* of the random sample $X_1, \cdots, X_n$. Again, we use lowercase letters to denote the observed values in a particular sample. That is, $x_{(1)}, \cdots, x_{(n)}$ are the observed values of the order statistics. The order statistics will be used in a number of places in this book.

Example 3.4: Aflatoxin is a toxic material that can be produced in grains by a certain type of mold. As a precaution to protect consumers, commercial lots of corn are sampled and tested for aflatoxin by the U.S. Department of Agriculture (USDA). Each test involves a series of operations and the end result is a set of replicate determinations of the amount of aflatoxin expressed in units of parts per billion (ppb), which are considered to be observed values on a random sample from an infinite population. A sample of $n = 15$ of these determinations contained the following observed values and corresponding order statistics. A dot plot of these observed values is shown in Fig. 3.6.

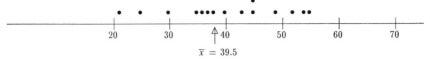

$$\overline{x} = 39.5$$

Figure 3.6   Dot Plot of Aflatoxin Data

i:	1	2	3	4	5	6	7	8
x_i:	48.5	37.8	20.1	35.9	36.4	29.1	24.1	39.6
$x_{(i)}$:	20.1	24.1	29.1	34.2	35.9	36.4	37.8	39.6

i:	9	10	11	12	13	14	15
x_i:	50.8	43.0	34.2	43.2	53.6	55.5	41.3
$x_{(i)}$:	41.3	43.0	43.2	48.5	50.8	53.6	55.5

In Chapter 2 we defined the mean and variance as measures of the location and spread, respectively, of a probability distribution on the real number line. We now define certain functions of a sample, that is, certain statistics, which measure features of the way a sample is distributed on the real number line (see Fig. 3.6).

3.4.1   Measures of Location

We consider first statistics that are *measures of location* of the sample. The most widely known and used measure of sample location is the sample mean.

> The *sample mean,* $\overline{X}$, of a sample $X_1, \cdots, X_n$ is
>
> $$\overline{X} = \frac{X_1 + \cdots + X_n}{n}$$

(3.4.1)

The sample mean is the centroid or point on which the real line will balance if a unit of mass is placed at each sample value. It is the value that is often called the "average" of the sample values. It can also be observed that the sample mean $\overline{x} = (x_1 + \cdots + x_n)/n$ of an observed sample is the mean of the discrete uniform probability distribution that assigns equal probability of $(1/n)$ to each of the observed sample points.

Example 3.4, continuation 1: The observed value of the sample mean for the aflatoxin data is

$$\bar{x} = (48.5 + 37.8 + \cdots + 41.3)/15 = 39.5.$$

This value is marked on the graph of Fig. 3.6. ∎

Recall that the ith order statistic, $X_{(i)}$, is the ith smallest sample value.

The *sample median*, X_{MED}, of a sample $X_1, \cdots, X_n$ is given by

$$X_{MED} = X_{(n+1)/2}, \text{ if } n \text{ is odd;}$$ (3.4.2)

$$= \frac{1}{2} [X_{(n/2)} + X_{(n/2+1)}], \text{ if } n \text{ is even.}$$

When n is odd, the sample median is the middle-order statistic, and when n is even it is the average of the two middle-order statistics.

Example 3.4, continuation 2: The sample median of the aflatoxin data is $x_{MED} = x_{(8)} = 39.6$. ∎

In the above development we used uppercase letters $X_1, \cdots, X_n$ to denote the random variables constituting a sample, and the corresponding lowercase letters $x_1, \cdots, x_n$ to denote the observed values of the sample random variables. We also use the corresponding lowercase letters to denote the observed values of the sample mean and sample median. Thus, $\bar{x}$ is the observed value of $\bar{X}$ and x_{MED} the observed value of X_{MED}.

The statistics $\bar{X}$ and X_{MED} are measures of the location of the center of the sample and are expressed in the same units of measurement as the sample members themselves. For example, if the sample members $X_1, \cdots, X_n$ are measured in inches, say, then $\bar{X}$ and X_{MED} are also in units of inches.

3.4.2 Measures of Spread or Dispersion

Some measures of the scatter or spread of the numbers in a sample are studied next. For many problems it is not sufficient to compute only measures of location since the degree of scatter or spread of the data about a "center" is also important. For example, suppose that two samples of ball bearings produced by different machines had the following diameters (in cm).

Machine 1: 0.81 0.80 0.85 0.76 0.78
Machine 2: 0.82 0.79 0.80 0.80 0.79

Both samples have means and medians equal to 0.80 cm. However, the bearings from machine 2 clearly have diameters grouped more closely about 0.80 cm. We introduce next some statistics which serve as measures of this *spread* or *dispersion* of a sample.

The *sample variance, S^2,* of a sample $X_1, \cdots, X_n$ is

$$S^2 = \frac{1}{n-1} \sum_{i=1}^{n} (X_i - \overline{X})^2$$

(3.4.3)

A formula that is sometimes convenient for computing S^2 by hand is obtained as follows.

$$(n-1)S^2 = \sum_{i=1}^{n} (X_i - \overline{X})^2 = \sum_{i=1}^{n} X_i^2 - 2\overline{X} \sum_{i=1}^{n} X_i + \sum_{i=1}^{n} \overline{X}^2$$

$$= \sum_{i=1}^{n} X_i^2 - 2 \left(\sum_{i=1}^{n} X_i \right)^2 / n + \left(\sum_{i=1}^{n} X_i \right)^2 / n$$

From this we obtain the

Sample Variance Computing Formula:

$$S^2 = \frac{1}{n-1} \left[\sum_{i=1}^{n} X_i^2 - \frac{\left(\sum_{i=1}^{n} X_i \right)^2}{n} \right]$$

(3.4.4)

Note that only the two quantities $X_1 + \cdots + X_n$ and $X_1^2 + \cdots + X_n^2$ are required in order to compute S^2 using (3.4.4).

Example 3.5:   We now compute the sample variances for some of the samples considered earlier in this section.

(a) Consider the sample variances for the ball bearing diameters for the two machines considered above. For the first machine we have

$$\sum_{i=1}^{5} x_i = 4.00, \; \sum_{i=1}^{5} x_i^2 = 3.2046, \; s_1^2 = \{3.2046 - (4.00)^2/5\}/4$$

$$= 0.00115.$$

For the second machine $s_2^2 = \{3.2006 - (4.00)^2/5\}/4 = 0.00015$.

Observe that the greater variability of the data for machine 1 is reflected in the magnitudes of these sample variances. In fact, the ratio is $(s_1^2/s_2^2) = 7.67$, so that the variance of the first sample is seven and two-thirds times as large as the variance of the second sample.

(b) As a computation exercise we compute the sample variance of the aflatoxin data of Example 3.5.

$$\sum x_i = 593.1, \; \sum x_i^2 = 24,919.07$$

$$s^2 = \{24,919.07 - (593.1)^2/15\}/14 = 104.85 \qquad \blacksquare$$

Sometimes when the sample values become available sequentially in time, that is, X_1 is the first observation observed, X_2 is the second, and so on; or for writing one-pass algorithms to compute the statistics, it will be convenient to use updating formulas for the sample mean and variance. Let $\overline{X}_n$ and S_n^2 denote the sample mean and variance computed from the first n observations. We call these statistics the *sequential* sample mean and variance. Observe that

$$\overline{X}_1 = X_1 \text{ and } S_2^2 = \frac{(X_1 - X_2)^2}{2}$$

Then the sample mean and variance can be computed from these starting values and the formulas in (3.4.5).

> **Updating Formulas** for sample mean and variance:
>
> $$\overline{X}_n = \frac{1}{n} [(n - 1) \overline{X}_{n-1} + X_n]$$ (3.4.5)
>
> $$S_n^2 = \left(\frac{n - 2}{n - 1} \right) S_{n-1}^2 + \frac{1}{n} (X_n - \overline{X}_{n-1})^2$$

These formulas are also numerically more stable than those of (3.4.3) and (3.4.4), and should be used to write computer algorithms rather than the "computing formulas" above—see Chan, Golub, and Le Veque (1983). Note that these formulas permit "one-pass" algorithms. Also, the defining formula of (3.4.3) will give better numerical results than the formula (3.4.4) by computer algorithm.

The observations will always be measured in units of some kind, such as inches, pounds, dollars, and so on. Whatever these units are, the sample variance will be expressed in units which are squares of these units. Now, for many purposes it is desirable to have a measure of spread that is expressed in the same units as the original observations, and measures of location such as $\overline{X}$ and X_{MED}. For this reason we define a measure of spread S with this property.

> The *standard deviation, S,* of a random sample $X_1, \cdots, X_n$ is
>
> $$S.D. = S = + \sqrt{S^2}$$ (3.4.6)

Example 3.6: Consider the sample variances for the ball bearing diameters computed in Example 3.5(a). The observed values of the standard deviations are $s_1 = \sqrt{0.00115} = 0.034$ cm and $S_2 = \sqrt{0.00015} = 0.012$ cm. ∎

We introduce one further measure of sample spread.

> The *sample range, R,* of a sample $X_1, \cdots, X_n$ is
>
> $$R = X_{(n)} - X_{(1)}$$ (3.4.7)

In words, the sample range is the length of the interval between the smallest and largest observations in the sample. The sample range is expressed in the same units of measurement as the original observations.

Example 3.7: The sample ranges for the two samples of ball bearing diameters considered above are

$$R_1 = (0.85 - 0.76) = 0.09, R_2 = (0.82 - 0.79) = 0.03$$

Thus, this measure of sample spread or dispersion also clearly shows that the first sample is more dispersed. ■

The principal advantage of the sample range is that it is easy to compute, at least for small samples. However, the range is usually considered a less reliable measure of spread than the standard deviation because it considers directly only the largest and smallest sample values. We shall also see later that for the important case when the data are from a normal parent distribution the range is less efficient than the sample standard deviation, in the sense that its sampling distribution has larger variance. However, the sample range has been widely used in classical statistical process control, largely because it is believed to be easier to compute, at least for small samples, and therefore results in fewer computing errors.

Example 3.8: A large quantity of water was taken from each of two sites in a certain ocean estuary. Subsequently, ten small specimens were taken from each and the salinity of each was assayed in parts per thousand, ppt, to give the following two salinity samples at the sites.

Location 1: 15.9 16.0 15.8 14.5 18.6 21.8 18.3 18.5 17.1 16.6
Location 2: 28.5 25.5 28.1 26.3 26.6 24.5 27.8 28.7 28.8 26.8

We shall now study the information in these two samples by plotting the data and computing the various statistics that have been introduced in this section.

Solution: As the first step in our analysis we make dot plots of the two samples as follows.

Sample 1

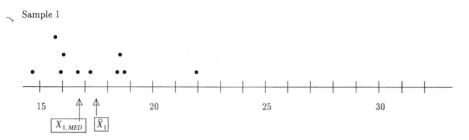

Sample 2

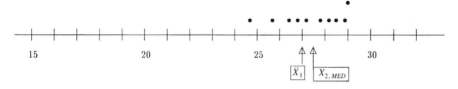

The measures of location for these samples are

$$\overline{X}_1 = 17.3, \; X_{1,MED} = (16.6 + 7.1)/2 = 16.9,$$
$$\overline{X}_2 = 27.2, \; X_{2,MED} = (26.8 + 27.8)/2 = 27.3.$$

The measures of spread are

$$S_1 = 2.07, \; R_1 = 21.8 - 14.5 = 7.3,$$
$$S_2 = 1.46, \; R_2 = 28.8 - 24.5 = 4.3.$$

By considering either the means or the medians of these two samples, it appears that the salinity at the second site is about 10 ppt greater
than at the first site. Also, by considering either the standard deviations
or the ranges, it appears that the variability or scatter in the first sample
is somewhat larger than in the second.   ■

We consider next the effect of linear transformations of the data upon
the various statistics that measure the location and spread of the data.

Linear Transformations: Put

$$Y_j = aX_j + b \text{ for } j = 1, \cdots, n; \; a > 0,$$ (3.4.8)

$$-\infty < b < \infty$$

Consider first the sample mean $\bar{Y}$.

$$\bar{Y} = \frac{1}{n} \sum_{i=1}^{n} Y_j = \frac{1}{n} \sum_{j=1}^{n} (aX_j + b) = a\bar{X} + b.$$

Recall that the order statistics satisfy $X_{(1)} \le X_{(2)} \le \cdots \le X_{(n)}$, and therefore we have immediately that $aX_{(1)} + b \le aX_{(2)} + b \le \cdots \le aX_{(n)} + b$. But these last values are the ordered values of $Y_1, \cdots, Y_n$, that is., $Y_{(j)} + b$ for $j = 1, \cdots, n$. From this we immediately obtain the following.

$$Y_{MED} = aX_{MED} + b$$

$$R_Y = Y_{(n)} - Y_{(1)},$$

$$= aX_{(n)} + b - aX_{(1)} - b,$$

$$= aR_X.$$

Finally, consider the sample variance

$$S_Y^2 = \frac{1}{n-1} \sum_{j=1}^{n} (Y_j - \bar{Y})^2,$$

$$= \frac{1}{n-1} \sum_{j=1}^{n} (aX_j + b - a\bar{X} - b)^2,$$

$$= \frac{1}{n-1} a^2 \sum_{j=1}^{n} (X_j - \bar{X})^2 = a^2 S_X^2.$$

We summarize these results in the following.

When a sample is transformed by a linear function as in (3.4.8), then the sample statistics are related as follows.

$$\bar{Y} = a\bar{X} + b, \text{ or } \bar{X} = (\bar{Y} - b)/a$$

$$Y_{MED} = aX_{MED} + b, \text{ or } X_{MED} = (Y_{MED} - b)/a$$

$$S_Y^2 = a^2 S_X^2, \text{ or } S_X^2 = S_Y^2/a^2$$

$$S_Y = aS_X, \text{ or } S_X = S_Y/a$$

$$R_Y = aR_X, \text{ or } R_X = R_Y/a$$

(3.4.9)

Observe certain points about the results displayed in (3.4.9). First, note that the new (Y) sample values of the location statistics are obtained by transforming the location statistics with the same linear transformation as was used on the sample members of the old (X) sample. Second, observe that S_Y and R_Y depend only on the constant a and not on the constant b. Indeed, if we let $a = 1$, then $S_Y^2 = S_X^2$ and $R_Y = R_X$. Thus, we see that sample variances and ranges are unchanged by the addition of a constant to each sample member.

Example 3.9: We illustrate these properties by direct computation using the data from the first sample in Example 3.8. First, we add 100 to each of these ten values to obtain: 115.9, 116.0, 115.8, 114.5, 118.6, 121.8, 118.3, 118.5, 117.1, 116.6. The mean and median of these values are

$$\bar{y} = 117.3 \text{ and } y_{MED} = (116.6 + 117.1)/2 = 116.9$$

The mean and median of the values before 100 was added to each were found in Example 3.8 to be 17.3 and 16.9. Direct computation of the sample range and standard deviation gives

$$R_y = 121.8 - 114.5 = 7.3, \text{ and } S_y = 2.07.$$

Thus the results stated in (3.4.9) are verified for this particular case. Next, we multiply each value in the first sample in Example 3.8 by five to obtain: 79.5, 80.0, 79.0, 72.5, 93.0, 109.0, 91.5, 92.5, 85.5, 83.0. Direct computation from these values gives $\bar{y} = 86.55$, $y_{MED} = 84.25$, $R_y = 7.3$, and $S_y = 10.36$, which verifies the result stated in (3.4.9), within the accuracy of the number of digits computed.   ■

In many cases the data in a sample may be measured and recorded in different but equivalent units of measurement. For example, a linear measurement may be taken in meters or centimeters, weights may be measured in pounds or ounces, and so on. In each case the measurements can be converted from one unit into the other by a simple scale transformation, that is, by multiplication by a particular constant. Thus, X m $= 100 \, X$ C, X lb $= 16 \, X$ oz, and so on. Thus, in view of (3.4.9), if it is required to compare the spread in two samples by comparing the sample ranges or standard deviations, then either the samples must be expressed in the same units of measurement, or we use the formulas of (3.4.9) to convert the statistics into the same units. In Chapter 11 it will be observed that many gauges are read in integers and converted to more meaningful units of measurement (inches, centimeters, and so on) by a linear transformation; see equation (10.2.1).

It is sometimes desirable or necessary to use a measure of sample variation that does not depend on the scale of measurement. We define next a measure of variation which has this property.

> The *coefficient of variation* of a sample is defined by $CV = 100(S/\overline{X})$ (3.4.10)

Since the mean and *s.d.* of the values $aX_1, \cdots, aX_n$ are $a\overline{X}$ and aS, the *CV* of these values is $100(aS/a\overline{X}s) = 100(S/\overline{X})$, and does not depend on the scale of measurement. The coefficient of variation is said to be *invariant* with respect to scalar transformations of the measurements. The coefficient of variation expresses the sample standard deviation as a percentage of the sample mean. This is desirable in some problems when the variation of a set of data relative to its magnitude is more relevant that its absolute variation as measured by, say, its sample standard deviation or range.

Example 3.10: Five piglets were weighed at two weeks and at 24 weeks after birth to give the following data in lb. Question: Has the variation among the piglets increased during growth?

> Two weeks: 4.1 3.5 5.2 4.4 3.9
> Twenty-four weeks: 251 222 320 272 242

Direct computation gives:

$$\overline{X}_2 = 4.22 \text{ lb}, \ S_2 = 0.64 \text{ lb}$$

$$\overline{X}_{24} = 261.4 \text{ lb}, \ S_{24} = 37.4 \text{ lb}$$

$$CV_2 = (0.64/4.22) \cdot 100 = 15.2\%$$

$$CV_{24} = (37.4/261.4) \cdot 100 = 14.3\%$$

As measured by the coefficient of variation, there has actually been very little change in the overall variation among these five pigs during this growth period. ∎

When a sample is presented in a frequency distribution table, as in Table 2.2, there is some loss of information, since the actual values of the observations within class intervals are not retained. In order to compute sample statistics from data that has been grouped into a frequency distribution table, we assign each observation the value of its class mark, m_i. For example, the sum, sum of squares, and sample size n of the observations are then

$$\sum_{i=1}^{k} f_i m_i, \sum_{i=1}^{k} f_i m_i^2, \text{ and } n = \sum_{i=1}^{k} f_i$$

and these give the following formulas for the sample mean and variance; see (3.4.1) and (3.4.4).

Sample Mean and Variance for Grouped Data:

$$\bar{x} = \frac{1}{n} \sum_{i=1}^{k} f_i m_i,$$

$$s^2 = \frac{1}{n-1} \left\{ \sum_{i=1}^{k} f_i m_i^2 - \left(\sum_{i=1}^{k} f_i m_i \right)^2 / n \right\}$$

(3.4.11)

Example 3.11: In order to illustrate the use of the formulas of (3.4.11), we consider the breaking strength data in Table 2.2. By direct computation using the data in Table 2.1 we obtain

$$\sum_{i=1}^{n} x_i = 1294.2, \sum_{i=1}^{n} x_i^2 = 21,239.52, \bar{x} = 16.18, s^2 = 3.83, s = 1.96.$$

If we compute the mean and variance from Table 2.2 using the formulas of (3.4.11) for grouped data, we obtain

$$\bar{x} \text{ (grouped)} = \{(11.5) (1) + (12.5) (3) + \cdots + (21.5) (1)\}/80$$

$$= 16.23,$$

$$\sum_{i=1}^{80} f_i m_i = 1299, \sum_{i=1}^{80} f_i m_i^2 = 21{,}406$$

$$s^2 = 3.97, \; s = 1.99.$$

Note how closely the means and standard deviations computed from the grouped and ungrouped data agree. ■

Sometimes a sample will have some numbers repeated, and in some cases, especially when the sample values are counts, a sample may consist of a few distinct values that are repeated with high frequency. When this is the case, the formulas in (3.4.11) can be used to compute the means and variances for the sample where $m_1, \cdots, m_k$ are replaced by the distinct values appearing in the sample. We illustrate these computations in the following example.

Example 3.12: The ages of 77 students in a statistics class were:

Age, x_i:	19	20	21	22	23	24
Frequency, f_i:	2	29	32	12	1	1

We compute the sample mean, sample variance, standard deviation, and median of this data.

$$\sum f_i x_i = (2)(19) + (29)(20) + \cdots + (1)(24)$$

$$= 1601, \text{ so } \bar{x} = (1601)/77 \doteq 20.79$$

$$\sum f_i x_i^2 = (2)(19)^2 + (29)(20)^2 + \cdots + (1)(24)^2 = 33{,}347$$

$$s^2 = \left\{ \sum f_i x_i^2 - \left(\sum f_i x_i \right)^2 \Big/ 77 \right\} \Big/ 76 = 0.7720, \; s = 0.88,$$

$$X_{MED} = X_{(\{77+1\}/2)} = X_{(39)} = 21$$

■

3.5 PROPERTIES OF THE SAMPLING DISTRIBUTIONS OF SAMPLE MEANS, VARIANCES, AND RANGES

As was noted in section 3.4, a statistic is a function of the random variables in a sample and is therefore itself a random variable, and, of course, has a probability distribution. This distribution is called the *sampling distribution* of the statistic. We now consider some properties of the sampling distributions of the sample mean and sample variance of a sample from an infinite population.

3.5.1 Sample Means and Variances from any Reference Distribution

Let $\overline{X} = (X_1 + \cdots + X_n)/n$ denote the mean of a sample on a random variable X, say, with mean $\mu = E(X)$ and variance $\sigma^2 = \text{Var}(X)$. We consider first the mean and variance of $\overline{X}$. By using the properties of the expectation operator we have:

$$\mu_{\overline{x}} = E(\overline{X}) = E\{(X_1 + \cdots + X_n)/n\}$$

$$= E\left(\frac{X_1}{n}\right) + \cdots + E\left(\frac{X_n}{n}\right)$$

$$= \frac{\mu}{n} + \cdots + \frac{\mu}{n} = \mu$$

$$\sigma_{\overline{x}}^2 = \text{Var}(\overline{X}) = \text{Var}\{(X_1 + \cdots + X_n)/n\}$$

$$= \text{Var}(X_1 + \cdots + X_n)/n^2$$

$$= (\sigma^2 + \cdots + \sigma^2)/n^2 = \frac{\sigma^2}{n}$$

These results express the mean and variance of the sampling distribution of the sample mean $\overline{X}$ in terms of the mean μ and variance σ^2 of the parent distribution from which the sample was drawn. To summarize

$$E(\overline{X}) = \mu_{\bar{x}} = \mu$$

$$\text{Var } (\overline{X}) = \sigma_{\bar{x}}^2 = \frac{\sigma^2}{n}, \quad SD(\overline{X}) \frac{\sigma}{\sqrt{n}}$$ (3.5.1)

The sample mean $\overline{X}$ is said to be an *unbiased* estimate of the parent distribution mean μ, because μ is the mean of the sampling distribution of $\overline{X}$. It should be observed that these results were obtained using only general properties of expectations and random samples, and do not depend on the form of the parent distribution, or even on whether the parent distribution is discrete or continuous. Note that $SD(\overline{X}) = \sigma/\sqrt{n}$ decreases as sample size n increases. Thus, if we choose n large enough, the standard deviation of the sample mean can be made as small as we desire. However, it should be noted that when n is chosen large in order to reduce the standard deviation of $\overline{X}$, large numbers of additional observations will eventually be required to achieve significant further reductions. To illustrate this point, suppose $\sigma = 10$ and consider the percent reduction (%r) of $SD(\overline{X}) = \sigma_{\bar{x}} = \sigma/\sqrt{n}$ for a few selected values of n.

n:	1	4	25	50	100	500	1000
$\sigma_{\bar{x}}$:	10	5	2	1.42	1	.45	.32
%r:	0	50	80	85.9	90	95.5	96.8

We can also show that S^2 is an unbiased estimate of σ^2 as follows. Recall for any random variable X that

$$\text{Var}(X) = E(X^2) - [E(X)]^2, \text{ or } \sigma^2 = E(X^2) - \mu^2,$$

and therefore $E(X^2) = \mu^2 + \sigma^2$

So, $E[(n - 1)S^2] = E\left(\sum_{i=1}^{n} X^2\right) - E\left(\sum_{i=1}^{n} X\right)^2 /n$

$$= n(\mu^2 + \sigma^2) - (n^2\mu^2 + n\sigma^2)/n = (n - 1)\sigma^2$$

and $E(S^2) = \sigma^2$, so S^2 is an unbiased estimator of σ^2, and, again, note especially that this result does not depend on the form of the parent distribution.

The sample variance S^2 computed from a sample from a distribution with variance σ^2 is an unbiased estimate of σ^2, that is   (3.5.2)

$$E(S^2) = \sigma^2$$

Recall that we use the symbol Z to denote a standard normal, $N(0, 1)$, random variable, and that $\Phi(z)$ is the distribution function of a $N(0, 1)$ random variable. The next property of a sample mean plays an important role in much work in quality improvement.

The Central Limit Theorem, CLT: If $\overline{X}$ is the mean of a sample on a parent random variable X with mean μ and finite variance σ^2, then for n large

$$Z = \frac{\sqrt{n}(\overline{X} - \mu)}{\sigma},$$ (3.5.3)

has a distribution that is closely approximated by a $N(0, 1)$ distribution.

This approximation statement means that

$$P(Z \le z) = P\left\{\frac{\sqrt{n}(\overline{X} - \mu)}{\sigma} \le z\right\} \doteq \Phi(z)$$

$$= \frac{1}{\sqrt{2\pi}} \int_{-\infty}^{z} e^{-z^2/2} dz \text{ for } -\infty < z < \infty$$

Note that the parent random variable can be continuous or discrete.

In applying the central limit theorem to evaluate probabilities of events involving $\overline{X}$, a decision must be made as to when the sample size n is large enough for the approximation to be adequate. There is no simple rule that can be followed in all cases because the goodness of the approximation depends on the form of the parent distribution. If the parent distribution is itself normal, then $\overline{X}$ is exactly a normal random variable for all sample sizes. The approximation tends to be better when the parent distribution is symmetric, when it is unimodal, and when the probability mass is all concentrated in a bounded interval. Since industrial data are usually unimodal, this means that the CLT should take effect rapidly, and that sample means of even small samples of industrial data will often be well approximated by a normal distribution. In fact, Shewhart studied industrial data of many types empirically and concluded that for most industrial data samples of size 4 or 5 are large enough for the normal approximation to the mean to be adequate for practical purposes. This is a principal reason why, as we shall discuss further in Chapter 4, Shewhart $\overline{X}$ control charts are often made using samples of size 4 or 5.

Example 3.13: The diameter measurements of certain parts have a mean of 2 cm and a standard deviation of 0.001 cm. A sample of five of these parts is regularly taken and the diameters are gauged. By using the central limit theorem, evaluate the probability that the mean of a sample of five of these parts will be in the interval 2 ± 0.001.

Solution: The mean $\overline{X}$ is approximately a $N(2, 0.001^2/5) = N(2, 0.000447^2)$ random variable. Thus we have

$$P(1.999 \leq \overline{X} \leq 2.001) = P\left(\frac{1.999 - 2}{0.000447} \leq Z \leq \frac{2.001 - 2}{0.000447}\right)$$

$$= \Phi(-2.24) - \Phi(-2.24)$$

$$= 0.98745 - 0.01255 = 0.974490 \qquad \blacksquare$$

3.5.2 Sample Means, Variances, and Ranges from Normal Distributions

In this subsection, $X_1, \cdots, X_n$ denotes a sample on a random variable with a $N(\mu, \sigma^2)$ distribution. Since $\overline{X}$ is a linear function of independent normal random variables, it follows immediately from (2.8.2) that $\overline{X}$ is itself also a normal random variable.

> If $\overline{X}$ is the mean of a random sample from a $N(\mu, \sigma^2)$ distribution, then $\overline{X}$ is itself a $N(\mu, \sigma^2/n)$ random variable. $\qquad$ (3.5.4)

This result should be compared with the central limit theorem, which says that for *n* *large* the sample mean has a probability distribution that is well approximated by a $N(\mu, \sigma^2/n)$ distribution. However, if the parent distribution is itself normal, then the sample mean is exactly normally distributed for all—even small—values of *n*.

Example 3.14: Suppose that X is a $N(\mu, 25)$ random variable, and $\overline{X}$ is the mean of a sample of n observations on the parent random variable X.

(a) Evaluate the probability that $\overline{X}$ is within 3 units of μ when $n = 5$.

(b) How many observations must be taken if we want $\overline{X}$ to be within 3 units of μ with probability at least 0.95?

Solution: (a) $\sigma^2 = 25$, $\mathrm{Var}(\overline{X}) = \dfrac{\sigma^2}{n} = \dfrac{25}{5} = 5$

$$P\{|\overline{X} - \mu| \le 3\} = P\{-3 \le \overline{X} - \mu \le 3\}$$

$$= P\left(\frac{-3}{\sqrt{5}} \le Z \le \frac{3}{\sqrt{5}}\right)$$

$$= 2\,\Phi\left(\frac{3}{\sqrt{5}}\right) - 1$$

$$= 2(0.9099) - 1 = \underline{0.8198}$$

(b) Required: $P\{-3 \le \overline{X} - \mu \le 3\} \ge 0.95$,

or, $P\left(\dfrac{-3\sqrt{n}}{5} \le Z \le \dfrac{3\sqrt{n}}{5}\right) \ge 0.95$, since $\mathrm{Var}(\overline{X}) = \dfrac{25}{n}$.

Then $\dfrac{3\sqrt{n}}{5} \ge 1.96 \Rightarrow n \ge \{(1.96)(5)/3\}^2 = 10.67$

$$\Rightarrow n = 11. \qquad \blacksquare$$

The next result is given here without proof.

If $X_1, \cdots, X_n$ is a sample from a $N(\mu, \sigma^2)$ parent distribution, then

(1) $\dfrac{(n-1)S^2}{\sigma^2}$ is a χ^2_{n-1} random variable,

and

(2) S^2 and $\overline{X}$ are independent statistics.

$(3.5.5)$

Example 3.15: Suppose S^2 is the sample variance from a sample on a $N(\mu, 30)$ distribution. Find a value c such that $P(S^2 > c) = 0.1$ when $n = 10$ and 60.

Solution: For $n = 10$

$$P(S^2 > c) = P\left(\frac{(n-1)S^2}{\sigma^2} > \frac{(n-1)c}{\sigma^2}\right) = P\left(\chi^2_9 > \frac{9c}{30}\right)$$

From Table A.2, $\dfrac{9c}{30} = \chi^2_{0.1,9} = 14.68$, and $c = 48.9$.

For $n = 60$ we use the inverse chi-squared distribution function on the Q-Charts disk.
Recall that in (2.9.2) the distribution function was written as

$$G_\nu(y) = P(\chi^2_\nu \le y)$$

and we write $G_\nu^{-1}(u)$ for the corresponding inverse distribution function. Then

$$P(S^2 > c) = P\left(\chi_{59}^2 > \frac{59c}{30}\right) = 1 - P\left(\chi_{59}^2 \leq \frac{59c}{30}\right)$$

$$= 0.1, \text{ and so}$$

$$P\left(\chi_{59}^2 \leq \frac{59c}{30}\right) = 0.99, \text{ and } \frac{59c}{30} = G_{59}^{-1}(0.99) = 87.166,$$

from the Q-Charts disk, and thus

$$c = (30/59)87.166 = 44.32 \qquad \blacksquare$$

The Student-t distribution was introduced in display (2.9.6). Recall that we standardize a $N(\mu, \sigma^2)$ random variable by subtracting its mean and dividing by its standard deviation to obtain $Z = (\overline{X} - \mu)\sqrt{n}/\sigma$, which is a $N(0, 1)$ random variable, and has a distribution that does not depend on either μ or σ. In order to perform this standardizing transformation, we require knowledge of the value of σ, which is not always available. When this is the case, replace σ by the sample standarde deviation S to obtain $T = (\overline{X} - \mu)\sqrt{n}/S$. This is called the *Studentized* sample mean and its distribution is given in (3.5.6). Note that this result requires the independence of $\overline{X}$ and S^2.

> If $\overline{X}$ and S^2 are the sample mean and variance of a sample $X_1, \cdots, X_n$ of $N(\mu, \sigma^2)$ random variables, then
>
> $$T = \frac{\sqrt{n}(\overline{X} - \mu)}{S} \qquad (3.5.6)$$
>
> is a Student-t random variable with $\nu = n - 1$ degrees of freedom.

We sometimes denote a Student-t random variable by T_ν if we wish to specifically note the value of the degrees of freedom parameter ν. The Student-t density function is given in display (2.9.6). It is readily seen that the density function satisfies $f(-t) = f(t)$, and is therefore a symmetric function about zero. Figure 2.9 shows the densities of two Student-t distributions and a $N(0, 1)$ density. The density of a Student-t random variable is similar in shape to that of a $N(0, 1)$ density, however, it is lower at zero and has thicker tails.

We consider next a setting where the Snedecor-F distribution is useful in applications. Let S_1^2 and S_2^2 denote the sample variances of independent samples of sizes n_1 and n_2 from $N(\mu_1, \sigma_1^2)$ and $N(\mu_2, \sigma_2^2)$ distributions, respectively. Then from the definition of display (2.9.9) we can write

$$F_{n_1-1,n_2-1} = \frac{S_1^2/\sigma_1^2}{S_2^2/\sigma_2^2} \tag{3.5.7}$$

That is, this ratio is a Snedecor-F statistic with $\nu_1 = n_1 - 1$ and $\nu_2 = n_2 - 1$. This quantity depends on the ratio of variances (σ_1^2/σ_2^2), and can be computed only when this value is known. An important special case occurs when $\sigma_2^2 = c\,\sigma_1^2$, for c a known constant, since then the F_{n_1-1,n_2-1} statistic of (3.5.7) becomes

$$F_{n_1-1,n_2-1} = c\,\frac{S_1^2}{S_2^2} \tag{3.5.8}$$

which is a value we can compute since it depends on no unknown parameters.

Example 3.16: Samples of sizes n_1 and n_2 are drawn from two normal distributions $N(\mu_1, \sigma_1^2)$ and $N(\mu_2, \sigma_2^2)$ with $\sigma_1^2 = \sigma_2^2$. For S_1^2 and S_2^2 the sample variances, find the upper and lower 0.05 significance points of the distribution of S_1^2/S_2^2 for (a) $n_1 = 8$ and $n_2 = 10$, and (b) $n_1 = 50$ and $n_2 = 80$.

Solution: (a) Here $\nu_1 = n_1 - 1 = 7$, and $\nu_2 = n_2 - 1 = 9$. Thus from Table A.4 we get $F_{0.05;7,9} = 3.29$. Also, from (2.9.11)

$$F_{0.95;7,9} = \frac{1}{F_{0.05;9,7}} = \frac{1}{3.68} = 0.272$$

(b) The needed values are not given in Table A.4, and we illustrate the more general procedure using the Q-Charts disk, which can be used whenever the values of either α, n_1, or n_2 are not given in either Table A.4 of this book or other available tables. Recall that in (2.9.9) we used the notation $H_{\nu_1,\nu_2}(f)$ for the Snedecor-F distribution function. With this notation we write

$$P\left(\frac{S_1^2}{S_2^2} \le c\right) = P(F_{49,79} \le c) = H_{49,79}(c) = 0.95;$$

thus, $F_{0.05;49,79} = H_{49,79}^{-1}(0.95) = 1.513$, from the Q-Charts disk. Here the symbol $H_{49,79}^{-1}(0.95)$ denotes the *inverse* Snedecor-F distribution function, and *not* a reciprocal function.

and
$$P\left(\frac{S_1^2}{S_2^2} > c\right) = P(F_{49,79} > c) = 0.95,$$

$$P(F_{49,79} \le c) = H_{49,79}(c) = 0.05$$

thus, $F_{0.95;49,79} = H_{49,79}^{-1}(0.05) = 0.645$, from the Q-Charts disk ∎

3.6 CONCEPTS OF STATISTICAL INFERENCE: ESTIMATION, PREDICTION

In our work in SPC we shall need an awareness of certain basic concepts of statistical inference, which we now review.

3.6.1 Estimation

We are often concerned with a sample $X_1, X_2, \cdots, X_n$ on a random variable X that has a distribution that is a member of a parametric class of distributions such as a normal $N(\mu, \sigma^2)$ distribution or a binomial $b(x; n, p)$ distribution. In order to consider a particular member of these classes, we must specify the value of one or more parameters such as (μ, σ) for the normal or p for the binomial. The general task in the field of parameter estimation is to use the sample $X_1, X_2, \cdots, X_n$ to infer information about parameters. This is generally done by either computing a value from the sample that is, in some sense, our best estimate of the value of the parameter when the sample was taken, or we sometimes compute a confidence interval for the parameter value. The confidence interval is assigned a confidence coefficient such as 0.90 and 0.95 of containing the value of the parameter. For example, we can compute a 0.95 confidence interval for a normal mean μ or binomial probability p using well-known formulas. The key point we wish to make is that the object of this *estimation* is a parameter that is itself a constant. Generally, if enough data are available we can expect to obtain an estimate of a parameter that is very close to the value of the parameter when the data were observed.

3.6.2 Prediction

In contrast to the problem of estimating the value of a parameter, we are generally concerned in SPC with predicting the value of a random variable. We can predict the value of a random variable under some conditions, the simplest of which is when we know its distribution completely. Then if a "best" guess or point predicted value of the random variable is needed, either the distribution mean or median could be chosen. Also, if an interval is required, the distribution can be examined in order to specify a *prediction interval* and a probability that a determination of the random variable will fall in the interval. Note that there is a sharp distinction between confidence intervals for parameters and prediction intervals for random variables.

To illustrate the concepts, suppose we have gauged ten parts made by a process with known standard deviation $\sigma = \sigma_0 = 0.011$ and found that the measurements have mean $\overline{X} = 10.00$. If the measurements are assumed to be normally distributed, then a 95% confidence interval for the process mean μ is given by

$$\overline{X} \pm \frac{\sigma_0}{\sqrt{n}} z_{.025} = 10.00 \pm \frac{0.011}{\sqrt{10}} 1.96$$

$$\Rightarrow (9.993, 10.007)$$

Note that the length of this confidence interval is 0.014.

Consider next a prediction interval. Suppose we have gauged enough parts to decide that the measurements are actually $N(\mu, \sigma^2) = N(10.00, 0.011^2)$ distributed. From this we can write a .95 prediction interval

$$(\mu \pm 1.96\ \sigma) = 10.00 \pm (1.96)(0.011)$$

$$\Rightarrow (9.978, 10.022)$$

The length of this prediction interval is 0.044, about three times the length of the above confidence interval for the mean μ.

Observe carefully the fundamental difference of confidence and prediction intervals. A confidence interval estimates the value a parameter had when the data were taken. By taking a large enough sample we can determine this value of the parameter to any desired degree of accuracy. However, a prediction interval is a fixed interval that another measurement will fall into with a stated probability. We *estimate* the value of a parameter, but we *predict* the value of a random variable.

PROBLEMS

3.1 The actual mileage obtained from 12 "40,000 mile"steel-belted radial tires was (in 1000-mile units);

| 23 | 28 | 24 | 18 | 21 | 15 |
| 19 | 16 | 30 | 22 | 31 | 27 |

(a) Make a dot plot of these observed values.

(b) Compute the order statistics, the sample mean, and the median.

(c) Compute the sample variance, standard deviation, and range.

3.2 The amount of time in minutes required for a worker to perform a task on an assembly line in each of 20 trials was

```
3.0 3.9 1.0 3.4 4.3 3.2 2.3 3.9 3.0 1.4
2.7 2.1 3.7 3.4 3.1 3.5 2.9 2.6 4.2 3.2
```

(a) Make a dot plot of these observed values.

(b) Compute the order statistics, the sample mean, and the median.

(c) Compute the sample variance, standard deviation, and range.

(d) Make a stem-and-leaf diagram of this data.

3.3 Determinations of the amounts of aflatoxin in batches of corn by the USDA gave the following data in parts per million (ppm):

35.4	56.7	32.6	56.4	38.4
53.3	22.3	47.4	49.1	45.9
40.6	43.5	50.5	22.5	51.6
41.9	46.6	43.6	30.2	75.9
48.0	31.5	40.9	33.6	67.3
79.4	38.3	51.5	56.9	43.1
32.3	51.4	50.0	36.0	54.9
40.6	42.7	49.2	42.5	47.6
49.3	49.0	46.7	47.2	59.0
44.6	42.4	63.0	38.7	31.6

(a) Make a frequency distribution for this data using six class intervals:

$$20 \rightarrow 29.95, \ 30 \rightarrow 39.95, \ \cdots, \ 70 - 79.95.$$

(b) Draw a histogram of the frequency distribution.

(c) Compute the mean and standard deviation from the ungrouped data.

(d) Compute the mean and standard deviation from the grouped data of your frequency distribution in (a). Compare these values with those obtained in (c).

3.4 Make a C&E diagram for a class in statistical process control where the "effect" is *learning*. Major "cause" branches should include: student, instructor, classroom, book(s), etc.

3.5 One hundred resistors had lives in hours, x, as given in the frequency table

Interval	Frequency
$100 \leq x \leq 200$	12
$200 \leq x < 300$	23
$300 \leq x < 400$	25
$400 \leq x < 500$	21
$500 \leq x < 600$	11
$600 \leq x < 700$	5
$700 \leq x \ 800$	2
$800 \leq x \ 900$	1

(a) Make a histogram for this frequency distribution.

(b) Compute the grouped mean $\bar{x}$ and standard deviation s.

(c) Using the values of $\bar{s}$ and s obtained in (b), compute the values of the density function, of a $N(\bar{x}, s^2)$ distribution at the values $x = 150, 250, \cdots, 850$. Plot these values on the same graph as the histogram in part (a), and draw, in a different color, a bell-shaped normal density function connecting these points. Compare these graphs to decide if resistor lives follow a normal distribution.

3.6 The reported monthly starting salaries of 70 randomly selected graduates of State University are given in the following table.

$1208	1028	1615	1400	1195	1630	1395
1040	840	1790	1060	1640	1200	1325
1280	1250	1100	1140	1345	1040	1275
2290	1625	1335	1410	1900	1750	1575
1290	2000	1560	1100	1400	1070	1440
1500	1150	1450	1800	1560	1525	1290
1675	970	2050	1280	1010	1490	930
2055	1960	1390	1875	2085	1675	1425
1425	1100	1510	1310	1500	1250	1090
1070	1080	1290	900	1345	1325	1400

(a) Construct a frequency distribution for this data using class intervals $800 \leq x < 1000$, $1000 \leq x < 1200$, and so on.

(b) Draw a histogram to display the data.

(c) Compute the sample mean, median, and standard deviation from the data.

(d) Compute the grouped sample mean and standard deviation from the frequency distribution constructed in part (a) above.

3.7 A wildlife biologist in Montana wished to compare the variability of doe weights of mule and whitetail deer in a particular deer management area. Random samples gave the following data (in lb):

Mule Deer Does:	110	130	135	160	175	140	150
Whitetail Does:	85	90	120	65	105	115	80

(a) Compute the means and variances of the two samples, and compare the spread of these samples.

(b) Compute the coefficients of variation and compare the spread of these samples using these scale-free measures of spread.

3.8   Given the frequency distribution of the ages of students in a statistics class:

Age (yr):	17	18	19	20	21	22	23	24
Frequency:	1	2	7	28	37	6	1	2

(a) Draw a histogram of this data.

(b) Compute the sample mean and standard deviation.

3.9   A sample of chief executives and laborers gave the following income data.

	Sample Size	Sample Mean	Sample S.D.
Executives	30	130,000	40000
Laborers	4000	12,000	3000

Compute the coefficients of variation to compare the variability of incomes.

3.10   A wildlife biologist conducted a creel census on Rock Creek and obtained the following data on the numbers of trout caught by licensed fishermen.

Number Fish:	0	1	2	3	4	5	6	7	8	9	10
Frequency:	8	18	23	16	14	16	9	5	2	4	9

Compute the sample mean, standard deviation, mode, and median.

3.11 An urn contains ten balls stamped with the numbers 0, 1, 2, $\cdots$, 9, and are otherwise identical. A sample of ten balls is drawn *with replacement*. For $\overline{X}$ the sample mean, use the central limit theorem to evaluate $P(\overline{X} > 5)$.

3.12 The ball bearings made by a certain machine have a mean diameter of 1.1 cm and standard deviation of 0.002 cm. If a random sample of ten of these bearings is taken, use the central limit theorem to evaluate the probability that the mean of this sample will differ from 1.1 cm by more than 0.001 cm.

3.13 An automobile manufacturer claims that his economy car averages 30 mpg with a standard deviation of 3 mpg. An independent testing group tests ten of these cars for mileage. If the manufacturer's claim is valid, use the central limit theorem to evaluate the probability that the average mileage for these ten cars will be less than 27 mpg.

3.14 To determine the percentage of one component in a compound, a chemist uses an analysis method which gives a number that is an observation on a random variable with mean equal to the true percentage μ of the ingredient in the compound, and sd of 2%. If $\overline{X}$ is the mean (in %) of n replicate analyses, evaluate $P(|\overline{X} - \mu| > 1)$ for $n = 5$, 15, and 30.

3.15 A sample of size $n = 10$ is drawn from a uniform $U(0, 1)$ distribution, that is, a distribution with density function

$$f(x) = 1 \text{ for } 0 < x < 1$$
$$= 0 \text{ elsewhere}$$

Use the central limit theorem to evaluate $P(|\overline{X} - 1/2| < 1/4)$.

3.16 A biochemist wishes to determine the amount of aflatoxin in a large bin of peanuts. He selects a small sample of peanuts and analyzes it for aflatoxin content using a method of analysis that has a standard deviation of 15 parts per million (ppm). If he is to make n replicate analyses, how large should he choose n if it is required to estimate the true mean aflatoxin content to within 5 ppm with probability 0.95? Assume that n is large enough for the central limit theorem to apply.

3.17 The weights of passengers who ride an elevator are randomly draw from a distribution with mean $\mu = 140$ lbs and sd $\sigma = 30$ lb. If the weight capacity of the elevator is 1600 lbs, what is the probability that it will be overloaded with ten passengers? Assume the CLT obtains.

3.18 Let $\overline{X}$ be the mean of a sample of size 25 from a $N(10, 25)$ distribution. Evaluate $P(9 \le \overline{X} \le 12)$.

3.19 Let $\overline{X}$ be the mean of a sample of size n from a $N(50, 25)$ distribution. Evaluate $P(45 \le \overline{X} \le 55)$ for each value of $n = 1$, 4, 9, and 16.

3.20 The diameters of ball bearings produced by a certain machine are normally distributed with mean 0.65 cm and sd 0.002 cm. A production inspector takes a sample of ten of these bearings and computes the sample mean. What is the probability that the mean will fall within 0.001 cm of 0.65 cm?

3.21 For S the sample standard deviation of a sample of size $n = 50$ from a $N(\mu, 25)$ distribution, find a value c such that $P(S > c) = 0.90$.

3.22 A sample of size $n = 10$ is drawn on a $N(\mu, 9)$ random variable. For $T = (\overline{X} - \mu)\sqrt{10}/S$, evaluate
(a) $P(T > 2.262)$ and $P(|T| > 1.833)$
(b) $P(S^2 > 2.088)$ and $P(S < 4.65)$.

3.23 A sample of size n is drawn on a $N(10, \sigma^2)$ random variable. For each value of $n = 15$, 30, and 50
(a) find a value for c such that $P(S^2 > c) = 0.05$, $\sigma^2 = 25$;
(b) find a value for c such that $P\left[\dfrac{(\overline{X} - 10)\sqrt{n}}{S} > c \right] = 0.01$.

3.24 A sample of size 5 is drawn from a $N(\mu, \sigma^2)$ distribution, and the sample mean $\overline{X}$ and variance S^2 are both computed. Evaluate c in each of the following.

(a) $P\left\{\sqrt{5}\left(\dfrac{\overline{X}-\mu}{\sigma}\right)>1.59\right\}=c$

(b) $P\left\{\sqrt{5}\left(\dfrac{\overline{X}-\mu}{S}\right)>c\right\}=0.05$

(c) $P\left(\dfrac{S^2}{\sigma^2}>c\right)=0.05$

3.25 A sample of size ten is drawn from a $N(\mu,\sigma^2)$ distribution, and the sample mean $\overline{X}$ and variance S^2 are both computed. Evaluate c in each of the following.

(a) $P\left(\dfrac{\overline{X}-\mu}{\sigma}>0.52\right)=c$

(b) $P\left(\dfrac{\overline{X}-\mu}{S}>c\right)=0.05$

(c) $P\left(\dfrac{S^2}{\sigma^2}>c\right)=0.05$

3.26 Independent samples of sizes $n_1=8$ and $n_2=10$ are drawn from $N(\mu_1,\sigma_1^2)$ and $N(\mu_2,\sigma_2^2)$ distributions and the sample variances S_1^2 and S_2^2 are computed. Then if $\sigma_1^2=\sigma_2^2$, evaluate c in each of the following.

(a) $P\left\{\dfrac{S_1^2}{S_2^2}>c\right\}=0.05,$

(b) $P\{S_1^2>3.29\,S_2^2\}=c,$

(c) $P\left\{\dfrac{S_1^2}{S_2^2}\le c\right\}=0.05,$

(d) $P\{S_1^2\le0.149\,S_2^2\}=c.$

3.27 Independent samples of sizes $n_1=10$ and $n_2=6$ are drawn from $N(\mu_1,\sigma_1^2)$ and $N(\mu_2,\sigma_2^2)$ distributions, and the sample variances S_1^2 and S_2^2 are computed. Then if $\sigma_1^2=2\sigma_2^2$, evaluate c in each of the following.

(a) $P\left\{\dfrac{S_1^2}{S_2^2}>c\right\}=0.05,$

(b) $P\{S_1^2>6.64\,S_2^2\}=c,$

(c) $P\left\{\dfrac{S_1^2}{S_2^2}\le c\right\}=0.05,$

(d) $P\{S_1^2\le9.54\,S_2^2\}=0.95.$

3.28 A sample of 15 measurements of hole diameters drilled by a certail drill press had a sample mean of $\bar{x} = 0.145$ cm. These hole diameters are known to be approximately normally distributed with a standard deviation of $\sigma = 0.002$.

(a) Compute a 95% confidence interval for the mean diameter, μ, of holes from this drill press.

(b) Suppose one more hole is to be drilled by this press. Give a 95% prediction interval for the diameter that this hole will have.

(c) Discuss the distinction between the intervals computed in parts (a) and (b).

■■■■■■ CHAPTER 4

Classical Shewhart Control Charts for Variables

In this chapter we will present some classical Shewhart control charting methods for variables. These methods have been widely used with good success. These charting techniques work best if the data are at least approximately normally distributed and there are enough data available to assume good parameter estimates. Thus, these techniques are most useful for high-volume manufacturing and other settings where data are plentiful. In later chapters we will consider methods that can be used in low-volume manufacturing when data are not available prior to the beginning of charting activities.

4.1 WORK PROCESS CONTROL AND QUALITY VARIABLES

A work process is a series of activities that converts inputs into production units of output by the combined contributions of men, methods, materials, machines, measurements, and environment—the so-called 5 m&e classification of inputs. The work processes that we are concerned with controlling can often be broken down into separate subprocesses or operations that are carried out sequentially in time. A flow chart of the work process is useful to display and study the process. Figure 4.1 shows a generic form of a process flow chart for drilling a mounting hole for a starter bracket.

We are primarily interested in the variation in the positions of a drilled mounting hole from a defined surface. Observe that there are $2 \times 3 \times 2 \times 2 = 24$ different process flow paths for this process. Actually, there are other factors that should also be accounted for since it is likely that some operations will involve more than one operator, machines will use more than one tool, or have multiple heads, etc. At the point of input or output, for each machine, or operation, or for the output for the entire system, we can consider defining a quality variable that reflects the stability of the process at that point.

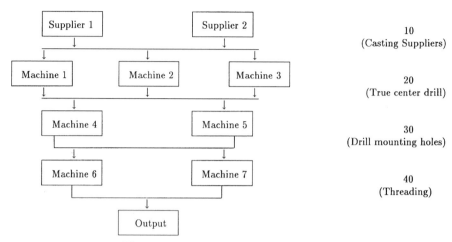

Figure 4.1   Generic Process Flow Chart

We obtain values of a quality variable X by either measurement or counting and the values we obtain will generally show some variation, so X can be considered a random variable. This random variable can be either continuous or discrete. Examples of continuous variables include measurements of parts dimensions such as the lengths of steel rods, the angles of gear teeth, the resistance of transistors, the percentage of a component in a chemical compound, the percentage of defectives in lots of purchased items, and so on. Discrete or counting variables could be the number of typographical errors on a page, the number of defective items in a subgroup of items, the number of effective items produced before the first defective, the number of warranty claims on an automobile in its first 12 months of service, or the number of false negative Pap smears by a laboratory per 1000 analyses. Such quality variables are important in the control of quality of services as well as for the manufacture of products.

Consider the values of a quality variable associated with units of product which can be denoted by a sequence of values

$$X_1, X_2, \ldots, X_n, \ldots \tag{4.1.1}$$

These values may be, for example, the lengths of steel rods measured consecutively as they are produced. No matter how precisely these rods are made, if they are measured with sufficient precision, it will be found that there is always some variation among the sequence of numbers obtained. Some variation will be present in sequences of determinations on any quality variable.

The variability in multiple determinations of a quality variable can be attributed to some set of sources or causes. For example, the variations in the lengths of rods can be attributed to a large number of known and unknown causes such as metallurgical variation in the stock, temperature of the metal during milling, the ambient temperature during milling, the type of lubricating fluid, as well as variation from different milling machines or operators, chipped or broken tools, measurement error, and so on. The number of known and unknown contributing causes is often large.

A process producing units of product with a particular related quality variable was defined by Shewhart, in general, to be a *stable* process or a process that is *operating in statistical control,* with respect to this variable, *if the values of the quality variable are predictable.* The values of a variable are predictable if the probability that the variable falls within prescribed limits can be stated. As mentioned in Chapter 1, the multitude of different sources or causes of variability in the sequence of values of a quality variable, as denoted in (4.1.1), were grouped by Shewhart into two classifications called *chance* and *assignable* causes of variation. Deming substitutes the terms *common* and *special* for *chance* and *assignable,* respectively. If a production process is operating with only common causes of variation, then we may be able to assume that the process generating the values X_i ($i = 1, 2, \ldots$) is stable or in-control. In order for a process to be stable, that is, to the predictable, it is often sufficient that the values X_i arise from a particular parametric model. Much of the work in statistical process control, SPC, has been based on the constant mean and variance model given in (4.1.2), which we shall call the *classical constant mean and variance stable model.*

A process producing the values X_i ($i = 1, 2, \cdots$) is said to be a *stable* or *in-control* process in the classical (Shewhart) sense if we can write $X_i = \mu + \epsilon_i$ for $i = 1, 2, \cdots$ where

1. μ is a constant,
2. the ϵ_i's are independently distributed random variables,
3. the ϵ_i's are distributed with common mean $E(\epsilon_i) = 0$, and common constant variance $\text{Var}(\epsilon_i) = \sigma^2$ for $i = 1, 2, \cdots$.

(4.1.2)

Note, in particular, that this does not require that the quality variable must have a normal distribution. If during a run of production units; $i = 1, 2, \ldots, n$, some special causes are affecting the production process, then the above model cannot adequately represent the process. Special causes may result in the process distribution parameters, and possibly its shape, also, shifting unpredictably. This is a state of chaos and the process is said to be unstable or "out of control," because we cannot assess the probability that values will fall outside limits. In most cases, when a change in the process distribution occurs it will entail a change in either the process mean μ or the process standard deviation σ, or both. In all cases, a change in the process distribution should be reflected by a change in the pattern of points in a runs plot such as that in Fig. 4.2. The plotted points may then show outliers or some other type of nonrandom patterns.

It should be noted that in practice the distinction between common and special causes is not always sharp. The concept of a stable or in-control system affected only by change or common causes is due to Shewhart and is nevertheless an extremely useful one. One useful way of thinking about common and special causes is that special causes are often sources of variation that can be removed by actions taken directly on the work process, probably by operators or other shop-floor workers. On the other hand, common causes are inherent in the process as it presently exists, and eliminating or reducing variation from them generally requires action from engineering or management such as redesigning the work process, purchasing new production equipment, and so on. Note that this implies that once special causes have been eliminated and a process is stable, further improvement by reduction in variation can only be accomplished by engineering or management actions on common causes. See, again, Deming's point 10.

In some problems we consider processes stable that can be represented by models less restrictive than the classical constant mean and

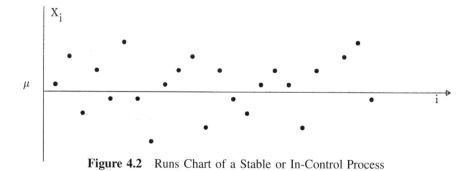

Figure 4.2   Runs Chart of a Stable or In-Control Process

variance model of (4.1.2). However, the Shewhart definition of predictability as the defining characteristic of a stable process will always hold. We will consider any process that can be modeled with a parametric model that can be used to predict future values to be a stable process, because such models satisfy Shewhart's concept of a stable model and are required for some processes. In the following subsections we discuss briefly some such models. SPC methods based on these types of models will be considered in later chapters.

4.1.1 Necessary Trends in the Data

There are some processes that produce data as in (4.1.1) but do not satisfy the conditions of (4.1.2) for an in-control process because the data show certain types of necessary trends. By necessary trends we mean trends that cannot be eliminated by management or engineering actions. There are two particularly important types of trends that arise due to two quite different types of failures of the assumptions of the model (4.1.2). One of these trends occurs when the assumption (1) that the mean is constant is incorrect, but the mean varies in a manner such that the observed values are predictable. This will be called a *regression type* predictable trend. Another type of necessary trend that is present in some types of data is an *autocorrelation type* trend, and is due to the failure of the assumption (2) of independently distributed errors ϵ_i.

When a regression type trend is present in the data, the mean is not constant but is a function of the index i, or, possibly, of some other variable(s). In this case we may be able to express the mean as a function of i and a set of parameters, say $\beta_0, \beta_1, \ldots, \beta_p$, as

$$\mu = g(i; \beta_0, \ldots, \beta_p) \qquad (4.1.3)$$

for g a general regression function depending (possibly) on parameters $\beta_0, \beta_1, \ldots, \beta_p$. The most common form for the regression function is a linear function, $g(i; \beta_0, \beta_1) = \beta_0 + \beta_1 i$. Figure 4.3 shows a plot of points with a linear regression trend. Note that σ is here the standard deviation about the regression line and, moreover, we will call σ the *process standard deviation* in this case. This model is often necessary for tool-wear processes, for example. Tool-wear processes are important in many manufacturing operations and will be considered in Chapter 12.

Another type of necessary trend that is present in some process data is due to autocorrelation that results in dependence among the errors, that is, the ϵ_i's. This dependence may be because values of measure-

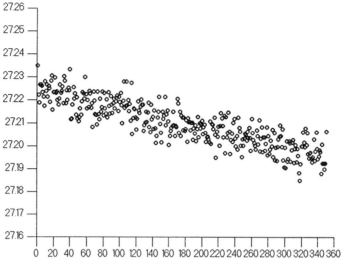

Figure 4.3   Runs Chart of Data with Linear Regression Trend

ments on parts made near the same point in time sometimes tend to be more alike than those on parts made at widely different times. The definition of autocorrelation is given in (4.1.4).

> For the sequence of values of (4.1.1), the *lag h autocorrelation* ρ_h is the correlation between the values X_i and X_{i+h}, that is
>
> $$\rho_h = \mathrm{Corr}(X_i, X_{i+h})$$

(4.1.4)

4.1.2   Other Nonconstant Means Models

In addition to the necessary trends models due to regression or auto-correlation, there are other models that can be used to predict values of the quality variable. Rather than being constant, the mean can, for example, sometimes be taken to be an additive function of components that can represent recognizable factors in the production process. In some applications the variance may not be constant but it may be reasonable to use a model with constant coefficient of variation. In later chapters we will consider some methods of process control based on these nonclassical SPC models. However, in this and the next several chapters, we consider statistical process control methods based on the classical constant mean and variance stable model of (4.1.2). In addition, we will sometimes also assume that the process distribution is a normal distribution.

4.2 OBSERVED AND EXPECTED MEAN SQUARES

In many manufacturing problems the purpose of on-line quality control is to produce units of product so that each measurement X_i of (4.1.2) is as near an ideal or *target value* τ as possible. Now, for an actual sequence of measurements $X_1, X_2, \ldots, X_n$, a measure of the variability of the data about the target value τ is given by the *observed mean square* about τ given by (4.2.1).

$$OMS = \frac{1}{n} \sum_{i=1}^{n} (X_i - \tau)^2 \qquad (4.2.1)$$

If a process is stable with constant values for the process mean and standard deviation, say $\mu = \mu_0$ and $\sigma = \sigma_0$, then we will call these values μ_0 and σ_0 the *nominal* values of μ and σ. The reader should note that these nominal values are not necessarily target or specification values of μ and σ. We also point out that the term *nominal value* is not always used in this way in the quality literature. Indeed, some writers use the terms *target value* and *nominal value* to mean the same value. We shall, however, maintain the above distinction in this book. When a process is operating in control according to (4.1.2) with nominal values μ_0 and σ_0 for the parameters, we can take the expected value of OMS to obtain the *expected mean square* about τ for the process as given in (4.2.2).

$$EMS = (\mu_0 - \tau)^2 + \sigma_0^2 \qquad (4.2.2)$$

We wish to operate a process in a manner such that the process is in control and its EMS is as small as possible. For a process operating in control, its EMS will be a minimum if the constant value μ_0 of the process mean is equal to the target value τ, for then the process expected mean square will be equal to the process variance σ_0^2. The process variance σ_0^2 represents the inherent variation in the measurements due to common causes beyond our control. We cannot reduce the overall variability measured by EMS below the value of σ_0^2 by adjusting the process mean. In order to reduce the value of σ_0^2 we would have to reduce the variability due to the system of common causes, in other words, to actually change the system of common causes. To accomplish this, it is necessary to either improve the present system by removing one or more of the common causes, or to find a way to reduce their effects; or to change to an entirely new manufacturing process by purchasing new technologically advanced manufacturing equipment, utilizing new or different scientific or engineering ideas or techniques, and so on. In many cases it will be found that the most cost-effective approach entails removing common causes from the existing system. Sometimes this can be accmplished with relatively little expense.

The measurements $X_1, X_2, \ldots$ are measured in units of measurement such as inches, pounds, degrees, ohms, feed conversion ratio (FCR), and so on. Whatever the unit of measurement for the observations X_1, $X_2, \ldots$; the values of OMS and EMS are always in units that are the squares of the units of measurement of the observations. For some purposes it is desirable to use an overall measure of the quality of a sequence of production units in units of measurement that are in the same units as the original data. For this purpose, we define the *root observed mean square* as

$$\text{ROMS} = \sqrt{\text{OMS}} = \sqrt{\frac{1}{n} \sum_{i=1}^{n} (X_i - \tau)^2} \qquad (4.2.3)$$

Similarly, we define the *root expected mean square*

$$\text{REMS} = \sqrt{\text{EMS}} = \sqrt{(\mu_0 - \tau)^2 + \sigma_0^2} \qquad (4.2.4)$$

The OMS is an unbiased estimator of EMS, and when the process is operating in control the mean of the distribution of OMS is given by (4.2.2). From this it is clear that to minimize variability we should operate the process with μ_0 equal to τ, for then the first term in (4.2.2) is zero and the overall variability of parts about target value has its minimum value σ_0^2, the process variance.

4.3 SHEWHART CONTROL CHARTS FOR VARIABLES—GENERAL DESCRIPTION

4.3.1 Applications of Shewhart Control Charts—Stability and Adjustment

The classical control charts of Shewhart (1931) have two principal applications. The first of these is to aid in recognizing special causes and bringing a process into a state of control. The second is to aid in the procedure of adjusting a stable process to keep it centered on a target value. We will call the charts used to bring a process into a stable state *stability* charts, and the activities involved in this application *statistical process control—SPC*. We will call the charts used as aids in adjusting a process in order to keep the process mean near a target value *adjustment* charts, and the activities involved in this application *statistical process adjustment—SPA*. In this book we are concerned primarily with SPC charts. These charts can be either variables charts or attributes charts. Variables charts are considered in this chapter, and attributes charts will be studied in Chapter 5.

4.3.2 Stability Charts (SPC) and Adjustment Charts (SPA)

Stability charts of SPC are used as aids to analyze a process and bring it into a state of control. A process is stable or operating in control *with respect to a particular quality variable,* in the sense of Shewhart, if the values of the variable are predictable. A sufficient condition for a variable to be predictable is for the variable to have a constant distribution. In practice, we usually consider it sufficient for a variable to have constant mean and variance to consider it predictable. The control chart is a powerful tool for bringing processes into control due to its capability to help identify special causes of variation so that they can either be eliminated, or production and charting can be organized so as to eliminate the variation from products. This use of control charts is the objective of SPC.

After stability charts have been used to stabilize a process, so that it is meaningful to speak of a process mean μ and variance σ^2, it will often be desirable to adjust the process mean to try to minimize the EMS of (4.2.2). If the process mean μ can be adjusted so that it is close to the target value τ in value, then the bias term $(\mu - \tau)^2$ will be small. If a process can be operated in a stable state with a zero bias, then there is no further way to reduce variation except to reduce the variation from common causes. Adjusting a process will generally involve making feedback or other adjustments to the process in order to produce production units with quality variable measurements close to a desired target value. Such adjustments can involve setting temperatures, fuel flow to a kiln, proportions of a mix, a cutting tool position, true position coordinates, and so on. Feedback adjustments should only be made to stable processes, because adjustments made in response to special causes will likely only create additional variability in the process. This means that generally a stabilization study should be performed before feedback adjustments are begun. Then the model established can be used to aid in designing the adjustment process. The charts that we call SPA charts are sometimes called by other names, including engineering process control (EPC) charts and automated process control (APC) charts. This book is largely concerned with SPC methods, but some material on SPA will be presented in later chapters.

4.3.3 A Generic Shewhart Control Chart

The Shewhart control chart operates as follows. Suppose m subgroups of n observations each are available and the data are denoted as in Table 4.1. We will consider the problem of choosing the subgroups later, but are concerned first with the basic charting technology, assuming that the sampling plan for choosing subgroups has been determined. A statistic, say W (such as $\bar{X}$, S, or R), which estimates an important parameter of the process is computed from each subgroup. The value of this statistic is plotted against a part number, time, or some other relevant ordering variable, on a chart that is marked with a center line (CL), an upper control limit (UCL), and a lower control limit (LCL). Assuming that the process is stable, the control limits are statistical *prediction* or *tolerance* limits for the distribution of the plotted statistic W. These control limits are usually taken to be at three standard deivations above and below the mean of the plotted statistic. That is, for $E(W) = \mu_W$ and $\text{Var}(W) = \sigma_W^2$, assuming both are known values, these classical *3-sigma* control limits are given in display (4.3.1).

$$
\begin{aligned}
UCL(W) &= \mu_W + 3\sigma_W \\
CL(W) &= \mu_W \\
LCL(W) &= \mu_W - 3\sigma_W
\end{aligned}
\qquad (4.3.1)
$$

TABLE 4.1   Notation for Subgroups and Statistics

Subgroup Number i	X_{i1}	X_{i2}	...	X_{in}	$\bar{X}_i$	S_i	R_i
1	X_{11}	X_{12}	...	X_{1n}	$\bar{X}_1$	S_1	R_1
2	X_{21}	X_{22}	...	X_{2n}	$\bar{X}_2$	S_2	R_2
⋮	⋮	⋮		⋮	⋮	⋮	⋮
m	X_{m1}	X_{m2}	...	X_{mn}	$\bar{X}_m$	S_m	R_m
					$\bar{\bar{X}}$	$\bar{S}$	$\bar{R}$

The "Statistics" heading spans the $\bar{X}_i$, S_i, and R_i columns.

When W is a normal random variable, the probability that it will fall above the upper control limit is 0.00135 and is the same that it will fall below the lower control limit. Thus, these 3-sigma control limits constitute a band of 0.99730 prediction intervals for future values of the statistic W. Even when W is not an approximately normal random variable, the 3-sigma control limits of (4.3.1) will still constitute a prediction interval that covers a large proportion of the distribution of the quality statistic W. Moreover, the mean of the normal distribution is also the distribution median so that the probabilities above and below the CL are both 0.5. For nonsymmetric distributions, the median and the mean are not the same value. For these distributions the probabilities above and below the mean will not be 0.5.

The 3-sigma charts are easy to construct and have been widely used with good success; however, there are situations where it is desirable to consider other approaches to constructing Shewhart-type charts. To describe a more general approach to constructing these charts, let w_α $(0 \leq \alpha \leq 1)$ denote the $(1 - \alpha)^{th}$ fractile of the distribution of W. That is, w_α satisfies the equation

$$P(W > w_\alpha) = \alpha$$

Then an α_L *lower probability limit,* an α_U *upper probability limit,* and a center line that has probability 0.5 both above and below it for the quality statistic W are given by

$$
\begin{aligned}
UCL(W) &= w_{\alpha_U} \\
CL(W) &= w_{0.5} \\
LCL(W) &= w_{1-\alpha_L}
\end{aligned}
\qquad (4.3.2)
$$

The interval $[w_{\alpha_L}, w_{\alpha_U}]$ is a $1 - \alpha_L - \alpha_U$ prediction interval for the distribution of W. We call this interval an $[\alpha_L, \alpha_U]$ *probability or prediction interval.* We frequently take $\alpha_L = \alpha_U = \alpha/2$, so that the probabilities of exceeding the control limits are the same for the two limits. The control limits for this chart are also frequently called $1 - \alpha$ probability limits.

Due to the form of the model (4.1.2) to represent measurements for an in-control process, control charts for subgroup means and ranges or standard deviations are of special importance. This is because when an assignable or special cause appears, it will usually induce a change in either the process mean μ or the process standard deviation σ, or both. If the process is operating with μ equal to τ, a desired target value, then a shift of μ away from τ will give an immediate increase in the term $(\mu_0 - \tau)^2$ of the EMS of (4.2.2). Changes of σ due to special causes are usually increases and will also therefore increase the EMS. Changes in μ and σ will be reflected in changes in the subgroup estimates of μ and σ. For this reason control charts for the subgroup mean $\bar{X}$, and for the subgroup range R or standard deviation S, are useful to detect changes in μ and σ.

If special causes of variation can be removed from an operating process until it can be modeled at least approximately by (4.1.2), then the process is considered stable or "in control" in the classical sense. This means that the values of the quality variable measured would all have the same value μ except for random deviations from it due to common causes that are part of the system as it presently exists. This variation due to the system of common causes is measured by the standard deviation σ.

The Decision Procedure

- The control limits from either (4.3.1) or (4.3.2) are drawn on a chart. The sequence of values $W_1, W_2, \cdots$ are plotted on this chart as the subgroups are obtained and these statistics are computed. If the process is in control as specified in display (4.1.2), the pattern of points on the chart should be that of identically and independently distributed statistics.

- If the pattern of points on the W chart is such that it would be highly unlikely for identically and independently distributed statistics, we will decide that the process is unstable or out-of-control and search for special causes. An important signal of the presence of a special cause is to have a point plot outside the control limits. Other particular anomalous patterns will be discussed later for particular charts.

- If all points are between the LCL and the UCL and otherwise no anomalous patterns are observed, we will decide that there is not evidence that the process is unstable. When enough points have been plotted with no signals of special causes observed, we decide that the process is stable or in control. *Note that this is the real purpose of SPC, namely, to establish when a process can reasonably be considered stable or in control.*

4.4 THE $\bar{X}$-, R-, AND S-CHARTS FOR BOTH σ AND μ "KNOWN"

In this section we introduce classical $\bar{X}$-, R-, and S-charts under the simplifying but unrealistic assumption that the process parameters μ and σ have known values. In practice it will never be the case that these parameters are known exactly, for they must always be estimated from data. Nevertheless, it is useful to first fix ideas by essentially assuming that a large sample of data is available, taken while the process was stable, that can be used to compute good estimates of these parameters.

4.4.1 The $\bar{X}$-Chart with both μ and σ "Known"

If the data of Table 4.1 are from a stable process, that is, if the individual subgroups can be modeled by (4.1.2), then we have

$$E(X_{ij}) = \mu, \ \text{Var}(X_{ij}) = \sigma^2, \ E(\bar{X}_i) = \mu, \ \text{Var}(\bar{X}_i) = \frac{\sigma^2}{n} \quad (4.4.1)$$

If the process distribution is normal, then the distribution of $\bar{X}_i$ itself is also normal. However, even if the process distribution is not itself normal, since data from an in-control process should be unimodal, the central limit theorem will take effect very quickly with increasing subgroup size, and so we can expect the subgroup means to be approximately normally distributed, even with rather small subgroups. Moreover, in his work Shewhart studied the normality of subgroup means for a number of types of industrial data and concluded that means of subgroups of size four or five are generally quite normal for most industrial data. Shewhart also observed that most types of industrial measurement data that are not normally distributed can be modeled quite satisfactorily with unimodal skewed distributions. We shall consider techniques for studying the normality of a sample of data in Chapter 9, and some transformation methods that will permit us to use charting methods based on an assumed normal process distribution for data from skewed process distributions.

Note that when μ or σ are assumed known, as in this section, we are tentatively assuming a stable process. We now consider a control chart for subgroup means. For this chart the center line is the mean μ_0 of the distribution of the observations. To obtain values for UCL and

LCL we make use of the (approximate) normality of the subgroup means $\bar{X}_i$. Then we can write

$$P(LCL \leq \bar{X}_i \leq UCL) = P\left[\frac{\sqrt{n}\,(LCL - \mu_0)}{\sigma_0} \leq Z\right.$$

$$\left. \leq \frac{\sqrt{n}\,(UCL - \mu_0)}{\sigma_0}\right] = 1 - \alpha$$

for Z a $N(0, 1)$ random variable. Then we put

$$-z_{\alpha/2} = \frac{\sqrt{n}\,(LCL - \mu_0)}{\sigma_0}, \text{ and } z_{\alpha/2} = \frac{\sqrt{n}\,(UCL - \mu_0)}{\sigma_0}$$

and, solving for UCL and LCL, we have the formulas of display (4.4.2) for the *upper* and *lower* $1 - \alpha$ control limits, where z_γ satisfies $P(Z > z_\gamma) = \gamma$, $0 < \gamma < 1$.

$$UCL(\bar{X}) = \mu_0 + z_{\alpha/2}\frac{\sigma_0}{\sqrt{n}}$$

$$CL(\bar{X}) = \mu_0 \qquad\qquad (4.4.2)$$

$$LCL(\bar{X}) = \mu_0 - z_{\alpha/2}\frac{\sigma_0}{\sqrt{n}}$$

The 3-sigma control limits of (4.3.1) are then given in (4.4.3).

$$UCL(\bar{X}) = \mu_0 + 3\frac{\sigma_0}{\sqrt{n}} = \mu_0 + A\sigma_0$$

$$CL(\bar{X}) = \mu_0 \qquad\qquad (4.4.3)$$

$$LCL(\bar{X}) = \mu_0 - 3\frac{\sigma_0}{\sqrt{n}} = \mu_0 - A\sigma_0$$

The constant $A = 3/\sqrt{n}$ is given in Table A.5 in the Appendix. For these 3-sigma control limits, the probability of being above UCL (or below LCL) is $\alpha/2 = 0.00135$, from the assumption that the distribution of $\overline{X}_i$ is normal.

Example 4.1: In order to fix ideas, we consider making an $\overline{X}$-chart for the soft drink fill data given in Table 4.2. Soft drink bottles are filled by an automatic filling machine. The mean amount of beverage in a bottle is $\mu_0 = 12$ oz and the filling machine is known to have a standard deviation of $\sigma_0 = 0.12$ oz. Note that we as *assuming* that the filling process is such that the mean of the process distribution is actually equal to a desired target value of 12 oz. This is, in fact, a large assumption and will often not be true. It is required to compute the 3-sigma control limits for this process if subgroups of five bottles are removed from the process every half hour and the contents weighed. Table 4.2 gives the values of the 20 subgroups of size $n = 5$. Plot the subgroup means on a 3-sigma $\overline{X}$ control chart.

TABLE 4.2   Soft Drink Beverage Fill Data (oz)

i	x_1	x_2	x_3	x_4	x_5	$\overline{x}$	S	R
1	11.91	11.85	12.04	12.02	11.98	11.96	0.079	0.91
2	12.29	12.00	11.85	11.85	11.98	11.99	0.180	0.44
3	11.93	11.95	12.07	11.88	12.03	11.97	0.077	0.19
4	12.09	12.11	12.07	11.82	12.00	12.02	0.118	0.29
5	11.93	12.12	12.06	11.97	12.17	12.05	0.100	0.24
6	11.77	11.93	11.83	11.93	12.01	11.89	0.094	0.24
7	11.91	12.03	12.07	11.85	11.99	11.97	0.089	0.22
8	11.84	11.79	12.07	11.95	12.05	11.94	0.124	0.28
9	12.28	11.98	12.13	11.72	12.16	12.05	0.215	0.56
10	12.05	11.90	12.08	11.83	11.92	11.96	0.105	0.25
11	12.19	12.05	11.97	11.80	11.88	11.98	0.151	0.39
12	12.22	12.11	11.93	11.82	11.97	12.01	0.157	0.40
13	11.88	11.95	11.95	12.34	12.11	12.05	0.185	0.45
14	11.95	11.84	12.01	11.87	11.87	11.91	0.070	0.17
15	12.24	11.77	11.96	12.12	11.88	11.99	0.188	0.47
16	11.87	12.07	11.88	12.23	12.16	12.04	0.163	0.36
17	12.17	12.12	12.00	11.93	11.87	12.02	0.126	0.30
18	11.88	12.00	12.06	11.88	11.90	11.94	0.082	0.18
19	11.93	11.92	12.01	12.01	12.03	11.98	0.051	0.11
20	11.98	12.02	11.95	12.01	11.97	11.99	0.029	0.07
					Sum:	239.71	2.383	8.81

Solution: $UCL(\overline{X}) = 12 + (3)(0.12)/\sqrt{5} = 12.16$

$CL(\overline{X}) = 12$

$LCL(\overline{X}) = 12 - (3)(0.12)/\sqrt{5} = 11.84$

An $\overline{X}$-chart for these data is shown in Figure 4.4. Note that the subgroup means tend to plot in a random pattern centered on the center line (CL) of the chart. All of the points are between the upper and lower control limits and the point pattern appears to be random. The process is operating in control. Recall that a process is operating in control if the model assumed in (4.1.2) is reasonable for the process. Note carefully that for a process to be stable or operating in control does not require that the parameters μ and σ have particular values, but only that they remain constant. However, the usefulness of the products of the process—in this case the fill levels of soft drink bottles—depends on the values of both of the parameters μ and σ. This chart exhibits the overall pattern of an in-control process with points more concentrated near the CL and becoming more sparse as we move away from the center line.   ■

If a control chart is made to determine if a process is stable and a special cause of variation exerts an influence, it will likely result in either a temporary or permanent change in the value of the process

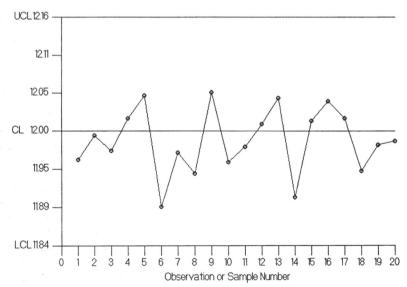

Figure 4.4   Three-sigma $\overline{X}$-Chart for μ for Soft Drink Fill Data

mean μ or the standard deviation σ, or both. These changes in the process parameters will be reflected in the point patterns of the statistics plotted on charts. Changes in the process mean will be reflected on the X̄-chart. Now, the overall variation in the process as measured by the mean squared error (4.2.2) is

$$EMS = (\mu - \tau)^2 + \sigma^2$$

and clearly a large difference in the values of μ and τ will give a large value of EMS. If the model (4.1.2) is reasonable, and σ is constant, then $E(\overline{X}) = \mu$ and the control chart for $\overline{X}$ will reflect changes in μ. Depending on the nature of the special cause involved, the process mean μ may change in different ways as a function of the product unit number or time. Thus we might write $\mu(j)$ or $\mu(t)$ to display this dependence. Sometimes μ may change suddenly by discrete amounts, while in other cases μ may change continuously. The change that often occurs when the machine or the operator is changed, and everything else remains unchanged, is likely to be a one-time discrete jump (or drop) in μ. The $\overline{X}$ control chart is valuable for detecting sudden changes in a process mean, especially when the changes are large. The sensitivity of the X̄-chart for detecting changes in μ will be considered in detail in later sections.

4.4.2 The 3-Sigma S-Chart for σ

In order to interpret $\overline{X}$-charts as reflecting behavior of the process mean μ, it is crucial that the process standard deviation σ remain constant. This is because the distribution of $\overline{X}$ depends on σ as well as μ. Since $\text{Var}(\overline{X}) = \sigma^2/n$, an increase in σ will cause the points on the X̄-chart to tend to be more spread out and therefore more points to fall outside the control limits, and this is likely to be misinterpreted to indicate the mean μ has changed. An unrecognized decrease in σ would result in an X̄-chart with reduced sensitivity to detect changes in μ. To assure that σ remains constant, we make charts of estimates of σ (or σ^2) to assure that these sequences of estimates indicate stable processes. To this end, when $\overline{X}$-charts are made they should always be accompanied by either S-charts or R-charts. We next consider the formulas required to construct these charts. An important point to keep in mind is that the distributions of S and of R depend only on the parameter σ, and *not* on μ.

To estimate σ from a single normal subgroup of size n, we observe that it can be shown, when the process distribution is normal, that the sample standard deviation has expectation

$$E(S) = \mu_s = \frac{\Gamma\left(\dfrac{n}{2}\right)}{\Gamma\left(\dfrac{n-1}{2}\right)} \sqrt{\frac{2}{n-1}} \, \sigma = c_4 \sigma \qquad (4.4.4)$$

where $\Gamma(\cdot)$ denotes the gamma function. Values of the constant

$$c_4 = \frac{\Gamma\left(\dfrac{n}{2}\right)}{\Gamma\left(\dfrac{n-1}{2}\right)} \sqrt{\frac{2}{n-1}}$$

are given in Table A.5 in the Appendix. Moreover, the standard deviation of the distribution of S is

$$\sigma_s = \sqrt{\text{Var}(S)} = \sqrt{E(S^2) - [E(S)]^2} = \sigma\sqrt{1 - c_4^2} \qquad (4.4.5)$$

Then 3-sigma control limits for subgroup standard deviations S_i, based on subgroups of constant size n, are given by (4.4.6).

$$\boxed{\begin{aligned} UCL(S) &= B_6\,\sigma_0, \text{ for } B_6 = c_4 + 3\sqrt{1 - c_4^2}, \\ CL(S) &= c_4\,\sigma_0 \\ LCL(S) &= B_5\,\sigma_0, \text{ for } B_5 = c_4 - 3\sqrt{1 - c_4^2}, \end{aligned}} \qquad (4.4.6)$$

Values of c_4, B_5, and B_6 are given in Table A.5.

Example 4.1, continuation 1: The value of σ was given as $\sigma_0 = 0.12$. From Table A.5 we read $c_4 = 0.94$, $B_5 = 0$, and $B_6 = 1.964$. Then we have

$$UCL(S) = B_6\,\sigma_0 = (1.964)(0.12) = 0.24$$

$$CL(S) = c_4\,\sigma_0 = (0.94)(0.12) = 0.11$$

$$LCL(S) = 0$$

The subgroup standard deviations given in Table 4.2 are plotted in Fig. 4.5 with these control limits. The pattern of points on this chart indicates a constant process standard deviation. ■

4.4.3 The 3-Sigma R-Chart for σ

When the process distribution is normal, it can be shown that the mean and standard deviation of the sample range R are as given in (4.4.7).

$$E(R) = d_2\,\sigma_0, \qquad SD(R) = d_3\,\sigma_0 \tag{4.4.7}$$

Here d_2 and d_3 are functions of n and values of these constants are given in Table A.5. Thus, if σ_0 is a known value for a process, we can write 3-sigma control limits for R as in (4.4.8).

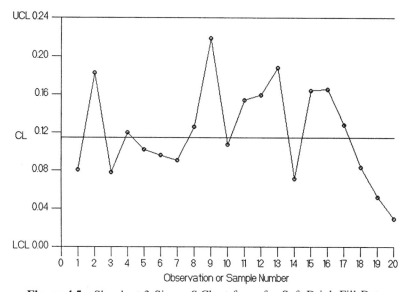

Figure 4.5 Shewhart 3-Sigma S-Chart for σ for Soft Drink Fill Data

$$UCL(R) = d_2\, \sigma_0 + 3d_3\, \sigma_0$$
$$= D_2\, \sigma_0, \text{ for } D_2 = d_2 + 3d_3,$$
$$CL(R) = d_2\, \sigma_0 \tag{4.4.8}$$
$$LCL(R) = d_2\, \sigma_0 - 3d_3\, \sigma_0$$
$$= D_1\, \sigma_0, \text{ for } D_1 = d_2 - 3d_3,$$

and values of D_1 and D_2 are given in Table A.5.

Example 4.1, continuation 2: From Table A.5 we read values $D_1 =$ 0, $d_2 = 2.326$, $D_2 = 4.918$; which give

$$UCL(R) = (4.918)(0.12) = 0.59$$
$$CL(R) = (2.326)(0.12) = 0.28$$
$$LCL(R) = 0$$

The sample ranges given in Table 4.2 are plotted in Fig. 4.6 with these control limits. It should be noted that, although the vertical scales

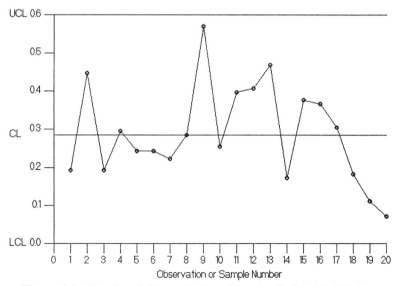

Figure 4.6   Shewhart 3-Sigma R-Chart for σ for Soft Drink Fill Data

of the two charts are different, the point patterns of the S-chart of Fig. 4.5 and the R-chart of Fig. 4.6 are very similar. This is, of course, what is to be expected since both the sample standard S and the sample range R are measures of spread of the sample. It is therefore not necessary to plot charts for both of these statistics. In the past the R-chart has generally been used more due to the belief that it is easier to make and therefore may result in fewer computing errors in making charts. The S statistic is somewhat more efficient in utilizing information, and since today most computations will be made with either hand calculators or computer software, we feel that the S-chart should be the preferred chart for controlling σ. For most of the examples in this book the S-chart will be used rather than the R-chart. For almost all cases, the two charts will give the same charting results, and there is not a really strong reason to prefer either chart.

Both the S-chart and the R-chart for this example show no evidence that the process variance was not constant while these data were being taken. Since the $\bar{X}$-chart of Fig. 4.4 also showed no indication that the process mean was not constant, we can conclude that there is no indication that this process is unstable. In the statement of the decision procedure above it was stated that when enough points have been plotted with no anomalous patterns, a decision will be made that the process is stable. A question then is: exactly how many points must be plotted with no out-of-control signals before the process can be declared an in-control process? There is not a simple answer to this question for all situations, and we will consider it further below; however, it should be noted that *Shewhart recommended that 25 subgroups of size five each would be sufficient.* ∎

4.4.4 The S-Chart with Probability Limits

By examining Table A.5 it is found that the constant B_5 used to compute the LCL of the subgroup standard deviation S in equation (4.4.6) is zero for $n \leq 5$; and the constant D_1 used to compute the LCL for the subgroup range R in equation (4.4.8) is zero for $n \leq 6$. Therefore, for $n \leq 5$ the S-chart has no lower control limit, and for $n \leq 6$ the R-chart has no lower control limit. For these values of subgroup size n, these charts have no ability to detect decreases in the process variance. There are applications where it is important to be able to detect a decrease in the process variance. It was mentioned above that an unnoticed decrease in σ will decrease the sensitivity of the $\bar{X}$-chart to detect changes in μ. Also, many companies are involved with quality improvement projects that are aimed at reducing variation in processes by eliminating or reducing the effects of common causes. It is important that the positive effects of such efforts be clearly recognized in charting programs for the psychological reinforcement of both management and personnel that comes from such feedback. Moreover, if the value of σ is decreased due to a special cause, then we would be very interested in having our chart signal the decrease in σ, so that we could study the special cause in order to take advantage of that information to decrease process variation. In other words, we are not interested only in "bad" special causes that result in increased process variation, but also in "good" special causes that decrease process variation.

The reason that both the S- and R-charts have no lower control limit for small values of subgroup size n is because they have skewed distributions of the general shape of the density function shown in Fig. 4.7. For these skewed distributions, the lower control limit of equations (4.3.1) is a negative number, which is essentially no lower control limit. It should also be observed that even for values of n large enough to give positive LCLs, the actual probabilities above the upper and below the lower control limits for an in-control process are unequal and, in general, unknown. Also, both the R-chart and the S-chart have poor sensitivity to detect decreases in σ, even when n is large enough to make LCL positive, as will be seen in section 4.7 when operating characteristic functions are studied.

An S-chart with probability limits in the form of equations (4.3.2) can be used to make a chart with general (α_L, α_U) probability limits. Recall that equation (3.5.5) stated that $(n - 1)S^2/\sigma^2$ is a χ^2_{n-1} random variable when S^2 is computed from a normal sample. Then we can write

$$P\left\{\chi^2_{1-\alpha_L,n-1} \le \frac{(n - 1)\,S^2}{\sigma^2} \le \chi^2_{\alpha_U,n-1}\right\} = 1 - \alpha_L - \alpha_U$$

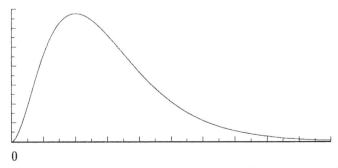

Figure 4.7 Density Function of a Positive Right Skewed Distribution

where $\chi^2_{\alpha,\nu}$ is defined by (2.9.3). For variance σ^2_0 known, the (α_L, α_U) probability limits for S are

$$UCL(S) = \sigma_0 \sqrt{\frac{\chi^2_{\alpha_U,n-1}}{n-1}}$$

$$CL(S) = \sigma_0 \sqrt{\frac{\chi^2_{0.5,n-1}}{n-1}} \qquad (4.4.9)$$

$$LCL(S) = \sigma_0 \sqrt{\frac{\chi^2_{1-\alpha_L,n-1}}{n-1}}$$

Example 4.1, continuation 3: We wish to plot the S's of this example on an S-chart with probability limits given by (4.4.9). Suppose that the values $\alpha_L = \alpha_U = 0.00135$ are to be used to make the control of false alarms comparable to that for a 3-sigma $\bar{X}$-chart. Then from Table A.2, we read

$$\chi^2_{\alpha_u,n-1} = \chi^2_{0.00135,4} = 17.800$$

$$\chi^2_{0.5,4} = 3.357$$

$$\chi^2_{1-\alpha_2,n-1} = \chi^2_{0.99865,4} = 0.106$$

and

$$UCL(S) = 0.12 \sqrt{\frac{17.800}{4}} = 0.253$$

$$CL(S) = 0.12 \sqrt{\frac{3.357}{4}} = 0.110$$

$$LCL(S) = 0.12 \sqrt{\frac{0.106}{4}} = 0.020$$

The probability chart for S with these control limits is given in Fig. 4.8. Of course, the point patterns are the same for this chart as for the 3-sigma chart of Fig. 4.5. Only the control limits are different. ∎

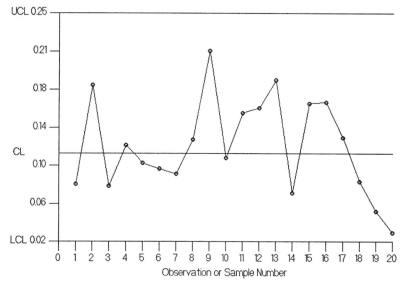

Figure 4.8   A (0.00135, 0.00135) Probability Chart for S for Soft Drink Fill Data

4.5   RUNS TESTS FOR 3-SIGMA $\overline{X}$ CONTROL CHART PATTERNS, μ AND σ KNOWN

When a point falls outside the control limits of the $\overline{X}$-chart, we study the process to determine if a special cause is responsible. In some cases, when a special cause is present it does not result in a point outside the control limits but does result in a nonrandom pattern of points. Such patterns of points represent more information about the process than single points because a single point reflects only the information in a single sample, while a pattern of points reflects information from several samples. Also, some types of special causes do not increase the probability of points falling outside the 3-sigma control limits, or increase it only slightly.

In order to insure objectivity and uniformity in the interpretation of control chart patterns, it is desirable in applications of charts to define a specific set of tests for detecting particular patterns of importance. A set of such tests for patterns on $\overline{X}$-charts given by Western Electric (1956) is often used. In order to distinguish "out-of-control" or "unstable" patterns, we discuss first "in-control" or "stable" patterns. An $\overline{X}$-chart of an in-control process is essentially a picture of a set of independent observations from a normal (bell-shaped) distribution. Shewhart (1931) pointed out that it is reasonable to assume that means of four or more observations of industrial measurements are normally distributed. Also, in Chapter 9 we will present some highly effective methods for studying the normality of one or more samples, and a method for transforming most nonnormal industrial measurements to normality. If the observations are plotted as a dot plot or histogram ignoring the ordering, then, except for sampling error, the graph should look like a bell-shaped normal density function. Thus, the points on the $\bar{X}$-chart should tend to concentrate around the center line and to be more sparse toward the control limits, with either no points or very few beyond the 3-sigma control limits.

Figure 4.9 displays eight types of unnatural patterns that may be important in some applications. These are essentially the charts given in Nelson (1984). The zones A+, B+, C+, A−, B−, and C− and the probabilities of these zones are shown in Fig. 4.10. Let A = (A+) ∪

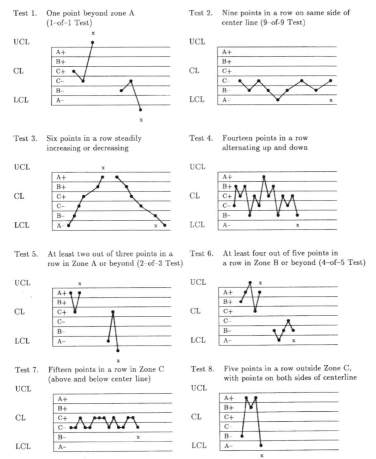

Figure 4.9 Some Runs Tests for Special Causes Applied to Shewhart $\bar{X}$-Charts

Zone	0.00135
A+	0.02135
B+	0.13601
C+	0.34131
C−	0.34131
B−	0.13601
A−	0.02135
	0.00135

Figure 4.10   Control Chart Zones and Normal Probabilities

(A−), and so on. Zone C contains all points within a distance of 1-sigma of the center line, zone B includes points that are within a distance of 2-sigma of the center line but not in zone C, and zone A contains those points not in B or C but within 3-sigma of the center line. We now give the probabilities that these tests will give false alarms when the points represent independently, identically distributed normal random variables. The probabilities that these tests will signal on one point are as follows.

Test 1 (1-of-1 Test): Probability $= 0.00270 \cong 1/370$

Test 2 (9-of-9 Test): Probability $= 2\left(\frac{1}{2}\right)^9 = \left(\frac{1}{2}\right)^8 = 0.00391$
$$= 1/256$$

Test 3: Probability $= 2/6! = 0.00277 \cong 1/360$

Test 4: Probability $= 0.0046 \cong 1/219$

Test 5 (2-of-3 Test): Probability $= 0.00304 \cong 1/329$

Test 6 (4-of-5 Test): Probability $= 0.00554 \cong 1/180$

Test 7: Probability $= (0.68262)^{15} = 0.00326 \cong 1/307$

Test 8: Probability $= (15/16)(0.31738)^5 = 0.00302 \cong 1/331$

Except for Test 4, these values are all readily obtained using elementary probability arguments. The probability of Test 4 was obtained by R. L. Marr using a recursive computer algorithm written for the purpose. When two or more of these tests are applied simultaneously, the overall probability of a false alarm is equal to the sum of the probabilities for patterns that are mutually exclusive, and is approximately the sum of the probabilities for the individual tests for all cases since the intersection probabilities are all small. Another point to be noted is that for a test of Fig. 4.9 that involves m consecutive points, the probabilities above refer only to one set of m consecutive points, and when applied to a long sequence of points the probabilities are much larger to get one or more false signals. For example, if Test 1 is applied to a chart with 100 points, then the probability of at least one signal is $1 - (1 - 0.0027)^{100} \cong 0.24$. Thus we can expect an average of about one false signal from Test 1 on four charts of this size. Similar considerations apply for the other tests, but for some of them the probabilities are more difficult to compute. We will further consider these properties for Tests 2, 5, and 6 in the next section after we have introduced operating characteristic (OC) and power functions, and run length distributions.

These tests can be used with $\bar{X}$-charts and, also, with any chart for which the plotted points are independent observations on a statistic that has an approximately normal in-control distribution. They can also be used on the Q-charts that will be developed in Chapters 7 and 8. Other charts of this type will be presented in later chapters. Note that Tests 1, 2, 5, and 6 are applied to the upper and lower halves of the chart separately, but that 3, 4, 7, and 8 are applied to the whole chart. also, observe that Tests 1 (1-of-1), 2 (9-of-9), 5 (2-of-3), and 6 (4-of-5) are all designed to detect monotone shifts in the process mean. Such monotone shifts could be either one-step shifts or drifting trends up or down. The Text 3 pattern suggests a process mean that is drifting up or down and Test 4 an alternating cyclic pattern for the mean.

Tests 7 and 8 are particularly relevant for SPC and are called tests for *stratification.* These patterns are likely to signify that the data have been taken from two or more populations with different means. Although we are assuming that μ and σ are "known" in this section, to discuss these two tests we assume that the estimated control limits given in (4.8.12) are being used. Readers may wish to skip this discussion until section 4.8 has been studied. The Test 7 pattern can arise when each subgroup includes observations from two or more populations, so that the subgroup mean $\bar{X}$ is actually estimating a weighted average of the population means of the different populations, and then the estimate of variance will be too large, which, in turn, causes the points to be too concentrated about the center line. To see how this occurs, suppose we have two machines and we take stratified subgroups of size $n = 2$ as shown in Fig. 4.11. Moreover, suppose the measurements from machine X are distributed with a $N(\mu_X, \sigma^2)$ distribution and those from machine Y are distributed with a $N(\mu_Y, \sigma^2)$ distribution, and $\mu_X < \mu_Y$. Further, suppose a subgroup consisting of measurements X and Y is taken. The subgroup mean and variance are

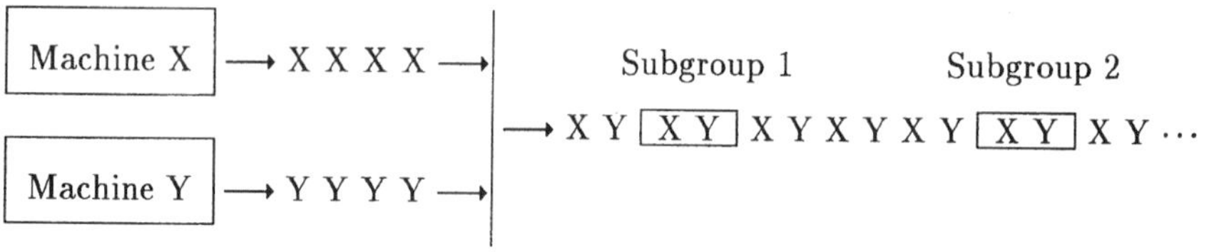

Figure 4.11   A Stratified Sampling Plan

$$\overline{X} = \frac{X + Y}{2}, \text{ and } S^2 = \frac{(X - Y)^2}{2}$$

and

$$E(\overline{X}) = \frac{E(X) + E(Y)}{2} = \frac{\mu_X + \mu_Y}{2} = \overline{\mu},$$

$$\text{Var}(\overline{X}) = \text{Var}\left(\frac{X + Y}{2}\right) = \frac{1}{4}[\text{Var}(X) + \text{Var}(Y)] = \frac{\sigma^2}{2}$$

So we see that the distribution of $\overline{X}$ has a mean $\overline{\mu}$ that is the average value of the means for machine X and machine Y; however, the variance of $\overline{X}$ is the same as for a subgroup of size 2 from either machine. The expected value of S^2 is

$$E(S^2) = E\left[\frac{(X - Y)^2}{2}\right] = \frac{1}{2}[E(X^2) + E(Y^2) - 2E(X)E(Y)]$$

$$= \frac{1}{2}[\sigma^2 + \mu_X^2 + \sigma^2 + \mu_Y^2 - 2\mu_X\mu_Y]$$

and

$$E(S^2) = \sigma^2 + \frac{(\mu_X - \mu_Y)^2}{2}$$

From this we see that this S^2 will tend to overestimate σ^2, and, of course, S/c_4 will tend to overestimate σ. This means that the control limits computed from (4.8.12) will tend to be too wide, which results in a pattern of points too close to the center line. This is why Test 7 is called a test for stratification. This discussion for two strata obviously generalizes to more than two strata. Also, the result does not depend on the variances being the same (see problem 4.24). To avoid this type of unstable pattern it is often necessary to make charts for each machine (strata) separately to assure it is stable, and then adjust, if possible, the individual machine means to a common target value. If this adjustment is successfully accomplished, we should not see the stratification pattern of Test 7 on our chart.

The pattern for Test 8 can also arise when the subgroups are from populations with different means. The particular pattern shown for Test 8 suggests that the first and fifth subgroups are from one population, and the second, third and fourth are from a different population with a larger mean. It is not necessary that all of the points be from the same strata, only that a disproportionate number be from different strata. For example, for Fig. 4.11, suppose we took alternating subgroups as follows:

$$XXXXY \quad XYYYY \quad XXXXY \quad XYYYY \quad XXXXY \quad XYYYY \quad \cdots$$

These subgroups would also tend to give alternating low and high points on the $\bar{X}$-chart.

The particular tests given in Fig. 4.9 are but a few of the many tests that can be designed on runs of consecutive points to detect an out-of-control state or changes in the process parameters. In some applications of $\bar{X}$-charts it may be desirable to design a special runs test to detect a pattern that reflects a troublesome condition specific to a particular process. However, when such a test is used, the performance of the test in giving false alarms when the process is stable, and sensitivity to detect out-of-control conditions, should be studied.

4.6 ASSESSING $\bar{X}$-CHART PERFORMANCE: OC AND POWER FUNCTIONS, RUN LENGTH DISTRIBUTIONS, μ AND σ BOTH KNOWN

4.6.1 Operating Characteristic and Power Functions for $\bar{X}$-Charts

Chart control limits and tests for out-of-control patterns are designed so that the probabilities of false alarms are small for a stable process. We also need to consider the performance of a chart when special causes result in variation of the parameter the chart is designed to "control." For the special case when the parameter changes by a one-step permanent shift, we will consider five functions, namely: the operating characteristic (OC) function, the power function, the average run length (ARL) function, the average total run length (ATRL) function, and the standard deviation of run length function (SDRL). The OC and power functions will be introduced in this section. The ARL, ATRL, and SDRL functions will be defined in the next section. In this section we assume that the subgroup mean is normally distributed.

To define these functions, we remind the reader that we use the term *nominal value* of a parameter somewhat differently from some writers. By the nominal value of a parameter, either the process mean μ or standard deviation σ, we mean the value of this parameter that was used to calculate the values of the control limits. It is assumed to be the actual correct value of the parameter for the process.

The *operating characteristic* (OC) function of a particular control chart test, such as one of those of Fig. 4.9, is a function which expresses the probability of not detecting a change of the parameter on one point as a function of its distance from its nominal value. The *power function* of a chart test is the probability that a given shift of a parameter from its nominal value will be detected on one point, and represents the same information as the OC function since the two always sum to one. These functions will be given more precise definitions for particular charts.

For the $\overline{X}$-chart with the $1 - \alpha$ probability limits of (4.4.2), we consider the problem of detecting a shift of the process mean from a nominal value $\mu = \mu_0$ to a new value $\mu = \mu_0 + \delta\sigma_0$, where, in general, δ can be either zero, positive, or negative. Then the operating characteristic (OC) function of the 1-of-1 test is the probability of not detecting this shift on one point, and is given by

$$\beta(n, \delta) = P\{LCL \le \overline{X} \le UCL | \mu = \mu_0 + \delta\,\sigma_0\}$$

and this in turn gives (4.6.1).

OC Function for a 1-of-1 Test on an $\overline{X}$-Chart:

$$\beta(n, \delta) = \Phi(z_{\alpha/2} - \delta\sqrt{n}) - \Phi(-z_{\alpha/2} - \delta\sqrt{n})$$ (4.6.1)

Note that $\beta(n, 0) = 2\Phi(z_{\alpha/2}) - 1 = 1 - \alpha$, which is the probability that no signal will be made when there has been no shift in the mean μ. For $z_{\alpha/2} \ge 3$ and larger values of δ, say $|\delta| \ge 1$, the OC function of (4.6.1) can be approximated by the somewhat simpler formula: $\beta(n, \delta) \cong \Phi(z_{\alpha/2} - |\delta| \sqrt{n})$. The power function is the probability that a shift will be detected and is given by (4.6.2).

> **Power Function for a 1-of-1 Test on an $\bar{X}$-Chart:**
>
> $$\text{Power}(n, \delta) = 1 - \beta(n, \delta)$$

(4.6.2)

In general, we would like to have the OC function $\beta(n, \delta)$ have a large value, $1 - \alpha$, when $\delta = 0$, so that the probability of a false signal, α, is small, and to have $\beta(n, \delta)$ be small when $\delta \neq 0$, so that the probability of a shift not being detected is small. Of course, exactly the opposite properties are desirable for the power function, namely, the power at $\delta = 0$ should be small so that the probability of a false signal is small, and the power at $\delta \neq 0$ should be large so that the probability of detecting a shift in the mean is large. For specific values of δ and n, we can use tables or algorithms for the normal distribution function to evaluate the OC function $\beta(n, \delta)$ and the power function $1 - \beta(n, \delta)$.

By choosing a range of values of δ we can construct a table of values of the OC function for the 3-sigma chart of (4.4.3) as given in Table 4.3 and shown in Fig. 4.12 for $n = 5, 10$. Examination of this table and figure shows that the $\bar{X}$-chart operated with Test 1 (the 1-of-1 test) only is not sensitive for detecting small values of δ (≤ 2, say) for the usual subgroup sizes of $n = 4$ or 5. For example, with $n = 4$ the probability of *not* detecting a shift in the process mean of one-half a standard deviation ($\delta = 0.5$) is given to be 0.977. There are two ways to improve the power of the chart to detect small shifts. First, the subgroup size n can be increased and the power will increase as a function of n; however, as is apparent from studying Table 4.3, the increase in power with increasing n is slow. For example, for $n = 30$ the probability of *not* detecting a change in the mean of $\delta = 0.6$ standard deviation is 0.387. There are other undesirable aspects of increasing subgroup size n much larger than the traditional values. Larger values of n can result in having large shifts detected more slowly, for example.

Second, the power to detect a mean shift can also be increased by applying some of the other tests in Fig. 4.9 simultaneously with Test 1. Tests that can be used simultaneously with Test 1 (1-of-1) to detect

TABLE 4.3   OC Function $\beta(n, |\delta|)$ for Test 1 (the 1-of-1 Test) on a 3-sigma $\overline{X}$-Chart

					$|\delta|$						
n	0.5	1.0	1.5	2.0	2.5	3.0	3.5	4.0	4.5	5.0	5.5
1	.994	.977	.933	.841	.691	.500	.309	.159	.067	.023	.006
2	.989	.944	.810	.568	.296	.107	.026	.004	.000	.000	.000
3	.984	.898	.656	.321	.092	.014	.001	.000	.000	.000	.000
4	.977	.841	.500	.159	.023	.001	.000	.000	.000	.000	.000
5	.970	.778	.362	.070	.005	.000	.000	.000	.000	.000	.000

					$|\delta|$						
	0.2	0.4	0.6	0.8	1.0	1.2	1.4	1.6	1.8	2.0	2.2
6	.994	.978	.937	.851	.709	.524	.334	.179	.079	.029	.008
8	.992	.969	.904	.770	.568	.347	.169	.064	.018	.004	.001
10	.991	.959	.865	.681	.436	.213	.077	.020	.004	.000	.000
12	.989	.947	.822	.590	.321	.124	.032	.006	.001	.000	.000
14	.988	.934	.775	.503	.229	.068	.013	.001	.000	.000	.000
16	.986	.919	.726	.421	.159	.036	.005	.000	.000	.000	.000
18	.984	.904	.675	.347	.107	.018	.002	.000	.000	.000	.000
20	.982	.887	.624	.282	.070	.009	.001	.000	.000	.000	.000
22	.980	.869	.574	.226	.045	.004	.000	.000	.000	.000	.000
24	.978	.851	.524	.179	.029	.002	.000	.000	.000	.000	.000
26	.976	.832	.476	.140	.018	.001	.000	.000	.000	.000	.000
28	.974	.811	.431	.109	.011	.000	.000	.000	.000	.000	.000
30	.972	.791	.387	.084	.007	.000	.000	.000	.000	.000	.000

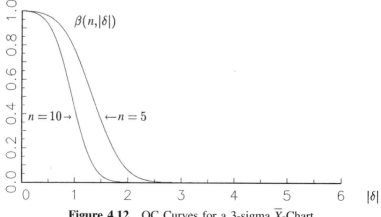

Figure 4.12   OC Curves for a 3-sigma $\overline{X}$-Chart

mean shifts are Test 2 (9-of-9), Test 5 (2-of-3), and Test 6 (4-of-5); however, in applying these tests to detect a mean shift, we should require that when more than one test signals, the tests must signal in the same direction from the center line to declare that a significant signal has been observed. Also, applying more than one test will increase the rate of false alarms. We will consider these approaches to increasing the sensitivity of $\bar{X}$-charts further after we have developed some immediate uses of the OC function, and introduced and ARL, ATRL, and SDRL functions.

4.6.2 The Run Length Distribution and ARL, ATRL, and SDRL Functions for Tests on an $\bar{X}$-Chart

Consider a 3-sigma $\bar{X}$-chart with subgroup size n and suppose that during operation of the process the mean shifts from a value of $\mu = \mu_0$ to a value of $\mu = \mu_0 + \delta\sigma_0$, and then remains constant at this new value. Then let Y denote the run length, that is, the number of subgroups that will be observed from the point when the shift occurred to the point when a signal first occurs in the form of a point above the upper control limit or below the lower control limit. The expected value or mean of Y is called the *average run length,* ARL, of the chart, and the standard deviation of the run length Y will here be called SDRL. Since the individual points on an $\bar{X}$-chart are values of independently and identically distributed statistics and the control limits LCL and UCL are assumed to be known constants, the variable Y is a *geometric* random variable with probability function, distribution function, ARL, and SDRL given by (see displays (2.7.4) and (2.7.5)) the equations (4.6.3). Note that the standard deviation, SDRL, of the distribution of run lengths is a simple function of the distribution mean, ARL, and that this relationship between the mean and standard deviation of the geometric distribution depends on the assumption that the process mean μ and process standard deviation σ are known.

$$
\begin{aligned}
&P(Y = y) = [\beta(n, \delta)]^{y-1}[1 - \beta(n, \delta)], \text{ and} \\
&P(Y \le y) = 1 - [\beta(n, \delta)]^y \text{ both for} \\
&\qquad y = 1, 2, \cdots \\
&ARL(n, \delta) = E(Y) = 1/[1 - \beta(n, \delta)]; \\
&SDRL(n, \delta) = \sqrt{ARL(n, \delta)[ARL(n, \delta) - 1]}
\end{aligned}
\tag{4.6.3}
$$

The OC function for the 1-of-1 test on a 3-sigma chart to detect a mean shift of 1.5σ when $n = 5$ is $\beta(5, 1.5) = \Phi(3 - 1.5\sqrt{5}) = 0.3617$. The probability of signaling on y or fewer points is thus $1 - (0.3617)^y$. These values for $y = 1, 2, \cdots, 6$ are given in the following table.

y:	1	2	3	4	5	6
Prob:	0.638	0.869	0.953	0.983	0.994	0.998

An important special case is for $\delta = 0$. Then, from (4.6.1), we have

$$\beta(n, 0) = \Phi(3) - \Phi(-3) = 0.9973$$

and thus

$$ARL(n, 0) = \frac{1}{1 - \beta(n, 0)} = \frac{1}{1 - 0.9973} = 370.4$$

and

$$SDRL(n, 0) = \sqrt{(370.4)(369.4)} = 369.9$$

Note, particularly, that for this case of a stable process, that is, no parameter shift, $SDRL \cong ARL - 0.5$ when $ARL \geq 3$. This is because $SDRL$ is the geometric mean of ARL and $ARL - 1$, and for $ARL \geq 3$ the geometric mean of these two numbers is approximately the same as their arithmetic mean. Also, note that while the formulas of (4.6.3) were obtained for a classical $\bar{X}$-chart, they will hold for any chart for which the plotted values are independently and identically distributed random variables, and the control limits are known exactly. Further, note that we have in general for a chart with these properties that $SDRL(n, \delta) \leq ARL(n, \delta)$, and $SDRL(n, \delta) \cong ARL(n, \delta) - 0.5$ for $ARL(n, \delta) \geq 3$.

By using the ARL formula in (4.6.3), the information in Table 4.3 can be displayed in a table of ARL values are shown in Table 4.4. Note that $ARL(n, 0)$ is 370 for all subgroup sizes n, which means that when there is *no change* in the process mean we will average one false signal in 370 plotted points. That is, we will get an average of one false signal in 370 subgroups. However, the ARL decreases with increases in either n or $|\delta|$. For small values of δ and subgroups of the

TABLE 4.4   ARL Function for Test 1 (the 1-of-1 Test) on a 3-Sigma $\bar{X}$-Chart

			$\|\delta\|$									
n	0	0.5	1.0	1.5	2.0	2.5	3.0	3.5	4.0	4.5	5.0	5.5
1	370	161.0	44.0	15.0	6.3	3.2	2.0	1.4	1.2	1.1	1.0	1.0
2	370	91.5	17.7	5.3	2.3	1.4	1.1	1.0	1.0	1.0	1.0	1.0
3	370	60.9	9.8	9.2	1.5	1.1	1.0	1.0	1.0	1.0	1.0	1.0
4	370	44.0	6.3	2.0	1.2	1.0	1.0	1.0	1.0	1.0	1.0	1.0
5	370	33.4	4.5	1.6	1.1	1.0	1.0	1.0	1.0	1.0	1.0	1.0

			$\|\delta\|$									
n	0	0.2	0.4	0.6	0.8	1.0	1.2	1.4	1.6	1.8	2.0	2.2
6	370	165.7	45.1	15.9	6.7	3.4	2.1	1.5	1.2	1.1	1.0	1.0
8	370	134.0	32.4	10.4	4.3	2.3	1.5	1.2	1.1	1.0	1.0	1.0
10	370	111.7	24.2	7.4	3.1	1.8	1.3	1.1	1.0	1.0	1.0	1.0
12	370	95.0	18.8	5.6	2.4	1.5	1.1	1.0	1.0	1.0	1.0	1.0
14	370	82.2	15.1	4.4	2.0	1.3	1.1	1.0	1.0	1.0	1.0	1.0
16	370	71.9	12.4	3.6	1.7	1.2	1.0	1.0	1.0	1.0	1.0	1.0
18	370	63.6	10.4	3.1	1.5	1.1	1.0	1.0	1.0	1.0	1.0	1.0
20	370	56.8	8.9	2.7	1.4	1.1	1.0	1.0	1.0	1.0	1.0	1.0
22	370	51.0	7.7	2.3	1.3	1.0	1.0	1.0	1.0	1.0	1.0	1.0
24	370	46.1	6.7	2.1	1.2	1.0	1.0	1.0	1.0	1.0	1.0	1.0
26	370	41.9	5.9	1.9	1.2	1.0	1.0	1.0	1.0	1.0	1.0	1.0
28	370	38.3	5.3	1.8	1.1	1.0	1.0	1.0	1.0	1.0	1.0	1.0
30	370	34.2	4.8	1.6	1.1	1.0	1.0	1.0	1.0	1.0	1.0	1.0

common sizes of 4 or 5 the ARL is rather large, and, on average, the sampled subgroups will contain a rather large number of units of production before a signal is given by the chart. For example, for $n = 5$ and $\delta = 1$, an average of 4.5 subgroups, or $4.5n = 22.5$ production units, will be required to detect the shift. Another point to observe is that the ARL(n, δ) is the average number of *points* or *subgroups* that will be observed between signals. However, for practical purposes in controlling a manufacturing process, a quantity that may be of more interest is the average total number of parts (units of production) that are in the subgroups between signals. We will call this value the *average total run length* (ATRL). In general, for a chart with constant subgroup size n

$$ATRL = n(ARL) \tag{4.6.4}$$

Now, the ARL is a strictly decreasing function of n for a fixed value of δ (>0); however, for a fixed δ it can be shown that the ATRL will take a minimum value at some integer n. Table 4.5 gives the absolute minimum value of ATRL and the corresponding subgroup size n that achieves this minimum ATRL for a range of values of δ. A number of points can be observed by studying Table 4.5. Note that the customary subgroup size of $n = 5$ is actually ideal for detecting a shift of $\delta = 1.5$ standard deviations in the process mean and $n = 4$ is ideal for detecting a shift of 1.6 or 1.7. To detect smaller shifts the best subgroup size increases rapidly as δ decreases. The values of ATRL and best subgroup sizes in Table 4.5 are an envelope representing the limits of the best performance we can expect to achieve with Test 1 on a 3-sigma $\overline{X}$-chart. The major point to be observed here is that clearly we cannot expect to improve the performance of classical $\overline{X}$-charts by simply increasing the subgroup size, and we will need to consider alternatives to this test to detect small changes in the process mean, say for $\delta < 1.5$.

Weiler (1952) studied the subgroup size problem in terms of the quantity that we call ATRL.

4.6.3 On ARLs and Stochastic Ordering

The relevance of ARL as a control criterion is dependent upon the result that the run length random variable Y has a geometric distribution. In later chapters we will consider other types of control charting schemes, and it will be necessary to consider criteria for comparing the performances of competing control schemes. Suppose that two competing control schemes have run length variables Y_1 and Y_2 and both

TABLE 4.5 Values of Subgroup Size n and Corresponding Minimum ATRL for a 3-Sigma $\overline{X}$-Chart

δ:	0	.1	.2	.3	.4	.5	.6	.7
ATRL:	$(370.4)n$	1762.1	440.5	195.8	110.1	70.5	48.9	36.0
n:	n	1108	227	123	69	44	31	23
δ:	.8	.9	1.0	1.1	1.2	1.3	1.4	1.5
ATRL:	27.5	21.8	17.6	14.6	12.2	10.5	9.0	7.8
n:	17	14	11	9	8	7	6	5
δ:	1.6	1.7	1.8	1.9	2.0	2.1	2.2	2.3
ATRL:	6.9	6.1	5.5	4.9	4.4	4.1	3.7	3.3
n:	4	4	3	3	3	3	2	2
δ:	2.4	2.5	2.6	2.7	2.8	2.9	3.0	3.1
ATRL:	3.1	2.8	2.7	2.5	2.4	2.2	2.0	1.9
n:	2	2	2	2	1	1	1	1

have geometric distributions, OC functions $\beta_1(\delta)$ and $\beta_2(\delta)$, and means $ARL_1(\delta)$ and $ARL_2(\delta)$, respectively. Next, suppose that

$$ARL_1(\delta = 0) = \frac{1}{1 - \beta_1(\delta = 0)} = \frac{1}{1 - \beta_2(\delta = 0)} = ARL_2(\delta = 0)$$

But for a fixed $\delta \neq 0$, suppose

$$ARL_1 = \frac{1}{1 - \beta_1} \leq \frac{1}{1 - \beta_2} = ARL_2$$

then

$$\beta_1 \leq \beta_2$$

and

$$P(Y_2 \leq y) = 1 - \beta_2^y \leq 1 - \beta_1^y = P(Y_1 \leq y) \text{ for all } y = 1, 2, \cdots$$

This says that the probability that scheme 1 will signal a shift on or before point y is larger than the probability that scheme 2 will signal on or before point y *for every* $y = 1, 2, \cdots$. Thus, these run length distributions are *stochastically ordered* for detecting shift. This property of geometric distributions, namely, that ordering of distribution means, ARLs, implies stochastic ordering of distributions is the basis for using ARLs for comparing competing control schemes. Note that unless both competing schemes are geometric, comparing ARLs is not necessarily a meaningful way to judge the schemes' relative performances.

In view of these considerations, we will use ARL as a criterion to judge performance of a charting method only when the run length distribution can be shown to be at least approximately a geometric distribution.

4.6.4 ARL for the Combined 1-of-1 and 4-of-5 Tests of Fig. 4.9

When considering the values of ARL and ATRL given in Tables 4.4 and 4.5, the question arises as to whether the performance of the X̄-chart could be improved by using one of the other runs tests of Fig. 4.9, or even others we could invent, to improve the sensitivity of the chart to detect changes in the process mean μ. The answer is yes, and has been studied by the present author in unpublished work, and by Champ and Woodall (1987). The 9-of-9, 2-of-3, and 4-of-5 tests of Fig. 4.9 combine information from consecutive runs of points, and we can consider using one or more of these tests as a supplement to the 1-of-1 test in order to attempt to increase the ability to detect small shifts in the process mean. We recommend that the 4-of-5 test be used with the 1-of-1 test and this combined test will here be called the 11-45 test. By this we mean, of course, that we will declare a signal if *either* the 1-of-1 test or the 4-of-5 test signals. If they both signal, then they must signal in the same direction.

This recommendation is based on consideration of the ARL of this combined 11-45 test; however, this requires some qualification. First, since the events of signals on consecutive points are no longer independent events, we do not know that the distribution of run lengths is a geometric distribution. Therefore, it is not enough to simply compare the means of run length distributions, unless both distributions are geometric, as discussed above. However, if the run length distribution of the 11-45 test would satisfy the relation between SDRL and ARL for a geometric distribution, viz., $SDRL = \sqrt{ARL(ARL - 1)}$, to a reasonable degree of approximation, then it would be reasonable to compare the ARL of the combined 11-45 test with ARLs of schemes with geometric run length distributions. The most favorable case is for $SDRL \cong \sqrt{ARL(ARL - 1)}$. Table 4.6 gives some values of the ARL and SDRL of the run length distribution for the 11-45 combined test. These values were obtained by simulation by the author; however, they agree well with the ARL values of Champ and Woodall (1987), obtained by using a Markov chain model for the process. Note that while the relationship $SDRL \cong \sqrt{ARL(ARL - 1)}$ is not satisfied exactly for these values, they do satisfy this relation to a reasonable approximation.

By comparing the values in Table 4.6 with those in Table 4.4 for $n = 1$, it is seen that the 11-45 test has much better sensitivity for detecting small shifts in μ, say for $\delta \leq 2$, then the 1-of-1 test alone, and virtually the same sensitivity for detecting larger shifts in μ. Note that the values of SDRL are essentially those for a geometric distribution for δ of 5 and 4; and for small values of δ it is smaller than it would be for a geometric distribution. This increased sensitivity comes at a

TABLE 4.6 ARL and SDRL Values for Combined 11-45 Test to Detect Shifts in a Process Mean

δ	0	0.25	0.5	1	1.5	2	3	4	5
ARL	164.20	113.83	45.89	12.16	5.555	3.47	1.83	1.18	1.02
SE(ARL)	0.257	0.251	0.099	0.023	0.008	0.004	0.002	0.001	0.0003
SDRL	162.43	112.47	44.30	10.16	3.68	1.89	1.02	0.46	0.15
SE(SDRL)	0.172	0.096	0.010	0.017	0.006	0.001	0.002	0.002	0.001

price, of course, because the ARL for $\delta = 0$ is decreased from 370 to 164. Nevertheless, we recommend the 11-45 test for most charting programs. It will be seen in later chapters that this combined test has appeal in a wide range of charting situations to be considered later. The values SE(ARL) and SE(SDRL) are standard errors of the estimates from the simulation.

4.7 THE OC, POWER, AND ARL FUNCTIONS FOR AN S-CHART, σ KNOWN

Consider next the performance of the S-chart to detect changes in the process standard deviation of a normally distributed process variable. Suppose a chart with the 3-sigma control limits (4.4.6) is used to detect a shift of σ from a nominal value of σ_0 to a value of $\delta\sigma_0$ ($\delta > 0$). If a point exceeds UCL we conclude that δ is greater than 1, and if a point is below LCL we conclude that δ is less than 1. If $\delta = 1$ (no change is σ) the OC function is

$$\beta(n, 1) = P(B_5\, \sigma_0 \leq S \leq B_6\, \sigma_0 | \sigma = \sigma_0)$$

$$\beta(n, 1) = P\{(n - 1)B_5^2 \leq \frac{(n - 1)S^2}{\sigma_0^2} \leq (n - 1)B_6^2\}$$

$$\beta(n, 1) = G_{n-1}\{(n - 1)B_6^2\} - G_{n-1}\{(n - 1)B_5^2\} \qquad (4.7.1)$$

for $G_\nu(\cdot)$ a χ_ν^2 distribution function.
For $\delta > 1$ the OC function is

$$\beta(n, \delta) = P\left\{\frac{(n - 1)S^2}{\delta^2\, \sigma_0^2} \leq \frac{(n - 1)B_6^2}{\delta^2}\,\Big|\, \sigma = \delta\sigma_0\right\}$$

$$\beta(n, \delta) = G_{n-1}\left\{\frac{(n - 1)B_6^2}{\delta^2}\right\} \qquad (4.7.2)$$

For $\delta < 1$ the OC function is

$$\beta(n, \delta) = 1 - G_{n-1}\left\{\frac{(n - 1)B_5^2}{\delta^2}\right\} \qquad (4.7.3)$$

For all values of $\delta > 0$, the power function is given by

$$\text{Power}(n, \delta) = 1 - \beta(n, \delta) \qquad (4.7.4)$$

Since the statistics S_1, S_2, $\cdots$ are independent and the control limits are constants, the run length distribution is geometric and ARL and SDRL are again given by

$$ARL(n, \delta) = \frac{1}{1 - \beta(n, \delta)}$$

$$SDRL(n, \delta) = \sqrt{ARL(n, \delta)[ARL(n, \delta) - 1]} \qquad (4.7.5)$$

The average total run length, assuming constant sample size n, is given by

$$ATRL(n, \delta) = n \times ARL(n, \delta) \qquad (4.7.6)$$

Since $B_5 = 0$ for $n \leq 5$, the chart has no ability to detect decreases in σ for $n \leq 5$. For any $n \in \{1, 2, 3, 4, 5\}$ and $\delta < 1$, we have $\beta(n, \delta) = 1$, or $\text{Power}(n, \delta) = 0$.

The values of the OC, Power, and ARL functions for $n = 5$ and a range of values of δ are given in Table 4.7. A graph of the OC function for $n = 5$ is shown in Fig. 4.13. Note that the ARL(5, 1), the case of no shift for σ, is only 256 which is considerably smaller than the ARL of 370 for an $\overline{X}$ 3-sigma chart. The probability of a false signal is 0.0039, which is much larger than the normal distribution value of 0.00135.

4.7.1 The S-Chart with Probability Limits

The probability limits for an S-chart were given in display (4.4.9). If we again consider a shift of σ from a nominal value of $\sigma = \sigma_0$ to a new value of $\sigma = \delta\sigma_0$, $0 \leq \delta$, then the OC function is given by (4.7.7). Again, the run length distribution is geometric and the power, ARL, SDRL, and ATRL functions are related to the OC function as given in

$$\beta(n, \delta) = 1 - \alpha_L - \alpha_U \text{ if } \delta = 1$$

$$\beta(n, \delta) = G_{n-1}\left(\frac{\chi^2_{\alpha_U, n-1}}{\delta^2}\right) \text{ if } \delta > 1$$

$$\beta(n, \delta) = 1 - G_{n-1}\left(\frac{\chi^2_{1-\alpha_L, n-1}}{\delta^2}\right)$$

$$\text{if } 0 < \delta < 1$$

$$(4.7.7)$$

TABLE 4.7   Values of the OC, Power, and ARL Functions for 3-Sigma S-Chart, $n = 5$

δ	OC	Power	ARL
<1	1.000	0.000	∞
1.0	.9961	.0039	256.41
1.1	.9874	.0126	79.37
1.2	.9700	.0300	33.33
1.3	.9420	.0580	17.24
1.4	.9035	.0965	10.36
1.5	.8562	.1438	6.95
1.6	.8027	.1973	5.07
1.8	.6872	.3128	3.20
2.0	.5741	.4259	2.35
2.2	.4729	.5271	1.90
2.4	.3869	.6130	1.63
2.6	.3159	.6840	1.46
2.8	.2582	.7418	1.35
3.0	.2118	.7882	1.27
3.5	.1317	.8683	1.15
4.0	.0848	.9152	1.09
4.5	.0565	.9435	1.06
5.0	.0388	.9612	1.04
5.5	.0275	.9725	1.03
6.0	.0199	.9801	1.02
10.0	.0028	.9972	1.00

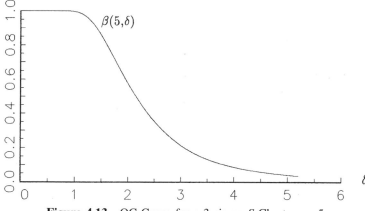

Figure 4.13   OC Curve for a 3-sigma S-Chart, $n = 5$

(4.7.4), (4.7.5), and (4.7.6). If we choose $\alpha_L = \alpha_U = 0.00135$, to correspond to the probabilities beyond $\pm 3\sigma$ under a normal curve, and $n = 5$, then the equations in (4.7.7) become, using Table A.2:

$$\beta(5, 1) = 0.99730$$

$$\beta(5, \delta) = G_4\left(\frac{17,800}{\delta^2}\right) \text{ for } \delta > 1$$

$$\beta(5, \delta) = 1 - G_4\left(\frac{0.106}{\delta^2}\right) \text{ for } 0 < \delta < 1$$

These formulas have been used to compute the values of the OC, Power, and ARL functions given in Table 4.8. These OC values in Table 4.8 are the probabilities that the chart does not signal in the *correct direction* of the shift in σ. Or, stated in terms of the power function, the power is the probability of a signal in the *correct direction,* and the ARL is the average number of subgroups until a correct signal is obtained. Note that the sensitivity of the chart to detect a small decrease in σ is poor; however, it is better than the 3-sigma chart, which has no ability to detect decreases in σ. Also, note that the ARL for $\delta = 0.9$ is larger than for $\delta = 1$.

Our discussion of the performance of the S-chart in terms of the OC, Power, and ARL functions largely relates to the increase or decrease in the mean of the distribution of S when σ changes from a nominal value of $\sigma = \sigma_0$ to a new value $\sigma = \delta\sigma_0$. Of course, this is because $E(S) = c_4\sigma$ and the chart centerline is at $c_4\sigma_0$, but after the shift the distribution mean is at $\delta c_4\sigma_0$. Thus the mean of the plotted values moves up or down on the chart according to whether $\delta > 1$ or $\delta < 1$. Recall that equation (4.4.5) stated that the standard deviation of the distribution of S is $SD(S) = \sigma\sqrt{1 - c_4^2}$. Thus, when σ shifts from σ_0 to $\delta\sigma_0$, then $SD(S)$ shifts from $\sigma_0\sqrt{1 - c_4^2}$ to $\delta\sigma_0\sqrt{1 - c_4^2}$. The importance of this is that a shift in the value of σ not only changes the mean of the distribution of S, but also causes a simultaneous increase ($\delta > 1$) or decrease ($\delta < 1$) in the spread of the pattern of plotted points. This change in the spread of the points on an S-chart can sometimes be more obvious than the shift in level of the point pattern, and is helpful supplementary information. This change in spread will occur on any chart made to control the process standard deviation σ. Another important implication of this is that the chart has poor sensitivity to detect small decreases in σ by having a point fall below the LCL, as can be seen by examining Table 4.8 for values of $\delta < 1$. In fact, the probability of a signal (power) at $\delta = 0.9$ is 0.00205, which is smaller

TABLE 4.8   Values of OC, Power, and ARL Functions for a (.00135, .00135) Probability S-Chart, $n = 5$

δ	OC	Power	ARL
0.05	0.00000	1.00000	1.00
0.10	0.03145	0.96855	1.03
0.15	0.38126	0.68174	1.47
0.20	0.61799	0.38201	2.62
0.30	0.88174	0.11826	8.46
0.40	0.95587	0.04413	22.66
0.50	0.98045	0.01954	51.18
0.60	0.99017	0.00983	101.73
0.70	0.99456	0.00544	183.82
0.80	0.99696	0.00324	308.64
0.90	0.99795	0.00205	487.80
1.00	0.99730	0.00270	370.37
1.10	0.99466	0.00534	187.27
1.20	0.98514	0.01486	67.29
1.30	0.96899	0.03101	32.25
1.40	0.94092	0.05908	16.93
1.50	0.90511	0.09489	10.54
1.60	0.86161	0.13839	7.23
1.80	0.75974	0.24026	4.16
2.00	0.65148	0.34852	2.87
2.20	0.54867	0.45133	2.22
2.40	0.45712	0.54288	1.84
2.60	0.37901	0.62099	1.61
2.80	0.31376	0.68624	1.46
3.00	0.26020	0.73980	1.35
3.50	0.16507	0.83483	1.20
4.00	0.10780	0.89220	1.12
4.50	0.07245	0.92755	1.08
5.00	0.05016	0.94984	1.05
5.50	0.03561	0.96539	1.04
7.00	0.01461	0.98539	1.01

than the probability of a signal at the stable case of $\delta = 1$! For this reason, the S Q-chart given in Chapter 7, with the 11-45 combined test, is much more sensitive than these classical S-charts for detecting decreases in σ.

4.8   ESTIMATING μ, σ, AND THE CONTROL LIMITS

In the preceding sections we have considered the process mean μ and standard deviation σ to be known values. In practice, in order for the process mean and standard deviation to be "known," we must have a large data set available that was taken while the process was operating in a stable state, that is, during a period while both the mean and variance were constant. In classical applications to parts manufacturing, where perhaps thousands, or even tens of thousands, of parts are made in each production run, large data sets can probably be accumulated. However, since most processes are not naturally stable, and the purpose of SPC is to stabilize the process, in practice this forces us to engage in a type of bootstrapping operation to establish control charts. Also, in many cases when we would like to consider charting today, large data sets are simply not available. The issue of the size of the data set needed to accurately estimate μ and σ, and, more importantly, the control limits, will be discussed in detail below. First, we consider formulas for estimating μ and σ.

Suppose that we have available m subgroups of size n each as shown in Table 4.1. then the following statistics given in Table 4.1 can be computed from the formulas for each subgroup.

$$\text{Sample mean} = \overline{X}_i = \frac{1}{n} \sum_{j=1}^{n} X_{ij} \tag{4.8.1}$$

$$\text{Sample range} = R_i = X_{i,\text{MAX}} - X_{i,\text{MIN}} \tag{4.8.2}$$

where $X_{i,\text{MAX}}$ is the largest value in the ith sample and $X_{i,\text{MIN}}$ is the smallest value.

$$\text{Sample variance } S_i^2 = \frac{1}{n-1} \sum_{j=1}^{n} (X_{ij} - \overline{X}_j)^2 \tag{4.8.3}$$

$$\text{Sample standard deviation} = S_i = \sqrt{S_i^2} \tag{4.8.4}$$

To estimate μ from all of the data in Table 4.1, we use the mean of the sample means given by

$$\overline{\overline{X}} = \frac{1}{m} \sum_{i=1}^{m} \overline{X}_i = \frac{1}{mn} \sum_{i=1}^{m} \sum_{j=1}^{n} X_{ij} \tag{4.8.5}$$

To estimate σ from a single normal sample in Table 4.1, we observed in (4.4.4) that the sample standard deviation can be shown to have expectation

$$E(S_i) = \mu_s = \frac{\Gamma\left(\dfrac{n}{2}\right)}{\Gamma\left(\dfrac{n-1}{2}\right)} \sqrt{\frac{2}{n-1}} \, \sigma = c_4 \sigma \qquad (4.8.6)$$

where $\Gamma(\cdot)$ denotes the gamma function. Values of the constant

$$c_4 = \frac{\Gamma\left(\dfrac{n}{2}\right)}{\Gamma\left(\dfrac{n-1}{2}\right)} \sqrt{\frac{2}{n-1}}$$

are given in Table A.5 in the Appendix. Moreover, the standard deviation of S_i, as noted in (4.4.5), is

$$\sigma_s = \sqrt{\mathrm{Var}(S_i)} = \sqrt{E(S_i^2) - [E(S_i)]^2} = \sigma\sqrt{1 - c_4^2} \qquad (4.8.7)$$

From (4.8.6) we see that an unbiased estimate of σ, computed from sample i, is given by

$$\hat{\sigma}_i = \frac{S_i}{c_4}$$

and the usual formula to estimate σ using all of the samples is the mean of these estimates

$$\hat{\sigma}_s = \frac{\overline{S}}{c_4} = \frac{1}{mc_4} \sum_{i=1}^{m} S_i \qquad (4.8.8)$$

Sometimes the sample ranges R_i are used to compute an estimate of σ. The variable $W = R_i/\sigma$ is called the *standardized* range and has a distribution that depends on n but is constant in σ. When the process distribution is normal, denote $d_2 = E(W) = \mu_W$ and we have

$$E(R) = \mu_R = d_2\,\sigma \qquad (4.8.9)$$

Values of d_2 are also given in Table A.5. For a normal process distribution the value R_i/d_2 is an unbiased estimate of σ based on only one sample and we use $\overline{R}/d_2$ to estimate σ using all of the samples.

$$\hat{\sigma}_R = \frac{\overline{R}}{d_2} = \frac{1}{md_2} \sum_{i=1}^{m} R_i \qquad (4.8.10)$$

The estimate $\overline{R}/d_2$ of σ and the estimate $\overline{S}/c_4$ are the same for $n = 2$, but for n of 3 or more the range estimate is more variable than the estimate using the standard deviation. The *relative efficiency* of the range estimate to the standard deviation estimate is defined as

$$RE(R, S) = (100) \frac{MSE(S)}{MSE(R)} = (100) \frac{\text{Var}(S)}{\text{Var}(R)}$$

and when the sample is from a normal distribution, this ratio has the following values:

n:	2	3	4	5	6	10
$RE(R, S)$:	100	99.2	97.5	95.5	93	85

Note that the loss of efficiency for $n = 5$ is about 4.5% and at $n = 10$ this loss is 15%. The traditional sample sizes for Shewhart $\overline{X}$-charts are $n = 4$ or 5, and for these values the loss of efficiency from using R rather than S is small and usually unimportant. This means, for example, for $n = 5$ from the above table, that by using the range estimate rather than the sample standard deviation estimate, we are wasting about 4.5% of the observations.

The reason for using R rather than the more efficient S to obtain an estimate of σ is historic. When these charting methods were first developed in the 1920s the computations were done by hand calculation with pencil and paper, sometimes by relatively untrained workers. It was felt that R was easier to calculate than S and could be computed routinely with fewer computational errors. Today there is little reason to use R and we recommend that S be used, especially when the charts are made with computer algorithms.

If σ_0 must be estimated from data as in Table 4.1, then σ_0 in the control limits formulas is replaced by either

$$\frac{\overline{S}}{c_4} \text{ or } S_{\text{pooled}} = \sqrt{\frac{1}{n_1 + n_2 + \cdots + n_m - m} \sum_{i=1}^{m} (n_i - 1)S_i^2} \qquad (4.8.11)$$

The "pooled" estimate should always be used to estimate σ_0^2 when the estimate is computed from samples of unequal sizes.

Example 4.2: To illustrate using these formulas, we compute estimates from the soft drinks data of Table 4.2. We have

$$\overline{\overline{X}} = \frac{1}{m} \sum_{i=1}^{m} \overline{X}_i = \frac{239.71}{20} = 11.986,$$

$$\overline{S} = \frac{1}{m} \sum_{i=1}^{m} S_i = \frac{2.383}{20} = 0.1192,$$

$$\overline{R} = \frac{1}{m} \sum_{i=1}^{m} R_i = \frac{5.81}{20} = 0.2905$$

From $n = 5$, we obtain from Table A.5 the values $c_4 = 0.9400$ and $d_2 = 2.326$. Then

$$\hat{\sigma}_s = \frac{0.1192}{0.9400} = 0.1268 \text{ and } \hat{\sigma}_R = \frac{0.2905}{2.326} = 0.1249$$

Note that these two estimates of σ agree well.   ∎

We are not just interested in estimating μ and σ, but, in fact, our real interest is in estimating the control limits LCL and UCL for the control charts for both μ and σ. The classical estimates that are used for LCL and UCL are "plus-in" estimates obtained by substituting estimates for both μ and σ for these parameters in the formulas that assume μ and σ are known. We consider next these classical formulas.

4.8.1   The $\overline{X}$-Chart Using $\overline{S}$ to Estimate σ

By substituting the estimate $\overline{\overline{X}}$ for μ and $\overline{S}/c_4$ for σ in the 3-sigma control limits formulas of (4.4.3), we obtain the formulas of (4.8.12).

$$
\begin{array}{c}
\widehat{UCL}(\overline{X}) = \overline{\overline{X}} + A_3\,\overline{S} \\[2mm]
\widehat{CL}(\overline{X}) = \overline{\overline{X}} \\[2mm]
\widehat{LCL}(\overline{X}) = \overline{\overline{X}} - A_3\,\overline{S}
\end{array}
\tag{4.8.12}
$$

where $A_3 = 3/c_4\sqrt{n}$ is a function of n only and is given in Table A.5. Note that we have placed a circumflex over these control limits to emphasize that they are estimates of the actual control limits given in (4.4.3).

Example 4.2, continuation 1: From Table A.3 we read $A_3 = 1.427$ and compute

$$\widehat{UCL}(\overline{X}) = 11.986 + (1.427)(0.1192) = 12.16$$

$$\widehat{CL}(\overline{X}) = 11.986$$

$$\widehat{LCL}(\overline{X}) = 11.986 - (1.427)(0.1192) = 11.84 \qquad \blacksquare$$

4.8.2 The $\overline{X}$-Chart Using $\overline{R}$ to Estimate σ

If we substitute $\overline{\overline{X}}$ for μ and $\overline{R}/d_2$ for σ in the control limits of (4.4.3), then we obtain formulas for the control limits given in (4.8.13). Here

$$
\begin{array}{c}
\widehat{UCL}(\overline{X}) = \overline{\overline{X}} + A_2\,\overline{R} \\[2mm]
\widehat{CL}(\overline{X}) = \overline{\overline{X}} \\[2mm]
\widehat{LCL}(\overline{X}) = \overline{\overline{X}} - A_2\,\overline{R}
\end{array}
\tag{4.8.13}
$$

Where $A_2 = 3/d_2\sqrt{n}$ and values of A_2 are given in Table A.5.

Example 4.2, continuation 2: From Table A.3 we read $A_2 = 0.577$. The limits from (4.8.13) are then

$$\widehat{UCL}(\overline{X}) = 11.986 + (0.577)(0.2905) = 12.15$$

$$\widehat{CL}(\overline{X}) = 11.986$$

$$\widehat{LCL}(\overline{X}) = 11.986 - (0.577)(0.2905) = 11.85$$

In this example the control limits obtained by the two methods using $\overline{S}$ and $\overline{R}$ differ slightly, but the difference is small. ∎

The estimated control limits for the 3-sigma S-chart when σ is estimated from S are given in (4.8.14).

$$\widehat{UCL}(S) = B_4\,\overline{S}, \text{ for}$$

$$B_4 = 1 + (3/c_4)\sqrt{1 - c_4^2},$$

$$\widehat{CL}(S) = \overline{S} \tag{4.8.14}$$

$$\widehat{LCL}(S) = B_3\,\overline{S}, \text{ for}$$

$$B_3 = 1 - (3/c_4)\sqrt{1 - c_4^2},$$

and values of B_3 and B_4 are given in Table A.5.

Example 4.2, continuation 3: From the data of Table 4.2, $\overline{S} = \dfrac{2.383}{20} = 0.119$, and, from Table A.5, $B_3 = 0$ and $B_4 = 2.089$. Then

$$\widehat{UCL}(S) = (2.089)(0.119) = 0.25, \qquad \widehat{CL}(S) = 0.12, \qquad \widehat{LCL}(S) = 0$$

Note that these estimates are reasonably close to the "true" values given earlier. ∎

The estimated control limits for the 3-sigma R-chart when σ is estimated from R are given in (4.8.15). These estimates of the control limits are obtained by substituting $\overline{R}/d_2$ for σ_0 in equations (4.4.8).

$$\widehat{UCL}(R) = \overline{R}(1 + 3d_3/d_2) = D_4\,\overline{R}$$

$$\widehat{CL}(R) = \overline{R} \tag{4.8.15}$$

$$\widehat{LCL}(R) = \overline{R}(1 - 3d_3/d_2) = D_3\,\overline{R}$$

The values of D_3 and D_4 are given in Table A.5. Estimates of probability limits are obtained from (4.4.2) and (4.4.9) by replacing μ and σ by their estimates.

Example 4.2, continuation 4: From Table 4.2 we have $\bar{R} = 8.81/20 = 0.44$ and from Table A.5 we read $D_3 = 0$, $D_4 = 2.114$. Then

$$\widehat{UCL}(R) = (2.114)(0.44) = 0.93, \qquad \widehat{CL} = 0.44, \qquad \widehat{LCL} = 0 \quad \blacksquare$$

4.8.3   Remark on the Problem of Estimating Control Limits

When the parameters μ and σ are assumed known, then the control limits of (4.4.3) are also known parameters of the process distribution. When the parameters μ and σ are not known, then in the classical approach to constructing a control chart given in this section we obtain estimates of μ and σ as described above, such as $\bar{X}$ and $\bar{S}/c_4$ or $\bar{R}/d_2$, and obtain *estimates* $\widehat{LCL}$, $\widehat{CL}$, and $\widehat{UCL}$ of LCL, CL, and UCL by substituting these estimats for μ and σ in the formulas for LCL, CL, and UCL of (4.4.3). In classical SPC applications these estimated control limits are then used just as though they are the true control limits. When the parameter estimates are based on m samples of size n each, for a fixed n of 4 or 5, how large must m be in order to assume the estimates $\widehat{UCL}$ and $\widehat{LCL}$ are essentially equal to UCL and LCL, respectively? Many writers on SPC recommend that m of 20 to 30 samples of size $n = 5$ are enough to treat the control limit estimates as the true control limits, *at least on a trial basis until more data are available.*

4.8.4   Stage 1 and Stage 2 Charts

Some writers have proposed starting a charting program for a particular process by formally implementing the program in two steps called Stage 1 and Stage 2 (see Hillier 1969). This approach has considerable appeal. Stage 1 consists of observing an initial calibration data set consisting of m subgroups of size n each. These data are then used to estimate the control limits for $\bar{X}$- and R- or S-charts. Then *retrospective* charts for $\bar{X}$ and R or S are made by plotting the sample statistics from these subgroups on charts with these estimated control limits. The hope is that this will lead to the identification of subgroups that were obtained when the process was in control. Data from these subgroups are then used to make new estimates of the control limits.

In Stage 2 the estimates of control limits established in Stage 1 are used to chart data from further production. This charting is often done on-line in real time. We recommend using at least $m = 30$ samples of size $n = 5$ each for Stage 1 retrospective charts; however, we will study this estimation and sample size problem in detail in section 4.11, and there develop results on which a more rational choice of m can be based.

4.9 EXAMPLES OF $\bar{X}$-, S-, AND R-CHARTS; STRATIFICATION AND RATIONAL SUBGROUPS

A new manufacturing process for piston wrist pins has been installed and $m = 50$ samples of size $n = 5$ pins each have been selected from the process in time order and diameter measurements made at the centers of the pins are given in Table 4.9. The last three columns of the table give values of $\bar{X}$, S, and R for each sample. The specifications for diameters for these wrist pins are 1.000 ± 0.003 in. That is, we wish to make all pins with diameters as near 1.000 in. as possible, and pins with diameters less than 0.997 in. or more than 1.003 in. are out of specification. We now proceed to use the sample information in Table 4.9 for a Stage 1 retrospective SPC charting program for the process. We wish to try to identify stable subgroups, and to use these subgroups to estimate control limits for charts to monitor Stage 2 daily operations.

Estimates of the process standard deviation σ and mean μ are computed first. From Table A.5, read $c_4 = 0.9400$ for $n = 5$ and estimate σ and μ by

$$\hat{\sigma} = \frac{\bar{S}}{c_4} = \frac{0.0615}{(50)(0.9400)} = 0.00128, \text{ and } \hat{\mu} = \bar{\bar{X}} = \frac{50.0028}{50} = 1.0001$$

The S-chart is studied first to decide if the process variance was constant while these data were being taken. Unless the variance is constant, we will not be able to interpret the $\bar{X}$-chart, as was discussed above. The control limits for the S-chart are computed next. From Table A.5 read $B_3 = 0$ and $B_4 = 2.089$. Here $\bar{S} = 0.0615/50 = 0.00123$ and we compute

$$UCL(S) = B_4\bar{S} = (2.089)(0.00123) = 0.0026 \text{ in.}$$

$$CL(S) = \bar{S} = 0.0012 \text{ in.}$$

$$LCL(S) = B_3\bar{S} = 0 \text{ in.}$$

TABLE 4.9 Wrist Pin Diameters

	Sample					$\overline{X}$	S	R
1	0.9986	0.9996	1.0009	0.9986	1.0002	0.9996	0.0010	0.0023
2	1.0000	0.9992	0.9987	1.0000	0.9999	0.9996	0.0006	0.0013
3	0.9996	1.0018	0.9988	1.0006	0.9993	1.0000	0.0012	0.0030
4	0.9999	1.0003	1.0001	1.0021	1.0004	1.0006	0.0009	0.0022
5	1.0011	1.0008	0.9995	0.9969	1.0001	0.9997	0.0017	0.0042
6	1.0000	1.0003	0.9982	0.9993	0.9997	0.9995	0.0008	0.0021
7	1.0019	1.0001	1.0005	0.9997	0.9995	1.0003	0.0010	0.0024
8	0.9997	1.0013	0.9968	1.0022	1.0014	1.0003	0.0021	0.0054
9	1.0005	1.0002	1.0007	1.0005	0.9994	1.0003	0.0005	0.0013
10	1.0013	0.9986	1.0002	0.9968	1.0023	0.9998	0.0022	0.0055
11	1.0006	0.9994	1.0004	0.9998	1.0000	1.0000	0.0005	0.0012
12	1.0000	1.0009	1.0012	0.9990	1.0002	1.0003	0.0009	0.0022
13	0.9985	0.9991	1.0010	1.0002	1.0002	0.9998	0.0010	0.0025
14	1.0004	0.9993	1.0008	1.0002	0.9963	0.9994	0.0018	0.0045
15	1.0010	1.0010	1.0004	1.0005	0.9995	1.0005	0.0006	0.0015
16	0.9995	1.0005	1.0011	1.0009	1.0007	1.0005	0.0006	0.0016
17	0.9992	1.0003	0.9986	1.0001	1.0006	0.9998	0.0008	0.0020
18	1.0001	1.0001	1.0042	0.9997	0.9999	1.0008	0.0019	0.0045
19	0.9991	0.9985	1.0008	0.9991	0.9997	0.9994	0.0009	0.0023
20	1.0006	1.0011	0.0998	1.0023	0.9998	1.0005	0.0013	0.0035
21	0.9980	1.0006	1.0044	1.0003	1.0005	1.0008	0.0023	0.0064
22	1.0005	0.9983	1.0007	1.0004	0.9994	0.9999	0.0010	0.0024
23	0.9990	0.9985	0.9992	1.0005	1.0019	0.9998	0.0014	0.0034
24	0.9998	0.9999	1.0003	1.0003	1.0010	1.0003	0.0005	0.0012
25	1.0002	0.9994	1.0003	0.9988	1.0006	0.9999	0.0007	0.0018
26	1.0011	0.9994	0.9986	0.9989	0.9999	0.9996	0.0010	0.0025
27	0.9993	1.0005	1.0002	1.0004	0.9991	0.9999	0.0007	0.0014
28	0.9970	1.0179	1.0003	1.0005	1.0002	1.0032	0.0084	0.0209
29	0.9991	0.9990	0.9995	1.0009	0.9998	0.9997	0.0008	0.0019
30	1.0009	1.0003	1.0015	0.9991	0.9986	1.0001	0.0012	0.0029
31	1.0011	1.0009	1.0003	0.9985	0.9981	0.9998	0.0014	0.0030
32	1.0008	1.0004	1.0010	0.9995	0.9998	1.0003	0.0006	0.0015
33	0.9976	1.0007	0.9985	1.0003	1.0004	0.9995	0.0014	0.0031
34	1.0020	1.0005	1.0000	0.9985	0.9994	0.9997	0.0008	0.0020
35	0.9984	0.9999	1.0014	1.0019	1.0008	1.0005	0.0014	0.0035
36	0.9982	0.9991	1.0002	1.0051	1.0012	1.0008	0.0027	0.0069
37	1.0014	1.0004	0.0998	1.0006	1.0003	1.0005	0.0006	0.0016
38	0.9987	0.9991	1.0011	1.0001	1.0006	0.9999	0.0010	0.0024
39	1.0010	0.9988	1.0006	1.0007	1.0009	1.0004	0.0009	0.0022
40	0.9999	1.0004	0.9995	0.9995	0.9993	0.9997	0.0004	0.0011
41	0.9986	1.0021	1.0000	0.9985	0.9998	0.9998	0.0015	0.0036
42	1.0001	1.0000	1.0000	0.9996	0.9994	0.9998	0.0003	0.0007
43	0.9987	1.0002	1.0005	0.9989	0.9993	0.9995	0.0008	0.0018
44	0.9991	1.0007	1.0007	1.0005	0.9992	1.0000	0.0008	0.0016
45	1.0006	0.9961	1.0009	1.0000	0.9983	0.9992	0.0020	0.0048
46	1.0002	1.0000	0.9996	0.9988	1.0003	0.9998	0.0006	0.0015
47	0.9993	0.9999	0.9996	0.9999	1.0006	0.9999	0.0005	0.0013
48	1.0017	1.0028	0.9985	0.9991	1.0000	1.0004	0.0018	0.0043
49	0.9989	1.0007	0.9997	0.9997	1.0001	0.9998	0.0007	0.0018
50	1.0012	0.9991	0.9994	0.9998	0.9987	0.9996	0.0010	0.0025
					SUM:	50.0028	0.0615	0.1515

The S-chart for the standard deviation σ is shown in Fig. 4.14. The chart shows that S_{28} is extremely large and S_{36} is slightly above the UCL; otherwise the process variance appears stable. We compute next the control limits for the sample means. From (4.8.12) we have

$$UCL(\bar{X}) = \bar{\bar{X}} + A_3 \bar{S} = 1.0001 + (1.427)(0.00123) = 1.0019 \text{ in.}$$

$$CL(\bar{X}) = \bar{\bar{X}} = 1.0001 \text{ in.}$$

$$LCL(\bar{X}) = \bar{\bar{X}} - A_3 \bar{S} = 0.9983 \text{ in.}$$

The 50 sample means from Table 4.9 are plotted with these control limits in Fig. 4.15.

Again, the value for sample number 28 is far outside the control limits. Examination of the values in sample 28 shows that the large values of $\bar{X}_{28}$ and S_{28} are due to an extremely large value of 1.0179 in for the second observation in the 28th sample. This type of extreme value is usually called an *outlier,* and it is likely due to a special cause. Machining processes are often prone to produce a few such outliers, which can be due to a variety of causes. Thus, in order to remove the effect of this subgroup on the estimates of μ, σ, and the control limits, we compute estimates from the other 49 samples only. Call these values $\bar{X}'$ and $\bar{S}'$ and we have

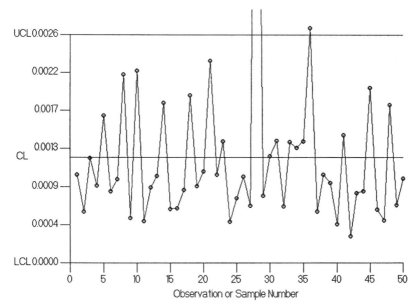

Figure 4.14 *S*-Chart for Wrist Pin Data, Stage 1 Analysis

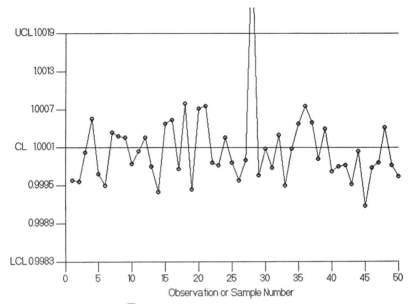

Figure 4.15 $\bar{X}$-Chart for Wrist Pin Data, Stage 1 Analysis

$$\bar{\bar{X}}' = 0.99999, \bar{S}' = 0.0011, \bar{R}' = 0.00267$$

Revised control limits for the S-chart are

$$UCL(S) = (2.089)(0.0011) = 0.0023 \text{ in,}$$

$$CL(S) = 0.0011 \text{ in,} \qquad LCL(S) = 0 \text{ in}$$

and from (4.8.11) revised control limits for the $\bar{X}$-chart are

$$UCL(\bar{X}) = 0.99999 + (1.427)(0.0011) = 1.0016 \text{ in,}$$

$$CL(\bar{X}) = 1.0000 \text{ in,} \qquad LCL(\bar{X}) = 0.9984 \text{ in}$$

The values of S_i and $\bar{X}_i$ from Table 4.9 are plotted with these new control limits in Figs. 4.16 and 4.17, respectively, with the values for sample number 28 omitted. Two points on the S-chart, S_{21} and S_{36}, are now on or above the UCL, but the S-chart looks pretty good for an operating process. The $\bar{X}$-chart in Fig. 4.17 now has all points well inside the control limits.

While we have plotted S-charts to study σ, the R-chart could also have been used and will here give essentially the same results as the S-chart, even though the R-chart wastes about 5% of the sample infor-

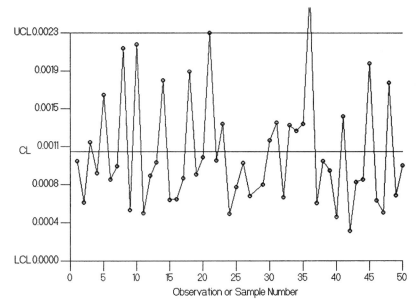

Figure 4.16   Revised S-Chart for Wrist Pin Data

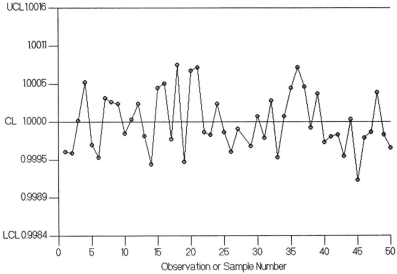

Figure 4.17   Revised $\bar{X}$-Chart for Wrist Pin Data

mation. With the ready availability of low-priced electronic calculators that automatically compute $\overline{X}$ and S, we feel that the S-chart should today be used in most cases rather than the R-chart, and we will usually make S-charts in our examples and problems. However, the R-chart is widely used in practice, and many experienced quality practitioners are accustomed to it and prefer to use it. To illustrate the computations, we now compute the R control limits for the wrist pin data. We have for that data, with R_{28} omitted, $\overline{R} = 0.1306/49 = 0.0027$, which gives control limits from (4.5.5) of

$$UCL(R) = D_4 \overline{R} = (2.114)(0.0027) = 0.0056 \text{ in.}$$

$$CL(R) = \overline{R} = 0.0027 \text{ in.}$$

$$LCL(R) = D_3 \overline{R} = 0 \text{ in.} \qquad \blacksquare$$

The charts made in the above example are Stage 1 *retrospective* charts, because they can be made only retrospectively after a set of calibration data have been collected in order to estimate the control limits. If the process is not stable while these calibration data are being taken, and usually it will not be, this can cause severe start-up problems in initiating a charting program. This is because shifts in the process parameters while the calibration data are being taken may cause the control limits to be badly estimated, and the charts to either give excessive numbers of false alarms or to be insensitive to detect parameter shifts on Stage 1 retrospective charts, or subsequently on Stage 2 charts.

The S- and R-charts are used to study the stability of the process standard deviation parameter σ, and the $\overline{X}$-chart to study the stability of the process mean μ. Observe that when the subgroups and observations in subgroups are taken in time order and μ changes in the period between sampled subgroups, then the change should be reflected immediately in the subsequent values of $\overline{X}_i$, but will not be reflected in the values of S_i. However, if there is a large change in μ while a subgroup is being taken, so that some observations in the subgroup are taken before the shift and others after the shift, then this change in μ should be reflected in the $\overline{X}$-chart for all points after the shift, and the S-chart point for *this one sample only.* That is, patterns on the S-chart for subsequent subgroups will be unaffected, while those for the $\overline{X}$-chart will reflect the changed value of μ.

When the model (4.1.2) is at least approximately correct, so that the observed values are approximately independent random variables with the same distribution mean μ and variance σ^2, we say that the process is *stable* and operating *in control,* and all of the sources or factors that contribute to the differences among the values are called *common or chance causes* of variation. Any other factors that enter and result in changes in the parameters μ and σ are called *special* or *assignable* causes of variation. In other words, common causes affect all points on the charts, while special or assignable causes affect only some of the points or, possibly, affect points differentially. A process is stable in the sense of Shewhart then if it has a constant system of chance causes.

It is helpful to consider some of the ways by which the mean μ and the standard deviation σ can change due to special causes. The mean μ can change from a nominal value μ_0 to a different value μ_1, say, by a sudden shift, and the change can be either permanent or temporary. If $|\mu_1 - T| > |\mu_0 - T|$, then the variability about target value is increased. If the shift is temporary and large there may be a small number, perhaps one or two, *outliers* produced before the mean shifts back to the former level. Such outliers may be due to many causes. In machining processes they may be due to having a chip fall against a cutting blade and foul up one or two parts before it wears or burns off. For data taken manually, outliers can result from reading or recording mistakes, and so on. Permanent mean shifts may be due to many causes such as changing machines, operators, operating methods, materials, measurement methods, or changes in the operating environment.

In addition to temporary or permanent sudden shifts of the mean, we can also have the mean change in many other patterns. For example, it may drift slowly either up or down. Drift can be caused by various factors. Tool wear causes drift in machining processes. In some types of rolling mills the constant pulling action can cause a drift in some types of measurements. Settling action of fluid in a tank can cause the percentage of a component in a sample from a fixed position to drift with time.

The variance of the process also can change either continuously or by discrete jumps, but changes in the variance are often increases. The variance of parts measurements tends to increase continuously over the life of a manufacturing machine due to wearout effects. A change of operators or machines may cause either an increase or decrease in the value of the process variance. Quality improvement programs frequently involve work on processes to remove common causes of variation and in this way to reduce the variance component of the expected mean square given in (4.2.2). For these applications it is clearly important that charts for the process variance have sensitivity to detect *decreases* in the process variance, in order to recognize improvement in the process resulting from process improvement efforts.

4.9.1 Sampling Plans, the Rational Subgroups Principle, Stratification

To this point we have been concerned with setting up and using Shewhart S-, R-, and $\overline{X}$-charts, but we have not considered the problem of designing the chart by deciding how the sample subgroups of product are to be selected. A key idea that dates from the pioneering work of Shewhart himself is the concept of a *rational subgroup*. To discuss this idea we recall the definition of the observed mean square about target value τ given in (4.2.1), but we write it using the notation of Table 4.1 as

$$OMS = \frac{1}{mn} \sum_{i=1}^{m} \sum_{j=1}^{n} (X_{ij} - \tau)^2 \qquad (4.9.1)$$

We can rewrite this as follows:

$$OMS = \frac{1}{m} \sum_{i=1}^{m} (\overline{X}_i - \tau)^2 + \frac{n-1}{mn} \sum_{i=1}^{m} S_i^2 \qquad (4.9.2)$$

Now, suppose we do not assume that the samples are all from the same distribution, but rather that sample i has mean μ_i and standard deviation σ_i. The expected value of OMS is then

$$E(OMS) = EMS = \frac{1}{m} \left[\sum_{i=1}^{m} (\mu_i - \tau)^2 + \sum_{i=1}^{m} \sigma_i^2 \right] \qquad (4.9.3)$$

So we see that the OMS can be written as the sum of two terms, where the first term is the average variation about target value of the sample subgroup means, and the second term is the average variation within subgroups about their respective subgroup means. The idea of selecting subgroups as rational subgroups entails selecting the subgroups to minimize the second term in the OMS formula above, that is, to minimize the within samples variation. Then the OMS—and its expected value EMS—can be reduced by centering the processes separately for the sources represented by the different subgroups. Observe that any action that can be taken to reduce any term in either sum of the EMS formula of (4.9.3) will reduce the overall variation from target value τ.

There are many operating and environmental factors which may effect either μ or σ. Such factors include operators, machines, temperature, days, shifts, time order of production, gauges, materials, lubricants, cooling oils, drill speeds, contaminants, and many others. For example, either the mean μ or the standard deviation σ may have different values for different operators or for different machines. Thus, we shall have to consider these factors carefully in order to conduct our process so as to minimize EMS. Generally, the values of the quality variable will have to be grouped or *stratified* according to the levels or values of these environmental or operating factors. Shewhart called these subgroups *rational subgroups*.

Studying the effects of various operating factors on one or more quality variables is a complex field that often requires comparison techniques from statistics, especially experimental design; however, control charts are also useful tools for this work. The observations must first be recorded on data sheets or entered into a data set in computer memory. The data sheet or set must contain sufficient information to identify each value as well as the levels or values of factors thought to (possibly) influence a quality variable.

4.9.2 Process Sampling Plans for Control Charts

A work process, such as that depicted by the process flow chart of Fig. 4.1, operates in time, and production units are naturally ordered in time. A principle strength of control charts is that they can be organized to take advantage of the information available from the time ordering of the data. This is accomplished in part by the way time is used in designing the process sampling plan. There are many possibilities of ways to design a sampling plan, and the plan must be suited to the particular process.

All of the six contributing factors to a work process—men, machines, material, methods, measurements, and environment—naturally vary somewhat over time. Therefore it is to be expected that the process distribution, and its mean and variance, will also vary somewhat over time. This implies, of course, that the assumptions of the model in display (4.1.2) of constant mean μ and standard deviation σ cannot be satisfied exactly by an operating process. In practice, we can reasonably expect the measurements of production units that are close together in time will have μ and σ very nearly the same, and units that are far apart are more likely to have different values of μ and σ. This point and the rational subgroups idea has important implications for designing our sampling plans. We consider a number of possible plans for sampling units of production. These are similar to those discussed by Kane (1989).

4.9.3 Consecutive Process Sampling

The samples are taken as consecutively produced production units. A sample plan consists of a pair (n, k) where n is the sample size and k is the number of units of production between samples. Units are selected as follows:

$$\cdots \times \times \times \times \times \times \times \times \otimes \otimes \otimes \otimes \otimes \times \times \times \times \times \times \times \times \otimes \otimes \otimes \otimes \otimes$$

$$\times \times \times \times \times \times \times \otimes \otimes \otimes \otimes \otimes \times \cdots$$

This is a $(n, k) = (5, 7)$ consecutive sampling plan. Sometimes, it will be more convenient to take a consecutive sample of size n at specified time points, such as every hour or at the midpoint of a production shift, for example.

4.9.4 Periodic Process Sampling

Suppose every m^{th} unit of production is sampled and a subgroup consists of n consecutively sampled units:

$$\cdots \times \times \times \times \otimes \times \times \times \times \otimes \times \times \times \times \otimes$$

$$\times \times \times \times \otimes \times \times \times \times \otimes \times \times \times \times \otimes \cdots$$

Sometimes the period may be specified in units of time rather than numbers of production units. For example, we might obtain a sample of size $n = 8$ from an 8-hour work shift by taking a unit at the end of each hour. It is often easier to sample using time rather than production order. If the production rate is constant, they are equivalent sampling methods.

4.9.5 Random Process Sampling

A specified proportion of the production units are to be sampled from a process. If one-sixth of the production units are to be sampled, then we can perform a random experiment for each unit to decide whether or not to sample it by tossing an honest die and the unit is taken if a snake-eye is thrown. Alternately, if we wish to sample 10% of the units from a production run of 1000 units, we can use a computer algorithm such as the one in the Q-Charts program to obtain a subset of 100 integers from the intergers 1; 2; 3; $\cdots$; 999; 1000. The record of sampled units might look like:

$$\cdots \times \times \times \times \times \otimes \times \times \times \times \times \times \times \times \times \times \times \times \otimes$$

$$\times \times \otimes \times \times \times \times \times \times \cdots$$

This is not a sampling plan that is very useful for process control charts. It is inconvenient to administer, and, worse, it does not give an attractive way to form the sampled units into subgroups.

This is essentially the plan used to sample completed production lots and is then treated as one sample per lot. In that case the units obtained are called a *representative* sample from the lot. Control charts can then be made from these sequences of samples from lots.

4.9.6 Stratified Process Sampling

Suppose a process can be partitioned into a number of strata. For example, there might be three parallel machines performing the same operation, or one machine with four spindles or heads, as in Fig. 4.18. These subgroups are usually taken periodically. In some cases, the subgroups may not always contain exactly one unit from each stratum when consecutively sampled units are combined into fixed size subgroups. This would be so if the four spindles produced at different rates. Recall that in section 4.5 we observed that this type of stratification can lead to the pattern of Test 7 of Fig. 4.9, that is, the points tend to hug the center line too closely. Further material on these important problems will be given in Chapter 7.

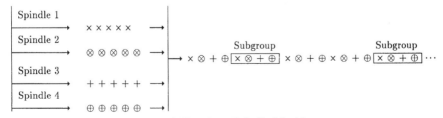

Figure 4.18 Four Spindle Machine

4.10 CHARTS FOR INDIVIDUAL MEASUREMENTS

Sometimes it will be required to make charts for individual measurements: $X_1, X_2, \cdots, X_t, \cdots$. It may be because the observations become available slowly in time or for other reasons cannot or should not be formed into subgroups. Modern automated gauging equipment often measures every part, and individual measurements charts retain all of the information from the original data. For a start-up process or one that has short runs, it is often desirable to measure every part in order to study the process, detect and eliminate or reduce the effects of assignable causes, estimate the process parameters, and bring the process into control as quickly as possible. For various reasons, some companies today make many individual measurements charts (see Palm 1992).

In setting up a charting system for individual measurements it should be borne in mind that the central limit theorem for means is not applicable and that the process distribution may not be normal. It is necessary to study the normality of the data. This can be done in many ways involving varying levels of sophistication and sensitivity. The individual measurements chart itself, given in this section, provides a rough graphical check on the normality of the data. If the individual measurements are approximately normal, then the points should be centered on the center line with the density of the points decreasing symmetrically as the distance from the CL increases. A more sensitive procedure is obtained by making a histogram of the data and, possibly, plotting the fitted normal density on it. More sensitive tests and graphical methods for studying normality of data will be given in Chapter 9.

As was discussed by Shewhart (1931), when individual industrial measurements are not normally distributed, the most common alternative shape is a unimodal distribution that is skewed either to the right or to the left, usually positive numbers skewed to the right. The density function of a unimodal distribution that is skewed to the right is shown in Fig. 4.7. Methods for charting processes with skewed distributions will be considered in Chapter 9.

We make control charts for individual measurements when the process standard deviation σ is "known," that is, when it is estimated from a prior data set. For this case when σ is assumed known, the control limits are obtained from (4.4.2) or (4.4.3) by putting $n = 1$. If μ and σ are unknown, then they must be estimated. For $X_1, X_2, \ldots,$ X_N a sequence of observations on the process available for estimating μ and σ, the mean $\bar{X}$ will be used to estimate μ and we often use the *moving range* to construct an estimate of σ. The average moving range, $\overline{MR}$, is given by (4.10.1).

$$\overline{MR} = \frac{1}{N-1} \sum_{j=2}^{N} |X_j - X_{j-1}| \qquad (4.10.1)$$

From (4.8.9), and the remark following it, the quantity

$$\tilde{\sigma} = \frac{\overline{MR}}{d_2} = \frac{\overline{MR}}{1.128} = 0.8865\overline{MR}$$

is an unbiased estimator of σ. thus, 3-sigma control limits are

$$\overline{X} \pm 3\tilde{\sigma} = \overline{X} \pm (30)(0.8865)\overline{MR} = \overline{X} \pm 2.6595\,\overline{MR} \quad (4.10.2)$$

The principal reason for using the moving range for subgroups of size two, rather than either ranges or sample standard deviations for larger subgroups, is that this method gives a better estimator of σ when the mean μ does not remain constant while the calibration data are being taken. Also, recall that for a sample of size $n = 2$ the range R and the standard deviation S are equivalent since $S^2 = R^2/2$. It should be noted, however, that when μ remains constant the sample standard deviation estimator, computed from all of the data available, is a more efficient estimator. In a subsection below, we will propose using a test for constancy of the mean based on the mean square successive difference to decide whether to use the moving range estimator or S computed from all the observations to estimate σ.

4.10.1 The Moving Range Chart

For a sequence of observations $X_1, X_2, \ldots, X_N$; the *moving range* MR_i is given by (4.10.4).

$$MR_i = |X_i - X_{i-1}| \text{ for } i = 2, \ldots, N \qquad (4.10.4)$$

When charts for individual measurements to study the constancy of the mean μ are made, we need also to consider the constancy of the standard deviation σ. As was the case for subgrouped data, unless the process standard deviation is constant, the chart to control the process mean μ cannot be interpreted as necessarily reflecting the constancy of μ, since an increase in σ will also tend to cause more points to fall outside the control limits. When the mean μ is not constant while the data are being taken, for example, if there is a regression trend in the data, we see from the above remarks that the moving range is a reasonable estimator of the variability about the trend line. The control limits are computed from the formulas in displays (4.4.8) and (4.8.15), with $\bar{R}$ replaced by $\overline{MR}$ of (4.10.1) above; and for $n = 2$ we read from Table A.5 the values $D_1 = 0$, $d_2 = 1.128$, $D_2 = 3.686$, $D_3 = 0$, and $D_4 = 3.267$. the moving range 3-sigma control limits are given in display (4.10.5). If an estimate of σ other than the $\overline{MR}$ estimate is used, then that estimate should replace σ in the "σ known" formulas to obtain "σ unknown" formulas.

σ known:

$$UCL(MR_i) = 3.686\sigma$$

$$CL(MR_i) = 1.128\sigma$$

$$LCL(MR_i) = 0$$

σ unknown (using $\overline{MR}$ estimate of σ):

$$\widehat{UCL}(MR_i) = 3.267\ \overline{MR}$$

$$\widehat{CL}(MR_i) = \overline{MR}$$

$$\widehat{LCL}(MR_i) = 0$$

(4.10.5)

An important point to keep in mind in interpreting moving range charts is that consecutive points are not independent, which means we have no valid way to interpret many patterns. For this reason, it is sometimes desirable to make a control chart by plotting only alternate points, that is, every other point, so that the plotted points are independent. When a chart is made this way it is equivalent to an S or S^2 chart made by grouping the observations into consecutive subgroups of size 2 each and constructing a chart.

Example 4.3: A machining process produces circular-shaped parts that are used in automatic transmissions. The inner diameter is gauged on each part and has target value 27.193 mm and the process standard deviation is known to be $\sigma = 0.003$ mm. The process mean is known to have some negative drift due to tool wear. In order to produce parts near nominal value, the process mean μ is reset to the value 27.194 mm after every subgroup of 25 consecutive parts. Measurements from 25 consecutive parts are given in Table 4.10. The estimate of the process mean is $\bar{x} = 27.192$.

For $n = 1$ we obtain the 3-sigma control limits

$$UCL(X) = \bar{x} + 3\sigma = 27.192 + (3)(.003) = 27.201 \text{ mm}$$

$$CL(X) = \bar{x} = 27.192 \text{ mm}$$

$$LCL(X) = \bar{x} - 3\sigma = 27.192 - (3)(.003) = 27.183 \text{ mm}$$

for individual measurements. These control limits were obtained from

TABLE 4.10   Collar Inner Diameters

Number	Observation	Moving Range
1	27.197	—
2	27.189	0.008
3	27.194	0.005
4	27.189	0.005
5	27.188	0.001
6	27.196	0.008
7	27.193	0.003
8*	27.212	0.019
9	27.196	0.016
10	27.191	0.005
11	27.188	0.003
12	27.189	0.001
13	27.196	0.007
14	27.192	0.004
15	27.191	0.001
16	27.190	0.001
17	27.193	0.003
18	27.189	0.004
19*	27.172	0.017
20	27.196	0.024
21	27.189	0.007
22	27.191	0.002
23	27.189	0.002
24	27.190	0.001
25	27.919	0.001
Average:	27.192	0.006

(4.4.3) for $n = 1$ by substituting the estimate $\bar{x}$ for μ. The 25 measurements from Table 4.10 are plotted in Fig. 4.19 with these limits. The chart shows that observation 8 is above the upper control limit and observation 19 is below the lower control limit. No other values are near the control limits.

From (4.10.5) with $\sigma = 0.003$ given we compute limits for the moving range chart

$$UCL(MR) = 3.686 \times \sigma = (3.686)(0.003) = 0.0111$$

$$CL(MR) = 1.128 \times \sigma = (1.128)(0.003) = 0.0034$$

$$LCL(MR = 0$$

The moving ranges of Table 4.10 are plotted in Fig. 4.20 with these limits. Note that on this chart the large observation 8 and the small observation 19 both cause *two* large points.   ∎

If there is an apparent large change in μ while the Stage 1 data are being taken, then we recommend that the ranges affected should be omitted from the estimate of σ. Nelson (1982) recommends omitting the ranges that are at least 3.5 times the average moving range, and

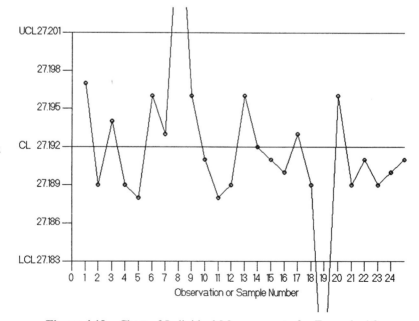

Figure 4.19   Chart of Individual Measurements for Example 4.3

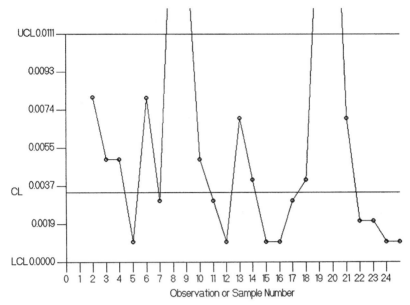

Figure 4.20   Moving Range Chart for Example 4.3

recalculating the average moving range. This appears to be a reasonable precaution to avoid overestimating σ and causing the chart to be insensitive to changes in μ. Also, it should be mentioned that some writers, such as Nelson (1982), recommend plotting *only* the chart of individual measurements and *not* plotting moving ranges separately. The basis of this recommendation is that the chart of individual measurements not only reflects changes in μ, but changes in the spread of points indicate changes in σ, and this chart essentially contains all of the information in the data.

If the individual observations are normally distributed, then the tests of Fig. 4.9 can also be applied to the chart for individual observations, and the probabilities for false signals when μ and σ are known and the process is stable are correct, since these probabilities depend upon the normality of the sample means. The combined 11-45 test is attractive here to improve the chart's sensitivity to detect small mean shifts. It should also be kept in mind that the sensitivity of these charts for detecting changes in either μ or σ is much less than that of charts based on sample means and standard deviations or ranges of subgroups of size 3 or more. For this reason, it may be desirable to group the individual observations into rational subgroups larger than two using time order as the grouping variable, when this is possible and reasonable.

A useful property of the individual measurements chart is that specification limits can be drawn on it to give information on the ability of the process to meet specifications, in addition to information on the stability of the process. In some applications, this may be considered very desirable; however, if this is done, caution must be exercised to assure that everyone interpreting the charts clearly understands the difference between control limits and specification limits. There is much potential here for problems arising from this practice.

4.10.2   The Mean Square Successive Difference Estimator of σ^2 and Testing for a Changing Mean

The mean square successive difference estimator of σ^2 is given by

$$MSSD = \frac{1}{2(n-1)} \sum_{i=1}^{n-1} (x_{i+1} - x_i)^2 \qquad (4.10.6)$$

It follows that MSSD is an unbiased estimator of σ^2. Further, like the moving range estimator $\overline{MR}$ of σ defined in (4.10.1), if the process mean μ is not constant while the individual observations $x_1, x_2, \ldots$ are being recorded, then this MSSD estimator will tend to be inflated less as an estimator of σ^2 than the sample variance S^2. When the process mean μ is constant, the statistics MSSD and S^2 are both unbiased estimates of σ^2 and the ratio

$$r = \frac{MSSD}{S^2} \qquad (4.10.7)$$

has been shown to have mean and variance given by (4.10.8).

$$E(r) = 1, \ \mathrm{Var}(r) = \frac{n-2}{(n-1)(n+1)} \qquad (4.10.8)$$

The ratio r is approximately normally distributed for $n \geq 20$. Now, if the process mean is not constant, then S^2 will tend to be larger than MSSD, so that we can make a hypothesis test for constancy for the process mean μ by rejecting in favor of the alternative if r is too small. The p-value for this test, say PV-MSSD, can be computed from

$$PV - MSSD = \Phi \left[(r - 1) \sqrt{\frac{(n - 1)(n + 1)}{n - 2}} \right] \quad (4.10.9)$$

These *p*-values give highly informative supplementary information for individual observations charts. Further discussion and references on MSSD are given in Hald (1952). We will discuss using this test for changing μ in examples for Q-charts for individual observations data in Chapter 7. If this value indicates that the mean is varying, by having a very small value, say PV-MSSD $\leq$ .05, then we should use either the moving average $\overline{MR}$ or MSSD estimate to construct charts; however, if this is not the case we may prefer to use the more efficient estimate based on *S*.

Example 4.4: The twenty-five consecutive observations in Table 4.10 give $\overline{X} = 27.192$, $S = 0.006422$, RMSSD $= 0.006218$, and PV-MSSD $= 0.37$. This does not signal a significantly nonconstant mean, which appears to imply that the two troublesome observations—points 8 and 19—are individual outliers, which does not imply a permanently shifted mean. Of course, these outliers would cause inflation of the estimate if they were used to estimate σ. ∎

4.11 ESTIMATING SHEWHART CHARTS CONTROL LIMITS FROM PAST DATA, SAMPLE SIZE CONSIDERATIONS

In the foregoing sections we have presented the classical SPC approach of taking *m* subgroups of size *n* each of past data as set out in Table 4.1, and using these data to estimate control limits for $\overline{X}$- and S-charts. In this section, we study these classical methods of estimating the control limits in some detail. In particular, we shall be especially interested in the numbers and sizes of subgroups required in order to obtain reliable estimates of the control limits. We observe that in much of the SPC literature, 20 to 30 subgroups of size four or five ($m = 20, 30$; $n = 4, 5$) are recommended as adequate to estimate control limits in Stage 1 applications. These recommendations are apparently based on empirical experience. Some of the material in this section follows the development of Quesenberry (1993). The presentation in this section will be somewhat more detailed and theoretical than the preceding sections, because some of this material is original and will be new to many quality practitioners. Readers who are not interested in the details of this study may wish to consult the recommendations resulting from it summarized in the subsection at the end of the section.

4.11.1   Estimating $\overline{X}$ Control Limits, Properties of Estimates

First, recall that if the process parameters μ and σ were actually known, then the true 3-sigma control limits for $\overline{X}$ would be given by (4.4.3) as

$$UCL = \mu + 3\,\frac{\sigma}{\sqrt{n}}, \qquad LCL = \mu - 3\,\frac{\sigma}{\sqrt{n}} \qquad (4.11.1)$$

Next, suppose the parameters μ and σ are unknown, but that m subgroups of size n each are available to estimate the control limits (4.11.1). The usual formulae for estimating UCL and LCL of (4.11.1) are

$$\widehat{UCL} = \overline{\overline{X}} + 3\,\frac{\overline{S}}{c_4\sqrt{n}}, \qquad \widehat{LCL} = \overline{\overline{X}} - 3\,\frac{\overline{S}}{c_4\sqrt{n}} \qquad (4.11.2)$$

We consider next the distribution of the estimate $\widehat{UCL}$. Note that $\overline{\overline{X}}$ is a normal random variable and $\overline{S}$ is also approximately normal since it is a mean of m independent random variables. Since $\widehat{UCL}$ is a linear combination of $\overline{\overline{X}}$ and $\overline{S}$, it is also normal, to good approximation. By directly evaluating the mean and variance of $\widehat{UCL}$, we have the distributional result of (4.11.3).

If $\widehat{UCL}$ of (4.11.2) is estimated using m subgroups of size n from a normal process distribution, then $\widehat{UCL}$ is approximately normally distributed with mean and variance

$$E(\widehat{UCL}) = \mu + \frac{3\sigma}{\sqrt{n}} = UCL,$$

$$VAR(\widehat{UCL}) = \frac{\sigma^2}{mn}\left(1 + \frac{9(1 - c_4^2)}{c_4^2}\right)$$

(4.11.3)

TABLE 4.11   Probabilities that $\widehat{UCL}$ is in Interval about UCL for $m = 30$ and $n = 5$

d:	0.01	0.05	0.10	0.2	0.3	0.4	0.6	0.8	1
P_d:	0.03	0.15	0.29	0.54	0.73	0.86	0.974	0.996	1.000

For $d > 0$, we consider next the probability that the estimate $\widehat{UCL}$ will be within a distance of $\pm\, d\sigma/\sqrt{n}$ of the actual value UCL. This probability is given by the formula in (4.11.4).

$$P_d = P\left\{ UCL - d\frac{\sigma}{\sqrt{n}} \le \widehat{UCL} \le UCL + d\frac{\sigma}{\sqrt{n}} \right\}$$

$$= 2\Phi(A) - 1, \text{ for } A = \frac{d\sqrt{m}}{\sqrt{1 + \frac{9(1 - c_4^2)}{c_4^2}}} \tag{4.11.4}$$

Note that this probability depends only on d, m, and n; and *not* on μ or σ. For example, for $m = 30$ and $n = 5$, often recommended values, $A = 3.7049\, d$. Table 4.11 gives some values of P_d for these values of m and n. The SD($\widehat{UCL}$) for $m = 30$ in units of $\sigma/\sqrt{n}$ is 0.27. This is used to sketch the density of $\widehat{UCL}$ in Fig. 4.21.

By studying Table 4.11 and Fig. 4.21 it is apparent that using $m = 30$ subgroups of size $n = 5$ each to estimate the control limits with the classical formulas will give a control chart with upper control limit sometimes too high and sometimes too low. A chart with upper control limit too high will have reduced sensitivity to detect increases in the mean μ, and a chart with upper control limit too low will result in

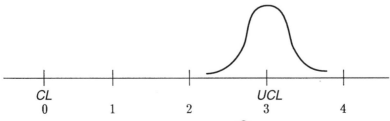

Figure 4.21   Density Function of $\widehat{UCL}$, $m = 30$, $n = 5$

excessive false alarms. Similar detailed results can be given for any values of m and n. By symmetry of the estimation problem, similar results are also true for the estimation of *LCL*.

4.11.2 Effects of Dependence of Signaling Events on the Run Length Distribution

Let A_i denote the event that the ith sample mean $\overline{X}_i$ either exceeds UCL or is less than LCL. Then $P(A_i) = P(\overline{X}_i - UCL > 0$ or $\overline{X}_i - LCL < 0) = 0.00270$ for $i = 1, 2, \cdots$. Since $\overline{X}_i$ and $\overline{X}_j$ are independent for $i \neq j$, clearly A_i and A_j are independent events and determining if $\overline{X}_i$ exceeds UCL or is less than LCL for $i = 1, 2, \cdots$ is a sequence of Bernoulli trials, that is, $A_1, A_2, \cdots$ is a sequence of Bernoulli trials.

Let B_i denote the event that the mean $\overline{X}_i$ either exceeds $\widehat{UCL}$ or is less than $\widehat{LCL}$. Then for a process with constant mean μ and variance σ^2 the probability of B_i is

$$P(B_i) = P(\overline{X}_i > \widehat{UCL} \text{ or } \overline{X}_i < \widehat{LCL}) \text{ for } i = 1, 2, \cdots$$

But since both $\overline{X}_i$ and $\widehat{UCL}$ are approximately normally distributed, the difference $\overline{X}_i - \widehat{UCL}$ is also approximately normally distributed and has mean and variance

$$E(\overline{X}_i - \widehat{UCL}) = \mu - \mu - \frac{3\sigma}{\sqrt{n}} = -\frac{3\sigma}{\sqrt{n}}$$

$$\text{Var}(\overline{X}_i - \widehat{UCL}) = \frac{\sigma^2}{n} + \frac{\sigma^2}{n}\frac{1}{m}\left[1 + \frac{9(1 - c_4^2)}{c_4^2}\right]$$

Using these values to standardize $\overline{X}_i - \widehat{UCL}$, we obtain

$$P(\overline{X}_i - \widehat{UCL} > 0) = 1 - \Phi\left[\frac{3}{\sqrt{1 + [1 + 9(1 - c_4^2)/c_4^2]/m}}\right]$$

Moreover, since $P(\overline{X}_i - \widehat{LCL} < 0) = P(\overline{X}_i - \widehat{UCL} > 0)$, and the events are mutually exclusive, the probability that a point will plot outside these estimated control limits is given in (4.11.5).

$$P(\text{False Signal}) = P(B_i)$$

$$= 2\left\{1 - \Phi\left[\frac{3}{\sqrt{1 + [1 + 9(1 - c_4^2)/c_4^2]/m}}\right]\right\} \quad (4.11.5)$$

Note the important point that this probability depends only on m and n, and therefore for fixed m and n this probability is a constant. Also, the argument of the standard normal distribution function Φ is less than 3, so that the probability of a false signal always exceeds 0.00270. In particular, for $m = 30$ and $n = 5$ (values often recommended), we have $c_4 = 0.9400$ and

$$\text{P(False Signal)} = 2\{1 - \Phi(2.8964)\} = 0.00378$$

We can readily use the formula of equation (4.11.5) to evaluate the probability of a false signal for any m and n; however, as we shall demonstrate, these probabilities have only limited value in assessing the properties of charts using $\widehat{LCL}$ and $\widehat{UCL}$ as control limits. Consider again the sequence of events $B_1, B_2, \cdots, B_i, \cdots$. From the above these events have constant probabilities for fixed m and n, and *if they were independent events* the sequence of trials comparing $\bar{X}_i$ with $\widehat{UCL}$ would be a sequence of Bernoulli trials, and the run length between occurrences of B_i would be a geometric random variable with probability $p = P(B_i)$, and the ARL would be $1/p$ or $1/P(B_i)$. However, the random variables $(\bar{X}_i - \widehat{UCL})$ and $(\bar{X}_i - \widehat{UCL})$ are *not independent* and the events B_i and B_j are *not independent* events for $i \neq j$. To verify this last statement, we note that the covariance of these random variables can be obtained by direct evaluation as follows.

$$\text{Cov}(\bar{X}_i - \widehat{UCL}, \bar{X}_j - \widehat{UCL}) = \text{Var}(\widehat{UCL}) = \frac{\sigma^2}{mn}\left(1 + \frac{9(1 - c_4^2)}{c_4^2}\right)$$

Then the correlation between these two random variables is

$$\text{Corr}(\bar{X}_i - \widehat{UCL}, \bar{X}_j - \widehat{UCL}) = \frac{\text{Cov}(\bar{X}_i - \widehat{UCL}, \bar{X}_j - \widehat{UCL})}{\sqrt{\text{Var}(\bar{X}_i - \widehat{UCL})\text{Var}(\bar{X}_j - \widehat{UCL})}}$$

$$= \frac{\text{Var}(\widehat{UCL})}{\text{Var}(\bar{X}_i - \widehat{UCL})} = \left[1 + m\left(1 + \frac{9(1 - c_4^2)}{c_4^2}\right)^{-1}\right]^{-1}$$

Note that this correlation is a function only of m and n, and is always positive. Table 4.12 gives some values of this correlation for selected values of m and n.

As we commented above, although for fixed m and n the probability $P(B_i)$ is constant for $i = 1, 2, \cdots$; because B_i and B_j are not independent, the sequence of trials comparing $\overline{X}_i$ with $\widehat{UCL}$ and $\widehat{LCL}$ is not a sequence of Bernoulli trials, and, therefore, the distribution of the run length between occurrences of the events B_i is *not* a geometric distribution. In other words, the ARL for the $\overline{X}$-chart with estimated control limits cannot be evaluated using the formula for the mean of a geometric distribution. This also means that the probability of a false signal, that is, a Type I Error, on one point, given in equation (4.11.5), has limited usefulness in assessing the overall performance of the chart of the stable case when the parameters μ and σ are constant. Therefore, to assess the performance of these charts we advocate studying the properties of the *distribution of run lengths.* Hillier (1964) gave a method for evaluating the probability of a Type I Error, a false signal on one sample, using estimated control limits for the case when the mean sample range $\overline{R}$ is used (rather than $\overline{S}$) to estimate σ in the control limits (4.11.1). However, he did not consider the dependence issue, and his formula, like that in (4.11.5), is of limited usefulness in assessing overall performance of that chart.

Proschan and Savage (1960) also considered the effect of the values of m and n on the probability of a Type I Error, and gave some tables of maximum values of m to control this error at level $\alpha = 0.01$ for a given value of n for the cases when either $\overline{R}$ or a pooled estimate of σ^2 are used to construct estimates of σ. However, these authors also do not address the issue of dependence, and therefore these results also have limited usefulness.

TABLE 4.12   Values of Corr$(\overline{X}_i - \widehat{UCL}, \overline{X}_j - \widehat{UCL})$ as a Function of m and n

m	n: 2	3	4	5	6	7	8	9	10
5	0.5511	0.4089	0.3434	0.3043	0.2796	0.2624	0.2497	0.2400	0.2323
10	0.3803	0.2570	0.2065	0.1794	0.1625	0.1510	0.1427	0.1364	0.1314
20	0.2348	0.1475	0.1152	0.0985	0.0884	0.0817	0.0768	0.0732	0.0703
30	0.1698	0.1034	0.0798	0.0679	0.0607	0.0560	0.0526	0.0500	0.0480
50	0.1093	0.0647	0.0495	0.0419	0.0374	0.0343	0.0322	0.0306	0.0294
80	0.0712	0.0414	0.0315	0.0266	0.0237	0.0217	0.0204	0.0194	0.0186
100	0.0578	0.0334	0.0254	0.0214	0.0190	0.0175	0.0164	0.0155	0.0149
200	0.0298	0.0170	0.0128	0.0108	0.0096	0.0088	0.0083	0.0078	0.0075
300	0.0200	0.0114	0.0086	0.0072	0.0064	0.0059	0.0055	0.0052	0.0050
500	0.0121	0.0069	0.0052	0.0044	0.0039	0.0035	0.0033	0.0031	0.0030

4.11.3 Using ARL and SDRL to Characterize the Run Length Distribution for $\bar{X}$-Charts

Suppose m subgroups of size n from a stable $N(\mu, \sigma^2)$ process are used to compute $\widehat{UCL}$ and $\widehat{LCL}$ of (4.11.2). Additional independent subgroups of size n are taken and the sample means are plotted on a chart with these limits. Next, suppose that at some point between subgroups the process mean shifts from the value $\mu = \mu_0$ to a new value $\mu = \mu_0 + \delta\sigma$. Then let Y denote the *run length,* which is the number of points plotted until a signal is given by having a point fall outside the control limits. Now, if the control limits of (4.11.1) were known constants, then the sequence of trials that consist of determining if $\bar{X}_i$ exceeds the known constant control limits would be a sequence of Bernoulli trials, and the run length Y between the events A_i would be a geometric random variable with mean, ARL, and standard deviation, SDRL, given by (4.11.6) [see equations (4.6.3)].

$$ARL = \frac{1}{1 - \beta(\delta)}, \; SDRL = \frac{\sqrt{\beta(\delta)}}{1 - \beta(\delta)} = \sqrt{ARL(ARL - 1)} \quad (4.11.6)$$

for $\beta(\delta) = 1 - P(A_i) = P(LCL \le \bar{X}_i \le UCL)$. In particular, for an $\bar{X}$-chart with known 3-sigma limits and $\delta = 0$, we have $1 - \beta(0) = 0.00270$, ARL = 370.4, and SDRL = 369.9.

The formulas of (4.11.6) characterize the distribution of run length for this case because the sequence of trials are Bernoulli trials. In particular, for this case of independent events note the simple formula relating SDRL To ARL. We suggest that a reasonable way to decide when m and n are large enough for $\widehat{LCL}$ and $\widehat{UCL}$ to be essentially equal to LCL and UCL is to determine when ARL and SDRL for the distribution of run length between events B_i satisfy (4.11.6), at least approximately. In particular, for $\delta = 0$ with 3-sigma limits we should have ARL = 370.4 and SDRL = 369.9 from (4.11.6).

To study the question of total sample size for the commonly used value of $n = 5$, we have generated ARLs and SDRLs by simulation for a range of values of m and δ. Table 4.13 gives the results of this simulation. For each entry in Table 4.13, m subgroups of size n were generated, the control limits $\widehat{LCL}$ and $\widehat{UCL}$ computed, and subgroups were generated from $N(\mu + \delta\sigma, \sigma^2)$ until a point outside $(\widehat{LCL}, \widehat{UCL})$ was found; the number of subgroups is one observation from the run length distribution. This procedure of computing a set of estimated control limits and one run of subgroups of size 5 each until a point outside the limits was obtained was repeated many times. For each

TABLE 4.13 ARL and SDRL for _m_ subgroups of Size _n_ = 5

_m_	$\|\delta\|$: 0	0.5	1.0	1.5	2.0
5	1347(40.5)	202.32(29.9)	9.91(0.58)	2.082(0.049)	1.159(0.012)
	9173	1888	41.15	3.11	0.538
10	611(17.1)	70.33(3.3)	6.68(0.31)	1.806(0.039)	1.097(0.008)
	3127	208.4	13.74	1.728	0.359
20	434(4.8)	46.68(1.40)	5.23(0.13)	1.658(0.026)	1.095(0.007)
	754	88.29	5.89	1.164	0.333
30	403(3.9)	43.74(1.00)	5.03(0.12)	1.599(0.024)	1.085(0.007)
	563	63.29	5.55	1.060	0.296
50	388.6(2.28)	39.21(0.81)	4.73(0.10)	1.625(0.024)	1.085(0.007)
	484.3	51.09	4.49	1.069	0.306
75	384.2(3.2)	35.65(0.65)	4.47(0.089)	1.581(0.023)	1.084(0.006)
	452.5	41.27	4.00	1.013	0.309
100	380.6(2.96)	34.18(0.61)	4.50(0.091)	1.584(0.023)	1.077(0.005)
	419.2	38.34	4.06	1.020	0.292
200	367.9(2.71)	35.05(0.59)	4.56(0.093)	1.529(0.028)	1.078(0.009)
	383.7	37.34	4.18	0.900	0.300
300	368.9(2.66)	34.46(0.56)	4.61(0.130)	1.544(0.030)	1.079(0.009)
	380.9	35.55	4.14	0.950	0.288
500	372.4(2.33)	34.39(0.54)	4.48(0.125)	1.527(0.029)	1.069(0.009)
	381.0	34.44	3.95	0.904	0.269
1000	365.5(3.6)	34.23(1.33)	4.60(0.125)	1.586(0.031)	1.077(0.009)
	369.5	32.63	3.96	0.970	0.288
∞	370.4	33.42	4.50	1.57	1.076
	369.9	32.92	3.97	0.95	0.286

table entry, enough replications of this procedure were made to obtain a sufficiently small estimated standard error of the estimate of ARL. The exact values for the known parameters case is given in the last row (for _m_ = ∞) for comparison. For each value of $\|\delta\|$ and _m_, the first value given is the estimated ARL and the entry beside it in parentheses is its estimated standard error. The value below ARL is the estimated value of SDRL. For example, for δ = 0 and _m_ = 30 the estimated ARL is 403, with a standard error of 3.9, and the SDRL is 563. These should be compared with the nominal values of approximately 370 when parameters are known.

Certain points should be noted in considering Table 4.13. First, a general effect of estimation of the control limits is to increase both ARL and SDRL from the nominal values given in the last row. Note that these increased values of ARL and SDRL are the _opposite_ of what would be expected from the evaluation of the probabilities in equation (4.11.5) for the stable case of δ = 0, if the events B_1, B_2, · · · were independent events. In particular, for _m_ = 30 and _n_ = 5 we obtained

P(False Signal) = 0.00378, so if the events $B_1, B_2, \cdots$ were independent we would have from the formulas for the geometric distribution mean and standard deviation ARL = $1/0.00378 = 264.6$ and SDRL = 264.0. However, the estimated values of ARL and SDRL in Table 4.13 are 403 and 563, respectively. This effect is due to the *dependence* of the events $B_1, B_2, \cdots$ that is in turn due to using estimated limits. Also, note that for smaller values of m there is a pronounced tendency for SDRL to exceed ARL. This is true even for large values of m for the $\delta = 0$ column, which represents the extremely important case of a stable or in-control process. However, from (4.11.5) we see that for a stable process the probability of a signal on a sample, event B_i, is constant over points for fixed values of m and n. Therefore, if the events $B_1, B_2, \cdots$ were independent, run length would be a geometric random variable and from (4.11.6) we know that SDRL = $\sqrt{\text{ARL}(\text{ARL} - 1)}$ < ARL. Thus, the values of SDRL and ARL in the $\delta = 0$ column of Table 4.13 must reflect the dependence of the events B_i. When SDRL is larger than ARL by a significant amount, there is dependence in the sequence of trials that consists of comparing the $\bar{X}_i$'s with the estimated control limits to determine if it exceeds either of them.

By considering the nature of the run length distribution, we can also see that when SDRL exceeds ARL, we can expect that the run length distribution will have, in comparison with the nominal geometric distribution, a large number of quite short runs that are balanced by a few very long runs. This is because when two probability distributions have the same mean, but the first, say, has a larger standard deviation, the first will have more probability in its tails. But since all run length distributions take only values that are positive integers, which are bounded below by 1, this means that the probability on the lower integers of the first distribution must be increased and be balanced by an increase in the probability on large integers in the right tail of the distribution. The net effect of the dependence caused by using estimated control limits $\widehat{\text{LCL}}$ and $\widehat{\text{UCL}}$ is that the run length distribution will, for a particular value of ARL, have an increased rate of very short runs between false signals. There will also be an increased number of extremely long runs between false signals; however, the ratio of the number of very short runs to the number of extremely long runs is itself large. This is clearly undesirable and we should remain constantly aware of this phenomenon in our charting activities. Studying Table 4.13 shows that there is a definite tendency of this type at the commonly recommended values of $m = 30$ and $n = 5$. At least a slight trend is still evident at $m = 100$, or even larger values.

Readers will note that the considerations just discussed are relevant to a much wider class of situations than the one considered here. For example, for many types of control procedures that signal on points when a defined event occurs, if the signaling events are *dependent,* then we should consider more properties of the run length distribution than just its mean, that is, ARL. Considering just the run length distribution mean and not its standard deviation can be misleading when judging a control procedure.

To study further the run length distribution of classical 3-sigma charts with estimated control limits, we have generated 10,000 observations from the runs distribution for $m = 20, 30, 50, 75,$ and 100 subgroups of size $n = 5$ from a stable $(\delta = 0)$ normal distribution. The generated empirical distribution functions for a range of values of x are given in Table 4.14. The values of the limiting geometric distribution function are given in the last column $(m = \infty)$. The standard errors for x near the median, roughly 200 or 220, are approximately $.5/\sqrt{10000} = 0.005$, and for values in the tails of the distribution the standard errors are much smaller.

The tendency of these classical charts to give too many false alarms after short runs is clearly seen in these values. For example, the estimated percentage increase in false alarm rates on the first $x = 20$ subgroups for $m = 20$ is $100(.073 - .0526)/.0526 = 38.8\%$, for $m = 30$ there is a 23.6% increase in false alarm rates, for $m = 50$ it is 16.0%, for $m = 75$ it is 12.2%, and at $m = 100$ it is essentially 0. By studying these results it is clear that using $m = 30$ subgroups of size $n = 5$ gives enough inflation in false alarm rates to be of concern. From the values in both Tables 4.13 and 4.14, we feel that in order to have the classical $\bar{X}$-chart perform essentially like a chart with truly known parameters, we must require $m = 100$ subgroups of size 5 each. Excessive false alarm rates after short runs are highly undesirable in an SPC charting program. When a charting program gives too many false alarms it will lead to frustration of those operating the program, because they will spend time searching for nonexistent assignable causes. The likely result will be that the charts are soon being ignored. At this point, management is likely to conclude that the SPC program is an expensive failure.

4.11.4 Characterizing the Run Length Distribution for Individual Measurements Charts

Consider a sequence of observations $X_1, X_2, \cdots, X_r, \cdots$ that are assumed to be identically and independently distributed with a $N(\mu, \sigma^2)$ process distribution. Now, if the process mean μ and standard de-

TABLE 4.14   Run Length Empirical Distribution Functions for 3-Sigma Charts for a Stable Process With Estimated Control Limits, $n = 5$

x m:	20	30	50	75	100	∞
20	0.073	0.065	0.061	0.059	0.052	0.0526
40	0.144	0.125	0.120	0.115	0.104	0.1025
60	0.205	0.187	0.175	0.165	0.157	0.1498
80	0.264	0.240	0.223	0.215	0.207	0.1945
80	0.264	0.240	0.223	0.215	0.207	0.1945
100	0.310	0.286	0.270	0.259	0.251	0.2369
120	0.355	0.328	0.316	0.302	0.291	0.2771
140	0.397	0.372	0.354	0.340	0.331	0.3150
160	0.435	0.408	0.393	0.378	0.364	0.3512
180	0.466	0.441	0.429	0.410	0.401	0.3853
200	0.497	0.472	0.459	0.444	0.430	0.4177
220	0.527	0.500	0.488	0.474	0.461	0.4483
240	0.549	0.525	0.517	0.498	0.491	0.4774
240	0.549	0.525	0.517	0.498	0.491	0.4774
260	0.575	0.553	0.540	0.527	0.519	0.5049
280	0.597	0.573	0.565	0.552	0.543	0.5309
300	0.616	0.594	0.589	0.574	0.565	0.5556
320	0.634	0.615	0.608	0.596	0.589	0.5790
340	0.653	0.635	0.628	0.618	0.611	0.6012
360	0.670	0.652	0.645	0.637	0.631	0.6222
380	0.685	0.668	0.663	0.653	0.648	0.6421
400	0.697	0.684	0.678	0.669	0.667	0.6609
420	0.711	0.698	0.693	0.686	0.684	0.6787
440	0.723	0.712	0.707	0.702	0.699	0.6957
460	0.734	0.726	0.720	0.718	0.715	0.7117
480	0.744	0.738	0.734	0.730	0.730	0.7269
500	0.754	0.749	0.746	0.744	0.744	0.7493
600	0.801	0.799	0.800	0.803	0.800	0.8025
700	0.833	0.837	0.839	0.844	0.845	0.8493
800	0.855	0.864	0.871	0.877	0.880	0.8850
900	0.876	0.886	0.895	0.900	0.902	0.9123
1000	0.893	0.903	0.913	0.920	0.921	0.9330
2000	0.969	0.977	0.985	0.988	0.990	0.9953
4000	0.992	0.996	0.998	0.9993	0.9990	0.99997
8000	0.99680	1.00000	1.00000	1.00000	1.00000	1.00000
12000	0.99970	1.00000	1.00000	1.00000	1.00000	1.00000
16000	0.99990	1.00000	1.00000	1.00000	1.00000	1.00000
20000	1.00000	1.00000	1.00000	1.00000	1.00000	1.00000

viation σ were known, then the control limits for a classical 3-sigma Shewhart chart for μ are given by

$$UCL = \mu + 3\sigma$$
$$LCL = \mu - 3\sigma$$

(4.11.7)

If the parameters μ and σ are unknown, but a sample $X_1, X_2, \cdots,$ X_N is available from the process, then the common practice is to estimate μ and σ by the sample $\overline{X}$ and the moving range $\overline{MR}$. The estimated control limits are given in (4.10.2) as

$$\widehat{UCL} = \overline{X} + 3\tilde{\sigma} = \overline{X} + 2.6595\ \overline{MR} \qquad (4.11.8)$$

$$\widehat{LCL} = \overline{X} - 3\tilde{\sigma} = \overline{X} - 2.6595\ \overline{MR}$$

We now consider how large the sample size N must be, that is, how many measurements must be made, in order for the estimated control limits of (4.11.8) to perform essentially like the "known" limits of (4.11.7). To study this issue we have performed a simulation study as follows and the results are summarized in Table 4.15. For each value of N and δ in Table 4.15 we first generated N observations from a $N(\mu, \sigma^2)$ distribution and computed $\widehat{LCL}$ and $\widehat{UCL}$ from (4.11.8). Then we generated a run of observations from a $N(\mu + \delta\sigma, \sigma^2)$ distribution until a value was found to fall outside these estimated control limits. This entire procedure was repeated many times to generate a large sample from the run length distribution. The values given for selected values of N and $|\delta|$ are the run length sample mean, sample standard deviation, and standard error of the sample mean. For example, the estimated ARL for $N = 100$ and $\delta = 0$ is 574.0 with standard error of 6.09 and estimated SDRL of 1217.5. The last row ($N = \infty$) gives the values of ARL and SDRL for the case when μ and σ are known, which for this case with $\delta = 0$ are ARL = 370.4 and SDRL = 369.9. This shows a considerable degree of dependence among the events for this sample size of $N = 100$.

The values in Table 4.15 for $|\delta| = 0$ show that the estimated control limits perform essentially like the limiting case only for very large sample size N of 2000, or so. By essentially the same argument as that given in the last subsection, there is a clear dependence of the events that consist of comparing the values X_i with the estimated control limits, even for N of 500 and 1000. This dependence will have the same type effect as that discussed above for $\overline{X}$-charts with estimated control limits. Namely, we can expect more false alarms after short runs and a few more very long runs between false alarms.

To study the run length distribution further for the important case with $\delta = 0$, we have generated 10,000 run lengths from each of the distributions for $N = 30, 50, 75, 100, 200, 300, 500, 1000,$ and 2000. The empirical distribution functions from this simulation for selected

TABLE 4.15 ARL and SDRL for Individual Measurements Charts

N	|δ|:	0	1	2	3	4	5	6
30		3306(181.4)	207(16.6)	11.98(0.63)	2.63(0.08)	1.29(0.013)	1.048(0.004)	1.0045(0.0011)
		38356	2782	40.11	4.88	0.79	0.241	0.0706
50		1106(43.5)	91.2(2.70)	8.70(0.27)	2.26(0.04)	1.25(0.017)	1.031(0.004)	1.0030(0.0012)
		8923	341	16.93	2.22	0.75	0.178	0.0547
75		663.4(8.74)	68.3(1.41)	8.15(0.17)	2.22(0.03)	1.21(0.012)	1.030(0.004)	1.0015(0.0009)
		1747.9	141.5	10.97	1.98	0.52	0.179	0.0387
100		574.0(6.09)	59.8(1.00)	7.16(0.14)	2.10(0.027)	1.20(0.012)	1.022(0.003)	1.0005(0.0005)
		1217.5	97.9	8.70	1.73	0.53	0.145	0.0224
200		458.7(3.40)	49.6(0.96)	6.70(0.12)	2.08(0.026)	1.196(0.011)	1.028(0.004)	1.0030(0.0012)
		679.8	61.0	7.34	1.63	0.498	0.167	0.00547
300		427.7(2.95)	47.2(0.84)	6.51(0.10)	2.04(0.024)	1.215(0.012)	1.0271(0.004)	1.0005(0.0005)
		561.4	53.3	6.46	1.51	0.516	0.162	0.0223
500		404.9(2.75)	46.4(0.80)	6.43(0.10)	2.03(0.023)	1.182(0.0010)	1.026(0.004)	0.0020(0.0010)
		484.8	50.6	6.05	1.48	0.460	0.164	0.0447
1000		387.5(2.45)	45.5(0.73)	6.46(0.10)	2.01(0.023)	1.200(0.011)	1.024(0.003)	1.0020(0.0010)
		409.1	46.0	6.01	1.43	0.497	0.153	0.0447
2000		379.1(2.81)	44.6(0.33)	6.37(0.04)	2.018(0.014)	1.189(0.005)	1.023(0.0015)	1.0012(0.0003)
		397.8	46.1	5.77	1.428	0.474	0.156	0.0346
∞		370.4	44.0	6.30	2.00	1.49	1.023	1.0014
		369.9	43.5	5.78	1.41	0.48	0.153	0.0374

values of x are given in Table 4.16. The last column ($N = \infty$) gives the values of the limiting geometric distribution when the parameters are known. For $N = 30$ there is an estimated increase in the false alarm rate on the first $x = 20$ points of $100(.1230 - .0526)/.0526 = 133.8\%$, for $N = 50$ it is 74.7%, for $N = 75$ it is 47.9%, for $N = 100$ it is 30.6%, for $N = 200$ it is 14.1%, and for $N = 300$ it is 7.0%.

4.11.5 Sample Size Recommendations

To this point we have considered chart performance only in terms of the chart's ability to signal a change in the process mean by having one point plot outside the control limits, that is, by a 1-of-1 test. However, when charts are used in SPC as aids to stabilize a process, and bring it into control, it is crucially important that we know the type of point pattern to expect when the process is stable. Only when we know the pattern to expect for a stable process can we recognize an anomalous pattern. Indeed, we expect to read more information from a chart than simply whether or not a point is outside 3-sigma control limits. However, when using estimated control limits, care must be exercised in interpreting many point patterns, especially those such as tests 1, 2, 5, 6, 7 and 8 of Fig. 4.9, which will in this circumstance be defined using *estimated zones*. For this reason, the actual probabilities of false alarms for these tests may be quite different from the nominal probabilities obtained assuming a normal distribution and constant zones defined in terms of known standard deviations from the known normal distribution mean. Indeed, in these applications the capability to recognize unexpected anomalous patterns is important and this ability may be destroyed by dependence of signaling events. In order to make sample size recommendations, we assume that control limits are to be established in a two-stage procedure that entails first estimating Stage 1 "trial" control limits based on a minimum number of subgroups, and then revising these to Stage 2 "permanent" limits when sufficient data are available. In Chapter 7, we shall recommend that the practice of beginning with Stage 1 "trial" limits be replaced by starting with Q-charts for the cases when the parameters are assumed unknown. This permits charting to proceed even while the calibration data are being taken and the false alarm rates are known. This also gives considerable protection against the risk of having the calibration data contaminated from an unrecognized shift in the parameters while the data are being taken. These Q-charts should be used until sufficient data are available to establish reliable limits that perform essentially like "known" limits. However, if the classical approach of first obtaining Stage 1 "trial"

TABLE 4.16 Run Length Empirical Distribution Functions for Individual Measurements Charts for a Stable Process with Estimated Control Limits

x	N: 30	50	75	100	200	300	500	1000	2000	∞
20	.1230	.0919	.0778	.0687	0.600	.0543	.0563	.0523	.0525	.0526
40	.217	.169	.149	.135	.120	.111	.110	.103	.103	.1025
60	.283	.231	.204	.194	.175	.165	.160	.150	.153	.1498
80	.332	.282	.256	.244	.220	.216	.205	.198	.197	.1945
100	.375	.326	.305	.290	.267	.263	.249	.244	.238	.2369
120	.410	.360	.343	.333	.306	.305	.290	.285	.278	.2771
140	.438	.396	.378	.371	.344	.342	.330	.320	.315	.3151
160	.463	.430	.411	.402	.376	.374	.365	.355	.351	.3512
180	.486	.456	.445	.433	.407	.406	.401	.390	.384	.3853
200	.508	.480	.473	.462	.435	.435	.432	.421	.418	.4177
220	.527	.504	.498	.489	.464	.463	.462	.451	.448	.4483
240	.542	.528	.520	.513	.492	.489	.489	.480	.479	.4774
280	.574	.563	.559	.556	.538	.538	.539	.528	.529	.5309
300	.589	.578	.576	.576	.560	.559	.563	.553	.553	.5556
340	.613	.608	.608	.612	.600	.600	.605	.599	.599	.6012
400	.645	.649	.647	.655	.648	.652	.658	.653	.656	.6609
500	.684	.694	.702	.714	.713	.728	.731	.732	.736	.7412
600	.715	.731	.756	.760	.763	.783	.787	.792	.798	.8025
700	.741	.762	.779	.792	.803	.825	.830	.837	.845	.8493
800	.761	.784	.804	.817	.836	.854	.861	.872	.877	.8850
900	.778	.803	.826	.839	.860	.882	.888	.901	.904	.9123
1000	.790	.819	.845	.857	.881	.902	.906	.921	.926	.9330
1500	.839	.874	.902	.914	.943	.955	.966	.973	.977	.9827
2000	.868	.905	.931	.943	.969	.978	.985	.990	.992	.9955
4000	.9201	.9532	.9731	.9814	.9939	.9980	.9993	.9998	1.0000	1.0000
8000	.9555	.9800	.9892	.9947	.9994	.9999	1.0000	1.0000	1.0000	1.0000
12000	.9689	.9895	.9946	.9978	.9999	.10000	1.0000	1.0000	1.0000	1.0000
16000	.9771	.9926	.9968	.9986	1.0000	1.0000	1.0000	1.0000	1.0000	1.0000
25000	.9842	.9958	.9989	.9994	1.0000	1.0000	1.0000	1.0000	1.0000	1.0000
40000	.9896	.9980	.9998	.9999	1.0000	1.0000	1.0000	1.0000	1.0000	1.0000
80000	.9947	.9994	.9998	1.0000	1.0000	1.0000	1.0000	1.0000	1.0000	1.0000
200000	.9985	.9999	1.0000	1.0000	1.0000	1.0000	1.0000	1.0000	1.0000	1.0000
400000	.9995	1.0000	1.0000	1.0000	1.0000	1.0000	1.0000	1.0000	1.0000	1.0000
600000	.9997	1.0000	1.0000	1.0000	1.0000	1.0000	1.0000	1.0000	1.0000	1.0000

control limits is to be followed, we make the following recommendations for sample sizes.

For the X̄ Chart: Based on the results discussed above, to establish "permanent" control limits that perform essentially like limits based on truly known parameters requires $m = 100$ subgroups of size $n = 5$ each. If Stage 1 "trial" limits are to be used initially rather than a Q-chart, then they should be based on at least 30 subgroups of size 5 each, and users should be aware that, for example, the effect of this will be to increase the false alarm rate on the first 20 subgroups in the charting program by about 24%. Note that this does not mean that this false alarm rate on any one particular chart is increased by 24%, but, rather, that the false alarm rate in the overall charting program is increased by this amount. We cannot know what this rate will be on any particular chart.

The simulation study reported here was only for $n = 5$. However, for other sample sizes we *speculate* that m should be taken roughly equal to $400/(n - 1)$ for "permanent" limits. This is based on requiring that the degrees of freedom for estimating σ be approximately equal to 400.

For the Individual Measurements X-Chart: To establish Stage 2 "permanent" individual measurements control limits, we recommend that a minimum sample size of $N = 300$ should be used. This gives an increase in false alarm rates on the first 20 values of about 7%. If Stage 1 "trial" limits are to be used for individual measurements charts, then they should be based on a sample of at least $N = 100$ measurements. This will give an increase in false alarms in the charting program, over nominal, in the first 20 values of about 31%.

4.11.6 On Estimated Control Limits for an S-Chart

The sample size recommendations in the last subsection were based on the issue of estimating control limits for the charts to control the process mean μ. We must also establish control limits for the charts to control σ. We give a small development here to point out the difficulties in estimating the control limits for an S-chart. If S is the standard deviation of a sample of size n from a normal distribution, then

$$E(S) = c_4\sigma, \text{ and } SD(S) = \sigma\sqrt{1 - c_4^2}$$

The upper 3-sigma control limit and center line for S are

$$UCL(S) = \sigma(c_4 + 3\sqrt{1 - c_4^2}) \quad \text{and} \quad CL(S) = c_4\sigma$$

and the distance between the upper control limit and the center line of the S-chart is

$$UCL(S) - CL(S) = 3\sigma\sqrt{1 - c_4^2}$$

An unbiased estimate of the upper control limit is

$$\widehat{UCL}(S) = \frac{\bar{S}}{c_4} (c_4 + 3\sqrt{1 - c_4^2})$$

This estimate is normally distributed, to close approximation. It has standard deviation

$$SD(\widehat{UCL}) = \left(\frac{c_4 + 3\sqrt{1 - c_4^2}}{\sqrt{m}\, c_4} \right) \sigma\sqrt{1 - c_4^2}$$

We express this standard deviation as a percentage of the distance between the center line of the S-chart and its upper control limit as follows:

$$SD(\%) = \frac{100\, SD(\widehat{UCL})}{[UCL(S) - CL(S)]} = 100 \left(\frac{c_4 + 3\sqrt{1 - c_4^2}}{3\sqrt{m}\, c_4} \right) \quad (4.11.9)$$

This quantity $SD(\%)$ is a highly relevant quantity that tells us about the accuracy of the estimated upper control limit. Note the important point that it depends only on m and n, and not on σ. For $n = 5$ this is

$$SD(\%) = 100 \left(\frac{0.94 + 3\sqrt{1 - 0.94^2}}{3(0.94)\sqrt{m}} \right) = \frac{69.63}{\sqrt{m}}$$

Evaluating this for this case of m subgroups of size $n = 5$, we get the following values:

m:	5	15	30	50	100	300	1000
SD(%)	31.1	18.0	12.7	9.8	6.96	4.02	2.20

   If we consider an interval of length, say, ± 3 standard deviations $= \pm SD(\widehat{UCL})$, as a prediction interval for the estimated control limit, for $m = 30$ this prediction interval will be of length $6(12.7) = 76.2\%$ of the distance between $CL(S)$ and $UCL(S)$. This suggests that the upper control limit for an S-chart estimated from 30 subgroups of size 5 will often be rather far from the true upper limit that would be used if the value of σ were known. Evaluations for other values of m are readily computed.

4.12 SUMMARY

In this chapter, we have introduced the basic concepts and some of the methods of classical statistical process control for variables. The intent here is to treat this material in somewhat more depth than the cookbook recipe format that is common in presentations of SPC material. In particular, we have given more attention to considerations involved in establishing charts, and especially to some of the problems that arise in the classical approach to estimating control limits. These issues will be considered further in later chapters.

PROBLEMS

4.1 Inner diameter measurements of certain automatic transmission parts are independent random variables with mean μ and standard deviation σ. The target value is $\tau = 22.147$ mm and the process standard deviation is $\sigma = 0.003$ mm. Compute the expected mean square, EMS, for this process for $\mu = 22.147$ to $\mu = 22.160$ in steps of size 0.001. Make a graph of EMS as a function of μ.

4.2 The following table contains 22 subgroups of size 5 from the production process described in problem 4.1. Compute control limits for an S-chart for this data using the formulas of (4.4.6). Plot the sample standard deviations for these subgroups on a chart with these limits. Discuss your results.

22.153	22.147	22.149	22.151	22.151
22.150	22.151	22.152	22.147	22.149
22.148	22.151	22.146	22.149	22.149
22.152	22.149	22.145	22.148	22.145
22.146	22.149	22.149	22.147	22.145
22.144	22.148	22.143	22.145	22.154
22.150	22.153	22.148	22.148	22.153
22.150	22.151	22.150	22.150	22.157
22.142	22.148	22.146	22.142	22.146
22.150	22.144	22.147	22.150	22.146

22.157	22.157	22.159	22.158	22.158
22.153	22.160	22.157	22.161	22.156
22.142	22.147	22.148	22.143	22.154
22.149	22.151	22.147	22.149	22.149
22.149	22.150	22.150	22.148	22.150
22.147	22.150	22.156	22.138	22.145
22.152	22.146	22.148	22.145	22.142
22.155	22.150	22.145	22.149	22.148
22.146	22.148	22.150	22.143	22.153
22.147	22.150	22.148	22.148	22.151
22.147	22.144	22.153	22.142	22.143
22.147	22.153	22.147	22.155	22.151

4.3 (a) Compute control chart limits for an $\overline{X}$-chart for the data of problem 4.2 using the formulas of (4.4.3) and a nominal value of $\mu_0 = 22.149$ (note that this is not the same as the target value of 22.147).

(b) Plot the sample means for these data on a chart with the limits found in (a). Discuss the results.

4.4 Compute (0.00135, 0.00135) probability limits for an S-chart for the wrist pin diameter data by using the S values given in Table 4.9. Omit sample number 28 to estimate σ.

4.5 Consider a runs test on an $\overline{X}$-chart that signals on point t when $\overline{X}_t$, $\overline{X}_{t-1}$, and $\overline{X}_{t-2}$ are all in zone B or beyond on the same side of the center line. Evaluate the marginal probability of a signal on point t, when the process is stable.

4.6 (a) Show that the probability given in section 4.5 for Test 3 of Fig. 4.9 is correct for a stable process.

(b) Show that the probability given in section 4.5 for Test 5 of Fig. 4.9 is correct for a stable process.

(c) Show that the probability given in section 4.5 for Test 6 of Fig. 4.9 is correct for a stable process.

(d) Show that the probability given in section 4.5 for Test 7 of Fig. 4.9 is correct for a stable process.

(e) Show that the probability given in section 4.5 for Test 8 of Fig. 4.9 is correct for a stable process.

4.7   Discuss some stratification situations that can lead to a chart pattern like that in Test 7 of Fig. 4.9.

4.8   Evaluate the OC function $\beta(n, \delta)$ of (4.6.1) for an (0.01, 0.01) probability chart for a normally distributed sample mean for $n = 4$ and $\delta = 0, \pm.25, \pm.5, \pm.75, \pm1, \pm1.25, \pm1.50, \pm1.75, \pm2$. Sketch the OC curve from these values.

4.9   A process has mean of 27.193 cm and standard deviation of .003 cm. How large must sample size n be for a 0.99 probability chart for $\overline{X}$ to have probability 0.5 to detect a shift in the process mean of .004 cm on one point?

4.10   Evaluate the OC function for a $1 - \alpha = 0.99$ probability chart for $\overline{X}$ when $n = 5$ and δ takes values: 0.0, 0.1, 0.3, 0.5, 1.0, 1.5, 2.0, 3.0. Draw the OC curve.

4.11   Give the general form of the OC function of an S-chart with (α_L, α_U) probability limits, where a point above UCL is interpreted as an increase in σ, a point below LCL is interpreted as a decrease in σ, and points on or between the control limits as no change in σ. Evaluate this function and the corresponding ARL function for $\alpha_L = \alpha_U = 0.01$, $n = 5$, and $\delta = 0.1, 0.2, 0.3, 0.6, 0.8, 1, 1.2, 1.5, 2, 3, 5$. Sketch the OC and ARL functions from these values. Assume σ is known.

4.12   A process has mean $\mu = 12.00$ oz and standard deviation $\sigma = 0.01$ oz. How large should the sample size be for an $\overline{X}$-chart to have probability 0.5 of not detecting a change in the mean to 12.01, by having one point fall outside 3-sigma control limits? Assume a normal process distribution.

4.13   We are planning to set up a 3-sigma $\overline{X}$ control chart for a process, and we would like to use a sample size n to minimize the average number of production units sampled before a signal is issued when the process mean shifts by 2.5 standard deviation units. How large should we take n?

4.14   Compute values of ARL for a 3-sigma S-chart based on subgroups of size $n = 4$ to detect shifts from a nominal value of $\sigma_0 = 2$ to values of $\sigma = 1, 2, 3, 5, 7, 9$, and 11. An increase in σ is signaled by one point above UCL. Decreases cannot be detected.

4.15   One hundred samples of size $n = 4$ each gave values of $\overline{\overline{X}} = 1.45$ and $\overline{S} = 0.02$. Compute 3-sigma trial control limits for an

S-chart for σ and an $\overline{X}$-chart for μ. Assume the process was stable while the data were being taken.

4.16 The following data are given in Ott and Schilling (1990), p. 61. These data are depth of cut measurements in mils of an air-receiver magnetic assembly from a lathe operation. Samples of $n = 5$ consecutively produced parts were taken every 15 minutes to obtain 25 samples. These data were taken to make an initial study of the stability of the lathing process. Study the stability of the process by making $\overline{X}$- and R-charts. Apply the 11-45 test for monotone shifts on the $\overline{X}$-chart.

1	160.0	159.5	159.6	159.7	159.7
2	159.7	159.5	159.5	159.5	160.0
3	159.2	159.7	159.7	159.5	160.2
4	159.5	159.7	159.2	159.2	159.1
5	159.6	159.3	159.6	159.5	159.4
6	159.8	160.5	160.2	159.3	159.5
7	159.7	160.2	159.5	159.0	159.7
8	159.2	159.6	159.6	160.0	159.9
9	159.4	159.7	159.3	159.9	159.5
10	159.5	160.2	159.5	158.9	159.5
11	159.4	158.3	159.6	159.8	159.8
12	159.5	159.7	160.0	159.3	159.4
13	159.7	159.5	159.3	159.4	159.2
14	159.3	159.7	159.9	158.5	159.5
15	159.7	159.1	158.8	160.6	159.1
16	159.1	159.4	158.9	159.6	159.7
17	159.2	160.0	159.8	159.8	159.7
18	160.0	160.5	159.9	160.3	159.3
19	159.9	160.1	159.7	159.6	159.3
20	159.5	159.5	160.6	160.6	159.8
21	159.9	159.7	159.9	159.5	161.0
22	159.6	161.1	159.5	159.7	159.5
23	159.8	160.2	159.4	160.0	159.7
24	159.3	160.6	160.3	159.9	160.0
25	159.3	159.8	159.7	160.1	160.1

4.17 The following measurements are from a process with a target value of 8.455 cm. Compute estimates of σ based on the sample standard deviation S, the moving range $\overline{MR}$, and the mean square successive difference MSSD. Compute the PV-MSSD and from this decide which is the better estimate of σ to use to construct control limits for the moving range and the individual observations. Make Stage 1 retrospective moving range and individual observations charts for these measurements. The values are given in row order from left to right.

8.454	8.458	8.455	8.454	8.456	8.467	8.459	8.461	8.459	8.457
8.459	8.446	8.461	8.458	8.459	8.451	8.457	8.464	8.458	8.454

4.18 A stable normal process has nominal mean of $\mu_0 = 10$ and standard deviation of $\sigma_0 = 0.5$. Consider making an $\overline{X}$ 3-sigma chart using subgroups of size n. Suppose the mean shifts to 10.5 at some point between samples during operation of the chart. We would like to choose n so that the average number of units of product made before the shift is signaled, by having a point beyond UCL, is a minimum. Compute the values of ATRL for each of the values $n = 1, 2, 3, 4, 5, 6, 8, 10, 11, 12, 14, 16$. What value of n gives a minimum? Compare your result with that given in Table 4.5.

4.19 The measurements in the following table are from a process with target value of 60.110 mm. The process is known to have a negative drift. Compute estimates of σ based on the sample standard deviation S, the moving range $\overline{MR}$, and the mean square successive difference MSSD. Compute the PV-MSSD and from this decide which is the better estimate of σ to use to construct control limits for the moving range and the individual observations. Make moving range and individual observations charts retrospectively for these measurements. The values are given in row order from left to right.

60.110	60.109	60.108	60.108	60.100	60.110	60.106	60.111	60.110	60.109	60.092	60.089
60.090	60.087	60.115	60.103	60.106	60.106	60.110	60.109	60.111	60.100	60.108	60.104

4.20 Roughly 200 to 300 units of product are made by a process in each run. Since there is no reason to think that either the mean or variance remain constant from run to run, it is necessary to establish charts for both the process mean and variance on each run. The quality manager has decided that, in order to start on-line charting as early as possible, the first 50 measurements of each run will be used as 10 subgroups of size 5 each to set up $\overline{X}$- and S- (or R-) charts. Discuss your opinion of this decision and the likely usefulness of the charts.

4.21 Evaluate the probability of a false signal using equation (4.11.5) for $n = 4$ and $m = 1, 2, 4, 6, 8, 10, 15, 20, 30, 50, 100$. Sketch a graph of this false signal probability as a function of m.

4.22 Compute the percentage change in the false alarm rate on $\overline{X}$-charts with estimated control limits with $n = 5$ and m and x as given in the following table. Use the empirical distributions of Table 4.15. Discuss the implications from these values.

x	m: 20	30	50	75	100
20					
60					
100					
200					

4.23 For this problem assume that m subgroups of size n each are available from a stable normal process distribution. For parts (b) and (c) let $m = 25$ and $n = 4$.

(a) Find the mean, variance, and (approximate) density function of $\widehat{LCL}$ of equation (4.11.2).

(b) Sketch the density function of $\widehat{LCL}$ on a line marked as follows (see Fig. 4.21):

$\qquad\qquad\quad LCL \qquad\qquad\qquad\qquad\qquad\qquad CL$

(c) Fill in the values of P_d for these values of m and n like Table 4.11.

d:	0.01 0.05 0.10 0.2 0.3 0.4 0.6 0.8 1
P_d:	

(d) Discuss the implications of this problem.

4.24 Suppose the observations in a subgroup of size n are independent with means μ_i and variances σ_i^2, $i = 1, 2, \cdots, n$. Then show that

$$\mathrm{Var}(\overline{X}) = \frac{1}{n^2} \sum_{i=1}^{n} \sigma_i^2, \quad \text{and}$$

$$E\left(\frac{S^2}{n}\right) = \mathrm{Var}(\overline{X}) + \frac{1}{n(n-1)} \sum_{i=1}^{n} (\mu_i - \overline{\mu})^2$$

for $\overline{\mu} = \dfrac{1}{n} \sum_{i=1}^{n} \mu_i$.

Note that this useful result shows that a pattern like that of Test 7 of Fig. 4.9, namely, points tending to be too near the center line, implies that the distribution means are different, and does not depend on having the distribution variances all having one constant value. In fact, the strength of the pattern depends directly on the amount of variation among the distribution means. The variation among the observation means causes S^2/n to overestimate the variance of $\overline{X}$.

CHAPTER 5

Classical Shewhart Control Charts for Attributes

In this chapter we present the classical Shewhart control charting methods for attributes, which have been widely used with good success. Most of these methods assume that sampling assumptions are such that either binomial or Poisson distributions can be used to analyze the data, and that enough data are available, or can be obtained, to assume that the distribution parameters are known values.

5.1 INTRODUCTION

In the presentation of control charts for variables in the last chapter, it was assumed that the variables measured were continuous in the sense that they could take any of the values in an interval of real numbers. Measurements of parts dimensions are examples of such quality variables. In this chapter we consider quality variables that are counting variables and assume only values $0, 1, 2, \cdots$; that is, they can take only a value of zero or a positive integer. Typically, such quality variables give the number of items that possess some particular attribute, or the number of times a particular attribute occurs on an item.

For manufactured or purchased items there are often stated specifications that a unit of product may or may not meet. Items that do not meet specifications are called "defectives," or, the modern terminology prefers "nonconformities" because it does not have quite as negative a connotation as "defectives." Whatever they are called, units of product that do not meet specifications must be reworked, sold as scrap, or sold as a lower grade of merchandise; and a loss is incurred. The specifications, or "specs," are sometimes expressed as upper or lower tolerance limits on a continuous variable on which we wish to exercise process control. In such cases the testing procedure may consist of "go" and "no-go" gauging so that the actual observed quality variable is a count of the number of no-go items produced. In other cases an item may be a defective or nonconforming item if it possesses some particular undesirable attribute.

There are also many applications of attributes charts in management. These may include counts of numbers of absences of employees, numbers of errors of workers performing clerical tasks, and so on. In many of these types of problems it may be reasonable to model the sequence of observed outcomes as a sequence of Bernoulli trials with probability parameter p. Depending on the details of the particular sampling situation assumed, this will often lead us to consider charts based on either a binomial or a Poisson distribution. In the following sections we consider "p-charts" based on the binomial distribution and "c-charts" and "u-charts" based on a Poisson distribution.

5.2   THE CLASSICAL 3-SIGMA p-CHART FOR FRACTION NONCONFORMING

Suppose that a randomly selected sample of n units of product is inspected and that X units are nonconforming to specifications. Let p denote the proportion of nonconforming items that the process was producing when the n sample items were produced, assuming that the process was stable, so that such a constant p exists. The proportion p or $100p$, to express it in percent, is called the *process fallout*. The *process yield* is $1 - p$ or $100(1 - p)$. If p remains constant during a production run, and nonconforming items are produced independently, then the number X of nonconformities in a sample of n items is a binomial random variable with probability function $b(x; n, p)$, distribution function $B(x; n, p)$, and mean and variance given in display (5.2.1); see also section 2.5.

$$b(x; n, p) = \binom{n}{x} p^x (1 - p)^{n-x},$$

$$x \in \{0, 1, \cdots, n\}$$

$$B(x; n, p) = \sum_{x'=0}^{[x]} b(x'; n, p)$$

$$E(X) = np, \ \mathrm{Var}(X) = np(1 - p)$$

(5.2.1)

We often are more interested in the observed proportion of noncon-formities $\hat{p} = X/n$ than the number of nonconformities X. The mean and variance of $\hat{p}$ are given in display (5.2.2).

$$
\begin{array}{l}
\text{Mean of } \hat{p} = E(\hat{p}) = p \\[6pt]
\text{Variance of } \hat{p} = \text{Var}(\hat{p}) = p(1 - p)/n
\end{array}
\tag{5.2.2}
$$

By the normal approximation to the binomial distribution, we know that for n sufficiently large, the random variables X and $\hat{p}$ are approx-imately normally distributed random variables. However, we will see below that for applications in SPC the approximation is rather poor. In the work here we will assume that $p \leq 0.5$, unless noted otherwise. This assumption is not really restrictive because in virtually all appli-cations p will be less than 0.5, usually much less. If p were greater than 0.5, we could replace p by $1 - p$, and carry on.

5.2.1 The *p*-Chart for *p* Known

We first consider setting control limits for a process for which the proportion of nonconforming product p is known to be $p = p_0$. Then the 3-sigma control limits of (4.3.1) for the proportion $\hat{p}$ of noncon-forming product in a sample of size n are given by (5.2.3).

$$
\begin{array}{l}
UCL(\hat{p}_i) = p_0 + 3\sqrt{\dfrac{p_0(1 - p_0)}{n}} \\[12pt]
CL(\hat{p}_i) = p_0 \\[12pt]
LCL(\hat{p}_i) = p_0 - 3\sqrt{\dfrac{p_0(1 - p_0)}{n}}
\end{array}
\tag{5.2.3}
$$

To operate the chart we take samples of size n and plot the estimated proportion $\hat{p}$ from each sample on the chart. Note that this assumes that the samples are all of the same size n. Also, the size n of the samples for a particular process must be chosen with care. For some values of p_0 and n the lower control limit will be negative and will not be useful for detecting decreases in the value of p. One criterion for choosing n is to take it large enough to make LCL positive. Thus, we require that

$$LCL = p_0 - 3\sqrt{\frac{p_0(1 - p_0)}{n}} > 0$$

or

$$n > \frac{9(1 - p_0)}{p_0} \tag{5.2.4}$$

Another criterion, which is usually more stringent by requiring a larger value of n, is to require that the probability that a change from the value $p = p_0$ to a new value $p = \delta p_0$ ($1 < \delta < 1/p_0$) be detected with probability at least 0.5 on each sample. The approximate sample size required to give a probability of 0.5 that a value $p = \delta p_0$ will be detected on one sample is given by formula (5.2.5).

$$n = \frac{9(1 - p_0)}{p_0(\delta - 1)^2} \tag{5.2.5}$$

The sample size given by the formula (5.2.5) will exceed that given by (5.2.4) unless $\delta > 2$. For $\delta = 2$, the formulas are the same. We give a few values of n from this formula in display (5.2.6). Note that large samples are necessary when p_0 is small and we wish to detect a small change. Also, the probability of detecting a shift in p from one sample is only $\frac{1}{2}$. It will often be found in practice that the p-charts require large sample sizes in order to achieve adequate power to detect small but important shifts.

p_0	.01	.01	.05	.05	.10	.10	.20	.20	.20
δ:	1.5	2	1.5	2	1.5	2	1.25	1.5	2
n:	3564	891	1069	171	324	81	576	144	36

(5.2.6)

5.2.2 The *p*-Chart When *p* Is Not Known

If it is required to establish a control chart for the proportion of defectives for a process for which p is unknown, then the first thing we must do is decide on at least a preliminary value, say n_0, of sample size to be used. In order to get started we will make use of any information available, even crude guesses, if necessary, to establish a preliminary estimate p_0' of the actual operating level p_0 of proportion defectives. It will often be worthwhile to take a preliminary sample to get an estimate p_0' of p_0, even if this preliminary sample is small. Then by specifying a value δ' for a proportional shift of significance, we can use (5.2.5) to obtain a value n_0 to use as our initial sample size. As we accumulate more information, we may decide to adjust this sample size.

Once a preliminary sample size n_0 has been established, we proceed to observe m samples of size $n = n_0$. Let X_i denote the number of nonconformities in sample i and we put

$$\hat{p}_i = \frac{X_i}{n}, \quad \bar{p} = \frac{1}{m}\sum_{i=1}^{m}\hat{p}_i \tag{5.2.7}$$

The sampling procedure should pay careful attention to the rational subgroups concept of sampling theory. We also require a method for determining a value for m, the number of samples to be taken. Some authors suggest taking m to be 20 or 25 in all cases; however, since the principal purpose in taking this sample is to estimate p_0 by $\bar{p}$ in (5.2.7), we now suggest a method for choosing m that takes this estimation purpose into consideration. We wish to take m large enough to make the probability almost one that the estimate $\bar{p}$ will be within $100\ \gamma$ percent $(\gamma > 0)$ of the true value p_0 of p. To obtain a formula for m we note that $\bar{p}$ is a mean of mn values and therefore is distributed approximately as a $N(p_0, p_0(1 - p_0)/mn)$ statistic. Thus we can set a confidence interval for p_0 using the normal distribution formula. If we take $z_{\alpha/2} = 3$, then the half-length of the confidence interval is $3\sqrt{p_0(1 - p_0)/mn}$. Setting this value equal to the desired half-length, γp_0, and solving for m gives the formula:

$$m = \frac{9}{n_0}\frac{(1 - p_0')}{p_0'\ \gamma^2} \tag{5.2.8}$$

Example 5.1: It is required to establish a *p*-chart for the proportion of nonconformities of a certain process. From records of customer complaints, opinions of operators familiar with the process, and so on, a preliminary estimate $p_0' = 0.18$ of the true proportion of defectives was established. A difference of $\delta = 1.67$ was selected as a shift to be detected by the 1-of-1 test with probability 0.5. Thus, the formula for sample size in (5.2.5) gives

$$n_0 = \frac{9\,(0.82)}{(0.18)(0.67)^2} = 91.33 \cong 90,$$

and we will use $n_0 = 90$.

Next, it was decided that m should be large enough to assure an estimate within 10% of its true value. For this value formula (5.2.8) gives

$$m = \frac{9(0.82)}{90(0.18)(0.1)^2} = 45.6 \cong 46$$

If we should decide that this is, perhaps, more samples than available resources will support, we might consider a few other values of γ in the formula. The following table gives a few values of m and γ.

γ:	.01	.05	.10	.12	.15	.20	.25
m:	4556	183	46	32	21	12	8

The reader should bear in mind that the value 100γ is the percent error that we are guarding against. For example, if the true value of $p_0 = 0.18$ and we take $m = 46$ samples, then the estimate $\bar{p}$ should be within 10% of 0.18 (or in the interval (0.162, 0.198)) with probability near one.

When m samples of size n have been obtained, we compute the estimate $\bar{p}$ of p_0 from equation (5.2.7), and then use this value for p_0 in the formulas of (5.2.3) to establish Stage 1 trial control limits for the process. Then to study the stability of the process producing non-conformities, we plot the sample proportions of nonconformities on a retrospective chart with these control limits. As further data are obtained while the process is stable, that is, as p remains constant, these trial limits will be revised using the additional data.   ■

Example 5.2: A set of $m = 25$ samples of size $n = 60$ each was observed and the data are given in Table 5.1. The estimate of p is $\bar{p} = 291/(25)(60) = 0.194$. This gives the following control limits

$$UCL = 0.194 + 3\sqrt{\frac{(0.194)(0.806)}{60}} = 0.347$$

$$CL = 0.194$$

$$LCL = 0.194 - 0.153 = 0.041$$

Next, we plot the $\hat{p}_i$ values from the calibration samples on a chart with these trial control limits in Fig. 5.1. The points on a *p*-chart for

TABLE 5.1   Binomial Nonconformities Data for Example 5.2

Sample Number	X_i	$\hat{p}_i$
1	9	0.150
2	5	0.083
3	7	0.117
4	7	0.117
5	14	0.233
6	10	0.167
7	10	0.167
8	15	0.250
9	8	0.133
10	13	0.217
11	13	0.217
12	26	0.433
13	12	0.200
14	18	0.300
15	12	0.200
16	12	0.200
17	10	0.167
18	14	0.233
19	10	0.167
20	13	0.217
21	12	0.200
22	9	0.150
23	10	0.167
24	7	0.117
25	15	0.250
	291	$\bar{p} = 0.194$

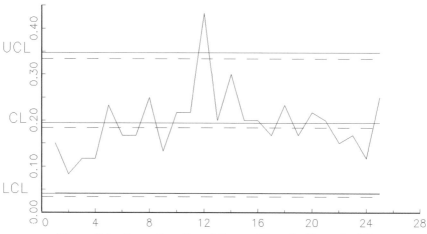

Figure 5.1 Proportion Out-of-Spec p-Chart for Example 5.2

a stable process should show a pattern roughly similar to that for an in-control $\overline{X}$-chart. That is, the points should be concentrated about the CL with the density of points becoming more sparse as the distance from CL increases with only a rare point outside the control limits. The chart of Fig. 5.1 looks good except for the point for sample 12. The value of $\hat{p}_{12}$ is 0.433, which is well above the UCL. Investigation revealed that certain special events (causes) occurred related to this sample and since it was not representative of the process it was dropped from the analysis. Dropping this point and recomputing, the following new values are obtained:

$$\overline{p}' = 265/1440 = 0.184$$

$$UCL'(\hat{p}_i) = 0.184 + 3\sqrt{(0.184)(0.816)/60} = 0.334$$

$$CL'(\hat{p}_i) = 0.184$$

$$LCL'(\hat{p}_i) = 0.034$$

The new limits are also shown on Fig. 5.1 as broken lines. The next step will be to use these new control limits for a Stage 2 application to monitor the process during production. If the process remains stable, we will accumulate further sample information and obtain a more precise estimate of p_0 and the corresponding control limits. ■

5.2.3 The p-Chart OC, Power, and ARL Functions

Suppose the binomial parameter p shifts from a nominal value p_0 to a new value δp_0, $\delta > 0$. Then the operating characteristic function for a p-chart with the 3-sigma control limits of (5.2.3) is the probability that one point will fall between the control limits expressed as a function of n and δ, and is denoted

$$\beta(\delta) = P(\text{one point is between control limits} \mid p = \delta p_0)$$

$$= P(LCL(\hat{p}_i) \le \hat{p}_i \le UCL(\hat{p}_i) \mid p = \delta p_0)$$

$$= \begin{cases} B(UCL(x_i); n, \delta p_0) - B(LCL(x_i) - 1; n, \delta p_0) & (5.2.9) \\ \text{if } LCL(x_i) \text{ is an integer} \\ B(UCL(x_i); n, \delta p_0) - B(LCL(x_i); n, \delta p_0) \\ \text{if } LCL(x_i) \text{ is not an integer} \end{cases}$$

where $UCL(x_i) = np_0 + 3\sqrt{np_0(1 - p_0)}$ and $LCL(x_i) = np_0 - 3\sqrt{np_0(1 - p_0)}$.

The binomial distribution function in the Q-Charts program can be used to evaluate this probability exactly. If np_0 is as large as 3 or 4, so that the normal approximation to the binomial is reasonable, then we can write this OC function as in (5.2.10) and use this for an approximate evaluation of the OC function.

$$\beta(\delta) \cong \Phi \left\{ \frac{p_0 - \delta p_0 + 3\sigma(p_0)}{\sigma(\delta p_0)} \right\}$$
$$- \Phi \left\{ \frac{p_0 - \delta p_0 - 3\sigma(p_0)}{\sigma(\delta p_0)} \right\} \quad (5.2.10)$$

where

$$\sigma(p) = \sqrt{p(1 - p)/n}$$

The p-chart power function is the probability of a signal expressed as a function of δ. The power and OC functions must sum to 1, and therefore $\text{Power}(\delta) = 1 - \beta(\delta)$. Since these points are independent, the number of points between signals is again a geometric random variable and average run length is $\text{ARL}(\delta) = 1/\text{Power}(\delta) = 1/[1 - \beta(\delta)]$.

Example 5.3: If the nominal value of p is $p_0 = 0.15$ and $n = 60$, then the OC, Power, and ARL functions for a range of values of δ are given in the following table.

```
        δ: 0.03333 0.06667 0.33333 0.66667
OC using (5.2.9): 0.25974 0.45284 0.95393 0.99999
OC using (5.2.10): 0.231   0.447   0.913   0.989
       Power: 0.74026 0.54715 0.04607 0.00180
         ARL: 1.35    1.83    21.7    555


        δ: 1.00000 1.33333 2.00000 2.66667
OC using (5.2.9): 0.99756 0.95730 0.45144 0.04129
OC using (5.2.10): 0.997   0.956   0.422   0.039
       Power: 0.02243 0.04270 0.54856 0.95871
         ARL: 411     23.4    1.82    1.04
```

For example, the exact formula (5.2.9) gives for this case

$$\beta(\delta) = P\{0.70 \le X_i \le 17.3 \mid n = 60, p = 0.15\delta\}$$

$$= P\{0 < X_i \le 17 \mid n = 60, p = 0.15\delta\}$$

$$\beta(1/3) = B(17; 60, 0.05) - B(0; 60, 0.05)$$

$$\beta(1/3) = 1.00000 - 0.04607 = 0.95393$$

by using the binomial distribution function algorithm on the Q-Charts disk. The normal approximation for this value is computed as follows.

$$\sigma(p_0) = \sigma(0.15) = \sqrt{(0.15)(0.85)/60} = 0.046,$$

$$\sigma(0.05) = \sqrt{(0.05)(0.95)/60} = 0.0281$$

$$\beta(0.05) = \Phi\left\{\frac{0.15 - 0.05 + 3(0.046)}{0.0281}\right\}$$

$$- \Phi\left\{\frac{0.15 - 0.05 - 3(0.046)}{0.0281}\right\}$$

$$= \Phi\{8.47\} - \Phi\{-1.36\} = 0.91$$

The values of the OC function from (5.2.9) are plotted for the OC curve in Fig. 5.2.

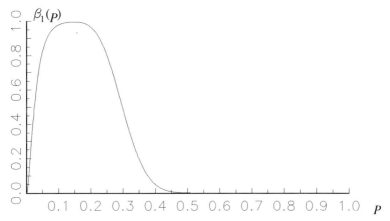

Figure 5.2   OC Curve for Binomial *p*-chart, $CL = 0.15$, $n = 60$

5.2.4 Exact *np* and Binomial Control Chart Limits

Sometimes it is desirable to plot the binomial count X itself rather than the sample proportion $\hat{p} = X/n$. Since $E(X) = np$, the center line of this chart will be $CL = np_0$ and the 3-sigma control limits are given in (5.2.11). Applications of this chart are similar to applications of the *p*-chart. These formulas for UCL and LCL generally give fractional values; however, since X takes only integer values, for some purposes it is convenient to use equivalent integer-valued control limits. The related equivalent integer-valued UCL is the largest integer that is less than or equal to the value of UCL given by the formula for UCL in (5.2.11), and the related integer-valued LCL is the smallest positive integer (or 0) that is greater than or equal to the value of LCL given by the formula in (5.2.11). We shall refer to these equivalent integer-valued control limits later in a number of contexts when we consider plotting integer-valued statistics.

$$
\begin{aligned}
UCL(X) &= np_0 + 3\sqrt{np_0(1 - p_0)} \\
CL(X) &= np_0 \\
LCL(X) &= np_0 - 3\sqrt{np_0(1 - p_0)}
\end{aligned}
\qquad (5.2.11)
$$

By using the binomial probability function $b(x; n, p)$ and an algorithm for the distribution function $B(x; n, p)$ of (5.2.1), we can directly evaluate the probabilities (α_L, α_U) of exceeding these control limits. Note first that the smallest lower control limit that can be violated is 1, since a value of LCL = 0 cannot be violated because a binomial random variable cannot take a negative value. For a stable process with constant $p = p_0$ and LCL = 1, the probability that a value falls below LCL is just the probability that a binomial random variable takes the value 0, that is, $(1 - p_0)^n$. Thus, if we specify a value of α_L, then the smallest sample size n required to give probability equal to or less than α_L is the smallest integer n satisfying (5.2.12).

$$n \geq \frac{ln(\alpha_L)}{ln(1 - p_0)} \tag{5.2.12}$$

Example 5.4: Suppose we wish to design an np control chart for a process with given operating fallout value of 1% and we would like to have $1 - \alpha$ probability limits be approximately the equivalent of 3-sigma normal control limits. That is, we would like to have probability approximately $\alpha_L = \alpha_U = 0.00135$ of a point beyond each control limit.

Solution: For $p_0 = 0.01$, formula (5.2.12) gives $n = 657.5$, and $.99^{658} = 0.00134$. By trying a few values in the distribution function algorithm, we find that a sample size of $n = 658$ has probability of 0.00123 of containing more than 15 nonconforming units. Therefore, if we take LCL = 1 and UCL = 15, the probability of a value of X outside these limits is $0.00134 + 0.00123 = 0.00257$, which is the best we can do in achieving the error rate of 0.00135 for each tail without taking larger samples.

   The control limits given by the formulas of (5.2.11) are LCL = -1.08 and UCL = 14.23. The equivalent integer-valued limits are LCL = 0 and UCL = 14. The probability of exceeding this UCL is $1 - B(14, 658, 0.01) = 1 - 0.99686 = 0.00314$. So the 3-sigma limits are here actually $(\alpha_L, \alpha_U) = (0, 0.00314)$ probability limits. These are rather poor approximations for $(0.00135, 0.00135)$ probability limits. Note carefully the improvement from using the binomial probability function and distribution function algorithm to design the control limits. We have a lower limit, and the false alarm rate for increasing p is close to the normal value of 0.00135. By using the binomial distribution itself, rather than the 3-sigma formulas, we can do a better job of designing charts for particular problems.   ■

5.2.5   Unequal Sample Sizes and the Standardized Binomial p-Chart

Let x_i denote a binomial random variable with probability function $b(x; n_i, p)$ of (2.5.1). Then the control limits of (5.2.3) and (5.2.11) vary with n_i. While some authors recommend charting the binomial proportion with varying control limits, we feel that this is a questionable practice for the same reasons that were discussed earlier for variables charts. If the only purpose of the chart is to compare each plotted point with its own 3-sigma control limits, then there is no problem with the chart. However, if there is to be an attempt to interpret point patterns, then the fact that the points are plotted in differing scales makes it difficult to interpret point patterns. To attempt to avoid these problems, we can consider plotting a *standardized* binomial random variable z_i given by (5.2.13).

$$z_i = \frac{x_i - n_i p_0}{\sqrt{n_i p_0 (1 - p_0)}}$$

(5.2.13)

Then $E(z_i) = 0$ and $\text{Var}(z_i) = 1$, so that *constant* control limits for a chart with 3-sigma limits for z are $\text{UCL}(z) = 3$, $\text{CL}(z) = 0$, $\text{LCL}(z) = -3$. The closeness of each of the probabilities of exceeding a control limit to the nominal normal value of 0.00135 depends, of course, upon the normality of the z_i statistics. However, it must be kept in mind that the linear transformation of (5.2.13) does not affect the shape of the distribution or the goodness of a normal approximation to this distribution.

The goodness of the normal approximation to the binomial distribution depends on both p and n, and is best for $p = 0.5$ and n large. In many of our charting applications, p is the proportion of nonconforming product and is usually a small value. For p so small, n must be very large in order for the normal approximation to the binomial to be good. This is of particular concern because for 3-sigma charts we are interested primarily in the tails of the binomial distribution, where the normal approximation is poor. We will give some further discussion and numerical results on the normal approximation for the binomial p-charts in Chapter 8.

From this discussion it appears that it would be desirable to consider transformations of x_i that transform to a distribution with a mean of zero and standard deviation of one, and also admit a better approximation by a normal distribution. To transform to a distribution that is more normal requires transforming with a *nonlinear* transformation. In

Chapter 8 we will consider certain nonlinear transformations of a binomial random variable and control charts based on them.

Example 5.5: To illustrate the computations to construct a standardized p-chart, we consider the first two samples from a process with $p = p_0 = 0.1$, which gave the following data.

i	n_i	x_i	$n_i p_0$	$\sqrt{n_i p_0(1 - p_0)}$	z_i
1	230	28	23	4.55	$(28 - 23)/4.55 = 1.10$
2	170	14	17	3.91	$(14 - 17)/3.91 = -0.77$

■

It will sometimes be required to estimate p from samples of varying sizes as follows: (n_1, x_1), (n_2, x_2), $\cdots$, (n_m, x_m), then we use the following estimator of p.

$$\overline{p} = \frac{\sum\limits_{i=1}^{m} x_i}{\sum\limits_{i=1}^{m} n_i}$$

5.2.6 Point Patterns on p- and np-Charts

Suppose that the binomial proportion p shifts from the nominal value $p = p_0$ to a different value $p = \delta p_0$. Consider how this shift will affect the point patterns on $\hat{p}_i$, X_i, and z_i charts. Since $E(X_i) = np$ and $E(\hat{p}_i) = p$, the plotted points should tend to plot lower or higher according to whether $\delta < 1$ or $\delta > 1$. Also, we know that $SD(X_i) = \sqrt{np(1 - p)}$ and $SD(\hat{p}_i) = \sqrt{p(1 - p)/n}$. However, since $\sqrt{p(1 - p)}$ is a strictly increasing function of p for $0 < p < 1/2$, we see that the *spread* of the points on either an np- or p-chart will increase or decrease with p. This increase or decrease in the spread of the points is itself an important sign of a shift in p.

When p changes from p_0 to δp_0, the mean of z_i changes from 0 to $n_i(\delta - 1)p_0/\sqrt{n_i p_0(1 - p_0)}$, which is positive or negative according to whether $\delta > 1$ or $\delta < 1$. The standard deviation of z_i is given by

$$SD(z_i) = \sqrt{\frac{\delta p_0(1 - \delta p_0)}{p_0(1 - p_0)}}$$

From this we see that when $0 < p_0 < 1/2$ and $1 < \delta < 1/2p_0$, then $SD(z_i) > 1$; and when $0 < p_0 < 1/2$ and $0 < \delta < 1$, then $SD(z_i) < 1$. Thus, since we generally assume $p < 1/2$, we see that the spread on the standardized z_i chart will also tend to increase or decrease with p.

There is another important implication of this property of the p-chart. This means that the chart will have poor sensitivity to detect a decrease in p by having a point plot below the lower control limit. This is because a decrease in p causes the mean of the plotted statistic to decrease, but the simultaneous decrease in the statistic's standard deviation results in probability being more concentrated about the mean and relatively little additional probability falling below *LCL*. In Chapter 8 a Q-Chart will be given that permits much more sensitive tests to detect decreases in p.

5.3 *c*-CHARTS FOR NUMBERS OF NONCONFORMITIES

In this section we consider charts based on the Poisson distribution. Let c denote the number of nonconformities—defects, imperfections, flaws, or whatever—that are found on a *standard inspection unit* of product. The number c could be the number of flaws in the paint of a standard inspection unit that is one automobile trunk lid, the number of breaks in the insulation of a standard inspection unit that is a 100-ft roll of insulated electrical wire, or the total number of nonconformities in a standard inspection unit that consists of 500 production units of product. In these problems, it will often be useful to consider c to be a Poisson random variable with probability function, distribution function, mean, variance, and standard deviation as follows.

$$
\begin{aligned}
f(c, \lambda) &= \frac{\lambda^c e^{-\lambda}}{c!}, \text{ and} \\
F(c, \lambda) &= \sum_{x=0}^{c} f(x; \lambda), \text{ both for} \\
c &= 0, 1, 2, \cdots \\
E(c) &= \lambda, \quad \mathrm{Var}(c) = \lambda, \\
SD(c) &= \sqrt{\lambda}
\end{aligned}
\tag{5.3.1}
$$

Recall that the Poisson distribution was studied in section 2.6 and these formulas were developed there. We now consider c-charts based on the Poisson distribution to control the number of nonconformities.

5.3.1 The Classical 3-Sigma c-Chart with λ Known

For a Poisson process operating in time, let λ denote the mean rate at which nonconformities occur per standard inspection unit. If this rate is known to be λ_0 for a particular inspection process, then 3-sigma control limits for the number of units c per inspection unit are given by display (5.3.2). In words, the LCL is taken to be zero if the value $\lambda_0 - 3\sqrt{\lambda_0}$ is negative.

$$
\begin{aligned}
UCL(c) &= \lambda_0 + 3\sqrt{\lambda_0} \\
CL(c) &= \lambda_0 \\
LCL(c) &= \text{Max } \{0, \lambda_0 - 3\sqrt{\lambda_0}\}
\end{aligned}
\tag{5.3.2}
$$

Suppose that we consider changing the size of an inspection unit by a factor of, say, n. Then the rate at which the defects would occur on an inspection unit would be n times the former rate λ_0. That is, the new rate would be $n\lambda_0$ and control limits for inspection units of this size are

$$
\begin{aligned}
UCL(c) &= n\lambda_0 + 3\sqrt{n\lambda_0} \\
CL(c) &= n\lambda_0 \\
LCL(c) &= \text{Max}\{0, n\lambda_0 - 3\sqrt{n\lambda_0}\}
\end{aligned}
\tag{5.3.3}
$$

Since c takes only integer values, we will actually use the equivalent integer limits discussed above. Note that for the LCL in (5.3.3) to be positive we must have

$$
n\lambda_0 > 9
\tag{5.3.4}
$$

It is often desirable to have $LCL(c)$ greater than zero and this means we must take the inspection unit to be large enough to satisfy (5.3.4).

5.3.2 Exact c-Chart Control Chart Limits

As for the binomial distribution, we can also use the probability and distribution functions for the Poisson distribution to determine (α_L, α_U) probability limits. The discussion preceding equation (5.2.12) obtains here also, and in this case if α_L is specified with an LCL of 1 and a nominal value of $\lambda = \lambda_0$, then the probability at zero is $p(0) = e^{-n\lambda_0}$. If this probability is to be less than α_L, then the size n of a sampling inspection unit must satisfy the inequality

$$n > \frac{-ln(\alpha_L)}{\lambda_0} \qquad (5.3.5)$$

The Q-Charts Poisson distribution function algorithm can be used to determine the UCL that gives a value as close as possible to α_U for this value of n. Consider the following example.

Example 5.6: Certain plastic bottles formed by a blow molding process are inspected for thin spots. The process has a history of producing about one defect in 50 bottles ($\lambda_0 = 1/50$). From (5.3.4) we obtain the value $n = 9/\lambda_0 + 1 = (50)(9) + 1 = 451$. Then $n\lambda_0 = 451/50 = 9.02$ and the 3-sigma control limits from (5.3.3) are

$$UCL(c) = 9.02 + 3\sqrt{9.02} = 18.02 \cong 18$$
$$CL(c) = 9.02$$
$$LCL(c) = 9.02 - 3\sqrt{9.02} = 0.010 \cong 1$$

Then the probabilities of exceeding these limits when $n\lambda_0 = 9.02$ are

$$P(c < 1) = P(c = 0) = e^{-9.02} = 0.00012$$

and using a Poisson distribution function algorithm gives

$$P(c > 18) = 1 - P(c \le 18) = 1 - 0.99752 = 0.00248$$

However, if we use LCL = 1 with $\alpha_L = 0.00135$ and formula (5.3.5) we obtain $n = 331$, and for this case $n\lambda_0 = 331/50 = 6.62$. For this value of the Poisson parameter, by using the Q-Charts algorithm again we obtain UCL = 15, $P(c < 1) = 0.00133$, and $P(c > 15) = 0.00139$.

Thus we see that by using the Poisson distribution itself we have obtained values of α_L and α_U much closer to the nominal value of

0.00135, and have accomplished this with a substantially smaller sample size n, which reduces the cost of sampling. ∎

5.3.3 The Classical 3-Sigma c-Chart with λ Not Known

If it is required to establish a c-chart for the number of defects for a process for which the value of the defect rate λ is not known, then we first define a standard inspection unit, and obtain at least a rough estimate λ_0' for the mean defect rate for this standard unit. Even a small preliminary sample is very helpful at this stage. If no other information is available from records for similar processes, preliminary samples, and so on, we may have to begin with "expert" guesses.

Once a preliminary estimate λ_0' of λ_0 is available, we can use it in conjunction with relations (5.3.4) and (5.3.5) to choose the size n of a sampling inspection unit, that is, a sampling inspection unit is n standard inspection units. Once the sampling inspection unit size is chosen, we can then observe m of these units to obtain an estimate

$$\bar{c} = \frac{1}{mn} \sum_{i=1}^{m} c_i \tag{5.3.6}$$

of the value of $\lambda = \lambda_0$ for this process, where c_i is the number of defects on the ith sampling inspection unit of size n.

We must also decide on a value of m. Suppose we would like to have confidence $1 - \alpha$ that our estimate $\bar{c}$ is within 100γ percent of the true value λ_0 of λ. Now, $\bar{c}$ itself is approximately a $N\left(\lambda_0, \frac{\lambda_0}{mn}\right)$ random variable, so that an approximate $1 - \alpha$ confidence interval for λ_0 is given by

$$\lambda_0' \pm z_{\alpha/2} \sqrt{\frac{\lambda_0'}{mn}}, \quad \text{then write} \quad z_{\alpha/2} \sqrt{\frac{\lambda_0'}{mn}} = \gamma\lambda_0'$$

and solving for m gives formula (5.3.7) for m.

$$m = \frac{z_{\alpha/2}^2}{n\lambda_0'\gamma^2} \tag{5.3.7}$$

Once the estimate $\bar{c}$ of λ_0 is available, we use it in place of λ_0' to set up the control chart. Note that equation (5.3.7) can also be used to select the total number of standard inspection units, mn.

Example 5.7: Consider setting up a control chart to monitor the number of defects in 100-ft rolls of insulated wire. We will use the 3-sigma control limits of (5.3.3). Since we do not know the defect rate, we decide to first inspect two rolls and they show five defects to give a preliminary estimate $\lambda_0' = 5/2 = 2.5$ defects per roll. Thus, to satisfy (5.3.4), we decide to inspect units of four rolls. Note that it is not necessary to inspect four complete rolls. We could inspect $n = 3.7 > 9/2.5 = 3.6$ rolls. Now that we have decided on the size of a sampling inspection unit, we need to choose the size m of a preliminary calibration sample. We estimate an average of ten defects per sampling unit of four rolls of wire. We decide to take m large enough to assure that the estimate of the defect rate will be within 20% of the true value. From (5.3.7) we find that

$$ m = \frac{9}{n\lambda_0'\lambda^2} = \frac{9}{(4)(2.5)(0.2)^2} = 22.5 $$

So we decide to take $m = 25$ sampling inspection units of four 100-ft rolls each. In choosing these inspection units we pay close attention to the rational subgroups idea. A sample of 25 inspection units of four rolls each gave the data in Table 5.2. The mean for these 25 samples is $\bar{c} = 9.04$ defects per four rolls of wire. The estimated 3-sigma control limits are

$$ UCL(c) = \bar{c} + 3\sqrt{\bar{c}} = 9.04 + 3\sqrt{9.04} = 18.06 $$
$$ CL(c) = \bar{c} = 9.04 $$
$$ LCL(c) = \bar{c} - 3\sqrt{\bar{c}} = 9.04 - 3\sqrt{9.04} = 0.02 $$

Since c is a discrete random variable that can assume only values in the set $\{0, 1, 2, \cdots\}$, when the *UCL* given by (5.3.3) is fractional we round to the next smaller integer, and when *LCL* is fractional we wound to the next larger integer. These equivalent integer control limits are

$$ UCL(c) = 18, \quad LCL(c) = 1 $$

TABLE 5.2 Insulated Wire Defects, Calibration Data

i:	1	2	3	4	5	6	7	8	9	10	11	12	13
c_i:	11	12	10	10	9	6	9	7	10	10	8	11	8
i:	14	15	16	17	18	19	20	21	22	23	24	25	
c_i:	13	7	10	7	9	9	10	6	10	5	10	9	Sum: 226

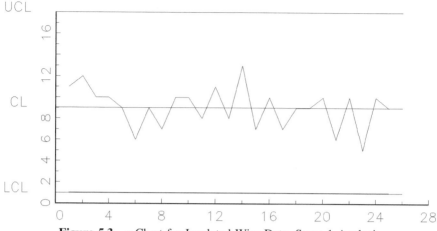

Figure 5.3 c-Chart for Insulated Wire Data, Stage 1 Analysis

These limits and the calibration data are shown in Fig. 5.3. An operating process control chart was kept by periodically sampling four rolls of wire for inspection and plotting the numbers of defects on a chart with control limits at $LCL = 1$ and $UCL = 18$. Table 5.3 shows data taken over a two-week period some time after the charting program was begun. Two samples were taken each day (one sample from each shift) of the ten work days during the two-week period. The c-chart for these data is shown in Fig. 5.4.

The chart for these operating data suggests an increase in the rate of nonconformities since the control limits were established. There is an apparent upward shift in the pattern of points and in the dispersion of the points. An increase in the Poisson parameter λ increases both the process mean and standard deviation. One point is above the UCL and two are on it. In fact, there is also some indication that the second week had a higher defect rate than the first week.   ■

Example 5.8: About 10% of the electronic boards from a process have wave soldering defects. We wish to establish a c-chart program for this process with 0.99 probability limits. We will use a $LCL(c)$ of one, and we first need to determine the number of boards that must be inspected

TABLE 5.3   Operations Data for Insulated Wire Control Chart

i:	1	2	3	4	5	6	7	8	8	10	11	12	13
c_i:	8	18	10	6	13	13	7	15	11	8	19	17	14

i:	14	15	16	17	18	19	20
c_i:	18	12	16	6	14	12	16

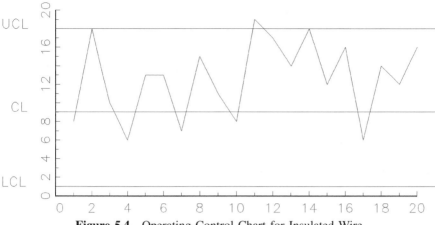

Figure 5.4 Operating Control Chart for Insulated Wire

for each determination of c in order to have the probability of zero defects be approximately equal to $\alpha_L = \alpha_U = 0.005$. The minimum number of boards required is then

$$n \geq \frac{-ln(0.005)}{0.1} = 52.98, \quad \text{so we take } n = 53$$

From this we decide to select $n = 53$ boards as the tentative sampling inspection unit, subject to investigating the upper control limit. For this value of n the Poisson parameter is 5.3 and we need to find the integer that has probability $\alpha_U = 0.005$ or less above it, or 0.995 or more below it. Since this Poisson distribution has standard deviation of $\sqrt{5.3} = 2.3$, we should expect the value to lie in the range of roughly 10 to 15. Again, using a Poisson distribution function algorithm we obtain the following values.

Integer, I:	10	11	12
$F(I)$:	0.98000	0.99159	0.99671

The best value for the UCL is 12. Therefore, we will use the values

$$LCL(c) = 1, \quad CL(c) = 5.3, \quad UCL(c) = 12.$$

The probability $\alpha_L + \alpha_U$ of one point falling outside these limits is

$$0.00499 + 0.00329 = 0.00828$$

From (5.3.4), in order to have a lower classical 3-sigma control limit we must have $n > 9/0.1 = 90$. By determining these exact probability limits, we can realize savings by using a smaller sample size than would be required in order to have a 3-sigma lower control limit.   ■

5.3.4 OC, Power, and ARL Functions for c-Charts

The OC function for a c-chart is given by

$$\beta(\lambda) = P\{LCL \leq c \leq UCL \mid \lambda\} \tag{5.3.8}$$

Assuming that c is a Poisson random variable with rate λ, and that the control limits are integers, we can express this as

$$\beta(\lambda) = F(UCL, \lambda) - F(LCL - 1, \lambda) \tag{5.3.9}$$

where F is the Poisson distribution function of (2.6.1). This probability can be evaluated using either tables or an algorithm for the Poisson distribution function. Also, the normal distribution can be used to obtain an approximate value of $\beta(\lambda)$ by using

$$\beta(\lambda) \cong \Phi\left(\frac{UCL + 0.5 - \lambda}{\sqrt{\lambda}}\right) - \Phi\left(\frac{LCL - 0.5 - \lambda}{\sqrt{\lambda}}\right) \tag{5.3.10}$$

Example 5.9: In Example 5.7 we obtained the control limits $UCL = 18$ and $LCL = 1$, for a c-chart for the number of defects in 100-ft rolls of insulated wire. The estimated value of λ was 9.04. Table 5.4 shows values of computations to compute the values of the OC function for selected values of λ. We have computed values of the OC function using the Poisson distribution function and the values are given in column (6) of Table 5.4. The normal approximation values are given in column (7). The values 18.5 and 0.5 in columns (4) and (5) are from using corrections for continuity in the approximation of the Poisson distribution by a normal distribution. The agreement is not very good, but may be adequate to sketch an OC curve by hand when tables or algorithms of the Poisson distribution function are not available.

An OC curve of this OC function is given in Fig. 5.5. This OC curve should be studied carefully because it summarizes the properties of this chart. Note, for example, that the probability of a point falling between

TABLE 5.4 OC, Power, and ARL Function Calculations for Example 5.9

(1) λ	(2) $P(c = 0)$	(3) $P(c \leq 18)$	(4) $\Phi\left(\dfrac{18.5 - \lambda}{\sqrt{\lambda}}\right)$	(5) $\Phi\left(\dfrac{0.5 - \lambda}{\sqrt{\lambda}}\right)$	(6) $(3) - (2)$ OC	(7) $(4) - (5)$	(8) Power	(9) ARL
1	0.368	1.000	1.000	0.309	0.632	0.691	0.368	2.72
2	0.135	1.000	1.000	0.145	0.865	0.855	0.135	7.41
3	0.050	1.000	1.000	0.075	0.950	0.925	0.050	20.
6	0.002	1.000	1.000	0.012	0.998	0.988	0.002	500.
10	0.000	0.993	0.996	0.001	0.993	0.995	0.007	142.86
12	0.000	0.963	0.970	0.000	0.963	0.970	0.037	27.03
14	0.000	0.882	0.885	0.000	0.882	0.885	0.118	8.47
16	0.000	0.742	0.734	0.000	0.742	0.734	0.258	3.88
18	0.000	0.562	0.547	0.000	0.562	0.547	0.438	2.28
20	0.000	0.381	0.367	0.000	0.381	0.367	0.619	1.62
22	0.000	0.236	0.228	0.000	0.236	0.228	0.764	1.31
24	0.000	0.128	0.131	0.000	0.128	0.131	0.872	1.15
26	0.000	0.065	0.071	0.000	0.065	0.071	0.935	1.07

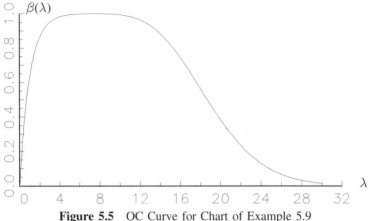

Figure 5.5   OC Curve for Chart of Example 5.9

the control limits is almost constant for $4 \leq \lambda \leq 12$, and is approximately 0.95 in this range. Only for λ about 24 is the probability down to about 0.1, and λ has to be about 30 for the OC function to take small values. This is not a very sensitive chart for detecting changes in λ! What can we do? One obvious thing we can do is to take a larger sample. We can also design supplementary runs tests to increase the chart's sensitivity to a change in λ, but this will also increase the rate of false alarms. The power function is again Power$(\lambda) = 1 - \beta(\lambda)$. The points plotted are again values of independent random variables, so the number of points plotted between values that fall outside the control limits is again a geometric random variable with mean = ARL = 1/Power(λ). The power for the chart of this example is given in column (8) of Table 5.4, and the ARL is given in column (9). These were computed from the OC values in column (6).   ∎

5.4   *u*-CHARTS FOR THE AVERAGE NUMBER OF DEFECTS PER STANDARD INSPECTION UNIT

Let c again denote the number of defects on a standard inspection unit, say 100 ft of insulated wire. Suppose c is a Poisson random variable with parameter λ. Then

$$E(c) = \lambda, \quad \mathrm{Var}(c) = \lambda$$

Suppose we would like to set up a control chart based on a sampling inspection unit that is n times as large as a standard inspection unit. If

λ is the rate of occurrence of defects based on a standard inspection unit, and if c is the observed number of defects observed on inspection units that are n times as large, then c is a Poisson random variable with mean and variance

$$E(c) = n\lambda, \quad \text{Var}(c) = n\lambda$$

For example, when λ is the defect rate on 100-ft rolls of wire, the number of defects on 250-ft rolls of wire would be a Poisson random variable with parameter 2.5λ and mean and variance both equal to 2.5λ.

Next, let u denote the average number of defects observed on n standard inspection units, for example, on n 100-ft rolls of wire. Then $u = c/n$, and we have

$$E(u) = \lambda, \quad \text{Var}(u) = \frac{\lambda}{n} \qquad (5.4.1)$$

Therefore, 3-sigma control limits for u for a process with nominal rate of λ_0 are

$$
\begin{aligned}
UCL(u) &= \lambda_0 + 3\sqrt{\frac{\lambda_0}{n}} \\[2mm]
CL(u) &= \lambda_0 \\[2mm]
LCL(u) &= \text{Max}\left\{0, \lambda_0 - 3\sqrt{\frac{\lambda_0}{n}}\right\}
\end{aligned}
\qquad (5.4.2)
$$

Note, particularly, in this development n can be any positive value, that is, we require only that $n > 0$. In particular, fractional values of n are permissible. However, it should not be inferred from these remarks that all values are equally valuable. For larger values of n we are taking larger samples with more information and shifts in the defect rate will be detected with higher probability.

If the defect rate per standard inspection unit is not given for the process, then we shall need to take a preliminary calibration sample in order to estimate λ for the process. If m inspection units of size n each are observed and c_i defects are observed on the ith unit, then we estimate λ by

$$\bar{u} = \frac{1}{mn} \sum_{i=1}^{m} c_i = \frac{1}{m} \sum_{i=1}^{m} u_i \qquad (5.4.3)$$

We next consider some guidelines for choosing m and n. First, we can choose n to make LCL > 0 for a 3-sigma chart. This gives

$$n > 9/\lambda_0 \qquad (5.4.4)$$

This depends on knowing the value of λ, which we often will not know. However, it can be used with even crude knowledge of the value of λ in order to start to design a chart. Once a value for n has been determined, we need to decide on the number of samples m to observe to obtain a good estimate $\bar{u}$ of λ. If we want to have confidence coefficient $1 - \alpha$ that the estimate $\bar{u}$ will be within 100γ percent of the true value, then m should satisfy

$$m \geq \frac{z_{\alpha/2}^2}{n\lambda_0 \gamma^2} \qquad (5.4.5)$$

We can also design an "exact" u-chart in a manner similar to that considered above for a c-chart. To design an exact u-chart recall that $c = nu$ is a Poisson random variable with mean and variance both equal to $n\lambda$. Then an exact (α_L, α_U) chart for c can be designed in the manner described above for designing an exact c-chart. The control limits for this chart can then be converted to exact probability limits for a u-chart by putting $UCL(u) = UCL(c)/n$, $CL(u) = CL(c)/n$, and $LCL(u) = LCL(c)/n$. In using the u-chart it should be kept in mind that while the u's being plotted take fractional values, they are still observed values of a discrete random variable and that this is an attributes chart.

Example 5.10: Consider designing a u-chart for the number of blemishes in the paint finish of plastic panels. We first design a 3-sigma c-chart, and then convert the limits to limits for u. The standard inspection unit will be one panel, and average rate per panel is approximately $\lambda_0' = 0.63$. Therefore we require

$$n > \frac{9}{0.63} = 14.3, \quad \text{or } n = 15$$

for a 3-sigma chart to have a lower control limit. However, to have a lower $\alpha_L = 0.00135$ probability limit we require that

$$e^{-n\lambda_0'} = e^{-0.63n} \leq 0.00135$$

or

$$n \geq \frac{ln(0.00135)}{-0.63} = 10.5, \quad \text{or } n = 11$$

We decide to inspect $n = 11$ panels as the size of our sampling inspection unit. Then the Poisson rate per sampling inspection unit is $n\lambda_0' = (11)(0.63) = 6.93$. If we take $LCL(c) = 1$ then the probability of a point below LCL is $e^{-6.93} = 0.00098$. To select an upper control limit with $\alpha_U = 0.00135$, approximately, we first note that an upper 3-sigma limit for c would be

$$6.93 + 3\sqrt{6.93} = 14.8$$

From a Poisson distribution function algorithm we find

$$P(c > 14) = 1 - P(c \leq 14) = 1 - F(14, 6.93)$$
$$= 1 - 0.994742 = 0.00526$$
$$P(c > 15) = 1 - F(15, 6.93)$$
$$= 1 - 0.997816 = 0.00218$$
$$P(c > 16) = 1 - F(16, 6.93)$$
$$= 1 - 0.999139 = 0.00086$$

At this point we observe that for $n = 11$ we cannot take a value of $UCL(c)$ that makes α_U close to the nominal value of 0.00135. If we take $UCL = 15$ then α_U is 0.00218 and $UCL = 16$ gives $\alpha_u = 0.00086$. We have to decide which false alarm rate we prefer. Of course, this choice also affects the sensitivity to detect shifts in λ. Suppose we choose $LCL(c) = 1$ and $UCL(c) = 16$. Then the control limits for the *u*-chart are

$$LCL(u) = 1/11 = 0.091, \quad CL(u) = 0.63,$$
$$UCL(u) = 16/11 = 1.45 \qquad \blacksquare$$

Example 5.11: Electric meter main boards are checked for defects of all types before they are installed in meters. Boards with defects are either repaired or scrapped. It is required to establish a charting program for defects as part of a major process improvement project. The standard inspection unit will be one board. A rough estimate of the number of defects per board is 0.6. (Note that this is for defects of *all* types, including minor nonconformities that do not affect functioning.) Calibration data of 25 samples of 60 boards each were taken and the data are given in Table 5.5. Note from equation (5.4.5) with $z_{\alpha/2} = 3$ that $mn = 1500$ boards are enough to assure that $\bar{u}$ is within 10% of the true value of λ with high probability. The value of $\bar{u}$ is 0.73. In order to plot points in more convenient units it was decided to plot on a standard inspection unit of size ten. Then the estimated defect rate per 10 boards inspection unit is 7.3, sample size is $n = 60/10 = 6$, and the control limits from (5.4.2) are

$$UCL(u) = 7.3 + 3\sqrt{\frac{7.3}{6}} = 10.6, \quad CL(u) = 7.3,$$

$$LCL(u) = 7.3 - 3\sqrt{\frac{7.3}{6}} = 4.0$$

These limits and the u's of Table 5.5 (multiplied by 10) are shown in Fig. 5.6. The process is stable.

Table 5.6 shows records of defects on samples of 60 boards per day taken on each of 22 subsequent working days over a five-week period. The control chart clearly indicates that the defects rate was higher for the second and third weeks. Three points of Fig. 5.7 (6, 13, and 14) of these operating data exceed the UCL. The process is not as stable during this operating period as it was when the initial data displayed in Fig. 5.6 were taken. Note that the points in Fig. 5.7 of these operating data are not only higher, but the spread also appears larger, which is an additional indicator of an increase in the Poisson defect rate. ∎

5.4.1 OC, Power, and ARL Functions for *u*-Charts

The OC function for a u-chart is given by

$$\beta(\lambda) = P\{LCL \leq u \leq UCL \mid \lambda\} \tag{5.4.6}$$

Assuming that $c = nu$ is a Poisson random variable with parameter $n\lambda$, then $\beta(\lambda)$ can be written as

TABLE 5.5   Defects on Sampling Inspection Units of 60 Main Boards

Sample Number	Sample Size	Number of Defects	u
1	60	38	.63
2	60	45	.75
3	60	48	.80
4	60	38	.63
5	60	41	.68
6	60	38	.63
7	60	48	.80
8	60	45	.75
9	60	45	.75
10	60	52	.87
11	60	38	.63
12	60	38	.63
13	60	50	.83
14	60	44	.73
15	60	48	.80
16	60	49	.82
17	60	44	.73
18	60	40	.67
19	60	43	.72
20	60	49	.82
21	60	54	.90
22	60	41	.68
23	60	40	.67
24	60	49	.82
25	60	30	.50

$$\bar{u} = 0.73$$

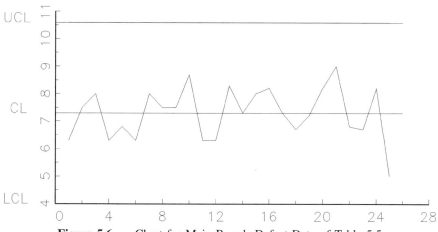

Figure 5.6   *u*-Chart for Main Boards Defect Data of Table 5.5

TABLE 5.6   Main Boards Defects Over 22 Days

Sample Number	Sample Size	Number of Defects	u
1	60	42	7.00
2	60	34	5.67
3	60	44	7.33
4	60	53	8.83
5	60	36	6.00
6	60	67	11.17
7	60	43	7.17
8	60	42	7.00
9	60	56	9.33
10	60	50	8.33
11	60	53	8.83
12	60	61	10.17
13	60	76	12.67
14	60	68	11.33
15	60	47	7.83
16	60	61	10.17
17	60	33	5.50
18	60	48	8.00
19	60	43	7.17
20	60	45	7.50
21	60	53	8.83
22	60	44	7.33

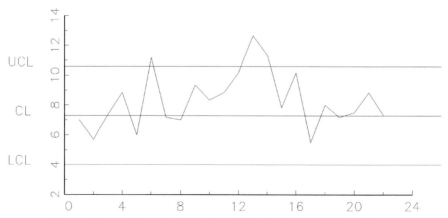

Figure 5.7 u-Chart for Main Boards Defect Data of Table 5.6

$$\beta(\lambda) = F(n(UCL); n\lambda) - F(n(LCL) - 1; n\;\lambda)$$

$$\text{if } n(LCL) \text{ is an integer} \qquad (5.4.7)$$

$$= F(n(UCL); n\lambda) - F(n(LCL); n\lambda), \quad \text{otherwise}$$

The OC function $\beta(\lambda)$ for a u-chart can also be evaluated approximately using a normal distribution approximation as follows.

$$\beta(\lambda) \cong \Phi\left\{\frac{n(UCL - \lambda)}{\sqrt{n\lambda}}\right\} - \Phi\left\{\frac{n(LCL - \lambda)}{\sqrt{n\lambda}}\right\} \qquad (5.4.8)$$

The Power function is Power$(\lambda) = 1 - \beta(\lambda)$ and the ARL function is ARL$(\lambda) = 1/$Power(λ).

Example 5.12: In Example 5.11 we obtained the following control limits for defects on sampling inspection units of ten electric meter main boards.

$$LCL = 4.0, \quad CL = \lambda_0 = 7.3, \quad UCL = 10.6, \quad n = 6,$$

$$n(LCL) = 24, \quad n(UCL) = 63.6$$

We calculate values of $\beta(\lambda)$, Power(λ), and ARL(λ) for selected values of λ in Table 5.7 using a Poisson distribution function algorithm and sketch the OC curve in Fig. 5.8. Note that the OC curve is almost

TABLE 5.7   OC Function Calculations for Example 5.12

(1) λ	(2) $n\lambda$	(3) $P\{c \le 23\}$	(4) $P\{c \le 63\}$	(5) $\beta(\lambda)$	(6) Power(λ)	(7) ARL(λ)
1	6	1.000	1.000	0.000	1.000	1.000
2	12	0.999	1.000	0.001	0.999	1.001
3	18	0.899	1.000	0.101	0.899	1.112
4	24	0.473	1.000	0.527	0.473	2.114
5	30	0.115	1.000	0.885	0.115	8.696
6	36	0.014	1.000	0.986	0.014	71.429
7	42	0.001	0.999	0.998	0.002	500.000
8	48	0.000	0.984	0.984	0.016	62.500
9	54	0.000	0.900	0.900	0.100	10.000
10	60	0.000	0.680	0.680	0.320	3.125
11	66	0.000	0.386	0.386	0.614	1.629
12	72	0.000	0.158	0.158	0.842	1.188
13	78	0.000	0.047	0.047	0.953	1.049

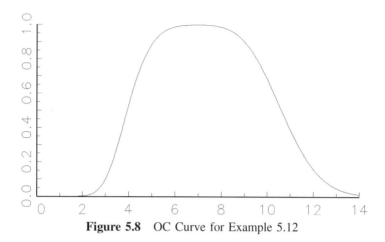

Figure 5.8 OC Curve for Example 5.12

constant in the interval 7.3 ± 1, and this chart has almost no sensitivity to detect shifts of λ to values in this interval. Indeed, this chart does not have good sensitivity to detect changes in λ unless the new values are outside the interval 7.3 ± 4. Recall that $c = nu$. ∎

5.5 c- AND u-CHARTS WHEN SAMPLE SIZES VARY—STANDARDIZED CHARTS

In some applications of either c- or u-charts it may be inconvenient or impossible to keep the sample size n constant. When this is the case, let n_i denote the ith sample size. Then the classical approach to charting in this situation involves either charting the statistics c and u with varying sample sizes, or standardizing the statistics by subtracting the mean and dividing by the standard deviation of each statistic before it is charted. The standardized statistics are then plotted with UCL = 3, CL = 0, LCL = −3. The closeness of the actual probabilities of exceeding these limits, (α_L, α_U), to the nominal normal values, (0.00135, 0.00135), depends on the goodness of the normal approximation to the Poisson distribution for each sample.

To standardize a c statistic, put

$$z_i = \frac{c_i - n_i\lambda_0}{\sqrt{n_i\lambda_0}} \tag{5.5.1}$$

These z_i statistics can then be plotted on a chart with control limits at ± 3.

The u statistic can also be standardized; however, it gives the same chart as (5.5.1) since

$$\frac{u_i - \lambda_0}{\sqrt{\lambda_0/n_i}} = \frac{\dfrac{c_i}{n_i} - \lambda_0}{\sqrt{\lambda_0/n_i}} = \frac{c_i - n_i\lambda_0}{\sqrt{n_i\lambda_0}}$$

In Chapter 8 we will present Q-Charts that generally perform better than these standardized charts in the sense that they give false alarm rates (α_L, α_U) that are closer to the nominal normal values than those of these standardized charts.

To estimate λ from samples (n_1, c_1), (n_2, c_2), $\cdots$, (n_m, c_m), use the estimator

$$\bar{c} = \frac{\displaystyle\sum_{i=1}^{m} c_i}{\displaystyle\sum_{i=1}^{m} n_i} \tag{5.5.2}$$

5.5.1 Point Patterns when λ Changes

Suppose λ changes from a nominal value of $\lambda = \lambda_0$ to a different value $\lambda = \delta\lambda_0$, $\delta > 0$. Then the means of the statistics c_i, u_i, and z_i change from nominal values of

$$E(c_i) = n_i\lambda_0, \quad E(u_i) = \lambda_0, \quad E(z_i) = 0$$

to new values

$$E(c_i) = n_i\delta\lambda_0, \quad E(u_i) = \delta\lambda_0, \quad E(z_i) = \frac{n_i(\delta\lambda_0 - \lambda_0)}{\sqrt{n_i\lambda_0}} = \sqrt{n_i\lambda_0}\,(\delta - 1)$$

Therefore, the point patterns for each of these statistics will tend to move up or down on the chart according to whether $\delta > 1$ or $\delta < 1$.

Also, the standard deviations of these statistics will shift from nominal values of

$$SD(c_i) = \sqrt{n_i\lambda_0}, \quad SD(u_i) = \sqrt{\frac{\lambda_0}{n_i}}, \quad SD(z_i) = 1$$

to new values

$$SD(c_i) = \sqrt{n_i\delta\lambda_0}, \quad SD(u_i) = \sqrt{\frac{\delta\lambda_0}{n_i}}, \quad SD(z_i) = \sqrt{\frac{\delta\lambda_0}{\lambda_0}} = \sqrt{\delta}$$

From these values we see that the spread of points on a chart of any one of these statistics will increase or decrease according to whether $\delta > 1$ or $\delta < 1$. This is an important point to keep in mind in interpreting charts to control a Poisson parameter.

Another implication of this, as was mentioned in section 5.2 for p-charts, is that these c- and u-charts will have poor ability to detect decreases in λ by having a point fall below LCL. This point will be considered further in Chapter 8 in connection with Q-Charts for attributes.

5.6 SUMMARY

In this chapter, we have presented some classical and modern material on charting methods for attributes data. The p- and np-charts based on the binomial sampling distribution and c- and u-charts based on the Poisson distribution were consdered. We have also discussed using binomial and Poisson distribution functions to design "exact" charts, that is, charts with exactly known probabilities of exceeding the control limits when the process is stable. The OC and Power functions were used to study the performance of these charts for the case when the parameters, p or λ, are known exactly.

PROBLEMS

5.1 The relation (5.2.4) was obtained by requiring that $LCL(\hat{p})$ exceed zero. Since p must also be less than or equal to one, we should also require that $UCL(\hat{p}) < 1$. Show that the condition (5.2.4) and the condition that $p_0 < 1/2$ is sufficient to assure that $UCL(\hat{p}) < 1$.

5.2   Show that the formula (5.2.5) is valid also for the sample size n required to detect a decrease in the value of p from p_0 to a value δp_0, $0 < \delta < 1$, with probability 0.5.

5.3   The following data are from 20 samples of size 450 each. The second row gives the number of nonconforming units from each sample. Analyze this data using a 3-sigma p-chart, and determine proposed (trial) control limits for Stage 2 applications of the p-chart.

i:	1	2	3	4	5	6	7	8	9	10
x_i:	9	11	10	12	2	14	8	4	9	0

i:	11	12	13	14	15	16	17	18	19	20
x_i:	0	3	7	13	23	8	2	8	6	9

5.4   The following table gives the number of nonconforming units from 20 samples from a production process. Analyze this data by constructing a standardized binomial p-chart. Note that three consecutive points are just above the lower control limit, and evaluate, that is, estimate, the probability of this pattern for a stable process. Recommend minimum sample sizes and a "trial" estimate $\hat{p}'$ of p to be used for a Stage 2 monitoring chart program. Assume that it is desired to detect a doubling of the probability parameter p on one point with probability at least 0.5.

Sample Number	Sample Size	x_i	$\hat{p}_i$
1	110	14	.127
2	112	12	.107
3	115	10	.087
4	95	10	.105
5	91	8	.088
6	105	6	.057
7	100	0	.000
8	90	0	.000
9	106	1	.009
10	132	10	.076

11	141	10	.071
12	128	9	.070
13	145	15	.103
14	120	13	.108
15	118	7	.059
16	119	9	.076
17	115	14	.122
18	112	11	.098
19	109	9	.083
20	107	10	.093
Sums:	2270	178	

5.5 A classical 3-sigma p-chart is to be used for a process with $p_0 = 0.1$ and $n = 100$.

(a) Use the exact formula of (5.2.9) and a binomial distribution function algorithm to evaluate the OC, Power, and ARL functions for the following values of p:

0.03 0.04 0.05 0.06 0.07 0.08 0.085 0.09 0.095 0.10 0.11 0.13

(b) Use the normal approximation formula of (5.2.10) to evaluate the OC, Power, and ARL functions for the same values of p as given in part (a) of this problem.

(c) Plot the ARL function using the values obtained in part (a).

5.6 It is required to design an np control chart for a process operating with nominal fallout value of 2% (i.e., $p_0 = 0.02$), and with (0.00135, 0.00135) probability limits.

(a) By taking LCL = 1, find the smallest possible value of sample size n and the best corresponding control limits. Evaluate the probabilities (α_L, α_U) of a point falling beyond these control limits when the process is stable, that is, when p is constant at 0.02.

(b) Determine classical 3-sigma limits for the sample size found in part (a) and evaluate the probabilities (α_L, α_U) of exceeding these limits.

(c) Compare the results obtained in parts (a) and (b).

5.7 The following table gives the number of nonconforming units from 20 samples from a production process. Analyze this data by constructing a standardized binomial p-chart, and recommend minimum sample sizes for a Stage 2 monitoring chart program.

i	n	x	i	n	x	i	n	x	i	n	x
1	210	8	6	187	9	11	205	9	16	231	17
2	175	8	7	197	31	12	195	11	17	217	12
3	181	17	8	201	16	13	207	8	18	211	13
4	198	7	9	199	33	14	223	11	19	201	10
5	189	6	10	200	4	15	227	7	20	203	7

5.8 It is required to design a probability control chart for a binomial proportion p with $n = 57$, $p = p_0 = 0.2$, $\alpha_L \leq 0.02$, and $\alpha_U \leq 0.02$. Find the best values of LCL and UCL for this problem. Evaluate the actual values of α_L and α_U for your chart.

5.9 A molding process that produces plastic cases for steel tapes has a history of producing about three nonconformities per 100 cases. It is required to set up a c-chart for this process.

(a) Show that a sampling inspection unit of 221 cases is adequate to permit an approximate 0.00135 lower probability control limit. Determine an approximate 0.00135 upper probability limit UCL.

(b) Compute the 3-sigma classical c-chart control limits for the same size sampling inspection unit of 221 cases.

(c) Evaluate the OC function for the chart with limits found in part (a) when the average rates of nonconforities per 100 cases are as follows: .1, 1, 2, 3, 4, 6, 7, 12. Sketch the OC chart for these values.

(d) Evaluate the OC function for the 3-sigma chart limits found in part (b) when the average rates of nonconformities per 100 cases are as follows: .1, 1, 2, 3, 4, 6, 8, 12. Sketch the OC chart for these values.

(e) Discuss and compare the two charts considered above for this problem.

5.10 The following table gives data that has been collected for a c-chart analysis. Compute approximate (0.005, 0.005) probability limits and determine if the process is in approximate control. Give recommended 3-sigma control limits for a Stage 2 monitoring program. All samples are size $n = 250$.

i	c	i	c	i	c	i	c
1	11	6	9	11	23	16	22
2	7	7	11	12	9	17	4
3	11	8	14	13	13	18	10
4	9	9	8	14	0	19	3
5	10	10	7	15	0	20	11

5.11 The following table gives the number of defects found on samples of $n = 200$ electronic boards.

i	c	i	c	i	c	i	c	i	c
1	16	6	22	11	19	16	25	21	31
2	22	7	22	12	24	17	24	22	29
3	23	8	19	13	20	18	21	23	29
4	16	9	18	14	20	19	24	24	29
5	18	10	19	15	24	20	25	25	35

Make a c-chart for these data and discuss results.

5.12 The following table gives lot sizes and the total number of defects found for lots produced on 25 consecutive work days. Make a standardized c-chart for these data. Interpret the chart.

i	n	c	i	n	c	i	n	c
1	190	19	10	312	31	18	264	46
2	210	24	11	167	18	19	197	30
3	211	20	12	278	28	20	276	34
4	214	20	13	345	42	21	432	55
5	210	16	14	191	21	22	326	53
6	186	21	15	321	36	23	263	35
7	232	14	16	478	58	24	241	31
8	457	57	17	354	66	25	265	47
9	236	23						

5.13 An automobile assembly plant inspects finished bodies for defective welds before primer painting operations. The average number of defective welds per body is $\lambda_0 = 1.7$. It is required to establish a u-chart to plot one point per day on a per-body basis. Is is desired to use a (0.00135, 0.00135) probability u-chart.

(a) Determine the minimum sample size n of cars that must be inspected each day.

(b) Compute the "exact" (0.00135, 0.00135) control limits for a u-chart using the sample size found in part (a).

(c) Suppose λ shifts from the nominal value of $\lambda_0 = 1.7$ to $\delta\lambda_0$ for $\delta = 0.59$, 1, and 1.47. Evaluate the probabilities, that is, the powers, of a chart with the control limits found in part (b) to detect these shifts. Also, compute the ARLs for these shifts. Note that the signals must be in the correct direction, that is, must violate the correct control limit.

(d) For the sample size determined in part (a), compute classical 3-sigma control limits for u.

(e) For the control limits found in part (d), evaluate the powers and ARLs to detect the shifts described in part (c). Compare these results with those found in part (c).

CHAPTER 6

MA, EWMA, and CUSUM Charts for Classical Stable Processes

In section 4.6 we considered the ARLs for a number of tests for changes in the process mean based on classical 3-sigma $\overline{X}$-charts. It was observed that for one-step shifts in the mean of less than about two standard deviations, Test 1 of Fig. 4.9, that is, the 1-of-1 test, has rather poor sensitivity for detecting such changes. Other runs tests such as Tests 2, 5, and 6 can be applied to improve this sensitivity; however, this will have the disadvantage that when two or more such tests are used simultaneously, the resulting rate of false alarms will increase.

The insensitivity of the 1-of-1 test on an $\overline{X}$ Shewhart chart for detecting small monotone shifts in a process mean has served to inspire work to develop other techniques with better sensitivity for detecting such shifts. The general idea common to these methods is to combine information from two or more samples in order to improve performance. In this chapter we present a number of charting schemes that combine information from two or more points. We will consider the *moving average* (MA) chart, the *geometric moving average* (GMA) chart, and the *cumulative sum* (CUSUM) chart. The GMA chart is often also called an *exponentially weighted moving average* (EWMA) chart. This name has been popular in recent quality literature, so we will use it here.

The material in this chapter is concerned with methods that are essentially alternatives to $\overline{X}$-charts for monitoring a process mean to detect monotone shifts. They are, in fact, special-purpose charts for detecting monotone shifts, and are not alternatives to Shewhart charts as general methods for detecting special causes and bringing processes into control. The reason is because the plotted statistics are dependent and due to this dependence it is difficult to interpret anomalous patterns other than the violation of a control limit. Some of these same statistics, viz., the MA and EWMA, have applications also for cases when some of the assumptions of the classical stable model, such as independence and constant means, are no longer valid. The EWMA will be considered in this context in Chapter 13.

6.1 THE MOVING AVERAGE (MA) CONTROL CHART

Consider again data with the structure of that in Table 4.1. For $\overline{X}_1$, $\overline{X}_2, \cdots, \overline{X}_t, \cdots$ the sequence of sample means, the sample means *moving average of span k at time t, M_t,* is given in (6.1.1). Note that this is the average of the nk most recently observed sample values at time t, for $t \geq k$. Now, if the data satisfy the model assumptions of display (4.1.2), then $E(M_t) = \mu$. However, if the process mean changed in value from $\mu = \mu_0$ to $\mu = \mu_0 + \delta\sigma$ for the last k_1 ($k_1 < k$) samples, with $t \geq k$, then $E(M_t) = \mu_0 + k_1\delta\sigma/k$.

$$M_t = \frac{\overline{X}_t + \cdots + \overline{X}_1}{t},$$

$$\text{for } t = 1, \cdots, k - 1$$

$$M_t = \frac{\overline{X}_t + \cdots + \overline{X}_{t-k+1}}{k},$$

$$\text{for } t = k, k + 1, \cdots \tag{6.1.1}$$

The variance of M_t is:

$$\mathrm{Var}(M_t) = \frac{\sigma^2}{tn}, t = 1, \cdots, k - 1$$

$$\mathrm{Var}(M_t) = \frac{\sigma^2}{kn}, t \geq k \tag{6.1.2}$$

The moving average M_t is an average of kn observations when $t \geq k$, and by the central limit theorem it is approximately normally distributed for the usual choices of n and k. However, two values M_t and M_{t+s} are independent only if $s \geq k$, that is, when the moving averages have no common sample means. One approach to constructing control limits for the moving average M_t is to define $(\alpha/2, \alpha/2)$ probability control limits as follows.

$$UCL(M_t) = \mu_0 + z_{\alpha/2} \frac{\sigma_0}{\sqrt{tn}}$$

$$LCL(M_t) = \mu_0 - z_{\alpha/2} \frac{\sigma_0}{\sqrt{tn}}$$

(6.1.3)

where t is replaced by k when $t \geq k$ and μ_0 and σ_0 are the known nominal values of μ and σ. A chart with these limits will have probability $\alpha/2$ of a single point falling above the UCL and the same value for a point below the LCL. For $t \geq k$, these limits are the same as for the $\bar{X}$-chart of (4.4.2) with n replaced by nk. From this observation it follows that the OC function which gives the probability that a single point will fall inside these limits when the mean has shifted from a nominal value of μ_0 to a new value $\mu_0 + \delta\sigma_0$, and nk observations have been taken since this shift, is given by (4.6.1) with n replaced by nk, that is, by

$$\beta(\delta) = \Phi(z_{\alpha/2} - \delta\sqrt{nk}) - \Phi(-z_{\alpha/2} - \delta\sqrt{nk})$$

$$\cong \Phi(z_{\alpha/2} - |\delta| \sqrt{nk})$$

(6.1.4)

We can use this formula to obtain a sample size formula to achieve a power of $1 - \beta$ to detect a permanent shift in mean of δ standard deviations on one point. The formula is

$$nk = \frac{(z_{\alpha/2} + z_\beta)^2}{\delta^2}$$

(6.1.5)

This is the total number of observations to be used for each point plotted; however, only n new observations are used for each point. The values of n and k and the distances between samples determine the design of the chart. These values are chosen to customize the MA chart for particular processes. For example, in some applications we may wish to take either n or k to be one.

Example 6.1: A process has nominal operating mean level of $\mu_0 = 22.00$ mm and $\sigma_0 = 0.030$ mm. We wish to use a 3-sigma MA chart and to have power of 0.99 to detect a change of 0.040 mm in the process mean on each plotted point. Determine values of n and k

needed for this chart, and make a chart using the data given in Table 6.1.

Solution: Here

$$\delta\sigma_0 = 0.040 \text{ and } \sigma_0 = 0.030 \text{ gives } \delta = 4/3$$

Then from (6.1.5): $nk = (3 + 2.33)^2 \left(\dfrac{3}{4}\right)^2 \cong 16$

Suppose we decide to take $n = k = 4$. The control limits will be given by the formulas of (6.1.3). Then the control limits are

$$UCL(M_1) = 22.0 + (3)\frac{(0.030)}{2} = 22.045,$$

$$LCL(M_1) = 22.0 - (3)\frac{(0.030)}{2} = 21.955$$

$$UCL(M_2) = 22.032, \quad LCL(M_2) = 21.968$$

$$UCL(M_3) = 22.026, \quad LCL(M_3) = 21.973$$

$$UCL(M_t) = 22.023, \quad LCL(M_t) = 21.977 \quad \text{for } t \geq 4$$

The moving average chart for the data of Table 6.1 is shown in Fig. 6.1. For comparison, we also plot in Figs. 6.2 and 6.3 the $\overline{X}$- and S-charts for the data in Table 6.1. The 3-sigma control limits for $\overline{X}$ are

$$UCL(\overline{X}) = UCL(M_1) = 22.045, \quad LCL(\overline{X}) = LCL(M_1) = 21.955,$$

and the 3-sigma control limits for S are (from (4.4.6))

$$UCL(S) = B_6\,\sigma_0 = (2.088)(0.030) = 0.062,$$

$$CL = c_4\sigma_0 = (0.9213)(0.031) = 0.027,$$

$$LCL(S) = B_5\,\sigma_0 = (0)(0.030) = 0$$

Discreteness in the data is apparent from the many values of the sample means that are equal.   ∎

TABLE 6.1   Data for Example 6.1

t	$\bar{X}_t$	S	R	M_t	LCL(M_t)	UCL(M_t)	EWMA
1	22.00	.027	.06	22.000	21.955	22.045	22.000
2	21.99	.016	.04	21.995	21.968	22.032	21.998
3	22.02	.026	.06	22.003	21.973	22.026	22.002
4	22.01	.042	.09	22.005	21.977	22.023	22.003
5	22.00	.039	.09	22.005	21.977	22.023	22.003
6	22.00	.026	.06	22.007	—	—	22.003
7	22.00	.053	.12	22.002	—	—	22.002
8	21.98	.028	.06	21.995	—	—	21.998
9	22.00	.026	.06	21.995	—	—	21.998
10	22.00	.022	.05	21.995	—	—	21.998
11	22.01	.026	.06	21.997	—	—	22.000
12	21.99	.013	.03	22.000	—	—	22.000
13	22.00	.024	.05	22.000	—	—	22.000
14	22.00	.033	.07	22.000	—	—	22.000
15	21.97	.018	.04	21.990	—	—	21.994
16	21.97	.017	.04	21.985	—	—	21.989
17	22.00	.013	.03	21.985	—	—	21.991
18	21.99	.035	.08	21.982	—	—	21.991
19	22.00	.019	.04	21.990	—	—	21.993
20	21.98	.021	.05	21.992	—	—	21.990
Mean	21.995	.026	.059				

It was noted above that even when the basic data are independent, M_t and M_{t+s} are independent only if $s \geq k$. To investigate the autocorrelation between M_t and M_{t+s}, we consider just the case for $t \geq k$. Then

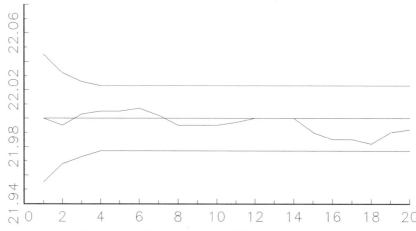

Figure 6.1   Moving Average Chart for Example 6.1

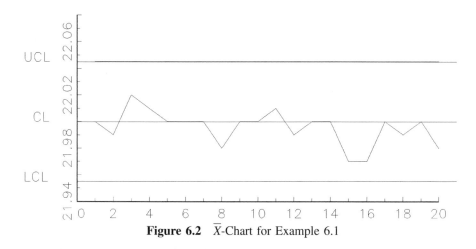

Figure 6.2 $\bar{X}$-Chart for Example 6.1

by direct algebraic manipulation we can show the result given in (6.1.6).

$$
\begin{aligned}
\text{Corr}(M_t, M_{t+s}) &\equiv \rho_{t,t+s} \\
&= 0 \quad \text{if } s \in \{k, k+1, \cdots\} \\
&= \frac{k-s}{k} \quad \text{if } s \in \{0, 1, \cdots, k-1\}
\end{aligned}
\tag{6.1.6}
$$

This shows that two values of a moving average with no common means have zero correlation and two that have $k - s$ common means

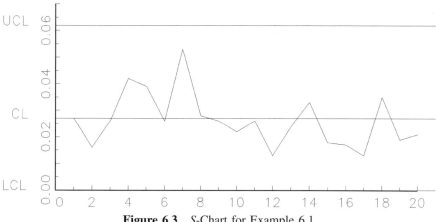

Figure 6.3 S-Chart for Example 6.1

have correlation $(k - s)/k$. For example, a moving average with $k = 12$ will have autocorrelation of $(12 - 1)/12 = 11/12 = 0.916$ between consecutive values M_t and M_{t+1}. This autocorrelation between elements of the sequence $M_t, M_{t+1}, \cdots$ causes this sequence to show nonrandom patterns of runs when plotted against the index. These effects appear as oscillations in the plots. Nelson (1983) has discussed this phenomenon in the quality literature. This is a principal reason why moving average plots are generally not used for stability studies to bring processes into control.

6.1.1 ARL and MA Chart Design

Due to the dependence of points, there is no simple exact relationship between the average run length, ARL, and the OC or power function of an MA chart, as there is for charts with independent points. The run length distribution cannot be taken to be an exact geometric distribution. Suppose we write the MA control limits as in (6.1.7).

$$UCL(M_t) = \mu_0 + K\,SD(M_t)$$
$$LCL(M_t) = \mu_0 - K\,SD(M_t)$$

(6.1.7)

where $SD(M_t)$ is obtained from (6.1.2). Assume that sample size n is constant. Then we need to consider choosing values for K for (6.1.7) and the span k, so that the moving average chart will be sensitive to detect small changes in the process mean. Suppose that we now consider the mean shifting from μ_0 to a new value $\mu_0 + \delta\sigma_{\bar{x}}$, where, of course, $\sigma_{\bar{x}} = \sigma_0/\sqrt{n}$. Then the chart with control limits (6.1.7) is determined by k and K, and we wish to choose these values so that the chart performs well, especially for small values of δ, say $\delta < 2$. A chart with $k = 12$, and $K = 2.7$ has been found to give good performance, and values of ARL for this chart are given in Table 6.2. The control limits for this chart are then:

$$\mu_0 \pm 0.78\sigma_{\bar{x}}$$

TABLE 6.2   ARL Values for MA Chart with $k = 12$, $K = 2.7$

δ	0.00	0.25	0.50	1.00	1.50	2.00	3.00	4.00	5.00
ARL	369.14	109.72	32.41	10.05	6.65	5.15	3.62	2.84	2.38
SE	0.70	0.24	0.12	0.015	0.006	0.004	0.003	0.003	0.004

The values in Table 6.2 were obtained by computer simulation. The values in the SE row are the estimated standard errors of the ARL estimates.

The ARL for this MA chart for $\delta = 0$ is approximately the same as for a 3-sigma $\bar{X}$-chart. However, this does not mean that the false alarm rates after short runs are exactly the same for these two charts. Due to the positive correlation of display (6.1.6), it cannot be claimed that the run length is a geometric distribution. However, it can be shown that it is approximately geometric; so the two ARLs are at least roughly comparable. The ARLs for small values of δ are much smaller than for an $\bar{X}$-chart. For example, the ARL($\delta = 0.5$) $\cong 32$, as compared with a value of 161 (see Table 4.4) for an $\bar{X}$-chart. However, for large values of δ (= 3, 4, 5) the $\bar{X}$-chart has smaller ARL than this MA chart. Thus, this MA chart gives better sensitivity for detecting small shifts in the process mean than an $\bar{X}$-chart, but poorer sensitivity for detecting large shifts, while maintaining roughly the same false alarm rates.

6.2 THE EXPONENTIALLY WEIGHTED MOVING AVERAGE (EWMA) CHART FOR A CLASSICAL STABLE PROCESS

The MA statistic of the last section assigns a weight of $1/k$ to each of the last k means. This weighting system has appeal for detecting a permanent shift of the process mean to a new value. However, if the mean can change in a continuous fashion, possibly due to related changes in environmental variables, or for other reasons, it may be desirable to chart a statistic that gives greater weight to more recent data.

Roberts (1959, 1966) proposed a chart using the geometric moving average, GMA, defined as

$$Z_t = \lambda \bar{X}_t + (1 - \lambda)Z_{t-1} \quad \text{for } t = 1, 2, \cdots \quad (6.2.1)$$

for $0 < \lambda \leq 1$, and Z_0 a starting value. By successive substitutions we can write

$$Z_t = \lambda \bar{X}_t + (1 - \lambda)\{\lambda \bar{X}_{t-1} + (1 - \lambda)Z_{t-2}\}$$
$$= \lambda \bar{X}_t + \lambda(1 - \lambda)\bar{X}_{t-1} + (1 - \lambda)^2\{\lambda \bar{X}_{t-2} + (1 - \lambda)Z_{t-3}\}$$

and, finally

$$Z_t = \lambda \sum_{i=0}^{t-1} (1 - \lambda)^i \overline{X}_{t-i} + (1 - \lambda)^t Z_0 \qquad (6.2.2)$$

[Aside: Recall that the sum of a geometric series is

$$1 + r + r^2 + \cdots + r^{t-1} = (1 - r^t)/(1 - r)$$

and thus the sum of the coefficients (weights) of the first term in (6.2.2) is

$$\lambda \sum_{i=0}^{t-1} (1 - \lambda)^i = \lambda\{[1 - (1 - \lambda)^t]/(1 - (1 - \lambda))]\} = 1 - (1 - \lambda)^t]$$

Because the weights in (6.2.2) decrease exponentially, the statistic Z_t is also called an *exponentially weighted moving average*—EWMA. These types of moving averages are useful for a number of different quality control problems. If the sequence of values (sample means here) are i.i.d. random variables, then the EWMA can be used to detect increases or decreases in the process mean, and to initiate corrective action when a shift is detected. This is the type of application that we consider in this section. In this application, the EWMA is a competitor to an $\overline{X}$-chart to trigger an adjustment to a process mean to keep it near a target value, that is, an SPA application. The EWMA chart in this application is much more sensitive for detecting small shifts of a process mean than an $\overline{X}$-chart using the 1-of-1 test; however, the $\overline{X}$-chart 1-of-1 test is more sensitive to detect large shifts in the process mean. In this regard the EWMA chart behaves similarly to an MA chart.

If μ is the process mean and σ^2 the process variance, we can write

$$E(Z_t) = \lambda \mu \sum_{i=0}^{t-1} (1 - \lambda)^i + (1 - \lambda)^t E(Z_0)$$

$$= \mu + (1 - \lambda)^t[E(Z_0) - \mu]$$

and $\qquad (6.2.3)$

$$\mathrm{Var}(Z_t) = \sigma^2_{\mathrm{EWMA}} = \frac{\lambda \sigma^2}{n} \frac{1 - (1 - \lambda)^{2t}}{2 - \lambda}$$

$$+ (1 - \lambda)^{2t} \mathrm{Var}(Z_0)$$

where the formula for the mean holds for all Z_0, but the variance formula assumes that Z_0 is independent of the sequence of means $\overline{X}_1$, $\overline{X}_2, \cdots$. Note that if $E(Z_0) = \mu$, then $E(Z_t) = \mu$ for all t. We consider the variance formula for two particular choices of the starting value Z_0.

First, when it is possible we shall start the process with Z_0 set equal to the target value τ of the process mean, which is a constant. If the nominal value of the process mean, namely μ_0, is equal to τ, then $E(Z_t) = \tau$ for all $t = 1, 2, \cdots$; which is the ideal value. Also, when Z_0 is a constant, the second term of the variance formula is zero. That is, for the starting value Z_0 a constant

$$E(Z_t) = \mu + (1 - \lambda)^t[Z_0 - \mu]$$

and

$$\text{Var}(Z_t) = \sigma_{\text{EWMA}}^2 = \frac{\lambda \sigma^2}{n} \frac{1 - (1 - \lambda)^{2t}}{2 - \lambda}$$

(6.2.4)

Note that σ_{EWMA} for this case is an increasing function of t. It may sometimes be desirable to start the process by putting $Z_0 = \overline{X}_1$ and define Z_t by (6.2.1). For this case we can then write

$$Z_t = \lambda \sum_{i=0}^{t-1} (1 - \lambda)^i \overline{X}_{t-i} + (1 - \lambda)^t \overline{X}_1$$

$$= \lambda \sum_{i=0}^{t-2} (1 - \lambda)^i \overline{X}_{t-i} + (1 - \lambda)^{t-1} \overline{X}_1$$

and from this we obtain formulas for the mean and variance as follows:

$$E(Z_t) = \mu \left(\lambda \sum_{i=0}^{t-2} (1 - \lambda)^i + (1 - \lambda)^{t-1} \right)$$

$$= \mu$$

and

(6.2.5)

$$\text{Var}(Z_t) = \sigma_{\text{EWMA}}^2$$

$$= \frac{\sigma^2}{n(2 - \lambda)} [\lambda + 2(1 - \lambda)^{2t-1}]$$

For this case σ_{EWMA} is a decreasing function of t. In all cases, as t becomes large, the mean and variance of Z_t converge to constants given in (6.2.6).

$$\lim_{t \to \infty} E(Z_t) = \mu,$$

$$\lim_{t \to \infty} \text{Var}(Z_t) = \sigma_{\text{EWMA}}^2 = \frac{\lambda \sigma^2}{n(2 - \lambda)}$$

(6.2.6)

Thus, for given $\mu = \mu_0$ and $\sigma = \sigma_0$, the 3-sigma asymptotic control limits for Z_t are

$$UCL(Z_t) = \mu_0 + 3\,\sigma_{\text{EWMA}}$$

$$= \mu_0 + 3\,\sigma_0 \sqrt{\frac{\lambda}{n(2 - \lambda)}}$$

$$UCL(Z_t) = \mu_0 + 3\,\sigma_{\text{EWMA}}$$

$$= \mu_0 - 3\,\sigma_0 \sqrt{\frac{\lambda}{n(2 - \lambda)}}$$

(6.2.7)

If the values of μ and σ are not known, then they must be estimated in order to use these formulas. From (6.2.2), observe that the weights for the sample means $\overline{X}_t, \overline{X}_{t-1}, \ldots$ are

$$w_{t-i} = \lambda(1 - \lambda)^i \quad \text{for } i = 0, 1, \ldots$$

Note that the most recent mean $\overline{X}_t$ always receives a weight of λ and that the preceding means receive weights that decrease exponentially in value. For example, for $\lambda = 0.20$ these weights are: 0.200, 0.160, 0.128, 0.102, 0.082, 0.066, 0.052, 0.042, 0.034, 0.027, 0.021, $\cdots$; while for $\lambda = 0.5$ these weights are 0.500, 0.250, 0.125, 0.063, 0.031, 0.016, 0.008, $\cdots$. Also, note that a large λ gives more weight to recent means, while a small λ gives more weight to older means.

Example 6.2: We construct an EWMA chart with $\lambda = 0.20$ for the problem given in Example 6.1 using the data of Table 6.1. Putting $Z_0 = \mu_0 = 22.00$ gives

$$Z_1 = \lambda \bar{X}_1 + (1 - \lambda) Z_0 = (0.2)(22.00) + (.8)(22.00) = 22.000$$

$$Z_2 = \lambda \bar{X}_2 + (1 - \lambda) Z_1 = (0.2)(21.99) + (.8)(22.00) = 21.998, \text{ etc.}$$

(See the last column in Table 6.1.)

From (6.2.7) and using σ_{EWMA} from (6.2.4) we compute 3-sigma limits

$$UCL(Z_t) = 22.000 + (3)(0.030) \sqrt{\frac{0.2[1 - (.8)^{2t}]}{(1.8)(4)}}$$

$$= 22.000 + 0.015 \sqrt{1 - .8^{2t}}$$

$$UCL(Z_1) = 22.009, \quad LCL(Z_1) = 21.991,$$

$$UCL(Z_2) = 22.012, \quad LCL(Z_2) = 21.988$$

$$UCL(Z_3) = 22.013, \quad LCL(Z_3) = 21.987,$$

$$UCL(Z_4) = 22.014, \quad LCL(Z_4) = 21.986$$

and the limiting values using (6.2.6) for large t are

$$UCL(Z_t) = 22.015, \quad LCL(Z_t) = 21.985$$

The reader should note the similarity of the patterns of points in Fig. 6.1 and 6.4. Both charts are weighted averages of the sample means before and including $\bar{X}_t$, so similar behavior is to be expected. ∎

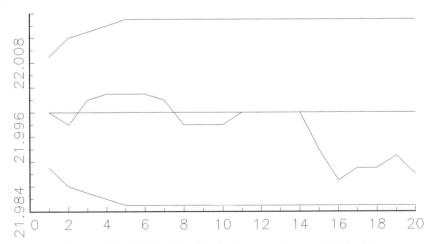

Figure 6.4 EWMA Plot for the Sample Means of Table 6.1

As was the case for the MA chart, the points on the EWMA chart are dependent and patterns are difficult, or impossible, to interpret.

6.2.1 Designing an EWMA Chart to Control ARL

In the discussion of EWMA charts thus far we have considered λ to be a given value. Of course, in practice, a value for λ must be selected. In this subsection we will present a method due to Crowder (1987a, 1987b, 1989) for selecting λ and designing EWMA charts. The control limits are expressed in terms of a nominal value μ_0 of the mean, the variance σ^2_{EWMA} given for different cases above, and a design constant K that is used as shown in display (6.2.8).

$$
\begin{aligned}
UCL(Z_t) &= \mu_0 + K\,\sigma_{\text{EWMA}} \\
LCL(Z_t) &= \mu_0 - K\,\sigma_{\text{EWMA}}
\end{aligned}
\tag{6.2.8}
$$

The chart is determined—designed—by the choice of the smoothing parameter λ and the constant K. The run length distribution is approximately geometric, and the ARL is usually used as a criterion for chart performance. Crowder (1987a) gave an algorithm for evaluating the ARL as a function of λ and K for a chart with the limit expressed in the form of (6.2.8). A version of this algorithm is given on the Q-Charts disk. Crowder (1989) suggested a method for designing an EWMA chart that follows the approach recommended by Lucas and Saccucci (1990). We are concerned with detecting a shift from a nominal value μ_0 of the mean to a new value $\mu_0 + \delta\sigma_{\bar{x}}$. This approach to designing an EWMA chart is set out as a four-step procedure as follows.

Steps to Design an EWMA Chart

1. Choose the smallest acceptable level of ARL when there is no shift ($\delta = 0$) in the process mean.
2. Decide what magnitude of shift δ is most important to detect quickly and is to have a specified ARL value for this shift. Then choose λ which produces a minimum ARL for that value. This choice can be made by reference to Figs. 6.5 and 6.6, which give approximately optimal values for a range of selected values of false alarm ARLs.

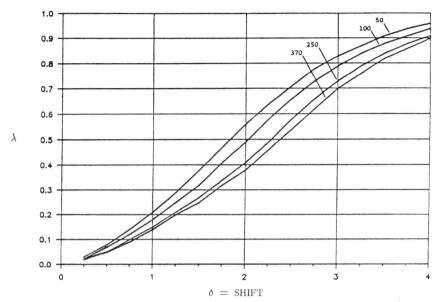

Figure 6.5 Optimal λ's for EWMA Charts, ARLs 50, 100, 250, 370 (© 1989 Re-produced with permission from the American Society for Quality Control)

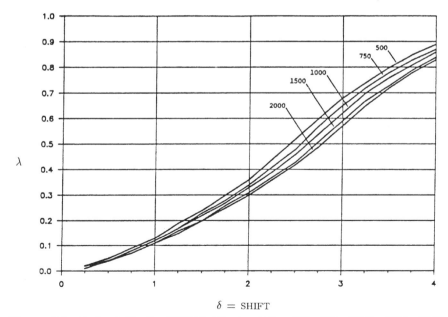

Figure 6.6 Optimal λ's for EWMA Charts, ARLs 500, 750, 1000, 1500, 2000 (© 1989 Reproduced with permission from the American Society for Quality Control)

3. Using the λ determined in step 2, find a value of K which satisfies the ARL constraint of step 1. This choice can be made using Figs. 6.7 and 6.8, which give values of K corresponding to λ for selected values of ARL(0).

4. Study the behavior of the chosen values by comparing the out-of-control ARLs for a net of values of (λ, K) giving the ARL(0) value chosen in step 1. This is called a *sensitivity analysis* and was suggested in a paper by Robinson and Ho (1978).

Example 6.3: We illustrate the four-step procedure by designing a chart with ARL(0) $\cong$ 370 and with minimum ARL for $\delta = 1.5$.

Step 1. The desired in-control false alarm rate is ARL(0) = 370.

Step 2. From Fig. 6.5, the optimal value of λ for a shift of $\delta = 1.5$ is $\lambda = 0.25$.

Step 3. Given $\lambda = 0.25$, Fig. 6.7 gives $K = 2.9$.

Step 4. Table 6.3 shows the "sensitivity analysis." ARLs are given for $\lambda = 0.20, 0.25$, and 0.30; and the required value of K to make ARL(0) approximately 370. The value $\lambda = 0.25$ gives the approximately minimum value of ARL(1.5). Note that when $\delta\ (> 0)$ is less than this value 1.5, for which the ARL is minimized, then ARL is an increasing function of λ, and when δ is greater than 1.5 the ARL is

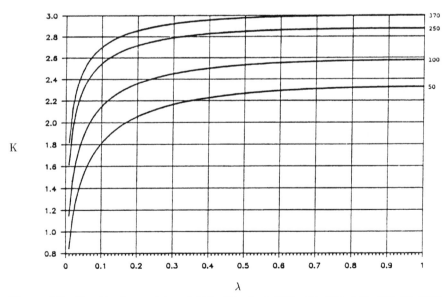

Figure 6.7   Combinations of λ and K for Nominal ARLs 50, 100, 250, 370 (© 1989 Reproduced with permission from the American Society for Quality Control)

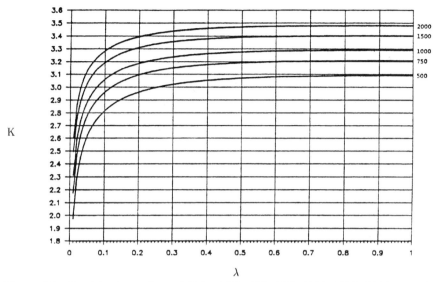

Figure 6.8 Combinations of λ and K for ARLs 500, 750, 1000, 1500, 2000 (© 1989 Reproduced with permission from the American Society for Quality Control)

a decreasing function of λ. These values were computed using the Q-Charts disk. ∎

We observe that there is a weak point in this approach to designing an EWMA control chart. This approach requires us to choose one value of $\delta > 0$ and optimize the chart for detecting a shift of this particular magnitude. However, there is not usually a particular value of δ that is more important than all others, and we may prefer a chart with good

TABLE 6.3 Sensitivity Analysis for Example 6.3

δ	(λ, K)		
	(0.20, 2.86)	(0.25, 2.90)	(0.30, 2.925)
0	371.10	372.56	370.39
0.25	121.22	136.13	149.09
0.50	36.20	41.26	46.54
1.00	9.80	10.27	10.90
1.50	5.23	5.18	5.21
2.00	3.59	3.47	3.39
3.00	2.31	2.19	2.09
4.00	1.81	1.67	1.55
5.00	1.41	1.27	1.18

overall or omnibus sensitivity for detecting shifts over a fairly wide range of magnitudes of shifts. EWMA charts do have good sensitivity for detecting a range of small shifts, especially for $\delta \leq 2$.

To help users find an EWMA chart that gives the optimal, or near optimal, EWMA performance to detect a shift of δ less than two, we give a few values δ, λ K, ARL($\delta = 0$) and ARL(δ) in Table 6.4. A particular chart can be selected from this table. Note that the ARL($\delta = 0$) values are all approximately 370.

Recall that δ here is the shift from $\mu = \mu_0$ to $\mu = \mu_0 + \delta\sigma_{\bar{X}} = \mu_0 + \delta\sigma/\sqrt{n}$. Thus, the ARL values in the last row of Table 6.4 can be compared to the values in the first row ($n = 1$) of Table 4.4 for the 1-of-1 test on an $\bar{X}$-chart for the same values of δ. For example, the classical 3-sigma $\bar{X}$-chart for $\delta = 0.5$ has ARL(0.5) = 161, while the EWMA has ARL(0.5) = 26.5.

Example 6.4: A process has nominal process mean of $\mu_0 = 1.5$ and standard deviation of $\sigma_0 = 0.1$. The following table gives the means, Z_t's, and so on, of ten samples of size $n = 5$ each. The computations to obtain these values are illustrated below.

t:	1	2	3	4	5
$\bar{X}_t$:	1.49	1.51	1.60	1.52	1.56
Z_t:	1.496	1.502	1.546	1.534	1.546
σ_{EWMA}:	0.020	.023	.024	.024	.024
UCL:	1.56	1.57	1.57	1.57	1.57
LCL:	1.44	1.43	1.43	1.43	1.43

t:	6	7	8	9	10
$\bar{X}_t$:	1.53	1.49	1.50	1.59	1.61
Z_t:	1.539	1.517	1.509	1.545	1.574
σ_{EWMA}:	.024	.024	.024	.024	.024
UCL:	1.57	1.57	1.57	1.57	1.57
LCL:	1.43	1.43	1.43	1.43	1.43

TABLE 6.4   A Selection of EWMA Charts with ARL($\delta = 0$) $\cong$ 370

δ:	0.25	0.50	0.75	1.00	1.25	1.50	1.75	2.00
λ:	0.02	0.05	0.08	0.15	0.20	0.24	0.33	0.37
K:	2.13	2.49	2.64	2.80	2.86	2.89	2.94	2.95
ARL(δ):	66.5	26.5	14.8	9.6	6.8	5.2	4.1	3.4

(a) Use the Crowder procedure to design an EWMA chart for these means with ARL of 370 when there is no shift in the process mean—that is, $\mu = \mu_0 = 1.5$—and with the best sensitivity for detecting a shift in the mean from 1.5 to 1.6.

(b) Compute the control limits and the geometric moving averages for this chart using a starting value of $Z_0 = 1.5$.

Solution:

(a) With $n = 5$ and $\sigma_0 = 0.1$ we have $\sigma_{\bar{x}} = \sigma_0/\sqrt{n} = 0.1/\sqrt{5} \cong$ 0.045. Therefore we have

$$\delta\sigma_{\bar{x}} = 1.6 - 1.5 \quad \text{or} \quad 0.045 \, \delta = .1 \Rightarrow \delta = 2.2$$

Reading Fig. 6.5 with $\delta = 2.2$ gives $\lambda \cong 0.45$. Reading Fig. 6.7 with ARL = 370 and $\lambda = 0.45$ gives $K \cong 2.9$. The Q-Charts disk gives ARL($\mu = 1.5$) = 298. Since this value is well below the required value of 370, we run a few slightly larger values of K and find that (λ, K) = (0.45, 2.97) gives ARL($\mu = 1.5$) = 370.7. We will use these values of λ and K. The sensitivity analysis in Table 6.5 shows that ARL($\mu = 1.6$ or $\delta = 2.2$) = 2.90 is the local minimum value.

(b) We will use $Z_0 = \mu_0 = 1.5$, a constant value; thus from (6.2.4) we have

TABLE 6.5   Sensitivity Analysis for Example 6.4

μ	δ	(μ, K) (.35, 2.945)	(.4, 2.96)	(.45, 2.97)	(.50, 2.978)
1.500	0.00	371.0	371.6	370.7	370.6
1.489, 1.511	0.25	162.0	174.4	185.4	196.2
1.477, 1.523	0.50	52.4	58.6	64.9	71.7
1.455, 1.545	1.00	11.7	12.7	13.9	15.2
1.433, 1.568	1.50	5.31	5.48	5.70	6.00
1.410, 1.590	2.00	3.35	3.35	3.37	3.42
1.401, 1.599	2.20	2.94	2.91	2.90	2.91
1.365, 1.635	3.00	2.01	1.95	1.89	1.85
1.320, 1.680	4.00	1.46	1.39	1.34	1.30
1.275, 1.725	5.00	1.13	1.10	1.07	1.06

$$\sigma_{EWMA} = \sigma_0 \sqrt{\frac{\lambda[1 - (1 - \lambda)^{2t}]}{n(2 - \lambda)}} = 0.1 \sqrt{\frac{0.45[1 - 0.55^{2t}]}{(5)(1.55)}}$$

$$= 0.024 \sqrt{1 - 0.55^{2t}}$$

These values are computed and given in the table above. Note that the limiting value of (6.2.6) is reached (to 3 digits) at $t = 3$. From (6.2.8) the control limits are

$$UCL(t = 1) = \mu_0 + K\sigma_{EWMA} = 1.5 + (2.97)(.020) = 1.56, \text{ etc.}$$

$$LCL(t = 1) = \mu_0 - K\sigma_{EWMA} = 1.5 - (2.97)(.020) = 1.44, \text{ etc.}$$

Computing values of Z_t from (6.2.1), with $Z_0 = \overline{X}_1$, we obtain

$$Z_1 = \lambda \overline{X}_1 + (1 - \lambda)Z_0 = (0.45)(1.49) + (0.55)(1.5) = 1.496$$

etc., to $Z_{10} = (0.45)(1.61) + (.55)(1.545) = 1.574$, see above table.

Comparing the values in the above table, we see that Z_{10} is too large, signaling an increase in the process mean. We note also that the control limits of a classical 3-sigma $\overline{X}$-chart are $\mu_0 \pm 3\sigma_0/\sqrt{n} = 1.5 \pm (3)(0.1)/\sqrt{5} = 1.5 \pm 0.13$ or UCL $= 1.63$ and LCL $= 1.37$, so that none of the means are significant for this chart, which is comparable since it also has ARL($\mu = 1.5$) $= 370$. ∎

In section 4.12 we saw that controlling ARL does not reliably control the false alarm rate after short runs for the case of Shewhart charts with estimated control limits, due to the dependence of signaling events. Since the EWMA statistics Z_t for $t = 1, 2, \cdots$ are also dependent, the question arises as to whether ARL is a reliable coefficient of EWMA chart performance. However, Crowder (1987b) has given results that suggest that the in-control run length distribution of an EWMA chart computed from statistics that are themselves nominally independent normal statistics is approximately a geometric distribution. However, it should be noted that this result depends on the assumption that the nominal values μ_0 and σ_0 are known. In practice, unless the estimates of these parameters are based on large samples, taken while the process is stable, the approximate geometric distribution of run lengths may not hold.

6.3 CUMULATIVE SUM (CUSUM) CHARTS

Shewhart charts for parameters have, as we have remarked before, relatively poor sensitivity for detecting small changes in the parameters, at least when the sample size is one of the commonly used values of 4 or 5, and only the 1-of-1 test of Fig. 4.9 is used. The moving average and geometric moving average charts studied in the last two sections were introduced because they use more of the data for each plotted point and have greater sensitivity for detecting small shifts of the process mean. The cumulative sum (CUSUM) chart, due to Barnard (1959), that we consider next also has better sensitivity than classical Shewhart charts to detect small monotone mean shifts. The CUSUM chart detects changes in the process mean by accumulating the sum of deviations of the observed sample means $\overline{X}_1, \cdots, \overline{X}_t$ from a reference value. We define the cumulative sum function about a *reference value* k at time t as

$$S_t = \sum_{i=1}^{t} (\overline{X}_i - k)$$

If the sample means are from a stable process with process mean μ, then

$$E(S_t) = (\mu - k)t$$

So the cumulative sum has a mean that is a linear function of t that passes through the origin and has a slope of $(\mu - k)$. If $\mu = k$ the slope is zero; if $\mu > k$ the slope is positive, and if $\mu < k$ the slope is negative. These observations are helpful in interpreting the patterns of points on a graph of the points (t, S_t) for $t = 1, 2, \cdots$. Thus, if $\mu = k$ the points should be scattered about zero, whereas if $\mu > k$ the points should show an upward trend and for $\mu < k$ a downward trend.

If the values (t, S_t) are plotted on a chart we can examine it to decide if one of these trends is present, but such a procedure is rather subjective. Two general methods have been developed for making objective decisions as to when significant increasing or decreasing trends are present in CUSUM charts. Barnard (1959) proposed the use of a V-*mask* chart. Charts called *decision interval* or *numerical charts* have also been developed and are especially well suited for use with modern automated gauging and control systems. In the following development, we show the relationship of the V-mask scheme to the numerical chart, but we will illustrate only the decision interval chart.

6.3.1 The CUSUM V-Mask Chart or Graphical Test

The CUSUM V-mask is overlaid on a graph of the points (t, S_t) as illustrated in Fig. 6.9. The vertex is pointing forward parallel to the t-axis with the most recent point a *lead distance d* from the vertex, and the sides of the mask at an *angle θ* with the horizontal. Each time a new point is obtained, the mask is moved forward. When a point falls outside the mask, a signal is given that the mean has increased (lower leg) or the mean has decreased (upper leg). The lead distance d and the angle θ determine the mask. The two-sided test can be operated as two simultaneous one-sided tests. To do so we define θ^+, d^+, θ^-, and d^-, and operate the two branches separately. We consider first one-sided CUSUM tests, and two-sided tests will be made as two simultaneous one-sided tests.

When a shift in the process mean is signaled by having a point fall outside a V-mask leg, we can obtain a crude estimate of the shift in the process mean as follows. Suppose the nominal mean is μ_0. From the chart we decide which point was the first observed after a mean shift, and then fit an eyeball line to the set of points consisting of this point and its successors. If ϕ_1 is the angle that this line makes with the horizontal, then since $\tan \phi_1$ is the slope of the line after the shift and $\mu_0 - k$ was the slope before the shift, the estimated mean shift is $\delta = \tan \phi_1 - (\mu_0 - k)$.

We consider first the V-mask chart for standardized values of the sample means. Put

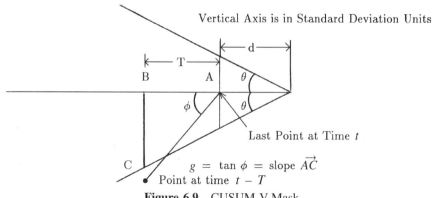

Figure 6.9   CUSUM V-Mask

$$q_t = \frac{\overline{X}_t - \mu_0}{\sigma_{\overline{x}}}, \quad t \in \{1, 2, 3, \cdots\} \tag{6.3.1}$$

Consider the V-mask as shown in Fig. 6.9. The last point plotted, at time t, is at A. Let T denote the number of points plotted from C to A, so that T is the length of the line $\overrightarrow{BA}$. Then the slope g of the line connecting the points plotted at times t and $t - T$ (in units of standard deviations per observation) is

$$g = \tan \phi \tag{6.3.2}$$

The V-mask test will signal on point t if

$$g = \tan \phi > \frac{\overrightarrow{CB}}{\overrightarrow{BA}} \tag{6.3.3}$$

or, in terms of the V-mask parameters, a signal is given when

$$g = \tan \phi > \frac{(T + d) \tan \theta}{T} \tag{6.3.4}$$

But this is for any value of $T \in \{1, 2, \cdots, t\}$, so that a signal occurs when at least one of the slopes over a span of T points exceeds $\{(T + d) \tan \theta\}/T$ for $T \in \{1, 2, \cdots, t\}$. That is, a signal occurs if one of the sums: $q_t, q_t + q_{t-1}, \cdots, q_t + q_{t-1} + \cdots + q_3 + q_2 + q_1$ exceeds $(T + d) \tan \theta$. In summation notation, a signal occurs at time t if

$$\sum_{j=0}^{T-1} q_{t-j} > (T + d) \tan \theta, \quad \text{for some } T \in \{1, \cdots, t\}$$

or, rewriting this we see that the process is out of control at time t if

$$\sum_{j=0}^{T-1} (q_{t-j} - \tan \theta) > d \tan \theta \tag{6.3.5}$$

for at least one value of $T \in \{1, 2, \cdots, t\}$.

6.3.2   The Decision Interval or Numerical CUSUM Test

In some applications it is convenient to have a numerical version of the CUSUM chart which can be applied directly without need to construct the V-mask. Today many potential applications involve automated gauging and computer control of processes where such a numerical procedure is particularly needed. In the following we use the relation (6.3.5) to establish a numerical procedure equivalent to the V-mask scheme. Define process parameters k_s and h_s in terms of θ and d as follows.

$$k_s = \tan \theta, \quad \theta = \tan^{-1} k_s \qquad (6.3.6)$$

$$h_s = d \tan \theta, \quad d = h_s / k_s$$

The value k_s is called the *reference value* and h_s is called the *decision interval*. Both k_s and h_s are expressed in units of measurement that are standard deviations of the observations. In other words, these two constants are in the same units of measurement as the q_t's.

To define a two-sided test we will make two simultaneous one-sided tests. Recall that the values θ and d in (6.3.6) are for charts from the q_t's, and this is why we label the corresponding values k_s and h_s with the subscript "s"—to emphasize that they are for *standard units*. We denote the reference values and decision intervals for these two tests by k_s^+, k_s^-, h_s^+, and h_s^-. Then the test is made using statistics S^+ and S^- given by

$$
\begin{aligned}
S_t^+(q) &= \text{Max}\{0,\ S_{t-1}^+ + q_t - k_s^+\} \\
S_t^-(q) &= \text{Min}\{0,\ S_{t-1}^- + q_t + k_s^-\}
\end{aligned}
\qquad (6.3.7)
$$

where $S_0^+ = S_0^- = 0$. We note that k_s^- is actually the absolute value of the reference value for testing for a decrease in the mean. The points (t, S_t^+) and (t, S_t^-) can be plotted on a chart with horizontal lines drawn at h_s^+ and $-h_s^-$, and a signal given when either S_t^+ exceeds h_s^+ or S_t^- is less than $-h_s^-$. After a signal, the sums S_t^+ and S_t^- are reset to 0. However, note that for computerized systems the plotted chart is unnecessary. A symmetric two-sided test has $h_s^- = h_s^+ = h_s$, say; and $k_s^+ = k_s^- = k_s$, say. We will consider using a nomograph or computer algorithm to evaluate h_s^+, h_s^-, k_s^+, and k_s^- in the following subsection.

TABLE 6.6 **Computations for a Standardized CUSUM Chart with:** $k_s^+\ k_s^-\ =$ 0.5, $h_s^+\ =\ h_s^-\ =\ 3.5$

t	q_t	$q_t - k_s^+$	$q_t + k_s^-$	S_t^+	S_t^-
1	-0.5	-1.0	0	0	0
2	1.2	0.7	1.7	0.7	0
3	3.5	3.0	4.0	3.7	0
4	2.8	2.3	3.3	6.0	0
5	-2.3	-2.8	-1.8	3.2	-1.8

Example 6.5: To illustrate the use of the formulas in display (6.3.7), consider the data in Table 6.6, which illustrates the computation of the cumulative sum statistics $S_t^+(q)$ and $S_t^-(q)$. Both of these values are shown plotted in Fig. 6.10. ■

In practice we sometimes prefer to work with the sample mean $\overline{X}_t$ rather than the standardized variable q_t discussed above. Then we require reference values k^+ and k^- and decision intervals h^+ and h^- for cumulative sums for these charts. To study the relationship between these values and those for the standardized values, substitute for q_{t-j} in the inequality (6.3.5) to obtain

$$\sum_{j=0}^{T-1} \left(\frac{\overline{X}_{t-j} - \mu_0}{\sigma_{\overline{x}}} - \tan \theta_s \right) > d_s \tan \theta_s$$

where d_s and θ_s denote the lead distance and angle of the V-mask chart

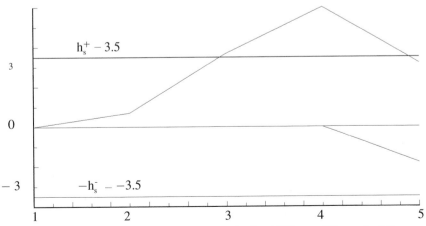

Figure 6.10 CUSUM Chart for Standardized Values of Example 6.5

for standardized values. Now, the lead distance d does not depend on the vertical scale, so that it is the same for equivalent charts based on q_t and $\overline{X}_t$. Rewrite the last inequality in the form

$$\sum_{j=0}^{T-1} [\overline{X}_{t-j} - (\mu_0 + \sigma_{\overline{x}} k_s)] > d \, \sigma_{\overline{x}} k_s = \sigma_{\overline{x}} h_s$$

By using the relation $d = h_s/k_s$, we can read values for k^+ and h^+ from this inequality. These values and those for k^- and h^-, obtained by a similar argument, are given in (6.3.8).

$$
\begin{array}{l}
k^+ = \mu_0 + \sigma_{\overline{x}} k_s^+, \; h^+ = \sigma_{\overline{x}} h_s^+ \\[2mm]
k^- = \mu_0 - \sigma_{\overline{x}} k_s^-, \; h^- = \sigma_{\overline{x}} h_s^-
\end{array}
\qquad (6.3.8)
$$

These relations can also be obtained by noting that h_s^+ and h_s^- are simply scale transformations of h^+ and h^-, while k_s^+ and k_s^- are standardized versions of k^+ and k^-. That is

$$k_s^+ = \frac{k^+ - \mu_0}{\sigma_{\overline{x}}}, \quad -k_s^- = \frac{k^- - \mu_0}{\sigma_{\overline{x}}}$$

$$h_s^+ = \frac{h^+}{\sigma_{\overline{x}}}, \quad h_s^- = \frac{h^-}{\sigma_{\overline{x}}} \qquad (6.3.9)$$

The test statistics are given by the formulas:

$$S_t^+(\overline{X}) = \text{Max}\{0, S_{t-1}^+ + \overline{X}_t - k^+\} \qquad (6.3.10)$$

$$S_t^-(\overline{X}) = \text{Min}\{0, S_{t-1}^- + \overline{X}_t - k^-\} \qquad (6.3.11)$$

where $S_0^+ = S_0^- = 0$. These statistics are plotted against t with upper and lower decision limits at h^+ and $-h^-$.

Example 6.6: Table 6.7 illustrates using the formulas (6.3.10) and (6.3.11) to compute S_t^+ and S_t^-. The numerical CUSUM chart for this data is shown in Fig. 6.11. ∎

To choose values of the constants k^+ and k^-, we specify a value μ_a of the mean that is the *acceptable quality level* (AQL) and another

TABLE 6.7   Means and Computations for Example 6.6

t	$\bar{x}_t$	$\bar{x}_t - k^+$	$\bar{x}_t - k^-$	S_t^+	S_t^-
1	12.07	−0.30	0.17	0.00	0.00
2	11.98	−0.12	0.08	0.00	0.00
3	11.90	−0.20	0.00	0.00	0.00
4	12.02	−0.08	0.12	0.00	0.00
5	12.19	0.09	0.29	0.09	0.00
6	12.06	−0.04	0.16	0.05	0.00
7	12.09	−0.01	0.19	0.04	0.00
8	11.81	−0.29	−0.09	0.00	−0.09
9	12.10	0.00	0.20	0.00	0.00
10	12.11	0.01	0.21	0.01	0.00
11	12.02	−0.08	0.12	0.00	0.00
12	12.18	0.08	0.28	0.08	0.00
13	12.17	0.07	0.27	0.15	0.00
14	12.22	0.12	0.32	0.27	0.00
15	12.03	−0.07	0.13	0.20	0.00
16	12.21	0.11	0.31	0.31	0.00
17	12.01	−0.09	0.11	0.22	0.00
18	12.07	−0.03	0.17	0.19	0.00
19	12.07	−0.03	0.17	0.16	0.00
20	12.12	0.02	0.22	0.18	0.00
	$\mu_0 = 12.00$	$k^+ = 12.10$	$k^- = 11.90$	$h^+ = 0.28$	$-h^- = -0.28$

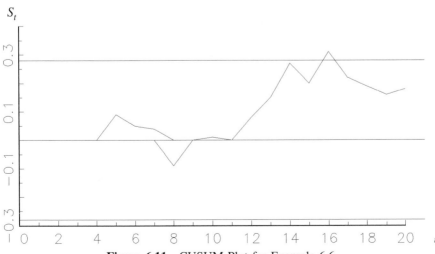

Figure 6.11   CUSUM Plot for Example 6.6

value, either $\mu_r^+ > \mu_a$ or $\mu_r^- < \mu_a$, that is the *rejectable quality level* (RQL). The value μ_r^+ is the RQL for the mean μ too large and μ_r^- is the RQL for the mean too small. The reference value in each case is usually taken as the midpoint between μ_a and the RQL. That is, we usually take

$$k^+ = \frac{\mu_a + \mu_r^+}{2}, \quad k^- = \frac{\mu_a + \mu_r^-}{2} \qquad (6.3.12)$$

The corresponding value for the standardized test is, from (6.3.9) with $\mu_a = \mu_0$,

$$k_s^+ = \frac{\mu_r^+ - \mu_a}{2\sigma_{\bar{x}}}, \quad k_s^- = \frac{\mu_a - \mu_r^-}{2\sigma_{\bar{x}}} \qquad (6.3.13)$$

In the formulas (6.3.8) the nominal value μ_0 is the same as the AQL = μ_a in the last formulas. We next consider using a nomogram to evaluate k_s and h_s and use the above relations to evaluate k and h.

6.3.3 The CUSUM ARL Function

We proceed as follows to use ARL as a criterion to determine values of the control parameters for a CUSUM scheme. First, we specify a value μ_a that we consider to be an *acceptable quality level* (AQL), a value μ_r that is just barely tolerable, and any value more extreme from μ_a in the same direction is rejectable, μ_r is called the *rejectable quality level* (RQL). The ARLs when $\mu = \mu_a$ and $\mu = \mu_r$ are denoted by L_a and L_r, respectively.

Kemp (1962) gave a nomogram that relates L_a and L_r to the quantities k_s and h_s. Kemp's nomogram is given in Fig. 6.12. The Q-Charts disk has an algorithm that computes L_a and L_r for given values of k_s and h_s. This algorithm is due to Vance (1986). If a two-sided scheme is made up of a scheme to detect increases in μ with ARL of $L^+(\mu)$ and one to detect decreases in μ with ARL of $L^-(\mu)$, then the ARL function $L(\mu)$ for the combined two-sided scheme is related to the ARLs for the one-sided schemes by

$$\frac{1}{L(\mu)} = \frac{1}{L^+(\mu)} + \frac{1}{L^-(\mu)} \qquad (6.3.14)$$

Example 6.7: Given that a process has standard deviation $\sigma = 0.015$ mm, we wish to have AQL $= \mu_a = 26.193$ mm, RQL $= \mu_r = 26.203$ mm, $L_a^+ = 500$, and $L_r^+ = 6$ for the one-sided control scheme. Design a numerical CUSUM scheme for this problem.

Solution: From Fig. 6.12 we read

$$k_s^+ = 0.66 \quad \text{and} \quad h_s^+ = 3.5$$

As a check we run these values in the Q-Charts algorithm and find that they give values of $L_a = 526$ and $L_r = 5.98$. Running $k_s^+ = 0.66$ and $h_s^+ = 3.47$ gives the closer values $L_a = 505$ and $L_r = 5.93$, so we will use these values. From (6.3.8) we obtain

$$k^+ = \frac{\mu_a + \mu_r}{2} = \mu_a + \frac{\sigma}{\sqrt{n}} k_s^+$$

and for this example

$$k^+ = 26.198 = 26.193 + \frac{(0.015)}{\sqrt{n}}(0.66)$$

Solving for n gives $n = 3.92$. We round up to the nearest integer and take $n = 4$. Then we have

$$h^+ = \sigma_{\bar{x}} h_s = \frac{\sigma}{\sqrt{n}} h_s = \frac{(0.015)}{2}(3.47) = 0.026$$

Thus the numerical CUSUM for sample means is defined by

$$n = 4, \quad k^+ = 26.198, \quad \text{and} \quad h^+ = 0.026$$

We next construct the ARL function $L(\mu)$ for this one-sided scheme. In addition to the values

$$L(26.193) = 505 \quad \text{and} \quad L(26.203) = 5.93$$

on the ARL chart, we can readily obtain additional values from the Q-Charts algorithm. To compute values of $L^+(\mu)$ we consider pairs of values of μ that are equally spaced above and below k^+, that is, values

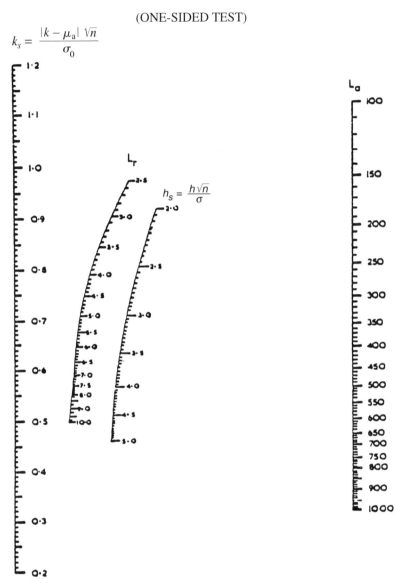

Figure 6.12 Kemp's nomogram for numerical CUSUM Parameters (© 1962: Reproduced from *Applied Statistics* with permission from The Royal Statistical Society)

at points $k^+ \pm i \times d$, for $i = 0, 1, 2, 3, \cdots$. Note that d is a spacing increment on the μ axis for plotting the ARL(μ) curve. The interval of most interest for plotting the curve will generally be from AQL of μ_a (= 26.193 here) to RQL of μ_r^+ (= 26.198 here). Therefore, we should evaluate $L(\mu)$ for μ taking at least eight values in the interval $[\mu_a, \mu_r^+]$. For this example, we put $d = (\mu_r^+ - \mu_a)/10 = (26.203 - 26.193)/10 = 0.001$. To evaluate $L(\mu)$ at $\mu = k^+ \pm i \times d$ we put

$$k_{s,i}^+ = \frac{k^+ - (k^+ - i \times d)}{\sigma_{\overline{X}}} = \frac{i \times d}{\sigma_{\overline{X}}}$$

$$= \frac{0.001i}{0.015/2} = 0.133i \quad \text{for } i = 0, 1, \cdots, 8.$$

We then use the values $(h_s^+, k_{s,i}^+)$ to obtain values of $L(k^+ - i \times d)$ and $L(k^+ + i \times d)$ either from Kemp's nomogram, when possible, or from an algorithm such as that given in Q-Charts. For example, for $i = 1$ we obtain $L^+(\mu = 26.197) = 33.5$ and $L^+(\mu = 26.199) = 15.0$. Other values for $i = 0, 2, 3, \cdots, 8$ are given in Table 6.8.

Next, suppose that we decide to operate the CUSUM chart as a two-sided test using the values above in the formulas (6.3.10) and (6.3.11). Then the ARLs will be determined from (6.3.14). Now, $L^+(\mu_a) = L^-(\mu_a)$, so that

$$L(\mu_a) = \left(\frac{1}{L^+(\mu_a)} + \frac{1}{L^-(\mu_a)} \right)^{-1} = \frac{L^+(\mu_a)}{2}, \text{ always,}$$

and here $L(\mu_a = 26.193) = L^+(26.193)/2 = 505/2 = 252$. To evaluate $L^-(\mu)$ for $\mu > \mu_a$, say $\mu = \mu_a + d$, and $d > 0$, then $L^-(\mu = \mu_a + d) = L^+(\mu_a - d)$. For example, $L^-(26.194) = L^+(26.192) = 1257$, from Table 6.7, and some of the ARLs for the symmetric two-sided scheme are

TABLE 6.8 Values of ARL Function for One-Sided CUSUM of Example 6.7, $k^+ = 26.198$

i	id	$\mu = k^+ - id$	h_s^+	k_s^+	$L^+(\mu = k^+ - id)$	$\mu = k^+ + id$	$L^+(\mu = k^+ + id)$
8	0.008	26.190	3.47	1.07	8314	26.206	3.98
7	0.007	26.191	3.47	0.93	3068	26.205	4.48
6	0.006	26.192	3.47	0.80	1257	26.204	5.08
5	0.005	26.193	3.47	0.66	505	26.203	5.9
4	0.004	26.194	3.47	0.53	230	26.202	7.0
3	0.003	26.195	3.47	0.40	112	26.201	8.6
2	0.002	26.196	3.47	0.27	60	26.200	10.9
1	0.001	26.197	3.47	0.13	33.5	26.199	15.0
0	0.000	26.198	3.47	0.00	21.5	26.198	21.5

$$L(26.194) = \left(\frac{1}{230} + \frac{1}{1257}\right)^{-1} \cong 194,$$

$$L(26.195) = \left(\frac{1}{112} + \frac{1}{3068}\right)^{-1} \cong 108,$$

$$\text{and } L(26.196) = \left(\frac{1}{60} + \frac{1}{8314}\right)^{-1} \cong 60$$

Table 6.9 gives the ARL values for this symmetric two-sided CUSUM chart. ∎

Example 6.8: As a second example, suppose we design a CUSUM chart to compete with the EWMA chart derived in Example 6.3 with $(\lambda, k) = (0.25, 2.90)$ and ARL(δ) given for selected values of δ in Table 6.3. That EWMA chart was designed for optimum performance to detect a shift of $\delta = 1.5$. For simplicity, we take $\mu_a = 0$, $\mu_r = 1.50$, and $\sigma_{\bar{x}} = 1$. We require $L_a = 740$ and $L_r = 5.18$. Then $k^+ = 0.75$ and we summarize the computations for the one-sided chart in Table 6.10, and from this chose $h_s^+ = 3.34$ and $k_s^+ = 0.75$. Note that here d is the actual deviation rather than a shift interval. The ARLs for the two-sided test are given in Table 6.11.

By comparing the values in Table 6.11 with those of the EWMA chart given in Table 6.3 for $(\lambda, K) = (0.25, 2.90)$, we see that the EWMA chart has slightly better performance for small values of δ and slightly worse performance for values of δ larger than 1.5. ∎

Example 6.9: Consider designing a CUSUM chart for the process described in Example 6.4 that is comparable to the EWMA chart with $(\lambda, K) = (0.45, 2.97)$ of that example. That is, we wish to design a

TABLE 6.9 Values of the ARL Function for Two-Sided CUSUM of Example 6.7, $k = 26.198$

$\mu = k - id$	h_s	k_s	$L(\mu = k - id)$	$\mu = k + id$	$L(\mu = k + id)$
26.190	3.47	1.07	60	26.206	3.98
26.191	3.47	0.93	108	26.205	4.48
26.192	3.47	0.80	194	26.204	5.08
26.193	3.47	0.66	252	26.203	5.9
26.194	3.47	0.53	194	26.202	7.0
26.195	3.47	0.40	108	26.201	8.6
26.196	3.47	0.27	60	26.200	10.9
26.197	3.47	0.13	33.5	26.199	15.0
26.198	3.47	0.00	21.5	26.198	21.5

TABLE 6.10 Computations of One-Sided ARL Function for Example 6.8, $k^+ = 0.75$

d	h_s^+	k_s^+	$k^+ - d$	$L^+(k^+ - d)$	$k^+ + d$	$L^+(k^+ + d)$
4.25	3.34	4.25	-3.50	(huge)	5.00	1.18
3.25	3.34	3.25	-2.50	(huge)	4.00	1.55
2.25	3.34	2.25	-1.50	(huge)	3.00	2.09
1.25	3.34	1.25	-0.50	22,524	2.00	3.39
1.00	3.34	1.00	-0.25	3,879	1.75	4.09
0.75	3.34	0.75	0	741	1.50	5.18
0.50	3.34	0.50	0.25	169	1.25	7.07
0.25	3.34	0.25	0.50	50	1.00	10.88
0.00	3.34	0.00	0.75	20.3	0.75	20.30

CUSUM chart for $\mu_a = 1.5$, $\mu_r = 1.6$, $L_a \cong (2)(370.7) = 741.4$, and $L_r \cong 2.90$. Using these values and Kemp's nomogram we read $h_s \cong 2.25$ and $k_s \cong 1.1$. Now, since $n = 5$ is given we cannot require both equations (6.3.8) and (6.3.12) to necessarily hold, because we would have two equations to solve for one free variable. However, here we obtain

$$k^+ = (1.5 + 1.6)/2 = 1.55 \quad \text{and}$$

$$k_s^+ = (k^+ - \mu_a)/\sigma_{\bar{X}} = \frac{0.05}{0.045} = 1.1,$$

so we will use these values of k^+ and k_s^+. From the algorithm we find that $(h_s^+, k_s^+) = (2.28, 1.1)$ give $L_a = 741$ and $L_r = 2.80$. Therefore we will use these values. This gives a chart defined by

$$n = 5, \ k^+ = 1.55, \ h^+ = \sigma_{\bar{X}} h_s^+ = (0.045)(2.28) = 0.103.$$

For a symmetric chart $h^- = h^+$ and $k^- = \mu_a - \sigma_{\bar{X}} k_s^- = 1.50 - 0.05 = 1.45$.

For selected deviations d from k^+, that give values of μ comparable to those in Table 6.5, we compute values for the one-sided chart in Table 6.12. The ARLs for the symmetric two-sided chart are given in Table 6.13.

TABLE 6.11 Two-Sided ARL Function for Example 6.8

δ:	0	0.25	0.50	0.75	1.00	1.50	2.00	3.00	4.00	5.00
ARL(δ):	370.5	162	50	20.3	10.9	5.18	3.39	2.09	1.55	1.18

TABLE 6.12   One-Sided Test ARLs for $n = 5$, $h^+ = 0.103$, $k^+ = 1.1$ CUSUM Chart

d	$k^+ - d$	$k^+ + d$	h_s^+	$k_s^+ = d/0.045$	$L(k^+ - d)$	$L(k^+ + d)$
.073	1.477	1.623	2.28	1.622	10408	2.05
.061	1.489	1.611	2.28	1.356	2659	2.37
.050	1.500	1.600	2.28	1.111	782	2.78
.039	1.511	1.589	2.28	0.867	246	3.38
.027	1.523	1.577	2.28	0.600	78.3	4.42
.005	1.545	1.555	2.28	0.111	15.5	9.35
.000	1.550	1.550	2.28	0.000	11.9	11.9

$$L(\mu = \mu_a = 1.5) = \frac{782}{2} = 391,$$

$$L(1.489) = L(1.511) = (2659^{-1} + 246^{-1})^{-1}$$

$$= 225, \text{ and so on.}$$

6.4   SUMMARY

The MA, EWMA, and CUSUM charts studied in this chapter are likely to be most useful for monitoring a process in order to retain control of a nominally stable process. They may also be used to decide when to adjust a process mean to reduce EMS about a target value τ. These charts have better sensitivity than Shewhart $\overline{X}$ and X-charts to detect small shifts in a mean, that is, for shifts less than, roughly, two standard deviations of the subgroup means. However, classical Shewhart charts for a normal mean are generally more useful for stability studies to find special causes and bring a process into a state of control, because they permit us to recognize many types of anomalous point patterns other than just monotone parameter shifts.

TABLE 6.13   Two-Sided Test ARLs

μ	$L(\mu)$	μ	$L(\mu)$
.1477	82	1.555	9.35
1.489	225	1.577	4.42
1.500	391	1.589	3.38
1.511	225	1.600	2.78
1.523	78	1.611	2.37
1.545	15.5	1.623	2.05
1.550	11.9		

There are also versions of these three types of charts for controlling parameters other than a normal process mean. However, we do not present these methods here. Some alternative EWMA and CUSUM type charts will be presented in later chapters.

The MA, EWMA, and CUSUM charts are competing charts to detect small shifts in a normal process mean. Roberts (1966) gave simulation results, which have been extended by other writers, that indicate that these three charts are competitive among themselves. The choice among the three is largely a matter of personal preference. We tend to prefer the EWMA chart, largely because we feel it is easy to design, understand, and apply; is particularly appealing to detect continuous monotone change in a mean, which we suspect is present in many processes; and has other important applications when some of the i.i.d. assumptions are not tenable, which we will consider in Chapter 13.

PROBLEMS

6.1 The values in the following table are the sample means for samples of size $n = 4$ from a process with nominal process mean of $\mu_0 = 12.00$ oz and standard deviation of $\sigma_0 = 0.092$ oz.

(a) Make a moving average (MA) chart for this data using $k = 12$ and $K = 2.7$.

(b) Plot the ARL(μ) curve for this MA chart to detect a shift of the process mean μ from $\mu_0 = 12.00$ oz to a new value of $\mu = 12.00 + d$ for $d = 0, 0.0115, 0.023, 0.046, 0.069, 0.092, 0.138, 0.184, 0.230$. (See Table 6.2.)

t:	1	2	3	4	5	6
$\bar{X}_t$:	11.979	12.033	11.909	12.019	12.009	12.048

t:	7	8	9	10	11	12
$\bar{X}_t$:	12.011	11.986	12.055	11.977	12.085	12.022

t:	13	14	15	16	17	18
$\bar{X}_t$:	12.061	12.024	12.042	11.964	12.025	12.082

t:	19	20	21	22	23	24
$\bar{X}_t$:	11.981	12.055	12.098	12.080	12.102	12.039

6.2 (a) Use the Crowder procedure to design an EWMA chart for the means in problem 6.1 with an ARL of 370 when there is no shift in the mean, and designed to have best control (minimum ARL) for detecting a shift to a mean value of 12.069.

    (b) Plot an EWMA chart using λ and K found in part (a). Use $Z_0 = \bar{X}_1$.

    (c) Use the Crowder algorithm to evaluate the $\text{ARL}(\mu)$ function and plot the $\text{ARL}(\mu)$ curve for $d = 0, 0.0115, 0.023, 0.046, 0.069, 0.092, 0.138, 0.184, 0.230$. Compare this curve with the curve obtained in problem 6.1(b).

6.3 For the problem described in problem 6.1, choose AQL $= \mu_a = 12.00$ and RQL $= \mu_r = 12.059$.

    (a) For these values design a numerical one-sided CUSUM scheme with approximate run lengths of $L_a = 741$ and L_r as close to 6 as possible. Recall that sample size of $n = 4$ was set in problem 6.1.

    (b) If the control parameters obtained in part (a) are used for both sides of a symmetric two-sided CUSUM control scheme, plot the ARL curve for this two-sided scheme.

    (c) Use the sample means given in problem 6.1 to plot a CUSUM chart using the values of k and h obtained in part (a).

6.4 A process has standard deviation of $\sigma = 0.1$ and we wish to choose AQL $= \mu_a = 10$, and RQL $= \mu_r = 10.08$.

    (a) Design a numerical one-sided CUSUM scheme with approximate run lengths $L_a = 700$, and $L_r = 5$. Compute values of the $\text{ARL}(\mu)$ function for $\mu = 9.99(0.01)10.09$ for this one-sided scheme.

    (b) If the same control parameters are used for both sides of a two-sided control scheme as those obtained in part (a), compute the $\text{ARL}(\mu)$ function for $\mu = 9.99(0.01)10.09$ for this two-sided scheme.

6.5 The following sample means are from samples of size $n = 5$ from a process with mean of 8.00 in and standard deviation of 0.10 in.

    (a) Use the Crowder procedure to design an EWMA chart with $\text{ARL}(\delta = 0) = 100$, and with the smallest possible ARL to detect a shift of the mean to 8.00 ± 0.022. Use the limiting value of $\text{Var}(Z_t)$ as $t \rightarrow \infty$.

    (b) Make an S^2 Shewhart chart with 0.98 probability limits to study the stability of the process variance.

(c) Make an EWMA chart using the results found in part (a) to study the stability of the process mean. Discuss your results.

Sample Number	$\bar{x}$	s^2
1	8.022	.01757
2	7.974	.00383
3	7.950	.00395
4	7.982	.00297
5	8.072	.01252
6	8.064	.00388
7	8.122	.00317
8	8.060	.00985
9	8.160	.00425
10	8.164	.00628
11	8.132	.00732
12	8.068	.01937

6.6 It is required to design an EWMA control chart when $n = 4$, in-control ARL $= 100$, and we are interested in having the shortest possible run length to detect a shift of two standard deviations of the mean of the distribution of the sample mean.

(a) Find "optimal" values for λ and k to satisfy these conditions. Do a sensitivity analysis to demonstrate the behavior of the ARL function near your "optimal" values.

(b) If the nominal value of the process mean is $\mu_0 = 10$, and the process standard deviation is $\sigma = 0.04$, compute the limiting values of UCL and LCL as $t \to \infty$.

6.7 A process has $\sigma = 0.03$, and we wish to have AQL $= 15.00$, RQL $= 15.04$, $L_a = 370$, and $L_r = 3$.

(a) Design a numerical CUSUM chart for this problem.

(b) Evaluate the ARL(μ) function of the scheme in part (a) for $\mu = 15.00(0.005)15.04$.

(c) Suppose a symmetric two-sided chart is operated using the values of n, k^+, and h^+ found in part (a). For this two-sided scheme evaluate $L(15.00)$, $L(15.05)$, and $L(14.95)$.

6.8 Verify the mean and variance formulas given in equations (6.2.5).

CHAPTER 7

Q-Charts for Variables

In this chapter we present a general approach to SPC charting that has been developed by the author. The charts considered are particular types of Shewhart, EWMA, and CUSUM charts. Those for controlling a process mean involve charting certain types of residuals from the classical constant means model of (4.1.2). These are flexible charting methods that permit the treatment of some important process control problems for which no analytically valid method was available before these were introduced. The material of this chapter is largely from Quesenberry (1991a, 1995a).

7.1 SOME CONSIDERATIONS IN USING CLASSICAL CHARTS FOR VARIABLES

7.1.1 Potential for Improvement

In Chapter 4 we considered the methodology of classical Shewhart charts for variables. However, there are some important applications where the assumptions on which these methods are based are clearly not satisfied, and this results in difficulties in using these methods. The classical Shewhart charts technology was largely developed for applications in parts manufacturing industries. In these high-volume manufacturing operations, the need to obtain large calibration data sets before actual charting operations can begin may not be a significant barrier to applications, because production runs are often very large, often in the thousands, or much larger. However, in all industries there are important work processes for which production runs are too short to permit valid applications of classical SPC methods. This is surely an important reason why SPC applications have not been developed in many important industries. Industries that have seen little or no development of applications of SPC technology include: most service industries including education, financial institutions such as banks, insurance and investment companies; food production and processing industries such as the poultry, beef, dairy, and other food animal production and processing industries; lumber and other materials producing industries; mining; transportation; and medicine. The SPC charting methods presented in this and the following chapters have the potential to permit the introduction of these powerful SPC techniques for improving work processes in these and many other business and industrial operations where they have had scant or no applications, as well as to improve the effectiveness of SPC applications in settings where they have long been in use.

7.1.2 The Problem of Nonconstant Control Limits

Recall that in section 4.3 a generic statistic W was used to introduce classical Shewhart charts, and that for a stable process the statistic W is assumed to have a constant or fixed distribution. In particular, the mean and variance of W are assumed to be constant for a process that is stable or in control. If $\mathrm{Var}(W_i)$ varies with i, for the sequence W_1, $\cdots$, W_i, $\cdots$ of values to be plotted, the control limits of (4.3.1) will also vary with i. One important circumstance when $\mathrm{Var}(W_i)$ will vary is, for subgroups data, when the subgroup size n is not constant; and in some applications it is inconvenient or impossible to keep a constant sample size. If the sample size n varies from sample to sample, then the control limits for $\overline{X}$, S, and R will also vary from sample to sample. Some writers propose plotting and using these varying control limits; however, we feel that this is a bad practice for the following reasons.

If the only use of the control chart is to compare each individually plotted point with its control limits, then there is not a problem with using varying control limits. However, especially in process stabilization applications, much of the usefulness of a Shewhart chart lies in the ability to recognize patterns of points. In a pattern the magnitudes of the individual points of the pattern are being compared. But with varying control limits *the points are plotted in different standard deviation scales,* and it is difficult or impossible to interpret patterns. As a simple example to illustrate the problem, consider the four points in Fig. 7.1. Note that even though the first and third plotted points are above the second and fourth points on the graph, *they are actually smaller values,* that is, they are closer to the center line as measured by their own (different) standard deviations. This inconstancy of standard deviation scales destroys the ability to interpret patterns. Nelson (1989) has also discussed this problem in interpreting charts with nonconstant control limits.

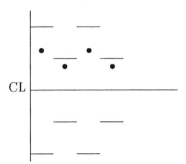

Figure 7.1 Points Plotted with Varying Control Limits

7.1.3 Nonnormal Distributions of the Plotted Statistics

Another problem with the 3-sigma charts is that for nonnormal statistics such as S and R the limits are crudely determined, especially for small values of n. There are no lower control limits for 3-sigma S- or R-charts for $n < 6$, even when the process distribution is itself normal, and therefore they have no ability to detect decreases in σ. The problem of having no lower control limit can be avoided, of course, by using probability limits as given in (4.4.9) for S. However, as discussed in the last paragraph of section 4.7, these S- and R-charts, even with probability limits, have poor sensitivity to detect decreases in σ.

7.1.4 Problems Charting with Low-Volume Production and Short Runs

Another consideration in using classical Shewhart charts is that these charts assume a high volume of production units. In order to compute control limits, we must accumulate quite a lot of data to estimate the process mean and variance in order to calculate control limits. The usual recommendation is that we should have 25 or 30 samples of size 4 or 5 to estimate the parameters. This requires roughly 100 or more observations before we can actually start charting. However, as we observed in section 4.11, even this much data does not assure good determinations of control limits for the $\overline{X}$- and S-charts. Also, even while these base-line data are being gathered, the process is probably running without any attempt to exercise process control. Now, it clearly would be advantageous to be able to chart a process from start-up in order, especially in the case of Stage 1 studies, to try to bring it into a stable, in-control state as early as possible, and save wasting production units. In Quesenberry (1991a, b, and c) an approach was proposed for charting both variables and attributes data from start-up in real time sequentially as data become available. Statistics that are computed sequentially and have known distributions when a process is stable are plotted to study the stability of a process.

Another problem appears when production is in a series of short runs—say no more than a few hundred production units, and possibly fewer than 100. Then, in view of our discussion in section 4.11, there will not be enough data to compute control limits for classical Shewhart charts. The development of product-oriented manufacturing layouts that use production flow control and just-in-time (JIT) delivery systems (cf. Suzaki, 1987) requires more short runs of components and assemblies than did classical mass production. Some writers have suggested replacing the process mean and standard deviation by their respective specification target values in order to chart short runs. This is sometimes called the "standards" approach to short runs. We feel that using specification target values for parameters to establish control limits is a mistake of the same kind as Deming (1986, p. 333) and others have warned against in using specification limits for control limits. The problem is that when a signal is obtained on such a chart it is not possible to know whether the signal is due to an unstable process, that is, a varying parameter, or whether it is due to using an incorrect parameter value to compute the control limits. In some cases, this will result in increased numbers of false alarms and time and expense spent searching for assignable causes that may not exist. In other cases, this will result in charts that are insensitive for detecting parameter shifts.

In this chapter we present a general approach to constructing control charts that can be helpful with the problems sketched in this section, and sometimes have other advantages. This approach entails transforming statistics to be plotted into exactly or approximately independently and identically distributed standard normal random variables that can be plotted in standard normal scale. This approach to charting can give economies in a number of ways.

Since all charts are in the same standard normal scale, it is possible to simplify the charts management program. Different quality variables can be plotted on the same chart, which may not only save in the number of required charts, but also may be helpful in interpretations. Even different statistics, say $\bar{X}$ and S, perhaps, can be plotted on the same chart. Since all statistics are plotted in the same standardized normal scale, the training programs for personnel at all levels are simplified.

7.2   INTRODUCTION TO NORMALIZED STATISTICS AND Q-CHARTS

Consider again a statistic W_i which we wish to chart in order to study the stability of a process or to monitor the value of a process parameter. As discussed in section 7.1, if the values of W_i are plotted on a chart with control limits at $E(W_i) \pm 3\ SD(W_i)$, then this charting procedure works moderately well if the distribution of W_i is at least approximately constant, and especially well if the distribution is constant and approximately normal. For many statistics W_i it is possible to transform a sequence W_1, W_2, $\cdots$ to a sequence Q_1, Q_2, $\cdots$ which are exactly or approximately independently and identically distributed as standard normal random variables, that is, to independent $N(0, 1)$ random variables. In this chapter, we consider ways to transform variables to obtain control charts for some of the more common problems. In Chapter 8 we will consider normalized charts for attributes. The charts that we propose will be referred to as Q-charts.

For statistics W_i that are themselves normally distributed, we only require the usual standardizing transformation, that is, subtract the mean and divide by the standard deviation. However, if W_i is not at least approximately normally distributed, then a nonlinear transformation is required. We propose here a general approach to these problems that utilizes the probability integral transformation—which will be discussed in Chapter 9. Suppose the statistic W_i has a distribution function G_i that is completely known and let Φ^{-1} denote the inverse of the standard normal distribution function. The transformation required to transform the sequence W_1, W_2, $\cdots$ to a sequence Q_1, Q_2, $\cdots$ of standard normal random variables is given in display (7.2.1).

$$
\boxed{
\begin{array}{l}
\text{Let} \\[4pt]
\qquad u_i = G_i(W_i) \\[6pt]
\qquad Q_i = \Phi^{-1}(u_i) \qquad \text{for } i = 1, 2, \cdots
\end{array}
}
\qquad (7.2.1)
$$

To transform the sequence of statistics W_1, W_2, $\cdots$ when the distribution functions are not completely known but depend on unknown parameters, we will propose methods that permit the estimation of the transforming function from the current data sequence and give a sequence Q_1, Q_2, $\cdots$ of values that are either exactly or approximately independent standard normal random variables. The actual computing and charting of these transformed statistics requires the use of at least a PC class computer, in most problems. However, algorithms are readily written and PCs are widely available in American business and industry today. All of the charts in this book have been made with algorithms written by the author. A menu-operated program designed especially to produce the charts described in this book is commercially available (see the tear-out page at the end of this book).

Since all of the Q-charts are for statistics expressed in a standard normal scale, it is convenient for many purposes to use a standardized chart which is the same for all Q-statistics. We will use a standardized Shewhart Q-chart form similar to those of Fig. 4.9 on which lines are drawn at ± 1, ± 2, and ± 3. This will make it convenient to apply runs rules such as those of Fig. 4.9, if desired.

If probability limits are desired, they can be computed as follows. Since the Q_1, Q_2, $\cdots$ are independent standardized normal random variables, the (α_L, α_U) probability limits are given in display (7.2.2), for q_α the upper α^{th} fractile of the standard normal distribution.

$$
\begin{aligned}
UCL(Q_i) &= q_{\alpha_U} \\
CL(Q_i) &= 0 \\
LCL(Q_i) &= -q_{\alpha_L}
\end{aligned}
\tag{7.2.2}
$$

7.3   Q-CHARTS FOR A NORMAL PROCESS, SUBGROUPED DATA

We consider now samples as in Table 7.1 that are observed in sequence and the ith sample has n_i observations for $i = 1, 2, \cdots$.

TABLE 7.1   Sample Subgroups and Statistics Notation

Sample				Sample Mean	Sample Variance
X_{11}	X_{12}	$\cdots$	X_{1n_1}	$\overline{X}_1$	S_1^2
X_{21}	X_{22}	$\cdots$	X_{2n_2}	$\overline{X}_2$	S_2^2
$\vdots$	$\vdots$		$\vdots$	$\vdots$	$\vdots$
X_{i1}	X_{i2}	$\cdots$	X_{in_i}	$\overline{X}_i$	S_i^2

Put

$$\overline{\overline{X}}_i = \frac{n_1 \overline{X}_1 + \cdots + n_i \overline{X}_i}{n_1 + \cdots + n_i},$$

and

$$S_{p,i}^2 = \frac{(n_1 - 1)S_1^2 + \cdots + (n_i - 1)S_i^2}{n_1 + \cdots + n_i - i}$$

Note particularly that the *sequential* mean $\overline{\overline{X}}_i$ and *pooled* variance $S_{p,i}^2$ are sequential statistics that estimate μ and σ^2 utilizing all of the information when the ith sample is available. The reason for using this weighted average of the sample means to estimate μ rather than the simple unweighted average is because the weighted average has a smaller variance (see Appendix 7A). An unbiased estimator of σ is then $\tilde{\sigma} = \dfrac{S_{p,i}}{c_4}$, where c_4 is for sample size $n_1 + n_2 + \cdots + n_i - i + 1$. This sample size is usually large enough to make c_4 approximately 1 (see Table A.5).

The Q-statistics for the sample mean $\overline{X}_i$ to control μ are given in the following for the four possible cases of knowledge about the parameters μ and σ.

Q-Statistics from Sample Means

Case *KK:* $\mu = \mu_0$, $\sigma = \sigma_0$, both known.

$$Q_i(\overline{X}_i) = \frac{\sqrt{n_i}\,(\overline{X}_i - \mu_0)}{\sigma_0} \qquad i = 1, 2, \cdots \qquad (7.3.1)$$

Case *UK:* μ unknown, $\sigma = \sigma_0$ known.

$$Q_i(\overline{X}_i) = \sqrt{\frac{n_i(n_1 + \cdots + n_{i-1})}{n_1 + \cdots + n_i}} \left(\frac{\overline{X}_i - \overline{\overline{X}}_{i-1}}{\sigma_0} \right)$$
$$i = 2, 3, \cdots \qquad (7.3.2)$$

Case *KU:* $\mu = \mu_0$ known, σ^2 unknown.

$$Q_i(\overline{X}_i) = \Phi^{-1} \left[H_{n_1 + \cdots + n_i - i} \left(\frac{\sqrt{n_i}\,(\overline{X}_i - \mu_0)}{S_{p,i}} \right) \right]$$
$$i = 1, 2, \cdots \qquad (7.3.3)$$

Case *UU:* μ unknown, σ unknown.

$$Q_i(\overline{X}_i) = \Phi^{-1}\left\{H_{n_1+\cdots+n_i-i}\right.$$

$$\left[\sqrt{\frac{n_i(n_1 + \cdots + n_{i-1})}{n_1 + \cdots + n_i}}\left(\frac{\overline{X}_i - \overline{\overline{X}}_{i-1}}{S_{p,i}}\right)\right]\right\} \quad (7.3.4)$$

$$i = 2, 3, \cdots$$

These sequences of Q-statistics for cases *KK, UK,* and *UU* are sequences of independently and identically distributed standard normal random variables, $N(0, 1)$, under the stable or in-control normality assumptions, and are approximately so for many other process distributions. A proof of this for (7.3.4) will be given in Appendix 7B. The statistics for case KU are normally distributed, $N(0, 1)$, and approximately independent. For this case see the discussion in Quesenberry (1995e).

The Q-statistics for the sample variance for the cases when the process variance is known and when it is unknown with data from samples as set out in Table 7.1 are as follows.

Q-Statistics from Sample Variances

Case *K:* $\sigma = \sigma_0$ known.

$$Q_i(S_i^2) = \Phi^{-1}\left\{G_{n_i-1}\left[\frac{(n_i - 1)S_i^2}{\sigma_0^2}\right]\right\}, \qquad i = 1, 2, \cdots \quad (7.3.5)$$

Case *U:* σ unknown.

Put

$$w_i = \frac{(n_1 + \cdots + n_{i-1} - i + 1)S_i^2}{(n_1 - 1)S_1^2 + \cdots + (n_{i-1} - 1)S_{i-1}^2} = \frac{S_i^2}{S_{p,i-1}^2},$$

$$i = 2, 3, \cdots$$

and

$$Q_i(S_i^2) = \Phi^{-1}[F_{n_i-1,n_1+\cdots+n_{i-1}-i+1}(w_i)],$$

$$i = 2, 3, \cdots$$
$$(7.3.6)$$

Under the assumption that the values in sample i are independent observations from $N(\mu_i, \sigma^2)$ distributions, the Q_i statistics of both (7.3.5) and (7.3.6) are sequences of independent normal $N(0, 1)$ random variables. This result will be demonstrated in Appendix 7B.

7.3.1 The $Q(\overline{X})$-Chart, μ and σ Both Known, Case KK

In this case we assume that the $\overline{X}_i$'s are independently and approximately normally distributed with known mean μ_0 and standard deviation of $\sigma_0/\sqrt{n_i}$. The assumption of approximate normality is reasonable due to the central limit theorem. The $Q_i(\overline{X})$ statistic is then given by (7.3.1). Note that the chart for this case is essentially the same as the classical $\overline{X}$-chart with known parameters studied in Chapter 4. The transformation is just the linear standardizing transformation and only changes the scale in which $\overline{X}$ is plotted.

Example 7.1: Measurements are taken on the production units made during five-minute intervals four times a day. The sample size varies and it was decided to use Q-charts for both sample means and variances. The process mean is given as 12.00 and the process variance is given as 0.0004. The sample means and variances and other computations are shown in Table 7.2. The standardized control chart for the process mean is shown in Fig. 7.2. Note that point 13 is beyond the 3-sigma control limit, and if test 5 of the tests of Fig. 4.9—for 2-out-of-3 beyond a 2-sigma line—is applied that point 19 signals for two points below the lower 2-sigma line. It is pretty apparent from these two signals and the pattern of points that an increase in process variance has occurred at about the 13th point. We will also see this clearly in the $Q(S^2)$-chart discussed below for this data. ∎

Recall that (α_L, α_U) probability limits were given in display (7.2.2). The plotted quantities Q_i are in units of measurement that are standard deviations of a normal distribution and, of course, are *not* the units of measurement in which the sample measurements were made. The fact that the plotted Q_i values are not in the original units of measurement is sometimes considered a disadvantage, because a graph may be more readily interpreted by some users if it is plotted in the original units of measurement of the data. However, it should be pointed out that it has long been common practice to rescale data before it is plotted, simply to give numbers that are easier to work with. Indeed, as will be considered in some detail in Chapter 10, most gauges give data in a transformed scale, so most QC operators are accustomed to dealing with transformed data.

TABLE 7.2 Data for Standardized Charts of Example 7.1

Sample Number, i	Sample Size, n_i	$\bar{X}$	S^2	$Q(\bar{X}) = \dfrac{\sqrt{n_i}(\bar{X} - 12)}{0.02}$	$\dfrac{(n_i - 1)S^2}{0.0004}$	u_i	$Q(S^2) = \Phi^{-1}(u_i)$
1	5	12.018	0.00032	2.01	3.20	0.475	-0.06
2	6	11.990	0.00028	-1.22	3.50	0.331	-0.44
3	3	12.003	0.00043	0.29	2.17	0.662	0.42
4	4	11.995	0.00030	-0.50	2.25	0.461	-0.09
5	3	12.004	0.00046	0.32	2.32	0.687	0.49
6	5	11.998	0.00032	-0.18	3.16	0.469	-0.07
7	10	11.990	0.00033	-1.50	7.46	0.393	-0.27
8	8	11.993	0.00042	-1.01	7.44	0.598	0.25
9	6	12.003	0.00099	0.39	12.43	0.968	1.85
10	7	12.007	0.00036	0.93	5.33	0.498	-0.01
11	7	12.000	0.00006	0.04	0.96	0.013	-2.23
12	5	11.999	0.00067	-0.09	6.79	0.853	1.05
13	8	12.024	0.00029	3.46	5.09	0.314	-0.48
14	4	12.014	0.00039	1.42	2.91	0.554	0.14
15	6	12.010	0.00039	1.24	4.92	0.536	0.09
16	5	12.008	0.00188	0.92	18.83	0.99781	2.85
17	6	11.982	0.00209	-2.24	26.25	0.99992	3.78
18	7	12.021	0.00132	2.76	19.74	0.99692	2.74
19	9	11.985	0.00062	-2.22	12.48	0.86896	1.12
20	4	12.009	0.00106	0.90	7.93	0.93810	1.54

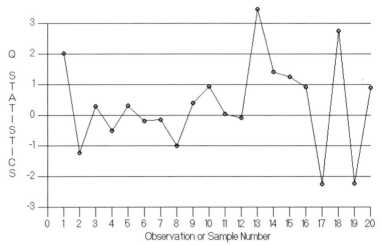

Figure 7.2   Shewhart $Q(\overline{X})$-Chart for Example 7.1

As mentioned above, another advantage of using standardized normal charts is that all the tests for patterns discussed in section 4.5, as well as many others that can be customized for particular processes, can be readily applied. It will be seen in later developments that for some important patterns this capability to make tests other than the classical 1-of-1 test on a Shewhart Q-chart, with known false alarm rates, is quite important. Also, charts for different variables and statistics can be, if desired, plotted on the same chart. In Chapter 8, Q-statistics for attributes will also be given for the problems of controlling parameters from binomial, Poisson, and geometric distributions. Q-statistics will also be given for other problems in later chapters. These Q-charts permit us to standardize much of our control charting methodology.

7.3.2   The $Q(S^2)$-Chart, σ Known

When sample size is not constant, the classic S and R 3-sigma charts will also have varying control limits. In addition, since S and R are positive random variables with skewed distributions, the classic ± 3-sigma control limits are crude, especially for small sample sizes. Indeed, as we have noted earlier, for small sample sizes ($n < 6$) the formulas give zero for a lower control limit due to the crudeness of the 3-sigma formula for *LCL*. We consider next a Q-chart for σ^2 based on the sample variance S^2. By assuming that the measurements in the samples are normally distributed, we consider transforming the sample variance S_i^2 to a Q-statistic. The formula for $Q(S^2)$ for this case is given in (7.3.5). Recall that $G_\nu(\cdot)$ is the distribution function of a chi-squared distribution with ν degrees of freedom and Φ^{-1} is the inverse of the standard normal distribution function.

These $Q_i(S^2)$ values can be plotted on a standardized Q-Chart like that of Fig. 7.2 or one with probability limits given by (7.2.2). Note, particularly, that these are control charts for σ. The $Q(S^2)$ chart for the data of Example 7.1 is given in Fig. 7.3. The values plotted are given in the last column of Table 7.2. We are interested in studying the stability of σ, and in detecting both increases in σ, which will be reflected by values of Q that are too large, and decreases in σ, which will be reflected in values of Q that are too small. Of course, it is important to detect an increase in σ because it means that there has been an increase in variability and a decline in quality. However, it is also important to be able to detect decreases in σ. As quality improvement programs are implemented on processes to recognize and eliminate or reduce the effects of common causes, it is useful to have analytical evidence of the positive effects for the positive psychological reinforcement of personnel. It may also aid in convincing management that the effort and expenses are bearing fruit in the form of improved quality. Moreover, it could happen that either by serendipity, or otherwise, some samples are taken under conditions for which the process variance is smaller than nominal. If this is true, then it would be desirable to have a charting program that would signal such an occurrence. Such information could be valuable in reducing the overall variability of the pro-

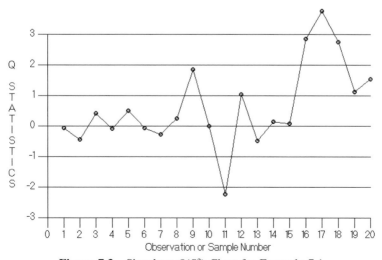

Figure 7.3   Shewhart $Q(S^2)$-Chart for Example 7.1

cess. Another point to note is that tests for patterns, based on the assumption that the plotted statistic is normally distributed, like or similar to those in Fig. 4.9, can be applied to these Q-charts for σ. This is a case for which this ability is especially important, as explained next.

The performance of this $Q(S^2)$ chart as judged by its ability to detect shifts in σ is readily evaluated. If the process standard deviation shifts from a known value $\sigma = \sigma_0$ to a new value $\sigma = \delta\sigma_0$, then the OC, power, and ARL functions for this $Q(S^2)$ chart using the 1-of-1 test are the same as for the S chart of section 4.7 with (0.00135, 0.00135) probability limits. Values of these three functions for selected values of δ are given in Table 4.8. In particular, the power function of the 1-of-1 test on this chart to detect a decrease represented by $\delta = 0.9$ is 0.00205, which is less than the false alarm probability for $\delta = 1$ of 0.00270. For the reasons discussed in the last paragraph of section 4.7, the sensitivity of this chart to detect decreases in σ by the 1-of-1 test is generally very poor. Quesenberry (1995a) studied this problem and showed that greatly improved sensitivity can be achieved by using the 4-of-5 test to detect decreases in σ. We recommend using the 4-of-5 test to detect decreases in σ on $Q(S^2)$ charts. In fact, if the increased false alarm rate is acceptable, ARL = 164, we recommend using both the 1-of-1 and 4-of-5 tests, the 11-45 combined test, to detect either increases or decreases in σ. The Q-EWMA chart and the Q-CUSUM charts, considered below, also give sensitive tests for detecting small decreases in σ.

Figure 7.3 is the $Q(S^2)$-chart for the sample variances given in Table 7.2, and clearly signals an increase in the variance at about the 16th point. We observed a signal on this point also on the $Q(\overline{X})$-chart. The 17th point is beyond the 3-sigma limit and the 4-of-5 test signals on the 19th and 20th points.

7.3.3 The Effects of Parameter Shifts on Chart Patterns

An increase or decrease in the process mean μ will cause the pattern of points on a $Q(\overline{X})$-chart to tend to move up or down on the chart, respectively, but will have no effect on the trends on a $Q(S^2)$ chart. Of course, if the shift occurs while the ith sample is being taken, it will tend to inflate $Q_i(S^2)$. However, a shift in the value of the process standard deviation σ has a number of consequences on the $Q(\overline{X})$- and $Q(S^2)$-charts. Since the standard deviation of $\overline{X}$ is $\sigma_{\overline{x}} = \sigma/\sqrt{n}$, a shift in the value of the process standard deviation from $\sigma = \sigma_0$ to $\sigma = \delta\sigma_0$, for $\delta > 0$, will cause a shift of $\sigma_{\overline{X}}$ from $\sigma_0/\sqrt{n}$ to $\delta\sigma_0/\sqrt{n}$, and this shift will be reflected in the spread of points on the $Q(\overline{X})$-chart. This is, of course, why we must have evidence that σ is stable in order to interpret any chart based on $\overline{X}$.

Consider next the effect of a shift from $\sigma = \sigma_0$ to $\sigma = \delta\sigma_0$, $\delta > 0$, on a $Q(S^2)$-chart. The mean of the sampling distribution of S^2 is, of course, $E(S^2) = \sigma^2$. So the shift causes $E(S^2)$ to shift from σ_0^2 to $\delta^2\sigma_0^2$. The standard deviation of the sampling distribution of S^2 is $SD(S^2) = \sigma^2\sqrt{2/(n-1)}$, assuming a normal process distribution. Thus, a shift from $\sigma = \sigma_0$ to $\sigma = \delta\sigma_0$ will cause $SD(S^2)$ to shift from $\sigma_0^2\sqrt{2/(n-1)}$ to $\delta^2\sigma_0^2\sqrt{2/(n-1)}$. That is, when σ changes by a multiple of δ, the standard deviation $SD(S^2)$ changes by a multiple of σ^2. This increase or decrease in $SD(S^2)$ will be reflected in the point pattern as an increase or decrease in spread on the chart. Note especially that a change from $\sigma = \sigma_0$ to $\sigma = \delta\sigma_0$ causes the spread on the $Q(\overline{X})$-chart to change by the same proportion δ, but it causes the spread on the $Q(S^2)$-chart to change by a factor δ^2. From these considerations, we see that there are three distinct point patterns on a $Q(\overline{X})$- and $Q(S^2)$-chart of a set of samples that signal an increase ($\delta > 1$) or decrease ($\delta < 1$) in the process variance σ^2, and they are: (1) an increase or decrease in the level of plotted points on a $Q(S^2)$-chart; (2) an increase or decrease in the spread of points on the $Q(S^2)$-chart; and (3) an increase or decrease in the spread of points on the $Q(\overline{X})$-chart. It is particularly useful in studying $Q(S^2)$-charts to remain aware of the increase or decrease in spread. These patterns are responsible for the poor performance of the 1-of-1 test and the good performance of the 4-of-5 test for detecting decreases in σ, that will be described below.

7.3.4   The Q($\overline{X}$)-Chart with Both μ and σ Unknown

In section 4.11 we recommended that 100 samples of size $n = 5$ from a stable process are needed in order to assume that the control limits are "known." We now consider charts that can be used before these many data are available. The Q-statistic formula for the mean chart for this case is given in equation (7.3.4). Recall that H_ν is a Student-t distribution function with ν degrees of freedom. These statistics Q_2, $Q_3, \cdots$ are independent standard normal, $N(0, 1)$, random variables. If these statistics are plotted on a Shewhart Q-chart, and the process is stable, then this chart will have the same types of expected point patterns as the Q-charts discussed above. If a shift in the process mean occurs, then the behavior of the points immediately following the shift will be similar to those for a Q-chart with known parameter values, but this tendency, of course, will depend on a number of things, including the magnitude of the shift and the number of samples that have been observed before the shift. However, there are important differences in the behavior of this chart and the chart made with "known" parameter values. Since the ith point is plotted by using all of the preceding samples to estimate the parameters, as additional samples are taken following a shift to a new value of the process mean, the following point should be kept in mind. The estimate $\bar{\bar{X}}_i$ will shift toward the new value of the process mean, and the resulting point pattern will shift eventually toward that of a stable process. Of course, if a shift in the mean occurs while the ith sample is being taken, then S_i^2 will tend to be inflated, and this will have some effect on the sensitivity of the chart.

The chart for $Q_2, Q_3, \cdots, Q_i$ permits the real-time charting of a normal process beginning with the second sample. It is particularly useful for charting a process at start-up, or for charting a process that has short production runs, since we do not have to first collect a large number of calibration samples to estimate the process parameters before an on-line, real-time, charting program can begin. We will consider some of the special issues of start-up processes and short runs further after we have introduced Q-charts for individual measurements in the next section.

7.3.5 Comments on Other Cases

The formulas (7.3.2) and (7.3.3) are for cases when a reliable estimate of one parameter, but not of the other, is available. The formula (7.3.2) is useful when a reliable estimate of σ is available from past data but a reliable estimate of μ is not available. Even if the process variance is known, the mean may not be, and the process is essentially a start-up process as far as information on the mean is concerned. This appears to be a practically important case for some applications when special causes present affect only the process mean, and not the process standard deviation; and therefore data can be accumulated for estimating the process standard deviation, but not for estimating the mean. We will consider a particularly important application of this case in Chapter 11 for adjusting a process. Charts illustrating the use of these formulas will be given in Example 7.3.

7.3.6 The $Q(\bar{X})$-Chart versus the Classical Retrospective $\bar{X}$-Chart

The $Q(\bar{X})$-chart for the case when the parameters are known is equivalent to the classical 3-sigma $\bar{X}$-chart made by plotting sample means on a chart with control limits given by (4.4.3). The performance of the classical 3-sigma $\bar{X}$-chart with known parameters was studied in Chapter 4, and those results hold also for the $Q(\bar{X})$-chart with known parameters. However, we noted in Chapter 4 that process parameters μ and σ are never really known, and that the classical charts with control limits estimated by "plug-in" methods often give poor results unless a very large data set taken while the process is in control is available.

Another problem is that one of the parameters μ or σ may shift while the calibration data set is being taken. Indeed, since most processes are unstable when charting programs are initiated, this is apparently a common event. It is of interest to compare the performance of the classical 3-sigma $\bar{X}$-chart with the corresponding $Q(\bar{X})$-chart for this case. Of course, the parameters can shift in many different ways, but we will consider the effect of a one-time permanent shift in the process mean while the data are being taken.

Suppose we take m samples of size n and the first m_1 samples are from a distribution with mean μ_0 and standard deviation σ_0, and the last $m - m_1$ samples are from a process distribution with mean $\mu_0 + \delta\sigma_0$ and standard deviation σ_0. Then the first m_1 sample means have distribution mean μ_0 and the last $m - m_1$ sample means have distribution mean $\mu_0 + \delta\sigma_0$, and both have standard deviation $\sigma_0/\sqrt{n}$. However, the statistic $\bar{\bar{X}}$ has mean $E(\bar{\bar{X}}) = \mu_0 + (m - m_1)\delta\sigma_0/m$, and standard deviation $\sigma_0/\sqrt{mn}$. In particular, if $m = 30$ and $m_1 = 15$, so that the shift occurs after observed value 15, then $\bar{\bar{X}}$ is an unbiased estimate of $\mu_0 + \dfrac{\delta\sigma_0}{2}$. This means that the sample means $\bar{X}_1, \cdots$ obtained before the shift and those obtained after the shift should tend to fall on opposite sides of the chart center line.

Example 7.2: To illustrate this behavior, we have generated $m_1 = 15$ samples of size $n = 5$ from a $N(5, 1)$ distribution, and then 15 more samples of size 5 from an $N(5.75, 1)$ distribution. From these values we obtained $\bar{\bar{X}} = 5.37$ and $\hat{\sigma} = 1.02$. Note that here $\bar{\bar{X}}$ is estimating the average value of the process mean before and after the mean shift. The $Q(\bar{X})$-chart of these data for the parameters unknown case is shown in Fig. 7.4, and the $Q(\bar{X})$-chart using these estimated parameter values in the KK formula is shown in Fig. 7.5. Recall that for this "known

Q-Chart for Mean, Parameters Unknown
XBARBAR = 5.370733, SIGMAHAT = 1.016495

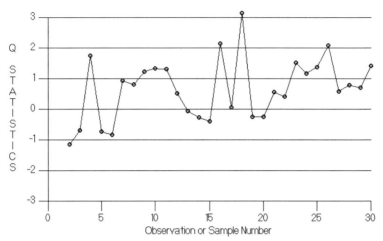

Figure 7.4 $Q(\overline{X})$-Chart for Example 7.2, Case UU

Q-Chart for Mean, Parameters Known
XBARBAR = 5.370733, SIGMAHAT = 1.016495

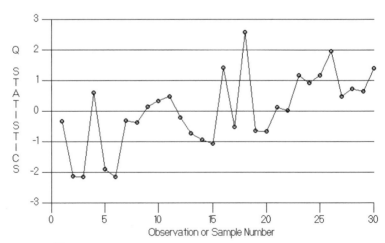

Figure 7.5 $Q(\overline{X})$-Chart for Example 7.2, Using Estimated Values in Case KK Control Limits

parameters" case the $Q(\overline{X})$-chart shows exactly the same pattern as the classical retrospective $\overline{X}$-chart itself.

The $Q(\overline{X})$-chart for the unknown parameters case gives a clear indication of the upward shift of the mean on about the 16th sample. The 19th mean is above the upper 3-sigma limit and the 4-of-5 test signals on the 26th point. We also note that the phenomenon discussed above of the tendency of the chart to eventually settle back to a stable process pattern is also evident. The retrospective $Q(\overline{X})$-chart using the estimated values of μ and σ shows a similar general pattern of plotted points. However, the pattern of points has been shifted down on the graph because $\overline{\overline{X}}$ now estimates an average of the value of the process mean before ($\mu = \mu_0 = 5$) and after ($\mu = \mu_0 + \delta\sigma_0 = 5.75$) the shift. As a result of this estimated value of the process mean, no points are outside control limits. The 4-of-5 test signals a decrease on the 6th point; however, this signal is misleading because it is due to an increase in μ at a *later* point. It also should be kept in mind that each point of Fig. 7.4 can be plotted as soon as the sample is observed, and trends may be detected when they occur, whereas Fig. 7.5 must be plotted retrospectively after the 30 subgroups have been observed. The $Q(\overline{X})$-chart for the unknown parameters case enables us to practice a more aggressive real-time, on-line form of SPC for this "start-up" or "short runs" case.

Of course, this is only one data set and further data sets taken under the same conditions will not show exactly the same patterns. However, we hope it will increase awareness of the inherent difficulties in using classical charting methods that always risk collecting calibration data from unstable processes in Stage 1 in order to begin a charting program.   ∎

Example 7.3: To illustrate the Q-Charts for the various cases, we have generated 15 samples of size 5 each from an $N(20, 1)$ distribution, and 15 more samples of size 5 each from an $N(21, 1)$ distribution. Q-charts for the process variance and the process mean are given in Figs. 7.6–7.13 to illustrate the use of the formulas (7.3.1)–(7.3.6).

Figure 7.6 is the $Q(S^2)$-Chart for σ when σ has a known nominal value of $\sigma_0 = 1$, formula (7.3.5); and Fig. 7.7 is the $Q(S^2)$-Chart for σ that does not assume a known value of σ, formula (7.3.6). Observe the similarity of the point patterns on these charts for a stable process variance. Also, note that the chart in Fig. 7.7 does not plot a point for the first sample, but the point patterns from the second sample on are very similar on the two charts. It can also be observed that in practice

SG Q-Chart for Variance, Sigma Known

XBarBar = 20.6468, SD = 1.008616

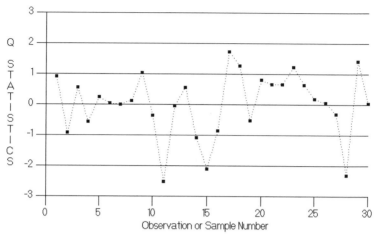

Figure 7.6 $Q(S^2)$-Chart for Example 7.3 with $\sigma_0 = 1$, Case K

we often do not really "know" σ, and the chart for this case would have to be made after the 30 or so samples have been collected using the estimate of $S_p = 1.01$, given on the line above the charts. Observe in the formulas (7.3.5) and (7.3.6) that these Q-statistics for the variance control chart do not depend on an assumption of a known value

SG Q-Chart for Variance, Sigma Unknown

XBarBar = 20.6468, SD = 1.008616

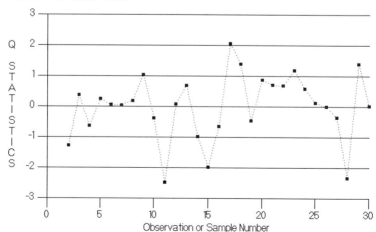

Figure 7.7 $Q(S^2)$-Chart for Example 7.3, Case U

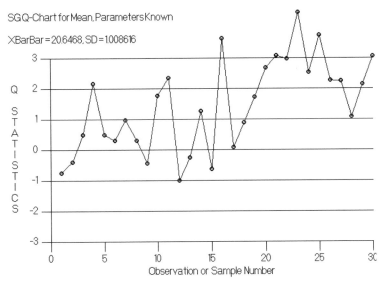

Figure 7.8 $Q(\overline{X})$-Chart for Example 7.3, Using $\mu = 20$ and $\sigma = 1$, Case KK

of the process mean μ. In fact, these charts are not affected if the mean changes from sample to sample. Also, recall that these are the charts for σ for which the 4-of-5 test is recommended for testing for a decrease in σ. Neither chart signals a decrease by this test. Finally, it

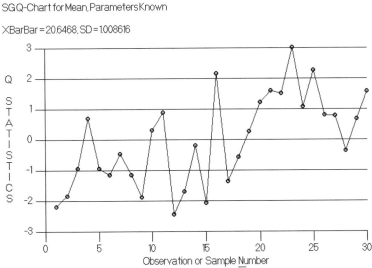

Figure 7.9 $Q(\overline{X})$-Chart for Example 7.3, Using $\overline{\overline{X}} = 20.65$ and $S_p = 1.01$ for "Known" Parameters, Case KK

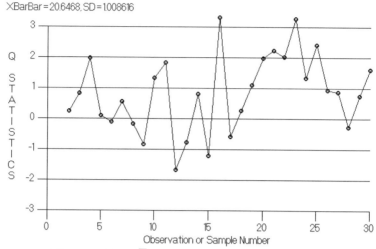

Figure 7.10 $Q(\overline{X})$-Chart for Example 7.3, Case UU

should be emphasized that the chart in Fig. 7.7 has the advantage that it can be made point-by-point, on-line, in real time as the samples arrive. That is, the first point on this chart corresponding to the second sample can be made as soon as the second sample is available, and similarly for the next point, and so on. This is a major advantage and

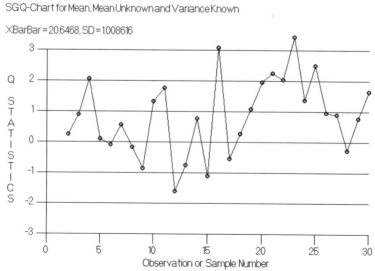

Figure 7.11 $Q(\overline{X})$-Chart for Example 7.3, Case UK

SG Q-Chart for Mean, Mean Known and Variance Unknown

XBarBar = 20.6468, SD = 1.008616

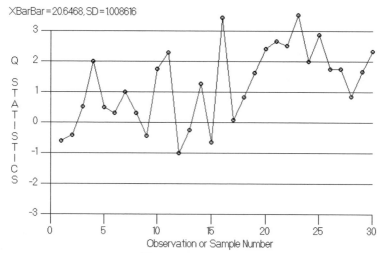

Figure 7.12 $Q(\overline{X})$-Chart for Example 7.3, Case KU

SG Q-Chart for Mean, Mean Known and Variance Unknown

XBarBar = 20.6468, SD = 1.008616

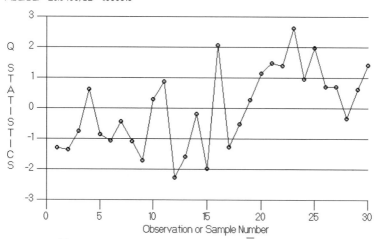

Figure 7.13 $Q(\overline{X})$-Chart for Example 7.3, Using $\overline{\overline{X}} = 20.65$ and σ Unknown, Case KU

permits charting short runs, and even start-up processes, without having prior data to estimate the process parameters.

We consider next the charts in Figs. 7.8, 7.9, and 7.10 to control the process mean. The chart in Fig. 7.8 is made from the known values of $\mu_0 = 20$ and $\sigma_0 = 1$ that were used to generate the first 15 samples. This chart clearly signals the shift in mean on the 16th sample. Now, in practice we never really know the true values of μ and σ, and have to estimate them from process data. Thus we have used the 30 samples to estimate μ by $\bar{\bar{X}} = 20.65$ and σ by $S_p = 1.01$ and used these values in the "known" parameters formula (7.3.1) to obtain the chart in Fig. 7.9. This is essentially the usual Stage 1 retrospective $\bar{X}$-chart. Note that Fig. 7.9 has a much weaker signal of the mean shift than Fig. 7.8. However, in practice Fig. 7.9 is the retrospective chart and will often be the only available chart with classical charting methods. Figure 7.10 is the Q-chart for this data assuming μ and σ both unknown. This chart can also be made point-by-point, on-line, in real time as the samples become available, starting with the second sample. This chart also has the advantage that it can be used to chart short runs and start-up processes without having to have prior data to estimate the parameters. For the data for this example, this chart performs better than the Stage 1 retrospective chart of Fig. 7.9 that uses parameters estimated from the present data since it clearly signals with a point above $UCL = 3$ on the 16th point, and the 4-of-5 test signals on points 23, 24, 25, and 26.

The reason the performance of the chart in Fig. 7.9 is poor is clearly due to the fact that $\bar{\bar{X}}$ is estimating an average of the values of μ before and after the shift from $\mu = 20$ to $\mu = 21$. Actually, this is an example of an important difficulty in the classical Stage 1 approach of first obtaining a calibration data set, and using it to estimate parameters. The problem is that when there is a shift in a parameter while the calibration data are being taken, the estimates of the parameters, one or both, are affected, and the control limits obtained from these estimated values can give misleading charts. The Q-charts that do not assume known parameter values give a valid approach to attempt to recognize the parameter shifts when they occur. Figure 7.11 shows the chart of the Q-statistic of equation (7.3.2) that uses the known value of $\sigma_0 = 1$, but assumes μ is unknown. Note that this chart is very similar to the chart of Fig. 7.10 that assumed no known parameters.

Figures 7.12 and 7.13 are charts of the Q-statistics of equation (7.3.3) that assume μ is known and σ unknown; however, Fig. 7.12 uses the correct nominal value of $\mu_0 = 20$, while Fig. 7.13 uses the value $\bar{\bar{X}} = 20.65$ estimated from all the data. The chart using $\bar{\bar{X}}$ has reduced sensitivity to signal a parameter shift. It does not signal by the 1-of-1 test, but does signal by the 4-of-5 test on points 23 and 24.

There is one point that we have commented on before, but we note again here. After a permanent parameter shift, such as the shift from $\mu = 20$ to $\mu = 21$ here, as further data are taken the charts will eventually settle back into a stable or in-control pattern. How quickly this happens depends on a number of variables, including the number of observations before the shift and the magnitude of the shift. To observe this phenomenon here, compare the chart patterns of Figs. 7.8 and 7.10 on points 16 through 30 and observe the decrease in the level of points in Fig. 7.10 as compared to those of Fig. 7.8. Finally, we should point out and emphasize that the charts we have made here are not competing charts, except for the charts of Figs. 7.9 and 7.10, and they were given here only for illustrative purposes. In applications, the parameters can be assumed "known" only when large data sets are available, taken while the process was stable. This would appear to be a rare situation, since most processes are not stable initially, and the actual purpose of SPC is to bring them into stable states.   ∎

Example 7.4: In this example we consider 30 samples of size 5 each. The data are given in Table 7.3. We are interested in beginning a charting program to identify assignable causes and bring the process into control by eliminating them, that is, a Stage 1 application. The Q-Charts for the variance and the mean, assuming no knowledge of the process parameters, are given in Figs. 7.14 and 7.15, respectively.

The chart for $Q(S^2)$ in Fig. 7.14 signals an increase in variance by having points 16 and 23 above the upper control limit and the 4-of-5 test signals on the 19th point. Also, note that there is a rather large, obvious increase in the spread of points on this chart. From the discussion above of the change in spread on an S-chart induced by a change in the process standard deviation, we know that this also implies an increase in the process standard deviation. Moreover, while the $Q(\bar{X})$-chart in Fig. 7.15 does not signal by having a point outside the control limits, there is a pattern of points from 16 on that appears to reflect an increase in σ.

In order to compare these Q-charts that can be made point-by-point, on-line, as the data are collected, with the competing charts from classical charting methods, we have used the "known parameters" formulas with the estimates $\bar{\bar{X}} = 5.00$ and $S_p = 0.0355$ computed from these 30 samples to plot the charts of Figs. 7.16 and 7.17. Of course, these charts cannot be made in real time and must be made retrospectively after the 30 samples are collected. The mean chart of Fig. 7.15 shows a pattern

TABLE 7.3   Data for Example 7.4

Sample Number	Sample Values				
1	5.001	4.959	4.996	4.979	4.986
2	4.981	5.019	4.951	5.026	4.972
3	5.006	4.976	4.999	5.018	5.018
4	5.011	4.953	4.973	5.000	5.005
5	5.012	4.990	5.010	5.016	4.988
6	4.986	5.010	5.006	5.021	4.966
7	4.985	4.980	4.962	4.991	5.020
8	4.999	4.966	4.969	4.995	4.974
9	5.014	5.024	5.044	4.965	5.008
10	5.012	4.987	5.002	4.992	4.983
11	4.981	4.968	5.000	5.018	4.998
12	4.998	4.969	4.984	4.984	4.966
13	5.006	4.989	4.991	4.971	5.018
14	5.014	4.999	5.025	4.998	4.959
15	5.026	4.962	5.004	5.017	5.021
16	5.058	5.056	5.018	4.912	5.031
17	5.005	5.021	4.959	5.064	4.974
18	4.909	4.993	5.024	5.023	5.048
19	4.994	5.010	4.993	5.018	5.104
20	4.977	4.901	4.944	4.978	5.008
21	5.016	5.005	5.025	5.051	5.026
22	4.976	5.026	4.958	5.043	4.991
23	4.979	5.168	5.052	4.993	4.999
24	4.937	4.928	5.059	5.067	4.989
25	5.003	5.026	5.029	5.078	5.022
26	5.002	5.010	4.997	5.001	4.991
27	4.983	4.973	4.940	4.979	5.027
28	5.059	5.070	5.012	4.971	5.030
29	5.034	4.966	5.047	5.044	4.981
30	5.101	4.968	5.028	5.057	5.007

of points from the 16th on that suggests the possibility of an increase in variance. The variance chart of Fig. 7.16 has only one point, the 23rd, outside the control limits; however, the increase in spread on this chart after the 15th point is apparent. Also, there is strong evidence of an increase in variance from the pattern on the first 15 points. In fact, all 15 points are below the center line and the spread is much smaller than for the later points. This pattern is indicative of an increase in variance after the 15th point, for then the estimate $S_p = 0.0355$ would

SG Q-Chart for Variance, Sigma Unknown

XBarBar = 5.00212, SD = 3.552056E-02

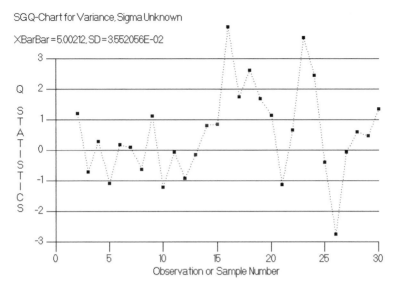

Figure 7.14 $Q(S^2)$-Chart for Example 7.4, Case U

SG Q-Chart for Mean, Parameters Unknown

XBarBar = 5.00212, SD = 3.552056E-02

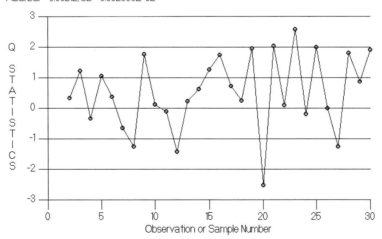

Figure 7.15 $Q(\overline{X})$-Chart for Example 7.4, Case UU

SG Q-Chart for Variance, Sigma Known

XBarBar = 5.00212, SD = 3.552056E-02

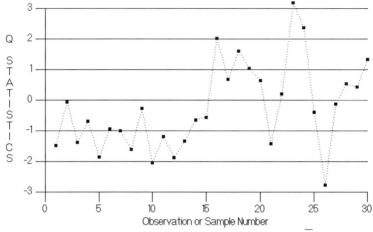

Figure 7.16 $Q(S^2)$ Retrospective Chart for Example 7.4, Using $\overline{\overline{X}}$ and S_p, Case KK

SG Q-Chart for Mean, Parameters Known

XBarBar = 5.00212, SD = 3.552056E-02

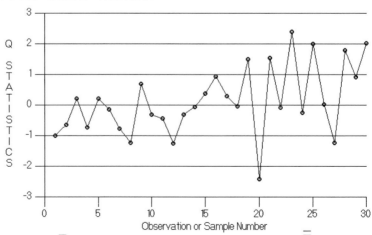

Figure 7.17 $Q(\overline{X})$ Retrospective Chart for Example 7.4, Using $\overline{\overline{X}}$ and S_p, Case KK

be larger than the true value of σ before the shift and smaller than the true value of σ after the shift. However, many SPC practitioners would likely be confused and liable to misinterpret this pattern. We believe the pattern of the $Q(S^2)$-chart of Fig. 7.14 gives a clearer signal of the variance shift. ∎

Example 7.5: To illustrate the pattern stratified subgroups make on the case UU mean Q-chart, we simulated 20 samples. Each sample consisted of six observations. Three were from an $N(5, 1)$ distribution and the other three were from an $N(6.5, 1)$ distribution. The sigma Q-chart is shown in Fig. 7.18, and it indicates a stable process variance. Figure 7.19 is the case UU chart for the process mean and it shows the typical Shewhart chart pattern of points too close to the center line that is indicative of this type of stratification. Figure 7.20 is the standardized version of the classical retrospective $\overline{X}$-chart, and it has the same pattern as the case UU chart in Fig. 7.19. Namely, the points tend to cluster too closely about the center line.

This type of stratification is an especially important pattern to recognize in SPC applications. Recall the discussion in section 4.5, and problem 4.24. The $Q(\overline{X})$-chart will often let us recognize stratification patterns early on and set about correcting them. In particular, recall that interpreting this stratification pattern does not depend on having the observations within subgroups have a constant variance. The ten-

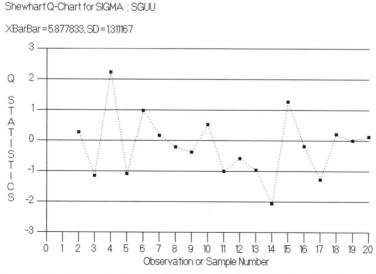

Figure 7.18 Sigma Q-Chart for Example 7.5, Case UU, Stratified Samples

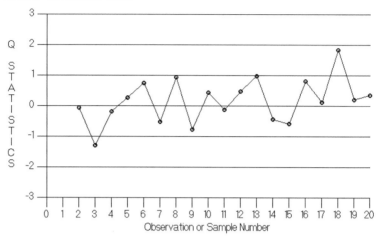

Figure 7.19 Mean Q-Chart for Example 7.5, Case UU, Stratified Samples

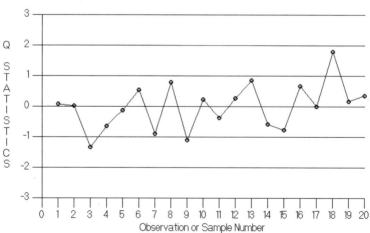

Figure 7.20 Mean Q-Chart for Example 7.5, Case KK Retrospective Chart, Stratified Samples

dency to have points tend to hug the center line too closely is caused by variation among the means of the observations in the subgroup. ■

7.3.7 Historical Data or Parameter Estimates Available

The presentation in this section has assumed data in the format of Table 7.1, and has essentially assumed that when historical data are available to estimate μ and σ, there are enough data to assume that μ and σ are known. This raises the question of how to proceed when some data are available, but not enough to assume μ and σ are known.

If historical data in the format of Table 7.1 are available, then one can proceed to use these data by simply adjoining new data to this data set, sample-by-sample, as they become available, and carrying on using the appropriate transformation from above. Sometimes the data set may not be available, but estimates of μ and σ are. Suppose that a mean estimate $\overline{X}_{h,a}$ of μ, and a mean-squared estimate $S_{h,b}^2$ of σ^2, is available, where "h" means "historical," a is the number of *observations* used to compute $\overline{X}_{h,a}$, and b is the number of *degrees of freedom* of the mean-squared estimate $S_{h,b}^2$.

The Q-statistics are computed as follows. Put

$$\overline{\overline{X}}'_i = \frac{a\overline{X}_{h,a} + (n_1 + \cdots + n_i)\overline{\overline{X}}_i}{a + n_1 + \cdots + n_i}, \quad \text{and}$$

$$(S'_{p,i})^2 = \frac{bS_{h,b}^2 + (n_1 + \cdots + n_i - i)S_{p,i}^2}{b + n_1 + \cdots + n_i - i}$$

Then the transformation formulas of (7.3.2), (7.3.3), (7.3.4), and (7.3.6) are replaced by the following.

Case UK: μ unknown, σ^2 known

$$Q_i(\overline{X}_i) = \sqrt{\frac{n_i(a + n_1 + \cdots + n_{i-1})}{a + n_1 + \cdots + n_i}} \left(\frac{\overline{X}_i - \overline{\overline{X}}'_{i-1}}{\sigma_0} \right), \tag{7.3.2'}$$

$$i = 1, 2, \cdots$$

Case KU: $\mu = \mu_0$ known, σ^2 unknown.

$$Q_i(\overline{X}_i) = \Phi^{-1}\left[H_{b+n_1+\cdots+n_i-i}\left(\frac{\sqrt{n_i}(\overline{X}_i - \mu_0)}{S'_{p,i}}\right)\right],$$

$$i = 1, 2, \cdots$$

(7.3.3')

Case UU: μ unknown, σ unknown.

$$Q_i(\overline{X}_i) = \Phi^{-1}\left\{H_{b+n_1+\cdots+n_i-i}\left[\sqrt{\frac{n_i(a + n_1 + \cdots + n_{i-1})}{a + n_1 + \cdots + n_i}}\right.\right.$$

$$\left.\left.\times\left(\frac{\overline{X}_i - \overline{\overline{X}}'_i}{S'_{p,i}}\right)\right]\right\}, \qquad i = 1, 2, \cdots$$

(7.3.4')

Case U: σ unknown.

Put $\qquad w_i = \dfrac{(b + n_1 + \cdots + n_{i-1} - i + 1)S_i^2}{bS_{h,b}^2 + (n_1 - 1)S_1^2 + \cdots + (n_{i-1} - 1)S_{i-1}^2}$

$$= \frac{S_i^2}{(S'_{p,i-1})^2}, \qquad i = 1, 2, \cdots$$

and

$$Q_i(S_i^2) = \Phi^{-1}[F_{n_i-1, b+n_1+\cdots+n_{i-1}-i+1}(w_i)],$$

$$i = 1, 2, \cdots$$

(7.3.6')

These Q-statistics can then be used for charts as described above. It should be noted that these formulas give us a lot of flexibility in using estimates from prior data to improve the sensitivity of our charts. One setting where these formulas are often useful is when a process must be restarted after it has been stopped to search for a special cause, or for some other reason. Then, in some cases, it may appear reasonable to use parameter estimates from before the stoppage.

7.3.8 Choosing the Transformations Case in Practice

In the transformations to $Q(\overline{X})$-statistics above, we have considered cases KK, UK, KU, and UU for $\overline{X}$-charts; where the letter in the first position indicates that μ is assumed known or unknown; and the second position letter indicates that σ is known or unknown. Now, in fact, neither the mean μ or standard deviation σ are ever really known exactly and must be estimated from data. Thus, in order to use any of the transformation formulas given in this chapter that have at least one parameter assumed known, we will in practice actually be substituting an estimated value for the "known" value. But this actually gives a competing method for estimating the Q-statistics transformations for the case of the parameters known. Moreover, this is a "plug-in" estimation method that has inferior inference properties to the unknown parameters cases that are UMVU estimating distribution functions. This suggests that, in practice, we should always use the unknown parameters cases. To fix ideas, we now consider this issue in more detail for a particular case.

Suppose that at a point in time we have i samples of size n in the format of Table 7.1. If $i \times n$ is large, say perhaps there are $i = 100$ samples of size $n = 5$ for a total of 500 observations, then we can estimate μ and σ by $\overline{X}_i$ and $S_{p,i}$ (or $\overline{S}$) and use these estimated values in the case KK formulas of (7.3.1) for μ_0 and σ_0 (the "plug-in" method of estimation) to compute $Q(\overline{X}_{i+1})$ of the next sample. Alternatively, we can simply use the case UU formulas of equation (7.3.4). Thus, these are, in fact, two competing methods for estimating the transformations of equation (7.3.1). But the case UU transformations have better inference properties for all data set sizes! For this reason, we recommend the use of the case UU formulas *all the time*.

For the same reason, the case U formula of (7.3.6) should be used for the chart for σ.

We also recommend, when the case UU Q-statistics are computed and charted sample-by-sample in real time, that a trailing window of samples be used as the data basis for the transformations. When the ith sample is observed, a trailing window of k samples consists of the data from the most recent k samples. This is a total of $n_{i-k+1} + \cdots + n_i$ observations. When the $(i + 1)^{st}$ sample of size n_{i+1} is observed, it is appended to the trailing window data set and the $(i - k + 1)^{st}$ sample is deleted.

The reason we recommend using only a limited number of samples as the basis of the transformations is because we think more recent data are more relevant. This is because, although we assume constancy of parameters, we know that in the long run they will not really remain constant. Using a trailing window database for Q-charts is for the same reason that control limits for classic Shewhart charts must be frequently updated. This trailing window approach automatically updates the data basis on every sample. Therefore, we are always using the most recent, and therefore hopefully the most relevant, basis data set for the transformations.

To use a trailing window of samples, we must decide how much data to use for the window. This issue will be discussed and recommendations given in section 7.7 after Q-charts for individual measurments, EWMA Q-charts, and CUSUM Q-charts have been introduced in the next three sections.

7.4   *Q*-CHARTS BASED ON INDIVIDUAL MEASUREMENTS

Many manufacturing processes today have the ability to measure or gauge every individual unit of production. In some systems the gauging is automated and can be sent directly to a computer for real-time analysis so that the data information can be used immediately. When a new process is started, or an old one is restarted, it may be helpful to chart the process from start-up to study its stability and to bring it into a stable state as quickly as possible. This is sometimes best accomplished by gauging every unit and making individual observations charts. Most of the considerations discussed in Chapter 5 for classical Shewhart individual measurements charts carry over to the charts considered in this section.

There are also many potential applications of individual measurements charting methods in nonmanufacturing areas, especially for the methods we present here that do not require large data sets from stable processes in order to set up the charts. In fact, as mentioned in the first paragraph of section 7.1, we believe that the principal barrier to the use of SPC methods, and the real reason such applications have not developed more than they have, is because of the requirement of large, clean, calibration data sets.

Let $X_1, X_2, \cdots$ denote observations made on a sequence of production units as they are produced in time, and assume that these values are independently and identically distributed random variables with a normal $N(\mu, \sigma^2)$ process distribution. The parameters μ and σ^2 are the process mean and variance and charts will be given for the cases when both, either, or neither of these parameters are assumed known in advance of the production run. Recall the definitions of the sequential mean $\overline{X}_r$ and variance S_r^2 given in section 3.4 and the updating formulas of display (3.4.5).

Q-Statistics for the Process Mean μ

Case KK: $\mu = \mu_0$ known and $\sigma = \sigma_0$ known.

$$Q_r(X_r) = \frac{X_r - \mu_0}{\sigma_0}, \qquad r = 1, 2, \cdots \qquad (7.4.1)$$

Case UK: μ unknown and $\sigma = \sigma_0$ known.

$$Q_r(X_r) = \sqrt{\frac{r-1}{r}} \frac{(X_r - \overline{X}_{r-1})}{\sigma_0}, \qquad r = 2, 3, \cdots \qquad (7.4.2)$$

Case KU: $\mu = \mu_0$ known and σ unknown.

$$Q_r(X_r) = \Phi^{-1}\left\{ H_{r-2}\left(\frac{X_r - \mu_0}{S_{r-1}} \right) \right\}, \qquad r = 3, 4, \cdots \qquad (7.4.3)$$

Case UU: μ unknown and σ unknown.

$$Q_r(X_r) = \Phi^{-1}\left\{ H_{r-2}\left[\sqrt{\frac{r-1}{r}} \left(\frac{X_r - \overline{X}_{r-1}}{S_{r-1}} \right) \right] \right\},$$
$$r = 3, 4, \cdots \qquad (7.4.4)$$

Note that for Case KK a value of Q_r corresponds to X_r for all values of $r = 1, 2, \cdots$. However, no value for Q_1 corresponding to X_1 is obtained for Case UK, and no values for Q_1 and Q_2 corresponding to X_1 and X_2 are obtained for Cases KU and UU. This is due to the appearance of unknown parameters in the model.

When the process is stable with a $N(\mu, \sigma^2)$ process distribution, then the statistics for cases KK, UK and UU are independently and identically distributed $N(0, 1)$ random variables. The statistics for case KU are normal, $N(0, 1)$, statistics and are approximately independent. See the discussion in Quesenberry (1995e) of case KU. Some of these properties will be demonstrated in Appendix 7B. From this it follows that the Q-statistics can be plotted on a Shewhart chart with control limits at ± 3. We will illustrate this procedure with examples after giving Q-statistics for the variance σ^2.

The Q-statistics for the process variance are as follows.

Q-Statistics for the Process Variance σ^2

Put $R_r = X_r - X_{r-1}$

Case K: $\sigma = \sigma_0$ known.

$$Q_r = \Phi^{-1}\left\{G_1\left(\frac{R_r^2}{2\sigma_0^2}\right)\right\} \qquad \text{for } r = 2, 4, 6, \cdots \quad (7.4.5)$$

Case U: σ unknown.

$$Q_r = \Phi^{-1}\left\{F_{1,\nu}\left(\frac{\nu R_r^2}{R_2^2 + R_4^2 + \cdots + R_{r-2}^2}\right)\right\} \qquad (7.4.6)$$

$$\text{for } r = 4, 6, \cdots ; \quad \nu = \frac{r}{2} - 1.$$

Note that for these two cases we obtain Q-statistics only for the even-numbered indices of the sequence of values $X_1, X_2, \cdots$. The statistic of (7.4.5) can, of course, be computed for all of the observations $r = 2, 3, \cdots$; and a statistic similar to that of (7.4.6) can be computed from all points. These sequences of statistics formed in this way are normally distributed; however, they are not *independent*. For this reason we advocate computing the statistics of (7.4.5) and (7.4.6) only for the observations with even-numbered indices, and plotting them on Q-charts. Also, the reader will note that we have not given formulas for the case when the process mean μ has a known value, say $\mu = \mu_0$, and formulas using this known value of μ can be readily given. The reason we do not advocate computing Q-statistics that depend on an assumed known value of μ to control the process variance is because if μ should change during a run, then this change in μ will cause a pattern on the chart to control σ that would incorrectly be interpreted as a change in σ.

7.4.1   Using Historical or Prior Estimates in the Transformations

Sometimes there may be historical data available for estimating the process mean μ and variance σ^2 when the run of parts with these measurements is begun. Suppose that these data are used to make a mean estimate $\overline{X}_{h,a}$ of μ and a mean-squared estimate $S_{h,b}^2$ of σ^2, where the subscript "h" means "historical," a is the number of *observations* used to compute $\overline{X}_{h,a}$, and b is the number of *degrees of freedom* of the mean-squared estimate $S_{h,b}^2$. By a "mean-squared" estimate we mean either a sample variance, a pooled estimate from several samples, or an MSE from an ANOVA table. When prior estimates $\overline{X}_{h,a}$ and $S_{h,b}^2$ of μ and σ^2 are available, the Q-statistics are computed as follows.

$$\overline{X}_{a+r}' = \frac{r\overline{X}_r + a\overline{X}_{h,a}}{r + a}, \quad \text{and} \quad (S_{b+r}')^2 = \frac{bS_{h,b}^2 + (r - 1)S_r^2}{b + r - 1}$$

Then the modified formulas for mean charts for Cases UK, KU, and UU are given in the following.

Case *UK*: μ unknown and $\sigma = \sigma_0$ known.

$$Q_r(X_r) = \sqrt{\frac{a + r - 1}{a + r}} \frac{(X_r - \overline{X}_{a+r-1}')}{\sigma_0},$$

$$r = 1, 2, 3, \cdots$$

(7.4.2)'

Case *KU*: $\mu = \mu_0$ known and σ unknown.

$$Q_r(X_r) = \Phi^{-1} \left\{ H_{b+r-2} \left(\frac{X_r - \mu_0}{S_{b+r-1}'} \right) \right\}, \qquad r = 1, 2, 3, \cdots \quad (7.4.3)'$$

provided $b \geq 1$.

Case *UU*: μ unknown and σ unknown.

$$Q_r'(X_r) = \Phi^{-1} \left\{ H_{b+r-2} \left[\left(\frac{a + r - 1}{a + r} \right)^{1/2} \left(\frac{X_r - \overline{X}_{r-1}'}{S_{b+r-1}'} \right) \right] \right\},$$

$$r = 1, 2, 3, \cdots$$

(7.4.4)'

provided $a \geq 1$ and $b \geq 1$.

The modified formula for a sigma chart for Case U is

Case *U*: μ unknown and σ unknown.

$$Q'(R_r^2) = \Phi^{-1} \left\{ F_{1,\nu} \left(\frac{\nu R_r^2}{2bS_{h,b}^2 + R_2^2 + R_4^2 + \cdots + R_{r-2}^2} \right) \right\}$$

(7.4.6)'

for $r = 4, 6, \cdots$; $\nu = b + \dfrac{r}{2} - 1$.

It can be shown by elementary arguments that the Q-statistics for each of the above cases are identically distributed $N(0, 1)$ random variables for a stable normal process. From the theory of conditional probability integral (CPIT) transformations developed by O'Reilly and Quesenberry (1973), (see also Quesenberry 1986), these distributional properties can also be shown, and that the statistics are *independent*. These distributional properties will be demonstrated in Appendix 7B.

Example 7.6: To illustrate the Q-charts for some of these formulas, we have generated a sample of $n = 50$ values from an $N(55, 1)$ distribution and then another 50 values from an $N(57, 1)$ distribution. To be realistic, we will act as though we know nothing about the process generating this data, and must make our decisions just from the data itself. This is usually the situation for a real process. Thus we first make graphs using the formulas for both μ and σ unknown. The chart for the variance is given in Fig. 7.21 and the chart for the process mean is given in Fig. 7.22. The chart for the variance appears as that of a stable process, so we can interpret the mean chart. The mean chart of Fig. 7.22 gives clear signals of the mean shift after observation number 50. Three consecutive points (51, 52, and 53) are in zone A, the 4-of-5 test signals on points 53, 62 and several later points, and later a long

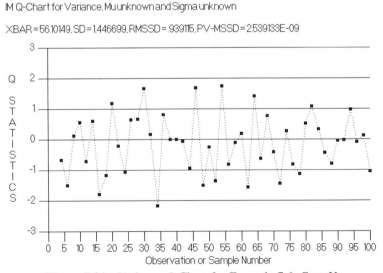

Figure 7.21 Variance Q-Chart for Example 7.6, Case U

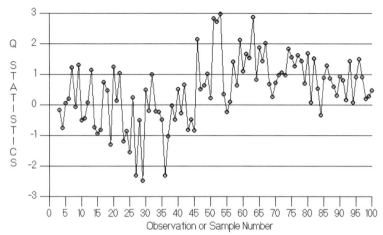

Figure 7.22   Mean Q-Chart for Example 7.6, Case UU

run of 28 points are above the center line. Also, on the chart title we note that the sample standard deviation of all 100 values is 1.45, the sample mean is 56.10, the mean square successive difference estimate of σ is 0.94, and the p-value of the MSSD test for a nonconstant mean is 2.5×10^{-9} (see subsection 4.10.2). This p-value is strong further evidence of a varying mean.

Next, to compare this charting analysis with the classical Stage 1 approach we use the parameter estimates from these data to make a chart using the formulas for the "known" parameter cases. Using the MSSD estimate of 0.94 for σ and the mean estimate of 56.10 for μ, we obtain the chart in Fig. 7.23 for the process variance and the chart in Fig. 7.24 for the process mean. The effect on the resulting estimate of μ is, of course, that the estimate is larger than the beginning nominal value of 55. This causes the process to appear to be out of control in the first 50 points with three points below LCL of Fig. 7.24, but from the pattern of points the shift is also apparent. It should also be borne in mind that the charts in Figs. 7.21 and 7.22 can be made in real time as the data are obtained for an operating process, so for this process the mean shift would have been detected almost immediately. This is an important advantage that will permit savings in many processes.

Further, it should be kept in mind that individual observations can sometimes be grouped into consecutive samples to make a subgroups chart. When such grouping is possible, that is, makes sense, this is a way to increase the power to detect smaller shifts of the process mean

IM Q-Chart for Variance, Mu known and Sigma known

XBAR=56.10149, SD=1.446699, RMSSD=.939115, PV-MSSD=2.539133E-09

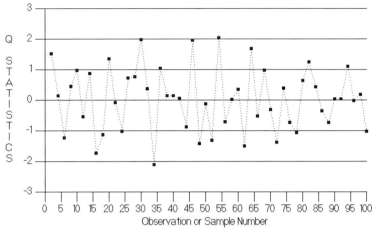

Figure 7.23 Variance Q-Chart for Example 7.6 Using Estimates $\mu = 56.10$ and $\sigma = 0.94$ in Case KK Formulas

IM Q-Chart for Mean, Mu known and Sigma known

XBAR=56.10149, SD=1.446699, RMSSD=.939115, PV-MSSD=2.539133E-09

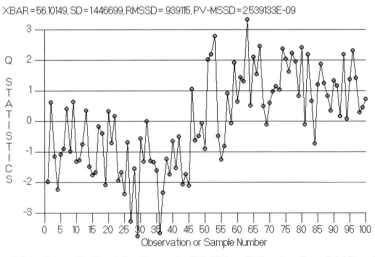

Figure 7.24 Mean Q-Chart for Example 7.6 Using Estimates $\hat{\mu} = 56.10$ and $\hat{\sigma} = 0.94$ in Case KK Formulas

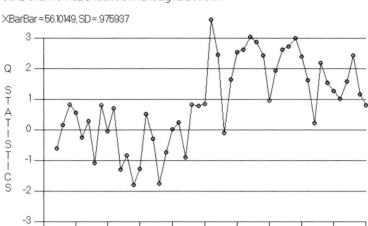

Figure 7.25   Mean Q-Chart for Consecutive Subgroups of Size 2

(or variance). To illustrate this process we have grouped the 100 observations first into 50 consecutive samples of 2 each, and the Q-chart for these samples for the process mean is given in Fig. 7.25. Similarly, the corresponding chart when the data are grouped into 20 consecutive samples of size 5 each is shown in Fig. 7.26. The power increase with

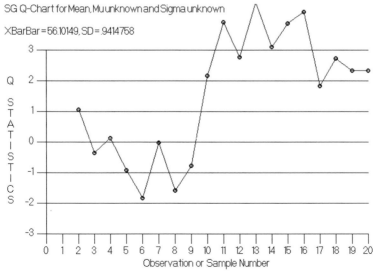

Figure 7.26   Mean Q-Chart for Consecutive Subgroups of Size 5

grouping is apparent. This improvement in power for the subgroups mean chart is due to the increased information for each point from a subgroup rather than just one observation, and also, importantly, to the fact that the variance estimate after the shift is not inflated from the shift (except for, possibly, one subgroup if the shift occurs while a subgroup is being taken), as it is for the individual measurements chart. ∎

In the discussion of Example 7.6 we pointed out that in the formulas for the cases KU and UU given in formulas (7.4.3) and (7.4.4), the sequential sample standard deviation S_r has the property that a shift in the process mean will tend to inflate S_r for points after the first point after the shift. We need to be aware of this phenomenon in our charting activities.

As a general precaution to try to recognize any type of variation in the process mean, we recommend always computing the PV-MSSD as supplementary information. If this p-value is at least as large as 0.1, we should not have a problem with S_r being inflated from variation in the process mean.

7.5 THE EWMA Q-CHART

It is apparent that the various types of Q-statistics considered here can be used as the input data to plot the MA, EWMA, and CUSUM charts considered in Chapter 6, and that these charts would have good sensitivity to detect smaller parameter shifts. We consider the EWMA Q-chart in this section. If the sequence of means $\overline{X}_1, \overline{X}_2, \cdots$, is replaced by a sequence of Q-statistics $Q_1, Q_2, \cdots$, then the formula (6.2.1) becomes

$$Z_t = \lambda Q_t + (1 - \lambda)Z_{t-1} \qquad \text{for } t = 1, 2, \cdots \qquad (7.5.1)$$

Since $\mu_Q = 0$ and $\sigma_Q = 1$ for a stable process, by taking the starting value $Z_0 = Q_1$ we have from (6.2.5) the mean and standard deviation given in (7.5.2).

$$E(Z_t) = 0$$

$$\text{Var}(Z_t) = \frac{1}{2 - \lambda} [\lambda + 2(1 - \lambda)^{2t-1}]$$

$$\rightarrow \sigma^2_{EWMA} = \frac{\lambda}{2 - \lambda},$$

$$\text{as } t \rightarrow \infty$$

$$(7.5.2)$$

The control limits of (6.2.8) are then

$$UCL(Z_t) = K \text{ Var}(Z_t) \rightarrow K \sqrt{\frac{\lambda}{2 - \sigma}},$$

$$\text{as } t \rightarrow \infty$$

$$(7.5.3)$$

$$LCL(Z_t) = -K \text{ Var}(Z_t) \rightarrow -K \sqrt{\frac{\lambda}{2 - \lambda}},$$

$$\text{as } t \rightarrow \infty$$

Thus we can apply the Crowder procedure to design a control chart. Suppose we design an EWMA Q-Chart as in Example 6.3 to obtain values of $(\lambda, K) = (0.25, 2.90)$. Then the limiting values of the control limits for the EWMA Q-Chart are

$$UCL = 2.9 \sqrt{\frac{.25}{1.75}} = 1.10, \qquad LCL = -1.10$$

Recall that the chart design in Example 6.3 chose the value of $\lambda = 0.25$ and $K = 2.9$ as the best values to detect a shift of $\delta = 1.5$ standard deviations in the mean of the plotted statistic. However, a shift of $\delta = 1.5$ standard deviations of the plotted statistics does not necessarily correspond to the same number of standard deviations of the Q's, except in cases where the Q-transformation is actually a linear function of a statistic that is itself normally distributed and parameters are "known." This case when the parameters of normally distributed sta-

tistics are known is particularly important, however, because it represents the limiting performance for the cases when one or more
parameters are unknown. For this case, if the process remains stable
for a long run the chart patterns and performance of charts for cases
with one or more unknown parameters will converge to the patterns
and performance of the corresponding chart with known parameters.
For most cases, this statement follows from the uniform strong consistency of UMVU distribution function estimators (see O'Reilly and
Quesenberry 1972).

Example 7.7: In this example we illustrate and compare some of the
EWMA Q-Charts and Shewhart Q-Charts using data generated with a
known structure. We have generated independent observations from
normal distributions with the following structure.

10 samples of varying size from an $N(50, 1)$ distribution.
5 additional samples from an $N(50.7, 1)$ distribution.
5 additional samples from an $N(50.7, 1.5)$ distribution.

These 20 samples are shown in Table 7.4. They vary in size from 4
to 7. We have plotted the EWMA Q-Chart and corresponding Shewhart
Q-Chart for each of 8 different cases, in order to provide some comparisons of the features of these charts, at least for this data set. The
EWMA Q-Chart uses the values $\lambda = 0.25$ and $K = 2.9$, which gives
a chart with ARL of approximately 372—see Example 6.3—for a stable process.

Figures 7.27 and 7.28 give the EWMA Q-Chart and the Shewhart
Q-Chart for the process variance for the limiting case when the process
mean μ and variance σ^2 are both assumed to be known exactly. Recall
that σ was increased from 1 to 1.5 for the last 5 subgroups. Both charts
signal for the first time on the 19th subgroup, but do not give any
indication of an increase in variance before the 16th subgroup. This is
useful to note for later reference in interpreting charts to control the
process mean μ. In fact, Fig. 7.30 signals the increase in the process
mean on observation 11 by signaling by the 4-of-5 test on point 13,
and at that time the variance appeared constant. It should be kept in
mind that these charts are made using the fact that the nominal values
of both $\mu_0 = 50$ and $\sigma_0 = 1$ are used to make them and cannot be
made when these parameters are not known exactly before the data are
taken, as will be the case in practice. Figures 7.31 and 7.32 give the
corresponding charts for controlling the variance for the case when the

TABLE 7.4 Data for Example 7.7

Sample	Sample Values						
1	50.84	50.44	49.16	51.15	49.85	50.44	
2	48.63	49.58	49.12	49.04			
3	49.61	49.07	50.27	49.91	50.45		
4	50.73	50.44	50.74	48.75	48.10	51.10	
5	48.60	50.71	49.73	49.55	49.86	51.13	
6	49.13	51.20	50.71	49.97	50.13		
7	50.35	48.41	50.52	51.12	50.37	52.41	48.80
8	49.84	49.57	50.78	48.88	49.89	49.40	50.00
9	49.44	50.14	50.63	49.76	50.59	48.95	
10	49.60	50.96	50.47	50.70	50.63	50.67	
11	51.72	49.37	50.54	50.93	51.12	51.70	52.05
12	51.85	51.32	50.68	52.14	48.62	49.24	
13	50.82	49.89	50.60	52.36	51.26	51.21	
14	50.10	51.08	49.79	50.95	50.07		
15	51.76	50.30	49.37	48.60	49.63	50.88	50.37
16	49.58	49.90	49.18	52.77	48.02	51.68	
17	53.07	52.93	50.66	52.29	51.73	49.40	
18	49.01	51.91	49.95	49.46	49.66	51.41	
19	51.43	52.51	46.94	50.93	53.23	50.69	52.12
20	51.87	50.45	51.23	51.10	47.63		

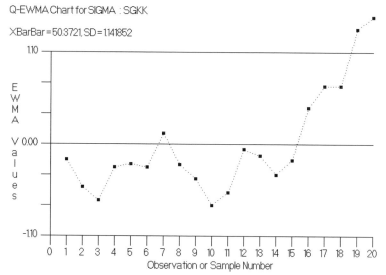

Q-EWMA Chart for SIGMA : SGKK

XBarBar = 50.3721, SD = 1.141852

Figure 7.27 EWMA $Q(S^2)$-Chart for σ, Case K

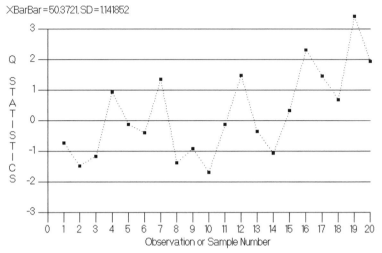

Figure 7.28   Shewhart $Q(S^2)$-Chart for σ, Case K

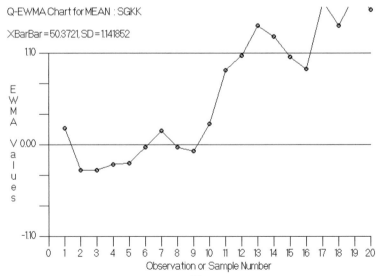

Figure 7.29   EWMA $Q(\bar{X})$-Chart for μ, Case KK

Shewhart Q-Chart for MEAN : SGKK

XBarBar = 50.3721, SD = 1.141852

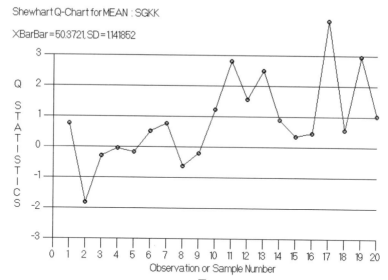

Figure 7.30 Shewhart $Q(\overline{X})$-Chart for μ, Case KK

Q-EWMA Chart for SIGMA : SGUU

XBarBar = 50.3721, SD = 1.141852

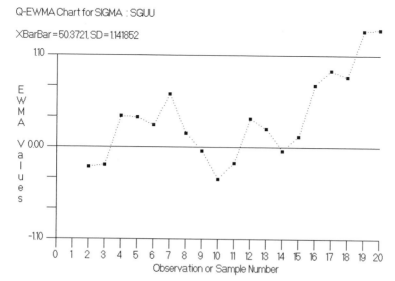

Figure 7.31 EWMA $Q(S^2)$-Chart for σ, Case U

Shewhart Q-Chart for SIGMA : SGUU

XBarBar = 50.3721, SD = 1.141852

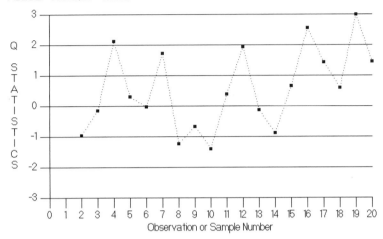

Figure 7.32   Shewhart $Q(S^2)$-Chart for σ, Case U

parameters are *not* known before the data are taken. These charts show the same patterns as those for the case with parameters known.

Figures 7.33 and 7.34 give the EWMA $Q(\overline{X})$- and Shewhart $Q(\overline{X})$-charts for the case UU. Comparison of the EWMA-Q charts in Fig. 7.29 and 7.33 illustrates the relative behavior of these charts when the

Q-EWMA Chart for MEAN : SGUU

XBarBar = 50.3721, SD = 1.141852

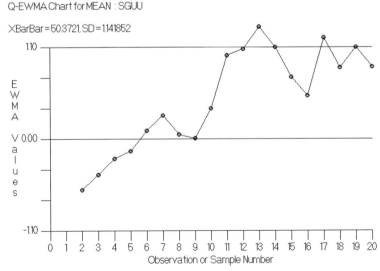

Figure 7.33   EWMA $Q(\overline{X})$-Chart for μ, Case UU

Shewhart Q-Chart for MEAN : SGUU

XBarBar = 50.3721, SD = 1.141852

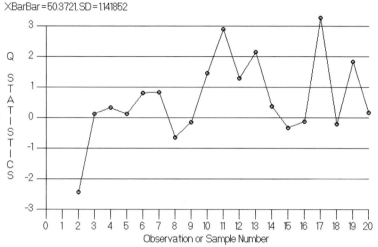

Figure 7.34 Shewhart $Q(\overline{X})$-Chart for μ, Case UU

parameters are both known or both unknown. While the Case UU EWMA chart signals on the 13th point, as does the Case KK chart, the subsequent behavior shows the tendency of the Q-statistics to return to the stable condition after a one-time parameter shift.

7.6 THE CUSUM Q-CHART

Consider next plotting a numerical CUSUM chart from a sequence of Q-statistics $Q_1, Q_2, \cdots$. Since the Q_i's for a stable process are independent standard normal statistics, the chart is determined by the reference value k_s and the decision interval h_s defined in equations (6.3.6). The CUSUM statistics S_t^+ and S_t^- were defined in (6.3.7) as follows.

$$S_t^+ = \text{Max}\{0, S_{t-1}^+ + Q_t - k_s\}$$
$$S_t^- = \text{Min}\{0, S_{t-1}^- + Q_t + k_s\}$$
(7.6.1)

with $S_0^+ = S_0^- = 0$.

The symmetric numerical CUSUM chart is made with control limits at $\pm h_s$. If $S_t^+ > h_s$ an increase in the parameter is signaled, and if $S_t^- < -h_s$ a decrease in the parameter is signaled. The values of k_s and h_s can be chosen using the methods of section 6.3.

In Example 6.8, a CUSUM chart was designed to have approximately the same ARL performance as the EWMA chart in the last section with $\lambda = 0.25$ and $K = 2.9$. The CUSUM chart obtained had $k_s = 0.75$ and $h_s = 3.34$. These values were chosen to give a CUSUM test with approximately the same ARL as the EWMA for the in-control case (for this CUSUM this is 370.5) and to detect a 1.5 standard deviation shift in a normal mean (for this CUSUM this is also 5.18, the same as for the EWMA test). As for the EWMA, this shift is in the mean of the distribution of the Q_t's, and not in a process mean, except for the KK case for a normal process mean.

Example 7.8: To illustrate the CUSUM Q-chart and compare it with the EWMA and Shewhart Q-charts, we have plotted the charts for $k_s = 0.75$ and $h_s = 3.34$ for the data of Table 7.4 in Figs. 7.35–7.38. These charts can be compared with the corresponding EWMA and Shewhart Q-charts for this data given in section 7.5.

The EWMA $Q(S^2)$-chart of Fig. 7.27 and the Shewhart $Q(S^2)$-chart of Fig 7.28 correspond to the CUSUM Q-chart of Fig 7.35. Recall that the standard deviation was increased by 50% on observations 16–20. Fig 7.27 (EWMA) and Fig 7.35 (CUSUM) both signal this increase on the 19th observation, and Fig 7.28 signals it by the 1-of-1 test on observation 19 as well as by the 4-of-5 test on observation 20. The charts for the other cases can be compared similarly. Overall, the different types of charts perform similarly. Note that the purpose of these examples is not intended as a global comparison of these competing charts, but merely to familiarize the reader with the details of the charts.

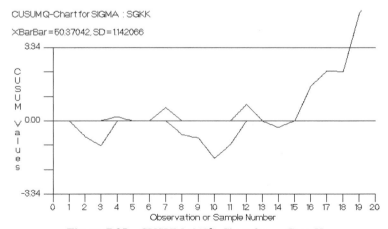

Figure 7.35   CUSUM $Q(S^2)$ Chart for σ, Case K

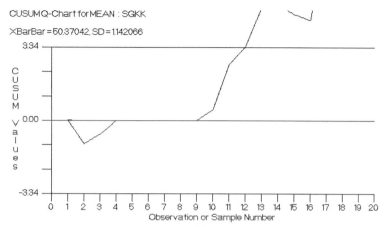

Figure 7.36 CUSUM $Q(\overline{X})$-Chart for μ, Case KK

Some general results from other work are given in the next section to aid in the choice and implementation of these charts. ∎

Hawkins (1987) proposed a CUSUM procedure that is essentially the same as the CUSUM Q-chart discussed here for case UU of individual measurements Q-statistics for the process mean, and an alternative chart for the variance. He also gives a particularly insightful discussion of the role and need for this general approach to SPC that does not require prior exact knowledge of process distribution parameters. Also see Hawkins (1981) for some related results.

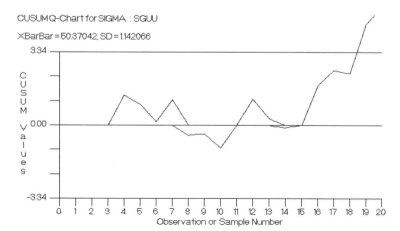

Figure 7.37 CUSUM $Q(S^2)$-Chart for σ, Case U

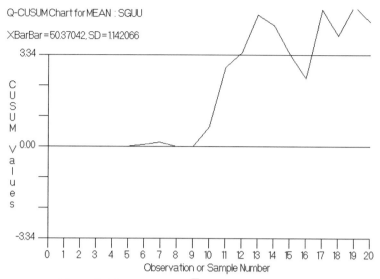

Figure 7.38   CUSUM $Q(\bar{X})$-Chart for μ, Case UU

7.7   SENSITIVITIES OF TRANSFORMATIONS, COMPETING TESTS, IMPLEMENTATION ISSUES

7.7.1   Case KK Charts

Since the Q-statistics for any of the cases considered above can be plotted on Shewhart, EWMA, CUSUM, or possibly other types of charts, some guidance is needed to make decisions as to exactly which charts to use for particular problems. Since the Q-statistics and charts for the case with both parameters known, case KK, are equivalent to those for classical charts, the known results for classical charts obtain for these charts also. In particular, since the 1-of-1 test has poor sensitivity for detecting small shifts in a process mean, this will, of course, be the same for the corresponding Q-charts for either means or standard deviations. Also, from our study of the power of the classical S^2 probability chart, we know that the 1-of-1 test on the $Q(S^2)$-chart for case KK will have poor power to detect decreases in σ. An EWMA Q-chart, a CUSUM Q-chart, or a 4-of-5 runs test on a Shewhart Q-chart will have much better sensitivity to detect small parameter shifts. Moreover, since case KK is the limiting case, as data accumulate, we can expect that the 1-of-1 test will perform poorly in detecting small parameter shifts for the cases with at least one unknown parameter, also.

7.7.2 Comparing Shewhart, EWMA, and CUSUM Charts to Detect Monotone Parameter Shifts

Quesenberry (1995a) studied the properties of the 1-of-1, 9-of-9, 4-of-5, and one additional test called a 3-of-3 test (that signals an increase in a parameter when three consecutive points are above 1, and signals a decrease when three consecutive points are below −1); as well as particular EWMA and CUSUM Q-charts. The EWMA chart had $\lambda = 0.25$ and $K = 2.9$, as derived in Example 6.3; and the CUSUM chart had $h_s^+ = 3.34$ and $k_s^+ = 0.75$; see Example 6.8. This paper studied the relative performance of these six tests to detect either a permanent increase or decrease in either μ or σ, assuming a normal process distribution; for the four cases KK, UK, KU, and UU; for both subgrouped and individual measurements Q-statistics. The paper considers statistical properties of the transformed statistics and gives results of a simulation study of the sensitivities of the tests using the four classes of transformations: KK, UK, KU, UU. The simulation study considered the number of signals from the next 30 measurements after a parameter shift, assuming varying numbers of measurements had been observed on a stable process before the shift. The overall conclusions can be summarized as follows.

- The classical 1-of-1 test has poor sensitivity, as expected, to detect shifts for some cases, including shifts less than two standard deviations of the process mean, and decreases in the process standard deviation. It is, however, the best possible test to detect a large shift in μ or large increase in σ on the first observation, or sample for subgrouped data, after the shift occurs, as discussed further below.
- The overall performance of the Q-EWMA and Q-CUSUM were comparable with each other and usually better than the four Shewhart chart tests to detect small one-step permanent parameter shifts.
- The 4-of-5 test is considered the best overall of the four Shewhart chart tests considered. It has false alarm rates comparable to the 1-of-1 test, the EWMA test, and the CUSUM test; and has good sensitivity to detect either increases or decreases in either μ or σ. This test is a good choice to use on the Shewhart charts to detect either increases or decreases in either μ and σ. If both this test and the classical 1-of-1 test are applied on the same chart, we will call this combined test the 11-45 test, then we remind the reader that

the overall rate of false alarms will be substantially increased. The ARL for the stable case is 165 (see Champ and Woodall 1987).

· The 3-of-3 test has false alarm rates roughly 2 1/2 times that of the 1-of-1 test; however, it has very good sensitivity for detecting parameter shifts quickly and in some applications, such as charting at start-up of a process, or short runs, this may be a good choice of test. This can be a reasonable trade-off in a start-up process before many data are available to improve sensitivity.

7.7.3 Outliers

Most of the foregoing discussion assumed that we are mainly concerned with detecting one-step permanent shifts, or at least monotone trends, in either a process mean or variance. One-step temporary shifts in a parameter, usually the mean, are sometimes a major concern. The observations produced by such shifts are often called "outliers" or "fliers." By this we mean that a process that is producing stably suddenly produces a small number, usually only one or two, values that are much larger or smaller than their preceding fellows. The fact that a process is outlier prone will likely be known by engineers and technicians familiar with the process. For example, machining processes are often outlier prone for a number of reasons.

It can be shown that the 1-of-1 test on the Shewhart Q-chart is optimal in most of the cases considered to detect a shift in a parameter value on the first observation after it occurs. It was shown in Quesenberry (1995f) (see Appendix 7C) that the 1-of-1 test on the Shewhart Q-chart for μ for individual observations is, in fact, essentially the classical two-sample t-test for equality of means, assuming unknown but equal variances. This test is the uniformly most powerful unbiased, UMPU, test for this two-sample testing problem. This means that the 1-of-1 test on the Shewhart Q-chart is the most powerful test possible for detecting a one-step shift on the first observation after it occurs. This also means it is the most powerful test possible to detect a single outlier. Moreover, if we consider the sequence $Q(X_r)$ of Q-statistics of equation (7.4.4) for $r = 1, 2, 3, \cdots, r, \cdots$; then the first point on the Q-chart for μ is for $r = 3$. The 1-of-1 test for the third point on this chart is a level 0.00270 t-test with one degree of freedom to test (7C.1) of Appendix 7C; for the fourth point it has two degrees of freedom; $\cdots$; for the rth point it has $r - 2$ degrees of freedom. As the degrees of freedom increase, the power of this t-test approaches that of a normal distribution test. This discussion obtains only for the sensitivity to detect a shift on the first point after it occurs. However, since detecting large shifts immediately is certainly crucial for most applications, especially Stage 1 studies, we feel that the 1-of-1 test on a Shewhart Q-chart should be part of stage 1 charting applications. This is the major reason for our recommendation below for including the 1-of-1 test with the 4-of-5 test for stage one applications of charting technology.

If outliers are automatically removed and not used in subsequent computations to compute Q-statistics, then the sensitivities to detect parameter shifts will be improved. However, the distribution theory for the stable case will also be disturbed. In many cases this disturbance of the stable case distribution theory is only slight, while the improvement of the chart sensitivity can be large. See Quesenberry (1986) for a more detailed discussion of these issues.

7.7.4 Restarting Charts

If a process is being charted and a special cause is signaled by one of the charts, then a search for a special cause of the signal may or may not be successful. Even if the special cause is identified, it may not be possible to remove it. In every case, we will at some point have the task of restarting the process. Questions then arise as to how the charts should be restarted. What data from before the signal should be used to restart the charts? The answer to this depends, of course, on the particular circumstances. In some cases, due to the nature of the special cause, it will be clear that the process mean and standard deviation after the special cause is removed or "fixed" are not necessarily the same as they were before the signal. When this is so, the case UU charts may have to be restarted from the beginning without using any prior data or estimates.

In other cases we may be able to use data from before the signal, or estimates computed from it using the formulas given in sections 7.3 and 7.4, that use estimates of μ and σ computed from historical data.

Consider the following hypothetical circumstances. Suppose we have charted a process from startup using the formula for case UU for subgroups means given in (7.3.4), and for subgroups variances given in (7.3.6). On the 31st point we get a strong signal that the mean has changed; however, the variance chart indicates a stable variance. We identify the special cause and feel that from its nature it would cause a mean shift but would not affect the process variance. We might then restart the charts using formulas (7.3.4)′ and (7.3.6)′. We would simply use $\bar{\bar{X}}_i$ for $\bar{X}'_i$ in the formulas, and let $S^2_{h,b}$ be the pooled estimate of σ^2 from the first 30 samples.

7.7.5   Sample Sizes, the Trailing Window Data Basis

The primary applications of Q-charts are as aids to guide us in recognizing assignable causes and bringing processes into control without requiring large prior data sets. In section 4.11, we considered the point that we never really know the true values of the parameters and must *always* use *estimated* control limits. In Tables 4.13 and 4.15 for subgrouped and individual measurements data, respectively, we saw that in order to have the classical charts behave like those with known limits, we must have quite a lot of data. For subgrouped data, we recommended at least 100 samples of size 5, and with individual observations at least 300 observations in order to have these charts comparable to charts with truly known control limits in the stable or in-control case. Of course, knowing the pattern of points for the stable case is crucial, because we must know this point pattern for an in-control process in order to recognize and interpret anomalous patterns. Note, particularly, that the need for large data sets is driven by the "plug-in" method of estimation of the control limits for classical charts. However, the Q-statistics for all cases are exactly or approximately independent standard normal statistics and require no prior data set *in order to maintain known false alarm rates.*

Thus, the only issues concerned with data set sizes for charts based on Q-statistics are those of the sensitivity of the resulting charts to detect variation in the parameter of interest. Now, the limiting case for the best performance that we can have for a particular chart is that of the chart for the case when the parameters are known, here case KK. In addition to studying the relative performance of the six tests for parameter shifts, Quesenberry (1995a) also considered the relative sensitivity of the tests when based on the Q-statistics for the four cases KK, UK, KU, and UU. For the cases with at least one unknown parameter (UK, KU, UU), the performance of the tests for these cases depends on how many data are available before a given parameter shift, and as more data are available the sensitivity for these cases approaches that of the KK case. In section 7.3 we recommended using the case UU transformations and a trailing window of data for subgrouped data charts. The results in Quesenberry (1995a) can then serve as a guide for recommending the size of the data basis for the trailing window.

First, it should be clear that the size of the data basis set for the trailing window will depend on the characteristics of the particular process being charted. Issues that influence how often the control limits for classical Shewhart charts should be updated obviously must also be considered here. The long-term stability of the process is a consideration. We believe that a basis data set of a total of at least 150 observations will give good charting results. When possible and convenient, we would use larger sets, perhaps of 300 or so. Experience with particular processes will provide the final verification of the best choice of the data set size.

It should also be remarked that for individual measurements charts, due to the possible presence of long-term trends that could influence the estimate of σ, when enough data are available it may be desirable to use the case KK formulas with σ estimated either by the moving range, $\overline{MR}$, or mean square successive difference, MSSD. However, if this is done the data set sizes required would be those for classical individual measurements charts, namely, 100 observations for "trial" limits and 300 for "permanent" limits.

7.7.6 Some General Recommendations for Variables *Q*-Charts

- Whenever possible, use subgroups charts, rather than individual measurements charts.
- Use supplementary runs tests in addition to the 1-of-1 test. The 11-45 combined test is particularly recommended for *all* *Q*-charts. This combined test gives an ARL for the stable case of about 165 (see Champ and Woodall 1987).
- Always respond to signals. A further comment is in order here. We have noticed that many SPC practitioners do not always respond immediately to all signals on classical Shewhart charts. Some say that they want to see persistent signals before they respond. This is a dangerous practice because when the chart is truly controlling the false alarm rate at a known value for the signal rules specified, this practice will result in a false alarm rate that is much smaller than the nominally stated rate, and in a correspondingly insensitive chart to detect true special causes. We suspect that this practice has come about because the operators involved have discovered by experience that the classical X- and $\overline{X}$-charts with control limits computed from commonly recommended sample

sizes frequently give too many false alarms (see Quesenberry 1993).

7.8 SOME EXAMPLES

7.8.1 Using *Q*-Charts with Multiple Operating Factors

There are generally a number of operating factors such as operators, machines, materials, production lots, etc., associated with the measurements on a quality variable. The number of such factors and the numbers of values for each factor is usually large. We are sometimes especially interested in using the flexibility of *Q*-charts in charting short runs, or small data sets; samples of varying size; and different variables on the same chart; in order to attempt to detect quickly operating factors that are assignable causes contributing variation to the process output. This flexibility can be especially useful in a low-volume manufacturing environment such as that described in Koons and Luner (1991). In this work, it is important to keep in mind that we are concerned with controlling the *process* itself.

Q-charts can be used in combination with process flow charts to study the stability of a process, and to attempt to identify assignable causes responsible for any instability observed. Consider the simple process flow diagram illustrated in Fig. 7.39. This simple process consists of input material from two suppliers that is subjected to a stamping operation and then to a finishing operation. Material from both suppliers is processed by one of three stamping machines, and then finished on one of three finishing heads. There are $2 \times 3 \times 3 = 18$

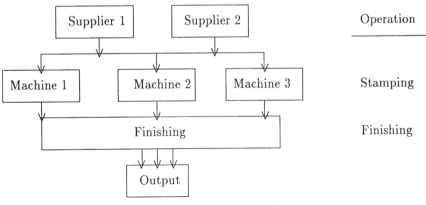

Figure 7.39   Process Flow Chart

distinct possible process flow paths. There are many possibilities for ways to use charts to study the stability of even this simple process. Initially, we might chart the final output to determine if the entire process is stable and producing product meeting specifications. If the results are not satisfactory, and we wish to improve the process, then we could consider charting material from particular production paths, or the incoming material from each supplier, or quality variables from each stamping machine, or from each finishing head. There are many possibilities.

Any of these charts can be made in real time, even if the number of observations on the quality variable is small, and can be made as operations are completed and measurements become available. Even though the Q-charts based on a small number of prior observations will not have high sensitivity to detect small parameter shifts, they will give a way to detect large instabilities in the process at a point in time before other valid charting methods are available.   ∎

Example 7.9: Process Flow Paths as Rational Subgroups.

Table 7.5 gives the values of a dimensional measurement made on output units from the process with flow chart shown in Fig. 7.39. The process flow path is given in the first three columns of each section column of Table 7.5. For example, the process flow path: 1 1 1 for a measurement means the measurement was taken on a unit of output of material from supplier 1, machine 1 and head 1. The data in Table 7.5 forms 14 different subgroups. Note that subgroups 6 and 8 are both for flow path 1 3 3. The values for these two groups were for production operations at separated times, and it was felt that this might possibly result in parameter shifts related to time.

We have made charts for the process standard deviation and mean for two cases. We first made individual measurements charts for σ and for μ by simply ignoring the subgrouping by flow paths. The IMUU charts (individual measurements, μ unknown and σ unknown) are given in Figs. 7.40 and 7.41. In this example, we apply the 1-of-1 and 4-of-5 tests to all the charts. The chart for σ does not signal and appears reasonably stable. The chart for μ also does not signal on these two tests, however, there are two issues that do require attention. First, note the PV − MSSD = 0.009 is a strong signal of a nonconstant mean, and, second, there are a number of groups of four or so consecutive points that are too close together. The first such group is for points 6, 7, 8, 9, and 10. These two points suggest there are mean differences in the flow paths.

TABLE 7.5 Data for Example 7.9

Point	Path	Value	Point	Path	Value	Point	Path	Value
1	1 1 1	20.86	6	1 3 3	20.22	10	2 1 2	18.44
	1 1 1	20.96		1 3 3	21.33		2 1 2	19.69
	1 1 1	19.54		1 3 3	20.46		2 1 2	20.42
	1 1 1	19.22		1 3 3	21.17		2 1 2	19.66
	1 1 1	21.83		1 3 3	21.84			
	1 1 1	20.02		1 3 3	22.56	11	2 2 2	21.68
				1 3 3	22.07		2 2 2	21.30
2	1 1 2	19.80					2 2 2	21.74
	1 1 2	19.62	7	1 2 3	21.06		2 2 2	21.91
	1 1 2	19.65		1 2 3	19.81		2 2 2	23.01
	1 1 2	19.38		1 2 3	21.52			
	1 1 2	20.49		1 2 3	20.61	12	2 2 3	20.69
	1 1 2	18.14		1 2 3	22.51		2 2 3	20.97
3	1 2 1	19.90	8	1 3 3	21.88		2 2 3	21.05
	1 2 1	21.71		1 3 3	22.39		2 2 3	20.43
	1 2 1	19.86		1 3 3	20.59	13	2 3 2	21.98
	1 2 1	20.80		1 3 3	21.58		2 3 2	21.24
	1 2 1	21.40		1 3 3	20.52		2 3 2	20.92
	1 2 1	21.63		1 3 3	23.23		2 3 2	23.91
4	1 2 2	22.02	9	2 1 1	20.09	14	2 3 3	23.23
	1 2 2	19.56		2 1 1	18.24		2 3 3	23.89
	1 2 2	21.35		2 1 1	21.41		2 3 3	21.70
	1 2 2	20.48		2 1 1	20.49		2 3 3	21.72
				2 1 1	19.86		2 3 3	20.91
5	1 3 2	20.86					2 3 3	23.30
	1 3 2	20.87					2 3 3	19.75
	1 3 2	22.25					2 3 3	23.19

In Fig. 7.42 and Fig. 7.43 we give the subgroups charts for this data set using the process flow paths as rational subgroups. Again, the chart for σ issues no signals by the 11-45 test. The subgroups chart for μ of Fig. 7.43 signals on points 6, 7, and 8 by the 4-of-5 test and on point 14 by the 1-of-1 test. The pattern of points for subgroups 2 through 11 is strongly suggestive of stratification; the points appear to be from two distinct distributions. Also, it should be noted that there were two separated subgroups for path 1 3 3 that were plotted as points 6 and 8, which give consistent results. At this point it is clear that we need to study the process to determine the special causes contributing to the differences in flow paths. Finishing operation number 3 appears as a likely candidate for study, because it is the finishing level of several of the points contributing to signals. ∎

Shewhart Q-Chart(s) for SIGMA : IMUU

XBAR = 2101876, SD = 1248339, RMSSD = 10633, PV-MSSD = 8.708771E-03

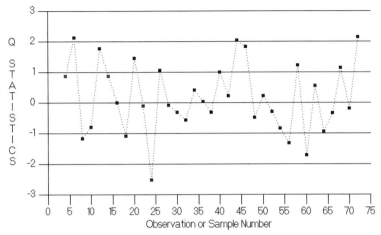

Figure 7.40 Individual Measurements Q-Chart for σ

Shewhart Q-Chart(s) for MEAN : IMUU

XBAR = 2101876, SD = 1248339, RMSSD = 10633, PV-MSSD = 8.708771E-03

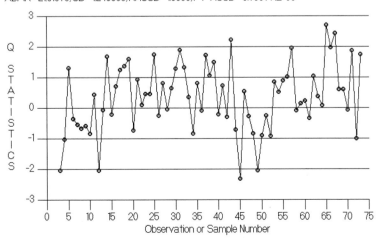

Figure 7.41 Individual Measurements Q-Chart for μ

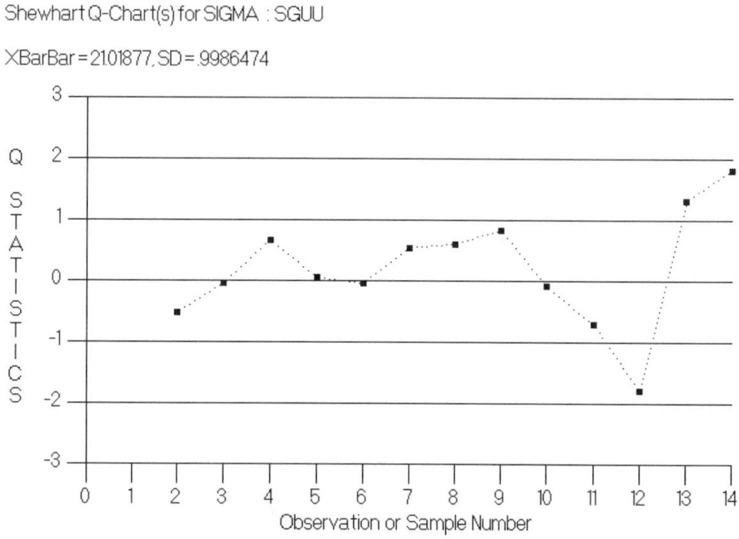

Shewhart Q-Chart(s) for SIGMA : SGUU

XBarBar = 21.01877, SD = .9986474

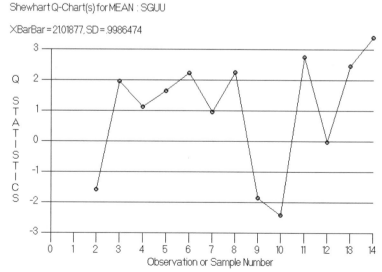

Figure 7.42   Subgroups Q-Chart for σ, Flow Paths as Rational Subgroups

Example 7.10: Feed Conversion Ratios, FCR, in Turkey Production.
     In the first paragraph of section 7.1, we stated a suspicion that the real reason classical SPC methods, which were developed largely for high-volume parts manufacturing industries, have not been used in

Shewhart Q-Chart(s) for MEAN : SGUU

XBarBar = 21.01877, SD = .9986474

Figure 7.43   Subgroups Q-Chart for μ, Flow Paths as Rational Subgroups

some industries is because the assumption that large data sets can be obtained, taken while a process is stable, is simply not met. The animal production industry and, in particular, the poultry industry, provide nice examples. In this example, we illustrate how feed conversion ratio (FCR) can be charted on Q-charts to give timely signals of the onset of costly special causes in turkey production operations.

Consider a flock of birds as one production unit. A typical flock would be 6000 heavy toms from one barn. When a flock is marketed, the feed conversion ratio, FCR, is an important quality variable. A production operation produces a time-ordered sequence of flocks with FCRs $X_1, X_2, \cdots, X_n$. Table 7.6 gives the FCRs for a sequence of 42 consecutively produced flocks from a farm.

Figures 7.44 and 7.45 give individual measurements Q-charts of the 42 values of Table 7.6. The chart for σ in Fig. 7.44 does not signal by the 11-45 test, suggesting a constant value of the variance of FCR. However, Figure 7.45 signals on points 33, 34, 35, 36, and 42; clearly signaling an increase in the mean FCR. Also, the PV $-$ MSSD $= 0.002$ is highly significant, also indicating a nonconstant mean. Thus there is strong evidence of an increase in the mean of the distribution of FCR at about the 29th flock.

Investigation by independent laboratory analysis showed an increase in blood pathogens indicating an onset of disease occurred in the 29th flock. Unfortunately, these charts were not being made flock-by-flock, as they could have been, as the flocks were marketed. Had the charts been made this way in real time, they would have given timely signals of the onset of disease soon after it occurred.

The onset of disease is apparently an important special cause in many, probably all, animal production processes. We believe that the special properties of Q-charts makes them useful potential management tools to help quickly recognize the onset of disease or many other special causes by charting FCR or other relevant quality variables. This example is from joint work with David Fernandez, Ph.D., D.V.M. ■

7.9 THE EXPONENTIAL Q-CHART

The exponential distribution, $EX(\alpha)$, was defined in section 2.10, and its relationship to a Poisson process was also discussed. Charts based on the exponential distribution are often very useful in charting to control a Poisson process rate parameter. If a Poisson process is operating in time with rate parameter α per unit of time, then the time between

TABLE 7.6 Feed Conversion Ratios of a Study Farm

Obs	1	2	3	4	5	6	7	8	9	10	11	12	13	14
FCR	2.46	2.65	2.68	2.53	2.60	2.59	2.54	2.61	2.62	2.63	2.68	2.61	2.64	2.65
Obs	15	16	17	18	19	20	21	22	23	24	25	26	27	28
FCR	2.55	2.50	2.57	2.58	2.66	2.59	2.55	2.54	2.62	2.59	2.72	2.56	2.59	2.62
Obs	29	30	31	32	33	34	35	36	37	38	39	40	41	42
FCR	2.65	2.67	2.68	2.73	2.71	2.68	2.67	2.80	2.63	2.72	2.67	2.66	2.65	2.86

Shewhart Q-Chart for SIGMA : IMUU

XBAR = 2.631191, SD = 7.600394E-02, RMSSD = 5.723295E-02, PV-MSSD = 2.024466E-03

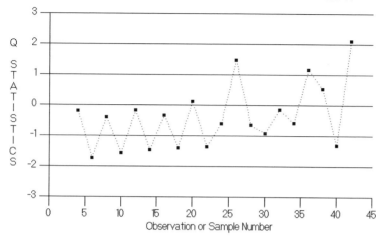

Figure 7.44 Shewhart Q-chart for σ for FCR Data of Table 7.6

events is an exponential $EX(\alpha)$ distribution. Let $X_1, X_2, \cdots, X_n$ denote times between occurrences of the event of interest. Then, if the parameter α is assumed to be known to be $\alpha = \alpha_0$, we define the exponential Q-statistics for this case, EXPK, as in display (7.9.1).

Shewhart Q-Chart for MEAN : IMUU

XBAR = 2.631191, SD = 7.600394E-02, RMSSD = 5.723295E-02, PV-MSSD = 2.024466E-03

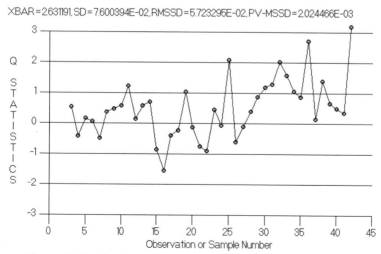

Figure 7.45 Shewhart Q-chart for μ for FCR Data of Table 7.6

$$u_n = 1 - e^{-\alpha_0 X_n}$$

$$Q_n = -\Phi^{-1}(u_n) \qquad (7.9.1)$$

$$\text{for } n = 1, 2, \cdots$$

If the value of α is unknown we define the Q-statistics for this case, EXPU, as in (7.9.2), where $\overline{X}_n$ is the usual sequential sample mean.

$$u_n = 1 - \left[1 - \frac{X_n}{n\overline{X}_n} \right]^{n-1}$$

$$Q_n = -\Phi^{-1}(u_n) \qquad (7.9.2)$$

$$\text{for } n = 2, 3, \cdots$$

If the values $X_1, X_2, \cdots, X_n$ are a sample from a stable exponential distribution, then the sequences of Q-statistics for cases EXPK and EXPU are independent standard normal statistics. This result is obvious from the classic probability integral transformation for the EXPK case. This result for the EXPU case follows from the conditional probability integral transformation of O'Reilly and Quesenberry (1973). See particularly Corollary 2.1 and Example 4.2 of that paper. (Note: the formula for $\tilde{F}_r(z)$ in that paper should have an exponent of $r - 1$ on the square brackets.)

These sequences of Q-statistics can be plotted on Shewhart, EWMA, or CUSUM Q-charts in the same manner as previously considered sequences of Q-statistics. We first consider the types of patterns we can expect on Shewhart charts in response to shifts in the parameter α.

Suppose α shifts from a nominal value of $\alpha = \alpha_0$ to a value $\alpha = \delta\alpha_0$ for $\delta > 0$. Recall, from display (2.10.2), that both the mean and standard deviation of the exponential distribution are $1/\alpha$. Thus, when α shifts from α_0 to $\delta\alpha_0$, both the mean and standard deviation will shift from $1/\alpha_0$ to $1/\delta\alpha_0$. If $0 < \delta < 1$, then both the mean and standard deviation will increase, but if $\delta > 1$ then both the mean and standard deviation will decrease. By examining the transformations (7.9.1) and (7.9.2) we see that an increase in the rate parameter α will result in an increase in the mean but a decrease in the standard deviation of the Q-statistics. Thus, an increase in α will tend to cause the pattern of points on a Shewhart Q-chart to move up on the chart and to have less vertical spread. A decrease in α will have exactly the opposite effects. The pattern of points will tend to move down on the chart and the vertical spread will tend to increase. We illustrate these points in the following Example 7.11.

Example 7.11: Suppose a production process produces a defective unit on average once in about 30 days and then shifts to producing defectives at a rate of about one in a week. To simulate such a process we have simulated 20 observations from an $EX(0.03)$ process and 20 more from an $EX(0.14)$ process. The chart for case U, EXPU, is given in Fig. 7.46. The increase on about point 21 is readily apparent because the point pattern moves up and the spread decreases. The 4-5 test signals immediately, and the 9-9 test signals several times later.   ■

Example 7.12: In Chapter 8, Example 8.9, we give a detailed discussion of the problem of charting nosocomial infections in hospitals. A chart of the data of Table 8.12 of small hospital data based on the geometric distribution is given in Fig. 8.21. Due to the approximation of the binomial distribution by the Poisson for small binomial p, the data from Table 8.12 can also be considered to be approximately exponentially distributed. We have charted that data in Fig. 7.47. The chart of Fig. 7.47 should be compared to the chart in Fig. 8.21. Note

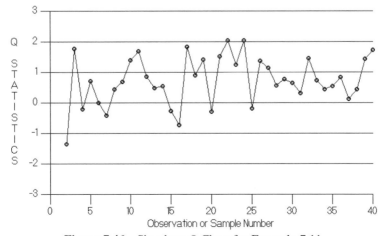

Figure 7.46   Shewhart Q-Chart for Example 7.11

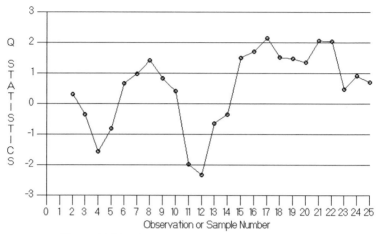

Shewhart Q-Chart for : EXPU
AlphaHat = 2.351834E-02

Figure 7.47 Shewhart Q-Chart for Example 7.12

that they are very similar charts. This is what we expect, of course. See the discussion of this chart in Example 8.9. ∎

7.10 SUMMARY

In this chapter we have presented an approach to control charting of either subgrouped or individual measurements data from a normal process distribution or from an exponential distribution that requires transforming statistics to sequences of independent standard normal statistics. This can be done with varying sample sizes and with a small data set, even when some of the process parameters are not known. A major advantage of this approach is that charting can be done on-line in real time, essentially from the beginning of a production run, with exactly known false alarm rates. The statistics in all cases can be charted on Shewhart, EWMA, or CUSUM charts. The 1-of-1 test on a Shewhart chart has the attractive property that it gives the most sensitive test possible to detect a one-step parameter shift on the first point after it occurs for most of the charts. These charting methods will make it possible to establish effective charting programs in industries where the large data sets of mass production required of classical SPC methods are not available.

An important point about this general approach to charting is as follows. Recall that the purpose of SPC charts is to study the stability or constancy of the parameter, μ, σ, α, or whatever. If the process is stable, the actual value of the constant parameter is not relevant to this notion of stability. In fact, it can be shown that the sequences of Q-statistics for the various cases considered in this chapter are independent of the parameter estimates we have recommended; see Quesenberry and Starbuck (1976), especially Theorem 3.1 and the discussion following it. A further advantage of Shewhart charts for individual observations from either a normal or exponential distribution is that when a process shows a stable chart, not only does this imply the absence of special causes of variation, but it also serves as a graphical verification of the form of the process distribution, that is, of normality or exponentiality of the process distribution.

APPENDIX 7A MINIMUM VARIANCE ESTIMATION OF A LINEAR FUNCTION

The choice of the formula (7.3.4) was due to the following inference considerations. Let y_j be independent random variables with $E(y_j) = \mu$ and $\mathrm{Var}(y_j) = \sigma_j^2$ for $j \in \{1, \cdots, m\}$. Then consider forming a linear estimate of μ of the form

$$L = \sum_{j=1}^{m} a_j y_j \qquad \text{with } \sum a_j = 1$$

We wish to determine the weights $(a_1, \cdots, a_m)$ so that $\mathrm{Var}(L)$ is a minimum. Then

$$\mathrm{Var}(L) = \sum_{j=1}^{m} a_j^2 \sigma_j^2 \quad \text{and} \quad \sum_{j=1}^{m} a_j - 1 = 0$$

Put
$$Q = \sum_{j=1}^{m} a_j^2 \sigma_j^2 - \lambda \left(\sum_{j=1}^{m} a_j - 1 \right)$$

Then $\dfrac{\partial Q}{\partial a_j} = 2 a_j \sigma_j^2 - \lambda = 0 \Rightarrow 2 a_j = \dfrac{\lambda}{\sigma_j^2}$ for $j = 1, \cdots, m$

and $2 \sum a_j = \lambda \sum \sigma_j^{-2} \Rightarrow \lambda = \dfrac{2}{\sum \sigma_j^{-2}}$

and
$$2\,a_j = \frac{2\,\sigma_j^{-2}}{\sum \sigma_j^{-2}}, \quad \text{or } a_j = \frac{\sigma_j^{-2}}{\sum \sigma_j^{-2}}$$

and we can summarize as follows.

If $y_1, \cdots, y_m$ are independent unbiased estimates of a parameter μ, then the minimum variance unbiased linear function estimate is

$$L = \sum_{j=1}^{m} a_j y_j, \quad \text{for } a_j = \frac{\sigma_j^{-2}}{\displaystyle\sum_{j=1}^{m} \sigma_j^{-2}}, \quad j = 1, \cdots, m.$$

Special Exercise: Show that the weights of the estimate (7.3.4) are of the form of these a_j's.

APPENDIX 7B DISTRIBUTIONAL PROPERTIES OF Q-STATISTICS

It was stated in the development that the Q-statistics are sequences of independent standard normal random variables. These results are obvious from the probability integral transformation for the cases with known parameter values. These results for individual measurements charts for the process mean μ follow immediately from the conditional probability integral transformations (CPIT) of O'Reilly and Quesenberry (1973), (see also Quesenberry 1986c). However, some readers may not have access to that paper, or may find it rather abstract. Quesenberry (1991a) gave elementary arguments for these cases, and a number of other cases as well. We give here those developments for these cases. We begin with two Lemmas that will be helpful in establishing the results.

Lemma 7B.1: Let Y_1 and Y_2 be independent $\chi^2_{\nu_1}$ and $\chi^2_{\nu_2}$ random variables. Then the ratio Y_1/Y_2 and sum $Y_1 + Y_2$ are independent random variables.

Sketch of Proof: Put

$$W_1 = \frac{\nu_2}{\nu_1} \frac{Y_1}{Y_2} \quad \text{and} \quad W_2 = Y_1 + Y_2$$

and W_1 is an F_{ν_1, ν_2} random variable while W_2 is a $\chi^2_{\nu_1 + \nu_2}$ random variable. By direct transformation, the density of (W_1, W_2) is found to be the product of these marginal densities.   ∎

Lemma 7B.2: If Y_i for $i = 1, 2, 3$ are independent $\chi^2_{\nu_i}$ random variables, then

$$W_1 = \frac{\nu_2 Y_1}{\nu_1 Y_2} \quad \text{and} \quad W_2 = \frac{\nu_1 + \nu_2}{\nu_3} \frac{Y_3}{Y_1 + Y_2}$$

are independent F_{ν_1, ν_2} and $F_{\nu_3, \nu_1 + \nu_2}$ random variables, respectively.

Proof: That W_1 and W_2 are F random variables is immediate. By Lemma 1, W_1 is independent of $Y_1 + Y_2$. Since W_1 is also independent of Y_3, it is independent of any function of Y_3 and $Y_1 + Y_2$.   ∎

Theorem 7B.1: The Q-Statistics given by equations (7.3.1), (7.3.2), (7.3.4), (7.3.5), and (7.3.6) are sequences of independent $N(0, 1)$ random variables when the samples are all from a stable normal process.

Proof: We will show only for (7.3.4) and (7.3.6). The other cases can be shown with similar arguments.

Equations (7.3.4): That the sequence of Q_i's are $N(0, 1)$ r.v.'s is immediate. We only need to show the independence. We will work in the $2i$-dimensional space of the distribution of $(\overline{X}_j, S_j^2)$ for $j = 1, 2, \cdots,$ i; when the first i pairs of sample statistics are available. Then it can be readily shown that the statistic $(\overline{X}_i, S_i^2)$ is a complete sufficient statistic for the process parameter (μ, σ^2). Put

$$A_i = \frac{\overline{X}_i - \overline{\overline{X}}_{i-1}}{S_{p,i}} \quad$$ and the result will be proved if it is shown that A_{i-1} and A_i are independent.

Consider the vector $T = (\overline{\overline{X}}_{i-1}, S_{i-1}^2, \overline{X}_i, S_i)$. Note that the distribution of A_j is a constant in the parameter (μ, σ^2), $j = 3, 4, \cdots, i$. From this and Basu's Theorem (Basu 1955) it follows that $(\overline{X}_{i-1}, S_{i-1}^2)$ is independent of A_{i-1} and obviously $\overline{X}_i$ and S_i are independent of A_{i-1}. Thus, T is independent of A_{i-1}, and, moreover, A_i is also independent of A_{i-1} since it is a function only of the components of T.   ∎

Equations (7.3.6): We need to show that the arguments

$$w_i = \frac{(n_1 + \cdots + n_{i-1} - i + 1)S_i^2}{(n_1 - 1)S_1^2 + \cdots + (n_{i-1} - 1)S_{i-1}^2} = \frac{S_i^2}{S_{p,i-1}^2},$$

$$i = 2, 3, \cdots$$

are independent $F_{n_i-1,n_1+\cdots+n_{i-1}-i+1}$ random variables. This follows from Lemma 7B.2 by recalling that $(n_i - 1)S_i^2$ are independent $\chi_{n_i-1}^2$ random variables for $i = 1, 2, \cdots$. ∎

Theorem 7B.2: The Q-Statistics given by equations (7.4.1)–(7.4.6) are sequences of independent $N(0, 1)$ random variables.

Proof: We will show for only some of the cases. The other cases can be shown with similar arguments.

Equations (7.4.4): For this case put

$$Y_1 = \frac{1}{\sigma^2} \sum_{i=1}^{r-1} (X_i - \overline{X}_{r-1})^2,$$

$$Y_2 = \left(\frac{r - 1}{r}\right) \frac{(X_r - \overline{X}_{r-1})^2}{\sigma^2},$$

$$Y_3 = \left(\frac{r}{r + 1}\right) \frac{(X_{r+1} - \overline{X}_r)^2}{\sigma^2}$$

Then Y_2 and Y_3 are both χ_1^2 random variables and Y_1 is a χ_{r-2}^2 random variable, and, moreover, all three are pairwise independent. To show independence of Y_1 and Y_2, consider

$$\text{Cov}(X_i - \overline{X}_{r-1}, X_r - \overline{X}_{r-1}) \quad \text{for } i \in \{1, \cdots, r - 1]$$

$$= E[(X_i - \overline{X}_{r-1})(X_r - \overline{X}_{r-1})]$$

$$= E(\overline{X}_{r-1}^2) - E(X_i \overline{X}_{r-1}) = \frac{\sigma^2}{r - 1} - \frac{\sigma^2}{r - 1} = 0$$

and since $(X_i - \overline{X}_{r-1})$ and $X_r - \overline{X}_{r-1})$ are normal they are independent. The other pairs can be shown to be independent in a similar way. Put

$$A_r^2 = \frac{(r-2)Y_2}{Y_1} = \left(\frac{r-1}{r}\right)\frac{(X_r - \overline{X}_{r-1})^2}{S_{r-1}^2} \quad \text{and}$$

$$A_{r+1}^2 = \frac{(r-1)Y_3}{Y_1 + Y_2} = \left(\frac{r}{r+1}\right)\frac{(X_{r+1} - \overline{X}_r)^2}{S_r^2}$$

and A_r is the argument of the Student-t distribution function of equation (7.4.1). That A_r and A_{r+1} are independent follows from Lemma 7B.2. That they have Student-t distributions is immediate. Therefore, Q_{r+1} and Q_r are independent $N(0, 1)$ random variables by the probability integral transformation.

Equations (7.4.6): We need to show that the arguments

$$B_\nu = \frac{\nu R_r^2}{R_2^2 + \cdots + R_{r-2}^2} \quad \text{for } \nu = \frac{r}{2} - 1 = 1, 2, \cdots$$

are independent $F_{1,\nu}$ random variables. This follows from Lemma 7B.2 by observing that the $R_r^2/2$ are χ_1^2 random variables for $r = 4, 6, \cdots$.

APPENDIX 7C   ON OPTIMALITY PROPERTIES OF Q-CHARTS 1-OF-1 TESTS

In section 7.7 it was noted that the classical 1-of-1 test on many of the Q-charts has the important property that they have the largest power possible to detect a parameter shift on the first observation after it occurs. We demonstrate this property now for a number of the Q-statistics. Consider first an individual observations chart and suppose $X_1, \cdots, X_{r-1}$ are from a stable $N(\mu_0, \sigma_0^2)$ distribution. Suppose X_r is observed and assumed to be from a $N(\mu_r, \sigma_r^2)$ distribution. Then the 1-of-1 test that signals when $Q(X_r)$ defined by one of the equations (7.4.1), (7.4.2), (7.4.3), or (7.4.4) either exceeds 3 or is less than -3 is actually an 0.00270 level test of the two sided hypothesis testing problem of (7C.1).

$$H_0: \mu_r = \mu_0$$

$$H_a: \mu_r \neq \mu_0 \tag{7C.1}$$

For each of the cases (KK, UK, KU, UU), it can be shown that this test is a uniformly most powerful unbiased (UMPU) test for the testing problem (7C.1). We consider in detail the statistic $Q(X_r)$ of (7.4.4). The test signals if

$$|Q(X_r)| = \left| \Phi^{-1} \left\{ H_{r-2} \left[\sqrt{\frac{r-1}{r}} \left(\frac{X_r - \overline{X}_{r-1}}{S_{r-1}} \right) \right] \right\} \right| > 3 \quad (7C.2)$$

But by symmetry of both the standard normal and Student-t distributions, (7C.2) is equivalent to requiring that

$$\left| \sqrt{\frac{r-1}{r}} \left(\frac{X_r - \overline{X}_{r-1}}{S_{r-1}} \right) \right| > t_{0.00135, r-2} \quad (7C.3)$$

for $t_{0.00135, r-2}$ the Student-t 0.00135 upper fractile. But the test of (7C.3) is the UMPU test for the hypothesis testing problem of (7C.1). (See Lehmann (1959), section 5.3, equations (28) and (30).) This shows that the 1-of-1 test made on the chart for case UU of individual observations is the most sensitive test possible to detect an outlier. The same statement holds for the other charts from the Q-statistics of (7.4.1), (7.4.2), and (7.4.3). The Q-charts from the subgroups formulas (7.3.1), (7.3.2), (7.3.3), and (7.3.4) have similar optimal properties, as do those for variances from (7.3.5) and (7.3.6).

PROBLEMS

7.1   The following table gives sample sizes, sample means, and sample variances collected from an operating process. Perform a Stage 1 analysis to determine the operating state of control of the process by plotting Q-charts for both the sample means and the sample variances for the two cases:

   (a) using $\overline{\overline{X}}$ and S_p^2 for μ and σ^2 and using the formulas for the "known" parameters case.

   (b) plot points on a Q-chart for subgroups 2, 3, 4, and 5 using formulas for the "unknown" parameters case.

Subgroup Number, i	Subgroup Size, n_i	$\overline{X}_i$	S_i^2
1	5	10.28	.0343
2	4	10.24	.0261
3	7	10.33	.0105
4	6	10.30	.0114
5	10	10.21	.0098
6	7	10.27	.0163
7	8	10.23	.0182
8	11	10.30	.0196
9	8	10.15	.0308
10	10	10.07	.0392
11	10	10.10	.0251
12	13	10.13	.0572
13	8	10.13	.0616
14	6	10.14	.0201
15	6	10.25	.0941
16	9	10.17	.0380
17	10	10.22	.0272
18	8	10.17	.0112
19	5	10.16	.0113
20	7	10.26	.0500
21	6	10.17	.0451

7.2 This is a problem that requires using the Q-Charts computer program. The data in the following table are from a process with a mean target value of 7.00, but the actual values of the process parameters are not known.

(a) Use the Case UU transformations to make Shewhart Q-charts for σ and μ.

(b) Use the Case KK transformations to make Shewhart Q-charts by using estimates from the entire data set for both σ and μ. Note that this chart for μ is essentially the same as the classical 3-sigma retrospective $\overline{X}$-chart.

(c) When parameters are not known, some writers have proposed using target values for them in order to chart short runs. Use the mean target value to make a chart by using the formulas for a Case KU, mean known and variance unknown, chart.

(d) Discuss your interpretation of the charts made in parts (a), (b), and (c) of this problem.

Sample	Observations					
1	6.92	6.80	6.90	6.88	6.87	
2	6.89	6.77	6.84	6.80	6.81	
3	6.83	6.87	6.93	6.92	6.92	
4	6.92	6.95	6.90	6.90	6.86	6.87
5	6.85	6.93	6.87	6.91	6.89	6.83
6	6.89	6.84	6.96	6.86	6.91	6.95
7	6.92	6.88	6.84	6.89	6.89	
8	6.85	6.94	6.92	6.81	6.92	
9	6.89	6.87	6.80	6.96	6.84	6.95
10	6.94	6.87	6.85	7.00	6.88	6.89
11	6.94	6.88	6.96	6.90	6.98	
12	6.94	7.01	7.03	6.97	6.85	
13	6.96	6.87	6.90	6.91	6.93	
14	6.89	7.01	7.03	7.03	6.92	
15	7.00	6.89	6.90	6.94	6.94	
16	6.94	6.95	6.94	6.92	6.91	6.92
17	6.95	6.99	6.95	6.91	7.01	6.97
18	6.95	6.90	6.88	7.00	6.92	
19	6.95	6.94	6.87	6.93	6.96	
20	6.92	7.02	6.99	6.99	6.98	
21	6.96	7.01	7.05	6.97	6.88	
22	7.03	7.07	6.91	7.01	6.96	
23	7.00	6.98	6.94	7.00	7.07	
24	6.96	7.00	6.87	6.97	6.94	6.96
25	6.96	7.09	6.92	6.92	6.97	7.02
26	6.96	6.97	6.98	6.98	7.01	7.00
27	6.88	6.97	7.01	7.05	6.99	7.00
28	7.05	7.03	6.98	6.94	7.03	7.02
29	6.92	7.07	7.02	6.92	6.94	
30	7.03	6.92	7.01	7.00	7.00	

7.3 The following table gives 40 values obtained in time order, by rows, from an operating process. Enter the first four values and make Q-Charts for the variance and mean. Enter the fifth value and replot the charts. Continue entering one value at a time and plotting the charts until all 40 points have been entered. Discuss your conclusions. Report only the charts after the 20th, 26th, and 40th values.

4.98	5.07	4.95	5.16	5.12	5.08	5.06	4.92	4.94	4.88
5.02	4.93	4.88	5.08	5.15	4.86	5.05	4.85	4.75	4.95
5.03	5.26	5.14	5.11	5.18	5.23	5.02	5.01	5.04	5.29
5.24	5.09	5.06	5.05	5.13	5.17	5.22	5.07	5.02	5.28

7.4 Analyze the data in file P74 on the data disk.

7.5 Analyze the data in file P75 on the data disk.

7.6 Use Q-charts to study the depth of cut data of Ott and Schilling given in problem 4.16.

7.7 For each of the EWMA Q-Charts below, assume that both μ and σ are unknown.

(a) Use the Crowder algorithm (described in Chapter 6) to find values of λ and K for an EWMA Q-Chart such that ARL(δ = 0) = 370, and the ARL(δ = 1) is a minimum. Use these values of λ and K in parts (c), (e), and (g) below. (P77)

(b) Make IM (individual measurements) Shewhart Q-Charts for both μ and σ.

(c) Make IM EWMA Q-Charts for both μ and σ.

(d) Make SG (subgroups) Shewhart Q-Charts using consecutive subgroups of size 2 each.

(e) Make SG (subgroups) EWMA Q-Charts using consecutive subgroups of size 2 each.

(f) Make SG (subgroups) Shewhart Q-Charts using consecutive subgroups of size 4 each.

(g) Make SG (subgroups) EWMA Q-Charts using consecutive subgroups of size 4 each.

(h) Discuss your conclusions from the charting in the previous parts of this problem.

7.8 Use Q-charts to work problem 4.15.

7.9 Use Q-charts to work problem 4.19.

CHAPTER 8

Q-Charts for Attributes

In this chapter, the *Q*-charts approach to control charting is extended to charts for attributes. The binomial *Q*-charts given here can, and should, be used in lieu of the usual *p*- or *np*-charts for the case when *p* is known, and the Poisson *Q*-chart can, and should, be used in lieu of the usual *c*- and *u*-charts for the case when λ is known. The binomial and Poisson *Q*-charts for the cases when the parameters are unknown provide the first distributionally sound approach to charting for the especially important case of charting short runs of attributes data. These methods provide a means of charting attributes for many problems in industries such as service, animal production, processing of many types, etc., for which valid control charting methods have not been available.

8.1 CONSIDERATIONS IN USING CLASSICAL CHARTS FOR ATTRIBUTES

8.1.1 Discussion of Parameters Known Case

Most of the discussion in section 7.1 of issues in using classical Shewhart charts for variables applies also to the use of attributes charts considered in Chapter 5. In particular, the difficulties that arise in interpreting patterns when sample sizes vary for variables charts also are present for attributes charts when sample sizes vary, and require the plotting of observations on statistics with varying standard deviations. There are many applications where charting attributes with varying sample sizes is required. For example, a common and often useful practice is to inspect all production units made during a fixed time period, such as one shift. The inspection might be by go–no go gauging. But the numbers of units made during different shifts will generally vary, producing binomial samples of varying sizes. As discussed in Chapter 5, one solution to this problem is to plot some form of standardized statistic that permits constant control limits. If the standardizing transformation also improves the normality and independence of the plotted statistics, then the effectiveness of 3-sigma control limits for the statistic will be improved. In this chapter we will present some methods for transforming both binomial and Poisson data that not only approximately standardize the data, but that also improve both the normality and independence of the plotted statistics, as compared with the classical attributes charts studied in Chapter 5.

8.1.2   Discussion of Parameters Unknown Case

The problem that arises when we need to chart a statistic without knowing the distribution parameter(s) is also present for attributes charts. This situation arises frequently for start-up processes and for low-production operations that produce short runs of attributes data. To set up a classical p-, c-, or u-chart we must first obtain in a Stage 1 study enough data from the process to obtain good estimates of the control limits. This requires large data sets, so the classical high-production control methods are not appropriate. When using these classical charts, there is no active real-time charting while the calibration data are being gathered and, of course, no control is being exercised. Further, when assignable causes of parameter shifts were present during the run when the calibration data were being taken, the result will be that the parameter estimates are actually estimates of an average of the values the process parameter(s) had during the run. Plugging these estimates into classical formulas, or even using them to obtain exact limits, can give misleading control limits. In this chapter, we shall use the same general approach as that used in Chapter 7 for variables to construct approximately standardized normal Q-statistics that permit us to begin plotting points almost from the time when data collection is begun. An especially important point to note is that some of the methods developed here can be applied in real time as the attributes data are obtained, almost from the beginning of operation of the process.

In section 7.1 it was stated that, in the view of the author, the apparent reason that SPC methods have been used very little in many important industries is that the required large data sets to estimate the control limits are frequently not available. This situation is essentially the same for attributes charts as for variables charts, and the charting methods presented in this chapter for attributes charting make possible effective SPC charting for problems in many industries where it has not been possible to use charting as an effective management tool.

8.2   BINOMIAL *Q*-STATISTICS AND SHEWHART *Q*-CHARTS

We consider the two cases for the binomial parameter p known and unknown. Recall that in section 5.2 a brief discussion and example were given to illustrate the design of a control chart for a binomial variable with exact probability limits, say (α_L, α_U). We now consider those ideas and the binomial distribution further in order to introduce the Shewhart Q-charts methodology for attributes. The material of this section is largely from Quesenberry (1991b).

8.2.1   The Binomial Shewhart *Q*-Chart for Known $p = p_0$, Case K

Suppose a manufacturing process has nominal fallout of $p = p_0$ of production units and it is required to design a control chart for p. For definiteness, suppose $p_0 = 0.1$ and for $\alpha_L = 0.00135$ we use the formula (5.2.12) to determine a sample size of $n = 63$. A graph of the binomial probability function $b(x; 63, 0.1)$ is shown in Fig. 8.1 and the actual values of the function are given in column 2 of Table 8.1. The values of the binomial distribution function $B(x; 63, 0.1)$ are shown in column 3 of Table 8.1. From these values we see that if we take LCL = 1 and UCL = 14, then the probabilities of exceeding these limits are

$$\alpha_L = P(X < LCL) = P(X = 0) = 0.00131$$

and

$$\alpha_U = P(X > UCL) = 1 - P(X \le UCL) = 1 - B(14; 63, 0.1)$$

$$= 0.00115.$$

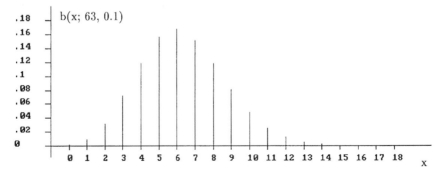

Figure 8.1   The Binomial $b(x; 63, 0.1)$ Probability Function

TABLE 8.1 Values of binomial and Q-binomial Probability and Distribution Functions

x	$b(x; 63, 0.1)$	$B(x; 63, 0.1)$	q
0	.00131	.00131	−3.01
1	.00917	.01048	−2.31
2	.03159	.04207	−1.73
3	.07136	.11343	−1.21
4	.11894	.23236	−.73
5	.15594	.38830	−.28
6	.16749	.55579	.14
7	.15154	.70732	.55
8	.11786	.82519	.94
9	.08003	.90522	1.31
10	.04802	.95323	1.68
11	.02571	.97894	2.03
12	.01238	.99132	2.38
13	.00540	.99671	2.72
14	.00214	.99885	3.05
15	.00078	.99963	3.38
16	.00026	.99989	3.72
17	.00008	.99997	4.01
18	.00002	.99999	4.32
19	.00001	1.00000	4.63

Thus, a chart for this binomial distribution with these probability limits has in-control probabilities for false signals close to those of a 3-sigma normal chart. The 3-sigma limits of equations (5.2.11) give

$$UCL = 6.3 + 3\sqrt{(6.3)(.9)} = 13.44, \quad \text{or } UCL = 13$$
$$LCL = 6.3 - 3\sqrt{(6.3)(.9)} = -0.84, \quad \text{or } LCL = 0$$

We now consider transforming a sequence of binomial random variables $x_1, x_2, \cdots$ to a sequence of approximately standardized, independent, normal values that we call Q-statistics. We assume that X_i has a binomial distribution function $B(x; n_i, p_0)$. Note, particularly, that we do not require that the sample sizes be equal. We then define Q-statistics $Q_1, Q_2, \cdots$ as in display (8.2.1). These values $Q_1, Q_2, \cdots$ are independent approximately standard normal statistics. They can be used to make Shewhart, EWMA, or CUSUM Q-charts. A Shewhart chart with approximate (α_L, α_U) probability limits can be made by putting $LCL = -q_{\alpha_L}$, $CL = 0$, and $UCL = q_{\alpha_U}$. For an in-control process, the Shewhart Q-charts have cell probabilities that are approximated much more closely by a normal distribution than those of p- or np-charts, or the standardized versions of those charts.

$$\boxed{\begin{aligned} u_i &= B(x_i; n_i, p_0) \\ Q_i &= \Phi^{-1}(u_i) \qquad \text{for } i = 1, 2, \cdots \end{aligned}}$$

(8.2.1)

To study the nature of this transformation, we consider again the binomial $b(x; 63, 0.1)$ distribution. The $b(x; 63, 0.1)$ probability function is shown in Fig. 8.1, and the transformed Q-binomial distribution is shown in Fig. 8.2. This Q-binomial distribution is, of course, a discrete distribution. It has the same probabilities of points as the binomial distribution and the points with positive probability appear in the same order on the horizontal axis; however, they are now in a standardized normal scale. For example, the probability at zero, namely $b(0; 63, 0.1)$, is now at the point $-q_{B(0; 63, 0.1)}$. In general, for x's with $B(x; 63, 0.1) \leq 1/2$, the probability at $-q_{B(x; 63, 0.1)}$ is $b(x; 63, 0.1)$; and for x's with $B(x; 63, 0.1) > 1/2$ the probability at $q_{B(x; 63, 0.1)}$ is $b(x; 63, 0.1)$.

When these Q-statistics are plotted on a control chart with (α_L, α_U) probability limits, it will be possible for a point to fall below the LCL only if inequality (5.2.12) is satisfied. Table 8.1 shows the probability and distribution functions for both the binomial and the Q-binomial distributions for $n = 63$ and $p = 0.1$. We shall denote this Q-binomial probability function by $Qb(q; n, p)$ and the corresponding Q-binomial distribution function by $QB(q; n, p)$. Note that for each value of x in the first column of Table 8.1, the value in the second column of the table is the binomial probability of this x, and this probability is assigned to the value of Q given in column 4, by the Q-binomial probability function $Qb(q; n, p)$.

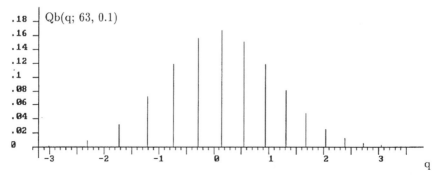

Figure 8.2   The Q-Binomial $Qb(q; 63, 0.1)$ Probability Function

TABLE 8.2 Fifty Observations from a $b(\cdot;\ 63,\ 0.1)$ Distribution

5	3	7	8	3	9	6	6	3	4	7	5	5	6	6	5	4	5	8	6	7	6	6	5	8
6	9	4	8	5	8	3	7	6	3	4	5	5	5	6	8	6	6	2	6	15	7	10	4	8

Example 8.1: To illustrate the use of the binomial Shewhart Q-chart for this case when the parameter p is known, we have drawn 50 samples from a $b(x;\ 63,\ 0.1)$ distribution. The data for these 50 samples are given in Table 8.2, and the Shewhart Q-chart from the formulas of (8.2.1) is shown in Fig. 8.3. We have drawn lines at ± 1, ± 2, ± 3. For $LCL = -3$ and $UCL = 3$, we see from Table 8.1 that these are actually (0.00131, 0.00329) probability limits.

For a stable process, the probabilities associated with the zones defined by the ± 1, ± 2, ± 3 standard deviation lines on these Shewhart Q-charts can be approximated by the standard normal probabilities. The goodness of the approximation depends on both n and p. For a fixed value of n, it is best for $p = 0.5$, and for a fixed value of p, it improves with increasing n. Here with $n = 63$ and $p = 0.1$ the approximation may be considered marginally adequate. The approximation will generally be better for zones on the positive side of the zero center line. When the approximation is good enough, special tests for point patterns, such as some of those of Fig. 4.9, can be applied to these Shewhart Q-charts, and the normal distribution probabilities are approximately correct.

For reasons that we will discuss in detail below, we recommend making the combined 11-45 test on these charts for detecting either

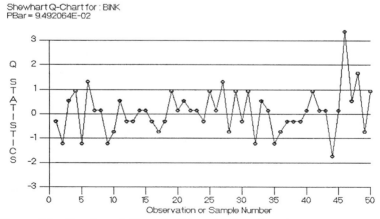

Figure 8.3 Shewhart Q-Chart for Binomial Samples with $p = 0.1$ Known

increases or decreases in p. The Q-chart of Fig. 8.3 signals by the 1-of-1 test on observation 46. ∎

8.2.2 The Binomial Shewhart Q-Chart for p Unknown, Case U

Some further notation is needed to treat the present case. Again, consider a sequence of values (n_i, x_i) for $i = 1, 2, \cdots$; and when the ith value is obtained a point is plotted on the Q-chart. Let

$$N_i = \sum_{j=1}^{i} n_j \quad \text{and} \quad t_i = \sum_{j=1}^{i} x_j$$

$$\text{for } i = 2, 3, \cdots$$

(8.2.2)

Then compute the Q-statistics by the equations (8.2.3), where $H(x; n, N_1, N_2)$ is the hypergeometric distribution function defined by (2.4.3).

$$u_i = H(x_i; t_i, n_i, N_{i-1})$$

$$Q_i = \Phi^{-1}(u_i) \quad \text{for } i = 2, 3, 4, \cdots$$

(8.2.3)

When the process is in control, that is, when $x_1, x_2, \cdots$ are independent binomial random variables with constant parameter p, the Q_i's are approximately independent with discrete Q binomial distributions. Therefore, the values $Q_2, Q_3, \cdots$ can be plotted on Shewhart, EWMA, or CUSUM Q-charts. The interpretation of this chart is similar to the interpretation of the chart for p known, but certain special considerations must be observed. We will see in examples below that for the same binomial data from an in-control process the pattern of points on a chart is very similar when the Qs are computed from the formulas of (8.2.3) and when they are computed from (8.2.1), using the correct value of the parameter p. Note that the equations (8.2.3) essentially solve the problem of charting short runs of binomial observations, since they do not require knowledge of the binomial parameter, and can be used for any sequence of binomial data. Points are plotted from the second binomial sample on, but no point is plotted for the first sample. This is because the transformation must be estimated from the present data sequence. The situation is similar to that in Chapter 7 for Shewhart Q-charts for variables when the parameters are not known.

Example 8.2: To illustrate the use of the binomial Shewhart Q-chart for unknown p, we consider again the data in Table 8.2 above. The Q-statistics have been computed using equations (8.2.3) and are shown in Fig. 8.4. The chart in Fig. 8.4 should be compared with the chart in Fig. 8.3. Note that these two charts for a stable or in-control binomial process have almost identical point patterns.   ∎

It is important to note that the Q-chart using the statistics computed in equations (8.2.1) and (8.2.3) can be made in real time, that is, when each binomial observation x_i is observed a point for it can be plotted immediately. It is not necessary to collect a large number of binomial samples before charting can begin. For the equations of (8.2.3), a point is plotted for each sample, beginning with the second. This strategy is ideal for detecting changes of p at the earliest possible time. However, the sample sizes should satisfy inequality (5.2.12), if the chart is to be an approximately (α_L, α_U) probability chart.

Example 8.3: To illustrate the responses of the two binomial Shewhart Q-charts to an increase in p for the cases when the initial nominal value of p is known and when it is not known, 20 samples have been drawn from a $b(x; 107, 0.06)$ distribution and then 10 more samples from a $b(x; 107, 0.08)$ distribution. Note that $n = ln(0.00135)/ln(0.94) = 107$ is the smallest sample size that gives positive probability below $LCL = -3$. The data are given in Table 8.3. The Q-chart for these data when the known value of $p = 0.06$ is used is shown in Fig. 8.5 and the Q-chart that does not assume a known value for p is shown in Fig.

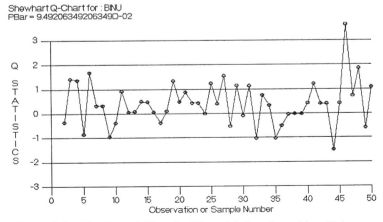

Shewhart Q-Chart for : BINU
PBar = 9.49206349206349D-02

Figure 8.4   Shewhart Q-Chart for Binomial Samples with p Unknown

TABLE 8.3   Data for Example 8.3

5	8	9	10	6	9	8	8	8	7	6	7	3	5	5	8	9	8	5	3	5	8	6	13	8	16	12	4	11	8	

8.6. Figure 8.5 shows the change in p from 0.06 to 0.08 from about observation 23 on.

To illustrate the use of the binomial Shewhart Q-chart for unknown p, we have plotted the Q-statistics for the formulas (8.2.3) in Fig. 8.6. The chart in Fig. 8.6 should be compared with the chart in Fig. 8.5. Note that the point patterns for the points before p shifts from 0.06 to 0.08 on observation 21 are very similar for both charts for p known and for p unknown. Also, the point patterns after the shift are also very similar but that eventually the pattern for Fig. 8.6 is less pronounced than that in Fig. 8.5. This is because, as was discussed in Chapter 7 for variables Q-charts, due to the increasing number of observations after the shift, the process is becoming stable at the new value of p. It should be noted, also, that the increase in p causes an obvious increase in the spread of the points on both charts, in addition to the upward shift.   ∎

8.2.3   Point Patterns with Changing p

In Chapter 5 it was noted that an increase or decrease of p from a value p_0 to a new value δp_0 results in point patterns that tend to be either higher or lower and to have greater or lesser spread according to whether $\delta > 1$ or $\delta < 1$. A shift in p will have the same effect on

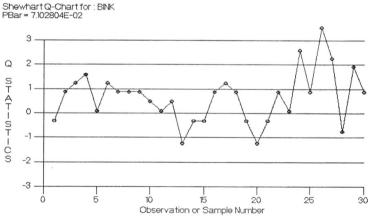

Figure 8.5   Binomial Shewhart Q-Chart for Example 8.2 Using $p = 0.06$ Known

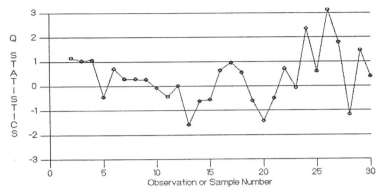

Figure 8.6   Binomial Shewhart Q-Chart for Example 8.3 with p Unknown

patterns on the binomial Shewhart Q-charts. It was also pointed out that this causes a p-chart to be insensitive for detecting decreases in p by having a point fall below the *LCL*. This is also the case for the Q-chart, for the same reason. However, it was shown in Quesenberry (1995b) that the 4-of-5 test of Fig. 4.9 is a much more sensitive test for detecting decreases in p. We recommend making both the 1-of-1 and the 4-of-5 tests, the 11-45 combined test, on these Binomial Shewhart Q-charts for increases and for decreases of p.

8.3 AN ARCSIN TRANSFORMATION, COMPARISONS WITH z- AND Q-CHARTS, SAMPLE SIZE ISSUES

If X is a $b(x; n, p)$ random variable, then y defined by (8.3.1) is approximately a $N(0, 1)$ random variable for large values of n.

$$y = 2\sqrt{n}\left[\sin^{-1}\left(\sqrt{\frac{X + 3/8}{n + 3/4}}\right) - \sin^{-1}(\sqrt{p})\right] \qquad (8.3.1)$$

This transformation is given in Johnson and Kotz (1969), and was discussed in the quality literature by Ryan (1989). This is a nonlinear transformation and approaches normality with increasing n more rapidly than the standardized value z_i of (5.2.13). When the values of y_1, y_2, $\cdots$ are plotted on a chart with $UCL(y) = 3$, $CL(y) = 0$, and $LCL(y) = -3$; the patterns will be similar to the patterns on a Q-chart using the formulas (8.2.1). Quesenberry (1990) gave some comparisons of the normal approximations for the three charts obtained by plotting the z's, y's, and Q's on nominally normal 3-sigma charts. We summarize these results briefly in the following.

Suppose that each of the statistics z, y, and Q are plotted on charts with lines drawn at 0, ± 1, ± 2, and ± 3. Then the vertical axis can be partitioned into cells in terms of Q as follows:

$$
\begin{array}{ll}
\text{Cell 1 is all values of} & Q < -3 \\
\text{Cell 2 is all values of} & -3 \le Q < -2 \\
\text{Cell 3 is all values of} & -2 \le Q < -1 \\
\text{Cell 4 is all values of} & -1 \le Q \le 0 \\
\text{Cell 5 is all values of} & 0 < Q \le 1 \\
\text{Cell 6 is all values of} & 1 < Q \le 2 \\
\text{Cell 7 is all values of} & 2 < Q \le 3 \\
\text{Cell 8 is all values of} & 3 < Q
\end{array}
\tag{8.3.2}
$$

When p and n are both known, it is possible to compute the probabilities that each of the statistics z, y, and Q will fall in each of these eight cells. In Table 8.4 we give the probabilities that will be in the eight cells of the statistics z, Q, and y for a few selected values of n and p. The first row gives the cell probabilities under a standard normal distribution for easy comparisons.

To illustrate reading Table 8.4, consider the entries for $n = 500$ and $p = 0.05$. The first row gives the cell probabilities for the z-chart. Since z is a standardized p-chart, given in equation (5.2.13), the cell probabilities for z are exactly the same values as those for the corresponding cells for a 3-sigma p-chart with lines drawn also at ± 1-sigma and ± 2-sigma. The cell probabilities can be compared with the standard normal distribution cell probabilities given as the first row of the table. Although this table contains only a few values of n and p, we think that a few points are apparent. The most important is that both the Q-chart and the arcsin y-chart have cell probabilities that are in general closer to the nominal normal values than the standardized p-chart. The cells 1 and 8 are especially important since the probability of cell 1 is the probability that a point will fall below the lower control limit LCL, and cell 8 is the probability that a point will fall above the upper control limit UCL, when the process is stable with a constant value of p. From this table, and from more extensive computations reported in Quesenberry (1990), it appears that there is no clear overall choice between Q- and y-charts from the comparison of cell probabilities with normal

TABLE 8.4 Cell Probabilities for z, Q, and y Binomial Charts

Cell:		1	2	3	4	5	6	7	8	
n	p	.00135	.02140	.13591	.34134	.34134	.13591	.02140	.00135	
500	.01	.00000	.00657	.11682	.49258	.25172	.10122	.02589	.00521	z
		.00000	.00657	.11682	.31623	.32331	.20598	.02920	.00190	Q
		.00657	.03318	.08363	.31623	.42807	.11908	.01260	.00065	y
700	.01	.00000	.00710	.16451	.42710	.23280	.14214	.02087	.00547	z
		.00088	.00622	.07362	.36824	.38256	.14214	.02407	.00228	Q
		.00088	.02820	.14254	.27734	.38256	.14214	.02545	.00089	y
900	.01	.00012	.02066	.18463	.38200	.21658	.15536	.03557	.00509	z
		.00119	.01959	.09369	.34052	.34900	.15536	.03836	.00230	Q
		.00119	.01959	.09369	.34052	.34900	.17456	.02046	.00099	y
100	.05	.00000	.00592	.11234	.49774	.25604	.09977	.02391	.00427	z
		.00000	.00592	.11234	.31772	.33003	.20580	.02672	.00146	Q
		.00592	.03116	.08118	.31772	.43606	.09977	.02773	.00046	y
200	.05	.00004	.00901	.11469	.45932	.28704	.10609	.02113	.00266	z
		.00040	.00864	.11469	.33097	.34177	.17972	.02113	.00266	Q
		.00234	.02411	.09730	.33097	.34177	.17972	.02264	.00116	y
400	.05	.00020	.01885	.13088	.40918	.28987	.12032	.02864	.00207	z
		.00062	.01843	.13088	.31804	.32472	.17660	.02864	.00207	Q
		.00172	.01733	.13088	.31804	.38101	.13199	.01793	.00110	y
500	.05	.00046	.01940	.15899	.37409	.27059	.14621	.02756	.00270	z
		.00114	.01871	.10738	.34412	.35218	.14621	.02871	.00155	Q
		.00261	.01725	.15899	.29250	.35218	.15683	.01878	.00086	y
100	.10	.00003	.00781	.10932	.46600	.29297	.10328	.01862	.00198	z
		.00032	.00751	.10932	.33413	.35053	.15829	.03791	.00198	Q
		.00194	.02177	.09344	.33413	.35053	.17758	.10979	.00081	y
200	.10	.00048	.01630	.12629	.41610	.29593	.11780	.02418	.00292	
		.00048	.01630	.12629	.32246	.33276	.17461	.02556	.00154	Q
		.00139	.03066	.11103	.32246	.38957	.11780	.02631	.00078	y
300	.10	.00057	.01655	.12680	.40450	.30624	.11995	.02297	.00242	z
		.00127	.01585	.12680	.32794	.33679	.16597	.02398	.00141	Q
		.00127	.02741	.11524	.32794	.38280	.11995	.02459	.00080	y
500	.10	.00055	.01808	.14783	.37111	.29658	.14080	.02328	.00177	z
		.00100	.01763	.11187	.34770	.35595	.14080	.02328	.00177	Q
		.00176	.02567	.13903	.31174	.35595	.14080	.02391	.00144	y

probabilities. A few general observations can be made, however. The Q-chart generally gives more accurate cell 8 probabilities but more often gives cell 1 probabilities smaller than the nominal 0.00135 value, while the y-chart frequently gives cell 1 probabilities larger than the nominal value and cell 8 probabilities that are too small.

However, these observations are by no means clear cut, due in part to the lumpiness of the distributions which can cause the cell probabilities to shift about somewhat erratically as a function of n. With this in mind it will be helpful in designing a chart to be able to evaluate at least the cell probabilities of cells 1 and 8. A binomial distribution function algorithm can be used to evaluate these probabilities.

8.4 BINOMIAL EWMA AND CUSUM Q-CHARTS, SAMPLE SIZES, BINOMIAL Q-CHARTS PERFORMANCE

The EWMA and CUSUM Q-charts can be made from a sequence of binomial Q-statistics Q_1, Q_2, $\cdots$ as described in sections 7.5 and 7.6. An EWMA Q-chart with $\lambda = 0.25$ and $K = 2.9$ for the binomial data of Table 8.3 is given in Fig. 8.7 for the case of p unknown, that is, case U. A corresponding CUSUM Q-chart with $k_s = 0.75$ and $h_s = 3.34$ is given in Fig. 8.8, also, for case U. Recall that these were the particular EWMA and CUSUM charts considered in examples in Chapter 7. These charts are competing charts to the binomial Shewhart Q-chart for case U of Fig. 8.6. All three of these charts signal an increase in p on the 26th point. We will discuss the relative performance of these charts and various runs tests on the Shewhart Q-chart in the next section.

8.4.1 Recommended Sample Sizes for Binomial Q-Charts

For case K ($p = p_0$ known) we recommend that the minimal sample size n should be the smallest value of n that satisfies equation (5.2.12) with $\alpha_L = 0.00135$. That is, the smallest n such that

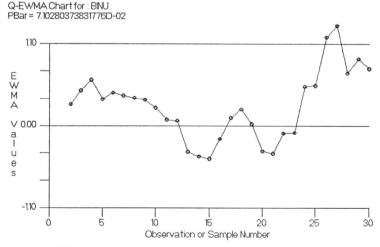

Figure 8.7 EWMA Q-Chart for Data of Table 8.3

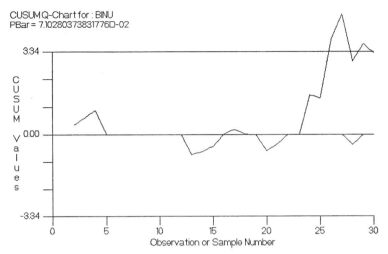

CUSUM Q-Chart for : BINU
PBar = 7.10280373831776D-02

Figure 8.8 CUSUM Q-Chart for Data of Table 8.3

$$n > \frac{-6.608}{ln(1 - p_0)} \tag{8.4.1}$$

This sample size assures that the binomial Shewhart Q-chart for Case K will have positive probability below -3 for the stable case. Moreover, an n that satisfies (8.4.1) will generally give a chart with the eight cell probabilities of Table 8.4 that are reasonably decent approximations to the normal cell probabilities.

When it is required to use a case U binomial Q-chart, we would use the same sample size criterion using equation (8.4.1). In this case p is unknown and we shall have to first obtain at least a crude estimate of p to use in equation (8.4.1). One approach to this problem is to take a preliminary sample, as large as possible, for the first sample and use the sample ratio from this to determine the minimal next sample size. We can continue to upgrade the estimates of p and the required sample size after each sample until the estimate of p appears stable.

It should be noted that the minimal sample sizes that satisfy (8.4.1) increase rapidly as p becomes small. A few values of n and p are given in the following table.

p	0.1	0.05	0.01	0.005	0.001
Minimum n	63	129	658	1319	6605

In some applications, these sample sizes will be impractically large. For these processes, two possible approaches to using Q-charts are as follows. The geometric Q-charts given in section 8.7 should be considered, particularly when p is small, say $p \leq 0.01$. Otherwise, we can use a binomial distribution function algorithm to design a chart with small n, and to evaluate its OC, Power, and ARL functions using one of the runs tests such as the 1-of-1 or 4-of-5 test.

8.4.2 Performances of Charts from Q-Statistics

Recall that we discussed at the end of section 5.2 the effect that a shift in the value of p has upon the plotted points on a classical p- or np-chart. We now consider the effect that such a shift will have on the binomial Q-statistics and the various charts that can be made from them. First, consider a sequence of binomial Q-statistics $Q_1, Q_2, \cdots ,$ $Q_c, \cdots$; and suppose that immediately after sample c (the shift point) is observed, p shifts from $p = p_0$ to $p = \delta p_0$, $\delta > 0$. Since the Q-statistics of (8.2.1) and (8.2.3) are strictly monotone functions of X_r, we can observe the effect of this shift on the distributions of the Q-statistics by studying the effect on the distribution of X_r. Now, the mean and standard deviation of X_r are $E(X_r) = n_r p$ and $SD(X_r) = \sqrt{n_r p(1 - p)}$. Thus, when p changes from $p = p_0$ to $p = \delta p_0$, then $E(X_r)$ shifts from $n_r p_0$ to $n_r \delta p_0$ and $SD(X_r)$ shifts from $SD(X_r) = \sqrt{n_r p_0(1 - p_0)}$ to $SD(X_r) = \sqrt{n_r \delta p_0(1 - \delta p_0)}$. But for $p < 0.5$, which is all of the values of p that are generally of interest, both the mean and standard deviation of X_r are strictly increasing functions of p. Thus, if p increases, $1 < \delta < 1/2p_0$, then both the mean and standard deviation of the distribution of X_r, and of Q_r, also increase. On the other hand, if p decreases, $0 < \delta < 1$, then both the mean and standard deviation of the distribution of X_r, and of Q_r, decrease.

This development implies that a 1-of-1 test on a binomial Q-chart, and, of course, also a classical p-chart, can be expected to have poor sensitivity to detect a *decrease* in p by having a value fall below the lower control limit. This is because a decrease in p causes the mean of the plotted statistic to decrease, but at the same time the distribution becomes more concentrated about the mean rather than placing correspondingly more probability below a lower control limit. From this development, we expect a classical p-chart and the Q-charts to have poor sensitivity to detect decreases in p by the 1-of-1 test. However, some of the other tests should perform relatively well to detect decreases in p.

Quesenberry (1995b), Q95b, gave results of a simulation study of the performance of the 1-of-1, 4-of-5, 9-of-9 and 3-of-3 tests on binomial Q-charts; and the EWMA and CUSUM Q-charts to detect either increases or decreases in p. The values of $\delta \in \{0.1, 0.5, 0.9, 1, 1.1, 1.5, 2, 3\}$ were used. For values of c in the set $\{1, 3, 5, 10, 20, 30, 50\}$, c samples were first generated from a binomial $b(x; n, p_0)$ distribution, and then 30 additional samples were generated from a $b(x; n, \delta p_0)$ distribution, for $n = 100$ and $p_0 = 0.1$. The Q-statistics for the sequence $(n_1, x_1), \cdots, (n_c, x_c), (n_{c+1}, x_{c+1}), \cdots, (n_{c+30}, x_{c+30})$ were computed for case K (p Known) of equations (3) and for case U (p Unknown) of equations (5). The six test statistics described above were computed for both sequences of Q-statistics. This procedure was replicated 5000 times and the proportion of times that each statistic signaled either an increase or a decrease in p on samples $c + 1, \cdots, c + 30$, for the first time, was recorded. In the following, when we speak of signal rates or false alarm rates we shall be referring to the rates on these specific 30 samples. The results of this study are summarized in the following points.

- For the stable case of $\delta = 1$, the false alarm rates for both case K and case U are approximately the same, and for case U this result does not depend on the value of c. This lends credence to the claim that the Q-statistics for both cases are approximately independent standard normal statistics.
- The overall performances of the EWMA and CUSUM charts were comparable with each other and better than the Shewhart chart tests to detect these one-step permanent parameter shifts. It would be good practice to regularly plot one of these charts. Although there is little difference in these two charts in performance, the personal preference of this author is the EWMA chart. The particular charts used here would work well in charting programs.
- The 4-of-5 test on the Shewhart chart is considered to be the best overall test of the Shewhart chart tests.
- The classical 1-of-1 test is a poor competitor for many of the cases considered. However, it is essentially the only test for detecting a single outlier on a chart for p. A nice compromise is to use the combined 11-45 test on Shewhart binomial Q-charts.
- If the increased rate of false alarms is considered tolerable in order to improve sensitivity to shifts, then the 3-of-3 test is a reasonable choice of test. This can be a reasonable trade-off in a start-up process before many data are available to improve sensitivity, that is, while c is small.

8.4.3   Performance of Tests with *p* Unknown

By considering results for small values of c, say $c = 1$, it was observed in Q95b that the tests based on Q-statistics for case U maintain essentially the same false alarm rates as the same tests based on Q-statistics for case K. This permits us to assess the effect on performances of the tests for $\delta \neq 1$ by comparing the U case results for the given values of c with those for the corresponding K case.

The worst case is, of course, for $c = 1$, when the shift in p occurs after only one binomial sample has been observed. For this case of $c = 1$ the tests for p unknown do not have high probabilities of detecting an increase until δ is 2 or 3. As c increases, the probabilities of detecting shifts increase to the limiting values for the K cases. For example, to detect $\delta = 1.5$ the probability of detection by the EWMA test was 0.262, for $c = 1$, for $c = 3$ it was 0.630, for $c = 5$ it was 0.808, for $c = 10$ it was 0.954, and for $c = 20$ it was 0.990, which is essentially the same as the limiting value for the K case. This general performance of the Q-charts tests for case U is, of course, exactly what we expect. For c small we are essentially making inferences with a small amount of data, and sensitivity is limited. However, the reader should be aware that for these cases there are no known competitors to these Q-charts that have known performance for a stable binomial process.

These simulation results were all based on using $n = 100$ and $p_0 = 0.1$. However, runs were also made for $p_0 = 0.01$ and 0.05, and the results were consistent with those for $p_0 = 0.1$. The results for p in this range of values depend largely on δ, rather than the nominal value of $p = p_0$.

It was stated in subsection 7.7.3 that a 1-1 test on an individual measurements variables mean Shewhart Q-chart is optimal for detecting a one-step parameter shift on the first plotted point after the shift. This was demonstrated for some cases in Appendix 7C. The 1-1 test on a binomial Q-chart also is optimal for detecting a one-step parameter shift on the first point after the shift, see Quesenberry (1995f).

8.4.4   Selecting the Case in Applications, Responding to Signals

The transformations and, of course, the results of the case K studies given above are based on the assumption that the binomial parameter has an exactly known value $p = p_0$. In practice, this is unrealistic because it is always necessary to estimate p from data. Given a calibration data set (n_1, x_1), (n_2, x_2), $\cdots$, (n_r, x_r); in order to use the case K formulas, the parameter p would be estimated by

$$
\bar{p} = \frac{\displaystyle\sum_{i=1}^{r} x_i}{\displaystyle\sum_{i=1}^{r} n_i} \tag{8.4.2}
$$

The Q-statistics of further samples (n_{r+1}, x_{r+1}), $\cdots$ would be computed using the case K formulas of equation (8.2.1) by replacing p_0 by $\bar{p}$. However, this is an alternative (to equation (8.2.3)) "plug-in" method of estimating the transformations, and as such has poorer properties than equation (8.2.3). The approximation of the distribution of the Q-statistics of equation (8.2.3), for the stable case, by the distribution of independent standardized normal statistics, will be better for any r than for the Q-statistics from (8.2.1) using $\bar{p}$ for p_0. For this reason, we recommend using the case U Q-statistics. In other words, we do not recommend ever switching to case K using an estimate $\bar{p}$ for p_0. When the backlog of data, obtained while the process is stable, of course, is large enough, the Q-statistics from (8.2.3) will be virtually the same as they would be with truly known p.

Suppose the data are being observed in real time and that p shifts value during the operation of the case U Q-chart. The chart either will or will not signal the change with some probabilities. The probability that the change is signaled will generally be less than one and this probability depends on a number of factors such as the amount of data obtained from the stable process before the shift, the magnitude and sign of the shift, sample size, and so on.

First, suppose the shift is not signaled. Then, if there are no further shifts, the chart pattern will eventually return to the stable normal pattern. This is reasonable behavior since the process is, in fact, stable after the shift.

Second, if the process signals the shift by one of the tests considered earlier, then, of course, we will search for an assignable cause. Suppose an assignable cause is found and removed so that it will no longer affect the process. Then, we must decide how to restart the process. If, by the nature of the assignable cause, we feel confident that the value of p will be the same as before the cause appeared, then the data from before its appearance can be used to restart the process. However, if there is doubt as to whether the value of p has changed, then we should restart the process without using prior data.

In using the case U statistics of equation (8.2.3), and the data are observed in real time, we recommend that a trailing window of data be used. When the rth sample (n_r, x_r) is observed, a trailing window of span k is the set of data: $(n_{r-k+1}, x_{r-k+1}), \cdots , (n_r, x_r)$. When the rth data point is plotted and the next point (n_{r+1}, x_{r+1}) is observed, this last observation will be appended to the data set and the observation (n_{r-k+1}, x_{r-k+1}) deleted. This dynamic approach to charting uses only the most recent k data observations, which are expected to be most relevant. This approach to charting requires a choice of k to design the charting procedure. We shall call the quantity (for a given k)

$$\sum_{i=0}^{k-1} n_{r-i} \tag{8.4.3}$$

the *window sample size* at the rth sample. We recommend that the window sample size should satisfy the following inequality

$$p_0 \sum_{i=0}^{k-1} n_{r-i} \geq 500 \tag{8.4.4}$$

for all $r = k, k + 1, \cdots$. This recommendation is based on observing in Table A.1 of Quesenberry (1995b) that for $c = 50$ with $np_0 = 10$ the case U tests have probabilities near those of case K to detect moderate to large shifts in p. If it is desired to have more sensitivity to detect smaller shifts, then a larger window should be used. If sample sizes have a constant value n, say, then this requirement can be expressed by requiring a span k that satisfies the following:

$$k \geq \frac{500}{np_0} \tag{8.4.5}$$

In practice, at the start-up of a process all data will be used until a good estimate of p is obtained to evaluate k from this last inequality.

8.5   POISSON Q-CHARTS

We consider the two cases of charting when the nominal value of the Poisson parameter $\lambda = \lambda_0$, the average rate of nonconformities, is known (case K) and when it is unknown (case U). Recall that in section

5.3 we considered designing a c-chart with exact probability limits. The concepts developed there are fundamental to the developments in this section.

8.5.1 The Poisson Shewhart Q-Chart for Known $\lambda = \lambda_0$, Case K

Suppose a stable process has a known nominal average rate of occurrence of defects of $\lambda = \lambda_0$ on a standard size inspection unit, and let c_i be the number of defects observed on a sampling inspection unit of size n_i standard units. Then c_i will have a Poisson distribution with probability and distribution functions as given in equations (2.6.1) with λ replaced by $n_i\lambda_0$. For definiteness, suppose we wish to design a chart for the case when $\lambda_0 = 1.7$ and we sample $n = 4$ standard inspection units. Then c has a Poisson probability function $f(c; 6.8)$ as shown in Fig. 8.9. The values of the Poisson probability function $f(c; 6.8)$ are given in column 2 of Table 8.5, and the values of the Poisson distribution function $F(c; 6.8)$ are given in column 3. From these values we see that if we take $LCL = 1$ and $UCL = 15$, then for

$$\alpha_L = P(c < LCL = 1) = 0.00111$$

$$\alpha_U = P(c > UCL = 15) = 1 - 0.99818 = 0.00182$$

these limits are exact $(\alpha_L, \alpha_U) = (0.00111, 0.00182)$ probability limits. These values are reasonably close to the 3-sigma normal chart values of $(0.00135, 0.00135)$, and are the closest we can come to those values for a sample size n this small.

The 3-sigma limits given by equations (5.3.3) are

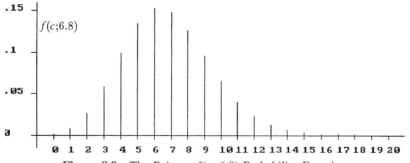

Figure 8.9 The Poisson $f(c; 6.8)$ Probability Function

$$UCL(c) = n\lambda_0 + 3\sqrt{n\lambda_0} = 6.8 + 3\sqrt{6.8} = 14.6, \text{ or } 14$$

$$CL(c) = n\lambda_0 = 6.8$$

$$LCL(c) = n\lambda_0 - 3\sqrt{n\lambda_0} = 6.8 - 3\sqrt{6.8} = -1.02, \text{ or } 0$$

and these are $(\alpha_L, \alpha_U) = (0, 0.00443)$ probability limits.

Next, suppose $(n_1, c_1), (n_2, c_2), \cdots$ is a sequence of values of sample sizes, that is, sizes of sampling inspection units, and the numbers of defects on these units. Then define Q-statistics as follows.

$$u_i = F(c_i; n_i\lambda_0)$$
$$Q_i = \Phi^{-1}(u_i) \qquad \text{for } i = 1, 2, \cdots$$

$$(8.5.1)$$

If the sequence of values $Q_1, Q_2, \cdots$ are plotted on a Poisson Shewhart Q-chart with control limits at ± 3, then in order to have approximately 0.00135 probability below LCL $= -3$, we require that

$$e^{-n_i\lambda_0} \le 0.00135 \quad \text{or} \quad n_i\lambda_0 \ge 6.7$$

Then the probabilities of the zones and of tests for patterns can be approximated by the probabilities for a standard normal distribution.

To study the nature of this transformation, we consider again the Poisson $f(c; 6.8)$ distribution. The $f(c; 6.8)$ probability function is shown in Fig. 8.9, and the transformed Q-Poisson probability function is shown in Fig. 8.10. This Q-distribution is, of course, a discrete distribution. It has the same probabilities of points as the Poisson distribution and the points with positive probability appear in the same order

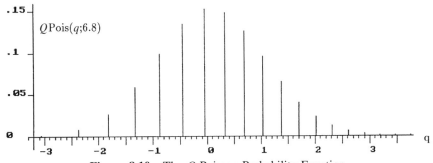

Figure 8.10   The Q-Poisson Probability Function

on the horizontal axis; however, they are now in a standardized normal scale. For example, the probability the Poisson distribution assigns to zero, namely $f(0; 6.8) = 0.00111$, is now at the point $-q_{f(0; 6.8)} = -3.06$. In general, for c's with $F(c; 6.8) \leq 1/2$, the probability at $-q_{F(c; 6.8)}$ is $f(c; 6.8)$; and for c's with $F(c; 6.8) > 1/2$ the probability at $q_{F(c; 6.8)}$ is $f(c; 6.8)$. Table 8.5 gives values of c, $f(c; 6.8)$, $F(c; 6.8)$ and the transformed value q.

For a stable process, when these Q-statistics are plotted on an (α_L, α_U) control chart, it will be possible for a point to fall below the LCL only if α_L, n and λ_0 satisfy equation (5.3.5). Table 8.5 gives the probability function of a Q-Poisson distribution for $n\lambda = 6.8$. We denote this distribution in general by $Q\text{Pois}(q; n\lambda)$. Note that for each value of c in the first column of Table 8.5, the value in the second column of the table is the Poisson probability of this c, and this probability is assigned to the value of q given in column 4 by the Q-Poisson probability function $Q\text{Pois}(q; n\lambda)$.

Example 8.4: To illustrate the use of the Poisson Shewhart Q-chart for a stable process when λ is known, we have drawn 60 samples of size $n = 4$ from an $f(c; 1.7)$ distribution. Note that $n = 4$ satisfies

TABLE 8.5 Poisson and Q-Poisson Probability and Distribution Functions

c	$f(c; 6.8)$	$F(c; 6.8)$	q
0	.00111	.00111	−3.06
1	.00757	.00869	−2.38
2	.02575	.03444	−1.82
3	.05837	.09281	−1.32
4	.09923	.19203	−.87
5	.13495	.32698	−.45
6	.15294	.47992	−.05
7	.14857	.62849	.33
8	.12628	.75477	.69
9	.09541	.85018	1.04
10	.06488	.91507	1.37
11	.04011	.95517	1.70
12	.02273	.97790	2.01
13	.01189	.98979	2.32
14	.00577	.99557	2.62
15	.00262	.99818	2.91
16	.00111	.99930	3.19
17	.00045	.99974	3.47
18	.00017	.99991	3.75
19	.00006	.99997	4.01

TABLE 8.6   Data for Examples 8.4 and 8.5, $\lambda = 1.7$, $n = 4$

8	11	8	8	4	11	4	7	7	3	12	6
6	2	8	4	11	4	7	7	3	12	6	6
2	8	5	8	4	9	7	3	12	6	6	2
8	5	8	4	9	10	7	4	10	6	2	8
5	8	4	9	10	7	4	10	13	9	3	7

inequality (5.3.5) for $\alpha_L = 0.00135$ and $\lambda_0 = 1.7$. The data are given in Table 8.6 in left-to-right row order. The Q-chart for these data is shown in Fig. 8.11. We have drawn lines at ± 1, ± 2, ± 3. For $LCL = -3$ and $UCL = 3$, we see from Table 8.5 above that these are actually (0.00111, 0.00182) probability limits, which are good approximations to the nominal normal (0.00135, 0.00135) probability limits.   ■

The probabilities associated with the zones defined by the ± 1, ± 2, ± 3 standard deviation lines can be approximated by the standard normal probabilities. The goodness of the approximation depends on both n and λ and tends to improve as $n\lambda$ increases. Here $n\lambda = 6.8$, and the approximation is pretty good. When the normal approximation to the Q-chart probabilities is good enough, special tests for point patterns, such as some of these of Fig. 4.9, can be applied to these Poisson Shewhart Q-charts, and the normal distribution probabilities are approximately correct. We will consider this approximation further in section 8.6.

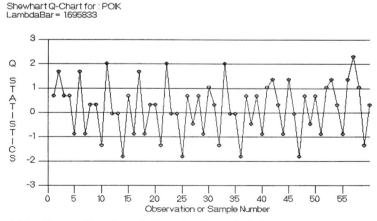

Figure 8.11   Poisson Shewhart Q-Chart for Example 8.4, Case K of $\lambda = 1.7$ Known

8.5.2 The Poisson Q-Chart for λ Unknown

Some further notation is needed to treat the present case. Again, we consider a sequence of pairs (n_i, c_i) for $i = 1, 2, \cdots$, and when the ith pair is obtained we compute a Q-statistic. Let $t_i = c_1 + c_2 + \cdots + c_i$ and $N_i = n_1 + n_2 + \cdots + n_i$ for $i = 1, 2, \cdots$; and compute the Q-statistics by the equations (8.5.2). Note that n_i is the number of standard inspection units and that it needs only be a positive number. Fractional values of n_i are permissible in settings where they are meaningful. Put

$$
\boxed{
\begin{aligned}
u_i &= B(c_i; t_i, n_i/N_i) \\
Q_i &= \Phi^{-1}(u_i) \qquad \text{for } i = 2, 3, \cdots
\end{aligned}
}
\qquad (8.5.2)
$$

where B is the binomial distribution function given in (2.5.5).

When the process is in control, that is, when $c_1, c_2, \cdots$ are independent Poisson random variables with constant parameter λ, the average rate for a standard inspection unit, the Q_i's are approximately independent with discrete Q-Poisson distributions, which can be approximated by standard normal distributions. Therefore, the values Q_2, $Q_3, \cdots$ can be plotted on a Shewhart Q-chart. The interpretation of this chart is similar to the interpretation of the chart for λ known, but certain special considerations must be observed. Note that the equations (8.5.2) essentially solve the problem of charting short runs of Poisson observations, since they do not require knowledge of the Poisson parameter. This chart permits plotting from the second Poisson sample on, but no point is plotted for the first sample. This is because the transformation must be estimated from the present data sequence. The situation is similar to that in Chapter 7 where Q-charts are given for a number of normal distribution processes with unknown parameters, and to that in section 8.2 above for an unknown binomial parameter p.

Example 8.5: To illustrate the use of the Poisson Q-chart for unknown λ, we consider again the data in Table 8.6 above. The Q-statistics have been computed using equations (8.5.2) and are shown in Figure 8.12. Recall that the 60 Poisson observations were drawn from an $f(c; 6.8)$ distribution, where $\lambda = 1.7$ and $n_i = 4$. The chart in Fig. 8.12 should be compared with the chart in Fig. 8.11. Note, particularly, that the point patterns on the two charts are very similar. This will generally

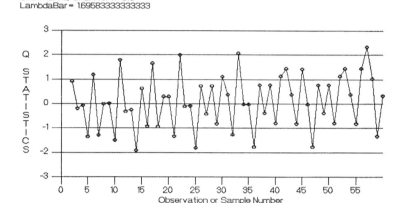

Shewhart Q-Chart for : POIU
LambdaBar = 1.69583333333333

Figure 8.12   Poisson Shewhart Q-Chart for Example 8.5, Case U of λ Unknown

be the case for charts made using the formulas for the two cases when the parameter λ is known and when it is unknown and the process is a stable Poisson process. ∎

It is important to note that the Q-chart using the statistics computed in equations (8.5.2) can be made in real time, that is, when each Poisson observation c_i is observed, a point for it can be plotted immediately. A point is plotted for each sample, beginning with the second. This strategy is ideal for studying a process in order to recognize special causes quickly and bring it into control at the earliest possible time.

Example 8.6: To illustrate the responses of these Shewhart Q-charts to a shift in the Poisson parameter λ, and the flexibility to permit varying sizes of the sampling inspection units, we have generated 30 observations for $\lambda = 1.7$ and varying sample sizes n_i. Twenty additional values were generated for $\lambda = 2.55$ (a 50% increase in λ). The data are given in Table 8.7. The Poisson Shewhart Q-chart using the known nominal value of $\lambda = 1.7$ obtained from the equations (8.5.1) is given in Fig. 8.13, and the Poisson Shewhart Q-chart obtained from the equations (8.5.2), that does not use a value for λ, is given in Fig. 8.14. Again, study of these charts shows that the patterns are very similar. However, as was noted for both variables Shewhart Q-charts and binomial Shewhart Q-charts, the pattern reflecting the shift in the parameter for the case when the parameter is not known becomes less distinct as the shift point becomes more remote. Both charts signal by the 4-

TABLE 8.7 Data for Example 8.6

i	n_i	c_i	i	n_i	c_i	i	n_i	c_i	i	n_i	c_i	i	n_i	c_i
1	4	4	11	4.5	7	21	5	8	31	5	7	41	4.4	20
2	4	3	12	4.5	10	22	5	11	32	5	9	42	4.4	15
3	4	3	13	4.5	10	23	5	12	33	5	14	43	4.4	11
4	4	7	14	4.5	6	24	5	5	34	5	16	44	4.4	18
5	4	6	15	4.5	9	25	5	7	35	5	17	45	4.4	11
6	4	10	16	4.5	5	26	5	8	36	5	15	46	4.4	6
7	4	7	17	4.5	9	27	5	8	37	5	15	47	4.4	8
8	4	6	18	4.5	5	28	5	10	38	5	9	48	4.4	15
9	4	7	19	4.5	11	29	5	5	39	5	13	49	4.4	11
10	4	4	20	4.5	3	30	5	14	40	5	11	50	4.4	10

of-5 test first on the 36th point and both charts signal by the 1-of-1 test on the 41st point.

We have also plotted the Poisson EWMA Q-chart in Fig. 8.15, using the Q-statistics for case K and the Poisson EWMA Q-chart in Fig. 8.16 using the Q-statistics for case U. Both of these charts signal first on the 34th point. ∎

8.6 COMPARISONS AMONG POISSON SHEWHART z-, Q-, AND y-CHARTS, SAMPLE SIZE RECOMMENDATIONS

If we consider the statistic u that is plotted on a u-chart, then recall that $E(u) = \lambda$ and $\text{Var}(u) = \lambda/n$. Then $c = nu$ is a Poisson random

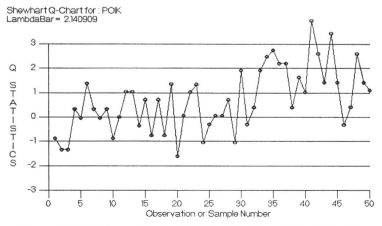

Figure 8.13 Poisson Shewhart Q-Chart for Example 8.6, Case K

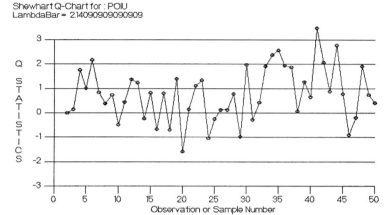

Figure 8.14 Poisson Shewhart Q-Chart for Example 8.6, Case U

variable with $E(c) = n\lambda$ and $\mathrm{Var}(c) = n\lambda$. The *standardized* value of u (or c) is

$$z = \frac{u - \lambda}{\sqrt{\lambda/n}} = \frac{c - n\lambda}{\sqrt{n\lambda}} \qquad (8.6.1)$$

and for n large z can be approximated by an $N(0, 1)$ random variable. However, this linear transformation does not improve the normal approximation. In general, to obtain a statistic that admits a better approximation by a normal distribution requires a nonlinear transformation. If we consider the eight cells defined in (8.3.2) and

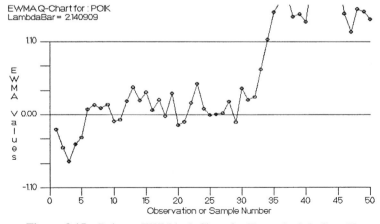

Figure 8.15 Poisson EWMA Q-Chart for Example 8.6, Case K

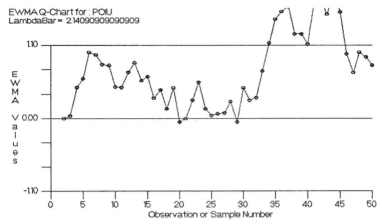

Figure 8.16 Poisson EWMA Q-Chart for Example 8.6, Case U

evaluate the actual probabilities that z of (8.6.1) falls in these cells using the Poisson distribution, then comparing these values with the normal probabilities gives an accurate evaluation of the normal approximation for a u-chart.

8.6.1 The Square-root Transformation

In addition to the Q transformation, another nonlinear normalizing transformation is the *square root* transformation given by

$$y = 2\sqrt{c} - 2\sqrt{n\lambda} \qquad (8.6.2)$$

This transformation and other related transformations have been studied by many writers. See Johnson and Kotz (1969) for a review of these transformations.

It is possible to compute the probabilities of the cells of (8.3.2) for nominally normal charts using the statistic z of (8.6.1), y of (8.6.2), and Q of (8.5.1). Table 8.8 gives these cell probabilities for selected values of $n\lambda$. By examining the cell probabilities for different values of $n\lambda$ it is clear that the statistics Q and y are both approximated more closely by a normal distribution than the standardized statistic z. The cell probabilities for the z statistic chart are the same as for the corresponding cells of a classical 3-sigma u-chart, or a 3-sigma c-chart. This table is read in essentially the same way as was Table 8.4.

The cells are again as given in display (8.3.2). The cell probabilities for the Q-statistic, especially for cells 1 and 8, are better approximated by the standardized normal probabilities than the standardized statistic

TABLE 8.8   Cell Probabilities for Poisson z-, Q-, and y-Charts

Cell	1	2	3	4	5	6	7	8	
$n\lambda$	.00135	.02140	.13591	.34134	.34134	.13591	.02140	.00135	
5.00	.00000	.00674	.11791	.49131	.25067	.10154	.02637	.00545	z
	.00000	.00674	.11791	.31584	.32169	.20599	.02981	.00202	Q
	.00674	.03369	.22460	.35093	.25067	.11968	.01300	.00070	y
6.00	.00000	.07135	.13385	.45510	.24093	.11014	.03899	.00363	z
	.00000	.01735	.13385	.29448	.29830	.21340	.04122	.00140	Q
	.00248	.05949	.08924	.29448	.40156	.13267	.01958	.00051	y
7.00	.00000	.00730	.16570	.42572	.23178	.14250	.02128	.00572	z
	.00091	.00638	.07447	.36795	.38078	.14250	.02459	.00241	Q
	.00730	.02234	.14336	.42572	.23178	.15669	.01245	.00036	y
8.00	.00000	.01375	.17748	.40131	.22334	.14993	.03046	.00372	z
	.00034	.01342	.08588	.35333	.36292	.14993	.03259	.00159	Q
	.00302	.03936	.14886	.40131	.29553	.09467	.01661	.00065	y
9.00	.00000	.00623	.10946	.47172	.28837	.10219	.01961	.00243	z
	.00123	.01999	.09446	.33996	.34736	.15553	.03904	.00243	Q
	.00623	.01499	.18555	.38063	.28837	.11312	.01067	.00044	y
10.00	.00005	.01029	.11981	.45290	.28142	.10849	.02359	.00345	z
	.00050	.00984	.11981	.32779	.33363	.18140	.02545	.00159	Q
	.00277	.02648	.19097	.36282	.28142	.12126	.01358	.00070	y
15.00	.00021	.01779	.16675	.38334	.25138	.14778	.02943	.00331	z
	.00086	.01715	.10046	.34719	.35382	.14778	.03103	.00172	Q
	.00279	.03465	.14731	.38334	.30713	.10532	.01860	.00086	y
20.00	.00026	.02113	.13513	.40258	.28413	.12244	.03165	.00269	z
	.00078	.02061	.13513	.31374	.31724	.17817	.03284	.00149	Q
	.00209	.03692	.11750	.40258	.28413	.13495	.02101	.00080	y
30.00	.00041	.02147	.13537	.39111	.29427	.12507	.02986	.00245	z
	.00092	.02095	.13537	.31847	.32159	.17038	.03082	.00149	Q
	.00195	.03334	.12196	.39111	.29427	.13528	.02122	.00089	y
40.00	.00073	.01860	.13207	.39051	.30596	.12406	.02516	.00290	z
	.00073	.01860	.13207	.32757	.33068	.16229	.02618	.00188	Q
	.00256	.02682	.12202	.39051	.30596	.13212	.01924	.00076	y
50.00	.00051	.01570	.12729	.39401	.31762	.12126	.02159	.00201	z
	.00092	.01530	.12729	.33769	.34093	.15428	.02159	.00201	Q
	.00269	.02107	.15604	.35772	.31762	.12759	.01638	.00089	y

z. The distribution of Q tends to give probabilities for cell 8 that are somewhat larger than the nominal normal value of 0.00135 and values for cell 1 that are smaller than than 0.00135, while just the opposite is the case for the y-statistic obtained by the square root transformation. Overall, the Q-statistic generally gives a reasonable approximation for values of $n\lambda \geq 7$. Note that the values in Table 8.8 can be used to evaluate the probabilities of false alarms for runs tests, for the values of $n\lambda$ given (see problem 8.10).

8.6.2 Recommended Sample Sizes for Poisson Q-Charts

For case K ($\lambda = \lambda_0$ known) we recommend that the minimal sample size n should be the smallest value of n that satisfies equation (5.3.5) with $\alpha_L = 0.00135$. That is, the smallest n such that

$$n > \frac{6.608}{\lambda_0} \tag{8.6.3}$$

This sample size assures that the case K Shewhart Poisson Q-chart will have positive probability below -3. Moreover, an n that satisfies (8.6.3) will generally give a chart with the eight cell probabilities of Table 8.8 that are decent approximations to the normal cell probabilities. It should be noted that the minimal sample sizes that satisfy (8.6.3) increase rapidly as λ becomes small. A few values of n and λ are given in the following table.

λ	>6.61	6.61	4	2	1
Minimum n	1	2	2	4	7

λ	0.5	0.2	0.1	0.05	0.01
Minimum n	14	34	67	133	661

For small fractional values of λ, the number of standard sampling units n required becomes impracticably large for most applications. For these processes, the Q-charts for an exponential distribution given in section 7.9 should be considered as an alternative approach to establishing control of a process. If this alternative is to be pursued, it would be well to define standard inspection units to be as small as practically feasible.

If the sample size required for equation (8.6.3) is too large to consider, we can, of course, make charts for smaller sample sizes, but there are certain consequences. First, the 1-of-1 test on a Poisson Shewhart Q-chart will have no power to detect a decrease in λ, and the 4-of-5 test should be used, in addition to the 1-of-1 test as recommended above, to detect increases or decreases. Of course, with any sample size a Poisson distribution function algorithm can be used to evaluate the probabilities of signals by any of the runs tests for any shift in value of λ, for case K.

When it is required to use a case U Poisson Q-chart, we would use the same sample size criterion using equation (8.6.3). In this case λ is unknown and we shall have to first obtain at least a crude estimate of λ to use in equation (8.6.3). One approach to this problem is to take a preliminary sample, as large as possible, for the first sample and use the observed rate per standard inspection unit from this sample to determine the minimal next sample size. We can continue to upgrade the estimates of λ and the required sample size after each sample until the estimate of λ appears stable.

8.6.3 Performances of Charts Tests from Poisson Q-Statistics

In section 5.5 it was noted that an increase or decrease of λ from a value λ_0 to a new value $\delta\lambda_0$ results in point patterns that tend to be either higher or lower and to have greater or lesser spread according to whether $\delta > 1$ or $\delta < 1$. A shift in λ will have the same effect on patterns on the Poisson Q-charts. It was also pointed out that this causes classical c- and u-charts to be insensitive for detecting decreases in λ by having a point fall below the LCL, that is, the 1-of-1 test for a decrease in λ. This is also the case for this Poisson Q-chart, for the same reason.

Quesenberry (1995c), Q95c, gave results of a simulation study of the performance of the 1-of-1, 4-of-5, 9-of-9, and 3-of-3 tests on Poisson Shewhart Q-charts; and the EWMA and CUSUM Q-charts to detect either increases or decreases in λ. This study was conducted in a similar manner to the study of binomial Q-charts discussed above, and the conclusions and recommendations for the Poisson Q-charts are very similar to those for binomial Q-charts. The study gave simulated signal rates on the next 30 samples for the various tests when λ shifts from λ_0 to $\delta\lambda_0$ after c samples. We summarize the results in the following points.

- For the stable case, the false alarm rates for both the K and U cases are approximately the same, and for the U case this result does not depend on the number of samples before the shift of λ. This lends credence to the claim that the Q-statistics for both cases are approximately independent standard normal statistics.
- The overall performances of the EWMA and CUSUM charts, using the same chart parameters as for the binomial study, were comparable with each other and better than the Shewhart chart tests to detect these one-step permanent parameter shifts. It would be good

practice to regularly plot one of these charts. Although there is little difference in these two charts in performance, the personal preference of this author is the EWMA chart. The particular charts used here would work well in charting programs.

· The 4-of-5 test on the Shewhart chart is considered to be the best overall test of the Shewhart chart tests.

· The classical 1-of-1 test is a poor competitor for many of the cases considered. However, it is essentially the only test for detecting a single outlier on a chart for λ. A nice compromise is to use the combined 11-45 test on Shewhart Poisson Q-charts.

· If the increased rate of false alarms is considered tolerable in order to improve sensitivity to shifts, then the 3-of-3 test is a reasonable choice of test. This can be a reasonable trade-off in a start-up process before many data are available to improve sensitivity, that is, while c is small.

In this study, c was the number of samples observed before λ shifts from λ_0 to $n\lambda_0$. By considering results for small values of c, say $c = 1$, it was observed in Q95c that the tests based on Q-statistics for case U maintain essentially the same error rates as the same tests based on Q-statistics for case K. This permits us to assess the effect on performances of the tests for $\delta \neq 1$ by comparing the case U results for selected values of c with those for the corresponding K case.

Finally, as was discussed earlier for variables and binomial Q-charts, the 1-1 test on the first point after a one-step shift of λ is an optimal test to detect the shift on this point (see Quesenberry 1995f).

8.6.4 Using Case U in Applications, Responding to Signals

The transformations and, of course, the results of the case K studies given above are based on the assumption that the Poisson parameter has an exactly known value $\lambda = \lambda_0$. In practice, this is unrealistic because it is always necessary to estimate λ from data. Given a calibration data set $(n_1, y_1), (n_2, y_2), \cdots, (n_r, y_r)$; to use the case K formulas the parameter λ is estimated by

$$\bar{\lambda} = \frac{\sum\limits_{i=1}^{r} y_i}{\sum\limits_{i=1}^{r} n_i} \tag{8.6.4}$$

The Q-statistics of further samples (n_{r+1}, y_{r+1}), $\cdots$ would be computed using the case K formulas of equation (8.5.1) by replacing λ_0 by $\bar{\lambda}$. However, this is an alternative (to equation 8.5.2) "plug-in" method of estimating the transformations, and as such has poorer properties than equation (8.5.2). The approximation of the distribution of the Q-statistics of equation (8.5.2), for the stable case, by the distribution of independent standardized normal statistics, will be better for any r than for the Q-statistics from (8.5.1) using $\bar{\lambda}$ for λ_0. For this reason, we recommend using the case U Q-statistics. In other words, we do not recommend ever switching to case K using an estimate $\bar{\lambda}$ for λ_0. When the backlog of data, obtained while the process is stable, of course, is large enough, the Q-statistics from (8.5.2) will be virtually the same as they would be with truly known λ.

Suppose that λ shifts value during the operation of the case U Q-chart. The chart either will or will not signal the change with some probabilities. The probability that the change is signaled will generally be less than one and this probability depends on a number of factors such as the amount of data obtained from the stable process before the shift, the magnitude and sign of the shift, sample size, and so on.

First, suppose the shift is not signaled. Then, if there are no further shifts, the chart pattern will eventually return to the stable normal pattern. This is reasonable behavior since the process is, in fact, stable after the shift.

Second, if the process signals the shift by one of the tests considered earlier, we will search for an assignable cause. Suppose that an assignable cause is found and removed so that it will no longer affect the process. Then, we must decide how to restart the process. If, by the nature of the assignable cause, we feel confident that the value of λ will be the same as before the cause appeared, then the data from before its appearance can be used to restart the process. However, if there is doubt as to whether the value of λ has changed, then we should restart the process without using prior data.

In using the case U statistics of equation (8.5.2), in most cases we recommend that a trailing window of data be used. When the rth sample (n_r, y_r) is observed, a trailing window of span k is the set of data: (n_{r-k+1}, y_{r-k+1}), $\cdots$, (n_r, y_r). When the rth data point is plotted and the next point (n_{r+1}, y_{r+1}) is observed, this last observation will be appended to the data set and the observation (n_{r-k+1}, y_{r-k+1}) deleted. This dynamic approach to charting uses only the most recent k data observations, which are expected to be most relevant. This approach to charting requires a choice of k to design the charting procedure. We shall call the quantity (for a given k)

$$\sum_{i=0}^{k-1} n_{r-i} \tag{8.6.5}$$

the *window sample size* at the rth sample. We recommend that the window sample size should satisfy the following inequality:

$$\lambda_0 \sum_{i=0}^{k-1} n_{r-i} \geq 500 \tag{8.6.6}$$

for all $r = k, k + 1, \cdots$. This recommendation is based on observing in Table A of Quesenberry (1995c) that for $c = 50$ with $\lambda_0 = 10$ the case U tests have probabilities near those of case K to detect moderate to large shifts in λ. If it is desired to have more sensitivity to detect smaller shifts, a larger window should be used. If sample sizes have a constant value n, say, then this requirement can be expressed by requiring a span k that satisfies the following:

$$k \geq \frac{500}{n\lambda_0} \tag{8.6.7}$$

In practice, at the start-up of a process, all data will be used until a good estimate of λ is obtained to evaluate k from this last inequality.

8.7 THE GEOMETRIC Q-CHART

From the developments in sections 5.2, 8.2, and 8.3, it is seen that charts based on the binomial distribution require impracticably large sample sizes for high-quality processes with small values of p, say $p \leq 0.01$. In the present section we consider Q-statistics based on a geometric distribution, which can be used for these very high quality processes. The geometric density, $g(x; p)$, and distribution, $G(x; p)$, functions were given in (2.7.4) and (2.7.5) as:

$$\begin{aligned}
g(x; p) &= p(1 - p)^{x-1} \quad \text{for } x \in \{1, 2, \cdots\} \\
G(x; p) &= 0, \, x < 1 \\
&= 1 - (1 - p)^{[x]} \quad \text{for } x \geq 1
\end{aligned} \tag{8.7.1}$$

where [·] is the greatest integer function.

A sampling method suitable for high-quality processes, and called *inverse* binomial sampling, was introduced by Haldane (1945), and can be described as follows. Suppose that a procedure for inspecting units of production from a process gives a constant average proportion p of nonconforming units. Moreover, suppose that the outcomes from inspections can be considered a sequence of Bernoulli trials. Then the number of units X observed to obtain a defective is a geometric random variable with the distribution and density functions of (8.7.1). If we let X_1 denote the number of units inspected to obtain the first nonconforming unit, X_2 the additional time to obtain the second, $\cdots$; $X_1, X_2, \cdots$, X_n is a sample on X. We consider plotting these values on a chart to control p. As usual, we will make charts for the case when p is assumed known in advance, case K; and p is assumed unknown in advance, case U. The material of this section is largely from Quesenberry (1995d). This section will be presented in somewhat more detail than the earlier sections on binomial and Poisson Q-charts because many readers will likely not have had an opportunity to see this material before.

8.7.1   An Exact Geometric Distribution Chart, $p = p_0$ Known

By using the distribution function of (8.7.1), we can design a Shewhart-type control chart for the geometric distribution. From the form of the distribution function, we see that if p increases, then the probability at or below any integer x is increased. So small values of X may indicate an increase in p, and, conversely, large values may indicate a decrease in p. This point should be kept in mind in the following developments.

To design an (α_L, α_U) probability chart, we wish to choose integers *LCL* and *UCL*, if possible, so that $P(X < LCL) = \alpha_L$ and $P(X > UCL) = \alpha_U$. For $\alpha_L > 0$, the smallest possible value of LCL is 2, and for this value we have $\alpha_L = P(X < LCL) = P(X < 2) = P(X = 1) = p_0$. That is, the smallest possible value of α_L is p_0, itself, and this is achieved when $\alpha_L = p_0$. In general, if α_L is given, and we are to design a chart with $P(X < LCL) = \alpha_L$, then we put

$$1 - (1 - p_0)^{LCL-1} = \alpha_L$$

and then

$$LCL = 1 + \frac{ln(1 - \alpha_L)}{ln(1 - p_0)}$$

This value of *LCL* is generally a fraction and we must round up or down to obtain an integer value of *LCL*. The exact probability of a point below *LCL* can be evaluated using the distribution function of (8.7.1). The *UCL* is to be chosen to give probability α_U of exceeding *UCL*. This can be done using the distribution function in (8.7.1). We require

$$P(X > UCL) = 1 - P(X \leq UCL) = 1 - \{1 - (1 - p_0)^{UCL}\} = \alpha_U$$

from this

$$UCL = \frac{ln(\alpha_U)}{ln(1 - p_0)}$$

and, again, this will generally be a fraction and must be rounded up or down. A chart for run length using these values of *LCL* and *UCL* will have probability of approximately α_L that a point will fall below *LCL*, and approximately α_U that a point will be above *UCL* when p remains constant at $p = p_0$. Of course, these probabilities can be evaluated exactly using the above distribution function.

Example 8.7: Suppose a process has fallout of $p = p_0 = 0.0001$ and we wish to choose $\alpha_L = \alpha_U = 0.00135$. Then

$$LCL = 1 + \frac{ln(0.99865)}{ln(0.9999)} = 14.5$$

so we choose $LCL = 14$ and the actual probability below *LCL* is

$$P(X < 14) = P(X \leq 13) = 1 - (1 - 0.0001)^{13} = 0.00130$$

To choose the *UCL*, we have

$$UCL = \frac{ln(\alpha_U)}{ln(1 - p)} = \frac{ln(0.00135)}{ln(0.9999)} = 66,073.2$$

So we take $UCL = 66073$, and the actual probability above *UCL* is

$$P(X > UCL) = 1 - P(X \leq UCL) = 1 - \{1 - (0.9999)^{66073}\}$$
$$= 0.00135$$

Then an "exact" geometric chart can be made by using LCL $= 14$ and UCL $= 66073$; and $\alpha_L = 0.00130$ and $\alpha_U = 0.00135$.   ■

Although charts can be designed as described here, for reasons that will be developed in the following, we feel that the Q-charts to be given next have important advantages. Also, it should be noted that Calvin (1983) proposed a charting method that is similar to the one just given. Goh (1987) also considered the chart proposed by Calvin. A number of other writers including Jackson (1972), Sheaffer and Leavenworth (1976), Bourke (1991), Kaminsky et al. (1992), Benneyan and Kaminsky (1995), and Benneyan (1995) have considered control charts based on the geometric or negative binomial distributions.

8.7.2   Geometric Q-Statistics for $p = p_0$ Known, Case K

As described above, let X_1 be the number of inspections to find the first defective, X_2 to find the second, and so on. Then we define Q-statistics as follows.

$$
\begin{array}{l}
u_i = G(x_i; p_0) = 1 - (1 - p_0)^{x_i} \\
Q_i = -\Phi^{-1}(u_i) \qquad \text{for } i = 1, 2, \cdots
\end{array}
\tag{8.7.2}
$$

When $p = p_0$ is constant, these Q_i's are independent approximately standard normal statistics. The approximate normality depends on p_0. Smaller values of p_0 give better approximations.

Another point of key importance is the behavior of the geometric distribution when $p = p_0$ shifts to a new value $p = \delta p_0$ for $0 < \delta < 1/p_0$. Recall that the parent geometric random variable X had mean $1/p$ and standard deviation $\sqrt{1 - p}/p$. Then the mean shifts from $1/p_0$ to $1/\delta p_0$ and the standard deviation shifts from $\sqrt{1 - p_0}/p_0$ to $\sqrt{1 - \delta p_0}/\delta p_0$. Thus, we see that if $1 < \delta < \dfrac{1}{p_0}$, then the mean of the run length distribution will decrease and the standard deviation will decrease even more. Then from (8.7.2) we see that an increase in p will cause the mean of the distribution of the Q-statistics to increase and the standard deviation to *decrease*. Similarly, if p decreases then the mean of Q will decrease and its standard deviation will *increase*. These responses of the mean and standard deviation of the Q-statistic to changes in p are crucially important in interpreting point patterns on charts of these geometric Q-statistics.

Suppose a sequence of Q-statistics $Q_1, Q_2, \cdots$ are computed from a sequence of run lengths $X_1, X_2, \cdots$; using the nominal value $p = p_0$ in the formulas of (8.7.2), and after the t_0^{th} value X_{t_0} is observed that p shifts to a new value $p = \delta p_0$ for $0 < p < 1/p_0$. Then for $\delta = 1$ (no shift) the Q_i's for $t = t_0 + 1, t_0 + 2, \cdots$ are independent approximately standard normal statistics. However, for $\delta > 1$ the Q_i's will tend to have means exceeding zero and standard deviations less than one. Similarly, for $\delta < 1$ the Q_i's will tend to have means less than zero and standard deviations greater than one. If these Q-statistics are plotted on Shewhart Q-charts, then these trends should be kept in mind in interpreting point patterns.

Example 8.8: To illustrate the effect of shifts in p on the pattern of points of the Q-statistics, we have generated ten values from a geometric distribution with $p = 0.0001$, and then ten more with $p = 0.001$. The values obtained are given in the following table. The Shewhart

p	Observations									
0.0001	13766	8903	35001	4645	1432	5056	29635	11084	2075	183
0.001	351	1301	469	1677	47	3298	925	2249	1461	1884

Q-chart is given in Figure 8.17, and illustrates the typical point pattern that results from an increase in p. From this, and the above discussion, it is apparent that the 1-of-1 test of Fig. 4.9 is not a sensitive test to detect an increase in p. The 4-of-5 test signals on a number of points and, as will be shown later, is especially sensitive for detecting increases in p. For the reason discussed above, the 1-of-1 test is a poor test to detect increases in p.

The Q-statistics can also be used to plot geometric EWMA or CUSUM charts, and these will often give good sensitivity to detect monotone changes in p. The EWMA chart for the Q-statistics for the above data is given in Fig. 8.18. This chart uses chart parameters $(\lambda, K) = (0.25, 2.90)$, which is the same chart we have used before for a number of problems. This EWMA chart clearly signals the increase in p. From the above discussion of the effect of shifts on the distribution of the Q-statistics, it can be anticipated that the EWMA chart will have good sensitivity to detect increases in p. Comparable CUSUM Q-charts also have good sensitivity to detect increases in p. ∎

Shewhart Q-Chart for : GEOK
PBar = 1.51465629259971D-04

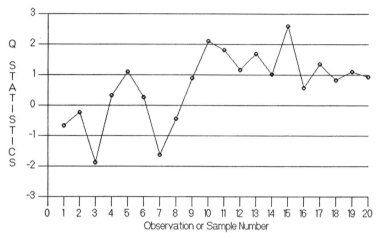

Figure 8.17   Shewhart Q-Chart for Data of Example 8.8, Using $p = p_0 = 0.0001$ Known

Q-EWMA Chart for : GEOK
PBar = 1.51465629259971D-04

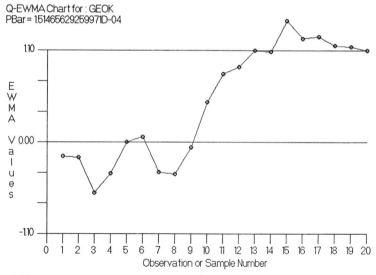

Figure 8.18   EWMA Q-Chart for Data of Example 8.8, $(\lambda, K) = (0.25, 2.90)$ Using $p = p_0 = 0.0001$ Known

8.7.3 Estimating *p* from a Geometric Sample

If $x_1, x_2, \cdots, x_n$ is a sample from the geometric distribution of (8.7.1), then the MVU estimate of p is

$$\bar{p} = \frac{n-1}{t-1} \qquad \text{for } t = x_1 + x_2 + \cdots + x_n \qquad (8.7.3)$$

8.7.4 Power Functions to Detect Changes in *p*

Suppose that p shifts from a value $p = p_0$ to a value $p = \delta p_0$, for $0 < \delta < 1/p_0$, and that the Q-statistics of (8.7.2) are plotted on a 3-sigma Shewhart chart. We now consider the probability, say P_I, that an increase in p will be signaled on one point, and the probability, say P_D, that a decrease will be signaled on one point for the 1-of-1, 9-of-9, and 4-of-5 tests of Fig. 4.9; and for a test that we call the 3-of-3 test. This 3-of-3 test signals an increase in p when three consecutive points are above 1 and signals a decrease in p when three consecutive points are below -1. It is possible to derive formulas for P_I and P_D. We have used these formulas to compute tables of P_D and P_I for these four tests for values of $p_0 = 0.01, 0.001, 0.0001, 0.00001, 0.000001, 0.0000001$; and for $\delta = I$ and $\delta = 1/I$ for $I = 1, 2, \cdots, 20$. These values are given in Table 8.9 for $p_0 = 0.0001$.

First, note that the row for $\delta = 1$ gives the values of these probabilities when the process is stable with $p = p_0$, its nominal value. Observe that these values are close to those for a normal distribution for all cases. For the 1-of-1 test this nominal value is 0.00135, for the 9-of-9 test it is $2^{-9} = 0.00195$, for the 4-of-5 test it is $\{1 - B[3; 5, \Phi(-1)]\} = 0.00277$, and for the 3-of-3 test it is $[\Phi(-1)]^3 = 0.00399$. For smaller values of p_0 these values are all closer to the nominal normal values. Indeed, for $p_0 \leq 0.00001$ these values are essentially equal to the nominal normal values.

It can be shown that when $p \geq 0.00135$ the 1-of-1 test has probability zero of a point larger than $UCL = 3$. This means, of course, that the 1-of-1 test has no power to detect a shift of p to a value in this range (see problem 8.9). Indeed, from Table 8.9 we see that this test is extremely insensitive to increases in p. This is exactly what we expect from the discussion in the two paragraphs just after equations (8.7.2).

Another important point that is apparent from studying all six tables for the values of p_0 given above is that while the various formulas for P_D and P_I depend on both p_0 and δ, with one exception the tables are virtually constant in p_0 for all six values of p_0. The exception is for

TABLE 8.9 Signal Probabilities on Points for Tests on Geometric Shewhart Q-Charts, $p_o = 0.0001$ Known, Case K

	1-of-1 test		9-of-9 test		4-of-4 test		3-of-3 test	
δ	P_D	P_I	P_D	P_I	P_D	P_I	P_D	P_I
0.050	0.7187	0.0001	0.7321	0.0000	0.9354	0.0000	0.7587	0.0000
0.053	0.7063	0.0001	0.7201	0.0000	0.9294	0.0000	0.7478	0.0000
0.056	0.6928	0.0001	0.7071	0.0000	0.9226	0.0000	0.7358	0.0000
0.059	0.6780	0.0001	0.6929	0.0000	0.9147	0.0000	0.7226	0.0000
0.063	0.6617	0.0001	0.6771	0.0000	0.9055	0.0000	0.7081	0.0000
0.067	0.6437	0.0001	0.6598	0.0000	0.8948	0.0000	0.6920	0.0000
0.071	0.6238	0.0001	0.6405	0.0000	0.8822	0.0000	0.6740	0.0000
0.077	0.6015	0.0001	0.6189	0.0000	0.8673	0.0000	0.6539	0.0000
0.083	0.5766	0.0001	0.5946	0.0000	0.8494	0.0000	0.6311	0.0000
0.091	0.5484	0.0001	0.5672	0.0000	0.8276	0.0000	0.6053	0.0000
0.100	0.5165	0.0001	0.5359	0.0000	0.8009	0.0000	0.5756	0.0000
0.111	0.4799	0.0001	0.5000	0.0000	0.7677	0.0000	0.5414	0.0000
0.125	0.4378	0.0002	0.4585	0.0000	0.7259	0.0000	0.5014	0.0000
0.143	0.3891	0.0002	0.4102	0.0000	0.6723	0.0000	0.4543	0.0000
0.167	0.3325	0.0002	0.3536	0.0000	0.6028	0.0000	0.3983	0.0000
0.200	0.2667	0.0003	0.2872	0.0000	0.5118	0.0000	0.3314	0.0000
0.250	0.1917	0.0003	0.2102	0.0000	0.3928	0.0000	0.2514	0.0001
0.333	0.1105	0.0004	0.1250	0.0000	0.2435	0.0000	0.1587	0.0002
0.500	0.0367	0.0006	0.0442	0.0000	0.0858	0.0002	0.0632	0.0006
1	0.00135	0.00130	0.00195	0.00195	0.00277	0.00276	0.00399	0.0040
2	0.0000	0.0026	0.0000	0.0751	0.0000	0.0279	0.0000	0.0249
3	0.0000	0.0039	0.0000	0.3007	0.0000	0.0905	0.0000	0.0661
4	0.0000	0.0052	0.0000	0.5595	0.0000	0.1861	0.0000	0.1242
5	0.0000	0.0065	0.0000	0.7516	0.0000	0.3007	0.0000	0.1935
6	0.0000	0.0078	0.0000	0.8680	0.0000	0.4194	0.0000	0.2687
7	0.0000	0.0091	0.0000	0.9319	0.0000	0.5315	0.0000	0.3454
8	0.0000	0.0104	0.0000	0.9655	0.0000	0.6306	0.0000	0.4201
9	0.0000	0.0116	0.0000	0.9826	0.0000	0.7142	0.0000	0.4908
10	0.0000	0.0129	0.0000	0.9913	0.0000	0.7823	0.0000	0.5561
11	0.0000	0.0142	0.0000	0.9956	0.0000	0.8362	0.0000	0.6153
12	0.0000	0.0155	0.0000	0.9978	0.0000	0.8781	0.0000	0.6683
13	0.0000	0.0168	0.0000	0.9989	0.0000	0.9100	0.0000	0.7151
14	0.0000	0.0180	0.0000	0.9995	0.0000	0.9340	0.0000	0.7561
15	0.0000	0.0193	0.0000	0.9997	0.0000	0.9519	0.0000	0.7919
16	0.0000	0.0206	0.0000	0.9999	0.0000	0.9651	0.0000	0.8228
17	0.0000	0.0219	0.0000	0.9999	0.0000	0.9748	0.0000	0.8494
18	0.0000	0.0231	0.0000	1.0000	0.0000	0.9819	0.0000	0.8722
19	0.0000	0.0244	0.0000	1.0000	0.0000	0.9870	0.0000	0.8918
20	0.0000	0.0257	0.0000	1.0000	0.0000	0.9907	0.0000	0.9084
21	0.0000	0.0270	0.0000	1.0000	0.0000	0.9933	0.0000	0.9226

$p_0 \le 0.001$, P_I for the 1-of-1 test is unstable in p_0. But this test is an extremely poor competitor, anyway.

If we consider the signal probabilities of the four tests to detect $\delta < 1$, then all of the tests are reasonably competitive, but the 4-of-5 test is, perhaps, slightly better. Of course, this is in part due to the fact that the 4-of-5 test has a larger in-control signal probability than either the 1-of-1 or 9-of-9 tests. When we consider these probabilities for the four tests to detect increases in p, that is, for $\delta > 1$, then the 9-of-9 test is clearly the winner. There is, however, a drawback for this test. We shall sometimes wish to use these tests for short runs, and this test cannot be used until nine points are plotted. Also, in general, the power functions of Table 8.9 for an x-of-y test assume y points have been plotted after the shift of p. This is the reason we have included the 3-of-3 test. The 3-of-3 test can, of course, be applied on the third point. However, it should also be noted that the 4-of-5 test is clearly more sensitive than the 3-of-3 test for detecting increases in p, and it can be applied starting with the fourth point.

Finally, we point out that these are the probabilities of signals on individual points, and do not give direct information on the performance of these tests when used on runs of points. However, they are suggestive of the relative performance to expect when the tests are used on sequences of points.

8.7.5 Geometric Q-Statistics for p Unknown, Case U

For this case we consider the sample of values $X_1, X_2, \cdots, X_n$ from the geometric distribution of (8.7.1), and denote $t = X_1 + \cdots + X_n$. Then the MVU estimating probability frunction $\tilde{g}(x; t, n)$ and distribution function $\tilde{G}(x; t, n)$ are given in (8.7.4), (see Lehmann 1983 and Patil 1963).

$$\tilde{g}(x; t, n) = \frac{(n-1)(t-n)\cdots(t-n-x+2)}{(t-x)\cdots(t-1)},$$

$$x \in \{1, 2, \cdots, t-n+1\}$$

$$\tilde{G}(x; t, n) = 0, \; x < 1$$

$$= \sum_{x'=1}^{[x]} \tilde{g}(x'; t, n),$$

$$1 \le x < t-n+1$$

$$= 1, \quad x \ge t-n+1$$

(8.7.4)

The Q-statistics are defined for this case by (8.7.5). When the process is stable, these Q_i's will be distributed approximately as independent standard normal random variables. Both the independence and the normality approximations are quite good after the first few points.

$$u_n = \tilde{G}(x_n; t, n)$$
$$Q_n = -\Phi^{-1}(u_n), \qquad n = 2, 3, \cdots$$

(8.7.5)

These Q-statistics can be used as the input to plot Shewhart, EWMA, and CUSUM Q-Charts to study the stability of the process. We apply the same tests on the Shewhart charts as those recommended above for the case of p having a known value. We will present information on the sensitivity of these charts after we consider the charts for the data given in Example 8.8.

Example 8.8, continuation 1:   Figures 8.19 and 8.20 give the Shewhart and the EWMA charts for this example for case U. Recall that these are charts of data from a geometric distribution, and the first 10 values were generated using parameter $p_0 = 0.0001$ and the last ten using $p_0 = 0.001$, a tenfold increase in p. Observe that the Shewhart Q-Chart of Fig. 8.19 that does not use the known value of p_0 has point

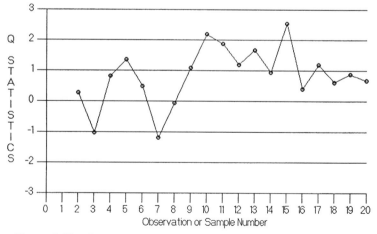

Shewhart Q-Chart for : GEOU
PBar = 1.51465629259971D-04

Figure 8.19   Geometric Shewhart Q-Chart for p Unknown, Case U

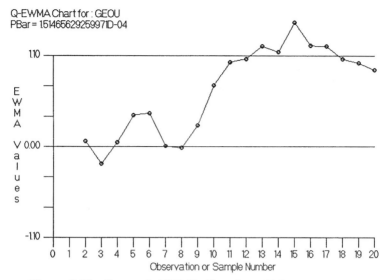

Q-EWMA Chart for : GEOU
PBar = 151465629259971D-04

Figure 8.20 Geometric EWMA Chart for p Unknown, Case U

patterns very similar to those of Fig. 8.17 that uses the known value, and it signals by the 4-of-5 test on the 12th point whereas the chart for case K signaled by the 4-of-5 test on the 13th point. Similarly, the chart of Fig. 8.20, after the shift in p, is similar to Fig. 8.18, and both charts signal on the 13th point. ∎

8.7.6 Performance of Geometric Q-Charts

In order to decide what charts and tests to recommend using the Q-statistics of (8.7.2) and (8.7.4), Quesenberry (1995d) made a simulation study as follows. For $c = 5, 10, 20, 40, 100$, c observations were generated from a geometric distribution with $p = p_0$; and then an additional 30 observations were generated from a geometric distribution with $p = \delta p_0$. The values $p_0 = 0.01$ and $\delta = 0.005, 0.01, 0.02, 0.05, 1, 2, 3, 5, 10$ were used for each value of c. The 9-of-9, 4-of-5, and 3-of-3 Shewhart tests; and the EWMA (with $\lambda = 0.25$ and $K = 2.90$, see Example 6.3), and CUSUM (with $k_s = 0.75$ and $h_s = 3.34$, see Example 6.8) tests were computed for the two sequences of Q-statistics—cases K and U—computed from each sample corresponding to observations $c + 1$ to $c + 30$. This was replicated 5000 times and the proportion of times that each test signaled an increase on observation $c + i$ ($i = 1, \cdots, 30$), for the first time, was recorded. The same procedure was used to study the abilities of the tests to signal decreases in p.

Consider first the performance of the tests when $\delta = 1$, that is, when the process is stable and p is constant. We give in Table 8.10 the proportion of signals obtained on the 30 observations immediately after observation c. The principal points to note in this table of false alarm rates are the relative stability of these values for different values of c, and the similarity of the rates for the charts for p known and for p unknown. This supports the claim that the Q-statistics with p unknown give essentially the same false alarm rates for these tests as the Q-statistics with p known. Note, particularly, that this supports the assertion that the Q-statistics for the p unknown case have approximately the same distributions as those for the case of p known, and, also, it lends credence to the claim that the Q-statistics for p unknown, but constant, are approximately independent.

Table 8.11 gives the simulated signal rates at which the tests *correctly* signal a change in p. By studying this table we note a number of points. It is apparent from these results, as we anticipated from the discussion above concerning the effect of changes in p on the mean and standard deviation of the geometric distribution that the relative performance of these tests is quite different for detecting increases and decreases in p.

TABLE 8.10   False Alarm Rates ($\delta = 1$) on 30 Consecutive Observations

	9-of-9		4-of-5		3-of-3		EWMA		CUSUM	
c	Case:K	U	K	U	K	U	K	U	K	U
				Increases Signaled						
5	.0256	.0278	.0530	.0460	.0973	.0901	.0200	.0228	.0196	.0214
10	.0288	.0312	.0526	.0460	.0938	.0872	.0180	.0155	.0178	.0179
20	.0300	.0302	.0468	.0464	.0884	.0874	.0187	.0191	.0157	.0153
40	.0268	.0300	.0500	.0482	.0926	.0886	.0213	.0187	.0201	.0191
70	.0276	.0282	.0548	.0548	.0990	.0998	.0195	.0205	.0171	.0183
100	.0262	.0284	.0496	.0466	.0926	.0892	.0226	.0235	.0237	.0201
				Decreases Signaled						
5	.0262	.0274	.0501	.0534	.0910	.0954	.0441	.0418	.0423	.0380
10	.0274	.0266	.0508	.0490	.0940	.0952	.0392	.0441	.0410	.0414
20	.0344	.0336	.0488	.0524	.0924	.0938	.0389	.0442	.0391	.0465
40	.0360	.0342	.0500	.0544	.0972	.0988	.0398	.0458	.0408	.0446
70	.0330	.0342	.0500	.0502	.0936	.0956	.0377	.0389	.0395	.0384
100	.0292	.0268	.0480	.0500	.0884	.0886	.0393	.0365	.0367	.0347

TABLE 8.11 Simulated Probabilities of Detecting a Shift in p, $p_0 = 0.01$

c	δ	9-of-9 Case: K	U	4-of-5 K	U	3-of-3 K	U	EWMA K	U	CUSUM K	U
5	0.1	0.980	0.159	1.000	0.447	1.000	0.547	1.000	0.776	1.000	0.844
	0.2	0.871	0.120	0.998	0.329	0.998	0.425	1.000	0.511	1.000	0.531
	0.5	0.324	0.067	0.670	0.140	0.735	0.214	0.897	0.153	0.879	0.148
	2	0.431	0.121	0.328	0.117	0.420	0.185	0.343	0.080	0.254	0.066
	2	0.431	0.121	0.328	0.117	0.420	0.185	0.343	0.080	0.254	0.066
	3	0.864	0.286	0.674	0.227	0.734	0.304	0.790	0.183	0.740	0.155
	5	0.997	0.579	0.975	0.452	0.975	0.510	0.996	0.405	0.999	0.412
	10	1.000	0.896	1.000	0.792	1.000	0.822	1.000	0.763	1.000	0.799
10	0.1	0.982	0.306	1.000	0.716	1.000	0.771	1.000	0.980	1.000	0.997
	0.2	0.873	0.224	0.999	0.556	0.999	0.631	1.000	0.857	1.000	0.881
	0.5	0.327	0.091	0.663	0.206	0.720	0.297	0.897	0.279	0.873	0.267
	2	0.436	0.192	0.317	0.144	0.415	0.226	0.336	0.108	0.246	0.085
	3	0.868	0.440	0.679	0.308	0.735	0.392	0.788	0.287	0.737	0.253
	5	0.997	0.797	0.974	0.641	0.978	0.691	0.996	0.650	0.998	0.649
	10	1.000	0.981	1.000	0.932	1.000	0.942	1.000	0.940	1.000	0.957
20	0.1	0.980	0.480	1.000	0.908	1.000	0.918	1.000	1.000	1.000	1.000
	0.2	0.871	0.358	0.998	0.769	0.998	0.813	1.000	0.982	1.000	0.986
	0.5	0.324	0.146	0.662	0.311	0.715	0.398	0.896	0.480	0.881	0.451
	2	0.425	0.242	0.326	0.200	0.412	0.277	0.337	0.170	0.255	0.133
	3	0.872	0.575	0.684	0.403	0.738	0.478	0.793	0.431	0.753	0.370
	5	0.999	0.914	0.975	0.759	0.978	0.793	0.996	0.818	0.998	0.815
	10	1.000	0.998	1.000	0.988	1.000	0.989	1.000	0.994	1.000	0.996
40	0.1	0.981	0.691	1.000	0.985	1.000	0.989	1.000	1.000	1.000	1.000
	0.2	0.872	0.540	0.998	0.922	0.998	0.928	1.000	0.999	1.000	1.000
	0.5	0.337	1.888	0.688	0.443	0.739	0.522	0.904	0.647	0.891	0.622
	2	0.450	0.321	0.332	0.237	0.418	0.326	0.348	0.223	0.269	0.168
	3	0.878	0.706	0.682	0.494	0.730	0.568	0.789	0.562	0.747	0.493
	5	0.998	0.979	0.974	0.863	0.975	0.884	0.997	0.935	0.998	0.938
	10	1.000	1.000	1.000	0.999	1.000	0.998	1.000	1.000	1.000	1.000
70	0.1	0.983	0.815	1.000	0.997	1.000	0.998	1.000	1.000	1.000	1.000
	0.2	0.867	0.642	0.998	0.964	0.998	0.968	1.000	1.000	1.000	1.000
	0.5	0.338	0.236	0.676	0.522	0.736	0.606	0.905	0.750	0.884	0.729
	2	0.436	0.358	0.331	0.261	0.427	0.350	0.340	0.251	0.258	0.193
	3	0.876	0.776	0.687	0.553	0.743	0.627	0.793	0.646	0.748	0.580
	5	0.998	0.987	0.977	0.916	0.978	0.930	0.997	0.973	0.998	0.980
	10	1.000	1.000	1.000	1.000	1.000	1.000	1.000	1.000	1.000	1.000
100	0.1	0.980	0.864	1.000	0.999	1.000	1.000	1.000	1.000	1.000	1.000
	0.2	0.870	0.699	0.998	0.983	0.999	0.985	1.000	1.000	1.000	1.000
	0.5	0.325	0.244	0.672	0.553	0.735	0.633	0.894	0.791	0.881	0.775
	2	0.443	0.380	0.327	0.277	0.415	0.363	0.324	0.268	0.247	0.203
	3	0.879	0.812	0.692	0.594	0.752	0.662	0.796	0.696	0.756	0.635
	5	0.998	0.991	0.977	0.933	0.974	0.935	0.997	0.981	0.998	0.985
	10	1.000	1.000	1.000	1.000	1.000	1.000	1.000	1.000	1.000	1.000

8.7.7 Remarks and Recommendations

- The EWMA and CUSUM tests are generally more sensitive to detect *decreases* in p, both for p known and unknown, although there are a few exceptions. Also, the performance of the EWMA and CUSUM tests are about equal. The EWMA and CUSUM tests are the *worst* tests to detect *increases* in p, especially for case U and c small.
- The 9-of-9 test is clearly the best test to detect increases in p, for p either known or unknown, but is poor for decreases. Also, it should be noted that although the 9-of-9 Shewhart chart test has generally higher probabilities to detect an increase in p on the first 30 observations after the shift, the 3-of-3 and 4-of-5 tests will generally give their signals more quickly.
- For case K and any fixed δ, all of the tests have detection probabilities that are constant in c (within sampling error), as they should. For case U and δ fixed ($\neq 1$), the detection probabilities are low for c small ($c = 5$) and increase with c. This is, of course, exactly what we know must happen because with c small there is little discrimination information available. It is worth noting, however, that even for $c = 100$ the probability of detecting either a twofold decrease ($\delta = 0.5$) or increase ($\delta = 2$) on the first 30 observations after the shift is clearly less for the p unknown case than for p known, for all of the tests.
- Of the three tests on Shewhart-type Q-charts, the 3-of-3 test appears best overall for both increases and decreases. However, this is in part because, as we see from Table 8.10, the 3-of-3 test has appreciably higher false alarm rates. In order to have increased sensitivity, the 3-of-3 test could be used at startup of a process. The increase in false alarms is probably a reasonable trade-off in order to increase sensitivity to detect an increase in p early on when the sample size available is small.
- If the false alarms rate for the 3-of-3 test is too much, and it is desired to make one test for both increases and decreases in p, then the 4-of-5 test is probably the best choice of test. It performs reasonably well for all cases, although it is usually not the best test for most cases.

Example 8.8, continuation 2:   Consider applying the tests discussed above to the Geometric Shewhart Q-charts of Figs. 8.17 and 8.19 to detect the increase in p. Then the 9-of-9 test signals on the 17th observation on both charts. The 4-of-5 test signals on the 13th observation on Fig. 8.17, and on the 12th observation on Fig. 8.19. The 3-of-3 test signals on the 12th observation on Fig. 8.17 and on the 11th observation on Fig. 8.19. Note the ability of the 3-of-3 and 4-of-5 tests to signal more quickly than the 9-of-9 test.

The Geometric EWMA Q-charts of Figs. 8.18 and 8.20 both signal on the 13th point. ∎

8.7.8 Remarks on Applications of Geometric Q-Charts to Time-ordered Events

The geometric Q-charts can sometimes be used successfully to study the stability of the rate at which defined events occur in time, and thereby give timely signals of changes in this rate of occurrence of the events. There are many potential applications that include events such as the occurrence of nosocomial infections in hospitals, the breakdown of machines, the deaths of birds in poultry flocks, of diseases in swine herds, the occurrences of defectives from a production line, and many others.

To model the time between the occurrences of the event of interest as a geometric distribution, we should observe the following points. First, we must define a time unit, say Δt, in which events occur, such as a day, week, hour, minute, second, or whatever. The observations are the counts of the numbers of time units required between occurrences of the event. Thus, the time line is partitioned into intervals equal to the time unit as follows:

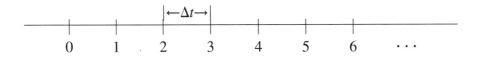

To model the number of trials between events as a geometric random variable, for the stable case, it is necessary that the occurrences in the intervals be essentially a sequence of Bernoulli trials. In order for this to be the case, we should have the conditions of display (8.7.6) satisfied.

> (1) The probability, p say, of an event on any time interval is the same for all intervals.
> (2) Events occur independently on different time intervals.
> (3) The probability of more than one event in a time interval is essentially zero.

$(8.7.6)$

These are just the conditions to assure the occurrences of events in the specified time intervals are essentially a sequence of Bernoulli trials.

In Example 8.9, we consider geometric charts for nosocomial infections in hospitals.

Example 8.9: In a very interesting paper, Finison, Spencer, and Finison (1993), FSF, discussed the problem of nosocomial infections and suggested using individual measurements charts to control these infections in hospitals. To describe the problem, we quote from these authors:

> A nosocomial infection, acquired as a by-product of hospitalization, is by definition not present or incubating at the time of admission. The infection may be due to diagnostic or therapeutic procedures, to exposure to the hospital environment or contact with health care workers. The spread of nosocomial infections is associated with lapses in aseptic technique, inadequate handwashing or environmental contamination of medical equipment and environmental surfaces.
>
> Nosocomial infections constitute a major medical problem, with approximately 20,000 people dying each year as a direct result of these infections. The national toll in additional hospital days is staggering and has been estimated at 8.7 million per year.
>
> The types of nosocomial infections defined by the Centers for Disease Control (CDC) include pneumonia, bacteremia, urinary tract infection, surgical wound infections, cutaneous wound infections, and gastrointestinal infections. In addition, most hospitals have endemic nosocomial problems with Methicillin-resistant *Staphylococcus aureas* (MRSA), *Clostridium difficile colitis*, and multiple-antibiotic resistant organisms.

FSF then give two data sets that are in units of days between infections (DBIs); one consists of 25 observations from a small hospital, and the other of 75 observations from a large hospital. These data are

TABLE 8.12 Clostridium Difficile Infections Data: Small Hospital

1	31	5	19	11	169	16	3	21	1
2	19	7	10	12	283	17	1	22	1
3	33	8	4	13	99	18	4	23	18
4	129	9	10	14	75	19	4	24	9
5	102	10	17	15	5	20	5	25	12

for *Clostridium difficile colitis*. The small hospital data are given in Table 8.12 and the large hospital data are given in Table 8.13.

8.7.9 Small Hospital Data, Discussion

Figure 8.21 shows the geometric Q-chart, case U, of the small hospital data. Although there is some suggestion of autocorrelation, the chart appears reasonably stable for the first 14 points. We apply the 11-45 combination test and the 4-of-5 test signals repeatedly after the 15th point. Clearly, there was an increase in the infection rate on about the 15th observation. The estimated probability of an occurrence of this infection on one day, from the first 14 observations, is $\hat{p} = 0.013$. This probability is small enough for the geometric chart to admit a good approximation by the normal distribution.

The case U chart is preferred here for two reasons. The data can be charted in real time, and, if this had been done, the increased infection rate on about the 15th day would have been immediately detected. This

TABLE 8.13 Clostridium Difficile Infections Data: Large Hospital

1	8	16	0	31	0	46	2	61	3
2	0	17	4	32	1	47	1	62	5
3	7	18	0	33	4	48	1	63	4
4	2	19	6	34	2	49	1	64	1
5	1	20	0	35	1	50	0	65	1
6	2	21	2	36	6	51	3	66	0
7	8	22	1	37	0	52	4	67	2
8	2	23	3	38	0	53	1	68	2
9	1	24	2	39	1	54	1	69	1
10	1	25	0	40	0	55	1	70	4
11	0	26	1	41	3	56	5	71	6
12	1	27	1	42	0	57	1	72	1
13	2	28	2	42	2	58	0	73	1
14	7	29	3	44	0	49	1	74	4
15	1	30	1	45	2	60	1	75	4

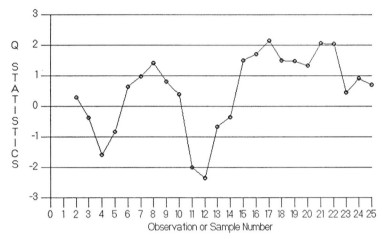

Shewhart Q-Chart for : GEOU
PBar = 2.25988700564972D-02

Figure 8.21   Clostridium Difficile Infections Chart: Small Hospital

is the ideal time to detect the increased infection rate, because when it is detected immediately it will generally be easier to both identify and correct the problem. Who isn't washing their hands or following proper sterile technique?

8.7.10   Large Hospital Data, Discussion

The *Clostridium difficile colitis* infection data of Table 8.13 are shown in a case U geometric (GEOU) *Q*-chart in Fig. 8.22. The interpretation of this chart is entirely different from that of the small hospital data. The points are clearly too crowded about the center line and discreteness of the data is apparent. The estimator of p is $\hat{p} = 0.327$, which is too large for the normal distribution to give a good approximation for the geometric. We observe also that there are 15 zero values among the 75 observations of Table 8.13. These zero values were recorded when two infections were observed on the same day. These data show that condition (3) of display (8.7.6) is clearly not satisfied. Basically, the sampling plan for the large hospital appears to be inadequate for modeling the times between infections by either a geometric distribution, or by the exponential distribution discussed in section 7.9.

   The difficulty with interpreting Fig. 8.22 appears to be due to using DBIs as the observed time unit. While DBIs are reasonable time units for the small hospital, they are too long for the large hospital where

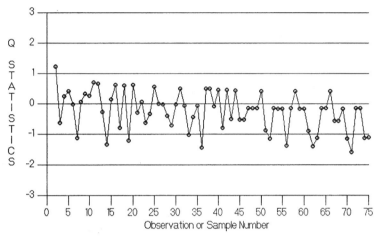

Shewhart Q-Chart for : GEOU
PBar = .327433628318584

Figure 8.22   Clostridium Difficile Infections Chart: Large Hospital

the rate of infections per day is, naturally, much higher. The question then, is what could be done to institute an effective charting program for a large hospital such as this one? We suggest two possible courses of action.

One course of action would be, if possible, to use a smaller time interval. Perhaps the data could be recorded by three eight-hour shifts per day. Of course, there may be difficulties in partitioning days into smaller time intervals. Hospitals and individuals tend to operate on daily cycles, and the rates may naturally vary among daily shifts. If rates vary during a day, then condition (1) of (8.7.6) would be violated.

A second, and preferred course of action, would be to partition the hospital into distinct functional areas such as obstetrics, surgery, etc., and chart each area separately. This approach has two major advantages. First, the daily occurrence rates should be small enough to give reliable charts. also, having charts for individual functional areas would simplify the task of identifying special causes.

One concern of managers may be the expense of maintaining charts in each functional area. However, the effort in maintaining such charts, using prepared software, is low. We need enter a value in a computer program only when infections are observed. When the infection rate is constant, that is, *endemic,* we will rarely have to plot a point. When the infection rate increases at the onset of an *epidemic,* the chart will give a timely warning. Also, it should be noted that if a hospital, or particular functional area, has a stable but high endemic rate and engages in a program to improve the rate, then the geometric chart has the ability to signal a significant decrease in the infection rate. This can be important for the reinforcement of the management and staff involved.   ∎

8.8   WEIGHTED SYSTEMS OF NONCONFORMITIES (WEIGHTED POISSON CHARTS)

In the presentation of classical c-charts and u-charts in Chapter 4, and of Poisson Q-charts in section 8.7, we counted defects of all types and made no distinctions among different types of defects. However, some nonconformities are more important than others, and it may be possible to make more effective control procedures by taking this into account in planning our control schemes. One way to do this is to use a weighting system that assigns weights to nonconformities according to relative importance. Weighted systems of nonconformities are also called *demerit* systems by some writers. In this section, we present a weighting system based on the Q-statistics for the Poisson distribution.

8.8.1   The Q-Chart Weighted System of Nonconformities

Suppose there are a total of k recognized types of defects or nonconformities. Further, let c_{ij} denote the number of nonconformities of type j counted on the ith sampling inspection unit of size n_i standard size inspection units, *that is the same for all k types of nonconformities.* Further, suppose that the c_{ij}'s can be modeled as independent Poisson random variables with rates $n_i\lambda_j$. The Q-statistics for the case when the λ_j's are known are defined by (8.8.1).

$$
\begin{aligned}
u_{ij} &= F(c_{ij};\, n_i\lambda_j) \\
Q_{ij} &= \Phi^{-1}(u_{ij}) \\
i &= 1, 2, \cdots; \qquad j = 1, \cdots, k
\end{aligned}
\tag{8.8.1}
$$

Let $w_1, w_2, \cdots, w_k$ be a set of k positive weights that reflect the relative importance of the k types of nonconformities. We also assume that these weights satisfy the relation

$$w_1^2 + w_2^2 + \cdots + w_k^2 = 1 \tag{8.8.2}$$

if the positive weights do not satisfy (8.8.2), then replace w_j by $w_j/\sqrt{\Sigma w_j^2}$. Weights that satisfy (8.8.2) are called *normed* weights. We define

$$Q_i = w_1 Q_{i1} + w_2 Q_{i2} + \cdots + w_k Q_{ik} \tag{8.8.3}$$

Since the Q_{ij}'s are distributed approximately as standard normal statistics, and Q_i is a linear function of these Q_{ij}'s, then Q_i is also approximately a standard normal statistic. The statistic Q_i, being a linear function of the Q_{ij}'s with positive weights, will be better approximated by a normal distribution than the individual normalized Poisson variables.

The choice of the weights $w_1, w_2, \ldots, w_k$ is subjective, but it should be possible in many applications to assign relative order-of-magnitude values in a reasonable scheme. A possible weighting scheme for four types of nonconformities is as follows.

Type 1 Nonconformities: These are the most serious nonconformities possible. A unit with a type 1 defect may not function at all, it may present a serious safety hazard or threaten a failure in service with calamitous consequences. Assign weight $w_1 = 100$.

Type 2 Nonconformities: This is a serious defect but is not as serious as a type 1 defect. A defect in this category might cause a failure in service of a less critical nature, or a reduced service life of the unit. Assign weight $w_2 = 50$.

Type 3 Nonconformities: This is a defect of moderate importance. A number of these nonconformities on a unit of product will cause the product to be viewed as shoddy and of poor quality. Assign weight $w_3 = 20$.

Type 4 Nonconformities: These are very minor nonconformities that usually do not affect the functioning of the product. They are often cosmetic but could affect the marketing of the product. Assign a weight of $w_4 = 1$.

The normed values of the weights $(w_1, w_2, w_3, w_4) = (100, 50, 20, 1)$ are $(0.880, 0.440, 0.176, 0.0088)$ where, for example, the first value was obtained as

$$\frac{w_j}{\sqrt{\Sigma w_j^2}} = \frac{100}{\sqrt{12901}} = \frac{100}{113.58} = 0.880$$

To estimate λ_j from m calibration samples, we use

$$\hat{\lambda}_j = \bar{c}_j = \frac{\displaystyle\sum_{i=1}^{m} c_{ij}}{\displaystyle\sum_{i=1}^{m} n_i} \qquad (8.8.4)$$

These estimates are then substituted for the λ_j's in (8.8.1).

If one (or more) of the Poisson parameters λ_j are not known, perhaps at the start-up of the process, or because we need to treat cases involving short runs, then we can use a transformation like that of (8.5.2) as follows.

$$\boxed{\begin{array}{l} u_{ij} = B(c_{ij}; \, t_{ij}, \, n_i/N_i), \qquad Q_{ij} = \Phi^{-1}(u_{ij}); \\[2mm] i = 2, 3, \cdots; \qquad j = \qquad\qquad 1, \cdots, k \end{array}} \qquad (8.8.5)$$

where $t_{ij} = c_{1j} + c_{2j} + \cdots + c_{ij}$ and $N_i = n_1 + \cdots + n_i$.

Then, Q_i is computed from these Q_{ij}'s using equation (8.8.3). Computing these Q-statistics and plotting the charts will generally require a computer algorithm for practical applications.

Example 8.10: Table 8.14 shows the data from a calibration sample consisting of the inspection data from all of the units of production made on each work day for a three-week period. There are four types of nonconformities and the normed values of the weights given above of $w_1 = 100$, $w_2 = 50$, w_3, 20, and $w_4 = 1$ are used. The estimates of the average rates are

$$\hat{\lambda}_1 = \frac{69}{5468} = 0.0126, \qquad \hat{\lambda}_2 = \frac{145}{5468} = 0.0265$$

$$\hat{\lambda}_3 = \frac{424}{5468} = 0.0775, \qquad \hat{\lambda}_4 = \frac{538}{5468} = 0.0984$$

We have plotted eight Q-charts in Figs. 8.23–8.30 to illustrate ways

TABLE 8.14 Defects Data and Computations for Weighted Q-Charts

Sample i	Sample Size, n_i	c_{i1}	c_{i2}	c_{i3}	c_{i4}
1	191	1	5	10	17
2	142	0	1	6	14
3	203	2	5	15	34
4	409	2	11	22	25
5	333	2	8	21	41
6	187	2	8	24	21
7	168	3	6	16	16
8	234	1	3	19	20
9	346	3	5	32	29
10	411	6	11	34	25
11	512	11	16	42	61
12	617	9	18	51	72
13	567	10	17	40	52
14	592	9	16	45	49
15	556	8	15	47	62
Totals:	5468	69	145	424	538

that the Q-statistics of (8.8.1) and (8.8.5) can be used to give immediate information useful for recognizing assignable causes and stabilizing processes. These are, of course, more charts than would be printed out in practice, but our purpose is to illustrate the flexibility and power of these charting methods. We discuss each of these charts briefly.

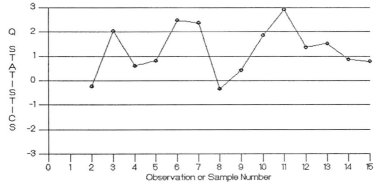

Figure 8.23 Weighted Poisson Defects Shewhart Q-Chart, λ's Unknown

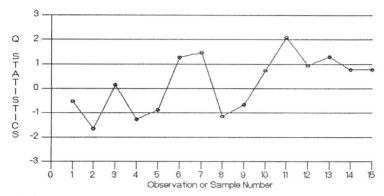

Figure 8.24   Weighted Poisson Defects Shewhart Q-Chart, λ's Known, that is, Estimated from the Data

Figure 8.23 is the Shewhart chart using equations (8.8.5) for the Q_{ij}'s that do not require prior estimates of the λ_j's. Note also that this chart, like all "unknown parameters" Q-charts, can be made point-by-point as each sample is obtained, and the points are not affected by any parameter shifts that occur after the sample is observed. Now, Fig. 8.23 has 12 of 14 points above 0, and increases are signaled by the 3-of-3 test on the 12th point and by the 4-of-5 test on the 13th point. This chart clearly signals a problem of an overall increase in the rate of defects.

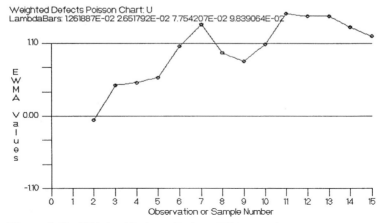

Figure 8.25   Weighted Poisson Defects EWMA Q-Chart, λ's Unknown

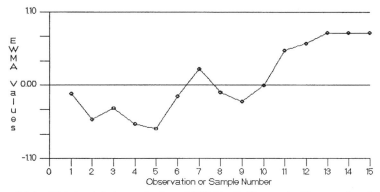

Figure 8.26 Weighted Poisson Defects EWMA Q-Chart, λ's Known, that is, Estimated from the Data

The patterns suggest the possibility that the overall rate was increasing monotonically, that is, growing with time.

Figure 8.24 is the Shewhart Q-chart using the formulas of (8.8.1) and using the estimates of the λ_j's for the "known" values in these formulas. Note the remarkable difference in this chart and Fig. 8.23! This chart issues no signals, and from it alone we would conclude the process is stable! The reason this chart gives different results from the chart that uses only prior data is that all of the data, including that observed after possible parameter shifts, are used to estimate the process parameters and control limits. This is the effect of "centering"

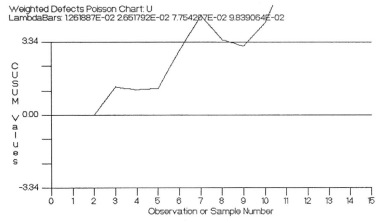

Figure 8.27 Weighted Poisson Defects CUSUM Q-Chart, λ's Unknown

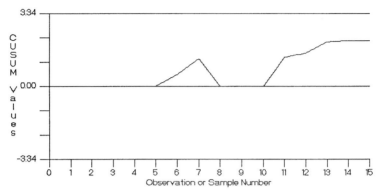

Figure 8.28   Weighted Poisson Defects CUSUM Q-Chart, λ's Known, that is, Estimated from the Data

plotted points about the center line, that we have noted for other charts, caused by using data taken while parameters were changing to make a retrospective chart.

Figures 8.25 and 8.26 are the weighted EWMA charts using the "unknown" λ's formulas for 8.25 and the estimated λ's in the "known" λ's formulas for 8.26. These two charts esssentially repeat the performances of the Shewhart charts in that Fig. 8.25 gives signals of an in-

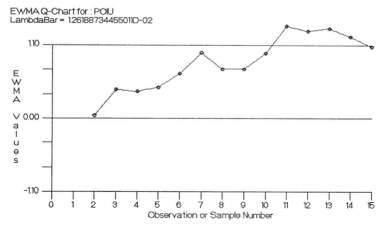

Figure 8.29   Poisson EWMA Q-Chart for First Defect, λ Unknown

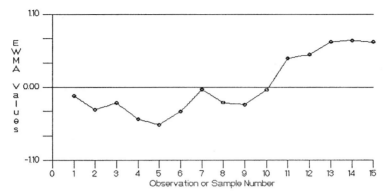

Figure 8.30   Poisson EWMA Q-Chart for First Defect, λ Unknown, that is, Estimated from the Data

creasing overall defects rate and 8.26 gives no signal of an increasing defects rate.

Figures 8.27 and 8.28 are the weighted CUSUM charts using the "unknown" λ's formulas for 8.27 and the estimates of the λ's in the "known" λ's formulas. These CUSUM charts tell the same story just described for the Shewhart and EWMA charts. The "unknown" λ's chart signals an increase in defects rates and the "known" λ's formulas using estimated λ's does not signal.

Finally, we have plotted Poisson Q-charts for each of the defect classes on Shewhart, EWMA, and CUSUM charts. From this it was apparent that most of the increase in the weighted defects statistic was due to the first defect class (with weight 100). Figures 8.29 and 8.30 give the Poisson EWMA chart for this defect. The chart for this defect is stable when estimated values of the λ's are used in Fig. 8.30, but the chart signals on the 11th sample for the unknown parameters case of Fig. 8.29.   ∎

8.9 SUMMARY

In this chapter we have extended the approach introduced in Chapter 7 for charting variables data to charting attributes data. Methods are given for transforming observations from binomial, Poisson, and geometric distributions to sequences of Q-statistics that are approximately independent standard normal statistics when the process distribution is stable. Transformations are given for the two cases when the distribution parameter is known and when it is unknown. The cases for parameters unknown are especially important for applications because they permit valid charting without requiring prior data sets. The ability to chart attributes without prior data should be particularly attractive for applications in many industries.

PROBLEMS

8.1 All units produced by a production process for four weeks (20 work days) were inspected to obtain the following table.

Day, i:	1	2	3	4
Production, n_i:	1451	1344	1272	2012
No. Defectives, x_i:	9	13	9	17
i:	5	6	7	8
n_i:	1433	1247	1332	1376
x_i:	11	14	9	5
i:	9	10	11	12
n_i:	1542	1555	1554	1439
x_i:	16	14	16	7
i:	13	14	15	16
n_i:	1287	1298	1449	2567
x_i:	17	13	15	28
i:	17	18	19	20
n_i:	1511	1523	1445	1487
x_i:	20	24	14	18

(a) Make and interpret a binomial Q-chart for these data by using the value $\bar{p}$ to estimate p in the "known p" formulas.

(b) Make and interpret a binomial Q-chart for these data using the "unknown p" formulas.

(c) Compare the charts obtained in parts (a) and (b). Discuss general advantages, disadvantages, etc., of each type of chart.

(d) For the charts found in parts (a) and (b), estimate the probabilities that a point will fall below the *LCL* and that a point will fall above the *UCL* on day 6 for a sample the size taken on day 6 (i.e., 1247) by using the appropriate estimating distribution functions to evaluate the probabilities, assuming the process is stable. Fill in the values obtained in a table like the following.

	Known p	Unknown p
Below LCL		
Above UCL		

(e) Fill in the values in the following table for the cases when $p = \bar{p}$ is used in the "p known formuls" and when p is assumed unknown.

			Known p			Unknown p		
i	n_i	x_i	u_i	Q_i	t_i	N_i	u_i	Q_i
1	1451	9			9	1451	—	—
2	1344	13			22	2795	.895	1.25
3	1272	9						
4	2012	17						

8.2 Electronic boards of a certain type have an average nonconformities rate of one for three boards.

(a) Determine the smallest number of boards n that can be inspected in each sample if it is required to set up a Poisson Shewhart Q-chart that is approximately equivalent to a ± 3-sigma classical normal chart, that is, an approximately (0.00135, 0.00135) probability Q-chart. When the process is stable, evaluate the probability that one point will fall below -3, and that one point will fall above 3. Evaluate the exact overall *ARL* for the 1-of-1 test on this chart for a stable process.

(b) Next, consider a setting up a Poisson Q-chart as follows. A sample of six boards is inspected, the observed count of nonconformities c is transformed into a Q-statistic and plotted on a Q-chart with $LCL = -3$ and $UCL = 3$. Make a table similar to that in Table 8.5 for this chart. When the process is stable, evaluate the probability that one point will fall below -3, and that one point will fall above 3. Evaluate the exact overall ARL for the 1-of-1 test on this chart for a stable process.

(c) Evaluate the probability that four out of five consecutive points will plot above 1 on the chart described in part (b) above: (i) when the process is stable, and (ii) when λ shifts from 1/3 to 2/3. Also, evaluate the probability that four out of five consecutive points will plot below -1 on the chart described in part (b) above: (i) when the process is stable, and (ii) when λ shifts from 1/3 to 1/6.

(d) The following data were obtained from the operation of the sampling scheme described in part (b). Use this data to estimate λ and use this estimate in the "known" λ formula to make a retrospective Shewhart Q-chart from this data.

1 1 2 2 1 0 2 3 3 2 3 2 3 3 1 3 4 6 3 5 7 4 3 3 4

(e) Make a Shewhart Q-chart from the data given in part (d), using the formulas for the parameter λ unknown case. Compare this chart with the chart obtained in part (d).

8.3 Make Shewhart Q-charts to study the stability of the process producing the data of problem 5.3. Interpret the results.

8.4 Make Shewhart Q-charts to study the stability of the process producing the data of problem 5.7. Interpret the results.

8.5 The electronic meter main boards produced during an 8-hour shift were inspected for numbers of nonconformities for 20 consecutive work days. The data are given in the following table.

i	n_i	c_i	i	n_i	c_i
1	344	39	11	281	34
2	331	51	12	307	28
3	421	42	13	255	23
4	357	46	14	233	26
5	271	31	15	405	30
6	452	58	16	266	30
7	376	47	17	288	28
8	278	32	18	324	39
9	198	38	19	333	31
10	222	29	20	399	33

(a) Make a Poisson Q-chart for these data using the "unknown λ" formulas.

(b) Make a Poisson Q-chart for these data by using $\bar{\lambda} = \Sigma c_i / \Sigma n_i$ in the "known λ" formulas.

(c) Interpret the charts in parts (a) and (b). From each chart try to decide if λ has shifted during these 20 days. Discuss.

8.6 The following table gives the run lengths between consecutive nonconforming units made by a certain process. The data are in left-to-right row order. Analyze the data using Q-charts to determine the state of control of the process.

184	3964	3551	322	1911	1268	150	478	623	1952
800	521	55	5	35	71		160	50	293	106

8.7 Make Shewhart, EWMA, and CUSUM Q-charts to study the stability of the process producing the data of problem 5.12. Interpret the results.

8.8 The following table gives the sizes of the sampling inspection units and the numbers of defects observed for each of five types of nonconformities. The weights for the five types are $(w_1, w_2, w_3, w_4, w_5) = (5, 40, 60, 10, 1)$. Use these data to set up weighted nonconformities charts of each of the two types given by using the transformations (8.8.1) and (8.8.5) to study the stability of the system. To use the transformations of (8.8.1) it will be necessary to estimate the λ_j's from the data set. Discuss your results.

Sample i	Sample Size, n_i	c_{i1}	c_{i2}	c_{i3}	c_{i4}	c_{i5}
1	1	11	1	2	6	20
2	1	8	4	0	8	12
3	1	4	2	0	8	13
4	2	20	0	3	19	35
5	2	22	1	2	14	34
6	2	17	2	3	8	43
7	2	27	2	2	9	47
8	1.5	14	5	4	12	62
9	1.5	15	3	5	11	53
10	1.5	15	4	3	14	49

8.9 Show that $p \geq 0.00135$ implies $P(Q_t > 3) = 0$, for Q_t given in (8.7.2).

8.10 Using Table 8.8 for $n\lambda = 8$, evaluate the probability of a false alarm on any one point on a Poisson chart, after at least five points have been plotted, by the 4-of-5 test by filling in the following table. Let p be the probability of one point above one on the chart indicated.

Statistic	p	$B(3; 5, p)$	$1 - B(3; 5, p)$
Std. Normal	0.15866		
z			
Q			
y			

8.11 A record of the numbers of days between *clostridium difficile colitis* infections found in a hospital are given in the following table. An infection control special initiative based on using geometric control charts was begun at about the time the twentieth case was found. Use the charts you consider appropriate to study this data. What conclusions are possible?

1	21	11	9	21	49	31	235
2	30	12	25	22	14	32	381
3	24	13	18	23	128	33	131
4	11	14	54	24	46	34	15
5	4	15	97	25	24	35	112
6	19	16	56	26	27	36	69
7	33	17	3	27	272	37	611
8	45	18	15	28	296	38	5
9	27	19	11	29	262	39	48
10	18	20	3	30	150	40	286

CHAPTER 9

Process Capability and Performance Analysis, Quadratic Loss Functions

Much of the work in quality improvement and, in particular, in statistical process control is based on an assumption of a normal distribution, or on the assumption of some other specific parametric model. An important part of process capability analysis involves methods for verifying the validity of parametric models, especially methods for checking the validity of normal or Gaussian distribution assumptions. There are many approaches to parametric modeling and analysis. These include graphical diagnostic methods, goodness-of-fit tests, model selection methods, and transformations. In this chapter we consider first some background material and selected topics from these areas. Capability indices for normal process distributions and approaches to treat nonnormal distributions are then considered.

9.1 SOME KEY BACKGROUND RESULTS

The empirical distribution function and the probability integral transformation both play important roles in the areas of goodness-of-fit testing and process capability analysis. Before proceeding, we introduce these concepts.

9.1.1 The Empirical Distribution Function

Given a sample $x_1, x_2, \cdots, x_n$ on a distribution with distribution function F, we wish to estimate the function F. By this it is meant that at every real number x it is required to find an estimating distribution function $\hat{F}(x)$, say, as an estimate of $F(x)$. Let $x_{(1)} \leq x_{(2)} \leq \cdots \leq x_{(n)}$ denote the order statistics. The *empirical distribution function* (EDF) is denoted by F_n and is defined as follows.

$$\text{Put } r(x) = \text{Max } \{i \mid x_{(i)} \leq x\}$$

$$= \text{(the number of observations} \leq x\text{)}$$

$$F_n(x) \equiv \frac{r(x)}{n} \qquad (9.1.1)$$

If $F(x)$ is known only to be either a discrete distribution function or an absolutely continuous distribution function, but nothing more is known about it, then the empirical distribution function is an excellent estimator of $F(x)$. It is a minimum variance unbiased estimator of $F(x)$ at every point x. A picture of the EDF for a particular sample is shown in Fig. 9.1. Note that the EDF is a step function with n steps of height $1/n$ each. It can be shown that as n becomes large the EDF converges to the process distribution function. These quoted properties of the EDF are important in the applications considered below.

9.1.2 The Probability Integral Transformation

The basic result can be summarized in a theorem as follows.

Theorem (PIT): Let X be a random variable with an absolutely continuous distribution function $F(x)$. Then $U = F(X)$ is a $U(0, 1)$ random variable. Conversely, if U is a $U(0, 1)$ random variable and $X = F^-(U)$, then X has distribution function $F(x)$.

This important result was discovered by Fisher (1931). Note that it shows how to transform any continuous distribution to a $U(0, 1)$ distribution, and how to transform a $U(0, 1)$ distribution to any continuous distribution. Thus, by combining the two results we can transform any

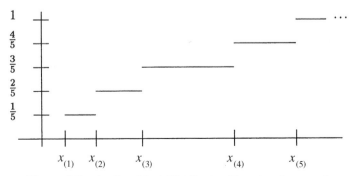

Figure 9.1 An Empirical Distribution Function for $n = 5$

continuous distribution to any other continous distribution. This is a helpful technique in many statistics problems, and there are many useful applications for it in statistical process control. This is a key result that we have made frequent use of in the development of results based on Q-statistics in the preceding chapters, and will be basic in developing some of the parametric modeling techniques in this chapter.

9.2   BASIC GRAPHICAL METHODS

The dot plots, histograms, and stem-and-leaf plots of a data set that were presented in Chapter 3 are all pictures of the data set. If the data set is itself a random sample from a continuous parent distribution, then these pictures are graphical estimates of the parent density function. Dot plots are useful for small data sets and histograms are used for large data sets, while stem-and-leaf plots are perhaps useful for intermediate-sized data sets.

As was discussed in section 3.2, a basic technique in using a histogram in parametric modeling is to draw the histogram and simply study it to see if its shape is similar to that of a particular parametric density function. In particular, if it is a symmetric bell-shaped graph we may decide that it is reasonable to therefore *assume* that the parent distribution is normal. A somewhat more objective procedure for checking normality is to draw the histogram and a fitted $N(\hat{\mu}, \hat{\sigma}^2)$ density function on the same graph in order to compare the shapes, where $\hat{\mu}$ and $\hat{\sigma}$ are estimates of μ and σ. This method was illustrated in Fig. 3.2 where a normal density was overlaid on a histogram.

It should be mentioned here that the background theory for using a histogram to choose a parametric density involves important theoretical properties of the histogram as a nonparametric graphical estimator of

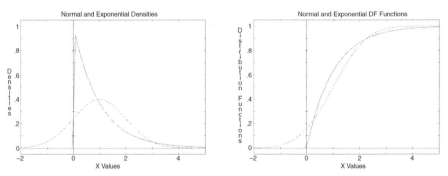

Figure 9.2   Normal and Exponential Densities and Distribution Functions

the parent density function. It can be shown that with increasing sample size the histogram will take the shape of the process density function.

It should also be noted that all of the Shewhart charts that are based directly on observations from an assumed distribution—individual observations from a normal, binomial, exponential, Poisson geometric, and so on—are themselves a form of graphical check on the form of the parent distribution, in addition to serving to signal special causes. If charts based on an assumed distribution are stable for runs of points, this is some verification of both the assumed form of the distribution as well as the absence of special causes from the process.

9.3   UNIFORM RESIDUALS PLOTS

In this section we consider a simple graphical technique based on the probability integral transformation that can be used to help decide if an observed set of values $x_1, \cdots, x_n$ is a random sample from a particular parametric class of distribution functions.

9.3.1   The General Case

We first suppose that it is required to decide if the sample is from a distribution with distribution function $G(x; \theta)$, say, for $\theta = (\theta_1, \cdots, \theta_p)'$ a vector of p parameters. Then, assuming that the vector θ is known, transform the sample members as follows.

$$u_j = G(x_j; \theta), j = 1, \cdots, n \qquad (9.3.1)$$

By the PIT theorem, when $G(x; \theta)$ is the correct distribution function, then $\mathbf{u} = (u_1, \cdots, u_n)'$ is a vector of independently and identically distributed uniform random variables. That is, $\mathbf{u}$ is a random sample from a $U(0, 1)$ distribution.

For $\mathbf{u}$ a vector of independently and identically distributed $U(0, 1)$ random variables, let $u_{(j)}$ denote the jth order statistic, that is, $u_{(j)}$ is the jth smallest member of the sample. Then it can be shown that $u_{(j)}$ is a beta random variable, $\beta(j, n - j + 1)$, and has mean and variance

$$E(u_{(j)}) = \frac{j}{n + 1}, \text{Var}(u_{(j)}) = \frac{j(n - j + 1)}{(n + 1)^2(n + 2)} \qquad (9.3.2)$$

Thus, if the points $(j/(n + 1), u_{(j)})$ are plotted on Cartesian axes the points will in all cases fall in the unit square, and when $G(x; \underset{\sim}{\theta})$ is the correct distribution function, the points will tend to follow the line connecting the points $(0, 0)$ and $(1, 1)$. In practice, we usually express the plot points in percentage and actually plot the points $(100j/(n + 1), 100u_{(j)})$.

In practice, the values of the parameters in the vector $\underset{\sim}{\theta}$ are not usually known, and then the transformations (9.3.1) cannot be carried through. However, if the sample size n is large, the sample in hand can be used to estimate the parameters by a vector of estimates $\underset{\sim}{\hat{\theta}}$, say. Then when $\underset{\sim}{\hat{\theta}}$ is substituted for $\underset{\sim}{\theta}$ in the transformations (9.3.1), the u_j's obtained are still approximately independently and identically distributed $U(0, 1)$ random variables. It is important to note that *the effect of using estimated parameters in the transformation (9.3.1) is that the plotted points will tend to follow the line connecting (0, 0) and (1, 1) more closely than when the true values of the parameters are used* (Quesenberry and Quesenberry 1982).

9.3.2   The Normal Distribution, Large Samples

The plotting technique described above is used for checking normality by putting

$$u_j = \Phi\left(\frac{x_j - \mu}{\sigma}\right); j = 1, \cdots , n \qquad (9.3.3)$$

In this case when n is large ($n \geq 30$), the sample mean $\bar{x}$ and standard deviation s are substituted for μ and σ. The resulting values are then ordered and used to plot the points $(100j/(n + 1), 100u_{(j)})$. When the observations are from the $N(\mu, \sigma^2)$ distribution used for the transformation in (9.3.3), the plotted points will tend to follow the line connecting the points $(0, 0)$ and $(100, 100)$. When the sample values are from some other distribution, the points will still fall in the square with corners at $(0, 0)$ and $(100, 100)$, but will show a pattern of deviation from the $(0, 0)$–$(100, 100)$ line that will be determined by the relationship of the density function of the true distribution to the density function of the normal distribution with the same mean and variance.

9.3.3   The Normal Distribution, any Size Sample

When n is small and the mean μ and variance σ^2 must be estimated from the sample, the large sample technique above will not be adequate. Then for a sample $x_1, x_2, \cdots , x_n$ we consider again the sequential statistics $\bar{x}_r$ and s_r and the updating formulas defined in (3.4.5). Then we consider the values $u_1, u_2, \cdots, u_{n-2}$ defined as follows:

$$u_{r-2} = H_{r-2}\left\{\sqrt{\frac{r-1}{r}}\left(\frac{x_r - \bar{x}_{r-1}}{s_{r-1}}\right)\right\} \quad r = 3, \cdots, n \quad (9.3.4)$$

where $H_\nu(\cdot)$ is the Student-t distribution function with ν degrees of freedom. These transformations were used in (7.4.4) to transform individual observations from a normal distribution with unkown parameters to Q-statistics. These transformations are *conditional probability integral transformations* (CPITs) for the univariate normal distribution. We will sometimes call the values $u_1, u_2, \cdots, u_{n-2}$ the *uniform residuals* from the $N(\mu, \sigma^2)$ distribution. This general class of transformations was introduced by O'Reilly and Quesenberry (1973). When the sample $x_1, \cdots, x_n$ is from a normal parent distribution, then the u's will be a sample from a $U(0, 1)$ distribution. Therefore, the ordered values from this "sample" can be plotted in a uniformity plot just as the u's from (9.3.3) were and will tend to follow the line connecting the origin and the point (100, 100), as did the u's from (9.3.3). Moreover, if the parent is not normal, then these u's will tend to follow a nonlinear pattern that depends on the form of its correct distribution, and is the same pattern that would be obtained if the transformation in (9.3.3) were used *with the correct values of μ and σ^2*. From this results we have a simple graphical technique for checking the assumption of normality for a sample of data.

A word of caution is in order concerning the transformation theory cited above. The reader should be aware that these transformation results depend on the assumption that the values $x_1, x_2, \cdots, x_n$ constitute a random sample and on the order in which the values appear. Different orderings will give different values $u_1, u_2, \cdots, u_n$. Thus, care must be exercised that the values are not ordered in any way that would disturb this distribution theory. In particular, the values must not be ordered by magnitudes before the transformations of (9.3.4) are made. Perhaps the best approach when the data are ordered in time (as they often will be) is to analyze in the order they were observed. Note carefully that the distributional results do not depend on the sample size n, except that n must exceed two. Note also that from each sample of size n we obtain only $n-2$ transformed values u_j.

9.3.4 Interpreting Uniform Residuals Plots

Figure 9.3 shows CPIT uniform residuals plots made for large samples ($n = 1000$) from four different parent distributions. The samples are

(a)   Normal Data

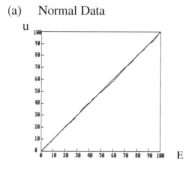

E

(b)   Double Exponential Data

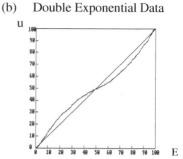

E

(c)   Uniform Data

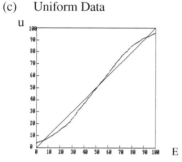

E

(d)   Exponential Data

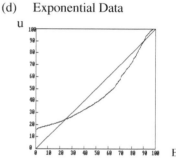

E

Figure 9.3   CPIT Uniform Residuals Plots, $n = 1000$

from normal, double exponential, uniform, and exponential distributions. An important point is that the transformation of (9.3.4) is location and scale invariant and this means that the patterns obtained in charts like those of Fig. 9.3 will be the same for any location and scale parameter values of the parent distribution. These charts essentially give patterns for the alternative distributions that have the *same mean and variance as the normal distribution with which they are compared.* To illustrate these ideas and the interpretation of the uniformity plots, we consider the plots of Fig. 9.3. First, note that the pattern of points for the data from a normal distribution in Fig. 9.3(a) follow the diagonal line, just as expected. Next, consider the uniform residuals plot of the exponential data in Fig. 9.3(d), and consider the graphs of the normal and exponential density and distribution functions given in Fig. 9.2. Note that the graph of the uniformity plot of exponential data in Fig. 9.3(d) takes a value of $u = 0.16$ when $E = 0$. This is the area below zero under the normal density curve, and the value of the normal distribution function at zero, of Fig. 9.2. By studying Fig. 9.2 we can readily interpret the graph for exponential data in Fig. 9.3(d). When the exponential density function is higher than the normal density function, as it is immediately above zero, then the data are more densely distributed and the resulting uniformity plot has a slope less than the nominal value of 1. When the densities are approximately equal, as they are near $x = 1$, then the uniformity plot has slope approximately 1. Keeping these principles in mind, the shapes of all of the uniformity plots in Fig. 9.3 can be readily interpreted.

It should be observed here that plots of the general pattern of Fig. 9.3(d) are of special importance in manufacturing operations. This is because, as will be discussed further below, there are many nonnormal quality variables that are nonnegative and follow unimodal right-skewed distributions. Data from these variables will tend to show uniform residuals plots similar to Fig. 9.3(d).

The plots in Fig. 9.3 were made using samples of size $n = 1000$ and the question arises as to how these plots will appear with smaller samples. With smaller samples the same patterns will show but will tend to be less distinct.

Example 9.1: The following table contains 60 values of an out-of-round measurement of parts from a production run. We wish to study these data in order to design an efficient process control scheme. The Q-Charts algorithm gives the uniform residuals plot shown in Fig. 9.4. Note that the data are all positive and the pattern is clearly that of a

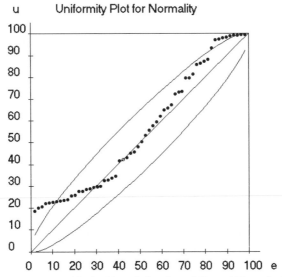

Figure 9.4 Uniform Residuals Plot of the Out-of-Round Data for Example 9.1

right skewed distribution. This is the form of distribution that Shewhart argued would obtain for most nonnormal industrial measurements. We will present a method for treating this important type of data in section 9.6.   ■

0.11	0.94	0.02	1.45	0.56	0.30
0.14	0.26	0.30	2.49	2.15	0.10
0.55	1.97	1.16	0.13	1.24	2.36
1.40	3.47	4.32	0.30	0.88	1.83
0.10	0.67	0.52	2.52	1.14	1.55
0.88	0.38	0.17	0.03	3.75	0.37
3.05	0.94	0.05	2.59	4.20	1.86
4.76	0.25	0.30	2.49	1.11	0.58
0.03	0.06	2.21	1.64	1.56	2.07
0.41	0.80	0.98	0.07	3.82	4.62

9.3.5 Uniform Residuals Plots with Many Small Subgroups

Much process control data is taken in the form of many small samples of size four or five. More generally, suppose that we have m samples of size n_i for $i = 1, 2, \cdots, m$. We will further assume that the observations in each of the samples were from units of production that were time-ordered. Then we perform the transformation of (9.3.4) on the ith sample to obtain $n_i - 2$ uniform residuals. For example, a sample of size four will have two uniform residuals and a sample of size five will have three uniform residuals. A sample must have at least three values in order to give any uniform residuals.

We can then pool all of these uniform residuals into a set of $N = n_1 + n_2 + \cdots + n_m - 2m$ values, and this set of N values can be plotted on a uniformity plot. This assumes that $n_i \geq 3$ for all $i = 1, 2, \cdots, m$. If $u_{(j)}$ denotes the jth smallest value in the pooled set of N values, then the point to be plotted is $(100j/(N + 1), 100u_{(j)})$. The following point is especially important. The interpretation of patterns on these pooled uniformity plots is the same as for patterns on plots for one (large) sample. A major advantage in this approach is that it does *not* assume that the process mean or variance are constant among samples. We are here checking only for normality, and varying means and variances do not vitiate the distribution theory. This technique is described in Quesenberry et al. (1976), and the reader should note that it provides a solution for an important goodness-of-fit testing problem that is common in SPC.

Example 9.2: The following table gives the values obtained in time order from a production process. The samples varied between 4 and 5 in size. A uniform residuals plot of this data is shown in Fig. 9.5. This plot shows that the process distribution that produced this data can reasonably be taken to be a normal distribution. This is, of course, the best of all distributional worlds. We will see below that the Neyman smooth test on these uniform residuals agrees with this conclusion of a normal process distribution.

Sample #	Measurements					Sample #	Measurements				
1	6.92	7.07	6.99	7.05	6.99	11	7.06	6.85	7.04	7.02	7.20
2	7.07	6.96	7.03	6.98	6.87	12	7.20	6.96	7.05	7.00	7.05
3	7.19	6.94	6.90	7.11	7.16	13	6.89	7.08	7.34	7.30	6.86
4	7.03	7.01	7.10	6.91	7.09	14	6.94	6.98	6.93	7.09	7.26
5	7.03	7.15	7.13	7.17	7.02	15	7.01	7.11	7.18	6.95	7.20
6	6.92	7.18	6.93	6.96		16	7.05	7.20	7.10	7.10	
7	6.76	7.00	6.92	6.86		17	6.80	7.05	6.98	7.28	
8	6.93	7.04	6.89	6.98		18	7.10	7.02	7.17	6.89	
9	6.93	7.07	7.10	6.97		19	7.03	7.19	7.22	7.20	7.15
10	6.97	7.03	7.09	6.89		20	6.96	7.15	7.29	7.07	7.06

■

9.4 CLASSICAL PROBABILITY PLOTS

The distribution of a random variable X is said to be a member of a *location-scale* parametric class of distributions if its distribution is indexed by parameters μ_X and σ_X, and if the distribution of $Z = aX + b$ ($a > 0$) is also a member of the class (with parameters $\mu_Z = a\mu_X + b$ and $\sigma_Z = a\sigma_X$). The parameter μ is a location parameter and σ is a scale parameter. The most important location-scale parametric class is the $N(\mu, \sigma^2)$ family. However, it should be noted that μ need not always be a mean and σ is not necessarily a standard deviation.

We consider now the technique that is generally called *probability plotting,* which is another graphical method for determining if a sample is from a particular parametric class of distributions. The uniformity

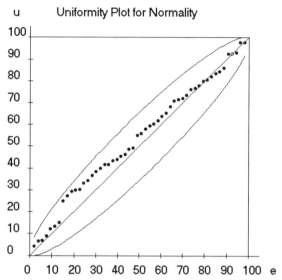

Figure 9.5   Uniform Residuals Plot of the Subgroups Data of Example 9.2

plots considered above are actually special types of probability plots. Suppose $x_1, \cdots, x_n$ is an observed sample on a random variable X with a continuous distribution function $F(x)$ that is a member of a location-scale class of continuous distributions, and, further, that we can write

$$F(x) = G[(x - \mu)/\sigma] = G(z), \; z = (x - \mu)/\sigma, \text{ or } x = \mu + \sigma z$$

Then G is the distribution function of the standardized variable z. But by the probability integral transformation, PIT, we know that we can write the relationship between x and z in an alternative form using the distribution functions F and G as follows:

$$z = G^{-1}(F(x)) = (x - \mu)/\sigma, \text{ or } x = F^{-1}(G(z)) = \mu + \sigma z$$

Now, we can transform the sample order statistics in the same manner:

$$z_{(i)} = G^{-1}(F(x_{(i)})) = (x_{(i)} - \mu)/\sigma, \text{ or } x_{(i)} = F^{-1}(G(z_{(i)})) = \mu + \sigma z_{(i)}$$

Since we do not know μ and σ, nor, therefore, F, we substitute the empirical distribution function F_n for F to obtain

$$z_{(i)} \cong G^{-1}(F_n(x_{(i)})) = G^{-1}(i/n),$$

or, $$(x_{(i)} - \mu)/\sigma \cong G^{-1}(i/n) \Rightarrow x_{(i)} \cong \mu + \sigma G^{-1}(i/n)$$

Thus, if the points $(G^{-1}(i/n), x_{(i)})$ are plotted on Cartesian coordinates, they should follow a straight line pattern with intercept μ and slope σ, with some additional "noise" introduced by using F_n for F in the transformation. To perform this plotting in applications we must be able to evaluate the inverse distribution function $G^{-1}(\cdot)$. Thus, we must have either a table or a computer algorithm to transform the unit interval $(0, 1)$ to the real line. To avoid this requirement, special graph paper can be used that is scaled on one axis in units of $G^{-1}(u)$ for $0 \le u \le 1$. Such paper is commercially available for the important parametric distributions. Commercial probability paper is usually scaled in percent rather than proportions so that $0 \le u \le 100$ is one scale. Also, in order to have the n sample points partition the interval $(0, 100)$ symmetrically for $i = 1, \cdots, n$; we usually use either $100(i - 0.5)/n$ or $100(i/(n + 1))$ in place of $100\, i/n$.

The most important application is for the normal distribution. For this case $G = \Phi$ and we illustrate the technique with a sample of aflatoxin data. The sample order statistics and the values of 100 $i/(n + 1)$ and $\Phi^{-1}(i/(n + 1))$ are given in Table 9.1. A probability plot using the $\Phi^{-1}(i/(n + 1))$ values is shown in Fig. 9.6. The line drawn is a least squares line. The points appear quite linear and suggest that the sample can be taken to be normal.

Note that the uniform residuals plots considered in the last section are more objective than these classical probability plots in that one can more readily judge if a plot of points follows the line that is the diagonal of a unit square, than to judge whether or not the plot of points follows *some undetermined* straight line.

9.5 GOODNESS-OF-FIT TESTS

Histograms, Shewhart charts, uniform residuals plots, and probability plots are useful graphical techniques for studying the form of a parent density function. However, these graphical methods are subject to the criticism that decisions based on them are subjective. For example, two people studying the same graph may well reach different conclusions, and this is unsatisfactory in many applications. A formal test of a

TABLE 9.1   Computations for Normal Probability Plot

i:	1	2	3	4	5	6	7
$\dfrac{i}{n+1}$:	0.048	0.095	0.143	0.190	0.238	0.286	0.333
$\Phi^{-1}\left(\dfrac{i}{n+1}\right)$:	−1.668	−1.309	−1.068	−0.876	−0.712	−0.566	−0.431
$x_{(i)}$:	31.6	35.4	36.0	38.7	40.6	41.9	42.5
i:	8	9	10	11	12	13	14
$\dfrac{i}{n+1}$:	0.381	0.429	0.476	0.524	0.571	0.619	0.667
$\Phi^{-1}\left(\dfrac{i}{n+1}\right)$:	−0.303	−0.180	−0.060	0.060	0.180	0.303	0.431
$x_{(i)}$:	43.1	46.7	47.2	47.6	48.0	49.2	50.0
i:	15	16	17	18	19	20	
$\dfrac{i}{n+1}$:	0.714	0.762	0.810	0.857	0.905	0.952	
$\Phi^{-1}\left(\dfrac{i}{n+1}\right)$:	0.566	0.712	0.876	1.068	1.309	1.668	
$x_{(i)}$:	51.1	54.9	56.9	58.2	59.0	63.0	

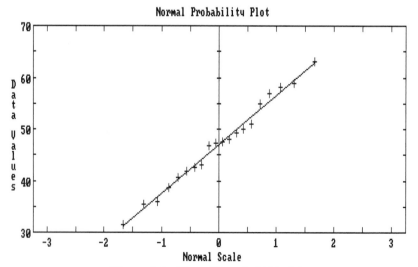

Figure 9.6   Plot of Data in Table 9.1

goodness-of-fit hypothesis has the merit that it is somewhat more objective.

We consider first the nature of a goodness-of-fit test. Suppose X_1, $X_2, \cdots, X_n$ is a sample from a continuous distribution with a density function f. Then suppose that $\mathcal{F}$ is a parametric family of density functions indexed by a vector of parameters $\theta = (\theta_1, \cdots, \theta_p)'$. For example, $\mathcal{F}$ might be the family of normal density functions. That is, $\mathcal{F}$ is the class of densities

$$f_{\mu,\sigma}(x) = f(x) = \frac{1}{\sigma\sqrt{2\pi}}\, e^{-\frac{1}{2}\left(\frac{x-\mu}{\sigma}\right)^2}, \ -\infty < x < \infty \qquad (9.5.1)$$

for $-\infty < \mu < \infty$, $\sigma^2 > 0$.

Then a goodness-of-fit hypothesis testing problem is to test

$$H_o: f \in \mathcal{F}$$
$$H_a: f \notin \mathcal{F} \qquad (9.5.2)$$

In particular, if $\mathcal{F}$ is the family of densities in (9.5.1), then the problem in (9.5.2) is called a *test of normality*. To make a test of this testing problem, we compute a statistic, say $T(X_1, \cdots, X_n)$, and define a critical region. Then if T falls in the critical region we will reject H_o of (9.5.2) in favor of H_a. Note carefully the nature of the null (H_o) and alternative (H_a) classes of distributions of the goodness-of-fit testing problem. The null hypothesis class is a parametric family indexed by p parameters. For the particular problem of testing normality $p = 2$, since there are two parameters (μ and σ). However, the alternative class of densities is an extremely large class. It contains all densities that are *not* in the null hypothesis class. Because the alternative class is so large there is no optimal solution to the problem of finding a test statistic for the goodness-of-fit testing problem. Actually, many tests have been proposed in the literature for testing the more important parametric distributions. We will give specific tests for testing simple uniformity, that is, for testing that a set of values $u_1, \cdots, u_n$ are from a $U(0, 1)$ distribution, and for testing normality.

9.5.1 The Neyman Smooth Test for Uniformity

In view of the probability integral transformations already studied, it is clear that to test many distributions we can first transform the sample to a $U(0, 1)$ sample under the null hypothesis. We can then consider testing the surrogate testing problem that $u_1, \cdots, u_n$ are from a distribution with a uniform density. Then we test the problem

$$H_o: f(u) = 1, 0 < u < 1$$
$$= 0, \text{ elsewhere} \qquad (9.5.3)$$
$$H_a: \text{Negation of } H_o$$

A test for (9.5.3) that has good power against a wide class of alternatives is the *Neyman smooth test.* We proceed to define this test.

Let $\pi_r(y)$ denote the rth degree Legendre polynomial, as given in (9.5.4) for $r = 0(1)4$.

$$
\begin{aligned}
\pi_0(y) &= 1, \\
\pi_1(y) &= \sqrt{12} \ (y - \tfrac{1}{2}) \\
\pi_2(y) &= \sqrt{5} \ [6(y - \tfrac{1}{2})^2 - \tfrac{1}{2}], \qquad (9.5.4) \\
\pi_3(y) &= \sqrt{7} \ [20 \ (y - \tfrac{1}{2})^3 - 3(y - \tfrac{1}{2})] \\
\pi_4(y) &= 210(y - \tfrac{1}{2})^4 - 45(y - \tfrac{1}{2})^2 + \tfrac{9}{8}
\end{aligned}
$$

Then to test that a sample $u_1, u_2, \cdots, u_n$ is a sample from $U(0, 1)$ distribution compute

$$t_r = \sum_{j=1}^{n} \pi_r(u_j) \qquad (9.5.5)$$

and the Neyman smooth statistic is

$$p_4^2 = \frac{1}{n} \sum_{r=1}^{4} t_r^2 \qquad (9.5.6)$$

Reject the simple uniformity null hypothesis H_o of (9.5.3) when p_4^2 is too large. The upper α fractiles of the distribution of p_4^2 are given in Table 9.2 for $\alpha \in \{0.10, 0.05, 0.01\}$ and $n = 2(1)20(10)50$ and ∞. Neyman (1937) showed that as n increases the limiting distribution of p_4^2 is a χ_4^2 distribution. The value for $n = \infty$ is $\chi_{.01,4}^2 = 13.28$. If this limit value is used for n as small as 20 or 30, the result is that the type

TABLE 9.2 **Significance Points for Neyman Smooth Statistic, p_4^2**

	α		
n	.10	.05	.01
2	7.19	9.52	16.14
3	7.34	9.51	15.80
4	7.46	9.50	15.43
5	7.53	9.49	15.12
6	7.57	9.48	14.86
7	7.60	9.47	14.65
8	7.62	9.47	14.47
9	7.63	9.46	14.32
10	7.64	9.46	14.19
11	7.65	9.45	14.09
12	7.65	9.45	14.00
13	7.66	9.44	13.93
14	7.66	9.44	13.87
15	7.66	9.43	13.82
16	7.66	9.43	13.78
17	7.66	9.43	13.74
18	7.67	9.42	13.71
19	7.67	9.42	13.69
20	7.67	9.42	13.67
30	7.68	9.40	13.58
40	7.68	9.40	13.52
50	7.69	9.40	13.48
∞	7.78	9.49	13.28

I error rate will be slightly larger than 0.01. In other words, the probability that we will reject the null hypothesis of uniformity when it is true will be a little larger than 0.01.

Example 9.3: The Q-Charts algorithm gives a Neyman smooth statistic P-value for normality of 0.00008 for the data of Example 9.1. Thus, this test agrees with the conclusion in that example from the uniform residuals plot in Fig. 9.4. ∎

9.5.2 The Anderson-Darling Test for Normality

There is a large literature that is concerned with testing that a sample came from a normal distribution. Many test statistics have been posed for this problem. There are a number of statistics that have attractive power properties against a wide range on nonnormal density function shapes. We present here the Anderson-Darling test which has good power properties and is convenient to use. This statistic is defined as follows. Let $x_{(1)}, \cdots, x_{(n)}$ denote the order statistics of a sample to be tested and put

$$y_i = \frac{x_{(i)} - \bar{x}}{s} \quad \text{and} \quad z_i = \Phi(y_i)$$

Then the Anderson-Darling statistic A^2 is given by

$$A^2 = \left\{ -\frac{1}{n} \sum_{i=1}^{n} (2i - 1) \left[\log z_i + \log (1 - z_{n-i+1}) \right] \right\} - n \quad (9.5.7)$$

The distribution of A^2 depends on the sample size n, but by making the following simple transformation of A^2 to a new *modified* value, the upper significance points are approximately constant in n.

$$A^2_{\text{MOD}} = A^2 \left(1.0 + \frac{0.75}{n} + \frac{2.25}{n^2} \right) \quad (9.5.8)$$

Selected significance points for A^2_{MOD} are given in Table 9.3. These points can be used for $n > 8$. The null hypothesis of normality is rejected at the α level if $A^2_{\text{MOD}} > A^2_{\text{MOD},\alpha}$. For smaller values of n this test is not valid and should not be used.

The A^2 statistic for the data in Table 9.1 is $A^2 = 0.16070$ and this gives $A^2_{\text{MOD}} = 0.168$. This is a small value that is below the $\alpha = .10$ significance point, so that the null hypothesis of normality is accepted, and this result is consistent with that of the probability plot of this data in Fig. 9.6.

Stephens (1986) gave a method for computing the observed significance level (p-value) of the A^2 statistic. This P-value for the data of Table 9.1 is 0.948, which indicates that this data can be fitted very well with a normal distribution. The Q-Charts algorithm computes this p-value for a sample.

Example 9.4: The Q-Charts algorithm gives an Anderson-Darling statistic p-value for normality of 0.00000 for the data of Example 9.1. Thus this test agrees with the conclusion in that example from the

TABLE 9.3 A^2_{MOD} **Significance Points**

α:	0.10	0.05	0.025	0.02	0.005
$A^2_{\text{MOD},\alpha}$:	0.631	0.752	0.823	1.035	1.159

uniform residuals plot in Fig. 9.4, and with the Neyman smooth test
p-value given in Example 9.3 in concluding that the data are not normally distributed.

The Neyman Smooth and Anderson-Darling P-values for the subgrouped data of Example 9.2 are NS-PV = 0.67 and AD-PV = 0.94,
respectively, which agree with the chart of Fig. 9.5.   ■

Before leaving this section we offer some further comments on the
general problem of goodness-of-fit testing and the special case of testing normality. First, we remark that the goodness-of-fit testing problem
of (9.5.2), and in particular the special case of testing normality, is
fundamentally a quite different type of decision problem from a test
on the value of a distribution parameter. In a test on a distribution
parameter the accepted strategy is to put the parameter values it is
desired to establish in the alternative hypothesis, and hope for a rejec-
tion of the null hypothesis. Then, if the null hypothesis is rejected, we
can claim that the alternative values are credible, and the α level of
the test assesses the probability of being incorrect in reaching this conclusion. However, for the goodness-of-fit problem of (9.5.2) this strategy is not possible. For this problem we are primarily interested in
establishing that the null hypothesis is true, for example, in showing
that a process distribution is normal, but the test level α relates only
to the mistake of rejecting normality when it is actually true. We will
rarely be able to assess the β value, which is the probability of ac-
cepting the null hypothesis and depends on the particular alternative
distribution that obtains. The Anderson-Darling test for normality, or
any other test for normality for that matter, will generally have good
power (say, .9 or more) for detecting nonnormal distributions only
when alternative distributions are extremely nonnormal in shape and
sample size is large. Since most nonnormal distributions of industrial
measurements are not severely nonnormal, as we will discuss further
below, it generally requires large samples in order for an acceptance
of the null hypothesis to give much confidence that the distribution is
really close to a normal shape. For these reasons, computing the p-
value of the Anderson-Darling test for normality is helpful in establishing that normality is a credible assumption for a data set.

9.6 TRANSFORMING SKEWED DATA TO NORMALITY

The assumption that measurements data are distributed in the form of
a normal distribution is important in applying many of the process
control charting techniques considered in earlier chapters. Some effi-

cient methods for deciding if a sample is from a normal distribution have been studied in preceding sections of this chapter. If a process is stable but the process distribution is not normal, then we may consider ways to establish control charts for the process. There is a large statistical literature concerned with the problem of a nonnormal distribution. One appealing approach to dealing with a nonnormal distribution is to try to transform the data to a normal distribution, so that normal-based methodology can be used with the transformed data. We present in this section a method of transforming nonnormal data to normality that will work well with much industrial measurements data. This ability to transform nonnormal data to normality, when it is possible, greatly broadens the class of processes to which normal-based methodology can be applied.

It was pointed out by Shewhart (1931) that most industrial measurements data that are not normal can, however, be modeled with a unimodal, skewed distribution. Indeed, the variables that have these skewed distributions such as total-indicator-runout (TIR), out-of-round, parallelism, surface finish, and many others; generally are positive quality variables with target values of zero and with only upper specification limits. For these types of variables a particularly simple *power transformation* as follows often can be used to transform the data to approximate normality.

$$z_i = x_i^\lambda, \lambda \neq 0$$
$$z_i = \log x_i, \lambda = 0$$

$$(9.6.1)$$

Given a calibration sample $x_1, x_2, \cdots, x_n$, we must find an estimate $\hat{\lambda}$ of λ. The transformations of (9.6.1) have been considered by a number of writers, including Tukey and Moore (1954) and Box and Cox (1964). Box and Cox propose a maximum likelihood estimate of λ. However, we will here use an estimate of λ based on the Anderson-Darling goodness-of-fit statistic. The method we propose is as follows. We will search for the value of λ, say $\hat{\lambda}$, for which the p-value of the Anderson-Darling statistic is a maximum. The Q-Charts algorithm can be used to find this value for a particular sample $x_1, x_2, \cdots, x_n$. We illustrate using the algorithm in the following example. The algorithm lets us specify a range of values of λ and then for 11 equally spaced values in this range it transforms the data set and computes the p-value of the Anderson-Darling statistic for each of the transformed data sets. We run the algorithm recursively until we have determined the value that gives a maximum p-value to sufficient accuracy.

Example 9.5: We consider the 60 measurements given in Example 9.1. Note that these data are positive with the smallest value of 0.02 just above zero. Also, the uniform residuals plot clearly indicates a right skewed distribution. We enter the data into the Q-Charts program and go to Menu F1.F4. Select item F3 "Find Normalizing Value LAMBDA," and when the query "Wish to evaluate PV's . . . (Y/N)" appears, press the Y key. When the query

$$\text{Range of Lambda: LOWER, UPPER} = ?$$

appears, type in a range with LOWER ≥ -10 and UPPER ≤ 9. For the present example we enter: -10, 10, and the 11 values returned include a p-value of approximately 6.06×10^{-3} at $\lambda = 0$ with much smaller values on both sides for $\lambda = -2$ and $\lambda = 2$. Press any key and run the algorithm successively with values as follows.

LOWER	UPPER	Maximum P-Value	Lambda of Maximum
-10	10	6.06×10^{-3}	0.0
0	2	0.252	0.4
.2	0.6	0.332	0.32
0.28	0.34	0.333	0.31

We would now use the transformation $y = x^\lambda = x^{0.31}$ to transform this type data for $\lambda \neq 0$. If $\lambda = 0$, we would put $y = \ln x$. Note that the p-value of 0.333 corresponding to this value of $\hat{\lambda} = 0.31$, while not extremely high, still indicates that the normality of this transformed data is much improved from the raw data. Figure 9.7 is a uniform residuals chart of these power transformed measurements. Note that the normality is much improved over the plot in Fig. 9.4. To study the stability of the process when these data were being observed we give in Fig. 9.8 the chart for the process variance, and in Fig. 9.9 the chart for the process mean. These charts indicate a stable process. Also, note that the estimated mean and standard deviation of the power transformed measurements are 0.97 and 0.37, respectively. We will use these values in the next section to compute estimates of the process fallout and yield.

The *estimate* $\hat{\lambda}$ obtained is, of course, the optimum value to use for λ for transforming this particular sample. However, if an estimate of λ

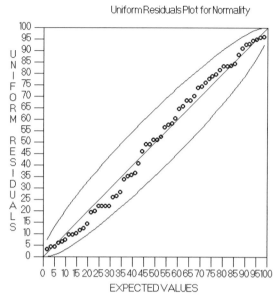

Figure 9.7   Uniform Residuals Chart for Power Transformed Data of Example 9.1

is computed for another sample it will generally be different from this particular estimate. The variation in these estimates depends on the amount of data available, as well as on other things, especially the stability of the process producing the data. The ultimate aim is to work to stabilize the process over long periods of production and to determine a stable value of λ to use in this context.   ∎

9.7 SPECIFICATION LIMITS, FALLOUT, YIELD, NATURAL TOLERANCE LIMITS, AND PROCESS CAPABILITY

The material in this book in earlier chapters has been concerned with applications of control charts to stabilize a process, that is, to study a process and bring it into control by eliminating assignable causes, or to monitor a stable process in order to recognize parameter shifts and take corrective actions. In this chapter we have presented some material useful for studying the shape or form of a process distribution, and thereby to design our charts more effectively. However, our work in charting and parametric modeling does not directly address the most central question in process control. This question asks how suitable the units of product are for their intended purpose. We need ways to assess the suitability of units of product for their intended purpose.

Shewhart Q-Chart for SIGMA : IMUU

XBAR = .9652374, SD = .3673151, RMSSD = .3362047, PV-MSSD = .1006505

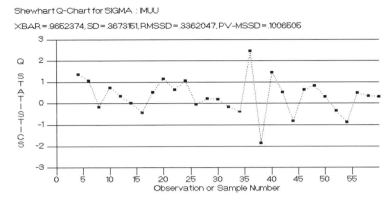

Figure 9.8 *Q*-Chart for Variance for the Transformed Data

A quality variable represents an important feature of a product. For a variable X measured on each unit of product, there is often a desired or *target value* τ that we would like to have the variable assume on each unit of product. Since the values of X observed on units of product will not be exactly equal to the target value on all units, we need objective ways to express how well a process is doing (process performance) and how well it is capable of doing by adjusting the process (process capability). The usual engineering approach to relating the values of a quality variable to the suitability of the product for its intended purpose is by using specification limits and target values.

For most processes there are specification limits for each quality variable. These are maximum and minimum values of the variable that are used in inspection of units or product. They should be set to satisfy two conditions. First, the target value and specification limits must be chosen so when a production unit is within specifications it will per-

Shewhart Q-Chart for MEAN : IMUU

XBAR = .9652374, SD = .3673151, RMSSD = .3362047, PV-MSSD = .1006505

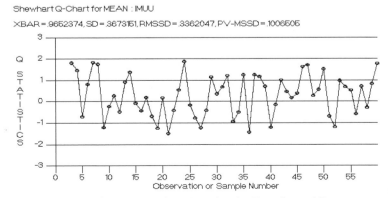

Figure 9.9 *Q*-Chart for Mean for the Transformed Data

form its intended purpose satisfactorily. Second, the manufacturing process to be used to make the unit must be capable of producing a large proportion of units within the specifications. Unfortunately, this second condition is not always observed and the spec limits may sometimes be set by criteria external to the production process: by design engineers, by management decision, by contract between a vendor and customer, or in some other way. Further, it must be kept clearly in mind that specification limits and control limits are quite different. Specification limits are values that are desired limiting bounds for the value of the quality variable, whereas control limits are prediction or tolerance limits for the distribution of either a quality variable or a computed statistic. Suppose that specification limits for a quality variable X are given by

$$\text{Upper Specification Limit} = USL = \tau + \Delta_U$$

$$\text{Lower Specification Limit} = LSL = \tau - \Delta_L$$

where τ is the process *target value,* Δ_U is the *upper allowance,* and Δ_L is the *lower allowance,* and both allowances are nonnegative. Some processes have only one specification limit and may or may not have a target value. For example, if the variable X is profit measured in units of dollars, then we might consider using a *LSL* of zero but want to maximize the value of X. Many quality variables such as measures of total-indicator-runout (TIR), out-of-roundness, taper, centering, etc., are nonnegative and have only an upper specification limit, and a target value and lower allowance both equal to zero. That is, we can consider $\tau = \Delta_L = 0$ for these types of variables.

9.7.1   Process Capability and Performance: Fallout And Yield

If the process that produces a quality variable is in control, then the term *process capability* refers to the potential ability of the process to produce within specifications, whereas *process performance* is the actual performance of the process in producing product within specifications. For a stable or in-control process, we can compute numbers which are useful numerical representations of these two different concepts. For a quality variable X, the *upper fallout,* the *lower fallout,* and the *fallout* are defined by

$$
\boxed{
\begin{aligned}
\text{Upper Fallout} &= P(X > USL) \\
\text{Lower Fallout} &= P(X < LSL) \\
\text{Fallout} &= P(X < LSL \text{ or } X > USL) \\
&= \text{Lower Fallout} + \text{Upper Fallout}
\end{aligned}
}
\qquad (9.7.1)
$$

The *yield* of a process is the probability that the quality variable falls between the specification limits, that is

$$
\text{Yield} = P(LSL \leq X \leq USL) = 1 - \text{Fallout} \qquad (9.7.2)
$$

and, of course, we would like to have the yield be large and the fallout be small. Process fallout and yield are, of course, equivalent measures of process performance. Both fallout and yield are often presented in percent rather than probability.

Next, suppose that a quality variable X is normally distributed with a mean μ and variance σ^2. If the process is centered so that the mean μ is equal to the process target value τ, then the yield is a measure of *process capability*, since this is the maximum yield the process is capable of when it is perfectly centered. Otherwise, when the process is not centered and $\mu \neq \tau$, the yield is a measure of actual *process performance*. To illustrate the computations, consider a process with a normal distribution with mean $\mu = 14$, $\sigma = 3$; and specifications $LSL = 5$, $\tau = 15$, and $USL = 24$, as in Fig. 9.10. Then we compute

$$
\text{Upper Fallout} = P(X > 24) = P\left(Z > \frac{24 - 14}{3}\right)
$$

$$
= P(Z > 3.33) \cong 0.00048
$$

$$
\text{Lower Fallout} = P(X < 5) = P\left(Z < \frac{5 - 14}{3}\right)
$$

$$
= P(Z < -3) \cong 0.00135
$$

$$
\text{Fallout} = 0.00048 + 0.00135 = 0.00183
$$

$$
\text{Yield} = 1 - \text{Fallout} = 1 - 0.00183 = 0.99817
$$

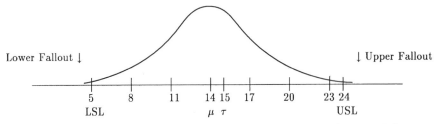

Lower Fallout ↓   ↓ Upper Fallout

5	8	11	14 15	17	20	23 24
LSL			μ τ			USL

Figure 9.10 Process Specifications, Target Value, Upper and Lower Fallout

9.7.2 Estimating Fallout from a Normal Distribution with Small Samples

It will often be the case that the number of observations available for estimating the process parameters μ and σ are not large enough to permit us to treat the estimates as though they are actually the correct values of the parameters, as we did in the computation above. We will discuss *short-term process capability* studies further below, but for these studies the sample size is often too small to ignore sampling variation in the parameter estimates. For example, the General Motors Supplier Development Manual (1989), p. 4, states that for a short-term process capability study a minimum of 50 consecutively produced parts must be measured. If measurements on a sample of n consecutively produced values gives $x_1, x_2, \cdots, x_n$; and it is known that the process distribution is approximately normal, then the best estimate (UMVU) of the process fallout values is computed as follows. Put

$$\tilde{F}(z) = 0 \text{ if } z < \bar{x} - \frac{n-1}{\sqrt{n}} s$$

$$= 1 \text{ if } z > \bar{x} + \frac{n-1}{\sqrt{n}} s$$

$$= H_{n-2}(A(z)) \quad \text{otherwise}$$

where

$$A(z) = \frac{\sqrt{n-2}\,(z - \bar{x})}{\sqrt{\dfrac{(n-1)^2}{n} s^2 - (z - \bar{x})^2}}$$

and H_ν is a Student-t distribution function.

> The estimates of fallout and yield are given by:
> Upper Fallout $= 1 - \tilde{F}\ (USL)$
> Lower Fallout $= \tilde{F}\ (LSL)$ (9.7.3)
> Fallout $=$ Upper Fallout $+$ Lower Fallout
> Yield $= 1 -$ Fallout

The function $\tilde{F}\ (z)$ can be evaluated using a Student-t distribution function algorithm.

We illustrate these computations in the following. Suppose a sample of size $n = 10$ had sample mean of $\bar{x} = 27.195$ and sample standard deviation of $s = 0.0041$, and the process had specification limits of $LSL = 27.183$ and $USL = 27.203$. Then

$$\bar{x} - \frac{n-1}{\sqrt{n}}s = 27.195 - \left(\frac{9}{\sqrt{10}}\right)(0.0041) = 27.1833$$

$$\bar{x} + \frac{n-1}{\sqrt{n}}\ s = 27.195 + \left(\frac{9}{\sqrt{10}}\right)(0.0041) = 27.2067$$

First, observe that since $LSL = 27.183 < 27.1833$, the estimated fallout below LSL is 0.

Next, since $USL = 27.203 < 27.2067$ we compute

$$A(USL) = \frac{\sqrt{8}\ (27.203 - 27.195)}{\sqrt{\left(\frac{81}{10}\right)(0.0041)^2 - (27.203 - 27.195)^2}} = 2.66$$

and the estimated fallout above USL is

$$\text{Upper Fallout} = 1 - H_8(2.66) = 1 - 0.98560 = 0.0144$$

So from these values of $\bar{x}$, s, LSL, and USL, and assuming a stable normal process distribution, we estimate zero percent fallout below LSL and 1.44% fallout above USL. We also note that the normal distribution analysis algorithm on the Q-Charts disk computes these values from the sample measurements.

We remind the reader that in order for these estimates of fallout and yield to be meaningful, *the process producing the measurements must be stable.*

9.7.3 Natural Tolerance Limits and Process Capability

The interval from $\mu - 3\sigma$ to $\mu + 3\sigma$ is called the *natural tolerance interval* for the process distribution and, of course, this is the 6-sigma interval that will contain 99.73% of the process output when the process distribution is normal, and, assuming the process is centered with $\mu = \tau = (LSL + USL)/2$, gives 99.73% yield. Even if the process distribution is not normal, this natural tolerance interval will still contain a large percentage of the process output due to the following considerations. From the Chebychev inequality of probability it is known that the proportion of output within the natural tolerance limits is greater than or equal to $8/9 = 0.89$ for any distribution whatever. However, this is an *extremely* conservative lower bound, and for distributions of quality variables we can reasonably expect that the probability within the natural tolerance limits will be *much larger* than 8/9.

The quantities μ, σ, $\bar{x}$, s, τ, LSL, and USL are all expressed in the same units of measurement as the observations. We wish to specify and study functions of these quantities that express the potential and actual ability of a process to produce quality units. We need to consider functions of the process parameters (μ and σ) and the specification values (LSL, USL, τ) that can serve as coefficients or indices of the capability and actual performance of a process to produce quality units. For such indices to be useful for different quality valuables, they must not depend on the units of measurement of the data. The upper fallout, lower fallout, fallout, and yield are expressed as proportions or probabilities and satisfy this requirement. They are also often expressed as percentages.

9.8 THE C_p CAPABILITY AND C_{PK} PERFORMANCE INDICES

An obvious way to study the ability of a stable process to produce within specifications is to compare the length of the natural tolerance interval, the *natural tolerance range,* 6σ, with the length of the specification range, $USL - LSL$. If the natural tolerance range is no larger than the specification range, then the process is capable of producing a large percentage of product within specifications. The *process capability index C_p* is the ratio of the specification range to the natural tolerance range, and the *capability ratio C_r* is the reciprocal of C_p.

$$C_p = \frac{USL - LSL}{6\sigma}, \quad C_r = \frac{1}{C_p} = \frac{6\sigma}{USL - LSL} \qquad (9.8.1)$$

The C_p index is a function only of the specification range, $USL - LSL$, and the process standard deviation σ, and does not reflect the location or centering of the process distribution. The C_p index essentially indicates how well a stable process is capable of performing, provided that the process is centered with the process mean midway between the specification limits. If the process distribution is normal with known values of μ and σ; the upper and lower allowances are equal so that $\tau = (USL + LSL)/2$; the process is centered with $\mu = \tau$; then a C_p of 1 gives a fallout beyond each specification limit of 0.135%. Note that this statement depends on these assumptions: (1) the process is stable, (2) the process distribution is normal, (3) the parameters, μ and σ, are known, and (4) the process is centered. When these assumptions are valid we can evaluate the fallout corresponding to values of C_p. A number of writers, including Montgomery (1991), have recommended minimum values that the indices should have for a process to be considered capable. Although a C_p of 1 for a centered normal process gives a small fallout value of 0.135% for each specification limit, the recommended values are generally larger than 1 in order to allow for the event that the distribution is not really exactly normal, the process is not precisely centered, the parameters are not exactly known, and the estimate is of short-term rather than long-term capability. We give in Table 9.4 some recommended values that are similar to those recommended by other writers. If the quality variable involves safety or is otherwise a critical parameter, than these values probably should be increased by perhaps 10%.

For some processes only a single specification limit is given. We can compute an estimate of fallout beyond the given specification limit using the methods described above. For one-sided specification bounds we define an *upper capability index* C_{PU} and a *lower capability index* C_{PL} as follows.

$$C_{PU} = \frac{USL - \mu}{3\sigma} \quad \text{and} \quad C_{PL} = \frac{\mu - LSL}{3\sigma} \qquad (9.8.2)$$

TABLE 9.4   Recommended Minimum Values for C_p

	Two-Sided	One-Sided
Operating Process	1.33	1.14
New Process	1.50	1.20

These indices are usually called *capability* indices. However, since they are standardized distances between the process mean and a specification limit, they are actually measures of process performance. Note that C_p is the average of C_{PU} and C_{PL}, that is

$$C_p = \frac{C_{PL} + C_{PU}}{2} \tag{9.8.3}$$

These indices are functions of μ and σ which are unknown parameters and must always be estimated. Estimates of these three indices are usually made by substituting estimates $\bar{\mu}$ and $\hat{\sigma}$ for μ and σ. That is

$$\hat{C}_p = \frac{USL - LSL}{6\hat{\sigma}}, \; \hat{C}_{PU} = \frac{USL - \hat{\mu}}{3\hat{\sigma}}, \; \hat{C}_{PL} = \frac{\hat{\mu} - LSL}{3\hat{\sigma}} \tag{9.8.4}$$

The mean estimate $\hat{\mu}$ is either $\overline{X}$ or $\overline{\overline{X}}$ and $\hat{\sigma}$ is based on a sample range R, or a pooled mean squared estimate S_ν, with ν degrees of freedom. We need to consider the sampling distribution of the estimate $\hat{C}_p$. Let $\hat{\sigma} = S_\nu/c_4$, and note that ν will often be large enough to make c_4 approximately equal to 1. For small ν the constant c_4 is read from Table A.5 using $n = \nu + 1$. Consider constructing a confidence interval estimate of C_p. If the process distribution is normal, then $\nu S^2/\sigma^2$ is a x_ν^2 random variable. Using the notation of section 2.9, we write

$$P\left[\chi^2_{1-\alpha/2,\nu} \leq \frac{\nu S^2}{\sigma^2} \leq \chi^2_{\alpha/2,\nu}\right] = 1 - \alpha$$

From this, after some manipulation, we obtain

$$P\left[\frac{\hat{C}_p}{c_4}\sqrt{\frac{\chi^2_{1-\alpha/2,\nu}}{\nu}} \leq C_p \leq \frac{\hat{C}_p}{c_4}\sqrt{\frac{\chi^2_{\alpha/2,\nu}}{\nu}}\right] = 1 - \alpha$$

So the values

$$\boxed{\frac{\hat{C}_p}{c_4}\sqrt{\frac{\chi^2_{1-\alpha/2,\nu}}{\nu}} \quad \text{and} \quad \frac{\hat{C}_p}{c_4}\sqrt{\frac{\chi^2_{\alpha/2,\nu}}{\nu}}} \tag{9.8.5}$$

are the end points for a $1 - \alpha$ confidence interval for C_p.

The formulas in (9.8.5) are used to compute a confidence interval for C_p after data have been collected and a mean squared estimate S^2 of σ^2 has been obtained. Now, suppose we would like to decide how many degrees of freedom, say ν', are required to make a confidence interval of a specified length δ, say. By setting the width of the CI in (9.8.5) equal to δ we obtain the equation

$$\frac{\hat{C}_p}{c_4} \frac{1}{\sqrt{1\nu'}} \left[\sqrt{\chi^2_{\alpha/2,\nu'}} - \sqrt{\chi^2_{1-\alpha/2,\nu'}} \right] = \delta$$

By using the formula in (2.9.4), and putting $c_4 = 1$, we obtain the following formula for the total number of degrees of freedom required to obtain a CI of length approximately δ.

$$\nu' = 2 \left(\frac{\hat{C}_p \, z_{\alpha/2}}{\delta} \right)^2 \tag{9.8.6}$$

Example 9.6: A sample of $n = 41$ observations gave an estimate $S = 0.0027$. The specification limits are $LSL = 17.184$ and $USL = 17.202$. Then

$$\hat{C}_p = \frac{17.202 - 17.184}{(6)\,(.0027)} = 1.11$$

From (9.8.5) we compute a 95% CI for C_p

$$\hat{C}_p \sqrt{\frac{\chi^2_{.975,40}}{40}} = (1.11) \sqrt{\frac{24.433}{40}} = 0.868$$

$$\hat{C}_p \sqrt{\frac{\chi^2_{.025,40}}{40}} = (1.11) \sqrt{\frac{59.342}{40}} = 1.352$$

So $(0.868, 1.352)$ is a 95% confidence interval for C_p. This interval is too wide to be useful. Consider the formula (9.8.6). To obtain a confidence interval of approximate width δ we require a total of

$$\nu' = \frac{2(1.11)^2(1.96)^2}{\delta^2} = \frac{9.466}{\delta^2}$$

degrees of freedom. The following gives the number of additional degrees of freedom ($\nu' - 40$) needed for a range of δ's.

δ:	.4	.3	.2	.1
$df = \nu'$:	20	66	197	907

∎

A one-sided $1 - \alpha$ confidence bound for C_p can be obtained from the formulas in (9.8.5) by using the formula for the corresponding end point of the confidence interval and replacing $\alpha/2$ in the formula by α. Because large values of C_p are desirable, we are usually interested primarily in a lower confidence bound for C_p. A $100(1 - \alpha)\%$ lower confidence bound for C_p is given by c for

$$c = \frac{\hat{C}_p}{c_4} \sqrt{\frac{\chi^2_{1-\alpha,\nu}}{\nu}} \tag{9.8.7}$$

Chou, Owen, and Borrego (1990) have used this formula (putting $c_4 = 1$) to compute a table of values of c. The equation (9.8.7) can be used to express $\hat{C}_p$ as a function of the other variables. If c_o is an accepted minimum value of C_p, such as one of the values in Table 9.4, then the process is capable when C_p exceeds c_o. If

$$\hat{C}_p \geq c_o \sqrt{\frac{\nu}{\chi^2_{1-\alpha,\nu}}} \equiv \hat{C}_{p,MIN} \tag{9.8.8}$$

then the process is capable at least $100(1 - \alpha)\%$ of the time. The quantity $\hat{C}_{p,MIN}$ is the minimum value of the computed value of $\hat{C}_p$ for which the process can be declared capable at the level c_o at least $100(1 - \alpha)\%$ of the time.

Example 9.7: Suppose we are to take a sample of size $n = 50$ from a new process, for which there is only an upper specification limit. We choose the minimum value of C_p to be $c_o = 1.20$, as in Table 9.4. For $\alpha = 0.05$, from the Q-Charts disk we obtain

$$\chi^2_{.95,49} = 33.90 \text{ and } \hat{C}_{p,MIN} = 1.20 \sqrt{\frac{49}{33.930}} \cong 1.44$$

Thus, if we take a sample of size 50 we can conclude that the process is capable 95% of the time provided the computed value of $\hat{C}_p$ is at least 1.44.

Chou et al. (1990) have given a table of values of $\hat{C}_{p,MIN}$ for $\alpha = 0.05$, and selected values of c_o and n. This table is given here in Table 9.5. The reader can verify the value of $\hat{C}_{p,MIN} = 1.44$ obtained in Example 9.7 from Table 9.5.

9.8.1 The C_{PK} Process Performance Index

Since C_P is a function of σ and not of μ, it is natural to consider measures of *performance* that relate both σ and μ to the specification limits. One performance index is C_{PK} given by

$$C_{PK} = \text{Min}\{C_{PL}, C_{PU}\} \qquad (9.8.9)$$

Unless the process mean is centered between LSL and USL, that is, $\mu = (LSL + USL)/2$, the values of C_{PL} and C_{PU} are unequal. From this and since from (9.8.3) we see that C_p is centered between C_{PL} and C_{PU}, it follows that $0 \le C_{PK} \le C_P$, and $C_{PK} = C_P$ only if $\mu = (LSL + USL)/2$.

The C_{PK} index can be introduced in an alternative way that reveals some of its properties. Let m denote the midpoint between the specification limits, that is, $m = (USL + LSL)/2$, and suppose that $C_{PK} = C_{PU}$, which means that USL is closer to μ and therefore $m \le \mu \le USL$. The distance of μ from m, scaled by the specification range, $(USL - LSL)/2$, is

$$k = \frac{2|\mu - m|}{USL - LSL} \qquad (9.8.10)$$

and this formula holds also when $LSL \le \mu \le m$. Then the two values C_P and C_{PK} are related by the formula

$$C_{PK} = (1 - k)C_P \qquad (9.8.11)$$

The factor k is a measure of the amount by which a process is off center. Since $0 \le k \le 1$, we see, again, that $0 \le C_{PK} \le C_P$ in all cases. A plug-in estimate $\hat{k}$ of k is obtained by replacing μ by an estimate $\hat{\mu}$. From the value of $\hat{k}$ or, equivalently, by comparing the values of $\hat{C}_p$ and $\hat{C}_{PK}$, we obtain a measure of the centering of a process.

The relationship between an acceptable minimum value, say c_1, of C_{PU} (or C_{PL}) and $\hat{C}_{PU}$ (or $\hat{C}_{PL}$) cannot be expressed in a simple formula

TABLE 9.5 The Minimum Value $\hat{C}_{p,MIN}$ of $\hat{C}_p$ for Which the Process is Capable, that is, $C_p \geq c_o$ 95% of the Time

c_o	n 10	20	30	40	50	75	100
0.7	1.15	0.96	0.90	0.86	0.84	0.81	0.79
0.8	1.32	1.10	1.02	0.99	0.96	0.93	0.91
0.9	1.48	1.23	1.15	1.11	1.08	1.04	1.02
1.0	1.65	1.37	1.28	1.23	1.20	1.16	1.13
1.1	1.81	1.51	1.41	1.36	1.32	1.27	1.25
1.2	1.97	1.64	1.54	1.48	1.44	1.39	1.36
1.3	2.14	1.78	1.66	1.60	1.56	1.51	1.47
1.4	2.30	1.92	1.79	1.72	1.68	1.62	1.59
1.5	2.47	2.06	1.92	1.85	1.80	1.74	1.70
1.6	2.63	2.19	2.05	1.97	1.92	1.85	1.81
1.7	2.80	2.33	2.18	2.09	2.04	1.97	1.93
1.8	2.96	2.47	2.30	2.22	2.16	2.08	2.04
1.9	3.13	2.60	2.43	2.34	2.28	2.20	2.15
2.0	3.29	2.74	2.56	2.46	2.40	2.32	2.27
2.1	3.46	2.88	2.69	2.59	2.52	2.43	2.38
2.2	3.62	3.02	2.82	2.71	2.64	2.55	2.49
2.3	3.78	3.15	2.94	2.83	2.76	2.66	2.61
2.4	3.95	3.29	3.07	2.96	2.88	2.78	2.72
2.5	4.11	3.43	3.20	3.08	3.00	2.89	2.83
2.6	4.28	3.56	3.33	3.20	3.12	3.01	2.95
2.7	4.44	3.70	3.46	3.33	3.24	3.13	3.06
2.8	4.61	3.84	3.58	3.45	3.36	3.24	3.17
2.9	4.77	3.97	3.71	3.57	3.49	3.36	3.29
3.0	4.94	4.11	3.84	3.70	3.61	3.47	3.40

c_o	n 125	150	200	250	300	350	400
0.7	0.78	0.77	0.76	0.76	0.75	0.75	0.74
0.8	0.89	0.88	0.87	0.86	0.86	0.85	0.85
0.9	1.01	1.00	0.98	0.97	0.97	0.96	0.96
1.0	1.12	1.11	1.09	1.08	1.07	1.07	1.06
1.1	1.13	1.22	1.20	1.19	1.18	1.17	1.17
1.2	1.34	1.33	1.31	1.30	1.29	1.28	1.27
1.3	1.45	1.44	1.42	1.40	1.39	1.39	1.38
1.4	1.56	1.55	1.53	1.51	1.50	1.49	1.49
1.5	1.68	1.66	1.64	1.62	1.61	1.60	1.59
1.6	1.79	1.77	1.74	1.73	1.72	1.71	1.70
1.7	1.90	1.88	1.85	1.84	1.82	1.81	1.81
1.8	2.01	1.99	1.96	1.94	1.93	1.92	1.91
1.9	2.12	2.10	2.07	2.05	2.04	2.03	2.02
2.0	2.24	2.21	2.18	2.16	2.14	2.13	2.12
2.1	2.35	2.32	2.29	2.27	2.25	2.24	2.23
2.2	2.46	2.43	2.40	2.38	2.36	2.35	2.34
2.3	2.57	2.54	2.51	2.48	2.47	2.45	2.44
2.4	2.68	2.65	2.62	2.59	2.57	2.56	2.55
2.5	2.79	2.77	2.73	2.70	2.68	2.67	2.66
2.6	2.91	2.88	2.84	2.81	2.79	2.77	2.76
2.7	3.02	2.99	2.94	2.92	2.90	2.88	2.87
2.8	3.13	3.10	3.05	3.02	3.00	2.99	2.97
2.9	3.24	3.21	3.16	3.13	3.11	3.09	3.08
3.0	3.35	3.32	3.27	3.24	3.22	3.20	3.19

such as (9.8.8), and the same is true for an acceptable minimum value, say c_k, of C_{PK} and $\hat{C}_{PK}$. However, Chou et al. (1990) have given tables that relate these minimum values that are given in Table 9.6 and Table 9.7. For further discussion of C_P, C_{PU}, C_{PL}, and C_{Pk}, see Kane (1986).

Example 9.8: Suppose a sample of size $n = 40$ from a stable process gives a mean of $\bar{x} = 18.004$ and standard deviation of $s = 0.009$. The specification limits are $LSL = 17.970$ and $USL = 18.030$. Then

$$\hat{C}_p = \frac{USL - LSL}{6s} = \frac{0.06}{6(0.009)} = 1.11$$

$$\hat{C}_{PL} = \frac{\bar{x} - LSL}{3s} = \frac{18.004 - 17.970}{3(0.009)} = 1.26$$

$$\hat{C}_{PU} = \frac{USL - \bar{x}}{3s} = \frac{18.030 - 18.004}{3(0.009)} = 0.96$$

$$\hat{C}_{PK} = \text{Min}\{\hat{C}_{PU}, \hat{C}_{PL}\} = \text{Min}\{0.96, 1.26\} = 0.96$$

$$\hat{k} = \frac{2\left|\bar{x} - \dfrac{USL + LSL}{2}\right|}{USL - LSL} = \frac{2\,|\,18.004 - 18.000|}{0.06} = 0.133$$

From the value $\hat{C}_P = 1.11$ and Table 9.5 we find a 95% lower confidence bound for C_P is 0.9. Also, 95% lower confidence bounds for C_{PL}, C_{PU}, and C_{PK} are approximately 1.0, 0.7, and 0.7, respectively, using Tables 9.6 and 9.7. From these values we note that the process is off center and both C_p and C_{PK} are too small to assure process capability and performance.   ∎

9.8.2 The C_{PM} Capability Index

Chan et al. (1988) proposed a quantity called C_{PM} which is the same as C_P except that σ in C_P is replaced by $\text{REMS} = \sqrt{\text{EMS}}$ from equation (4.2.4). That is

$$C_{PM} = \frac{USL - LSL}{6\sqrt{EMS}} = \frac{USL - LSL}{6\sqrt{\sigma^2 + (\mu - \tau)^2}} \tag{9.8.12}$$

The authors call this a *capability* index; however, it should be noted that it is a measure of performance and not just potential performance.

TABLE 9.6 The Minimum Value $\hat{C}_{PU,MIN}$ of $\hat{C}_{PU}$ (or $\hat{C}_{PL}$) for Which the Process is Capable, that is, $C_{PU} \geq c_1$(or $C_{PL} \geq c_1$)] 95% of the Time

c_1	n	10	20	30	40	50	75	100
0.7		1.21	1.00	0.93	0.89	0.87	0.83	0.81
0.8		1.37	1.13	1.05	1.01	0.98	0.94	0.92
0.9		1.53	1.26	1.18	1.13	1.10	1.06	1.03
1.0		1.69	1.40	1.30	1.25	1.22	1.17	1.15
1.1		1.85	1.53	1.43	1.37	1.34	1.29	1.26
1.2		2.01	1.67	1.56	1.50	1.46	1.40	1.37
1.3		2.17	1.80	1.68	1.62	1.58	1.52	1.48
1.4		2.33	1.94	1.81	1.74	1.70	1.63	1.60
1.5		2.50	2.08	1.94	1.86	1.81	1.75	1.71
1.6		2.66	2.21	2.06	1.98	1.93	1.86	1.82
1.7		2.82	2.35	2.19	2.11	2.05	1.98	1.93
1.8		2.98	2.48	2.32	2.23	2.17	2.09	2.05
1.9		3.15	2.62	2.44	2.35	2.29	2.21	2.16
2.0		3.31	2.76	2.57	2.47	2.41	2.32	2.27
2.1		3.48	2.89	2.70	2.60	2.53	2.44	2.39
2.2		3.64	3.03	2.83	2.72	2.65	2.55	2.50
2.3		3.80	3.16	2.95	2.84	2.77	2.67	2.61
2.4		3.97	3.30	3.08	2.97	2.89	2.79	2.73
2.5		4.13	3.44	3.21	3.09	3.01	2.90	2.84
2.6		4.29	3.57	3.34	3.21	3.13	3.02	2.95
2.7		4.46	3.71	3.46	3.33	3.25	3.13	3.07
2.8		4.62	3.85	3.59	3.46	3.37	3.25	3.18
2.9		4.79	3.98	3.72	3.58	3.49	3.36	3.29
3.0		4.95	4.12	3.85	3.70	3.61	3.48	3.41

c_1	n	125	150	200	250	300	350	400
0.7		0.80	0.79	0.78	0.77	0.76	0.76	0.75
0.8		0.91	0.90	0.88	0.87	0.87	0.86	0.86
0.9		1.02	1.01	0.99	0.98	0.97	0.97	0.96
1.0		1.13	1.12	1.10	1.09	1.08	1.07	1.07
1.1		1.24	1.23	1.21	1.20	1.19	1.18	1.17
1.2		1.35	1.34	1.32	1.30	1.29	1.29	1.28
1.3		1.46	1.45	1.42	1.41	1.40	1.39	1.39
1.4		1.57	1.56	1.53	1.52	1.51	1.50	1.49
1.5		1.68	1.67	1.64	1.63	1.61	1.60	1.60
1.6		1.80	1.78	1.75	1.73	1.72	1.71	1.70
1.7		1.91	1.89	1.86	1.84	1.83	1.82	1.81
1.8		2.02	2.00	1.97	1.95	1.93	1.92	1.92
1.9		2.13	2.11	2.08	2.06	2.04	2.03	2.02
2.0		2.24	2.22	2.19	2.16	2.15	2.14	2.13
2.1		2.35	2.33	2.29	2.27	2.26	2.24	2.23
2.2		2.46	2.44	2.40	2.38	2.36	2.35	2.34
2.3		2.58	2.55	2.51	2.49	2.47	2.46	2.45
2.4		2.69	2.66	2.62	2.60	2.58	2.56	2.55
2.5		2.80	2.77	2.73	2.70	2.68	2.67	2.66
2.6		2.91	2.88	2.84	2.81	2.79	2.78	2.76
2.7		3.02	2.99	2.95	2.92	2.90	2.88	2.87
2.8		3.13	3.10	3.06	3.03	3.01	2.99	2.98
2.9		3.25	3.21	3.17	3.14	3.11	3.10	3.08
3.0		3.36	3.32	3.27	3.24	3.22	3.20	3.19

TABLE 9.7 The Minimum Value $\hat{C}_{PK,MIN}$ of $\hat{C}_{PK}$ for Which the Process is Capable, that is, $C_{PK} \geq c_k$ 95% of the Time

c_k $\quad$ n	10	20	30	40	50	75	100
0.7	1.31	1.06	0.97	0.93	0.90	0.85	0.83
0.8	1.47	1.19	1.10	1.05	1.02	0.97	0.94
0.9	1.64	1.33	1.22	1.17	1.13	1.08	1.06
1.0	1.80	1.46	1.35	1.29	1.25	1.20	1.17
1.1	1.96	1.60	1.48	1.41	1.37	1.31	1.28
1.2	2.12	1.73	1.61	1.54	1.49	1.43	1.39
1.3	2.29	1.87	1.73	1.66	1.61	1.55	1.51
1.4	2.45	2.01	1.86	1.78	1.73	1.66	1.62
1.5	2.62	2.14	1.99	1.90	1.85	1.78	1.73
1.6	2.78	2.28	2.12	2.03	1.97	1.89	1.85
1.7	2.94	2.42	2.24	2.15	2.09	2.01	1.96
1.8	3.11	2.55	2.37	2.27	2.21	2.12	2.07
1.9	3.27	2.69	2.50	2.40	2.33	2.24	2.19
2.0	3.44	2.83	2.63	2.52	2.45	2.35	2.30
2.1	3.60	2.96	2.75	2.64	2.57	2.47	2.41
2.2	3.76	3.10	2.88	2.77	2.69	2.59	2.53
2.3	3.93	3.24	3.01	2.89	2.81	2.70	2.64
2.4	4.09	3.38	3.14	3.01	2.93	2.82	2.75
2.5	4.26	3.51	3.27	3.14	3.05	2.93	2.87
2.6	4.42	3.65	3.39	3.26	3.17	3.05	2.98
2.7	4.59	3.79	3.52	3.38	3.29	3.16	3.09
2.8	4.75	3.92	3.65	3.50	3.41	3.28	3.21
2.9	4.92	4.06	3.78	3.63	3.53	3.40	3.32
3.0	5.08	4.20	3.90	3.75	3.65	3.51	3.43

c_k $\quad$ n	125	150	200	250	300	350	400
0.7	0.82	0.80	0.79	0.78	0.77	0.77	0.76
0.8	0.93	0.91	0.90	0.89	0.88	0.87	0.87
0.9	1.04	1.02	1.01	0.99	.098	0.98	0.97
1.0	1.15	1.13	1.11	1.10	1.09	1.08	1.08
1.1	1.26	1.24	1.22	1.21	1.20	1.19	1.18
1.2	1.37	1.35	1.33	1.32	1.31	1.30	1.29
1.3	1.48	1.47	1.44	1.42	1.41	1.40	1.49
1.4	1.59	1.58	1.55	1.53	1.52	1.51	1.50
1.5	1.71	1.69	1.66	1.64	1.63	1.62	1.61
1.6	1.82	1.80	1.77	1.75	1.73	1.72	1.72
1.7	1.93	1.91	1.88	1.86	1.84	1.83	1.82
1.8	2.04	2.02	1.99	1.96	1.95	1.94	1.93
1.9	2.15	02.13	2.09	2.07	2.06	2.04	2.03
2.0	2.26	2.24	2.20	2.18	2.16	2.15	2.14
2.1	2.38	2.35	2.31	2.29	2.27	2.26	2.25
2.2	2.49	2.46	2.42	2.40	2.38	2.36	2.35
2.3	2.60	2.57	2.53	2.50	2.48	2.47	2.46
2.4	2.71	2.68	2.64	2.61	2.59	2.58	2.56
2.5	2.82	2.79	2.75	2.72	2.70	2.68	2.67
2.6	2.93	2.90	2.86	2.83	2.81	2.79	2.78
2.7	3.05	3.01	2.97	2.94	2.91	2.90	2.88
2.8	3.16	3.12	3.08	3.04	3.02	3.00	2.99
2.9	3.27	3.23	3.18	3.15	3.13	3.11	3.10
3.0	3.38	3.34	3.29	3.26	3.23	3.22	3.20

©1989 Reproduced with permission from the American Society for Quality Control.

The authors suggest a plug-in estimate of C_{PM} obtained by replacing the parameters μ and σ by $\bar{x}$ and s, respectively.

$$\hat{C}_{PM} = \frac{USL - LSL}{6\sqrt{s^2 + (\bar{x} - \tau)^2}} \tag{9.8.13}$$

We will not discuss the C_{PM} index further here. Interested readers should refer to the article by Chan et al. (1988). We will, however, consider the reciprocal of C_{PM} in the next section in some detail. We think that the reciprocal of C_{PM} is a more practical index because it has better inference properties.

9.8.3 Remarks on Computing Capability and Performance Indices in Practice

The above discussion of statistical inference issues in estimating either fallout or capability and performance indices has been in terms of a single sample. In actual practice it may sometimes be necessary to obtain a sample of values $x_1, \cdots, x_n$ for this purpose. However, this should often not be the case for the following reason.

We have emphasized the point that for these estimates to be meaningful it is necessary that the process be stable. This means that we must have a charting record of the process to establish that the process is, or was, in control. If such records are available, we can, of course, use the data to compute estimates of process capability. The data will often be subgrouped data rather than a single sample of individual measurements. With subgrouped data we can follow one of two approaches to estimating capability and performance.

If we feel very confident, based on a charting program, that both the process mean and standard deviation are constant, then we can pool all of the data into one large sample, and carry on. A more conservative approach would be to use the estimate of variance obtained by pooling the subgroups sample variances. If this pooled estimate of variance is used, then a question arises as to what should be used for sample size n to enter Tables 9.5, 9.6, and 9.7. We suggest using the degrees of freedom for the pooled mean squared estimate as a conservative value for n.

9.9 THE TAGUCHI QUADRATIC LOSS FUNCTION

The general approach of this section is due to Taguchi (1981), Chapter 2.

9.9.1   Variation Losses with Symmetric Specifications

In the preceding sections we have considered using target values and specification limits in inspection of units of products and in defining process capability. For X a quality variable with symmetric specification limits

$$\tau \pm \Delta, \text{ perhaps } 5 \pm 0.003 \text{ in, say}$$

we would declare a unit unacceptable if X is outside this interval, and acceptable if it is in the interval. This amounts to using a loss function, $L(x)$, defined as follows:

$$L(x) = 0, \text{ if } \tau - \Delta \leq x \leq \tau + \Delta$$

$$= \infty, \text{ otherwise}$$

This implies that we consider all values of X within specifications as being of equally good quality, and all values outside as bad, unacceptable quality. This is not a reasonable reflection of reality in many applications. The target value τ is presumably the ideal value for the functioning of the unit, and we would, if it were possible, make all parts with X equal to τ. Since this is not possible, we should prefer a loss function that gives less weight to points that are nearer target than to points that are farther away. We would like a loss function $L(x)$ that has the following four properties.

(a) $L(x) \geq 0$ for all x, and is expressed in dollars.
(b) $L(\tau) = 0$, because there should be no loss at $x = \tau$.
(c) $L'(\tau) = 0$, so the loss function has a minimum at $x = \tau$.
(d) $L(x)$ is expandable in a Taylor series about τ.

Then we write $L(X)$ in a Taylor series as follows:

$$L(X) = L(\tau) + \frac{L'(\tau)}{1!} (X - \tau) + \frac{L''(\tau)}{2!} (X - \tau)^2 + \cdots \quad (9.9.1)$$

Since $L(\tau) = L'(\tau) = 0$, we can write

$$L(X) \cong k(X - \tau)^2 \quad (9.9.2)$$

since this is the dominant term of the expansion. The value k is called the *loss parameter* or *loss constant*.

Now, if the value of an inspected unit is $X = \tau \pm \Delta$, then the unit is either trashed or reworked. Let C denote the cost (loss) of this rejected unit, expressed in dollars. Note that this is the overall production cost per unit. Then we have from (9.9.2)

$$k(\tau + \Delta - \tau)^2 = k\Delta^2 = C$$

and

$$k = \frac{C}{\Delta^2} \qquad (9.9.3)$$

As a simple example, suppose a transmission component has specifications of

$$\tau \pm \Delta = \tau \pm 6GS$$

where GS is "gauge scale." The overall cost to produce one component is $C = \$60$. If the measurement is at $\tau \pm 6$ the loss is therefore \$60. Then

$$k = \frac{C}{\Delta^2} = \frac{60}{36} = 1.67$$

The loss function is then

$$L = 1.67(X - \tau)^2$$

This is the loss from having one unit outside of tolerance. The *average loss* due to variation, *ALV*, is obtained by taking the expectation of (9.9.2) to obtain

$$ALV = E[k(X - \tau)^2] = k(EMS) = k[\sigma^2 + (\mu - \tau)^2] = k\,\sigma^2(1 + \delta^2)$$

$$(9.9.4)$$

where $\delta = (\mu - \tau)/\sigma$ is the standardized deviation of the process mean from process target value. The $EMS = \sigma^2 + (\mu - \tau)^2 = \sigma^2(1 + \delta^2)$ was discussed in sections 4.2 and 4.9.

Suppose that for this example $\tau = 20$ and from prior data we have estimates $\hat{\sigma} = 2$ and $\hat{\mu} = 19.5$. Then the average loss, *ALV*, is estimated by

$$\widehat{ALV} = 1.67\,[4 + (19.5 - 20)^2] = \$7.10 \text{ per unit of product}$$

If we wish to consider just the capability of a process to produce economically, and therefore assume $\mu = \tau$, or $\delta = 0$, then the *potential average loss* due to variation for such a process is

$$PALV = k\sigma^2 \qquad (9.9.5)$$

For this example, the process has an estimated potential average loss of

$$\widehat{PALV} = 1.67\sigma^2 = (1.67)(4) = \$6.67 \text{ per unit of product.}$$

To illustrate a possible use of this potential average loss function, suppose the company manufacturing these units is considering buying new equipment which will reduce σ from 2 to 1. Moreover, this equipment is estimated to produce at least 5,000,000 units over its life at an average cost of \$64 per unit. Thus, k for this new equipment would be

$$k_{new} = \frac{64}{36} = 1.78$$

and the potential average loss per unit would be

$$PALV = k_{new}\sigma_{new}^2 = (1.78)(1) = \$1.78$$

Thus, the potential savings per unit is

$$\$7.10 - \$1.78 = \$5.32 \text{ per unit.}$$

The potential savings over the estimated life of the new equipment would be

$$(5,000,000)(\$5.32) = \$26,600,000.$$

9.9.2 Losses with 100% Inspection

The loss function of (9.9.2) is for any value of the variable X and the average loss function of (9.9.4) assumes no restrictions on X, that is, that the units of product are not being inspected. However, this is not realistic in some applications because it is sometimes the practice to inspect all of the units (100% inspection) and ship only units within specifications. We need to assess the effect of 100% inspection on the loss due to variation. To assess this effect requires considering the conditional distribution of X given that $LSL \leq X \leq USL$. Let Y denote a random variable that has this conditional distribution. See density function in Fig. 9.11.

We investigate this distribution when:

X is a $N(\mu, \sigma^2)$ random variable
$\Delta_L = \Delta_U = \Delta$, the upper and lower allowances are equal
$\mu = \tau$, the process is "centered"

The density function of Y is

$$f(y) = I_{[\tau - \Delta, \tau + \Delta]}(y) \frac{1}{\sigma\sqrt{2\pi}} \frac{e^{-\frac{1}{2}\left(\frac{y-\tau}{\sigma}\right)^2}}{d}$$

where $I_{[a,b]}(y)$ is the indicator function of the interval $[a, b]$, $d = 2\Phi(\Delta/\sigma) - 1$, and $\Phi(\cdot)$ is the standard normal distribution function. The mean of this conditional distribution is clearly τ. We require the variance of this distribution, with 100% inspection, say $\mathrm{Var}(y) = \sigma^2_{100\%\text{ins}}$.

$$\sigma^2_{100\%\text{ins}} = E(Y - \tau)^2 = \frac{1}{d\sigma\sqrt{2\pi}} \int_{\tau - \Delta}^{\tau + \Delta} (y - \tau)^2 e^{-\frac{1}{2}\left(\frac{y-\tau}{\sigma}\right)^2} dy$$

Which, after some manipulation, we can rewrite as

$$\sigma^2_{100\%\text{ins}} = \sigma^2 \left[1 - \sqrt{\frac{2}{\pi}} \frac{\Delta}{d\sigma} e^{-\Delta^2/2\sigma^2} \right] \tag{9.9.6}$$

Note that this is a function only of the ratio Δ/σ of tolerance Δ to the

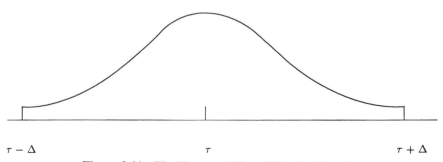

$\tau - \Delta$ $\qquad\qquad\qquad\qquad$ τ $\qquad\qquad\qquad\qquad$ $\tau + \Delta$

Figure 9.11   The Truncated Normal Density Function

standard deviation σ. Of course, the *PALV* for this case with 100% inspection is

$$PALV = k\sigma^2_{100\%ins} \qquad (9.9.7)$$

In the above example, the loss parameter was $k = 1.67$, $\sigma = 2$, and $\Delta = 6(= 3\sigma)$. Then $\Delta/\sigma = 3$ and

$$\sigma^2_{100\%ins} = \sigma^2 \left(1 - \sqrt{\frac{2}{\pi}} \frac{3e^{-9/2}}{d} \right) = 4 \left(1 - \frac{0.026591}{0.99730} \right) = 3.893$$

Therefore

$$PALV \text{ (with inspection)} = (1.67)(3.893) = \$6.50$$

Note that this compares with an *ALV* without inspection of $6.67, so inspection has resulted in a reduction in cost per unit from variation of only $6.67 − $6.58 = $0.17.

Actually, the losses, that is, costs, due to inspection itself should also be counted. Then the *potential average loss from variation and inspection, PALVI*, can be written as, say

$$
\boxed{
\begin{aligned}
PALVI = & \text{ (inspection cost per unit)} \\
& + \text{ (loss per defective found)} \\
& \times \text{ (fraction defective)} \\
& + k\sigma^2_{100\%ins}
\end{aligned}
}
\qquad (9.9.8)
$$

Suppose in the example the inspection cost per unit is $1.00, and the loss per defective is $70.00. From (9.9.8) we have it that the potential average loss from variation with 100% inspection is

$$PALVI = 1.00 + (70.00)(.00270) + (1.67)(0.97071)(4) = \$7.67$$

The lesson is that, at least for a normal process distribution with good process capability, it is sometimes not good practice to try to improve quality by inspection. This result is general and does not really depend on the special assumptions of this example. *Improvement in production cost must come from reduction in process variation,* and not from reduction in the conditional variance from inspection.

9.9.3 Variation from Losses with Nonsymmetric Specifications

Recall that the expected mean square, *EMS*, and observed mean square, *OMS*, were considered in section 4.2. Let X be a stable process variable with mean μ and variance σ^2, target value τ, and upper and lower tolerances Δ_U and Δ_L, respectively. That is

$$LSL = \tau - \Delta_L \quad \text{and} \quad USL = \tau + \Delta_U$$

Let $X_1, X_2, \cdots, X_n$ be a sample on X and let $X_{1,U}, \cdots, X_{y,U}$ denote the members of the sample, y in number, that fall on or above the target value τ; and let $X_{1,L}, \cdots, X_{n-y,L}$ denote the $n - y$ values that are below τ, but in both cases are indexed in the same order as the original sample. Next, we define the *upper observed mean square, UOMS*, and the *lower observed mean square, LOMS*, as

$$UOMS = \frac{1}{n} \sum_{i=1}^{y} (X_{i,U} - \tau)^2$$

$$LOMS = \frac{1}{n} \sum_{i=1}^{n-y} (X_{i,L} - \tau)^2$$

(9.9.9)

Small Example to Illustrate Notation   Suppose $\tau = 5.5$, $n = 5$, $X_1 = 5.6$, $X_2 = 5.5$, $X_3 = 5.3$, $X_4 = 5.8$, and $X_5 = 5.4$. Then $y = 3$; $X_{1,U} = 5.6$, $X_{2,U} = 5.5$, $X_{3,U} = 5.8$; $X_{1,L} = 5.3$, and $X_{2,L} = 5.4$. Then

$$UOMS = \frac{1}{n} \sum_{i=1}^{3} (X_{i,U} - \tau)^2 = \frac{1}{5}[(5.6 - 5.5)^2$$

$$+ (5.5 - 5.5)^2 + (5.8 - 5.5)^2] = 0.02$$

$$LOMS = \frac{1}{n} \sum_{i=1}^{2} (X_{i,L} - \tau)^2 = \frac{1}{5}[(5.3 - 5.5)^2$$

$$+ (5.4 - 5.5)^2] = 0.01 \quad \blacksquare$$

Let $f(x)$ denote the density function of the process variable X, which can be any density function. Next partition *EMS* into the *lower expected mean square, LEMS*, and the *upper expected mean square, UEMS*, as follows:

$$EMS = LEMS + UEMS \qquad (9.9.10)$$

$$LEMS = \int_{-\infty}^{\tau} (x - \tau)^2 f(x) \, dx$$

$$UEMS = \int_{\tau}^{\infty} (x - \tau)^2 f(x) dx$$

$$(9.9.11)$$

Then the following result is proved in Appendix 9.

UOMS and LOMS are unbiased estimates of UEMS and LEMS, respectively.

$$(9.9.12)$$

Note also that UOMS and LOMS can be expressed in the following forms:

$$UOMS = \frac{1}{n} \sum_{i=1}^{y} (X_{i,U} - \overline{X})^2 + \hat{p}(\overline{X} - \tau)^2$$
$$+ 2\hat{p}(\overline{X} - \tau)(\overline{X}_U - \overline{X})$$

$$(9.9.13)$$

$$LOMS = \frac{1}{n} \sum_{i=1}^{n-y} (X_{i,L} - \overline{X})^2 + (1 - \hat{p})(\overline{X} - \tau)^2$$
$$+ 2(1 - \hat{p})(\overline{X} - \tau)(\overline{X}_L - \overline{X})$$

$$(9.9.14)$$

where $\hat{p} = y/n$, $\overline{X}_U$ is the mean of the y values above τ, and $\overline{X}_L$ is the mean of the values below τ.

A number of interesting points can be observed in (9.9.13) and (9.9.14). The first terms on the right-hand side of these equations estimate variation due to the overall variance σ^2. The second terms estimate variation due to lack of centering of the mean μ at the target τ. The third terms are interaction terms that require some study. First, since $\overline{X}_L \leq \overline{X} \leq \overline{X}_U$ the third terms are of opposite signs. In fact, since

$$OMS = UOMS + LOMS = \left(\frac{n-1}{n} \right) S^2 + (\overline{X} - \tau)^2$$

the sum of the third terms in (9.9.13) and (9.9.14) is zero, which can also be readily shown algebraically.

We see that $UOMS$ and $LOMS$ partition the total observed variation about target value into components that are unbiased estimates of the process variation above ($UEMS$) and below ($LEMS$) target value. This partitioning permits us to define and estimate average losses due to lower and upper variation as follows.

$$ALV_L = k_L \ LEMS, \ ALV_U = k_U \ UEMS$$

where

$$k_L = \frac{C_L}{\Delta_L^2}, \ k_U = \frac{C_U}{\Delta_U^2}$$

$$ALV = ALV_L + ALV_U$$

(9.9.15)

The values C_L and C_U are the costs at $X = \tau - \Delta_L$ and $X = \tau \ \Delta_U$. Sometimes $C_L = C_U = C$, say.

Unbiased estimates of ALV_L and ALV_U are obtained by replacing $LEMS$ and $UEMS$ by $LOMS$ and $UOMS$ in (9.9.15). That is

$$\widehat{ALV}_L = K_L LOMS, \ \widehat{ALV}_U = k_U UOMS$$

and

$$\widehat{ALV} = \widehat{ALV}_L + \widehat{ALV}_U$$

(9.9.16)

are unbiased estimates of ALV_L, ALV_U, and ALV.

Example 9.9: A process variable with $\tau = 5.00$, $\Delta_L = 0.06$, $\Delta_U = 0.05$, and $C_L = C_U = \$21$, gave the following sample of 20 values.

4.97	5.01	4.98	4.98	5.00	5.00	4.99	4.99	4.98	4.98
4.99	5.01	5.02	5.01	4.96	4.99	4.96	4.99	4.97	4.96

$$UOMS = \frac{1}{20}[(5.01 - 5.00)^2 + (0.00)^2 + (0.00)^2 + (0.01)^2$$

$$+ \cdots + (0.01)^2] = \frac{1}{20}(0.0007) = 0.000035$$

$$LOMS = \frac{1}{20}[(4.97 - 5.00)^2 + (4.98 - 5.00)^2 + \cdots$$

$$+ (4.96 - 5.00)^2] = \frac{1}{20}(0.0087) = 0.000435$$

$$\overline{X} = 4.987, \quad OMS = LOMS + UOMS = 0.00047$$

Now,

$$k_L = \frac{21}{(0.06)^2} = 5833, \quad k_U = \frac{21}{(.05)^2} = 8400.$$

Then

$$\widehat{ALV_L} = (5833)(0.000435) = \$2.54$$

$$\widehat{ALV_U} = (8400)(0.000035) = \$0.29$$

$$\widehat{ALV} = \widehat{ALV_L} + \widehat{ALV_U} = \$2.83 \qquad \blacksquare$$

Note that the mean estimate is $\overline{X} = 4.987$ and $S = 0.02$ indicates also that the process is off center below $\tau = 5$, and it is adding a significant cost.

Although this is an unbiased estimate of ALV, a question arises as to how good it is. In order to obtain a confidence interval and results for sample size determination, we next assume a normal process distribution of X.

9.9.4 Special Results for a Normal Process Distribution

We consider next confidence interval estimation and sample size determination issues for *EMS* and *ALV*, under the assumption that $X_1, \cdots, X_n$ is a sample from a $N(\mu, \sigma^2)$ process distribution. Then the sum

$$\sum_{i=1}^{n}\left(\frac{X_i - \tau}{\sigma}\right)^2 = \sum_{i=1}^{n}\left[\left(\frac{X_i - \mu}{\sigma}\right) + \left(\frac{\mu - \tau}{\sigma}\right)\right]^2$$

is a noncentral chi-squared random variable with n degrees of freedom and noncentrality parameter

$$\lambda = n\left(\frac{\mu - \tau}{\sigma}\right)^2 = n\delta^2, \text{ for } \delta = \frac{\mu - \tau}{\sigma}$$

Denote this noncentral chi-squared random variable by $\chi_n'^2$.

We shall use the result in (9.9.17) due to Sankaran (1959). It should be noted that this distribution depends only on the sample size n and the standardized deviation of the mean from target δ.

For $\chi_n'^2$ a noncentral chi-squared random variable with n degrees of freedom and noncentrality parameter λ, then

$$Z = \left(\frac{\chi_n'^2}{n + \lambda}\right)^h$$

is approximately a $N(m, V)$ random variable for

$$h = 1 - \frac{2}{3}\frac{(n + \lambda)(n + 3\lambda)}{(n + 2\lambda)^2}$$

$$m = 1 + h(h - 1)\frac{n + 2\lambda}{(n + \lambda)^2} - h(h - 1)(2 - h)$$

$$\times (1 - 3h)\frac{(n + 2\lambda)^2}{2(n + \lambda)^4}$$

$$V = h^2 \frac{2(n + 2\lambda)}{(n + \lambda)^2}\left[1 - (1 - h)(1 - 3h)\right.$$

$$\left.\times \frac{n + 2\lambda}{(n + \lambda)^2}\right]$$

(9.9.17)

Using this approximation, we obtain the result in (9.9.18).

$$P\left\{\frac{OMS}{\left[m + z_{\alpha/2}\sqrt{V}\right]^{1/h}} \leq EMS \leq \frac{OMS}{\left[m - z_{\alpha/2}\sqrt{V}\right]^{1/h}}\right\} \cong 1 - \alpha$$

(9.9.18)

This result is summarized as follows.

An approximate $1 - \alpha$ confidence interval for *EMS* is given by the values:

$$\left(\frac{OMS}{A_{\alpha/2}}, \frac{OMS}{B_{\alpha/2}}\right) \qquad (9.9.19)$$

for $A_{\alpha/2} = (m + z_{\alpha/2}\sqrt{V})^{1/h}$, $B_{\alpha/2} = (m - z_{\alpha/2}\sqrt{V})^{1/h}$

We are primarily concerned that *EMS* (and *ALV*) not be too large. A $100(1 - \alpha)\%$ upper confidence bound for EMS is given by c_α for

$$c_\alpha = \frac{OMS}{B_\alpha}, \quad B_\alpha = (m - z_\alpha\sqrt{V})^{1/h} \qquad (9.9.20)$$

Suppose that we specify an *acceptable performance level* of *EMS*, say EMS_{APL}. This is the highest level that we consider tolerable. Then if we set EMS_{APL} equal to c_α in (9.9.20), we can write

$$\widehat{OMS}_{MAX} \equiv (EMS_{APL})(m - z_\alpha\sqrt{V})^{1/h} = (EMS_{APL})B_\alpha \geq OMS \quad (9.9.21)$$

When this inequality is satisfied, the process is performing at a level of EMS_{APL} or better $100(1 - \alpha)\%$ of the time. Now, the quantity $\widehat{OMS}_{MAX}$ is a function of EMS_{APL}, σ, δ, and n. However, since $EMS = \sigma^2(1 + \delta^2)$, in general, we will specify EMS_{APL} by specifying an acceptable performance level for $\delta = (\mu - \tau)/\sigma$, the standardized deviation of the process mean from target. We denote this value by δ_{APL}. Values of B_α for $\alpha = 0.05$ are given in Table 9.9 for selected values of n and $100\delta^2$.

The partitioning results of (9.9.10) were for any distribution. For the normal distribution assumed in this subsection, more detailed results are possible. For this normal distribution, *UEMS* and *LEMS* are multiples of σ^2 that depend only on the standardized deviation δ as given in (9.9.22).

If X has a $N(\mu, \sigma^2)$ process distribution and target value τ, then

$$UEMS = \sigma^2 \left\{ (1 + \delta^2)\Phi(\delta) + \frac{\delta e^{-\delta^2/2}}{\sqrt{2\pi}} \right\}$$

$$= \sigma^2 U_\delta$$

$$LEMS = \sigma^2 \left\{ (1 + \sigma^2)\Phi(-\delta) - \frac{\delta e^{-\delta^2/2}}{\sqrt{2\pi}} \right\}$$

$$= \sigma^2 L_\delta$$

The inflation of EMS due to lack of centering, $1 + \delta^2$, can be written as $1 + \delta^2 = U_\delta + L_\delta$

(9.9.22)

Table 9.8 gives values of $1 + \delta^2$, U_δ, and L_δ computed from the formulas of (9.9.22) for $\delta = 0(0.1)2$. Note that $U_{-\delta} = L_\delta$, so that

TABLE 9.8   Inflation Factors of EMS, LEMS, and UEMS as Functions of δ, Normal Distribution

δ	$1 + \delta^2$	L_δ	U_δ
0.0	1.000	0.500	0.500
0.1	1.010	0.585	0.425
0.2	1.040	0.681	0.359
0.3	1.090	0.788	0.302
0.4	1.160	0.908	0.252
0.5	1.250	1.040	0.210
0.6	1.360	1.187	0.173
0.7	1.490	1.348	0.142
0.8	1.640	1.524	0.116
0.9	1.810	1.716	0.094
1.0	2.000	1.925	0.075
1.1	2.210	2.150	0.060
1.2	2.440	2.392	0.048
1.3	2.690	2.652	0.038
1.4	2.960	2.931	0.029
1.5	3.250	3.227	0.023
1.6	3.560	3.542	0.018
1.7	3.890	3.877	0.013
1.8	4.240	4.230	0.010
1.9	4.610	4.602	0.008
2.0	5.000	4.994	0.006

we need not consider negative values of δ separately. To illustrate the interpretation of the formulas in display (9.9.22) and the values in Table 9.8 computed from them, consider the line in Fig. 9.12. For these values of τ, μ, and σ, we have $\delta = (\mu - \tau)/\sigma = -0.5\sigma/\sigma = -0.5$. Thus for these values $EMS^- = \sigma^2(1 + \delta^2) = 1.25\ \sigma^2$. In other words, the EMS is inflated by 25% from having the mean be one-half a standard deviation above target. Note also that the two component terms of the inflation factor due to lack of centering, that is, due to bias, $1 + \delta^2$, are $U_\delta = 0.210$ and $L_\delta = 1.040$ from Table 9.8. This also means that for any value of the loss constant k the loss or cost of variation from not having the process centered is increased 25%.

To obtain a confidence interval for the average loss from variation, ALV, we simply multiply the limits for EMS in (9.9.19) by the loss parameter k. Also,

$$\widehat{ALV}_{MAX} = k(\widehat{OMS}_{MAX}) \tag{9.9.23}$$

is the maximum value that the estimate $\widehat{ALV}$ can have to assure that ALV is less than an *acceptable cost level, $k \times EMS_{\text{APL}}$.*

Example 9.10: A process has

$$\text{Target value: } \tau = 5.00$$

$$\text{Allowances: } \Delta_L = \Delta_U = \Delta = 0.09$$

$$\text{Costs or losses: } C_L = C_U = \$8.00$$

The process has been charted in an SPC program and is stable with an estimated variance of approximately $\sigma^2 = 0.0009$. If a 5% increase in production cost is considered acceptable performance, we evaluate $\widehat{OMS}_{MAX}$ for $n = 20, 50, 100, 200, 400$. From Table 9.9 we read the vaues of B_α for $\alpha = 0.05$.

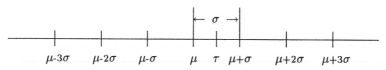

Figure 9.12   Configuration of τ, μ, and σ that give $\delta = -0.5$

TABLE 9.9 B_α to Compute $\widehat{OMS}_{MAX}$ and $\widehat{ALV}_{MAX}$, $\alpha = 0.05$

$100\delta^2$	δ	n:10	20	30	40	50	75	100	125
1	0.1000	0.3942	0.5435	0.6175	0.6637	0.6963	0.7482	0.7801	0.8021
2	0.1414	0.3953	0.5446	0.6185	0.6647	0.6971	0.7490	0.7808	0.8028
3	0.1732	0.3963	0.5456	0.6194	0.6655	0.6979	0.7497	0.7814	0.8033
4	0.2000	0.3972	0.5466	0.6203	0.6663	0.6987	0.7504	0.7820	0.8039
5	0.2236	0.3982	0.5475	0.6211	0.6671	0.6994	0.7510	0.7825	0.8044
6	0.2449	0.3991	0.5484	0.6219	0.6679	0.7001	0.7516	0.7830	0.8049
7	0.2646	0.4000	0.5492	0.6227	0.6686	0.7007	0.7521	0.7836	0.8053
8	0.2828	0.4009	0.5500	0.6234	0.6692	0.7014	0.7527	0.7840	0.8058
9	0.3000	0.4017	0.5508	0.6241	0.6699	0.7020	0.7532	0.7845	0.8062
10	0.3162	0.4025	0.5516	0.6248	0.6705	0.7026	0.7537	0.7850	0.8066
11	0.3317	0.4034	0.5523	0.6255	0.6712	0.7032	0.7542	0.7854	0.8070
12	0.3464	0.4042	0.5531	0.6262	0.6718	0.7037	0.7547	0.7858	0.8074
13	0.3606	0.4049	0.5538	0.6268	0.6724	0.7043	0.7552	0.7863	0.8078
14	0.3742	0.4057	0.5545	0.6275	0.6729	0.7048	0.7556	0.7867	0.8082
15	0.3873	0.4065	0.5552	0.6281	0.6735	0.7053	0.7561	0.7871	0.8085
16	0.4000	0.4072	0.5559	0.6287	0.6740	0.7058	0.7565	0.7874	0.8089
17	0.4123	0.4079	0.5565	0.6293	0.6746	0.7063	0.7569	0.7878	0.8092
18	0.4243	0.4086	0.5572	0.6298	0.6751	0.7068	0.7573	0.7882	0.8095
19	0.4359	0.4093	0.5578	0.6304	0.6756	0.7073	0.7577	0.7885	0.8099
20	0.4472	0.4100	0.5584	0.6310	0.6761	0.7077	0.7581	0.7889	0.8102
21	0.4583	0.4107	0.5590	0.6315	0.6766	0.7082	0.7585	0.7892	0.8105
22	0.4690	0.4114	0.5596	0.6320	0.6771	0.7086	0.7589	0.7896	0.8108
23	0.4796	0.4121	0.5602	0.6326	0.6776	0.7091	0.7593	0.7899	0.8111
24	0.4899	0.4127	0.5608	0.6331	0.6780	0.7095	0.7596	0.7902	0.8114
25	0.5000	0.4134	0.5614	0.6336	0.6785	0.7099	0.7600	0.7906	0.8117
26	0.5099	0.4140	0.5619	0.6341	0.6789	0.7103	0.7604	0.7909	0.8120
27	0.5196	0.4146	0.5625	0.6346	0.6794	0.7108	0.7607	0.7912	0.8123
28	0.5292	0.4153	0.5630	0.6351	0.6798	0.7112	0.7611	0.7915	0.8126
29	0.5385	0.4159	0.5636	0.6355	0.6803	0.7116	0.7614	0.7918	0.8128
30	0.5477	0.4165	0.5641	0.6360	0.6807	0.7119	0.7617	0.7921	0.8131
31	0.5568	0.4171	0.5646	0.6365	0.6811	0.7123	0.7621	0.7924	0.8134
32	0.5657	0.4177	0.5651	0.6369	0.6815	0.7127	0.7624	0.7927	0.8136
33	0.5745	0.4183	0.5656	0.6374	0.6819	0.7131	0.7627	0.7930	0.8139
34	0.5831	0.4188	0.5662	0.6378	0.6823	0.7135	0.7630	0.7932	0.8141
35	0.5916	0.4194	0.5666	0.6383	0.6827	0.7138	0.7633	0.7935	0.8144
36	0.6000	0.4200	0.5671	0.6387	0.6831	0.7142	0.7636	0.7938	0.8146
37	0.6083	0.4205	0.5676	0.6391	0.6835	0.7145	0.7639	0.7940	0.8149
38	0.6164	0.4211	0.5681	0.6395	0.6839	0.7149	0.7642	0.7943	0.8151
39	0.6245	0.4216	0.5686	0.6400	0.6843	0.7152	0.7645	0.7946	0.8153
40	0.6325	0.4222	0.5690	0.6404	0.6846	0.7156	0.7648	0.7948	0.8156
41	0.6403	0.4227	0.5695	0.6408	0.6850	0.7159	0.7651	0.7951	0.8158
42	0.6481	0.4232	0.5700	0.6412	0.6854	0.7162	0.7654	0.7953	0.8160
43	0.6557	0.4238	0.5704	0.6416	0.6857	0.7166	0.7657	0.7956	0.8163
44	0.6633	0.4243	0.5709	0.6420	0.6861	0.7169	0.7659	0.7958	0.8165
45	0.6708	0.4248	0.5713	0.6424	0.6864	0.7172	0.7662	0.7961	0.8167
46	0.6782	0.4253	0.5717	0.6427	0.6868	0.7175	0.7665	0.7963	0.8169
47	0.6856	0.4258	0.5722	0.6431	0.6871	0.7179	0.7668	0.7965	0.8171
48	0.6928	0.4263	0.5726	0.6435	0.6875	0.7182	0.7670	0.7968	0.8173
49	0.7000	0.4268	0.5730	0.6439	0.6878	0.7185	0.7673	0.7970	0.8176
50	0.7071	0.4273	0.5735	0.6442	0.6881	0.7188	0.7675	0.7972	0.8178

TABLE 9.9 **(Continued)**

$100\delta^2$	δ	n:150	200	250	300	350	400
1	0.1000	0.8186	0.8420	0.8581	0.8701	0.8795	0.8870
2	0.1414	0.8192	0.8425	0.8586	0.8705	0.8799	0.8874
3	0.1732	0.8197	0.8430	0.8590	0.8709	0.8802	0.8878
4	0.2000	0.8202	0.8434	0.8594	0.8713	0.8806	0.8881
5	0.2236	0.8207	0.8438	0.8598	0.8716	0.8809	0.8884
6	0.2449	0.8211	0.8442	0.8601	0.8720	0.8812	0.8887
7	0.2646	0.8216	0.8446	0.8605	0.8723	0.8815	0.8890
8	0.2828	0.8220	0.8450	0.8608	0.8726	0.8818	0.8892
9	0.3000	0.8224	0.8453	0.8611	0.8729	0.8821	0.8895
10	0.3162	0.8228	0.8457	0.8614	0.8732	0.8823	0.8897
11	0.3317	0.8231	0.8460	0.8617	0.8734	0.8826	0.8900
12	0.3464	0.8235	0.8463	0.8620	0.8737	0.8828	0.8902
13	0.3606	0.8238	0.8466	0.8623	0.8740	0.8831	0.8904
14	0.3742	0.8242	0.8469	0.8626	0.8742	0.8833	0.8907
15	0.3873	0.8245	0.8472	0.8628	0.8745	0.8835	0.8909
16	0.4000	0.8248	0.8475	0.8631	0.8747	0.8837	0.8911
17	0.4123	0.8252	0.8478	0.8633	0.8749	0.8840	0.8913
18	0.4243	0.8255	0.8480	0.8636	0.8751	0.8842	0.8915
19	0.4359	0.8258	0.8483	0.8638	0.8754	0.8844	0.8917
20	0.4472	0.8261	0.8486	0.8641	0.8756	0.8846	0.8919
21	0.4583	0.8264	0.8488	0.8643	0.8758	0.8848	0.8921
22	0.4690	0.8266	0.8491	0.8645	0.8760	0.8850	0.8922
23	0.4796	0.8269	0.8493	0.8648	0.8762	0.8852	0.8924
24	0.4899	0.8272	0.8496	0.8650	0.8764	0.8854	0.8926
25	0.5000	0.8275	0.8498	0.8652	0.8766	0.8855	0.8928
26	0.5099	0.8277	0.8500	0.8654	0.8768	0.8857	0.8929
27	0.5196	0.8280	0.8503	0.8656	0.8770	0.8859	0.8931
28	0.5292	0.8282	0.8505	0.8658	0.8772	0.8861	0.8933
29	0.5385	0.8285	0.8507	0.8660	0.8774	0.8862	0.8934
30	0.5477	0.8287	0.8509	0.8662	0.8776	0.8864	0.8936
31	0.5568	0.8290	0.8511	0.8664	0.8777	0.8866	0.8937
32	0.5657	0.8292	0.8514	0.8666	0.8779	0.8867	0.8939
33	0.5745	0.8295	0.8516	0.8668	0.8781	0.8869	0.8940
34	0.5831	0.8297	0.8518	0.8670	0.8783	0.8871	0.8942
35	0.5916	0.8299	0.8520	0.8671	0.8784	0.8872	0.8943
36	0.6000	0.8302	0.8522	0.8673	0.8786	0.8874	0.8945
37	0.6083	0.8304	0.8524	0.8675	0.8787	0.8875	0.8946
38	0.6164	0.8306	0.8526	0.8677	0.8789	0.8877	0.8948
39	0.6245	0.8308	0.8528	0.8679	0.8791	0.8878	0.8949
40	0.6325	0.8310	0.8529	0.8680	0.8792	0.8880	0.8950
41	0.6403	0.8313	0.8531	0.8682	0.8794	0.8881	0.8952
42	0.6481	0.8315	0.8533	0.8684	0.8795	0.8883	0.8953
43	0.6557	0.8317	0.8535	0.8685	0.8797	0.8884	0.8955
44	0.6633	0.8319	0.8537	0.8687	0.8798	0.8885	0.8956
45	0.6708	0.8321	0.8539	0.8689	0.8800	0.8887	0.8957
46	0.6782	0.8323	0.8540	0.8690	0.8801	0.8888	0.8958
47	0.6856	0.8325	0.8542	0.8692	0.8803	0.8889	0.8960
48	0.6928	0.8327	0.8544	0.8693	0.8804	0.8891	0.8961
49	0.7000	0.8329	0.8545	0.8695	0.8806	0.8892	0.8962
50	0.7071	0.8331	0.8547	0.8696	0.8807	0.8893	0.8963

n	$B_{0.05}$	EMS_{APL}	$\widehat{OMS}_{MAX}$	$\widehat{ALV}_{MAX}$
20	0.5475	0.000945	0.000517	$0.51
50	0.6994	0.000945	0.000661	$0.65
100	0.7825	0.000945	0.000729	$0.73
200	0.8438	0.000945	0.000797	$0.79
400	0.8884	0.000945	0.000840	$0.83

For $n = 20$ we compute $EMS_{APL} = (1 + \delta^2) \times \sigma^2 = 1.05 \times \sigma^2 = (1.05) \times (0.0009) = 0.000945$, and $\widehat{OMS}_{MAX} = EMS_{APL} \times B_{0.05} = (0.000945) \times (0.5475)$. The loss constant is

$$k = \frac{c}{\Delta^2} = \frac{8.00}{(0.09)^2} = 987.6.$$

A sample of size $n = 100$ observations was taken and gave the following estimates.

$$\bar{x} = 4.99, \ S = 0.029$$

$$LOMS = 0.000675, \ UOMS = 0.000259$$

$$OMS = 0.0000933$$

$$\widehat{ALV} = (987.6)(0.000933) = \$0.92$$

Note that this value of OMS is larger than the value of $\widehat{OMS}_{MAX} = 0.000739$ given above for $n = 100$, and this value of $\widehat{ALV} = \$0.92$ exceeds the value of $\widehat{ALV}_{MAX} = \$0.73$ given above. The process is not operating within the 5% increase over potential considered acceptable. ∎

9.9.5 The C_Q Performance Ratio, Definition, and Properties

In section 9.8, C_{PM} were defined as a measure of product performance. However, this index has the undesirable feature that it is essentially the reciprocal of the square root of the expected mean square. While EMS can be partitioned in a natural way into lower and upper components of variation about τ, $LEMS$, and $UEMS$, and all three of these expected mean squares admit natural unbiased estimates of OMS, $LOMS$, and

UOMS, respectively, the reciprocal of *EMS* does not have comparable properties. Thus we define a performance ratio that is the reciprocal of C_{PM} index.

The process *performance ratio* C_Q is a general measure of process performance defined by

$$C_Q^2 = \frac{36\ EMS}{(USL - LSL)^2} = \frac{36[\sigma^2 + (\mu - \tau)^2]}{(USL - LSL)^2} \qquad (9.9.24)$$

Since $E(OMS) = EMS$, we estimate C_Q^2 by

$$\hat{C}_Q^2 = \frac{36\ OMS}{(USL - LSL)^2} = \frac{36 \sum\limits_{i=1}^{n} (x_i - \tau)^2}{n(USL - LSL)^2} \qquad (9.9.25)$$

From display (9.9.12), *UOMS* and *LOMS* partition the total observed variation about target value into components that are unbiased estimates of the process variation above (*UEMS*) and below (*LEMS*) target value. This partitioning permits us to define and estimate performance ratios for variation above target value, C_{QU}, and below target value, C_{QL}. This is particularly useful when the upper and lower allowances, Δ_U and Δ_L, are not equal. Define

$$C_{QU}^2 = \frac{9\ UEMS}{\Delta_U^2}$$

$$C_{QL}^2 = \frac{9\ LEMS}{\Delta_L^2}$$

and $\qquad\qquad\qquad\qquad\qquad\qquad\qquad\qquad (9.9.26)$

$$\hat{C}_{QU}^2 = \frac{9\ UOMS}{\Delta_U^2}$$

$$\hat{C}_{QL}^2 = \frac{9\ LOMS}{\Delta_L^2}$$

From (9.9.12) it follows that

$$E(\hat{C}_{QL}^2) = C_{QL}^2 \quad \text{and} \quad E(\hat{C}_{QU}^2) = C_{QU}^2 \qquad (9.9.27)$$

Moreover, when $\Delta_U = \Delta_L = (USL - LSL)/2$, that is, $\tau = (LSL + USL)/2$, then

$$
\begin{aligned}
\text{and} \qquad C_{QU}^2 + C_{QL}^2 &= C_Q^2 \\
\hat{C}_{QU}^2 + \hat{C}_{QL}^2 &= \hat{C}_Q^2
\end{aligned}
\qquad (9.9.28)
$$

The equations (9.9.28) show that C_{QL} and C_{QU} ($\hat{C}_{QU}$ and $\hat{C}_{QL}$) are related to C_Q ($\hat{C}_Q$) in the same relationship (Pythagorean relation) as the sides of a right triangle are related to the hypotenuse. Therefore, the performance and centering of a process can be conveniently summarized by a sketch of the C_Q *performance triangle.*

If a normal process distribution is assumed, the equation in (9.9.18) can be used to give a $1 - \alpha$ confidence interval for C_Q as in (9.9.29).

$$
\boxed{
\begin{array}{l}
\text{An approximate } 1 - \alpha \text{ confidence interval for } C_Q \text{ is} \\
\text{given by} \\[6pt]
\qquad \left(\dfrac{\hat{C}_Q}{\sqrt{A_{\alpha/2}}}, \dfrac{\hat{C}_Q}{\sqrt{B_{\alpha/2}}} \right) \\[12pt]
\text{for } A_{\alpha/2} = (m + z_{\alpha/2}\sqrt{V})^{1/h}, \; B_{\alpha/2} = (m - z_{\alpha/2}\sqrt{V})^{1/h}
\end{array}
}
\qquad (9.9.29)
$$

Recall that m, h, and V are defined in display (9.9.17).

We are primarily concerned that C_Q not be too large. A $100(1 - \alpha)\%$ upper confidence bound for C_Q is given by c for

$$c = \frac{\hat{C}_Q}{\sqrt{B\alpha}}, \quad B_\alpha = (m - z_\alpha \sqrt{V})^{1/h} \tag{9.9.30}$$

Suppose that we specify a value of C_Q, say $C_{Q, APL}$, that is an *acceptable performance level*. This is the highest level that we consider tolerable. Then if we set $C_{Q, APL}$ equal to c in (9.9.30), we can write

$$\hat{C}_{Q, MAX} \equiv C_{Q, APL}(m - z_\alpha \sqrt{V})^{1/2h} = \sqrt{B_\alpha} \, C_{Q, APL} \geq \hat{C}_Q \tag{9.9.31}$$

When this inequality is satisfied, the process is performing at a level of $C_{Q, APL}$ or better $100(1 - \alpha)\%$ of the time. The values of B_α can be obtained from Table 9.9 for $\alpha = 0.05$ and selected values of n and δ.

To decide what are reasonable values of C_Q, note from (9.2.24) that when the process is centerd with $\mu = \tau$ then C_Q is the same as the capability ratio C_r given in (9.8.1), which is the reciprocal of the capability ratio C_p. Whereas large values of C_p are desirable, small values of C_r and C_Q are desirable, and therefore the reciprocals of the values in Table 9.4 are reasonable upper bounds for C_r and C_Q. These values can be used as values of $C_{Q,APL}$ in (9.9.31).

Example 9.11: A process has

$$\text{Target value: } \tau = 7.35 \text{ cm}$$

$$\text{Allowances: } \delta_L = \Delta_U = 0.02 \text{ cm}$$

A sample of size $n = 100$ gave $\bar{x} = 7.353$, $s = 0.005$, $LOMS = 0.000029675$, and $UOMS = 0.000004325$. From these values we compute

$$\hat{\delta} = \frac{\bar{x} - \tau}{s} = \frac{7.353 - 7.35}{0.005} = 0.6$$

$$\hat{C}_{QL}^2 = \frac{9(0.000029675)}{(0.02)^2} = 0.67, \ \hat{C}_{QL} = 0.82$$

$$\hat{C}_{QU}^2 = \frac{9(0.000004325)}{(0.02)^2} = 0.10, \ \hat{C}_{QU} = 0.32$$

$$\hat{C}_Q^2 = \hat{C}_{QL}^2 + \hat{C}_{QU}^2 = 0.67 + 0.10 = 0.77, \ \hat{C}_Q = 0.88$$

To sketch the C_Q performance triangle, put $\theta = \sin^{-1}(\hat{C}_{QU}/\hat{C}_Q) = \sin^{-1}(0.32/0.88) = 21.3°$. This performance triangle is then as follows.

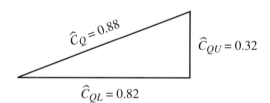

Suppose we use the value 1.33 from Table 9.4 and put $C_{Q, APL} = 1/1.33 = 0.75$. For $\delta = 0.6$ then $100\delta^2 = 36$, and for this value and $n = 100$ we read $B_{0.05} = 0.7838$ from Table 9.9. Then

$$\hat{C}_{Q, MAX} = \sqrt{B_{0.05}} \ C_{Q, APL} = \sqrt{0.7938} \ (0.75) = 0.67$$

Since the observed value of $\hat{C}_Q = 0.88$ exceeds this vaue, this condition is not being met by the process at present. From the performance triangle it is apparent that the process is substantially off center. The process is centered above the target value, of course. ∎

9.9.6 Results for Right Skewed Positive Distributions

Shewhart (1931) asserted that most industrial measurements that are not normally distributed have positive right skewed distributions. Such measurements include: Brinell hardness, surface finish smoothness, out-of-round, and so on. Suppose the distribution is of the general shape of Fig. 9.13. Actually, it is only required to assume that measurements must be as large or larger than a target value τ, and not necessarily nonnegative, because we can subtract τ from the measurements and work with these differences, which are nonnegative.

Thus we assume a sample $X_1, X_2, \cdots, X_n$ on a nonnegative random variable X with a right skewed distribution as shown in Fig. 9.13. Note that Δ is the upper tolerance bound.

Note that since zero is the target value and also is the lower terminal of the distribution, the term $(\tau - \mu)^2$ is always a significant part of $EMS = (\tau - \mu)^2 + \sigma^2$. Thus, we must consider the average loss from variation, ALV; and not just the potential average loss from variation, $PALV$, because $PALV$ cannot be achieved by centering the distribution.

Let C denote the loss from having a unit of product exceed the $USL = \Delta$. The loss parameter is $k = C/\Delta^2$ and

$$ALV = k \times EMS = k(\mu^2 + \sigma^2)$$

This is estimated by

$$\widehat{ALV} = k \times OMS = \frac{k}{n} \sum_{i=1}^{n} X_i^2 \qquad (9.9.32)$$

We wish to find an upper confidence bound for EMS and ALV. By

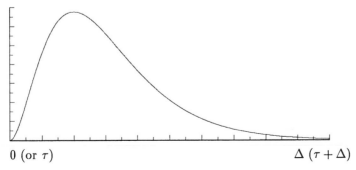

Figure 9.13 Right-Skewed Positive Distribution

the Central Limit Theorem, the *OMS* is itself distributed with a normal $N(E(X^2), VAR(X^2)/n)$ distribution, for n sufficiently large. Since X has a unimodal distribution on positive numbers, X^2 also has a unimodal distribution and normality will obtain fairly quickly. We will use this normal distribution to obtain confidence bounds for *EMS* and *ALV*. To do so we consider the situation when prior samples and values of *OMS* are available.

Prior Samples Available

Suppose that m samples of size n have been taken and estimates OMS_1, OMS_2, $\cdots$, OMS_m from these samples are available. Then let $\widehat{OMS}$ and S^2_{OMS} denote the sample mean and variance from this sample from the distribution of *OMS*. Then an approximate $100(1 - \alpha)\%$ confidence interval for *EMS* is given by (9.9.33).

$$\widehat{OMS} \pm t_{\alpha/2,\, m-1}\frac{S_{OMS}}{\sqrt{m}} \qquad (9.9.33)$$

A $100(1 - \alpha)\%$ upper confidence bound for EMS is given by (9.9.34)

$$\widehat{OMS} + t_{\alpha,\, m-1}\frac{S_{OMS}}{\sqrt{m}} \qquad (9.9.34)$$

Confidence intervals and an upper confidence bound for the average loss from variation, *ALV*, can be obtained by multiplying the confidence bounds in (9.9.33) and (9.9.34) by the loss parameter k.

Example 9.12: Five samples of size $n = 50$ measurements each were taken on a total indicator runout (TIR) measurement. The target value is $\tau = 0$, the specification (upper) is $\Delta = 3.50$, and measurements have a right skewed distribution. Units that exceed $\Delta = 3.50$ are scrapped at a cost (loss) of $C = \$61$ per unit. The values of OMS from the five runs were: 2.39, 2.30, 1.83, 2.73, 1.30. Compute 95% upper confidence bounds for EMS and ALV.

Solution: For $n = 50$ the normal approximation for the distribution of OMS should be reasonable.
Then

$$\widehat{OMS} = 2.11, \quad S_{OMS} = 0.56$$

and from (9.9.34) a 95% upper confidence bound for EMS is

$$\widehat{OMS} + t_{.05,\,4} \frac{S_{OMS}}{\sqrt{5}} = 2.11 + (2.132) \frac{(0.56)}{\sqrt{5}} = 2.65$$

The loss parameter is

$$k = \frac{C}{\Delta^2} = \frac{61}{3.5^2} = 4.98$$

Therefore, a 95% upper confidence bound for ALV is (4.98) (2.64) = \$13.15. ∎

9.9.7 Short-Term and Long-Term Process Capability and Performance

In our discussion so far we have considered process capability and performance under the assumption of a stable process, that is, under the assumption that the process mean and variance are constant. However, we know that in practice this assumption is only approximately true. In particular, over time the mean is likely to change somewhat due to many causes. This variation in the mean will be manifested by increasing the OMS from data taken over a given period of time. Thus any estimates of process capability and performance from data taken over short periods of time will generally tend to make a process look better than those taken over a longer time period. In particular, a customer of the process should be interested in capability and performance over the period when the units of product he receives are being made. A long-term customer is definitely interested in long-term performance.

9.10 SUMMARY

In Chapter 9 we presented material useful for studying both the capability and performance of a process to meet product specifications. This includes both graphical and analytical goodness-of-fit methods for evaluating the functional form of the distribution of a stable process variable. Methods of estimating the fallout and a number of other capability and performance statistics are given. The Taguchi quadratic loss function approach is given as a way to assign monetary value to the loss due to variation, including a technique for partitioning the resulting expected mean square, EMS, into lower and upper components and estimating the components. Transformation methods for treating non-normal, right skewed distributions are given.

APPENDIX 9A

Theorem 9A.1: The statistics *UOMS* and *LOMS* defined in display (9.9.9) are unbiased estimates of *UEMS* and *LEMS* defined in display (9.9.11).

Proof: We will show for *UOMS*, and *LOMS* is done similarly.
Put

$$p = P(X \geq \tau)$$

and observe that $X_{1,U}, \cdots, X_{y,U}$ are a sample from the conditional distribution with density function

$$I_{[\tau,\infty)}(x) \frac{f(x)}{p}$$

Then

$$nE(UOMS) = nE_y[E(UOMS|y)]$$

$$= E_y\left[E\left(\sum_{i=1}^{y} (X_{i,U} - \tau)^2 \Big| y\right)\right]$$

$$= E_y\left[y \int_{\tau}^{\infty} (x - \tau)^2 \frac{f(x)}{p} dx\right]$$

$$= n \int_{\tau}^{\infty} (x - \tau)^2 f(x) dx$$

and so E($UOMS$) = $UEMS$.   ■

PROBLEMS

9.1   The data for this problem are given in data file 91. These are
individual measurments data from a process with specification
limits LSL = 16.97 and USL = 17.03.

   (a) Plot a histogram with overlaid normal density function.

   (b) Make a normal uniform residuals plot of the data.

   (c) Compute the p-value of the Anderson-Darling statistic for
this data.

   (d) Compute the fallout below LSL and above USL.

   (e) Discuss the results from the parts (a) through (d) above.

9.2   Show that the equation (9.8.11) holds. (Hint: Consider the two
cases when $C_{PK} = C_{PU}$ and $C_{PK} = C_{PL}$ separately.)

9.3   The data for this problem are given in data file 93. This is a
sample of 30 values.

   (a) Make Q-charts for both the process variance and mean.

   (b) Make a normal uniform residuals plot of the sample

   (c) Compute an Anderson-Darling test of normality p-value for
this data.

   (d) Compute a power transformation to improve the normality
of this data.

   (e) Make a normal uniform residuals plot of the power transformed data.

   (f) Make Q-charts for both the process variance and mean from
the transformed data.

   (g) Discuss all of your results thoroughly.

9.4   The following data are also given in data file 94.

   (a) Make a normal uniform residuals plot of the following sample (given in left to right row order).

   (b) Compute an Anderson-Darling test of normality p-value for
this data.

   (c) If the specification limits are LSL = 7.70 and USL = 8.30,
estimate the fallout by (i) using the large-sample "plug-in"
method and (ii) using the MVU method for small (all)
samples.

7.89	7.95	7.95	7.91	8.09	7.85	7.85	7.92	7.57	8.10
7.78	8.08	7.95	7.86	8.16	7.95	8.29	7.98	8.14	7.98
8.07	8.22	8.11	7.89	7.91	8.00	7.98	7.97	8.12	7.92
8.20	8.10	7.99	8.05	8.22	8.12	7.98	8.10	8.02	8.11
7.93	8.01	8.00	8.03	8.15	7.75	8.13	7.93	8.05	8.12
8.17	7.91	8.15	7.96	7.94	7.95	7.97	7.98	8.09	8.05

9.5   The data for this problem are given in data file P95. There are 17 subgroups (samples) that vary in size.

(a) Make subgroups Q-charts for both the process variance and mean.

(b) Make a subgroups normal uniform residuals plot of the sample.

(c) Compute an Anderson-Darling test of normality p-value for this data.

(d) Compute a power transformation to improve the normality of this data.

(e) Make a subgroups normal uniform residuals plot of the power transformed data.

(f) Make subgroups Q-charts for both the process variance and mean from the transformed data.

(g) Do any further analyses that you feel are helpful and discuss all of your results.

9.6   A sample of $n = 50$ observations gave a sample standard deviation of $s = 0.013$ and $\bar{x} = 7.991$. If $LSL = 7.96$ and $USL = 8.04$ then:

(a) Compute $\hat{C}_p$.

(b) Compute a 95% confidence interval for C_p.

(c) Compute the total sample size required, that is, these 50 plus additional observations, if the confidence interval is to have length approximately 0.2.

9.7   Suppose we are to take a sample of size $n = 60$ from a new process, for which there is only an upper specification limit. We choose the minimum value of C_p to be $c_o = 1.30$. Compute the value of $\hat{C}_{p,MIN}$ required in order to be 95% confident that this minimum value of C_p is being met.

9.8   A sample of $n = 30$ values on a process variable with $LSL = 4.988$ and $USL = 5.012$ gave the following sample values.
$\bar{x} = 4.99818$ and $S = 0.00299$
Anderson-Darling Normality test p-value $= 0.675$
Neyman-Smooth Normality test p-value $= 0.719$
$PV - MSSD = 0.241$

(a) Compute $\hat{C}_p$, $\hat{C}_{PU}$, $\hat{C}_{PL}$, and $\hat{C}_{PK}$.

(b) Compute 95% lower confidence bounds for C_p, C_{PL}, C_{PU}, and C_{PK}.

(c) Discuss the general status of the process using the information in parts (a) and (b), and the p-values given in the statement of the problem.

9.9   A sample of size $n = 50$ from a stable process gave $\bar{x} = 3.02$ and $s = 0.007$. The specification limits are $LSL = 2.969$ and $USL = 3.031$. Compute estimates of C_P, C_{PL}, C_{PU}, and C_{PK}. Also, find a 95% lower confidence bound for each of these indices. Discuss the capability and performance of this process.

9.10   The data in file P910 are allegedly from a stable normal process.

(a) Make charts to decide if you believe the process is stable. For the following parts, assume the process is stable. The upper and lower specification limits are $USL = 23.00$ and $LSL = 17.00$. Target value is $\tau = 20.00$.

(b) Compute estimates of the upper and lower fallout for this process.

(c) Compute estimates of C_P, C_{PL}, C_{PU}, and C_{PK}.

(d) Compute 95% lower confidence bounds for C_P, C_{PL}, C_{PU}, and C_{PK}.

(e) Discuss the capability and performance of this process.

9.11   A process has a normal $N(\mu, \sigma^2)$ quality variable with
Target $= \tau = 8.00$
$\Delta_L = \Delta_U = \Delta = 0.12$
$\mu = \tau$
$\sigma = 0.03$
$C = $ cost (loss) per unit $= \$50$
Assume a quadratic loss function.

(a) Evaluate the loss parameter k.
(b) Evaluate the average loss per production unit due to variation assuming no inspection.
(c) Evaluate the average loss from variation per production unit with 100% inspection if inspection costs are $2.00 per unit.
(d) Discuss these results.

CHAPTER 10

Measurement Assurance

10.1 MEASUREMENT SYSTEM STABILITY, ACCURACY, PRECISION

It has been observed in a number of places in earlier chapters that the sources of variability of quality variables can be classified into six general categories: men, machines, materials, methods, measurements, and environment. When measurements are made for the purpose of studying the stability of a work process, or for any purpose, it is important that the errors of measurement be small. If the errors are not small, the effectiveness of process control will be reduced. Indeed, instability of variation due to the measurement process can easily be misinterpreted as variation in the production process, and can lead to expensive unnecessary efforts to improve a process. Similarly, unrecognized measurement error can lead to a decision to redesign a product that is already a good one. The issues we consider in this chapter are concerned with the quality control of a measurement process.

The first issue in evaluating the effectiveness of a measurement process is to consider the purpose or intent in taking the measurements. The intended use of the measurements is often to study the stability and capability of a production process. Sometimes the purpose is to determine if particular specifications are being met, and then an understanding of the purpose of the specifications will be needed in evaluating the measurement process. Understanding the measurement intent permits the statement of an operational definition of the measurement, which, in turn, leads to the development of detailed gauging methodology. Note, particularly, that gauging methodology is an important part of the measurement system along with the gauge itself.

The measurement process is itself a work process, or system. As such, it is subject to control like any work process. In order to consider characteristics of a measurement process, the process must be stable. Only when the measurement process is stable is there a distribution of measurements that can be modeled by a probability distribution. A stable measurement process is characterized by its *accuracy* and *precision* (see Fig. 10.1).

Accuracy and precision are characteristics of the distribution of measurements from the measurement process. The location of the distribution of measurements determines the accuracy of a measurement process. If the process distribution is centered on a "true" value, it is an accurate process. The precision of a measurement process is the spread or dispersion of the distribution of measurements. The smaller the spread the more precise is the measurement process.

10.2 SOURCES OF ERROR IN A GAUGING PROCESS

A measurement system consists of units (parts) to be measured, measurement devises (gauges), observers (operators), and a defined methodology that is used to obtain a measurement. When a measurement is obtained by a measurement system, it will often not be the same as the "true" value for the part due to a number of "sources" or "causes" of error in measurements. We will consider here a number of issues concerned with the adequacy of a measurement (gauging) system as follows.

Linearity
Accuracy
Various Sources of Variation for the Measurement System:
  Repeatability (Test–Retest)
  Reproducibility (Gauge Operators)
  Others
Adequacy of Measurement System Variation for:
  Specified Tolerances

Accurate, Precise   Accurate, Not Precise

Not Accurate, Precise   Not Accurate, Not Precise

Figure 10.1 Accuracy and Precision, τ = Target Value

Production Process Variation
Measurement Sensitivity or Resolution and:
  Estimating Process Capability
  Control Charts

A measurement system or gauge analysis is a procedure for obtaining data and analyzing it to study the effectiveness of the measurement system. Figure 10.2 is a flow chart that recommends a sequence of steps for analyzing linearity, accuracy, repeatability, and reproducibility. We consider data sets with the following structure.

Let n parts be selected from the production process that are made with production operators, methods, tooling, materials, etc. These parts can be selected in one of two ways as follows:

- *Purposive selection:* The parts are selected so that the measurements will cover the specified tolerance range, or the natural tolerance range, if it is known. We will select parts, if possible, with some measurements near the upper specification (natural) tolerance limit, the lower specification (natural) tolerance limit, the target value, and others spread out more or less evenly between these.
- *Random sampling:* The parts are selected randomly from the production process. They should be taken over a long enough time interval so that they will reflect long-term production variation.

Each of these n parts is measured twice and the measurements can be presented as in Table 10.1. The details of the gauging process will depend on the use we will make of these data, as specified below.

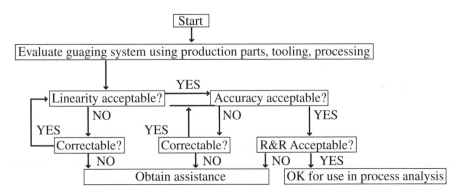

Figure 10.2 Flow Chart for Gauge Analysis

TABLE 10.1 Notation for Two Measurements on Each of n Parts, that is, Paired Measurements

Part Number	First Measurement	Second Measurement	Difference
1	x_1	y_1	$d_1 = x_1 - y_1$
2	x_2	y_2	$d_2 = x_2 - y_2$
3	x_3	y_3	$d_3 = x_3 - y_3$
⋮	⋮	⋮	⋮
n	x_n	y_n	$d_n = x_n - y_n$

Compute the sample and mean variance: $\bar{d}$ and S_d^2

10.2.1 Observed Values and Coded Values

Gauges are designed to read in some unit of measurement. The gauge often reads in coded values and these are converted to standard units by the equation:

$$\text{Observed Value (OV)} = \text{Offset} + \text{Gauge Scale (GS)} \quad (10.2.1)$$
$$\times \text{ Coded Value (CV)}$$

If the values are from a stable production process, such that the observed value has a distribution with mean μ_{OV} and standard deviation σ_{OV}, then the mean μ_{CV} and standard deviation σ_{CV} of the coded value are related to those of the observed value as given in (10.2.2).

$$\mu_{OV} = \text{Offset} + GS \times \mu_{CV}, \quad \text{and} \quad \sigma_{OV} = GS \times \sigma_{CV} \quad (10.2.2)$$

In this chapter, unless noted otherwise, we will assume that all coded values have been expressed as observed values.

10.2.2 Linearity

As noted in Fig. 10.2, we recommend that the analysis of a gauge begin with an analysis of linearity. To study linearity, and accuracy, it is best if the parts were selected by purposive selection. All of the x measurements of the first sample are made by the same operator using the production gauge under study. The methodology for obtaining these measurements requires that the parts be arranged in random order, which can be achieved in a number of ways. The parts can be labeled from 1 to n, and then identical balls numbered from 1 to n placed in a box, randomly mixed, and drawn out one-by-one to determine an ordering. Alternatively, and more easily, a computer algorithm such as that given on the Q-Charts disk can be used to obtain a random ordering of the integers 1 to n. The y measurements of the second sample are obtained using a "standard" or "master" gauge. These measurements taken by a master gauge are operationally defined as the "true" values for the parts. For studying linearity, it is important to have some parts, if possible, with true values at or near both the upper and lower specification limits, and the target value, τ. This is why purposive sampling of parts is preferred.

To study the linearity of the production gauge, we make a scatter plot of the values (x_i, y_i) for $i = 1, 2, \cdots, n$. If the production gauge agreed exactly with the master, then the plotted points would all fall on the line $y = x$. However, due to measurement variation the points generally will not fall exactly on the line, but the points should satisfy the equation (10.2.3).

$$y_i = x_i + \epsilon_i \text{ and the } \epsilon_i\text{'s are independent with} \quad (10.2.3)$$

$$E(\epsilon_i) = 0 \quad \text{and} \quad \text{Var}(\epsilon_i) = \sigma_\epsilon^2$$

If these plotted points tend to drift away from the $y = x$ line in a recognizable pattern, there is a linearity problem. We illustrate a plot of points with a linearity problem in Example 10.1.

Example 10.1: Fifteen parts were selected (purposive selection) and gauged in random order by one operator. The specification tolerance range is 5–30. The parts were also measured by a master gauge and the data are given in Table 10.2, and a scatter plot of the data is given in Fig. 10.3. These data show a pattern that does not follow the $x = y$ line. The x-values tend to be less than the y-values when the values are small, but tend to exceed the y-values for large values. Near the middle of the tolerance range the x and y values agree well. This is a fairly typical type of violation of linearity. It also illustrates why gauges should be calibrated at the specification limits, not just at target value. ■

10.2.3 Accuracy

A production gauge is accurate if a scatter plot of the measurements from it and those of the master gauge are scattered randomly about the line $y = x$, with approximately the same proportion of points above the line and below it, with no long runs of points either above or below

TABLE 10.2   Data for Linearity Example 10.1

Part	Operating Gauge, x	Master Gauge, y	Difference $d = x - y$
1	12	14	−2
2	20	20	0
3	29	27	2
4	5	9	−4
5	20	19	1
6	27	24	3
7	16	16	0
8	3	5	−2
9	15	16	−1
10	7	9	−2
11	15	14	1
12	18	18	0
13	30	27	3
14	10	11	−1
15	23	22	1

$\sum d_i = -1, \sum d_i^2 = 55$

$\bar{d} = 0.02, S_d = 1.01$

the line. If $E(d_i) = E(x_i - y_i) = b \neq 0$ for all i, then the gauge is inaccurate with a bias b. When this is the case the mean $\bar{d}$ is an estimate of the bias b. A simple, effective way to study accuracy of a gauge with data of the structure described above in the discussion of linearity

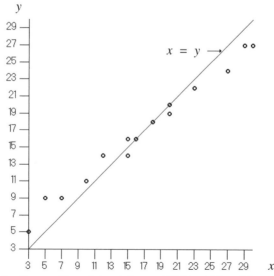

Figure 10.3   Scatter Plot of (x, y) Data of Table 10.2, a Linearity Problem

is to plot the same type of (x, y) scatter plot discussed there, with parts taken from the process by purposive selection as for the plot for linearity. However, the type of anomalous pattern on this chart that indicates an accuracy problem is quite different from the pattern that signifies a linearity problem. An accurate gauge will give a plot with points scattered randomly about the 45° line. The proportion of points above the line and below it should be approximately the same, and there should not be long runs of points on the same side of the line. An example of points from a gauge with an accuracy problem is given in Example 10.2.

Example 10.2: Table 10.3 gives measurements on 13 parts from a process with $LSL = 3$ and $USL = 15$. The data are plotted in Fig. 10.4, and show a definite tendency for the x value to exceed the y value throughout the range of values. Also, the estimate of bias is $\bar{d} = 1.31$. However, there does not appear to be a linearity problem, since the data are randomly scattered about a 45° line shifted to the right of the $x = y$ line. ∎

As commented above, if there is not a linearity problem and the bias is constant, then $\bar{d}$ is an estimate of the bias of the gauge. If it is required to have a formal procedure to decide if $\bar{d}$ is close enough to zero to proclaim the production gauge accurate, then we can compute a confidence interval using the following formula:

TABLE 10.3   Data for Accuracy Example 10.2

Part	Study Gauge Reading, x	Master Gauge Reading, y	Different $d = x - y$
1	8	6	2
2	12	10	2
3	6	7	−1
4	11	8	3
5	10	6	4
6	5	3	2
7	10	8	2
8	9	10	−1
9	13	12	1
10	6	5	1
11	8	8	0
12	7	4	3
13	9	10	−1

$\sum d_i = 17, \sum d_i^2 = 55$

$\bar{d} = 1.31, S_d = 1.65$

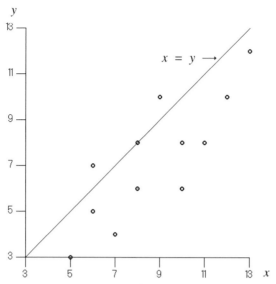

Figure 10.4   Scatter Plot of (x, y) Data for Example 10.2, an Accuracy Problem

$$\bar{d} \pm \frac{t_{\alpha/2, n-1} S_d}{\sqrt{n}} \qquad (10.2.4)$$

If this confidence interval contains zero, we consider the gauge accurate, but if it does not contain zero we will conclude at the $100(1 - \alpha)\%$ level that there is a significant bias.

For the data of Table 10.2 with $\alpha = 0.05$, this formula gives a 95% apparent confidence interval of

$$0.02 \pm (2.145)(1.01)/\sqrt{15} = 0.02 \pm 0.56,$$

or $(-0.54, 0.58)$ for the gauge bias. Since this interval contains zero (indeed, zero is almost the center of the interval), we might be tempted to conclude that the gauge is unbiased. This conclusion is not reasonable, however, because we saw in Example 10.1 that there is a linearity problem. Thus, computing and interpreting an estimate of bias is worse than meaningless, it is misleading.

Next, consider the data of Table 10.3, and with $\alpha = 0.05$ we obtain from Table A.3 $t_{0.025, 12} = 2.179$. Then we get

$$1.31 \pm (2.179)(1.65)\sqrt{13} = 1.31 \pm 1.00,$$

or (0.31, 2.31) for a 95% confidence interval for the gauge bias. Since there was no indication of a linearity problem, we will interpret this as a legitimate estimate of bias for this gauge. Since the interval contains only positive values, well above zero, this is strong evidence of a positive bias. We will then adjust the gauge to try to eliminate this bias. A gauge should not be adjusted unless there is such evidence that there is not a linearity problem and that there is a significant bias. Adjusting a gauge without such evidence will tend to increase the variability of the measurement process.

10.2.4 Repeatability

Suppose that both the x and the y measurements are made with the same gauge by the same operator. The n parts are arranged in random order, and the x measurements made. The parts are rearranged in a new random order before the y measurements are made. It is important that the operator not know the values of the first measurements on the individual parts when the second measurements are made. If the operator knows the x value for a part when the y value is being taken, then the y value will likely be influenced. This will vitiate the analysis.

Now, the ith part has a true value, say a_i, which we would like to know, but because of measurement errors the values we actually obtain from measurement can be expressed as

$$x_i = a_i + e_{xi} \quad \text{and} \quad y_i = a_i + e_{yi} \tag{10.2.5}$$

where the values e_{xi} and e_{yi} are the measurement errors on the first and second measurements. We assume that the $2n$ values of e_{xi} and e_{yi} for $i = 1, \cdots, n$ are all independent random variables with mean 0 and variance σ^2. The variance σ^2 is the variance when the same part is measured repeatedly by the same operator with the same gauge. The standard deviation σ is the variability due to the gauge and associated methods of using it, and is called the *repeatability* of the gauge. The variance σ^2 is also sometimes called the Test–Retest variance, since it is also the variance of measurements obtained by measuring and then remeasuring each part with all other sources of variation in the measurement system held constant.

The n quantities a_i for $i = 1, \cdots, n$ are the true values for the parts and their interpretation depends on how the parts were taken from the production process. If the parts were taken by purposive selection, then these data will not be useful for studying the variability of the production process. However, they will be most useful for estimating the repeatability, σ^2, of the measurement system because this allows for the possibility of variation in the measurement process related to measuring different values of the a_i's. For this case of purposive selection, we denote $\xi_p = (a_1 + \cdots + a_n)/n$, that is, ξ_p is just the mean of the a_i values.

On the other hand, if the n parts were obtained by random sampling from a *stable* production process, then we can reasonably consider the true parts values $a_1, \ldots, a_n$ to be a random sample from the production process distribution of parts. For this case, let ξ_p denote the mean of this parts distribution and σ_p^2 its variance, that is, σ_p^2 is the *parts variance*. Note, particularly, the difference in the interpretation of ξ_p depending on how the parts were obtained from production. In either case, we put $\alpha_i = a_i - \xi_p$. When the parts were obtained by random selection, the quantity α_i is called the *parts effect*. In either case, the model of (10.2.5) can be rewritten in the following equivalent form.

$$x_i = \xi_p + \alpha_i + e_{xi} \quad \text{and} \quad y_i = \xi_p + \alpha_i + e_{yi} \qquad (10.2.5')$$

The analysis and interpretation of the data depend also, of course, on how the measurements are made on the parts. In this subsection, we expressly assume the measurements are made as follows.

- The n parts are labeled (arranged) randomly and measured by the one operator using the same gauge to obtain the first, that is, the x reading.
- The n parts are rearranged randomly and measured again by the same operator using the same gauge to obtain the second, that is, the y reading. Then, we have from either (10.2.5) or (10.2.5') the following results.

$$E(d_i) = E(x_i - y_i) = E(e_{xi} - e_{yi}) = 0 \quad \text{and}$$

$$\text{Var}(d_i) = \text{Var}(e_{xi} - e_{yi}) = 2\sigma^2$$

and $E(\bar{d}) = 0$ and $E(S_d^2) = 2\sigma^2$

Thus, we will estimate the *repeatability* $= \sigma$ for this case by

$$\hat{\sigma} = \frac{S_d}{\sqrt{2}} \qquad (10.2.6)$$

It is often useful to express repeatability as a percent of the specified Tolerance $= UCL - LCL$, as follows.

$$\% \text{ Repeatability} = 100 \, \frac{5.15 \times \hat{\sigma}}{\text{Tolerance}} \qquad (10.2.7)$$

By custom, the value 5.15 is used here because an interval of length 5.15 standard deviations centered on the mean of a normal distribution covers 0.99 of the probability.

10.2.5 Reproducibility

Next, suppose that both measurements are made with the same gauge, but with different operators. For this case we assume that the measurements are obtained as follows.

· The n parts are labeled (arranged) randomly and measured by the same operator using the same gauge to obtain the first, that is, the x readings.
· The n parts are rearranged randomly and measured again by a second operator using the same gauge to obtain the second, that is, the y readings.
· The two operators are selected randomly from the set of operators that will, or may, use this gauge in production.

For this case, we need to add terms to the right-hand sides of the equations of the model of (10.2.5) to represent the effects of operators on the measurement process. Suppose we denote these terms by b_x and b_y, and assume that these are independently and identically distributed random variables with common mean and variance—due to operators—of ξ_o and σ_o^2, respectively. The standard deviation σ_o due to operators is called the *reproducibility* of the gauge. Then the model of (10.2.5) becomes the following for this case.

$$x_i = a_i + b_x + e_{xi} \quad \text{and} \quad y_i = a_i + b_y + e_{yi} \qquad (10.2.8)$$

We define *operator effects* by $\beta_x = b_x - \xi_o$ and $\beta_y = b_y - \xi_o$. Then (10.2.8) can be rewritten as follows.

$$x_i = \mu + \alpha_i + \beta_x + e_{xi} \quad \text{and} \quad y_i = \mu + \alpha_i + \beta_y + e_{yi} \qquad (10.2.8')$$

where $\mu = \xi_p + \xi_o$ is the overall mean, and is constant for all observations. From (10.2.8') we obtain the following results.

$$d_i = x_i - y_i = \beta_x - \beta_y + e_{xi} - e_{yi}$$

$$\bar{d} = \beta_x - \beta_y + \bar{e}_x - \bar{e}_y$$

$$E\left(\frac{\bar{d}^2}{2}\right) = \sigma_o^2 + \frac{\sigma^2}{n}, \quad E\left(\frac{S_d^2}{2}\right) = \sigma^2$$

By equating these statistics to their expectations and solving, we obtain the estimates of Repeatability, Reproducibility, and Repeatability & Reproducibility (R&R) in (10.2.9).

$$\text{Repeatability} = \hat{\sigma} = \frac{S_d}{\sqrt{2}}$$

$$\text{Reproducibility} = \hat{\sigma}_o = \sqrt{\frac{\bar{d}^2}{2} - \frac{S_d^2}{2n}}$$

$$R\&R = \hat{\sigma}_{R\&R} = \sqrt{\hat{\sigma}_o^2 + \hat{\sigma}^2}$$

$$= \sqrt{\frac{1}{2}\left(\bar{d}^2 + \frac{(n-1)}{n} S_d^2\right)}$$

(10.2.9)

The percent repeatability is computed as before from (10.2.7). The percentages of Reproducibility and R&R are computed by the following formulas.

$$\% \text{ Reproducibility} = 100 \frac{5.15 \times \hat{\sigma}_o}{\text{Tolerance}}$$

$$\% R\&R = 100 \frac{5.15 \times \sqrt{\hat{\sigma}_o^2 + \hat{\sigma}^2}}{\text{Tolerance}}$$

$$= 100 \frac{5.15 \times R\&R}{\text{Tolerance}}$$

(10.2.10)

Note the interpretation of these three quantities. They represent respectively the percentages of specification tolerance taken up by these components of gauge variation. In particular, % R&R is the percent of tolerance taken up by both of these sources of gauging variation. Clearly, we want this percent to be small, but how small should it be? Kane (1989) recommends the scale given in Table 10.4 for evaluating a measurement process. The SPC Manual of the Automotive Division of the American Society for Quality Control, ASQC (1986), also recommends considering more than 30% unacceptable.

10.2.6 Sample Sizes

The sample size n depends on the parameters of the gauging system under study. However, we make the following general suggestions as a guide. Sample size n should always be at least ten, and, if resources permit, it should be larger. A sample of size $n = 30$ will usually give good results.

Example 10.3: Twelve parts are gauged by two operators. The gauge reads in integers from 1 to 35 and the tolerance is 30, in the gauge scale. The data are given in the following table.

Part	Operator A	Operator B	Difference, d	
1	14	15	−1	
2	12	9	3	
3	15	14	1	
4	16	14	2	
5	15	15	0	
6	13	14	−1	
7	13	11	2	
8	16	15	1	
9	14	12	2	
10	13	14	−1	$\bar{d} = 0.83$,
11	14	14	0	$S_d = 1.40$
12	15	13	2	

TABLE 10.4   Evaluation of the Percentage R&R for a Measurement Process

0–10%	Excellent
10–20%	Good
20–30%	Marginal
More than 30%	Unacceptable

$$\text{Repeatability} = \hat{\sigma} = \frac{S_d}{\sqrt{2}} = 0.99,$$

$$\text{Reproducibility} = \hat{\sigma}_o = \sqrt{\frac{\overline{d}^2}{2} - \frac{S_d^2}{2n}} = 0.51$$

$$R\&R = \sqrt{\hat{\sigma}^2 + \hat{\sigma}_o^2} = \sqrt{(0.99)^2 + (0.51)^2} = 1.11$$

Then

$$\% \text{ Repeatability} = 100\,\frac{(5.15)(0.99)}{30} = 17.0\%$$

$$\% \text{ Reproducibility} = 100\,\frac{(5.15)(0.51)}{30} = 8.8\%$$

$$\% \text{ R\&R} = 100\,\frac{(5.15)(1.11)}{30} = 19.1\%$$

Note that this value of % R&R is toward the upper bound of the "good" range in Table 10.4. Most of the measurement system variation is from the repeatability component. In fact, % R&R is only slightly larger than the % Repeatability component.   ∎

The measurement system analysis presented to this point in this subsection is actually valid whether the parts were selected from production by purposive selection or by random sampling. However, it will generally be more useful if the parts are purposely selected to cover the natural and specification tolerance ranges. This is true because we have only estimated parameters (standard deviations) of the measurement process, and compared these with specification tolerance ranges, to judge the performance of the measurement system. However, it will often be the case that it is not enough to study the performance of a gauge relative to the specification tolerance, because we are interested in knowing whether it is adequate for measuring the products of the particular stable production process under study. To answer this question we need to compare the measurements system variation to the parts variation.

10.2.7 Estimating Parts Variation, the Intraclass Correlation Coefficient, and Discrimination Ratio

In this subsection we consider measurements made on parts that were randomly sampled from the production process. The data are modeled by equation (10.2.8′), where now α_i is the random parts effect with mean zero and variance σ_p^2. If we consider the variance of the individual measurements, x_i and y_i, and we denote their variance by σ_m^2, then

$$\sigma_m^2 = \sigma_p^2 + \sigma_{R\&R}^2 \tag{10.2.11}$$

or, in words

Measurement Variance = Parts Variance

+ Measurement System Variance

First, observe that equation (10.2.11) is a Pythagorean relationship that permits us to interpret σ_m, σ_p, and $\sigma_{R\&R}$ as the sides of a right triangle as follows.

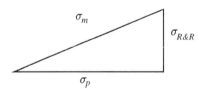

From this and (10.2.11) itself, clearly the ratio of parts variance to the measurement variance is useful for judging the adequacy of the measurement system for these particular measurements of these parts. This quantity is called the *parts intraclass correlation coefficient, ρ_I,* and is given by (10.2.12).

$$\rho_I = \frac{\sigma_p^2}{\sigma_m^2} = 1 - \frac{\sigma_{R\&R}^2}{\sigma_m^2} \tag{10.2.12}$$

From equation (10.2.11), clearly ρ_I takes values in the interval between 0 and 1. See Kendall and Stuart (1961) and Wheeler (1989) for discussions of this quantity.

To estimate ρ_I, we will obtain estimates $\hat{\sigma}_p^2$ of σ_p^2 and $\hat{\sigma}_m^2$ of σ_m^2 and substitute these estimates in (12.2.12) to obtain

$$r_I = \hat{\rho}_I = \frac{\hat{\sigma}_p^2}{\hat{\sigma}_m^2} = 1 - \frac{\hat{\sigma}_{R\&R}^2}{\hat{\sigma}_m^2} \tag{10.2.13}$$

The estimate r_I is called the *sample parts intraclass correlation coefficient.* In theory it is also bounded between zero and one. However, if it is computed from the last expression in (10.2.13), and depending on just how the estimates $\hat{\sigma}_{R\&R}^2$ and $\hat{\sigma}_m^2$ are computed, it is possible that it can be negative. This is an indication that measurement system variation is so large relative to parts variation that $\hat{\sigma}_{R\&R}^2$ exceeds $\hat{\sigma}_m^2$ due to sampling variation. In this case the negative value of r_I should be replaced by zero, that is, put $r_I = 0$.

Consider next obtaining an estimate $\hat{\sigma}_p^2$, and recall that we are now assuming that the parts were obtained by random sampling. Define $w_i = (x_i + y_i)/2$ for $i = 1, \cdots, n$. Denote the sample variance of these w_i's by S_w^2. Then, from the model in (10.2.8′) we obtain

$$E(S_w^2) = \sigma_p^2 + \frac{1}{2}\sigma_{R\&R}^2$$

The estimate $\hat{\sigma}_{R\&R}^2$ is obtained from (10.2.9), and we obtain unbiased estimates of σ_p^2 and σ_m^2 as follows.

$$\hat{\sigma}_p^2 = S_w^2 - \frac{1}{2}\hat{\sigma}_{R\&R}^2$$
$$\hat{\sigma}_m^2 = \hat{\sigma}_p^2 + \hat{\sigma}_{R\&R}^2 = S_w^2 + \frac{1}{4}\left(\bar{d}^2 + \frac{(n-1)}{n}S_d^2\right) \tag{10.2.14}$$

While ρ_I and r_I clearly reflect the relative magnitudes of parts and measurements variation, it is difficult to interpret the magnitudes of these quantities. This is because they are ratios of quantities that are themselves expressed in units of measurement that are squares of the actual measurement units of the data. To give a more readily interpreted quantity, Wheeler (1989) defined a function of ρ_I called the *discrimination ratio, D_p,* as follows.

$$\text{Discrimination Ratio} = D_p = \sqrt{\frac{1 + \rho_I}{1 - \rho_I}} = \sqrt{\frac{2\sigma_m^2}{\sigma_{R\&R}^2} - 1} \quad (10.2.15)$$

An estimate of D_p is given by

$$D_r = \hat{D}_p = \sqrt{\frac{1 + r_I}{1 - r_I}} = \sqrt{\frac{2\hat{\sigma}_m^2}{\hat{\sigma}_{R\&R}^2} - 1} \quad (10.2.16)$$

The discrimination ratio is a strictly monotone increasing function of ρ_I that maps the interval $[0, 1]$ to numbers exceeding 1. The magnitude of this quantity represents essentially the number of distinct categories that the measurements being taken can be used to group products into when variation in the measurement system is taken into account. For example, a discrimination ratio of 1 means that the measurements have no value to detect variation for this particular product. See Wheeler (1989) for discussion of this interpretation of the discrimination ratio.

The discrimination ratio is thus useful for deciding the usefulness of a measurement system for detecting variation in a particular product, and can be used to decide whether it is more desirable to concentrate efforts to improve the production process, or if the measurement system must be improved in order to study the variation in the production process. We recommend that the measurement be considered inadequate if the discrimination ratio is less than about 2, and that the measurement process needs improvement when it is less than 4. These are essentially the recommendations of Wheeler (1989).

Example 10.4: A production process had specification target value of $\tau = 3.000$ cm and specification tolerance range centered on τ of 0.009 cm. It was suspected that the %(R&R) was too large and the gauging system inadequate. A new better gauge was very expensive and it was decided to study the measurement system to determine the adequacy of the gauging system. Twenty parts were taken from production randomly over a period of two weeks, in order to assure that reasonably long term parts variation would be represented. These 20 parts were gauged once each by two operators

x	y	d	w
3.001	3.001	0.000	3.0010
3.002	3.003	−0.001	3.0025
2.999	2.999	0.000	2.9990
2.999	2.999	0.000	2.9990
2.999	3.000	−0.001	2.9995
3.000	3.001	−0.001	3.0005
2.996	2.997	−0.001	2.9965
3.003	3.004	−0.001	3.0035
3.002	3.002	0.000	3.0020
2.999	2.999	0.000	2.9990
2.999	3.000	−0.001	2.9995
2.997	2.997	0.000	2.9970
3.000	3.000	0.000	3.0000
3.000	3.001	−0.001	3.0005
2.998	2.998	0.000	2.9980
3.001	3.002	−0.001	3.0015
3.004	3.005	−0.001	3.0045
3.000	3.000	0.000	3.0000
3.002	3.003	−0.001	3.0025
3.001	3.001	0.000	3.0010

$$d = x - y, \quad w = \frac{x + y}{2}$$

$$\overline{d} = -0.0005, \quad S_d^2 = 0.000000263$$

$$\overline{w} = 3.00035, \quad S_w^2 = 0.0000042$$

$$(\text{Repeatability})^2 = \frac{S_d^2}{2} = 0.000000132$$

$$\text{Repeatability} = 0.000363$$

$$(\text{Reproducibility})^2 = \frac{\overline{d}^2}{2} - \frac{S_d^2}{2n} = 0.000000118$$

$$\text{Reproducibility} = 0.000344$$

$$\text{R\&R} = \hat{\sigma}_{\text{R\&R}} = \sqrt{0.000000132 + 0.000000118} = 0.0005$$

$$\%(\text{R\&R}) = \frac{100(5.15)(0.0005)}{0.009} = 28.61\%$$

$$\hat{\sigma}_p^2 = S_w^2 - \frac{1}{2}\,\hat{\sigma}_{R\&R}^2 = 0.00000407, \quad \hat{\sigma}_m^2 = \hat{\sigma}_p^2 + \hat{\sigma}_{R\&R}^2 = 0.00000408$$

$$\hat{D}_p = \sqrt{\frac{2\hat{\sigma}_m^2}{\hat{\sigma}_{R\&R}^2} - 1} = 5.63$$

selected randomly from the operators who use this gauge for these parts in production, and the values are given in the x and y columns of the accompanying table. The computations of the required estimates are illustrated with the table. We note first that if the adequacy of the gauging system is to be judged with respect to the specification range, the estimated %(R&R) = 28.61% indicates an inadequate measurement system. However, the estimated discrimination ratio of $\hat{D}_p = 5.63$ indicates that the gauge is acceptable for measuring parts from this production process. Therefore, we would likely be better advised to spend our time and money to improve the production system, rather than investing in a more expensive gauge. However, we note that reproducibility is a large component of R&R, and we might be able to improve this component without purchasing an expensive new gauge. Perhaps a more carefully specified gauging methodology and more operator training and emphasis on the importance of consistency could reduce reproducibility for less than the cost of a new gauge.   ∎

10.3 AN ANALYSIS OF VARIANCE (ANOVA) FOR GAUGES

The gauge analyses given in the last section assumed that each part is measured twice to give paired data of the structure of that of Table 10.1. The analyses given in section 10.2 are attractive in part because they can be performed with a hand calculator and the charts plotted by hand on graph paper. However, due to the fact that the reproducibility sampling plan permits the use of only two operators, the operator variance σ_o^2, that is, reproducibility, may not be well estimated. In this section we present an approach to analyzing a gauge that is more flexible and often more informative by permitting more operators and replications of the basic plan. To this end, suppose that we are to perform a gauge analysis using the following:

n - number of parts
J - number of operators

K - number of replicated measurements made on each part by each operator

y_{ijk} - the kth measurement made by operator j on part i

As before, the ith part has a true value a_i, which is impossible to know. Thus, the measured value y_{ijk} can be expressed as

$$y_{ijk} = a_i + \epsilon_{ijk}; \quad i = 1, \cdots, n;$$

$$j = 1, \cdots, J; \quad k = 1, \cdots, K \qquad (10.3.1)$$

For parts drawn by random sampling from a stable manufacturing process, or otherwise from a large population, the a_i's can reasonably be assumed to be random variables. For this case, denote the *parts mean* by $\xi_p = E(a_i)$ and the *parts variance* by $\sigma_p^2 = \text{Var}(a_i)$. For parts drawn by purposive selection, we denote $\xi_p = (a_1 + \cdots + a_n)/n$. For parts drawn by either random sampling or purposive selection, the quantity $\alpha_i = a_i - \xi_p$ will be called the *parts effect*.

Unless we note otherwise, from here on we assume the parts were obtained by random sampling, and have $E(\alpha_i) = 0$ and $\text{Var}(\alpha_i) = \sigma_p^2$. Then the $(i, j, k)^{\text{th}}$ measurement can be written

$$y_{ijk} = \xi_p + \alpha_i + \epsilon_{ijk}; \quad i = 1, \cdots, n;$$

$$j = 1, \cdots, J; \quad k = 1, \cdots, K \qquad (10.3.2)$$

Consider next the deviation ϵ_{ijk} of the measured value y_{ijk} from the true value a_i for the ith part. This can be modeled as follows.

$$\epsilon_{ijk} = \xi_o + \beta_j + e_{ijk}; \quad i = 1, \cdots, n;$$

$$j = 1, \cdots, J; \quad k = 1, \cdots, K \qquad (10.3.3)$$

where ξ_o is the sum of constant gauge and gauge operator biases, β_j is the gauge operator effect, and e_{ijk} is the replication error, also called the test–retest error. Suppose the e_{ijk} are i.i.d. $N(0, \sigma^2)$. If the gauge operators are randomly selected from a population of gauge operators, then it is reasonable to consider the β_j's to be i.i.d. $N(0, \sigma_o^2)$ random variables.

Combining (10.3.2) and (10.3.3) gives

$$y_{ijk} = \mu + \alpha_i + \beta_j + e_{ijk}; \quad i = 1, \cdots, n;$$
$$j = 1, \cdots J; \quad k = 1, \cdots, K \qquad (10.3.4)$$

that is

Measurement = Overall Mean + Part Effect + Operator Effect

+ Replication Error

where

Overall Mean = $\mu = \xi_p + \xi_o$ = Parts Mean + Gauge Bias

+ Operator Bias

This model represents measurements made with a single gauge. The model provides a useful guide for studying the *components of variance* of the measurements. From (10.3.4) it follows that

$$E(y_{ijk}) = \mu = \xi_p + \xi_o; \quad i = 1, \cdots, n;$$
$$j = 1, \cdots, J; \quad k = 1, \cdots, K \qquad (10.3.5)$$

Since all measurements have the same constant mean, $\mu = \xi_p + \xi_o$, it is not possible to construct an unbiased linear estimate of the (gauge + operator bias) = ξ_o from data of this structure taken with a single gauge. No linear function of the observations will separate ξ_p and ξ_o. The parts mean ξ_p and gauge bias ξ_o are said to be *confounded*.

Also, from (10.3.4) it follows that the variance of an individual measurement is

$$\mathrm{Var}(y_{ijk}) = \sigma_p^2 + \sigma_o^2 + \sigma^2; \quad i = 1, \cdots, n;$$
$$j = 1, \cdots, J; \quad k = 1, \cdots, K \qquad (10.3.6)$$

or

Measurement Variance = Parts Variance + Reproducibility

+ Repeatability

As noted earlier, the variance component σ^2 due to replications when the part and operator are constant is called the gauge *repeatability*, and the variance component due to operators, σ_o^2, is called the gauge *reproducibility.*

The model (10.3.4) is the two-factor, random effects, additive model of experimental design. The term "additive" refers to the fact that both the part effects and operator effects are assumed to contribute to measurement values in an additive fashion. However, this assumption will not always be valid, and when it is not the model is generalized by including an interaction term $(\alpha\beta)_{ij}$ as follows.

$$y_{ijk} = \mu + \alpha_i + \beta_j + (\alpha\beta)_{ij} + e_{ijk}; \quad i = 1, \cdots, n;$$

$$j = 1, \cdots, J; \quad k = 1, \cdots, K \qquad (10.3.7)$$

where $(\alpha\beta)_{ij}$ is the effect from having part i measured by operator j. The nJ values $(\alpha\beta)_{ij}$ are assumed to be i.i.d. $N(0, \sigma_{p\times o}^2)$ random variables. Note that the mean of y_{ijk} assuming model (10.3.7) is the same as given in (10.3.5). However, the variance now becomes

$$\text{Var}(y_{ijk}) = \sigma_p^2 + (\sigma_o^2 + \sigma_{p\times o}^2) + \sigma^2; \quad i = 1, \cdots, n;$$

$$j = 1, \cdots, J; \quad k = 1, \cdots, K$$

For this model with an interaction term, we define

$$\text{Reproducibility} = \sigma_o^2 + \sigma_{p\times o}^2$$

If we put

$$\sigma_m^2 = \text{Var}(y_{ijk}) = \text{Measurement Variance,}$$

and

$$\sigma_{R\&R}^2 = (\sigma_o^2 + \sigma_{p\times o}^2) + \sigma^2$$

then we can write

$$\sigma_m^2 = \sigma_p^2 + \sigma_{R\&R}^2 \qquad (10.3.8)$$

or   Measurement Variance = Parts Variance

$$+ \text{ Measurement System Variance}$$

the same relationship as was given in equations (10.2.11) and (10.3.6).

In practice, it will be necessary to conduct experiments for particular measurement systems to determine if the nonadditive model that permits interaction is required, rather than the simpler additive model. The principal advantage of the additive model, when it is reasonable, is that, as will be seen below, it permits a more precise estimate of the repeatability of the system.

10.3.1 The ANOVA Identity and Table, Point Estimates of Components of Variance

Consider next the total variation in the set of nJK values y_{ijk} about their mean. The "dot" notation will be used to denote means as follows.

$$y_{ij\cdot} = \sum_{k=1}^{K} \frac{y_{ijk}}{K}, \quad y_{i\cdot k} = \sum_{j=1}^{J} \frac{y_{ijk}}{J}, \quad y_{\cdot jk} = \sum_{i=1}^{n} \frac{y_{ijk}}{n}$$

$$y_{i\cdot\cdot} = \sum_{j=1}^{J} \sum_{k=1}^{K} \frac{y_{ijk}}{JK}, \quad \cdots, \quad y_{\cdots} = \sum_{i=1}^{n} \sum_{j=1}^{J} \sum_{k=1}^{K} \frac{y_{ijk}}{nJK}$$

Define the following sums of squares:

$$SSTotal = SS_T \equiv \sum_{i=1}^{n} \sum_{j=1}^{J} \sum_{k=1}^{K} (y_{ijk} - y_{\cdots})^2$$

$$SSParts = SS_p \equiv JK \sum_{i=1}^{n} (y_{i\cdot\cdot} - y_{\cdots})^2$$

$$SSOperators = SS_o = nK \sum_{j=1}^{J} (y_{\cdot j\cdot} - y_{\cdots})^2$$

$$SS(Parts \times Operators) = SS_{p\times o}$$

$$\equiv K \sum_{i=1}^{n} \sum_{j=1}^{J} (y_{ij\cdot} - y_{i\cdot\cdot} - y_{\cdot j\cdot} + y_{\cdots})^2$$

$$SSError = SS_E = \sum_{i=1}^{n} \sum_{j=1}^{J} \sum_{k=1}^{K} (y_{ijk} - y_{ij\cdot})^2$$

It can be shown by direct algebraic manipulation that these five sums of squares satisfy the following analysis of variance, ANOVA, identity.

$$SS_T = SS_p + SS_o + SS_{p\times o} + SS_E \qquad (10.3.10)$$

This equation is summarized in the *analysis of variance* (ANOVA) Table 10.5. The degrees of freedom column gives the number of independent linear contrasts associated with each sum of squares. When the model (10.3.7) components are normally distributed, then the sums of squares of the ANOVA table are chi-squared random variables, and the mean squares column entries have expected values given in the last column of the table.

The usual method of obtaining point estimates of σ^2, σ_p^2, σ_o^2, and $\sigma_{p\times o}^2$ is to equate each individual mean square to its expected value (EMS), and solve for the variance component required. The estimates obtained by subtraction are sometimes negative. This means that the estimated value is small (near zero), and with the size sample used there is enough probability below zero of the sampling distribution to give some negative estimates. A negative value is replaced by zero. By this method we obtain the estimates given in Table 10.6.

The *F*-ratio for parts $\times$ operators is used to test the null hypothesis that $\sigma_{p\times o}^2$ is zero. This ratio

$$F = \frac{MS_{p\times o}}{MS_E}$$

is a Snedecor-*F* ratio with $[(n-1)(J-1), nJ(K-1)]$ degrees of freedom when $\sigma_{p\times o}^2 = 0$. In order to have good power for detecting a value of $\sigma_{p\times o} > 0$, the α level of this *F*-test should be fairly large, perhaps $\alpha = 0.20$. The *p*-value for this *F*-test is the probability that a Snedecor-*F* random variable will exceed the computed value of the *F*-ratio. If the *p*-value of the *F* test is computed, the null hypothesis that $\sigma_{p\times o} = 0$ is rejected in favor of the alternative hypothesis that $\sigma_{p\times o} > 0$ when the *p*-value is less than or equal to α.

If the hypothesis H_o: $\sigma_{p\times o} = 0$ is not rejected, then the additive model of (10.3.4) is probably adequate to represent the measurement processes. When this is the case the $MS_{p\times o}$ and MS_E of Table 10.5 both are unbiased estimates of σ^2, the repeatability variance. The ANOVA table for this additive model is given in table 10.7. The formulas for unbiased estimates of the variance components for this additive model are given in Table 10.8.

Example 10.5: One part was sampled randomly from production on each of ten days and three operators measured each of the ten parts twice. The measurements are given in Table 10.9. The ANOVA for the nonadditive model is given in Table 10.10. The (square roots of) the

TABLE 10.5   ANOVA for n Parts Measured K Times Each by J Operators, With Interaction

Source of Variation	Sum of Squares	Degrees of Freedom	Mean Squares	F Ratio	Expected Mean Squares (EMS)
Parts	SS_p	$n-1$	$MS_p = \dfrac{SS_p}{n-1}$		$\sigma^2 + K\sigma_{p\times o}^2 + JK\sigma_p^2$
Operators	SS_o	$J-1$	$MS_o = \dfrac{SS_o}{J-1}$		$\sigma^2 + K\sigma_{p\times o}^2 + nK\sigma_o^2$
Parts $\times$ Operators	$SS_{p\times o}$	$(n-1)(J-1)$	$MS_{p\times o} = \dfrac{SS_{p\times o}}{(n-1)(J-1)}$	$\dfrac{MS_{p\times o}}{MS_E}$	$\sigma^2 + K\sigma_{p\times o}^2$
Error	SS_E	$nJ(K-1)$	$MS_E = \dfrac{SS_E}{nJ(K-1)}$		σ^2
Total	SS_T	$nJK-1$			

TABLE 10.6   Variance Components Estimates, Nonadditive Model

Variance Component	Estimate
σ^2 (Repeatability)	MS_E
$\sigma^2_{p \times o}$	$\dfrac{MS_{p \times o} - MS_E}{K}$
σ^2_p (Parts)	$\dfrac{MS_p - MS_{p \times o}}{JK}$
σ^2_o	$\dfrac{MS_o - MS_{p \times o}}{nK}$
$\sigma^2_o + \sigma^2_{p \times o}$ (Reproducibility)	$\dfrac{MS_o + (n - 1)MS_{p \times o} - (n)MS_E}{nK}$
$\sigma^2 + \sigma^2_o + \sigma^2_{p \times o}$ (R&R)	$\dfrac{MS_o + (n - 1)MS_{p \times o} + n(K - 1)MS_E}{nK}$

variance components estimates are given in Table 10.11. Note that the
p-value of the F-test for significance of the interaction term in the
model is large enough, p-value $= 0.240$, to consider the additive model
adequate to represent these data. The target value for these measurements is $\tau = 2.234$ cm and the tolerance limits are $LSL = 2.229$ cm
and $USL = 2.239$ cm. The tolerance range is Tolerance $= USL - LSL$
$= 0.01$ cm.

The estimated percentages of tolerance range are obtained using the
estimates in Table 10.11 as follows:

$$\% \text{ (Parts)} = 100 \times \frac{(5.15)(0.000677)}{0.01} = 34.9\%$$

$$\% \text{ (Repeatability)} = 100 \times \frac{(5.15)(0.000275)}{0.01} = 14.2\%$$

$$\% \text{ (Reproducibility)} = 100 \times \frac{(5.15)(0.000160)}{0.01} = 8.2\%$$

$$\% \text{ (R\&R)} = 100 \times \frac{(5.15)(0.000318)}{0.01} = 16.4\%$$

It was remarked above that since the p-value of the F-test for interaction is p-value $= 0.240$, the additive model should be adequate. The
ANOVA for the additive model is given in Table 10.12. The estimates
of the square roots of the variance components for the additive model
are given in Table 10.13. From these values the percentage of tolerance
is computed for these components as follows:

TABLE 10.7   ANOVA Table for Additive Model for n Parts Measured K Times Each by J Operators

Source of Variation	Sum of Squares	Degrees of Freedom	Mean Squares	Expected Mean Squares
Parts	SS_p	$n - 1$	$MS_p = \dfrac{SS_p}{n - 1}$	$\sigma^2 + JK\sigma_p^2$
Operators	SS_o	$J - 1$	$MS_o = \dfrac{SS_o}{J - 1}$	$\sigma^2 + nK\sigma_o^2$
Residuals	$SS_R = SS_{p \times o} + SS_E$	$nJK - n - K + 1$	$MS_R = \dfrac{SS_R}{nJK - n - J + 1}$	σ^2
Total	SS_T	$nJK - 1$		

TABLE 10.8 Variance Components Estimates, Additive Model

Variance Component	Estimate
σ^2 (Repeatability)	MS_R
σ_p^2 (Parts)	$\dfrac{MS_p - MS_R}{JK}$
σ_o^2 (Reproducibility)	$\dfrac{MS_o - MS_R}{nK}$
$\sigma^2 + \sigma_o^2$ (R&R)	$\dfrac{MS_o - (nK - 1)MS_R}{nK}$

$$\% \text{ (Repeatability)} = 100 \times \frac{(5.15)(0.000288)}{0.01} = 14.8\%$$

$$\% \text{ (Reproducibility)} = 100 \times \frac{(5.15)(0.000119)}{0.01} = 6.1\%$$

TABLE 10.9 Measurements for Example 10.5
P = Part, O = Operator, R = Replication, M = Measurement

P	O	R	M	P	O	R	M	P	O	R	M
1	1	1	2.2333	4	2	1	2.2325	7	3	1	2.2341
1	1	2	2.2337	4	2	2	2.2328	7	3	2	2.2344
1	2	1	2.2332	4	3	1	2.2322	8	1	1	2.2345
1	2	2	2.2338	4	3	2	2.2331	8	1	2	2.2345
1	3	1	2.2336	5	1	1	2.2340	8	2	1	2.2355
1	3	2	2.2339	5	1	2	2.2344	8	2	2	2.2353
2	1	1	2.2338	5	2	1	2.2345	8	3	1	2.2348
2	1	2	2.2341	5	2	2	2.2345	8	3	2	2.2353
2	2	1	2.2342	5	3	1	2.2345	9	1	1	2.2331
2	2	2	2.2340	5	3	2	2.2349	9	1	2	2.2326
2	3	1	2.2345	6	1	1	2.2346	9	2	1	2.2332
2	3	2	2.2344	6	1	2	2.2340	9	2	2	2.2335
3	1	1	2.2338	6	2	1	2.2345	9	3	1	2.2330
3	1	2	2.2341	6	2	2	2.2349	9	3	2	2.2333
3	2	1	2.2340	6	3	1	2.2342	10	1	1	2.2343
3	2	2	2.2337	6	3	2	2.2339	10	1	2	2.2341
3	3	1	2.2342	7	1	1	2.2338	10	2	1	2.2345
3	3	2	2.2335	7	1	2	2.2343	10	2	2	2.2346
4	1	1	2.2327	7	2	1	2.2341	10	3	1	2.2341
4	1	2	2.2324	7	2	2	2.2341	10	3	2	2.2338

TABLE 10.10 Gauge ANOVA for Example 10.5, Nonadditive Model

Source	SS	df	MS	F-Ratio	P-Value
Parts	0.0000256	9	0.000002845		
Operators	0.0000007	2	0.000000366		
Parts by Operators	0.0000018	18	0.000000100	1.33	0.240
Error	0.0000023	30	0.000000076		
Total	0.0000304	59			
Grand Mean = $y\ldots$ = 2.23395					

$$\% \text{ (Parts)} = 100 \times \frac{(5.15)(0.000677)}{0.01} = 34.9\%$$

$$\% \text{ (R\&R)} = 100 \times \frac{(5.15)(0.000312)}{0.01} = 16.1\%$$

Comparing these estimates with those obtained above for the nonadditive model shows the results are virtually the same.

Using Table 10.4 as a guide the gauging variation is an acceptable percentage of specification tolerance. The values of %(Repeatability) and %(Reproducibility) give guidance as to where the gauging variation comes from, and therefore where improvement of the gauging system can be considered. From these values, it appears that a large part of the gauging variation is due to the gauge itself and the methodology for using it, rather than to differences in the ways that the operators implement the methods of using the gauge. The 16.1% for R&R (by the additive model) is in the "good" category; however, any reduction that can be made in this value, probably by improving repeatability, will improve the sensitivity of charting. Also, any reduction in R&R will result in improved estimates of process capability, and the im-

TABLE 10.11 Variance Components Estimates for Example 10.5 based on the Nonadditive Model

Variance Component	Estimate of Square Root of Variance Component
σ^2 (Repeatability	0.000275
$\sigma^2_{p\times o}$	0.000111
σ^2_o	0.000115
σ^2_p (Parts)	0.000677
$\sigma^2_o + \sigma^2_{p\times o}$ (Reproducibility)	0.000160
$\sigma^2 + \sigma^2_o + \sigma^2_{p\times o}$ (R&R)	0.000318

TABLE 10.12   Gauge ANOVA for Example 10.5, Additive Model

Source	SS	df	MS
Parts	0.0000256	9	0.000002845
Operators	0.0000007	2	0.000000366
Residuals	0.0000041	49	0.000000083
Total	0.0000304	59	

Grand Mean $= y \ldots = 2.23395$

proved estimates will indicate higher capability! This is a particularly welcome result. The computations for this example were made using the algorithm on the Q-Charts disk.

Since the parts were selected randomly from production over a two-week period, we can also compute a discrimination ratio from these data. First we compute an estimate, using equation (10.3.8) and the additive model estimates from Table 10.13,

$$\hat{\sigma}_m^2 = \hat{\sigma}_p^2 + \hat{\sigma}_{R\&R}^2 = (0.000678)^2 + (0.000312)^2 = 0.000000557.$$

Then

$$\hat{D}_p = \sqrt{\frac{2\hat{\sigma}_m^2}{\hat{\sigma}_{R\&R}^2} - 1} = 3.23.$$

From the guidelines stated earlier, the gauging system is marginally acceptable for gauging parts from this production system.   ■

10.3.2   Using Control Chart Estimates of Measurement Variance with Purposive Selection of Parts

Purposive selection of parts is desirable to assure that the parts represent the full natural tolerance range, and this enhances the overall va-

TABLE 10.13   Variance Components Estimates for Example 10.5 based on the Additive Model

Variance Component	Estimate of Square Root
σ^2 (Repeatability)	0.000288
σ_p^2 (Parts)	0.000678
σ_o^2 (Reproducibility)	0.000119
$\sigma^2 + \sigma_o^2$ (R&R)	0.000312

lidity of the measurement system analysis. However, with purposive selection of parts, the subsequent analysis of the data by either the method of section 10.2 for paired data, or the ANOVA techniques of this section, there will be no valid estimates of either parts variance, σ_p^2, or measurements variance, σ_m^2, available from this study. Therefore, to judge the meaning of the magnitudes of repeatability, reproducibility, and R&R, we can refer them only to the specified tolerance; by computing % repeatability, % reproducibility, and % R&R.

However, if the process producing the parts is being charted, and both the mean chart and the variance chart indicate a stable process, then we can use the estimate of variance from the charting program as an estimate of σ_m^2. Indeed, this is likely to be a better estimate than one obtained from the measurement system analysis, because it will often have more degrees of freedom for the estimate. This estimate and the estimate of $\sigma_{R\&R}^2$ from the gauge study can be used to estimate D_p using (10.2.16). This approach also has the important advantage of assuring that the process is stable, which is necessary for D_p to having meaning.

10.4   GAUGE SENSITIVITY OR MEASUREMENT RESOLUTION

Recall that in section 10.2 the relation between the observed value, OV, and coded value, CV, was given in equation (10.2.1) as

$$OV = \text{Offset} + GS \times CV$$

Suppose a certain dimensional measurement has target value of $\tau = 3.005$ in. and specification limits of 3.005 ± 0.003 in. Then we might put Offset $= 3.000$ and GS $= 0.001$. Then the gauge might read as zero or a positive integer. A coded value of 5 gives an observed value of 3.005 inch. The gauge scale, GS, is the units a gauge is read in, and is the *sensitivity* or *resolution* of the gauge. A gauge that reads in a scale of 0.001 in. is more sensitive than a gauge read in a scale of 0.01 in., say.

It is common to have problems with data due to insufficient gauge sensitivity. Problems from insensitivity of gauge data are due in part to the facts that we humans have ten fingers and walk on our hind legs. These facts were responsible for the development of the decimal system. Now, we generally expect the digits we read, record, and use on a gauge to be accurately determined, at least with high probability. Because we work in the decimal system, any time we require one

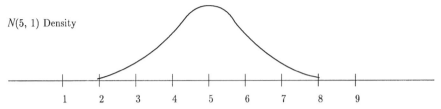

$N(5, 1)$ Density

Figure 10.5   Case 1 of a Normal distribution Centered on a Gauge Mark

additional correct digit we require a gauge that is ten times more sensitive. For example, a gauge that reads in a scale of 0.001 in. is ten times more sensitive than one that reads in 0.01 in. Now, for our purposes it will often be the case that we do not really require such huge improvements in gauge sensitivity. Moreover, since more sensitive gauges are often expensive, we are interested in studying the issue of gauge sensitivity in order to make objective gauge purchase decisions.

Suppose that the process mentioned above is stable and OV has a $N(3.005, 0.001^2)$ distribution. Now, if CV is read as zero or a positive integer the normal distribution is transformed, that is, grouped, into a discrete distribution. This is illustrated in Fig. 10.5 where the normal density is drawn on the CV scale, with the mean centered on a scale mark. Note that, for example, the probability of a CV of 5 is

$$P(CV = 5) = P(-0.5 < Z < 0.5) = 0.38292$$

for Z a $N(0, 1)$ random variable. We see that for this example, with probability almost one, the only values that will be read from the gauge are 1, 2, 3, 4, 5, 6, 7, 8, 9. The probabilities of these values are given in Table 10.14. By symmetry, the mean of this discrete distribution is 5. By direct computation, the standard deviation is $SD(CV) = 1.041$. Points to note are that this discrete distribution has the same mean but a larger standard deviation than the normal process distribution. Also, it should be carefully noted that the equations (10.2.2) relate the mean and variance of the corresponding discrete distribution of OV to those of this discrete distribution of CV, and $\sigma_{OV} = 0.001 \times 0.001041 = 0.001041$ in.

TABLE 10.14   The Probability Function for Case 1 Centering of the Normal Distribution

CV	1	2	3	4	5	6	7	8	9
P(CV)	0.00023	0.00598	0.06060	0.24173	0.38292	0.24173	0.06060	0.00598	0.00023

$$E(CV) = 5, SD(CV) = 1.041$$

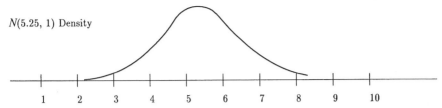

$N(5.25, 1)$ Density

Figure 10.6 Case 2 of a Normal distribution Centered (1/4) *GS* Above a Gauge Mark

When using a gauge we often will not know the location of the mean of the process distribution relative to the gauge scale marks, and this will generally affect the relationship of the mean and standard deviation of the gauge distribution to those of the process distribution. We will study three possible locations of the mean of a normal process distribution relative to the gauge scale marks:

- Case 1 is the case for the normal mean equal to a gauge scale interval boundary, and shown in Fig. 10.5 for $GS/\sigma = 1$. The corresponding probability distribution is given in Table 10.14.
- Case 2 is the case for the normal mean at a point $\frac{1}{4}$ the interval width above an interval boundary, and shown in Fig. 10.6 for $GS/\sigma = 1$. The corresponding probability distribution is given in Table 10.15.
- Case 3 is the case for the normal mean at the center of a gauge scale interval, and shown in Fig. 10.7 for $GS/\sigma = 1$. The corresponding probability distribution is given in Table 10.16.

Now, if the normal density in Fig. 10.5 was shifted somewhat to the right or left, then the values of the mean and variance would not be the same, in general. The most extreme shift would be for the Case 3 situation of a normal distribution with mean centered between two integers as shown in Fig. 10.7. The probability function for this configuration is given in Table 10.16. The mean of this distribution is 5.5 and the standard deviation is 1.04.

Both Case 1 and Case 3 result in discrete distributions that are symmetric about the mean of the normal distribution, so the mean of a

TABLE 10.15 **The Probability Function for Case 2 Centering of the Normal Distribution**

CV	1	2	3	4	5	6	7	8	9	10
P(CV)	0.00009	0.00289	0.03708	0.18657	0.37208	0.29564	0.09343	0.01164	0.00057	0.00001

Mean = 5.25, SD = 1.04

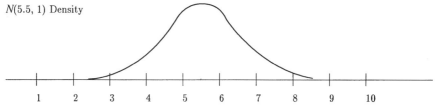

$N(5.5, 1)$ Density

Figure 10.7   Case 3 of a Normal distribution Centered between Two Gauge Marks

sample from either of these distributions is unbiased for the normal distribution mean. Note, particularly, the standard deviations for these two discrete gauge distributions are larger than the standard deviation of the underlying normal process distribution. The mean and standard deviation computed from Table 10.15 for the nonsymmetric gauge distribution are 5.25 and 1.04; and this mean is the same, to two decimal places, as that of the normal distribution. Also, the standard deviation for this nonsymmetric gauge distribution is the same as those for the two symmetric distributions above.

Important points to note here are as follows. Even though the process distribution is normal, the values obtained by the gauge constitute a sample from a discrete distribution. It follows from this observation that we should not, in general, use inference procedures that assume the data are from a normal distribution. For the two cases shown in Figs. 10.5 and 10.7, the mean of the discrete distribution is the same as the mean of the underlying process normal distribution. However, these are the special cases of the process distribution centered on a scale mark or halfway between two scale marks. For all other centerings, the mean of the discrete distribution would not be exactly the same as that of the normal distribution. The worst cases, that is, the most asymmetric distributions, are for the mean of the normal to be either one-fourth or three-fourths of the way between two scale marks. A question that arises then is how much are these estimates for the mean and variance affected by the centering of the process distribution on a scale mark? The fact that the standard deviations for the three different centerings are the same is an interesting and useful property that we will see below holds more generally.

TABLE 10.16   The Probability Function for Case 3 Centering of the Normal Distribution

CV	1	2	3	4	5	6	7	8	9	10
P(CV)	0.00003	0.00132	0.02140	0.13591	0.34134	0.34134	0.13591	0.02140	0.00132	0.00003

Mean = 5.5, SD = 1.04

The estimate of the standard deviation of a normal distribution based on the sample range, viz., $\bar{R}/d_2$, is invalid and should not be used with gauge data whenever sensitivity is a problem. It is invalid because d_2 is correct only for a normal distribution, and *not* for these discrete gauge distributions. This means that the classical control chart formulas that use estimates of the process standard deviation based on the sample range, viz., $\bar{R}/d_2$, are invalid, and should not be used.

Now, although estimates of the standard deviation based on sample ranges are invalid, the sample variance, S^2, is an unbiased estimate of the variance of the discrete gauge distribution that is actually being sampled. Although S is a biased estimate of the standard deviation of this gauge distribution, the bias is small. Thus, the sample mean and standard deviation are adequate estimates of the mean and standard deviation of this discrete gauge distribution.

For the three cases considered and sketched in Figs. 10.5, 10.6, and 10.7, we have taken the gauge scale to be equal to one standard deviation σ of the normal process distribution, that is, $GS/\sigma = 1$. Now, if the gauge scale (GS) is small enough relative to σ, then using estimates based on the normal distribution assumption would be approximately correct. A question, then, is how large should GS be relative to the normal standard deviation σ in order for the sample standard deviation S from the gauge data to be a reasonable estimate of σ? The answer to this question depends on the use we intend to make of the estimate. We consider here two particular uses of S, viz., to estimate process capability, and to make SPC charts.

10.4.1 Estimating the Normal Distribution Parameters and Process Capability from Gauge Data

If GS/σ is small enough, then distribution theory for the assumed normal process distribution can be used both to establish control charts and to evaluate process capability. In order to study the effect of the gauge scale to standard deviation ratio, GS/σ, on the means and standard deviations of the discrete gauge distributions for different centerings of the normal distribution, we have computed these means and standard deviations for the three cases described above for GS/σ taking values from 0.1(0.1)3. These values are given in Table 10.17. Several particular points can be observed from this table. For the largest value of $GS/\sigma = 3$, the values of the standard deviations of the gauge distributions vary widely depending on the location of the normal distribution in a scale interval, and the gauge mean of 0.643 for the asymmetric Case 2 is substantially different from the related normal mean of 0.75. Data from a scale this crude has little value for process

TABLE 10.17   Means and Variances of Discrete Gauge Distributions

GS $\frac{}{\sigma}$	Normal Mean				
	Case 1	Case 2			Case 3
	SD Gauge	Mean Normal	Mean Gauge	SD Gauge	SD Gauge
0.10	1.000	0.025	0.025	1.000	1.000
0.20	1.002	0.050	0.050	1.002	1.002
0.30	1.004	0.075	0.075	1.004	1.004
0.40	1.007	0.100	0.100	1.007	1.007
0.50	1.010	0.125	0.125	1.010	1.010
0.60	1.015	0.150	0.150	1.015	1.015
0.70	1.020	0.175	0.175	1.020	1.020
0.80	1.026	0.200	0.200	1.026	1.026
0.90	1.033	0.225	0.225	1.033	1.033
1.00	1.041	0.250	0.250	1.041	1.041
1.10	1.049	0.275	0.275	1.049	1.049
1.20	1.058	0.300	0.300	1.058	1.058
1.30	1.068	0.325	0.325	1.068	1.068
1.40	1.078	0.350	0.350	1.079	1.079
1.50	1.089	0.375	0.375	1.090	1.090
1.60	1.101	0.400	0.400	1.102	1.102
1.70	1.112	0.425	0.424	1.114	1.116
1.80	1.123	0.450	0.449	1.127	1.131
1.90	1.132	0.475	0.472	1.141	1.149
2.00	1.141	0.500	0.495	1.155	1.168
2.10	1.148	0.525	0.517	1.169	1.191
2.20	1.152	0.550	0.538	1.185	1.216
2.30	1.154	0.575	0.557	1.200	1.245
2.40	1.154	0.600	0.575	1.216	1.276
2.50	1.151	0.625	0.591	1.233	1.311
2.60	1.145	0.650	0.605	1.250	1.348
2.70	1.136	0.675	0.618	1.267	1.387
2.80	1.126	0.700	0.628	1.284	1.428
2.90	1.112	0.725	0.637	1.301	1.471
3.00	1.097	0.750	0.643	1.318	1.516

control or process capability analysis, because the biases in the estimates computed from it will depend on the centering of the process distribution relative to scale marks, which we usually will not know.

However, note that for GS/$\sigma \leq 2$, the standard deviations for the three cases are approximately the same, and, moreover, the gauge distribution mean of the asymmetric Case 2 is reasonably close to that of the normal distribution. This means, of course, that the location of the normal distribution relative to the scale intervals has little effect on the standard deviation and mean of the gauge distribution. Thus, when

$GS/\sigma \le 2$ the mean of a sample of gauge data is an almost unbiased estimate of the process normal distribution mean, and the sample standard deviation is a biased overestimate of the process normal distribution standard deviation by a factor given in Table 10.17 that does not depend much upon the centering of the normal distribution relative to the scale marks.

Note also that when an estimate S of the process standard deviation is computed from gauge data, the factors given in Table 10.17 can be used to adjust the estimate for the bias due to the discreteness of the gauge data. If the standard deviation from gauge data, without this adjustment, is used to compute an estimate of either process capability or process performance then this will result in a tendency to *underestimate* capability or performance, since the estimates tend to overestimate the process standard deviation. We consider an example to illustrate using these factors.

Example 10.6: A gauge reads in a scale of GS = 0.01 in. It is required to use this gauge to estimate the process capability index C_p of a dimension from a process with a stable normal process distribution with specification tolerance interval $\tau \pm \Delta = 0.60 \pm 0.025$ in. We proceed as follows.

First, a sample of 50 parts produced under the full range of operating conditions are gauged with this gauge and the sample has a mean of $\bar{x} = 0.61$ in. and standard deviation of $S = 0.007$ in. From this we compute an initial estimate of GS/σ and $GS/S = 0.01/0.007 = 1.43$. By interpolating in the Case 1 SD column of Table 10.17 we obtain a correction factor of approximately 1.081. This gives an adjusted estimate of σ of $\tilde{\sigma} = S/1.081 = 0.007/1.081 = 0.0065$. Using this value we compute an improved estimate of GS/σ as $0.01/0.0065 = 1.54$, a correction factor of 1.094 and an improved estimate of σ of $\tilde{\sigma} = .007/1.094 = 0.0064$.

Note that if we used $S = 0.007$ without adjusting S as an estimate of σ, then we obtain an estimate

$$\tilde{C}_p = \frac{\text{Tolerance}}{6S} = \frac{0.05}{6(0.007)} = 1.19$$

of C_p. By using the adjusted estimate we obtain an estimate

$$\tilde{C}_p = \frac{0.05}{6(0.0064)} = 1.30$$

This is an improvement of $100(1.30 - 1.19)/1.19 = 9.2\%$. The same percentage improvement would result from estimates of C_{PL}, C_{PU}, and C_{PK}. ∎

The issue of correcting estimates for the effects of grouping data has been studied by many writers. Perhaps the best known of the recommendations are *Sheppard's corrections* (see Kendall and Stuart 1958). The Sheppard correction that expresses the approximation of the gauge distribution standard deviation in terms of the process standard deviation σ is the following:

$$SD(\text{Gauge Distribution}) = \sigma\sqrt{1 + (GS/\sigma)^2/12} \qquad (10.4.1)$$

The quantities given by the radical are approximations to the correction factors given in Table 10.17, and are adequate for our purposes (see problem 10.9). By using this formula to obtain the first correction factor in Example 10.6 we obtain $\sqrt{1 + 1.43^2/12} = 1.082$.

10.4.2   Shewhart Q-Charts from Gauge Data

As discussed above, in using gauge data for any purpose we should remain aware that the data are actually a sample from a discrete distribution. In particular, if the data are to be used to make Shewhart charts, the subgroup size n and the ratio GS/σ are crucial parameters to the effectiveness of the charts for both the chart for the standard deviation and the chart for the mean. For a normal process distribution and a given subgroup size n, if GS/σ is small enough, then the discreteness of the distribution of the plotted statistic can be ignored and normal distribution methods used to establish satisfactory charts. The question is: how small must GS/σ be in order for the charts to be made and interpreted as though the data were truly normal?

Table 10.17 sheds some light on this question, since from it we can see the bias of S as an estimate of σ and the bias of $\overline{X}$ as an estimate of μ. For case 2, the worst possible case, the bias in $\overline{X}$ for $GS/\sigma = 2$ is only $100(0.500 - 0.495)/0.500 = 1\%$, and for smaller values of GS it is smaller. The bias in S as an estimate of σ is about $+4\%$ when $GS/\sigma = 1$. For $GS/\sigma \leq 0.9$ the bias is smaller.

An important point to note is that in forming Shewhart, or, for that matter, any types of charts, we should use the sample standard deviation S computed from the gauge data to estimate the standard deviation and *not* the adjusted estimate discussed in the last subsection. The reason for this is that the data being charted are actually from the

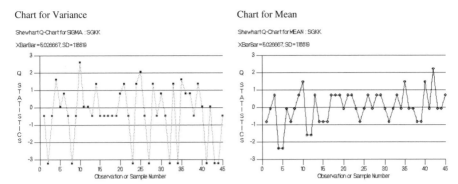

Figure 10.8 Sample Size 5, GS/σ = 2

discrete gauge distribution, and not from the normal process distribution.

To study further the effects of GS/σ and n upon the charts for the case of a stable normal distribution, we have generated data sets and charts for a range of values of these parameters and plotted charts. Some of these charts are given in Figs. 10.8–10.16. Each figure gives the Shewhart Q-charts for both the variance and the mean for fixed values of both n and Gs/σ, and for the cases with known mean and variance.

Figures 10.8–10.12 give charts made from a sample of size $n = 5$ and GS/$\sigma \in \{2, 1.5, 1.25, 1, 0.9\}$. These charts are all made from the same data set of 45 subgroups of size $n = 5$ each. A principal problem for GS/σ large, say GS/$\sigma = 2$, is that we obtain some subgroups with all values the same, and thus these subgroups give $S = 0$. These values all plot at -3.2 on the sigma Q-charts. A reasonable criterion is to require that GS/σ and n be such that there will be few or no zero

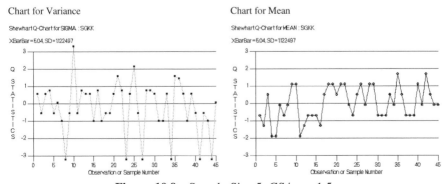

Figure 10.9 Sample Size 5, GS/σ = 1.5

Chart for Variance

Chart for Mean

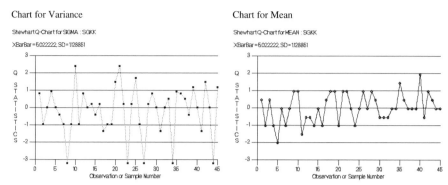

Figure 10.10   Sample Size 5, GS/σ = 1.25

values of S due to the rounding of the data by the gauge. These charts in Figs. 10.8, 10.9, and 10.10 for n = 5 and GS/σ = 2, 1.5, and 1.25, respectively, show a considerable degree of discreteness of the data by both the sigma and the mean charts. The charts of Fig. 10.12 for n = 5 and GS/σ = 0.9 are reasonably acceptable, and those for GS/σ = 1 are marginally so. From these charts and others we have studied, we think a subgroup size of n = 5 should require SG/σ of no more than 0.9, or, possibly, 1.

Figures 10.13–10.16 give comparable charts for n = 10 and GS/σ $\in$ {2, 1.5, 1.25, 1}. The data set for n = 10 is a new set. Clearly, the increased sample size makes better charts. Thus, for n = 10 a value of GS/σ of 1, or, possibly, 1.25 should give acceptable results. The reader will note that, at least to a crude approximation, the adequacy of the sensitivity of a gauge can be judged by the point patterns indicating discreteness of the data obtained.

One way to solve a problem of gauge insensitivity is to purchase a replacement gauge with greater sensitivity. However, this is often an

Chart for Variance

Chart for Mean

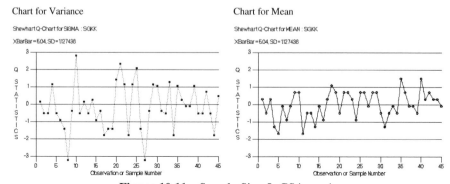

Figure 10.11   Sample Size 5, GS/σ = 1

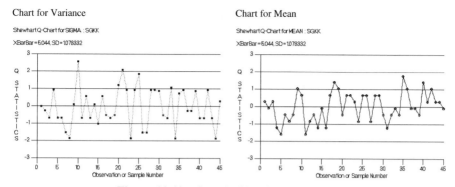

Figure 10.12 Sample Size 5, GS/σ = 0.9

expensive approach and may not be necessary in some cases. For a gauge with a given sensitivity GS/σ, the effectiveness of charts is generally improved by increasing the subgroup size n. For example, note the improvement for GS/σ = 1.25 in Fig. 10.15 for n = 10 over the charts in Fig. 10.10 for n = 5. It may sometimes be more cost effective to take data in larger subgroups, rather than purchase a new more sensitive gauge.

There is one further point that we would make for use in gauging activities. As a particular gauge is used for a particular measurement and information on the value of the process mean μ is accumulated, we shall usually be attempting to center the mean on the target value τ, that is, to make $\mu = \tau$, if possible. Now, we recommend that the gauge scale marks be translated so that the target τ falls on a scale mark. This is done by the choice of the Offset in equation (10.2.2).

Another possibility for improving the charts made from data from a gauge of marginal sensitivity is to interpolate values on the gauge, when possible. For example, if a gauge reads in integers, say; 1, 2,

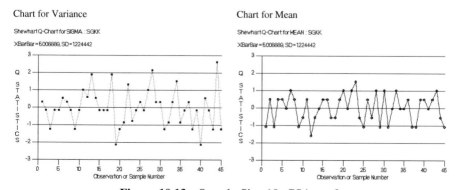

Figure 10.13 Sample Size 10, GS/σ = 2

Chart for Variance   Chart for Mean

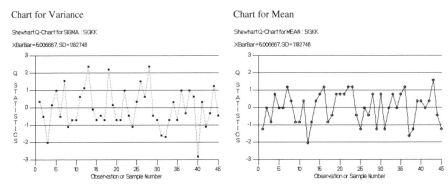

Figure 10.14   Sample Size 10, GS/σ = 1.5

$\cdots$, 9, 10; then we can try to read an additional digit such as 5.5, or 6.7, etc. Even if the last digit recorded cannot be read with certainty, the value 5.5 is likely to be closer to the true value than simply recording a value of 5 or 6. The extra digit need only be recorded when it is though to be at least a little closer to the "true" value than an integer would be. Interpolating values helps to overcome the problems due to the crudeness of the decimal scale discussed at the beginning of this section.

Also, it should be noted that as production processes are stabilized by eliminating assignable causes, and process capability improved by working on the common cause system, for a given gauge the ratio GS/σ will increase. Thus, in a sense, by improving the process we are creating gauge sensitivity problems. Fortunately, this may sometimes be a nice problem to have. At this point the process capability may be good enough to eliminate, or greatly reduce, the need for a charting program.

Chart for Variance   Chart for Mean

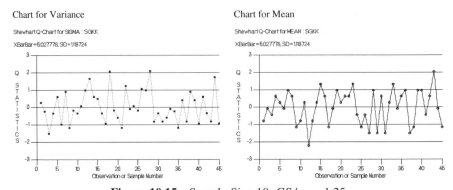

Figure 10.15   Sample Size 10, GS/σ = 1.25

Chart for Variance

Chart for Mean

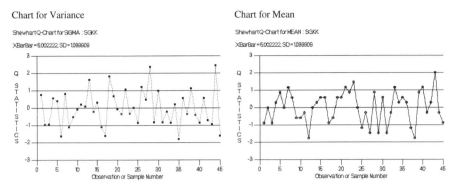

Figure 10.16 Sample Size 10, GS/σ = 1

10.5 GAUGE STABILITY

A measurement system is a work process and the products are the measurements obtained. As such it must be a stable process in order for its outcomes to be predictable. In this section we consider charting methods to study the stability of a gauging system. These methods assume samples consisting of two measurements on each part in the format of the data given in Table 10.1.

10.5.1 Gauge Repeatability Control Charts

Suppose we periodically select a new sample of parts and measure each part twice. Let n_i parts be selected at the ith period to give data $(x_{i1}, y_{i1}), \cdots, (x_{in_i}, y_{in_i})$. Then let $d_{i1} = x_{i1} - y_{i1}, \cdots, d_{in_i} = x_{in_i} - y_{in_i}$. We make subgroups Q-charts from the sequence of samples $d_{i1}, \cdots, d_{in_i}$ for $i \geq 1$. The interpretations of the charts depend on how the measurements are made.

First, note that it is not necessary, in general, for the sample sizes to be a constant value. In fact, it is recommended that n_1 should usually be larger than subsequent subgroups of measurements. We consider now some alternative ways the x and y measurements can be taken.

Case 1 Let both the x and y measurements be made by the same gauge operator using the same process gauge under study. Then the Shewhart variance Q-chart for subgroups can be made using either the case UU or the case KK formulas. Only the variance chart has a meaningful interpretation, and it is a chart to study the stability of the repeatability of the gauge.

Example 10.7: The stability of the repeatability of a gauge was studied as follows. A gauge operator was selected randomly from operators who use the gauge in production. An initial set of 30 parts was selected from production on one day and each day thereafter ten parts were selected. The parts in each sample are put in random order and each part gauged by the operator to obtain the x measurement. The parts are then put in a new random order and gauged again by the same operator to obtain the y measurement. For the first sample, a record as follows was kept of the random orders: $1 \rightarrow 7, 2 \rightarrow 16, \cdots, 30 \rightarrow 14$. This means that the part gauged first initially was gauged seventh in the second gauging, and so on. This was to assure that the operator did not recognize the parts during the second gauging operation. If the operator recognizes individual parts during the second gauging operation, then he may recall the values obtained on the first gauging, and such knowledge would vitiate the analysis. The values $d_i = x_i - y_i$ were recorded for the individual samples. Figure 10.17 shows the Q-chart for sigma from the first twenty samples taken on consecutive days.

We will apply the 11-45 combined test to these Q-charts. A major advantage of these Q-charts is that this gives a sensitive test for detecting either increases or decreases in repeatability. Figure 10.17 indicates a stable process. This is a chart to study the stability of the variances of the differences d from day-to-day. Since this variance is stable, the estimate $SD = 2.21$ given in the figure is an estimate of

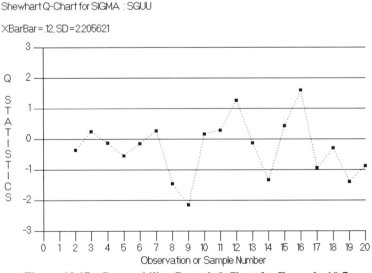

Figure 10.17   Repeatability Control Q-Chart for Example 10.7

$\sqrt{2}\ \sigma$, and from equation (10.2.6) an estimate of σ = repeatability is $\hat{\sigma} = \dfrac{SD}{\sqrt{2}} = \dfrac{2.21}{\sqrt{2}} = 1.56$. This is expressed in gauge scale units, GS. ∎

Example 10.8: Another study of repeatability stability was carried out on another gauge in a manner as described in Example 10.7. The first subgroup contained values obtained on 30 parts and all the subgroups thereafter were of size 10. The Q-chart for the variance of the differences, d, is given in Fig. 10.18. This chart indicates a stable process for the first 15 days, but the 1-of-1 rule signals on the 16th day and the 4-of-5 rule signals on the points 16–20. Note that for this example it is not reasonable to construct an estimate of repeatability from the data from these 20 days, because repeatability does not have a constant value. ∎

Case 2 We now consider studying the stability of a measurement system that may use more than one gauge and more than one operator. The difference in this case and case 1 above is that we now permit the use of different gauges and different operators. The restriction here is that all of the first, x, measurements made on each sample of parts must be made with the same gauge and same operator; and all of the second, y, measurements made on each sample of parts must also be made with the same gauge and same operator. Either the gauge or operator, or

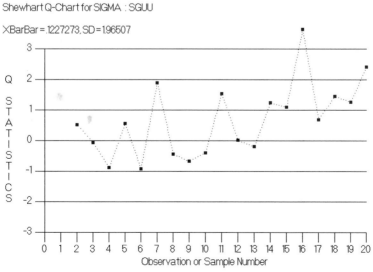

Figure 10.18 Repeatability Control Q-Chart for Example 10.8

both, for the second measurement may be different from those of the first measurement.

From these measurements, we will form samples of differences, and plot both sigma and mean Q-charts. The sigma Q-chart is again a valid chart for repeatability. If repeatability is stable, then signals on the mean chart indicate variation due to changing gauges or operators, or both. It should also be noted that runs tests such as the 4-of-5 test are valid only when the operator and gauge assignments in subgroups are the same for all points in the run. We illustrate this case in Example 10.9.

Example 10.9: A measurement system has two gauges and three operators. A gauge stability study was conducted by selecting a sample of parts from production each Friday for 21 weeks. The first sample consisted of 30 parts and subsequent samples were all of size 10. It was desired to study possible different effects of operators and gauges, in addition to repeatability. Table 10.18 shows the operator and gauge assignments for the samples.

The chart for studying repeatability is given in Fig. 10.19. This chart shows that the measurement process repeatability was stable during this period. Therefore, it is possible to at least attempt to interpret a chart for the sample means in terms of operator and gauge factors involved.

The mean Q-chart is shown in Fig. 10.20. Note from Table 10.18 that the baseline data of sample one was taken with operator 1 and gauge 1 making all measurements. Samples 2–6 involve switching to gauge 2 for the second measurement, but operator 1 is still making all measurements. There is, perhaps, a slight indication of a difference in the gauges. Samples 7–11 involve changing to operator 2 from the baseline data of sample 1, but do not give signals. Points 12–16 represent comparisons of measurements made by operator 1 with gauge 1 to measurements made by operator 3 with gauge 2. These points issue

TABLE 10.18   Operator (O) and Gauge (G) Used

Samples	x Measurement		y Measurement	
	O	G	O	G
1	1	1	1	1
2–6	1	1	1	2
7–11	1	1	2	1
12–16	1	1	3	2
17–21	2	2	3	2

Shewhart Q-Chart for SIGMA : SGUU

XBarBar = -1088, SD = 1708954

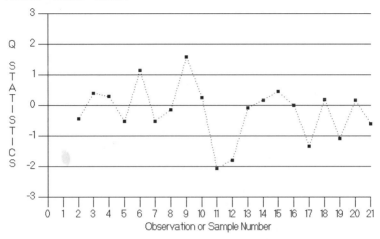

Figure 10.19   Repeatability Control Q-Chart for Example 10.9

Shewhart Q-Chart for MEAN : SGUU

XBarBar = -1088, SD = 1708954

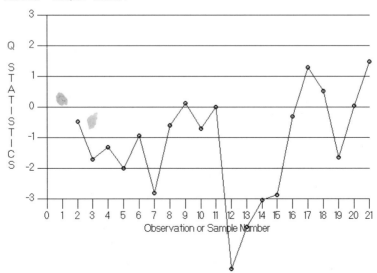

Figure 10.20   Mean Control Q-Chart for Example 10.9

the only strong signals, and an investigation of these differences should be made. An interaction effect is a possibility. ∎

10.5.2   Gauge Bias Control Charts

The charting methods discussed thus far in this section address just the issue of stability of a gauging process. These charting methods have required taking new samples of parts periodically and making two measurements on each part. We now consider purposive selection of a sample of n parts with measurements spaced over the natural tolerance range. The parts are then gauged by a master gauge and the values obtained: $y_1, \cdots, y_n$ will be considered the constant "true" values for these parts. These n parts are regauged periodically by the same operator to obtain values $x_{i1}, \cdots, x_{in}$ for $i = 1, 2, \cdots$ by the production gauge under study, and form the differences $d_{i1} = x_{i1} - y_1, \cdots, d_{in} = x_{in} - y_n$. Note that $x_{i1}, \cdots x_{in}$ are new values for each point to be charted, but the values $y_1, \cdots, y_n$ from the master gauge are obtained only once, that is, in the beginning of the study. Then when the mth measurements are available

$$\bar{d}_i = \frac{1}{n} \sum_{j=1}^{n} d_{ij} \quad \text{and} \quad \bar{\bar{d}} = \frac{1}{m} \sum_{i=1}^{m} \bar{d}_i$$

are both estimates of the gauge bias. Also, since the y_j's are constants we have

$$\mathrm{Var}(d_{ij}) = \mathrm{Var}(x_{ij} - y_j) = \mathrm{Var}(x_{ij})$$

and it follows that the sample standard deviations from the individual d samples and the pooled sample standard deviation from these samples are estimates of the gauge repeatability.

From these remarks it follows that statistics from the subgroups of d values can be charted on sigma and mean Q-charts in a number of ways that reveal different aspects of the gauging process. These values can be used to make mean charts for the cases UU, UK, KU, and KK for subgroups of equations (7.3.1)–(7.3.4). The sigma chart is a chart to study the stability of repeatability. The mean charts for cases that assume the mean is unknown, that is, cases UU and UK, are charts for the stability, or, constancy, of the gauge bias. Mean charts that assume the mean is known—cases KU and KK—and that use a "known" value of zero, are charts for the constancy of the mean *at the value zero*.

Example 10.10: Ten parts were selected with measurements that cover the natural tolerance range of the production process distribution. These parts were gauged with a master gauge to obtain values $y_1, \cdots, y_{10}$. The parts were gauged again with a process gauge each work day for 30 days. Each day the parts were arranged in random order to avoid having operator memory influence the values. Note that larger sample sizes will help with this problem of operator memory. The differences $d_1 = x_1 - y_1, \cdots, x_{10} - y_{10}$ were the subgroups values for charting.

Figure 10.21 gives the sigma chart. This is a repeatability chart, and its shows a stable process. Note the estimates $\bar{d} = 0.36$ and $S_d = 1.63$, computed from the 30 samples.

Figure 10.22 shows the case UU mean chart. If the bias is constant, this chart should reflect a stable process, which it does, indeed.

Figure 10.23 is the case KU chart, that is, for the mean having "known" value of zero and sigma unknown. The chart shows that the bias has a positive value since there are a number of signals of a positive bias. The estimate of the bias is $\bar{d} = 0.36$.

The corresponding charts made retrospectively using the estimate $S_d = 1.63$ for sigma give the same conclusions. ∎

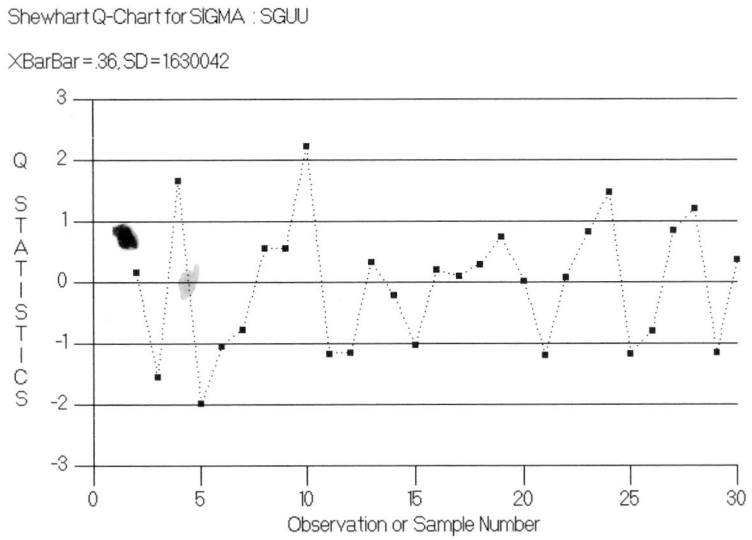

Shewhart Q-Chart for SIGMA : SGUU

XBarBar = .36, SD = 1630042

Figure 10.21 Repeatability Control Q-Chart for Example 10.10

Shewhart Q-Chart for MEAN : SGUU

XBarBar = .36, SD = 1630042

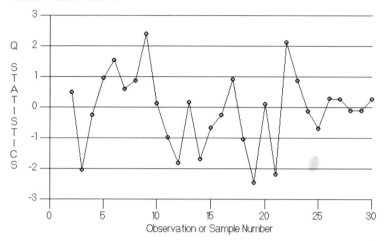

Figure 10.22   Chart for Mean Stability, Example 10.10

10.6   SUMMARY

In this chapter we have considered some concepts and methods of measurement assurance. Sources of error in a measurement process studied included linearity and accuracy of a gauge, and the repeatability

Shewhart Q-Chart for MEAN : SGKU

XBarBar = .36, SD = 1630042

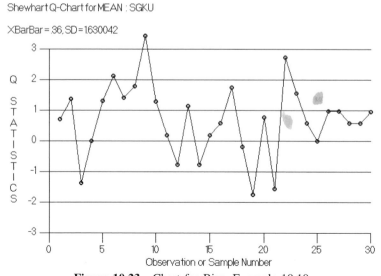

Figure 10.23   Chart for Bias, Example 10.10

and reproducibility of a stable measurement process. The adequacy of a measurement process for the purpose of assuring that specifications are met, and for control charting to assure process stability, was considered. The role of measurement resolution was considered in some detail and some methods were given for charting to assure the stability of the measurement process itself.

Further detailed discussion of issues of measurement assurance can be found in Eisenhart (1963), Cameron (1977), Kane (1989), and Wheeler (1989).

PROBLEMS

10.1 A gauge that reads in units of 0.01 in. (GS = 0.01 in.) is used to measure a part dimension from a process with $LSL = 7.61$ in. and $USL = 7.81$ in. The gauge reads in integers and the coded values (CV) are related to observed values (OV) by the formula:

$$OV = 7.61 + (0.01)CV$$

Thirty production parts selected to cover the specification range were measured by this production gauge and by a master gauge. The values obtained were as follows.

Gauge, x:	5	6	6	7	7	7	8	8	8	9	9	10	10
Master, y:	4	6	7	5	8	10	6	8	9	8	10	7	9

Gauge, x:	10	10	10	11	11	12	12	12	12	13	13
Master, y:	10	11	12	9	11	11	12	13	14	10	13

Gauge, x:	14	14	14	15	16	17
Master, y:	13	15	16	14	14	16

Determine if this gauge has a linearity or accuracy problem.

10.2 It was decided to study the repeatability of the gauge described in problem 10.1. Thirty new parts covering the production range were selected, randomly ordered, and measured by one operator. The parts were then placed in a new random order and measured again by the same operator. Care was taken to assure that the operator could not identify the parts from the first gauging, which could invalidate the study. The values from the first, *x*, gauging and the second, *y*, gauging were as follows.

x	5	15	9	11	11	7	10	13	7	14	8	10	12
y	6	15	10	14	7	9	10	12	7	13	6	9	12

x	11	8	12	11	13	14	13	9	10	9	6	9	12
y	10	9	11	11	14	16	10	13	12	10	6	8	9

x	8	7	11	14
y	8	10	12	13

Note that the *LSL*, *USL*, and the relationship between observed values and coded values were given in problem 10.1. Evaluate the repeatability of the gauge expressed in units of in. Also, evaluate the % Repeatability.

10.3 A certain part dimension has a target value of 0.265 in., LSL = 0.255 in., and USL = 0.275 in. Values from a gauge are given in integers, and these values are related to observed values by:

$$OV = 0.250 + (0.001)(CV)$$

An R&R study was made of a gauge that gave values from operators *x* and *y* as follows from 30 parts.

x	*y*	*x*	*y*	*x*	*y*	*x*	*y*	*x*	*y*
12	14	11	9	17	18	12	16	11	16
10	12	18	14	14	19	18	20	15	17
19	17	18	17	14	16	15	14	24	24
14	13	15	14	13	19	16	18	13	14
12	13	12	12	12	11	14	17	16	13
16	20	15	15	13	14	11	13	12	15

Evaluate % Repeatability, % Reproducibility, and % (R&R) for this gauge study.

10.4 A certain part dimension has target value of 1.45 in., LSL = 1.40 in., and USL = 1.50 in. A gauge used to measure this dimension reads in integers and the relationship between observed values (OV) and coded values (CV) is given by:

$$OV = 1.35 + (0.01)(CV)$$

Thirty parts were taken from production under conditions that represent what is believed to be the range of production conditions for these parts, and gauged by two operators (operator x and operator y) to obtain the following gauge readings.

x	y	x	y	x	y	x	y	x	y	x	y
11	10	11	11	8	7	6	6	8	7	10	10
9	8	7	6	13	13	12	12	9	9	14	14
9	8	9	8	10	10	11	10	8	6	10	10
5	4	6	6	10	9	10	10	12	12	12	12
9	9	10	9	9	9	10	9	10	10	5	4

Estimate the Repeatability, Reproducibility, and %(R&R). Comment on your results.

10.5 Fifteen parts were sampled randomly from production by taking one part each day on each of five days per week for three weeks. The specification tolerance range is 0.30 in., and is centered on specification target value. Using the production gauge for this process, two gauge operators—selected randomly from the set of operators who regularly use this gauge—gauged each part once to obtain the following table of data, expressed in inches.

x	y	d	w	
3.001	3.001	−0.000	3.0010	$\overline{d} = -0.00627$,
2.997	3.010	−0.013	3.0035	
2.980	2.996	−0.016	2.9880	$\hat{S}_d^2 = 0.0000938$
2.991	2.997	−0.006	2.9940	$\overline{w} = 2.99835$,
3.013	3.028	−0.015	3.0205	
2.986	2.991	−0.005	2.9885	$\hat{S}_w^2 = 0.0001063$
3.004	2.997	0.007	3.0005	
2.987	3.002	−0.015	2.9945	
2.981	2.991	−0.010	2.9860	
2.998	2.996	0.002	2.9970	
2.999	3.007	−0.008	3.0030	
2.993	3.019	−0.026	3.0060	
3.011	3.011	−0.000	3.0110	
3.013	3.005	0.008	3.0090	
2.985	2.982	0.003	2.9835	

(a) Compute estimates of Repeatability, Reproducibility, R&R, and % R&R.

(b) Compute an estimate of the discrimination ratio, $\hat{D}_p$.

(c) Discuss these results and give your recommendations.

10.6 A certain part dimension has specification limits of 3.24 ± 0.05 cm. To study the effectiveness of a particular gauge for taking these measurements, six parts were gauged three times each by three operators. Observed values obtained are given in the following table.

P	O	R	x	P	O	R	x	P	O	R	x
1	1	1	3.246	3	1	1	3.247	5	1	1	3.242
1	1	2	3.244	3	1	2	3.247	5	1	2	3.237
1	1	3	3.243	3	1	3	3.248	5	1	3	3.241
1	2	1	3.255	3	2	1	3.249	5	2	1	3.242
1	2	2	3.249	3	2	2	3.252	5	2	2	3.239
1	2	3	3.251	3	2	3	3.252	5	2	3	3.241

1	3	1	3.243	3	3	1	3.245	5	3	1	3.237
1	3	2	3.244	3	3	2	3.245	5	3	2	3.236
1	3	3	3.246	3	3	3	3.250	5	3	3	3.237
2	1	1	3.243	4	1	1	3.235	6	1	1	3.232
2	1	2	3.242	4	1	2	3.235	6	1	2	3.235
2	1	3	3.240	4	1	3	3.235	6	1	3	3.233
2	2	1	3.246	4	2	1	3.242	6	2	1	3.233
2	2	2	3.245	4	2	2	3.236	6	2	2	3.232
2	2	3	3.249	4	2	3	3.235	6	2	3	3.235
2	3	1	3.240	4	3	1	3.234	6	3	1	3.232
2	3	2	3.242	4	3	2	3.232	6	3	2	3.230
2	3	3	3.238	4	3	3	3.230	6	3	3	3.232

P = Part, O = Operator, R = Replication, x = Value
Evaluate:
% Repeatability
% Reproducibility
% (R&R)
% Parts

10.7 A part dimension has specification limits of 0.446 $\pm$ 0.004 inch. To study the performance of a gauge, ten parts were gauged twice each by four operators to obtain the values in the following table.

P	O	R	x	P	O	R	x	P	O	R	x
1	1	1	0.447	4	2	2	0.447	7	4	1	0.444
1	1	2	0.447	4	3	1	0.447	7	4	2	0.443
1	2	1	0.447	4	3	2	0.447	8	1	1	0.446
1	2	2	0.447	4	4	1	0.446	8	1	2	0.447
1	3	1	0.447	4	4	2	0.447	8	2	1	0.446
1	3	2	0.447	5	1	1	0.446	8	2	2	0.446
1	4	1	0.447	5	1	2	0.446	8	3	1	0.446
1	4	2	0.447	5	2	1	0.447	8	3	2	0.446
2	1	1	0.445	5	2	2	0.446	8	4	1	0.446
2	1	2	0.445	5	3	1	0.446	8	4	2	0.446
2	2	1	0.445	5	3	2	0.446	9	1	1	0.444
2	2	2	0.445	5	4	1	0.446	9	1	2	0.444

2	3	1	0.445	5	4	2	0.446	9	2	1	0.444			
2	3	2	0.445	6	1	1	0.447	9	2	2	0.444			
2	4	1	0.445	6	1	2	0.446	9	3	1	0.444			
2	4	2	0.446	6	2	1	0.446	9	3	2	0.444			
3	1	1	0.445	6	2	2	0.447	9	4	1	0.444			
3	1	2	0.446	6	3	1	0.446	9	4	2	0.444			
3	2	1	0.445	6	3	2	0.446	10	1	1	0.449			
3	2	2	0.446	6	4	1	0.447	10	1	2	0.448			
3	3	1	0.445	6	4	2	0.447	10	2	1	0.448			
3	3	2	0.445	7	1	1	0.443	10	2	2	0.448			
3	4	1	0.445	7	1	2	0.443	10	3	1	0.448			
3	4	2	0.445	7	2	1	0.443	10	3	2	0.448			
4	1	1	0.447	7	2	2	0.443	10	4	1	0.448			
4	1	2	0.447	7	3	1	0.443	10	4	2	0.448			
4	2	1	0.447	7	3	2	0.443							

P = Part, O = Operator, R = Replication, x = Value
Evaluate:
% Repeatability
% Reproducibility
% (R&R)
% Parts
Discuss the capability of this measurement system.

10.8 A dimensional measurement has specification limits 2.71 ± 0.02 in. A gauge used for this measurement reads in units of 0.01 in., i.e., Gauge Scale = GS = 0.01. A sample of n = 100 parts was gauged by one operator using this gauge and gave a sample standard deviation of S = 0.0047 in.

(a) Compute an estimate of the process capability index, C_p, using S to estimate σ.

(b) Compute an approximately unbaised estimate $\hat{\sigma}$ of the process standard deviation σ.

(c) Compute an estimate of the process capability index, C_p, using $\hat{\sigma}$ to estimate σ.

(d) Discuss these results.

10.9 Verify that the Sheppard's correction factor $\sqrt{1 + (GS/\sigma)^2/12}$ of equation (10.4.1) gives an adequate approximation to the correction factors of Table 10.17 by computing its value for GS/σ = 0.1, 0.3, 0.5, 1, 1.5, 2, 2.5, 3.

CHAPTER 11

Regression SPC Models

In Chapter 4 it was mentioned that in order for a process to be stable by the definition of Shewhart, it is only necessary that the process be predictable. In this chapter we consider regression models and methods based on them for processes that have either means or variances that are not constant. They are nevertheless predictable processes since the models considered can be used to predict future values of the quality variable.

11.1 SPC FOR THE SIMPLE LINEAR REGRESSION MODEL

The material in earlier chapters has treated statistical process control of processes when the constant mean and variance model of display (4.1.2) is adequate to model the process when no special causes are active. It was mentioned in section 4.1 that some processes have natural trends that cannot be removed, but can be modeled by regression models. Such processes will here be said to have *necessary trends,* that is, trends that cannot be removed by management or engineering actions. However, if the quality variable y can be modeled as a regression function of a variable x, then, of course, this regression model can be used to predict values of y. When this is so, the process is stable or in-control by Shewhart's definition.

We assume that the data consist of a sequence of pairs (x_i, y_i), called *cases,* for $i = 1, 2, \cdots$. Then we assume that the simple linear regression model of (11.1.1) is valid for this data.

$$
\begin{aligned}
&y_i = \beta_0 + \beta_1 x_i + \epsilon_i \\
&x_i \text{ is a fixed value} \\
&\epsilon_i\text{'s are i.i.d. } N(0, \sigma^2) \text{ random variables} \\
&\beta_0, \beta_1, \text{ and } \sigma^2 \text{ are parameters}
\end{aligned}
\tag{11.1.1}
$$

We assume that the cases

$$(x_1, y_1), (x_2, y_2), \cdots, (x_i, y_i), \cdots$$

are observed sequentially in time order. We will consider two cases initially, namely, when prior estimates are available that are based on enough data to assume the parameters β_0, β_1, and σ are "known," and when prior data are not available. We will later consider the intermediate case when prior estimates are available, but cannot be taken to be the exact values of the parameters.

11.1.1   The Parameters "Known" Case, Case K

For this case we set Q_i equal to the standardized residuals as follows:

$$Q_i = \frac{\epsilon_i}{\sigma} = \frac{y_i - \beta_0 - \beta_1 x_i}{\sigma} \qquad (11.1.2)$$

for $i = 1, 2, \ldots$.

These Q_i's can then be plotted on Shewhart, EWMA, or CUSUM Q-charts.

11.1.2   The Parameters "Unknown" Case, Case U

When the ith case (x_i, y_i) is observed, we define the sequential statistics given in Table 11.1. The updating formulas are convenient for computations.

If the model (11.1.1) is correct, then the sequence of statistics Q_4, Q_5, $\cdots$ is a sequence of independent standard normal statistics. See O'Reilly and Quesenberry (1973) and Quesenberry (1990) for proofs and further discussion of these statistics. Marr and Quesenberry (1991) call these statistics the normalized uniform residuals, NU residuals, from a regression model. These Q-statistics can also be plotted on a Shewhart Q-chart, or as a CUSUM or EWMA Q-chart. Note that these charts can be made in real time case-by-case as the data become available.

The reader will note that the values $\hat{\beta}_{0,i}$ and $\hat{\beta}_{1,i}$ are the usual least squares estimates of β_0 and β_1 from the first i cases, and that the value B_i is a Studentized version of the ith residual from this fitted model. We recommend making two charts as in SPC analysis of the data. When each case (x_i, y_i) arrives, we will plot the case on an (x, y) runs

TABLE 11.1 Sequential Statistics and Updating Formulas

Sequential Statistics	Updating Formulas
$\bar{x}_i = \dfrac{1}{i}\sum_{j=1}^{i} x_j$	$\bar{x}_i = \dfrac{1}{i}[(i-1)\bar{x}_{i-1} + x_i]$
$\bar{y}_i = \dfrac{1}{i}\sum_{j=1}^{i} y_j$	$\bar{y}_i = \dfrac{1}{i}[(i-1)\bar{y}_{i-1} + y_i]$
$S_{xy}^{(i)} = \sum_{j=1}^{i} (x_j - \bar{x}_i)(y_j - \bar{y}_i)$	$S_{xy}^{(i)} = S_{xy}^{(i-1)} + \dfrac{i-1}{i}(x_i - \bar{x}_{i-1})(y_i - \bar{y}_{i-1})$
$S_{xx}^{(i)} = \sum_{j=1}^{i} (x_j - \bar{x}_i)^2$	$S_{xx}^{(i)} = S_{xx}^{(i-1)} + \dfrac{i-1}{i}(x_i - \bar{x}_{i-1})^2$
$S_{yy}^{(i)} = \sum_{j=1}^{i} (y_j - \bar{y}_i)^2$	$S)_{yy}^{(i)} = S_{yy}^{(i-1)} + \dfrac{i-1}{i}(y_i - \bar{y}_{i-1})^2$
$\hat{\beta}_{1,i} = \dfrac{S_{xy}^{(i)}}{S_{xx}^{(i)}}$	
$\hat{\beta}_{0,i} = \bar{y}_i - \hat{\beta}_{1,i}\bar{x}_i$	
$K_i = \dfrac{iS_{xx}^{(i)}}{(i-1)S_{xx}^{(i-1)}}$	
$SSE_i = S_{yy}^{(i)} - S_{xy}^{(i)}\hat{\beta}_{1,i}$	
$B_i = \dfrac{\sqrt{i-3}(y_i - \hat{\beta}_{0,i-1} - \hat{\beta}_{1,i-1}x_i)}{\sqrt{(SSE_{i-1})K_i}}$	
$u_i = H_{i-3}(B_i)$ for $i = 4, 5, \cdots$	
$Q_i = \Phi^{-1}(u_i)$ for $i = 4, 5, \cdots$	

plot, and plot the Q-statistic Q_i on a Shewhart Q-chart. We illustrate this in the next example.

Example 11.1: To illustrate this simple linear regression Q-chart, we consider a data set given by Mandel (1969). The data are given in Table 11.2. These data are records of pieces of mail handled in a U.S. Post Office (the x variable) and the number of manhours used (the y variable), recorded for 26 four-week periods for the fiscal years 1962 and 1963. Mandel fits a simple linear regression model using these data and advocates drawing control limits parallel to this regression line and at $2\hat{\sigma}$ above and below it, for $\hat{\sigma}^2$ the usual mean square estimate of σ^2.

Notably, Mandel argues, from examining a scatter plot of all of the data, that the cases 7 for both fiscal years should be omitted from the regression analysis because they covered the Christmas period when a lot of temporary employees are used, who would be expected to have lower efficiency. He also noted that point 6 for fiscal year 1963 violated the linear trend of the scatter plot, and that investigation showed that

TABLE 11.2   Data on Mail Processing Hours and Volume for the ABCD Post Office (Fiscal Years 1962–1963)

Four-Week Accounting Period	Pieces of Mail Handled, x (in millions)	Manhours used, y (in thousands)
Fiscal Year 1962		
1	157	572
2	161	570
3	168	645
4	186	645
5	183	645
6	184	671
7	268	1053
8	180	675
9	175	670
10	193	710
11	184	656
12	179	640
13	164	599
Fiscal Year 1963		
1	154	569
2	157	564
3	164	573
4	188	667
5	191	700
6	180	765
7	270	1070
8	180	637
9	172	650
10	184	655
11	179	665
12	169	599
13	160	605

this was caused by an abnormal amount of machine down-time. This point and the two points for period 7 (the Christmas season) were then dropped from his subsequent analysis. The remaining 23 cases were then used to fit a simple linear regression model and plot the regression control chart as the regression line with parallel control limits at $2\hat{\sigma}$ above and below it. It is noteworthy that Mandel used the scatter plot, and not the "regression control chart" to decide which points were signaling special causes.

We have also plotted these data on a scatter plot as shown in Fig. 11.1a. We note that in this plot case 6 of fiscal year 1963 (the 19th point, overall) appears to violate the linear trend; however, the two period 7 cases, while far removed from the other points, do not appear

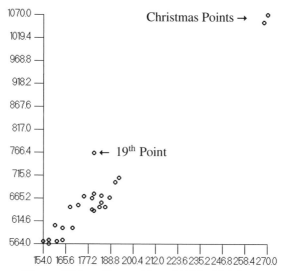

Figure 11.1a   Scatter Plot of Table 11.2 Data

to violate the linear trend. We do not drop any points at this stage of our analysis, and proceed to plot Q-charts of these data. The case U Q-chart is given in Fig. 11.1b. This chart shows clearly that point 19 is an outlier. Since Mandel noted that an abnormal amount of machine down-time during this period was responsible, we now delete this ob-

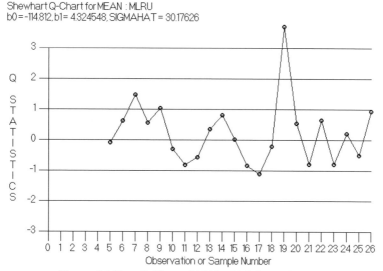

Figure 11.1b Q-Chart of Table 11.2 Data, Case U

servation from the data set and make the Q-chart in Fig. 11.1c from the other 25 cases. This chart shows no anomalous patterns.

Some further comment is in order. From the scatter plot it is apparent that the two period 7 Christmas season points are highly influential points in determining the regression line, and they should not be omitted from the analysis.

A major strength of this case U Q-chart is that it could have been made case-by-case in time order as the cases became available. Had this been done with these data, the sixth period of 1963 would have been immediately recognized as an outlying case.　　　　■

11.2 THE TOOL-WEAR PROBLEM

Measurements of dimensions of parts made by some manufacturing processes show necessary trends that can be modeled adequately by a simple linear regression model with independent errors, at least over some subintervals of tool life. This is true for some machining operations that involve cutting, drilling, or grinding operations that use lathes, drills, or grinding wheels to shape parts. The tool itself—the lathe insert, drill bit, or grinding wheel—is subject to wear and, if adjustments are not made during the life of the tool, the dimensions of parts may change in predictable patterns. However, the dimensions of

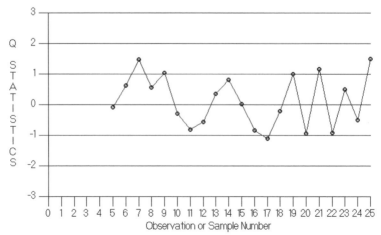

Shewhart Q-Chart for MEAN : MLRU
b0 = -120.7552, b1 = 4.334918, SIGMAHAT = 22.02826

Figure 11.1c Q-Chart of Table 11.2 Data with Case 19 Deleted, Case U

parts will be predictable only if there are no special causes affecting the process. Therefore, our first purpose is to chart the process as an aid to find special causes, and stabilize the process by removing them. Quesenberry (1988) considered statistical process adjustment (SPA) of a linear trend tool-wear process. In Chapter 12 we will consider SPA for this model, and in Chapter 13 we will consider SPC and SPA for these processes when the errors are autocorrelated.

For a tool-wear process, we now tentatively assume that the simple linear regression model of display (11.1.1) is valid with $x_i = i$. The linear relationship is then

$$y_i = \beta_0 + \beta_1 i + \epsilon_i \qquad (11.2.1)$$

where the ϵ_i's are independent. This is a very special case of the simple linear regression model of equation (11.1.1). However, it is a particularly important special case because processes that entail wear on tools are common and important in manufacturing. Moreover, many manufacturing processes can be modeled quite adequately over at least part of the tool's life by the simple model of (11.2.1).

Note that in this model the parameter β_1 has an immediate and readily understood interpretation. It is simply the wear rate on the tool per part made. The parameter σ is essentially the same here as it was for the constant mean model. It represents the variation due to common causes for this process. It was seen in Quesenberry (1988) that the ratio σ/β_1 of inherent variation to tool wear rate is itself an important parameter for designing an SPA procedure.

Example 11.2: Table 11.3 gives the measurements made on the first 50 parts made just after the cutting tool was changed. A runs plot of these data is given in Fig. 11.2a. The plot clearly suggests that a linear model is reasonable for these data. We do note that observation 31 appears to be high. The Shewhart Q-chart for these data is given in Fig. 11.2b. This chart shows that the measurement for part number 31 is definitely an outlier. It is slightly more than four standard deviations above the center line. An examination of part 31 showed that the large measurement was due to a sand hole in the casting being machined, and was not due to the machining operation itself. Therefore, the measurement from this 31st part was dropped from the data set and the Q-chart for this deleted data set is given in Fig. 11.2c. A number of things can be observed by comparing Figs. 11.2b and 11.2c. Of course, the charts are exactly the same for the first 30 measurements. However, when the large observation 31 is removed, the spread of the points in

TABLE 11.3 Data for Example 11.2, in mm

Part	Obs.	Part	Obs.	Part	Obs.	Part	Obs.	Part	Obs.
1	7.150	11	7.157	21	7.155	31	7.184	41	7.158
2	7.154	12	7.154	22	7.154	32	7.158	42	7.160
3	7.151	13	7.153	23	7.158	33	7.160	43	7.163
4	7.150	14	7.151	24	7.157	34	7.161	44	7.161
5	7.154	15	7.161	25	7.164	35	7.159	45	7.171
6	7.147	16	7.152	26	7.158	36	7.165	46	7.160
7	7.155	17	7.159	27	7.161	37	7.162	47	7.167
8	7.156	18	7.157	28	7.158	38	7.162	48	7.167
9	7.154	19	7.150	29	7.156	39	7.162	49	7.167
10	7.152	20	7.160	30	7.155	40	7.163	50	7.161

Fig. 11.2c is smaller for points 32–50 than on Fig. 11.2b for these points. This is because the large observation 31 inflated the estimate of variance on these points on Fig. 11.2b. The chart in Fig. 11.2c indicates that this process is a stable linear tool-wear process in the variable measured (an outer diameter dimension).

The Shewhart charts also give estimates $\hat{\beta}_0$ ($b0$ on chart), $\hat{\beta}_1$ ($b1$ on chart) and $\hat{\sigma}$ (SIGMAHAT on chart) of β_0, β_1, and σ as follows. These are computed from the entire data set.

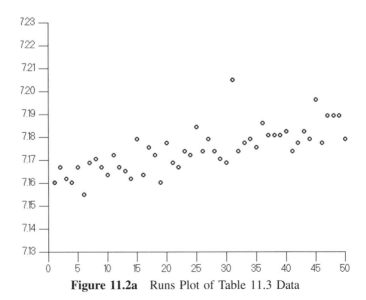

Figure 11.2a Runs Plot of Table 11.3 Data

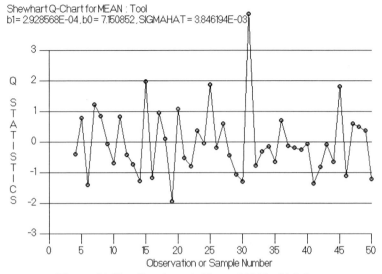

Figure 11.2b   Shewhart Q-Chart of Table 11.3 Data

	$\hat{\beta}_0$	$\hat{\beta}_1$	$\hat{\sigma}$
Figure 11.2b	7.15	0.00029	0.0038
Figure 11.2c	7.15	0.00028	0.0031

The effect of removing observation 31 is appreciable on $\hat{\sigma}$, but small on $\hat{\beta}_0$ and $\hat{\beta}_1$. ■

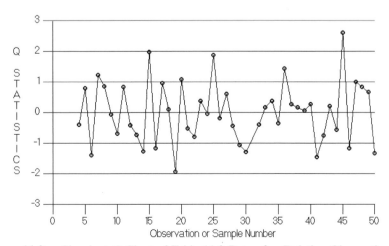

Figure 11.2c   Shewhart Q-Chart of Table 11.3 Data after Deleting Observation 31

11.2.1 Outliers in Tool-Wear Processes

In the last example, we saw an outlier from the simple linear regression tool-wear model. This is a rather common occurrence, for many tool-wear processes are prone to give outlying observations due to causes that are generally recognized, but may be difficult to identify in particular instances. Even though many machining operations have chip guards, it is not at all unusual to have a chip fall against a cutting blade and spoil the part before it burns or falls off. Sand holes or other abnormalities from casting operations can cause extreme outliers. The Q-statistics plotted on Q-charts have ideal properties for detecting outliers in the data stream in real time and on line.

11.2.2 Inherent Lack of Potential Process Stability

Tool-wear processes are complex by nature and it may sometimes be difficult or even impossible to bring a process to an acceptably stable state by working with the process itself in isolation. For example, the wear rate per part β_1 may not be constant due either to variation among tools from the same batch of tools, or among batches; or due to variation among castings being machined or ground. Tools may vary in hardness, sharpness, or in other ways; while castings may also vary in hardness, or in the amount of stock that must be removed in a machining process. If the amount of stock to be removed varies, the wear rate β_1 will necessarily vary accordingly, increasing variation in the machining operation. To bring tool-wear process to an acceptably stable state may require bringing upstream processes in foundries and tool making into better control. This, in turn, will likely involve contract relations with suppliers.

11.3 SPC FOR THE MULTIPLE LINEAR REGRESSION MODELS

In this section we consider charting Q-statistics for the univariate multiple linear regression model with independent normal errors. The formulas used here are given in Quesenberry (1986). They were originally given in O'Reilly and Quesenberry (1973). Notation is defined in Table 11.4.

Suppose the cases are a sequence $(\mathbf{x}_i', y_i)$ for $i = 1, 2, \cdots$, which are from the ith part in order of production. Then we assume the regression model of display (11.3.1).

TABLE 11.4 Notation and Q-Statistics Formulas for Multiple Linear Regression

Notation	Formulas
$\mathbf{y}_n = (y_1, \cdots, y_n)'$	a vector of independent random variables
	$\hat{\beta}_i = (\mathbf{X}_i'\mathbf{X}_i)^{-1}\mathbf{X}_i'\mathbf{y}_i$, the least squares estimates of β from the first i cases
$\mathbf{X}_n = [X_{ij}]$	an $n \times p$ matrix of independent variables of full rank $(n > p)$
	$S_i^2 = \mathbf{y}_i'[I - \mathbf{X}_i(\mathbf{X}_i'\mathbf{X}_i)^{-1}\mathbf{X}_i']\mathbf{y}_i$, the sum of squares for residuals from the first i cases
$\beta = (\beta_0, \cdots, \beta_{p-1})'$	a vector of p coefficient parameters
	$B_i = \dfrac{\sqrt{i - p - 1}(y_i - \mathbf{x}_i'\hat{\beta}_i)}{\sqrt{[1 - \mathbf{x}_i'(\mathbf{X}_i'\mathbf{X}_i)^{-1}\mathbf{x}_i]S_i^2 - (y_i - \mathbf{x}_i'\hat{\beta}_i)^2}}$
$\mathbf{x}_i' = (x_{i,1}, \cdots, x_{i,p})$	the ith row of $\mathbf{X}_n$
$\mathbf{X}_i$	the matrix consisting of the first i rows of $\mathbf{X}_n$
	$u_{i-p-1} = H_{i-p-1}(B_i), \ i = p + 2, \cdots, n$
	$Q_i = \Phi^{-1}(u_{i-p-1}), \ i = p + 2, \cdots$

$$y_i = \mathbf{x}_i'\beta + \epsilon_i = \beta_0 x_{i,1} + \cdots + \beta_{p-1} x_{i,p} + \epsilon_i,$$

$$i = 1, 2, \cdots$$

(11.3.1)

ϵ_i's are independent $N(0, \sigma^2)$ random variables for $i = 1, 2, \cdots$

Under the model assumptions, the statistics Q_{p+2}, Q_{p+3}, $\cdots$ are independent standard normal statistics and can be plotted on Shewhart, CUSUM, or EWMA Q-charts. These charts will reflect the adequacy and stability of the model.

In some tool-wear processes the simple linear regression model is not adequate because even if there is a predictable trend, it may be nonlinear. In many of these cases a quadratic or higher degree polynomial may give an adequate fit to the process. That is, a model of the form of equation (11.3.2) may give an adequate fit for the data.

$$y_i = \beta_0 + \beta_1 i + \cdots + \beta_p i^p + \epsilon_i \qquad (11.3.2)$$

The Q-statistics for this model can be computed using the formulas of Table 11.4. For tool-wear processes, however, we generally expect the regression function to be monotone, so the degree p of the polynomial is usually taken to be either 1 or 2.

Example 11.3: Table 11.5 gives 100 measurements made on consecutively made parts. Figure 11.3a is a runs chart of these data. This runs chart shows a fairly clear curvilinear trend with a slope that itself appears to be increasing on the last 25 or so points. The Q-chart for the simple linear regression model ($p = 1$) is shown in Fig. 11.3b. This chart of residuals also indicates a curvilinear trend and strongly signals on the last seven points by both 1-of-1 and 4-of-5 tests. Also, the 11th point signals by the 1-of-1 test and the 65th by the 4-of-5 test.

The quadratic regression Q-chart is shown in Fig. 11.3c. It indicates a considerably better fit by the quadratic model, as we could expect from the runs chart. The last seven points issue no signals, and the 11th no longer signals, however, the 65th still signals by the 4-of-5 test. The quadratic model, fitted from all the data, is

$$y_i = 3.858 + 0.0000099i + 0.0000059i^2$$

TABLE 11.5   Data for Example 11.3

Part	Obs.	Part	Obs.	Part	Obs.	Part	Obs.	Part	Obs.
1	3.863	21	3.865	41	3.858	61	3.892	81	3.878
2	3.858	22	3.861	42	3.862	62	3.895	82	3.896
3	3.853	23	3.872	43	3.879	63	3.857	83	3.890
4	3.848	24	3.879	44	3.886	64	3.896	84	3.891
5	3.856	25	3.865	45	3.880	65	3.902	85	3.914
6	3.856	26	3.851	46	3.852	66	3.875	86	3.909
7	3.859	27	3.875	47	3.873	67	3.881	87	3.887
8	3.852	28	3.862	48	3.856	68	3.882	88	3.911
9	3.849	29	3.861	49	3.882	69	3.888	89	3.890
10	3.854	30	3.852	50	3.886	70	3.876	90	3.916
11	3.874	31	3.865	51	3.877	71	3.886	91	3.887
12	3.846	32	3.849	52	3.859	72	3.891	92	3.932
13	3.859	33	3.878	53	3.861	73	3.897	93	3.907
14	3.863	34	3.861	54	3.885	74	3.895	94	3.921
15	3.860	35	3.879	55	3.867	75	3.890	95	3.903
16	3.855	36	3.882	56	3.880	76	3.887	96	3.921
17	3.871	37	3.875	57	3.890	77	3.894	97	3.914
18	3.858	38	3.885	58	3.879	78	3.874	98	3.932
19	3.843	39	3.866	59	3.880	79	3.881	99	3.922
20	3.866	40	3.876	60	3.880	80	3.890	100	3.944

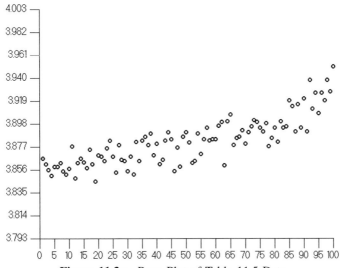

Figure 11.3a   Runs Plot of Table 11.5 Data

Shewhart Q-Chart for MEAN : TOOL
b0 = 3.847865, b1 = 6.102014E-04, SIGMAHAT = .0118339

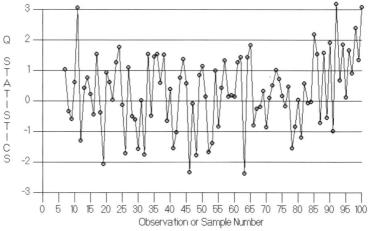

Figure 11.3b   Simple Linear Regression Q-Chart of Table 11.5 Data

The slope of this line for part i is the wear rate for this i^{th} part, and is given by

$$\text{Slope} = \text{wear rate for part } i = WR_i = \frac{dy_i}{di} = 0.0000099 + 0.0000118i$$

Shewhart Q-Chart for MEAN : TOOL
b0 = 3.858069, b1 = 9.925639E-06, b2 = 5.943325E-06, SIGMAHAT = .011012

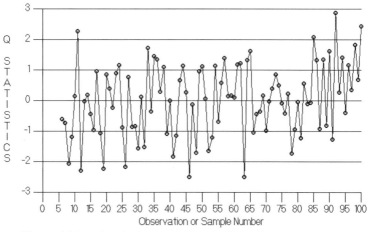

Figure 11.3c   Quadratic Regression Q-Chart of Table 11.5 Data

We can make several useful observations at this point. First, observe that although this model was fitted from all of the 100 cases, the points on the Q-charts were computed from the cases observed up to and including that case. Thus, the charts can be plotted point-by-point, on-line, in real time, as the parts are made.

Next, the data indicate that the process is operating reasonably well in control, because it can be modeled by a quadratic model, which can in turn be used to predict the values of measurements on future parts before they are made. This is the very nature of Shewhart's concept of stability. We note also that through about 80% of the tool life a simple linear regression model will do an adequate job of representing the process mean. This is fairly typical of many tool-wear processes, namely, that they show a pretty constant wear rate through much of the tool's life, until heat build-up friction due to increasing surface contact and dulling causes an increasing wear rate. ∎

11.4 SPC FOR SUBGROUPED GROWTH DATA

In this section we consider SPC methods for some types of growth data that cannot be treated using the classical constant mean and variance model, nor by the classical regression model considered in earlier sections of this chapter. The material of this section was developed for applications in the food animal production industry. However, we believe the methods discussed here will be found useful for other types of growth data.

Suppose it is required to monitor the stability of growth of a production unit of animals during a particular time period, perhaps a barn of 1000 swine or a house of 6000 heavy tom turkeys. At particular times during the growth period a random sample of animals is taken and weighed. At times x_i a sample of n_i animals are weighed and y_{ij} is the weight of the jth animal, $j = 1, 2, \cdots, n_i$. In some cases it will be possible to model these data with a linear regression model with non-constant variance as follows.

$$y_{ij} = u_i + \epsilon_{ij} = \beta_0 + \beta_1 x_i + \epsilon_{ij} \qquad (11.4.1)$$

for $i = 1, 2, \cdots, k; j = 1, 2, \cdots, n_i$, and we assume the ϵ_{ij}'s are independent with $E(\epsilon_{ij}) = 0$ and $\mathrm{Var}(\epsilon_{ij}) = \sigma_i^2$.

From the ith sample we compute $\bar{y}_i$ and S_i^2.

11.4.1 Constant Coefficient of Variation Models

For subgrouped data of the structure of y_{ij}, $i = 1, \cdots, k$; $j = 1, \cdots,$ n_i the *coefficient of variation* for each subgroup is defined as

$$\gamma_i = \frac{\sigma_i}{E(y_{ij})} = \frac{\sigma_i}{\mu_i} \qquad (11.4.2)$$

The *sample coefficient of variation* for the ith subgroup is defined by

$$C_i = \hat{\gamma}_i = \frac{S_i}{\bar{y}_i} \qquad (11.4.3)$$

A property of some growth data is that the variation tends to increase with time, and the standard deviation increases in proportion to the mean. Suppose this is the case, so that we would have

$$\sigma_i = \gamma E(y_{ij}) = \gamma(\beta_0 + \beta_1 x_i) \qquad (11.4.4)$$

When this is the case, the C_i's are all estimates of γ, and their weighed mean

$$\bar{C} = \frac{\displaystyle\sum_{i=1}^{k} n_i C_i}{\displaystyle\sum_{i=1}^{k} n_i} \qquad (11.4.5)$$

is an overall estimate of γ.

To check the condition of a constant coefficient of variation, we can plot the k points $(\bar{y}_i, S_i)$ on a scatterplot and study the plot for linearity. Note that this can be done sequentially in time as the samples become available.

11.4.2 The Coefficient of Variation Q-Chart

To simplify notation in the following development, we will suppress the subscripts on n_i, C_i, $\bar{y}_i$, S_i, μ_i, and σ_i and simply write n, C, $\bar{y}$, S, μ, and σ. We require an expression for the distribution function of C, say $F(c)$.

Then write

$$F(c) = P(C \leq c)$$
$$= P(S - c\bar{y} \leq 0)$$

Put $W = S - c\bar{y}$ and for n large W is approximately normal with

$$E(W) = c_4\sigma - c\mu$$

If the ϵ's are normally distributed, then

$$\text{Var}(W) = \sigma^2 \left(1 - c_4^2 + \frac{c^2}{n} \right)$$

Therefore

$$F(c) \cong \Phi \left[\frac{c/\gamma - c_4}{\sqrt{1 - c_4^2 + c^2/n}} \right]$$

From this we define a Q-statistic for the ith sample coefficient of variation in (11.4.6).

$$Q_i(C_i) = \frac{C_i/\gamma - c_4}{\sqrt{1 - c_4^2 + \dfrac{C_i^2}{n_i}}} \tag{11.4.6}$$

In applications, if a prior estimate of γ is not available, we can make a retrospective chart by replacing γ by $\bar{C}$ given above.

Example 11.4: A random sample of size 20 swine was taken from a barn of approximately 1000 swine on nine dates from 6-3-94 to 8-4-94. In this case x_i is the number of days from the first day, and is given in row two of Table 11.6. The chart in Fig. 11.4a is a scatter plot of $\bar{y}_i$ vs time and, except for one point, the growth over this period appears very linear. Investigation revealed that there was a problem with the weight scale on this date that apparently affected the weights of this fifth subgroup. Figure 11.4b is a scatter plot of $\bar{y}_i$ vs S_i for the nine subgroups, and shows a general linear trend.

The coefficient of variation Q-chart is shown in Fig. 11.4c, and it indicates a stable coefficient of variation. ∎

TABLE 11.6   Swine Weights and Summary Statistics

i:	1	2	3	4	5	6	7	8	9
x_i(day):	0	11	20	27	35	40	49	55	62
	92	88	118	129	157	112	176	185	171
	83	79	90	99	153	162	181	180	191
	63	96	126	129	142	156	174	163	179
	62	115	100	99	144	117	173	173	172
	79	93	118	131	167	156	144	188	180
	62	99	117	129	177	133	148	166	180
	67	88	93	119	152	135	163	150	164
	65	82	113	141	149	149	159	175	186
	84	85	99	113	173	161	173	189	154
	88	72	109	126	149	134	153	170	207
	75	101	116	116	152	143	154	168	187
	68	95	109	117	157	103	146	177	182
	77	71	95	107	176	162	110	172	167
	72	76	105	127	150	122	170	177	173
	83	97	110	104	148	120	134	115	160
	76	88	116	124	140	127	147	143	156
	90	97	118	120	156	141	143	140	178
	80	95	105	112	129	147	157	172	148
	79	81	87	134	139	123	163	133	170
	77	95	114	91	144	143	158	172	153
$\bar{y}_i$:	76.1	89.6	107.9	118.3	152.7	137.3	156.3	165.4	172.9
S_i:	9.3	10.8	10.8	13.2	12.6	17.6	16.9	19.5	14.6
C_i:	0.122	0.121	0.100	0.112	0.083	0.128	0.108	0.118	0.084
$Q_i(C)$:	0.84	0.78	−0.39	0.28	−1.36	1.18	0.06	0.61	−1.31

11.4.3   Charting for Stability of the Model of Equations (11.4.1) and (11.4.4)

When equations (11.4.1) and (11.4.4) for the individual observations y_{ij} are valid, the sample means $\bar{y}_i$ satisfy (11.4.7).

$$\bar{y}_i = \beta_0 + \beta_1 x_i + \bar{\epsilon}_i \qquad (11.4.7)$$

and the coefficient of variation of $\bar{y}_i$ is given by (11.4.8).

$$\gamma_{\bar{y}_i} = \frac{\gamma}{\sqrt{n_i}} \qquad (11.4.8)$$

To make a chart we assume that the subgroups means $\bar{y}_i$ are approximately normally distributed. Since these are means of moderately large

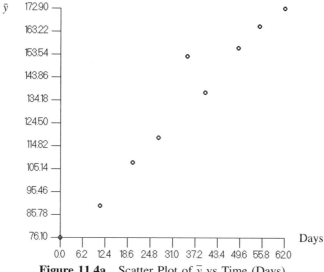

Figure 11.4a   Scatter Plot of $\bar{y}$ vs Time (Days)

samples, this assumption is not very restrictive. Then $\bar{y}_i$ is approximately a

$$N(\beta_0 + \beta_1 x_i, \ \gamma^2(\beta_0 + \beta_1 x_i)^2/n_i)$$

statistic. We define Q-statistics for this case in (11.4.9).

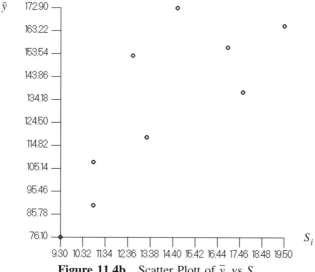

Figure 11.4b   Scatter Plott of $\bar{y}_i$ vs S_i

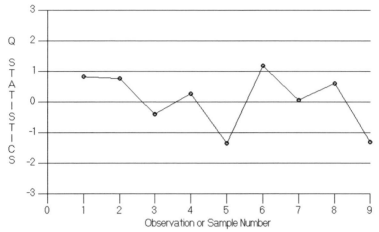

Figure 11.4c $Q(C_i)$-Chart of Example 11.4, Coefficient of Variation Q-Chart

$$Q_i(\bar{y}_i) = \frac{\sqrt{n_i}[\bar{y}_i - (\beta_0 + \beta_1 x_i)]}{\gamma|\beta_0 + \beta_1 x_i|} \qquad (11.4.9)$$

11.4.4 Estimating the Growth Model Parameters

In the foregoing development the parameters γ, β_0, and β_1 were assumed known. In many applications this is a reasonable assumption, for if we are regularly producing say, barns of swine, then we can use estimates of these parameters from previous barns. However, given a data set, such as that in Table 11.6, we require methods to estimate these parameters. Now, the approach to estimate γ was illustrated above in Example 11.4. We first compute the C_i's from all subgroups available, then make a Q-chart using the formula in (11.4.6), using the weighted mean estimate $\bar{C}$ of (11.4.5) for the constant γ.

When the $Q(C)$ chart implies a constant coefficient of variation, we next require estimates of the regression coefficients β_0 and β_1. However, since the variances are different for different subgroups, we shall use weighted regression estimates of these coefficients (see, e.g., Seber 1977, or any book on regression analysis). For our coefficients we define weights in (11.4.10).

$$w_i = \frac{n_i}{(\beta_0 + \beta_1 x_i)^2} \qquad (11.4.10)$$

Using these weights, estimates β_0^* and β_1^* are computed from the cases $(\bar{y}_i, x_i)$ for $i = 1, \cdots, k$ from the formulas of (11.4.11). All sums are for $i = 1, \cdots, k$.

$$
\begin{aligned}
\text{Put } d &= \left(\sum w_i \right)\left(\sum w_i x_i^2 \right) - \left(\sum w_i x_i \right)^2 \\
\beta_0^* &= \frac{1}{d} \left[\left(\sum w_i x_i^2 \right)\left(\sum w_i \bar{y}_i \right) \right. \\
&\qquad \left. - \left(\sum w_i x_i \right)\left(\sum w_i x_i \bar{y}_i \right) \right] \\
\beta_1^* &= \frac{1}{d} \left[\left(\sum w_i \right)\left(\sum w_i x_i \bar{y}_i \right) \right. \\
&\qquad \left. - \left(\sum w_i x_i \right)\left(\sum w_i \bar{y}_i \right) \right]
\end{aligned}
\tag{11.4.11}
$$

The weights w_i depend, of course, on the coefficients β_0 and β_1 that we wish to estimate. We recommend using an iterative procedure as follows. First, obtain initial estimates, say $\hat{\beta}_0$ and $\hat{\beta}_1$, using the unweighed least squares formulas given in Table 11.1. These values are used to estimate weights from (11.4.10) by

$$
\hat{w}_i = \frac{n_i}{(\hat{\beta}_0 + \hat{\beta}_1 x_i)^2}
$$

which are used in the formulas of (11.4.11) to obtain weighted estimates. When these estimates are obtained, they can be used to define new weights and update the estimates again. This is continued until the estimates are stable. In practice it will usually be found that only one or two interactions are required. In fact, even the first weighed estimates are often found to agree well with the ordinary least squares estimates.

Example 11.4, continued: Since the scatter plot in Fig. 11.4a indicates a linear relationship of the sample means to time, and the coefficient of variation Q-chart of Fig. 11.4c indicates a stable coefficient of variation, we now proceed to estimate the coefficients β_0 and β_1. The ordinary least squares estimates computed from the cases $(\bar{y}_i, x_i)$ are

$$\hat{\beta}_0 = 76.54 \quad \text{and} \quad \hat{\beta}_1 = 1.63$$

The weights are then computed from

$$w_i = \frac{20}{(76.54 + 1.63 \, x_i)^2}$$

Using these weights and the formulas of (11.4.11), we find that

$$\beta_0^* = 76.54 \quad \text{and} \quad \beta_1^* = 1.63.$$

So, for this data the first iteration weighted least squares estimates agree with the ordinary least squares estimates. Using these estimates of β_0 and β_1, and the estimate $\bar{C} = 0.108$ of γ obtained above, we compute the following $Q(\bar{y}_i)$ statistics. These values are plotted in Fig. 11.4d.

i:	1	2	3	4	5	6	7	8	9
Q_i:	−0.24	−0.12	−0.47	−0.77	5.87	−1.29	−0.03	−0.19	−1.09

The subgroup five point is highly significant by the 1-of-1 test, just as we expected, because the special cause associated with it was already known. We can improve the parameter estimates somewhat by omitting this case and estimating the parameters from the other eight cases. This gives the following estimate of the model.

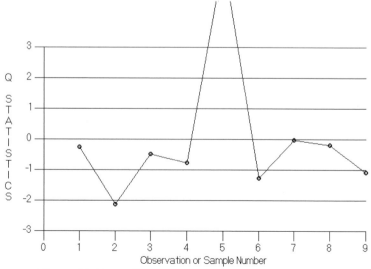

Figure 11.4d $Q(\bar{y}_i)$-Chart of Example 11.4 Growth Data

$$y = 74.53 + 1.62\,x$$

We can use this model to predict the weight of randomly selected individual hogs from this barn, or, the average weight of the entire herd. For example, if we assume the model will hold for eight more days, that is, to $x = 70$, then the predicted average weight per hog is

$$\bar{y} = 74.53 + (1.62)(70) = 188 \text{ lb}$$

Moreover, by assuming the parameters are essentially the true values (based on large subgroup sizes), we can also compute prediction intervals if the individual weights are normally distributed. The $1 - \alpha$ prediction interval for an individual hog weight at time x is

$$\boxed{\begin{array}{c} \beta_0 + \beta_1 x \pm z_{\alpha/2}\gamma(\beta_0 + \beta_1 x) \\ = (\beta_0 + \beta_1 x)(1 \pm \gamma z_{\alpha/2}) \end{array}} \qquad (11.4.12)$$

In this example a 0.95 prediction interval at time $x = 70$ days is

$$188[1 \pm (0.108)(1.95)]$$

or   (148 lb, 228 lb)   ∎

11.4.5   Further Remarks on the Growth Model

There are a number of points that should be noted about the SPC procedure based on the linear growth model in this section.

When a farm is regularly harvesting production units, it will be useful to consider the parameters γ, β_0, and β_1 "known" from earlier units. Then the SPC charts will not only provide a basis for deciding if the growth model is valid, but will also detect parameter variation due to special causes, such as the onset of diseases, diet changes, etc.

If it is required, or at least desired, to perform real-time charting based on data from the same production unit, then we suggest using a forward-weighted sampling scheme that entails taking larger subgroup sizes on the early sampling dates. The first three or four subgroups should be at least 20 each, and, when practically and economically feasible, as large as 30 or 40. Then the above formulas can be used to compute a new Q-statistic in real time when each following subgroup is taken. This can be particularly useful for identifying special causes at an early date.

We have discussed this growth model SPC process in relation to an example of data from swine production. However, we believe that this approach is promising for use in other types of food production, especially food animals, such as poultry. Example 11.4 is based on joint work of Quesenberry and John Roberts, D.V.M., Ph.D.

11.5   SUMMARY

Classical SPC considers models with constant means and variances. However, Shewhart's definition of a stable or in-control process requires only that the values of the relevant quality variable be predictable. Clearly, if a quality variable can be modeled by a regression model or a normal model with constant coefficient of variation, then values of this variable can be predicted using these models. Therefore we have given in this chapter some SPC methods for these models. These SPC methods for regression models have real potential for useful applications in manufacturing, especially for machining processes. The charting methods for constant coefficient of variation variables have considerable potential for use in food production industries.

PROBLEMS

11.1   The 50 values in Table P11.1 are dimensional measurements from a tool-wear process. Make the following charts to study the stability of this process.

  (a) A scatter plot of measurements y vs the part #.

  (b) IMUU Shewhart charts for both the variance and the mean. Give estimates of the mean and variance for this model.

  (c) A simple linear regression tool-wear Shewhart chart. Give estimates of the parameters for this model, that is, for β_0, β_1, and σ.

  (d) Any other charts you feel are useful.

  (e) Discuss your results.

11.2   Make plots like those in Figs. 11.1a, 11.1b, and 11.1c of the data given in Table 11.2. Discuss your results.

TABLE P11.1

Part #	y	Part #	y	Part #	y
1	21.500	18	21.501	35	21.502
2	21.499	19	21.499	36	21.501
3	21.501	20	21.499	37	21.501
4	21.501	21	21.498	38	21.507
5	21.499	22	21.501	39	21.505
6	21.499	23	21.502	40	21.506
7	21.498	24	21.505	41	21.504
8	21.503	25	21.501	42	21.504
9	21.500	26	21.503	43	21.501
10	21.500	27	21.500	44	21.504
11	21.499	28	21.505	45	21.506
12	21.497	29	21.503	46	21.504
13	21.502	30	21.504	47	21.507
14	21.498	31	21.505	48	21.504
15	21.503	32	21.499	49	21.503
16	21.503	33	31.504	50	21.502
17	21.504	34	21.508		

Combining Statistical Process Control and Statistical Process Adjustment Methods

For many manufacturing processes it is not enough to bring the process into control so that it can be modeled by a parametric model. There is often a target value τ that we would like to have the process mean as near to as possible. This is necessary to minimize the expected mean square (EMS) and therefore to also minimize the average loss from variation (ALV). In this chapter we will consider using models that have been validated by SPC methods, either previously or concurrently, to determine an adjustment procedure for keeping a process mean near a target value, and thereby minimize the EMS about target τ.

12.1 PROCESS STABILITY AND PROCESS ADJUSTMENT FOR THE CLASSICAL CONSTANT MEAN AND VARIANCE MODEL

As we have discussed in earlier chapters, the principal purpose of SPC is to help in identifying special causes of variation so that they can be dealt with by engineering or management actions, and to validate a particular model for the process. We call the charts used for this purpose "stability" charts. If a charting program based on a particular parametric model indicates a stable process, then two important things have been accomplished. Of course, one is that special causes have been eliminated from the process, and also, this is an indication of the validity of the model used for the charting program. Even when a process has been brought to a stable or in-control state for a classical constant mean and variance process, it may still be subject to improvement if the mean μ is not the same as the target value τ for the process. The expected mean square for such a process is

$$EMS = \sigma^2 + (\mu - \tau)^2 = \sigma^2 (1 + \delta^2) \qquad (12.1.1)$$

for $\delta = (\mu - \tau)/\sigma$, and both EMS and the inflation factor $1 + \delta^2$ of EMS due to bias are minimized for $\mu = \tau$. We would like to operate the process so that δ^2 is small. A small value of EMS will assure a small average loss from variation. Of course, unless the process is stable there is no mean μ, variance σ^2, or EMS to consider. These are parameters defined for a particular process distribution. Without process stability there is no distribution to define these parameters.

If a process is stable with respect to a particular parametric model for a quality variable, then we would like to adjust the process so as to minimize the bias term in (12.1.1). Of course, we should use our knowledge of this model in adjusting the process.

In the next section we study the effect of sample means adjustments of the process mean and obtain certain basic results in terms of process parameters and specifications. These results will provide guidance in establishing process adjustment methods.

12.2 SAMPLE MEAN ADJUSTMENT OF A CONSTANT MEAN AND VARIANCE PROCESS

Consider a process that produces parts with a quality variable y defined on individual parts. Suppose that from an SPC charting program we know that, except for adjustments we make to the process, the process variance is constant and the process mean is constant except for an occasional shift due to a special cause. Further, we assume that a procedure is available for adjusting the process mean that does not otherwise affect the process, and that the full effect of the adjustment obtains on all parts made after the adjustment. In particular, the adjustment does not affect the process variance. However, we will allow the possibility that the adjustment process itself is not deterministic, but involves a random adjustment error.

We consider defining an *adjustment scheme* that consists of two parts:

(1) a rule to determine when to adjust the process
(2) a rule that tells us how much to adjust the process

There will be, in general, the possibility of making several adjustments to the process during a production run of parts. Hereafter, when we refer to a run of parts we shall mean the parts made after one adjustment and before the next adjustment. Suppose there are k adjustments and $k + 1$ runs of parts between adjustments during the life of one tool, that there are n_r parts made during the rth adjustment run, and that m_r of these parts are gauged. Let $y_{r,i}$ for $i = 1, 2, \cdots$ denote the measurements made on the gauged parts during the rth run. Then we assume the model in display (12.2.1).

(a) $y_{r,i} = \mu_r + \epsilon_{r,i}$ for $i = 1, \cdots, n_r$; $r = 1, \cdots, k + 1$

(b) The $\epsilon_{r,i}$'s are independent random variables with $E(\epsilon_{r,i}) = 0$, $\text{Var}(\epsilon_{r,i}) = \sigma^2$.

(c) The adjustment after run r affects only μ_r, and *not* σ^2.

(d) Let a_r denote the adjustment errors, which are independent with $E(a_r) = 0$, $\text{Var}(a_r) = \sigma_a^2$ for $r = 1, \cdots, k$.

(12.2.1)

We consider two particular adjustment schemes: the first scheme makes an adjustment after a fixed number of units are made and a fixed number of these units are measured, and the second will apply a rule after each measured part to decide when to adjust the process mean.

12.2.1 An Adjustment Scheme

We now consider an adjustment wherein we sample a subsequence of the parts made during the rth run for gauging. When the ith measurement of the rth run, $y_{r,i}$, is observed, we will use the measurements obtained to this point to determine the adjustment increment. The adjustment increment we consider is

$$d_{r,i} = \bar{y}_{r,i} - \tau \quad \text{for} \quad \bar{y}_{r,i} = \frac{1}{i} \sum_{j=1}^{i} y_{r,j} \qquad (12.2.2)$$

Since Bias $= \mu_r - \tau$, note that $d_{r,i}$ is an unbiased estimate of the Bias. The process mean is decreased by $d_{r,i}$ if $d_{r,i}$ is positive, and is increased by $|d_{r,i}|$ when $d_{r,i}$ is negative. To assess the effect of adjustment, we will consider the expected mean square of the next part produced when the adjustment is made and when it is not made.

Let μ_r denote the process mean during the rth run of parts. This mean is a function of the first mean, μ_1 (the set-up mean), all previous adjustments, and, possibly, some special causes. Now, if no adjustment were made immediately after $y_{r,i}$ is observed, from (12.2.1) the measurement on the next part made is

$$y_{r,i+1} = \mu_r + \epsilon_{r,i+1}$$

then $\qquad E(y_{r,i+1}) = \mu_r, \quad \text{Var}(y_{r,i+1}) = \sigma^2$

and $\qquad EMS(y_{r,i+1}|WOA) = \sigma^2 + (\mu_r - \tau)^2 \qquad (12.2.3)$

where WOA means "without adjustment."

On the other hand, if an adjustment is made ("with adjustment," WA) the measurement on the next part made is given by

$$y_{r+1,1} = \mu_r - d_{r,i} + \epsilon_{r+1,1} + a_r$$
$$= \mu_r - \bar{y}_{r,i} + \tau + \epsilon_{r+1,1} + a_r$$

where a_r is the adjustment error. Then

$$E(y_{r+1,1}) = \tau \quad \text{and} \quad \text{Var}(y_{r+1,1}) = \left(\frac{i+1}{i}\right)\sigma^2 + \sigma_a^2$$

and the expected mean square is

$$EMS(y_{r+1,1}|WA) = \left(\frac{i+1}{i}\right)\sigma^2 + \sigma_a^2 \qquad (12.2.4)$$

Thus the effect of this process adjustment is seen by comparing (12.2.3) and (12.2.4). First, note that the EMS with adjustment is not necessarily smaller than without adjustment. Unless the EMS(WA) is smaller than EMS(WOA), the adjustment should not be made. An adjustment should be made only if

$$\left(\frac{i+1}{i}\right)\sigma^2 + \sigma_a^2 < \sigma^2 + (\mu_r - \tau)^2$$

or, equivalently, if

$$\frac{\sigma^2}{i} < (\mu_r - \tau)^2 - \sigma_a^2 \qquad (12.2.5)$$

This last inequality has a nice interpretation. It says that no adjustment should be made unless the variance of the sample mean used to determine the adjustment is smaller than the square of the bias less the adjustment variance. Moreover, since the left-hand side of (12.2.5) is positive, in order for the inequality to hold, the right-hand side must also be positive. Thus we must also have it that

$$\sigma_a^2 < (\mu_r - \tau)^2 = (\text{Bias})^2 \qquad (12.2.6)$$

if an adjustment is to be made. This inequality also has an interesting interpretation. It says that no adjustment should be made unless the absolute value of the bias exceeds the adjustment standard deviation.

When (12.2.6) is satisfied, the inequality (12.2.5) essentially sets a lower bound on the sample size needed in order for the adjustment to improve the process. We rewrite (12.2.5) as

$$i > \frac{\sigma^2}{(\mu_r - \tau)^2 - \sigma_a^2} = \frac{1}{\delta_r^2 - \dfrac{\sigma_a^2}{\sigma^2}} \qquad (12.2.7)$$

for $\delta_r = (\mu_r - \tau)/\sigma$, and δ_r^2 is the proportional increase, the inflation factor, in EMS due to bias. To see this, write

$$EMS = \sigma^2 + (\mu_r - \tau)^2 = \sigma^2(1 + \delta_r^2)$$

Equation (12.2.7) says that unless the number of observations on which the adjustment is based, the number of parts gauged, is this large, no adjustment should be made.

Note that (12.2.7) implies a further smaller lower bound for the minimum number of measurements required for adjustment to improve the process. For all cases, even if $\sigma_a^2 = 0$ and there is no adjustment error, we should require that

$$i > \frac{\sigma^2}{(\mu_r - \tau)^2} = \frac{\sigma^2}{(\text{Bias})^2} = \frac{1}{\delta_r^2} \qquad (12.2.8)$$

This is a universal lower bound for the minimum sample size required. Unless the sample size exceeds this value, no adjustment should be made. Recall that we considered δ_r^2 before in section 9.9. There we considered an acceptable performance level denoted by δ_{APL}. Table 9.8 gives values of inflation factors of the expected mean square, $(1 + \delta_r^2)$, the lower expected mean square, L_δ, and the upper expected mean square, U_δ, when the process distribution is normal.

We can use the inequality of (12.2.8) to develop an adjustment strategy. The following approach may be reasonable for some processes. Bias in the initial set-up is often a problem, and we are eager that any large bias be adjusted out quickly. For a given process we may specify the magnitude of the largest standardized bias we expect at set-up, or, alternatively, the percentage inflation of EMS we consider tolerable. For example, suppose for a particular process we specify an increase of more than 25% in EMS at start-up as intolerable. This gives $\delta_1^2 = 0.25$, and we would make an initial adjustment on the ith part made and gauged for

$$i > \frac{1}{\delta_1^2} = \frac{1}{.25} = 4, \quad \text{or } i = 5 \text{ parts}$$

After the initial adjustment we would use a smaller value of δ_r^2; that is, for $r = 2, 3, \cdots$; which will increase the number of gauged parts required to make an adjustment. Note that adjusting on $(i + 1)$ measured parts is always adequate to adjust for an inflation factor of $\delta_r^2 = \frac{1}{i}$. Adjusting on 11 gauged parts protects against an inflation factor of $\delta_r^2 = 0.1$, that is, a 10% inflation factor of EMS.

Finally, when the number of gauged parts in a particular run has become large enough, we can use feedback information to decide when to adjust as follows. How many measurements does this require? We think that perhaps 20 or more measurements are needed to avoid having estimation error unduly inflate EMS. If the number of gauged parts is 20 or more, and $\sigma_a = 0$, we can estimate δ_r by

$$\hat{\delta}_{r,i} = \frac{\overline{y}_{r,i} - \tau}{\sigma} = \frac{d_{r,i}}{\sigma}$$

where $\overline{y}_{r,i}$ is the mean of the gauged parts, and adjust when i exceeds $(1/\hat{\delta}_{r,i}^2 + 1)$.

We summarize the adjustment given in this subsection in Table 12.1, and will illustrate using the relations developed here in section 12.3.

12.2.2 Adjusting on Samples of Size One

Adjusting a process on the value of a single observation, sample size one, is of special importance. For practical reasons it may be necessary to consider adjusting a process on samples of size one. This may be because observations become available very slowly, or for other rea-

TABLE 12.1   A Feedback Adjustment Scheme for a Classical Constant Mean and Variance Process

During the rth run of parts, if the following inequalities are satisfied
$$(\text{Bias})^2 = (\mu_r - \tau)^2 > \sigma_a^2$$
and

$$i > \frac{\sigma^2}{(\text{Bias})^2 - \sigma_a^2} = \frac{1}{\delta_r^2 - \frac{\sigma_a^2}{\sigma^2}}$$

then the process mean is to be adjusted by an increment
$$d_{r,i} = \bar{y}_{r,i} - \tau$$
after the ith gauged part.

sons. It should be observed that there are processes other than manufacturing where feedback type adjustments are made. The Federal Reserve may adjust interest rates based on inflation data for one month. A naval gun may be adjusted from the impact of a single round.

For $i = 1$ in (12.2.7), we obtain the result that the process should not be adjusted unless

$$(\mu_r - \tau)^2 > \sigma^2 + \sigma_a^2 \tag{12.2.9}$$

In words, this says that no adjustment should be made on a single observation unless the square of the bias exceeds the sum of the process variance and the adjustment variance. If adjustments are made from single observations when (12.2.9) is not satisfied, the result is an increase in expected mean square of subsequent observations.

This result is helpful in interpreting an experiment described in Deming (1986).

12.2.3   Remarks on Deming's Funnel Experiment

Deming (1986) describes an experiment in which a ball is dropped through a funnel above a plane. A target point is marked on the plane and each time the ball is dropped the position of the funnel is subsequently adjusted by the coordinate distances of the ball's strike point from the target point. This is the equivalent, in each coordinate, to adjusting on a mean of $i = 1$ measurements. From $\text{Var}(y_{r+1,1}|\text{WA})$ above we see that the variance after adjustment is $2\sigma^2 + \sigma_a^2$. Thus, the variance is more than doubled. From (12.2.9), the expected mean square is increased unless $|\mu_i - \tau| > \sqrt{\sigma^2 + \sigma_a^2}$. Actually, if the funnel is far enough from the target, at least the first adjustment will reduce EMS of subsequent trials.

12.2.4 Estimating the Adjustment Variance, σ_a^2, for the Constant Mean Model

To use the foregoing results, we require estimates of σ^2 and σ_a^2. To compute these estimates we suppose that data from $p + 1$ runs are available from a particular tool, and that the SPC charting program indicates that the process was stable while these runs were being made. An estimate of σ^2 can be obtained as a pooled estimate of variance from these runs. This estimate is available from the SPC charting program. Call this estimate S_{pooled}^2. If estimates are available from more than one tool, then they can be pooled across tools.

To compute an estimate of σ_a^2, assume that the same number m of parts are gauged from each run. Then it will be shown in Appendix 12A that the adjustment increment d_r for the rth run can be expressed as

$$d_r = \bar{y}_r - \bar{y}_{r-1} + a_{r-1} = \mu_r - \mu_{r-1} + \bar{\epsilon}_r - \bar{\epsilon}_{r-1} + a_{r-1}$$

for $r = 2, 3, \cdots, p$ (12.2.10)

In order to compute an estimate of σ_a^2, we also assume that records are available from a run of parts made while the process was stable, and that the means μ_r were constant during this run. Then d_r can be written as in (12.2.11).

$$d_r = \bar{\epsilon}_r - \bar{\epsilon}_{r-1} + a_{r-1} \quad \text{for } r = 2, \cdots, p \quad (12.2.11)$$

From this it can be shown (see Appendix 12A) that the sample variance S_d^2 computed from the values $d_2, \cdots, d_p$ has expectation

$$E(S_d^2) \cong \sigma_a^2 + \left(\frac{p-2}{p-1}\right) \frac{2\sigma^2}{m} \quad (12.2.12)$$

Then an approximately unbiased estimate of σ_a^2 is given by

$$\hat{\sigma}_a^2 = S_d^2 - \left(\frac{p-2}{p-1}\right)\left(\frac{2S_{pooled}^2}{m}\right) \quad (12.2.13)$$

This formula assumes a constant number m of measurements are made during each run. If the number m_r of measurements vary somewhat, but not too much, an approximate formula can be obtained by replacing m by the average, $\bar{m}$ say, in (12.2.12). Also, if the number measured in each run is really large, then S_d^2 itself may be an adequate estimate of σ_a^2. It will, of course, be slightly positively biased. This can be studied for particular processes when S_d^2 and S_{pooled}^2 have been obtained.

Note, particularly, that the formula in (12.2.12) is based on the assumption that the process is stable during runs and that the means μ_r are constant for $r = 1, \cdots, p$. If the process is unstable the estimate will be inflated. To assure the process is stable, we should chart the process with SPC charts over these runs.

Small Example   Data from $p = 21$ runs with $m = 40$ parts measured in each run gave estimates

$$S_d = 0.00084 \quad \text{and} \quad S_{\text{pooled}} = 0.003$$

We compute an estimate $\hat{\sigma}_a$

$$\hat{\sigma}_a = \sqrt{(0.00084)^2 - \left(\frac{19}{20}\right)\frac{[2(0.003)^2]}{40}} = 0.00053 \qquad \blacksquare$$

12.3   SPC AND STATISTICAL PROCESS ADJUSTMENT (SPA) OF A CLASSICAL STABLE PROCESS

12.3.1   A Generic Procedure

We wish to operate a process that is stable and has minimum EMS. We propose using two simultaneous control charts for each run of parts as follows:

Chart A. A chart such as an *MR, R, S², Q(S²)* or other chart for the process variance σ^2.

Chart B. A chart such as a *Q(X), Q(X̄)* or other chart for the process mean μ. These must be stability charts to detect nonconstancy of μ. The actual nominal value of $\mu = \mu_r$ for each run must not affect the chart patterns.

If either chart A or chart B signals, this is evidence the process is unstable and a search for a special cause is made and, hopefully, found and eliminated. When charts A and B indicate the process is stable, we will implement the following steps for action.

- We first decide what is the largest inflation factor δ^2 we are willing to tolerate. Then put $i = 1/\delta^2 + 1$, and proceed to gauge i parts.
- When the ith measurement is made, let $\bar{y}_i$ denote the mean of the gauged observations in this run to this point, and adjust the process by $d_i = \bar{y}_i - \tau$.

Note that after an adjustment is made, it may be necessary, depending on the nature of the special cause(s), to restart the A and B charts as Q-charts using data generated after the process interruption. The formulas given in $(7.4.3)'$, $(7.4.4)'$, and $(7.4.6)'$ are useful for the charting program.

It may sometimes be useful to make another chart such as a Shewhart, EWMA, or CUSUM; either classical or Q-chart, designed to detect a monotone shift in the process mean μ under the assumption that the mean has a "known" nominal value of $\mu_{r,0} = \tau$, the target value. These charts are designed to detect a difference in the true process mean μ_r and its nominal value $\mu_{r,0} = \tau$. Comparing this type chart with the B chart will give information on whether the process mean has shifted during operation, or whether it was off at set-up. If the process is stable and operating on target, the charts should agree closely. In the following we call this chart C.

Example 12.1: A rough finishing operation produces units with target value $\tau = 5$ mm. The process has recently been serviced and cannot be assumed to be in control. Also, it is generally not possible to set up the process with the process mean μ centered on the target value of $\tau = 5$. Therefore, we wish to use feedback information to simultaneously bring the process into a controlled state and to center the process. A value of the inflation factor of $100\delta^2 = 12.5\%$ was decided, from previous experience, to be about the largest value likely to occur for this process. Therefore, an initial run of $i = 1/0.125 + 1 = 9$ parts were made and gauged.

The A chart was made as an IMUU $Q(S^2)$ chart for σ, the B chart as an IMUU $Q(X)$ chart for μ, and a third C chart as an IMKU $Q(X)$ chart for μ with the "known" value of μ set equal to $\tau = 5.00$. The measurements obtained were:

> *First Run:*
>
> 5.20 5.45 5.43 5.35 4.93 5.03 5.26 4.92 5.66

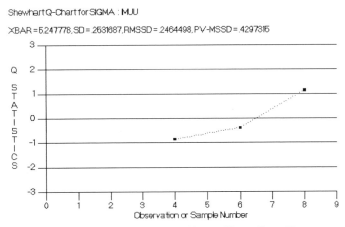

Figure 12.1a First Run Sigma Chart, Case U

The Q-charts for these nine measurements are given in Figs. 12.1a, 12.1b, and 12.1c. The chart for control of σ in Fig. 12.1a has only three plotted points, but there is no indication of an unstable process variance. The IMUU chart for μ in Fig. 12.1b also indicates a constant mean μ for these nine observations. The IMKU $Q(X)$ chart for the mean with the "known" value of the mean μ set equal to the target value of $\tau = 5.00$ is given in Fig. 12.1c. This chart signals strongly on the 9th point, and it is apparent that the pattern of points tend to be higher on this chart than on the case UU chart in Fig. 12.1b. This indicates that the process mean needs to be adjusted down.

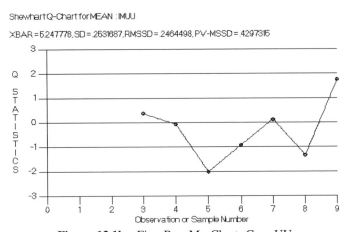

Figure 12.1b First Run Mu Chart, Case UU

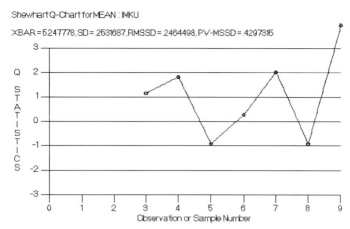

Figure 12.1c First Run Mu Chart, Case KU

The sample mean and standard deviation from these nine observations are given on the figures as $\bar{y} = 5.25$ and $s = 0.25$. Therefore, the adjustment made to the process mean is to adjust it down by $d = 5.25 - 5.00 = 0.25$ mm.

With the mean having been adjusted down by 0.25 mm, we decide to choose the acceptable proportional increase in EMS to be $\delta^2 = 0.055$, which gives a required sample size of 19. The 19 measurements from the second run were:

Second Run:

4.75 5.19 5.12 4.71 5.05 4.82 4.69 4.91 4.87 4.84

4.93 5.09 4.83 4.71 5.04 4.92 4.93 5.16 4.31

The A, B, and C charts for these 19 observations are given in Figs. 12.2a, 12.2b, and 12.2c. Again, the A chart is evidence that σ is constant, and the B chart indicates a constant mean, although point 19 is almost on the lower control limit. Chart C gives a strong signal on point 19 with the point below -3, and the general pattern of points appears to indicate a mean below the target value of $\tau = 5.00$. In fact, the estimate of the mean is $\bar{y} = \hat{\mu} = 4.89$. We can now obtain a direct estimate of δ for this second run, and decide from it whether or not to adjust the process mean. The sample standard deviations from the first and second runs are $s_1 = 0.253$ and $s_2 = 0.208$, based on samples of

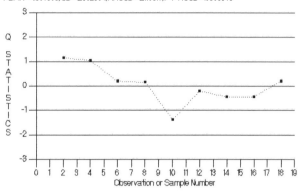

Figure 12.2a   Second Run Sigma Chart, Case K

sizes $n_1 = 9$ and $n_2 = 19$, respectively. The pooled estimate of σ^2 is then

$$s^2_{\text{pooled}} = \frac{(n_1 - 1)s_1^2 + (n_2 - 1)s_2^2}{n_1 + n_2 - 2}$$

$$= \frac{(8)(0.253)^2 + (18)(0.208)^2}{26} = 0.0496$$

The estimate $\hat{\delta}^2$ of δ^2 is then

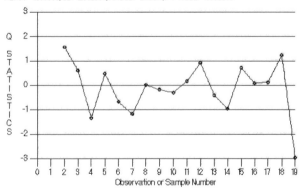

Figure 12.2b   Second Run Mu Chart, Case UK

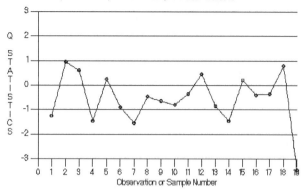

Figure 12.2c Second Run Mu Chart, Case KK with Mu = Target

$$\hat{\delta}^2 = \frac{(\bar{y} - \tau)^2}{s^2_{\text{pooled}}} = \frac{(4.89 - 5.00)^2}{0.0496} = 0.253$$

and the lower bound for i is

$$\frac{1}{\hat{\delta}^2} = \frac{1}{0.253^2} = 15.6, \quad \text{or } i = 16$$

Thus, the second run of 19 gauged parts is enough measurements to support a process mean adjustment. We then adjusted the mean up by $|d| = 0.11$ mm.

After this adjustment, we decide to take $\delta^2 = 0.01$, that is, to adjust to correct 1% inflation in EMS due to lack of centering. This requires that we take the next sample of size $\delta^{-2} = 100$. After this adjustment we gauged the next 100 points. The A chart again indicated a stable process variance, and is omitted here to save space. The B and C charts are given in Figs. 12.3a and 12.3b. Observe that these two charts are very similar, in fact, after the first 20 or so points they are virtual overlays of each other. This is exactly what we like to see, for it indicates a stable process mean with process mean very nearly equal to the process target value. However, we note that the estimated mean from the observations from this third run is $\bar{y}_i = \hat{\mu}_3 = 5.014$ mm and the standard deviation is $s_3 = 0.224$. We now compute an estimate $\hat{\delta}^2$ of δ^2 for this third run. The pooled estimate of σ^2 from all three runs is

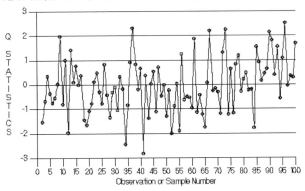

Figure 12.3a   Third Run Mu Chart, Case UK

$$s^2_{pooled} = \frac{(99)(0.224)^2 + (26)(0.0496)}{125} = 0.0501$$

$$\hat{\delta}^2 = \frac{(\bar{y} - \tau)^2}{s^2_{pooled}} = \frac{(5.014 - 5.00)^2}{0.0501} = 0.0039$$

The required sample size is then

$$\frac{1}{\hat{\delta}^2} = \frac{1}{.0039} = 256.4, \text{ or } 257$$

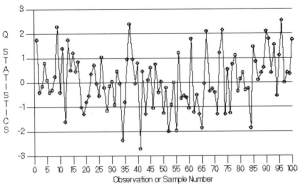

Figure 12.3b   Third Run Mu Chart, Case KK with Mu = Target

Thus we will not attempt to adjust the process at this point. If after we have gauged 157 additional parts the estimate of δ^2 is essentially the same, we might decide to adjust it further. Note that this is really fine-tuning the process. In this we have essentially assumed that the adjustment variance is zero. It if it not, further adjustment may well increase the EMS, rather than decrease it.   ■

12.4 STATISTICAL PROCESS ADJUSTMENT FOR A LINEAR TOOL-WEAR PROCESS WITH INDEPENDENT ERRORS

12.4.1 Introduction

The tool-wear problem was considered in Chapter 11 and SPC methods were given that can be used to study the stability of a tool-wear process with either a linear or quadratic regression model. A linear regression model can be used for some tool-wear processes, at least over some intervals of tool life. As for constant mean and variance processes, we do not consider adjusting the process, except in conjunction with an SPC program. Unless a process is stable, that is, can be modeled so that the process is predictable, we do not recommend a method for adjusting the process.

We assume that over the life of a tool a number of adjustments will be made, and consider the data from, say, the general r^{th} run of parts made between adjustments. The relevant data from the rth run are the production number of each part made, the number of the part gauged, and the measurement itself. These numbers can be represented, for example, as in Table 12.2.

The form of the data available from the rth run ($r = 1, 2, \cdots$) is

$$(x_{r,1}, y_{r,1}), (x_{r,2}, y_{r,2}), \cdots, (x_{r,m_r}, y_{r,m_r}) \qquad (12.4.1)$$

We may measure (gauge) only the second or tenth parts made, or, possibly, one part every five minutes or hour. In every case $x_{r,i}$ is the

TABLE 12.2 Notation for Data from r^{th} Run of Parts

Production Part #:	1	2	3	4	5	6	7	8	9	$\cdots$
Measurement # i:		1		2		3		4		$\cdots$
Gauged Part # $x_{r,i}$:		2		4		6		8		$\cdots$
Measurement $y_{r,i}$:		$y_{r,1}$		$y_{r,2}$		$y_{r,3}$		$y_{r,4}$		$\cdots$

number of parts made when the ith part is gauged, and $y_{r,i}$ is the measurement on this part. Of course, if all units are measured, then $x_{r,i} = i$, and if n_r units are made in the rth run we would have data:

$$(1, y_{r,1}), (2, y_{r,2}), \cdots, (n_r, y_{r,n_r})$$

We will initially assume (subject to checking in the SPC program and otherwise) the tentative model of display (12.4.2), assuming data as in (12.4.1).

(a) $y_{r,i} = \beta_{0,r} + x_{r,i}\beta_1 + \epsilon_{r,i}$ for $i = 1, \cdots, m_r$; $r = 1, \cdots, k + 1$
(b) The $\epsilon_{r,i}$'s are i.i.d. $N(0, \sigma^2)$ for $i = 1, 2, \cdots$.
(c) The adjustment after run r affects only $\beta_{0,r}$, and *not* β_1 or σ^2.   (12.4.2)
(d) Let a_r denote the adjustment errors, which are independent with $E(a_r) = 0$, $\text{Var}(a_r) = \sigma_a^2$ for $r = 1, \cdots, k$.

Assuming that the process appears to be stable with respect to the model of (12.4.2), we consider two particular adjustment schemes. The first adjustment scheme will apply a rule after each measured part to decide when to adjust the process mean, and how much to adjust it. The second scheme makes an adjustment after a fixed number n of units are made and a fixed number m of these units are measured.

The analysis of data based on the model in (12.4.2) will depend on what is known about the parameters $\beta_{0,r}$, β_1, and σ^2. We cannot know the value of $\beta_{0,r}$ before the run, and must always be concerned with estimating it from the present run. However, if we are conducting an SPC charting program, as we must be to assure a stable process according to the simple linear model of (12.4.2), then we can obtain good estimates of β_1 and σ^2 from this SPC program.

12.4.2 A Feedback Decision and Adjustment Scheme

We next consider using feedback measurements to decide when and by how much to adjust the process mean. We assume an adjustment procedure is available that does not otherwise affect the process. By considering the model in (12.4.2) and the runs structure of the data of

(12.4.1), we formulate rules for adjusting the process mean as the data are observed sequentially in time.

We consider the rth run of parts for $r = 1, \cdots, k$. Suppose that m_r of the n_r parts made during the rth run are gauged to give the values $y_{r,1}, y_{r,2}, \cdots, y_{r,m_r}$. Also, let $x_{r,i}$ for $i = 1, 2, \cdots, m_r$ denote the order of manufacture of the ith measured part from the rth run. To illustrate this notation, suppose that $n_r = 10$ parts are made during the third run and that the second, fourth, and seventh are gauged. Then $m_r = 3$, $x_{3,1} = 2$, $x_{3,2} = 4$, and $x_{3,3} = 7$. When part $x_{r,i}$ is made and gauged, we will have the cases in display (12.4.3) available for analysis.

$$(x_{r,1}, y_{r,1}), (x_{r,2}, y_{r,2}), \cdots, (x_{r,i}, y_{r,i}) \qquad (12.4.3)$$

If all parts in the rth run are gauged, then $m_r = n_r$ and $x_{r,i} = i$ for $i = 1, \cdots, n_r$.

For the cases in (12.4.3) the model of (12.4.2)(a) is written

$$y_{r,j} = \beta_{0,r} + x_{r,j}\beta_1 + \epsilon_{r,j} \text{ for } j = 1, 2, \cdots, i$$

If we define sequential means as follows:

$$\bar{y}_{r,i} = \frac{1}{i} \sum_{j=1}^{i} y_{r,j}, \quad \bar{x}_{r,i} = \frac{1}{i} \sum_{j=1}^{i} x_{r,j}$$

$$\bar{\epsilon}_{r,i} = \frac{1}{i} \sum_{j=1}^{i} \epsilon_{r,j} \qquad \text{for } i = 1, 2, \cdots, m_r$$

then

$$\bar{y}_{r,i} = \beta_{0,r} + \bar{x}_{r,i}\beta_1 + \bar{\epsilon}_{r,i} \qquad \text{for } 1, 2, \cdots, m_r$$

Note that these are the sequential means for the y's, x's, and ϵ's for the first i parts that are actually measured from the rth run. Then the (potential) compensation increment we propose is given in (12.4.4).

$$d_{r,i} = \bar{y}_{r,i} + (x_{r,i} + 1 - \bar{x}_{r,i})\beta_1 - \tau \qquad (12.4.4)$$

If $d_{r,i}$ is positive, the process mean is decreased by $d_{r,i}$, and if it is negative the process mean is increased by $|d_{r,i}|$. We judge the effectiveness of the adjustment by its effect on the expected mean square of the first part made after the adjustment. If no adjustment is made, this part is denoted $y_{r,i+1}$. However, if an adjustment is made, then this part is denoted $y_{r+1,1}$. Then, if no adjustment were made after the ith measured part, we would have

$$y_{r,i+1} = \beta_{0,r} + (x_{r,i} + 1)\beta_1 + \epsilon_{r,i+1}$$

So, without adjustment (WOA), we have

$$E(y_{r,i+1}|WOA) = \beta_{0,r} + (x_{r,i} + 1)\beta_1, \quad \text{Var}(y_{r,i+1}|WOA) = \sigma^2$$

and

$$EMS(y_{r,i+1}|WOA) = \sigma^2 + [\beta_{0,r} + (x_{r,i} + 1)\beta_1 - \tau]^2$$

$$= \sigma^2(1 + \delta^2)$$

where

$$\delta = \frac{\beta_{0,r} + (x_{r,i} + 1)\beta_1 - \tau}{\sigma} = \frac{\text{Bias}}{\sigma}$$

and

$$\text{Bias} = \beta_{0,r} + (x_{r,i} + 1)\beta_1 - \tau$$

So δ is the standardized bias on the $(i + 1)^{\text{st}}$ part of the rth run if no adjustment is made. As for the constant mean case, δ^2 is the proportional increase in EMS due to bias on this part when no adjustment is made. But, with adjustment (WA), the value on the next part is

$$y_{r+1,1} = y_{r,i+1} - d_{r,i} + a_r = y_{r,i+1} - \bar{y}_{r,i} - (x_{r,i} + 1 - \bar{x}_{r,i})\beta_1 + \tau + a_r$$

where a_r is the adjustment error, recall (12.4.2), part (d). Then

$$E(y_{r+1,1}|WA) = \tau, \quad \text{Var}(y_{r+1,1}|WA) = \left(\frac{i + 1}{i}\right)\sigma^2 + \sigma_a^2$$

and

$$EMS(y_{r+1,1}|WA) = \left(\frac{i + 1}{i}\right)\sigma^2 + \sigma_a^2$$

An adjustment should be made only if the expected mean square with adjustment is less than the expected mean square without adjustment. That is, only if

$$\left(\frac{i + 1}{i}\right)\sigma^2 + \sigma_a^2 < \sigma^2 + [\beta_{0,r} + (x_{r,i} + 1)\beta_1 - \tau]^2$$

or, equivalently, if

$$\frac{\sigma^2}{i} < [\beta_{0,r} + (x_{r,i} + 1)\beta_1 - \tau]^2 - \sigma_a^2 = (\text{Bias})^2 - \sigma_a^2 \quad (12.4.5)$$

As for the constant mean model, this says that no adjustment should be made unless the variance of the sample mean used to determine the adjustment is smaller than the square of the bias less the adjustment variance. Moreover, since the left-hand side of (12.4.5) is positive, in order for the inequality to hold the right-hand side must also be positive. Thus, we require that

$$\sigma_a^2 < [\beta_{0,r} + (x_{r,i} + 1)\beta_1 - \tau]^2 = (\text{Bias})^2 \qquad (12.4.6)$$

if an adjustment is to be made. This says that no adjustment should be made unless the absolute value of the bias exceeds the adjustment standard deviation.

The inequality (12.4.5) essentially sets a lower bound on the sample size needed in order for the adjustment to improve the process. We rewrite this inequality as

$$i > \frac{\sigma^2}{(\text{Bias})^2 - \sigma_a^2} = \frac{1}{\delta^2 - \frac{\sigma_a^2}{\sigma^2}} \qquad (12.4.7)$$

which says that unless the number of observations on which the adjustment is based, the number of parts gauged, is this large, no adjustment should be made.

Note that (12.4.7) implies a further smaller lower bound for the minimum number of measurements required for adjustment to improve the process. For all cases, even if $\sigma_a^2 = 0$, that is, there is no adjustment error, we should require that

$$i > \frac{\sigma^2}{(\beta_{0,r} + (x_{r,i} + 1)\beta_1 - \tau)^2} = \frac{\sigma^2}{(\text{Bias})^2} = \frac{1}{\delta^2} \qquad (12.4.8)$$

and δ^2 is the proportional increase, the inflation factor, in EMS due to bias, that is, to having the mean off target. This is a universal lower bound for the minimum sample size required. Unless the sample size exceeds this value, no adjustment should be made. Recall that we considered δ^2 before for constant mean models in sections 9.9 and 12.2.

As in section 12.2, we can use the inequality of (12.4.8) to develop an adjustment strategy. The following approach may be reasonable for some processes. Bias in the initial set-up is often a problem, and we are especially eager that any large initial bias be adjusted out quickly. For a given process we may specify the magnitude of the largest standardized bias we expect at set-up, or, alternatively, the percentage inflation of EMS we consider tolerable. For example, suppose for a particular process we specify an increase of more than 25% in EMS at start-up as intolerable. This gives $\delta^2 = 0.25$, and we would make an initial adjustment on the ith part made and gauged for

$$i > \frac{1}{\delta^2} = \frac{1}{.25} = 4, \text{ or } i = 5 \text{ parts}$$

After the initial adjustment we would use a smaller value of δ^2, which will increase the number of gauged parts required to make an adjustment. Note that adjusting on $(i + 1)$ measured parts is always adequate to adjust for an inflation factor of $\delta^2 = \frac{1}{i}$. Adjusting on 11 gauged parts protects against in inflation factor of $\delta^2 = 0.1$, that is, a 10% inflation factor of EMS.

Finally, when the number of gauged parts in a particular run has become large enough, we can use feedback information to decide when to adjust as follows. Again, we think perhaps 20 or more measurements are enough to avoid having estimation error unduly increase EMS. If the number of gauged parts is this large, we can estimate δ by

$$\hat{\delta} = \frac{d_{r,i}}{\sigma}$$

where $d_{r,i}$ is the adjustment increment given in (12.4.4). If $\sigma_a = 0$, we adjust the process when i exceeds the smallest integer greater than $(1/\hat{\delta}^2 + 1)$.

We summarize the adjustment results given in this subsection in Table 12.3.

TABLE 12.3   Feedback Adjustment Scheme for a Simple Linear Regression Tool-Wear Process

During the rth run of parts, if the following inequalities are satisfied

$(\text{Bias})^2 = [\beta_{0,r} + (x_{r,i} + 1)\beta_1 - \tau]^2 > \sigma_a^2$

and

$i > \dfrac{\sigma^2}{(\text{Bias})^2 - \sigma_a^2} = \dfrac{1}{\delta^2 - \dfrac{\sigma_a^2}{\sigma^2}}$

then the process mean is to be adjusted by an increment

$d_{r,i} = \bar{y}_{r,i} + (x_{r,i} + 1 - \bar{x}_{r,i})\beta_1 - \tau.$

12.4.3 Adjustment Based on a Constant Run Size

Suppose the SPC program indicates the linear regression model on production part number of (12.4.2) with independent errors is reasonable for the process, so we wish to use this model to determine an adjustment procedure for the process. Moreover, suppose a constant number $n = mk$ parts are made in each run between adjustments, and that every k^{th} part is gauged to give a total of m measurements. For example, we might make 30 parts in each run between adjustments and gauge the 5th, 10th, 15th, 20th, 25th, and 30th parts. Then we would have $m = 6$ measurements made on every 5th (k^{th}) manufactured part. Since adjustments are made after fixed run sizes, we need only decide upon the magnitude of the adjustment to be made at the end of the rth run. To choose an adjustment increment for this special case, we assume that n is an odd integer, and we will adjust to eliminate bias on the $[(3n + 1)/2]^{th}$ part made from the beginning of the rth run. This is the part made in the center of the next run. Now, if no adjustment were made (without adjustment, WOA) the value on this part, from (12.4.2), would be

$$y_{r,(3n+1)/2} = \beta_{0,r} + \left(\frac{3n + 1}{2}\right) \beta_1 + \epsilon_{r,(3n+1)/2} \qquad (12.4.9)$$

Thus, to eliminate bias on this part we will adjust by d_r for

$$d_r = \hat{\beta}_{0,r} + \left(\frac{3n + 1}{2}\right) \beta_1 - \tau$$

for
$$\hat{\beta}_{0,r} = \bar{y}_r - k \left(\frac{m + 1}{2}\right) \beta_1, \quad \text{and}$$

$$\bar{y}_r = \beta_{0,r} + k \left(\frac{m + 1}{2}\right) \beta_1 + \bar{\epsilon}_r$$

So d_r can be written

$$d_r = \bar{y}_r + \left(\frac{2n + 1 - k}{2}\right) \beta_1 - \tau \qquad (12.4.10)$$

When all parts are gauged ($m = n$, $k = 1$) this becomes

$$d_r = \bar{y}_r + n\beta_1 - \tau \qquad (12.4.11)$$

which is exactly the increment studied and recommended in Quesenberry (1988), and was there called d_3. If n is an even integer, the formula for d_r is

$$d_r = \bar{y}_r + \left(n - \frac{k}{2}\right)\beta_1 - \tau \qquad (12.4.10')$$

From (12.4.9), if no adjustment were made, the expected mean square of $y_{r,(3n+1)/2}$ would be

$$EMS(WOA) = \sigma^2 + \left[\beta_{0,r} + \left(\frac{3n+1}{2}\right)\beta_1 - \tau\right]^2 \qquad (12.4.12)$$

If an adjustment is made (WA), then the value on this part is

$$y_{r+1,(n+1)/2} = \epsilon_{(3n+1)/2} - \bar{\epsilon}_r + \tau + a_r \quad \text{and}$$

$$\bar{\epsilon}_r = \frac{1}{m}\sum_{i=1}^{m}\epsilon_{r,i}.$$

The expected mean square with this adjustment is

$$EMS(WA) = \sigma^2 + \frac{\sigma^2}{m} + \sigma_a^2 \qquad (12.4.13)$$

Thus we should require that EMS(WA) be less than EMS(WOA). We require that

$$\frac{\sigma^2}{m} < \{\beta_{0,r} + [(3n+1)/2]\beta_1 - \tau\}^2 - \sigma_a^2 = (\text{Bias})^2 - \sigma_a^2 \quad (12.4.14)$$

This implies that m should satisfy

$$m > \frac{\sigma^2}{\{\beta_{0,r} + [(3n+1)/2]\beta_1 - \tau\}^2 - \sigma_a^2} = \frac{\sigma^2}{(\text{Bias})^2 - \sigma_a^2} \quad (12.4.15)$$

We must first select a value of n. To select n we use a result from Quesenberry (1988) for the special case when $m = n$. This requires a run size of n given by

$$n = \left(\frac{6\sigma^2}{\beta_1^2}\right)^{1/3} = (6\theta^2)^{1/3} \tag{12.4.16}$$

for $\theta = \sigma/\beta_1$, the *noise-to-wear* ratio.

For run size n given by (12.4.16), we choose m to satisfy (12.4.15). If σ_a is small, we can choose m to satisfy (12.4.17).

$$n \geq m > \frac{\sigma^2}{(\text{Bias})^2} = \frac{1}{\delta^2} \tag{12.4.17}$$

for $\delta = \dfrac{\text{Bias}}{\sigma}$.

We cannot know the expected mean square on the $[(n + 1)/2]^{\text{nd}}$ part of run $r + 1$. However, we know that on this part

$$EMS = \sigma^2(1 + \delta^2)$$

so that δ^2 is, as before, the proportional increase in EMS due to bias. Thus we can specify the proportional increase in EMS that is an acceptable performance level. However, because $m \leq n$, this restricts the maximum sample size m that can be chosen, and in turn, the maximum percentage increase in EMS due to bias that we can protect against.

Example: Quesenberry (1988) gives an example for which the noise-to-wear ratio is estimated as

$$\hat{\theta} = -41.3$$

From this we compute the optimal run length from (12.4.16) as

$$n = [6(-41.3)^2]^{1/3} = 22$$

Thus, the smallest percentage proportional increase in EMS due to bias that we can protect against is

$$\delta^2 = \frac{100}{22} = 4.5\%.$$

Of course, if m is chosen less than n, the proportional increase allowed will be higher. ∎

12.4.4 Estimating the Adjustment Variance, σ_a^2, for the SLR Model

To estimate the adjustment variance σ_a^2, we assume that a record of adjustments $d_2, d_3, \cdots, d_p$ are available from runs with the sampling structure described in section 12.4.3. That is, each run consists of n manufactured parts where $n = mk$ and every k^{th} part is measured.

Then it can be shown with a proof that parallels the proof of Appendix 12A for the constant mean case that the adjustment increment d_r for the rth run can be written as

$$d_r = \bar{y}_r - \bar{y}_{r-1} + a_{r-1} = \beta_{0,r} - \beta_{0,r-1} + \bar{\epsilon}_r - \bar{\epsilon}_{r-1} + a_{r-1} \quad (12.4.18)$$

for $r = 2, \cdots, p$.

To compute an estimate of σ_a^2, assume that records are available from a run of parts made while the process was stable, and that the intercepts $\beta_{0,r}$ were constant during this run. Then d_r can be written as in (12.4.19).

$$d_r = n\beta_1 + \bar{\epsilon}_r - \bar{\epsilon}_{r-1} + a_{r-1} \quad \text{for} \quad r = 2, \cdots, p \quad (12.4.19)$$

Note that (12.4.19) is essentially the same as (12.2.11) given earlier for the constant means model. Thus if a sample variance S_d^2 is computed from the adjustment increments $d_2, d_3, \cdots, d_p$, then, as for the constant means case, we have

$$E(S_d^2) = \sigma_a^2 + \left(\frac{p-2}{p-1}\right)\frac{2\sigma^2}{m} \quad (12.4.20)$$

Then, as in (12.2.13), an unbiased estimate of σ_a^2 is given by

$$\hat{\sigma}_a^2 = S_d^2 - \left(\frac{p-2}{p-1}\right)\left(\frac{2S_{\text{pooled}}^2}{m}\right) \quad (12.4.21)$$

Note carefully that to obtain this formula to estimate σ_a^2, we are assuming that a record from a run of parts if available that were made when the linear regression model was adequate to model the process, and no special causes disturbed the process while these parts were being made.

12.5 ESTIMATING σ^2 AND β_1 FROM PROCESS DATA

The developments above essentially assumed that good estimates of σ^2 and β_1 are available. We need to consider the problem of estimating these parameters from production data. We consider the measurements made on a subset of a sequence of runs of parts made between adjustments to the process. The data from all of the cases above can be considered in the form of display (12.5.1).

$$
\begin{aligned}
&\text{Run 1: } (x_{1,1}, y_{1,1}), (x_{1,2}, y_{1,2}), \cdots, (x_{1,m_1}, y_{1,m_1}) \\
&\text{Run 2: } (x_{2,1}, y_{2,1}), (x_{2,2}, y_{2,2}), \cdots, (x_{2,m_2}, y_{2,m_2}) \\
&\quad \vdots \qquad \vdots \qquad\quad \vdots \qquad\qquad \vdots \\
&\text{Run } r\text{: } (x_{r,1}, y_{r,1}), (x_{r,2}, y_{r,2}), \cdots, (x_{1,m_r}, y_{1,m_r}) \\
&\quad \vdots \qquad \vdots \qquad\quad \vdots \qquad\qquad \vdots
\end{aligned}
\tag{12.5.1}
$$

$$
\bar{x}_r = \frac{1}{m_r} \sum x_{r,i}
$$

$$
\bar{y}_r = \frac{1}{m_r} \sum y_{r,i}
$$

$$
S_{xx,r} = \sum (x_{r,i} - \bar{x}_r)^2
$$

$$
S_{yy,r} = \sum (y_{r,i} - \bar{y}_r)^2
$$

$$
S_{xy,r} = \sum (x_{r,i} - \bar{x}_r)(y_{r,i} - \bar{y}_r)
\tag{12.5.2}
$$

$$
\hat{\beta}_{1,r} = \frac{S_{xy,r}}{S_{xx,r}}
$$

$$
SSE_r = S_{yy,r} - S_{xy,r} \hat{\beta}_{1,r}
$$

$$
\hat{\sigma}_r^2 = \frac{SSE_r}{m_r - 2}
$$

For $r = 1, 2, \cdots$

The estimate β_1 and σ^2 from the data set (12.5.1), we first compute estimates from each run using the ordinary least squares formulas. For the rth run, the quantities computed are given in (12.5.2). All sums are for $i = 1$ to m_r.

Suppose data are available from k runs. Then pooled estimates are computed from the formulas in (12.5.3).

$$
\text{For } w_r = \frac{S_{xx,r}}{\sum\limits_{i=1}^{k} S_{xx,i}}, \text{ put}
$$

$$
\hat{\beta}_{1,\text{pooled}} = \sum_{i=1}^{k} w_i \hat{\beta}_{1,i}, \quad \text{and} \tag{12.5.3}
$$

$$
\hat{\sigma}^2_{\text{pooled}} = \frac{\sum\limits_{i=1}^{k} SSE_i}{\sum\limits_{i=1}^{k} m_i - 2k}
$$

These estimates will be utilized in section 12.6.

12.6 COMBINING SPC AND SPA FOR SIMPLE LINEAR REGRESSION TOOL-WEAR PROCESSES

In practice it is desirable to integrate the SPC charts considered in section 11.1 and the statistical process adjustment methods of section 12.4. We consider first the formulas required for constructing the SPC Q-chart for the type of data one obtains from a process subjected to process mean adjustments.

12.6.1 SPC Plus SPA when β_1 and σ^2 Are Known

When the variance σ^2 and wear rate β_1 are assumed known in advance, we consider first computing the Q-statistics from data taken during one run between adjustments. The notation for the data is given in (12.4.3).

For these data we define, for $i = 1, 2, \cdots, m_r$;

$$\bar{y}_{r,i} = \frac{1}{i} \sum_{j=1}^{i} y_{r,j}, \quad \bar{x}_{r,i} = \frac{1}{i} \sum_{j=1}^{i} x_{r,j}$$

Note that these are the sequential means for the y's and x's for the parts that were actually measured up to the ith measured part. Then the sequential Q-statistics from the rth run are defined in (12.6.1).

$$Q_i = \sqrt{\frac{i-1}{i}} \, \frac{[y_{r,i} - \bar{y}_{r,i-1} - (x_{r,i} - \bar{x}_{r,i-1})\beta_1]}{\sigma} \qquad (12.6.1)$$

for $i = 2, 3, 4, \cdots, m_r$. We obtain $m_r - 1$ Q-statistics from the rth run for plotting, that is, the number of measured parts minus one.

When the linear regression model of (12.4.2) is valid, this is a sequence of independent $N(0, 1)$ statistics. These can be plotted on Q-charts to study the stability of the process with respect to the model. While this SPC chart indicates a stable process, we can use the SPA methods developed in section 12.4 to adjust the process.

12.6.2 SPC Plus SPA with β_1 and σ^2 Estimated

We consider first the case when there are data from just one run of parts made before the first adjustment after a tool change, when no prior data are available. In the notation of (12.4.3), the data available from the parts that are actually measured are denoted as

$$(x_{1,1}, y_{1,1}), (x_{1,2}, y_{1,2}), \cdots, (x_{1,i}, y_{1,i}), \cdots$$

The formulas from Table 11.1 can be used to compute a sequence of Q_i statistics for $i = 4, 5, \cdots$. These statistics can be plotted on an SPC Q-chart to study the stability of the process and the adequacy of the simple linear regression model.

Moreover, while this chart implies a stable process, we will compute compensation increments and apply the adjustment methods given in section 12.4. To do this, we will require external estimates of β_1 and σ^2, at least until enough data are available to compute good estimates of these parameters.

Next, we consider the case when parts from the rth run are being made, and some are gauged, and data from earlier runs are available for $r \geq 2$. We will then use pooled estimates of β_1 and σ^2 obtained from the formulas of (12.5.3) by pooling estimates from all prior runs and from the data available from the present (r^{th}) run. Denote these estimates by $\hat{\beta}_{1,\text{pooled}}$ and $\hat{\sigma}_{\text{pooled}}$. Moreover, denote the sample mean and sum of squares of the x variable from the first i measured parts from run r by

$$\bar{x}_{r,i} \quad \text{and} \quad S_{xx,r}^{(i)}$$

Then the Q-statistics formulas for the SPC Q-chart are given in (12.6.2) for $i = 2, 3, \cdots$; using notation from (12.5.2).

Put

$$B_i = \frac{y_{r,i} - \bar{y}_{r,i-1} - (x_{r,i} - \bar{x}_{r,i-1})\hat{\beta}_{1,\text{pooled}}}{\hat{\sigma}_{\text{pooled}} \sqrt{\dfrac{i}{i-1} + \dfrac{[x_{r,i} - \bar{x}_{r,i-1}]^2}{\displaystyle\sum_{j=1}^{j-1} S_{xx,j} + S_{xx,r}^{(i-1)}}}}$$

$$u_i = H_\nu(B_i) \text{ for } i = 2, 3, \cdots, m_r$$

$$Q_i = \Phi^{-1}(u_i) \text{ for } i = 2, 3, \cdots, m_r$$

$$\text{and } \nu = \sum_{j=1}^{r-1} m_j - 2r + j - 1$$

(12.6.2)

When the model of (12.4.2) is valid, the Q_i's are independent $N(0, 1)$ statistics. That the Q_i's are $N(0, 1)$ statistics is almost immediate. The independence can be shown by an argument that parallels the proof of equations (7.4.4) in Theorem 7B2. The formula for the Q's given in Table 11.1 is a special case of that in (12.6.2), or, to put it differently, the formulas of (12.6.2) are essentially a generalization of those in Table 11.1. These formulas permit us to make a real-time, on-line, SPC chart to decide if the linear regression model is reasonable for a process, and to attempt to recognize special causes. These charts are very sensitive to outliers and therefore provide a useful outliers screen.

Again, while this chart indicates a stable process, we can apply the adjustment rule of Table 12.3, with β_1 and σ^2 replaced in the rule by these pooled estimates at each step for $i = 1, 2, \cdots$.

The material in this and the last section on SPC and adjustment for a simple linear tool-wear process has assumed independent model residuals. Due to inertia, or possibly other reasons, for some processes it will be necessary to assume that the residuals are autocorrelated. We will consider statistical process control and statistical process adjustment (SPC and SPA) for linear tool-wear processes with autocorrelated errors in Chapter 13.

12.7 SPC AND SPA FOR A LINEAR TOOL-WEAR PROCESS WITH INDEPENDENT ERRORS

We wish to operate a tool-wear process so that it is stable and has small EMS about target value. The Q-chart given in section 11.1 for a simple linear regression model with independent errors will be our SPC stability chart. Since this model assumes independent errors, we will routinely compute and examine the Marr–Quesenberry test statistic for lag 1 autocorrelation, $MQ(1)$, given in Chapter 13. When the model appears reasonable and the process stable, we will use the model to adjust the process as described in section 12.4. We illustrate some of this in Example 12.2.

Example 12.2: The data given in column (1) of Table 12.4 are measurements made on 100 consecutively produced parts from a process with $LCL = 23.820$ mm, $\tau = 23.855$ mm, and $UCL = 23.890$ mm. No adjustments were made to the process during this run of parts. A runs plot of these data is given in Fig. 12.4a, and a Q-chart of these data based on the simple linear regression model is shown in Fig. 12.4b. The process is very stable with respect to this model and the parameter estimates are

$$\hat{\beta}_0 = 23.850, \quad \hat{\beta}_1 = -0.00058, \quad \hat{\sigma} = 0.0106$$

Although the adjustment schemes discussed in section 12.4 are designed for use in real-time applications, for illustration we consider applying adjustments retroactively to these data sequentially as they would be in real time. We will use the estimates $\hat{\beta}_1$ and $\hat{\sigma}$ as though they were obtained from prior data.

TABLE 12.4   Data for Example 12.2

(1)	(2)	(1)	(2)	(1)	(2)	(1)	(2)
23.859	23.859	23.818	23.8388	23.830	23.8652	23.792	23.8411
23.847	23.847	23.850	23.8708	23.829	23.8642	23.820	23.8691
23.847	23.847	23.849	23.8698	23.804	23.8392	23.792	23.8411
23.861	23.861	23.812	23.8328	23.828	23.8632	23.789	23.8381
23.831	23.831	23.851	23.8718	23.830	23.8652	23.789	23.8381
23.851	23.8599	23.823	23.8438	23.826	23.8612	23.805	23.8541
23.845	23.8539	23.850	23.8758	23.805	23.8402	23.802	23.8511
23.851	23.8599	23.842	23.8678	23.818	23.8562	23.809	23.8581
23.831	23.8399	23.832	23.8578	23.840	23.8782	23.805	23.8656
23.861	23.8699	23.821	23.8468	23.807	23.8452	23.803	23.8636
23.829	23.8379	23.822	23.8478	23.813	23.8512	23.802	23.8626
23.842	23.8509	23.829	23.8548	23.813	23.8512	23.808	23.8686
23.831	23.8399	23.820	23.8458	23.819	23.8572	23.800	23.8606
23.850	23.8589	23.812	23.8378	23.802	23.8402	23.790	23.8506
23.839	23.8479	23.838	23.8638	23.801	23.8392	23.811	23.8716
23.832	23.8409	23.836	23.8618	23.816	23.8542	23.791	23.8516
23.835	23.8439	23.817	23.8428	23.813	23.8512	23.805	23.8656
23.846	23.8549	23.815	23.8408	23.819	23.8572	23.784	23.8446
23.842	23.8628	23.821	23.8468	23.797	23.8352	23.814	23.8746
23.840	23.8608	23.811	23.8462	23.817	23.8552	23.800	23.8606
23.843	23.8638	23.832	23.8672	23.797	23.8461	23.778	23.8386
23.829	23.8498	23.812	23.8472	23.798	23.8471	23.811	23.8742
23.840	23.8608	23.844	23.8792	23.812	23.8611	23.784	23.8472
23.837	23.8578	23.829	23.8642	23.815	23.8641	23.789	23.8522
23.843	23.8638	23.837	23.8722	23.805	23.8541	23.794	23.8572

Since all units were measured the adjustment increment from (12.4.4) is

$$d_{r,i} = \bar{y}_{r,i} + \left(\frac{i+1}{2}\right)\hat{\beta}_1 - \tau$$

$$= \bar{y}_{r,i} + \left(\frac{i+1}{2}\right)(0.00058) - 23.855$$

$$= \bar{y}_{r,i} + 0.00029i - 23.85529$$

We will use the rule suggested in section 12.4.3 and make the first adjustment to protect against an inflation of EMS of 25% due to bias. Therefore, we make the first adjustment after the first $(1/.25) + 1 = 5$ parts. The following adjustments will be made on constant run size. To determine this run size, we use (12.4.16) and obtain

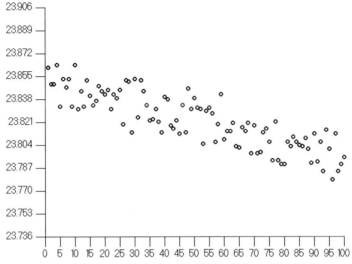

Figure 12.4a Runs Chart for Data of Example 12.2

$$n = \left(\frac{6(0.0106)^2}{(0.00058)^2}\right)^{1/3} = 12.6, \quad \text{or } n = 13$$

So we will adjust the process after the 5th, 18th, 31st, $\cdots$, 96th parts. The data from this "controlled" process are given in column (2) of Table 12.4. A runs plot of these "controlled" data is given in Fig. 12.4c. These data are well centered on the target value of $\tau = 23.855$ (note that the vertical scale is smaller in Fig. 12.4c than in Fig. 12.4a).

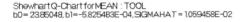

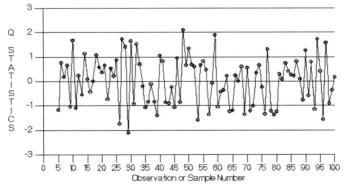

Figure 12.4b Q-Chart for Data of Example 12.2

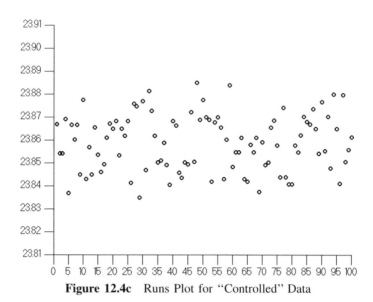

Figure 12.4c   Runs Plot for "Controlled" Data

The observed mean square (OMS) for the original data is

$$OMS = \frac{1}{100} \sum (y_i - \tau)^2 = \frac{1}{100} \sum (y_i - 23.855)^2 = 0.00154$$

and for the "controlled" data the OMS is

$$OMS = 0.00013.$$

Thus, the controller has reduced OMS by 91.6%.

Although the controlled data are not assumed to be from a stable constant mean process, we have plotted these data in an IMUU Q-chart in Fig. 12.4d, and the chart appears quite stable. There is a 4-of-5 signal on observation 81. Note that the mean of these data is 23.852, and the standard deviation is 0.0113. Note that this standard deviation is only $0.0113 - 0.0106 = 0.0007$ mm larger than the standard deviation about the linear regression line. This means that we have eliminated most of the component of EMS due to bias because the variance about the original regression line is the limiting value that we can achieve for EMS by compensator actions.   ∎

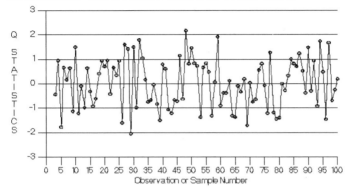

Figure 12.4d *Q*-Chart for "Controlled" Data

12.8 SUMMARY

SPC is concerned with charting a process with a control chart based on a particular parametric model in order to identify and remove special causes that disturb the process and invalidate the model, and, thereby, to validate the model. This model can then be used to predict values of the quality variable and to decide when and how much to adjust the process in an SPA program in order to minimize EMS and the average loss due to variation. This general approach which entails first using SPC methods to bring a process into control with respect to a particular parametric model, and then using SPA based on the model to center the process, will be called the SPC-SPA *paradigm.*

In this chapter we have given an SPC-SPA paradigm for both the constant mean and variance i.i.d. model, and the classical regression model with normal errors.

APPENDIX 12A

To show that d_r can be expressed as in (12.2.10), we proceed as follows. For this case, when a constant number m of parts are gauged from each of p runs, the values on the parts are expressed as

$$y_{r,i} = \mu_r + \epsilon_{r,i}; \quad i = 1, 2, \cdots; \quad r = 1, \cdots, p$$

before any adjustments are made. After the first run and adjustment are made, the values on the last $p - 1$ runs are

$$y_{r,i} - \bar{y}_1 + \tau + a_1; \quad i = 1, 2, \cdots; \quad r = 2, \cdots, p$$

After the second run of parts are made, the adjustment computed is

$$d_2 = \bar{y}_2 - \bar{y}_1 + a_1$$

and the values on all remaining runs are

$$y_{r,i} - \bar{y}_2 + \tau + a_2$$

continuing, after the rth run the adjustment increment is

$$d_r = \bar{y}_r - \bar{y}_{r-1} + a_{r-1} \text{ for all } r = 2, 3, \cdots, p \qquad ■$$

To establish the approximate formula of (12.2.12), we proceed as follows. We shall use the following Lemma.

Lemma 12A.1   Let $X_1, \cdots, X_p$ be identically distributed random variables with mean μ and variance σ^2. Then the sample variance computed from the usual formula has expectation

$$E(S_x^2) = \sigma^2 + \mu^2 - \frac{2}{p(p-1)} \sum_{i=2}^{p} \sum_{j=1}^{i-1} E(X_i X_j) \qquad ■$$

Then, for $d_r = \bar{\epsilon}_r - \bar{\epsilon}_{r-1} + a_{r-1}$ as in (12.2.11), we have

$$E(d_r) = 0, \quad \text{Var}(d_r) = \sigma_a^2 + \frac{2\sigma^2}{m}$$

and
$$E(d_r d_j) = 0 \text{ if } j = 1, \cdots, r - 2$$

$$= \frac{\sigma^2}{m} \text{ if } j = r - 1$$

Using these results in Lemma 12A.1, we obtain

$$E(S_d^2) = \sigma_a^2 + \left(\frac{p-2}{p-1}\right)\frac{2\sigma^2}{m}$$

PROBLEMS

12.1 Do an analysis of the data given in Table P11.1 for problem 11.1 similar to that in Example 12.4. Recommend a specific adjustment scheme for the process.

CHAPTER 13

Some SPC Methods for Autocorrelated Processes

In earlier chapters we have considered statistical process control and adjustment methods based on an assumption that either the individual measurements are a sequence of independent random variables, or, more generally, that the measurements can be modeled by a regression model with independent errors. For some processes this assumption will not be justified, as has been discussed by many authors including Montgomery (1991) and Farnum (1994). In this chapter we will consider first some methods for analyzing data to determine if the independence assumption is reasonable. When analysis indicates that independence is not a reasonable assumption, we consider some alternative methods for treating autocorrelated processes based on either low-order autoregressive models for stationary processes, or exponentially weighted moving averages for some nonstationary processes.

13.1 STUDYING THE INDEPENDENCE ASSUMPTION

13.1.1 Autocorrelation of Regression Residuals

We consider the problem of testing that the errors ϵ_i of the multiple regression model of (11.3.1) are independent against the alternative of nonzero lag k autocorrelation. The lag k autocovariance is defined as

$$\gamma_k = \text{Cov}(\epsilon_i, \epsilon_{i+k}) \tag{13.1.1}$$

where the sequence $(\epsilon_i)_{i \geq 1}$ is assumed to be stationary in the sense that γ_k of (13.1.1) is constant in i for all $k = 0, 1, 2, \cdots$. Then γ_0 is the variance of ϵ_i for $i = 1, 2, \cdots$; and the lag k autocorrelation, ρ_k, is defined by

$$\rho_k = \frac{\gamma_k}{\gamma_0} \tag{13.1.2}$$

A plot of ρ_k against k is called a *correlogram*. The material of this section is largely from Marr and Quesenberry (1991), M-Q91. In that paper the Q_i statistics of Table 11.4 were called NU—for *normalized uniform*—residuals, and it was noted that the sequence (Q_i) tends to track the errors (ϵ_i). This was used to form statistics for testing the lag k autocorrelation testing problems given in Table 13.1. The test for any one of these hypotheses testing problems was called a NU test for autocorrelation.

To define the test statistic for these testing problems, we first define a sum of products lag k statistic as follows. For a vector of Q-statistics, $\mathbf{Q} = (Q_1, Q_2, \cdots, Q_n)'$, form the statistic

$$S_{\mathbf{n}}^{(k)} = \sum_{i=1}^{n-k} Q_i Q_{i+k} \quad \text{for} \quad k < n \tag{13.1.3}$$

Then it can be shown that $S_n^{(k)}$ is asymptotically normal and has mean of 0 and variance $n - k$ under the null hypothesis $H_0: \rho_k = 0$. Now, in order to make tests with data from processes subject to adjustments or other interventions, so that data are from different regression regimes, suppose we have J sequences of Q-statistics of lengths given by the vector $\mathbf{n} = (n_1, n_2, \cdots, n_J)'$. Then we define a statistic by (13.1.4).

$$S_{\mathbf{n}}^{(k)} = S_{(n_1, n_2, \cdots, n_J)}^{(k)} = \sum_{i=1}^{J} S_{n_i}^{(k)} \tag{13.1.4}$$

The statistic $S_{(n_1, n_2, \cdots, n_J)}^{(k)}$ has mean and variance

$$E(S_{(n_1, n_2, \cdots, n_J)}^{(k)}) = 0, \quad \text{Var}(S_{(n_1, n_2, \cdots, n_J)}^{(k)}) = n_+ - kJ,$$

$$\text{with } n_+ = n_1 + n_2 + \cdots + n_J$$

TABLE 13.1 Lag k Autocorrelation Testing Problems

(1)		(2)		(3)	
$H_0: \rho_k = 0$			$H_0: \rho_k = 0$		$H_0: \rho_k = 0$
$H_a: \rho_k > 0$			$H_a: \rho_k < 0$		$H_a: \rho_k \neq 0$

and is asymptotically normally distributed. Note that this variance is the total number of product terms summed to form the statistic. The standardized version of this statistic will here be called the *normalized uniform* test statistic for lag k autocorrelation and denoted NU(k).

$$NU(k) = \frac{S^{(k)}_{(n_1, n_2, \cdots, n_J)}}{\sqrt{n_+ - kJ}} \qquad (13.1.5)$$

This test statistic is approximately a standard normal statistic when $\rho_k = 0$, and can be used in the usual way by referring to standard normal tables or algorithms for the right-tailed, left-tailed and two-tailed testing problems of Table 13.1. *P*-values are easily computed from standard normal distribution function tables or algorithms and can be used to summarize the tests. M-Q91 gives tables of significance points for $\alpha = 0.05$, 0.025 and 0.01, and $k = 1, 2, \cdots, 6$ when $J = 1$. The normal approximation *p*-value is adequate for practical applications for all values of $n_+ - kJ$, but for very small values of $n_+ - kJ$ it is conservative in the sense that the actual *p*-value will be smaller than the one computed.

An estimate of ρ_k is given by

$$\hat{\rho}_k = \frac{S^{(k)}_{(n_1, n_2, \cdots, n_J)}}{n_+ - kJ} \qquad (13.1.6)$$

Computing this estimate assumes, of course, that ρ_k is itself constant over the J regression regimes. If this is not so we would be estimating an average of its value in different regimes.

In manufacturing, due to inertial elements in processes, concern is often about positive autocorrelation. Thus, we will often wish to report the *p*-values of the test statistics for positive autocorrelation. We will call this value NU(k)pv, which is given (approximately) by

$$NU(k)pv = 1 - \Phi[NU(k)] \qquad (13.1.7)$$

More detailed study and discussion of the NU(k) statistic is given in M-Q91 and Marr and Quesenberry (1989). The following example is taken from Example 1 of M-Q91.

Example 13.1: Table 13.3 gives data from four runs between compensator settings of a machining process. There were 346 measurements on parts made by one cutting tool and the process was controlled by an automated compensator that gave run lengths from 1 to 78. There were many short runs of just a few values and runs from only four compensator settings (87, 107, 112, 72) were long enough to use to study autocorrelation. A simple linear regression model was fitted to each run and the runs of Q_i residuals computed. The part numbers and Q_i residuals are also given in Table 13.3.

Note that no Q residuals are given for parts number 19 and 102. This is because $Q_{19} = -6.21$ and $Q_{102} = -6.12$ and these measurements are clearly outliers. The Q residuals should always be used to screen for outliers, which are quite common in many tool-wear processes. If these values are not deleted from the data, they will vitiate the residuals computed after them for a particular compensator setting. Omitting them will also disturb the null hypothesis distribution theory; however, the effect will be slight.

Table 13.2 gives the estimates of the linear regression coefficients for each of the four compensator settings. The numbers in parentheses are the estimated standard errors of the estimates.

In M-Q91 all of the residuals in Table 13.3 were plotted in a normal probabilities plot and the p-value of an Anderson–Darling test for normality was given as 0.4164. These results support a conclusion that the data are reasonably normal.

Table 13.4 summarizes the analysis of these data for autocorrelation. The runs sums of products $S_{n_i}^{(k)}$ are given under the compensator settings. For example, for setting 72 we compute from the last seven Q_i's in Table 13.3:

$$S_7^{(1)} = (1.758)(.342) + (.342)(-.034) + (-.034)(.282)$$

$$+ (.282)(-.016) + (-.016)(.277) + (.277)(.041)$$

$$= .582$$

$$S_7^{(6)} = (1.758)(.041) = .072$$

TABLE 13.2 Estimates of Regression Coefficients in Example 13.1

Compensator Setting	Intercept, β_0	Slope, β_1
87	26.797(.002)	.00030(.00003)
107	26.791(.018)	.00031(.00058)
112	26.736(.032)	.00075(.00027)
72	25.448(.880)	.00443(.00286)

TABLE 13.3 Data for Example 13.1

\multicolumn{4}{c}{Part}				\multicolumn{4}{c}{Part}				\multicolumn{4}{c}{Part}			
Set.	Diam.	#i	Q_i	Set.	Diam.	#1	Q_i	Set.	Diam.	#1	Q_1
87	26.791	1	—	87	26.808	43	−.432	107	26.820	95	.100
87	26.793	2	—	87	26.810	44	−.127	107	26.823	96	.530
87	26.798	3	—	87	26.808	45	−.499	107	26.818	97	−1.019
87	26.800	4	−.342	87	26.810	46	−.182	107	26.824	98	.648
87	26.791	5	−2.455	87	26.810	47	−.222	107	26.824	99	.243
87	26.806	6	1.127	87	26.808	48	−.598	107	26.824	100	−.056
87	26.794	7	−1.167	87	26.808	49	−.606	107	26.821	101	−1.154
87	26.802	8	.242	87	26.811	50	−.096	107	26.828	103	.831
87	26.796	9	−.869	87	26.808	51	−.663	107	26.826	104	−.241
87	26.803	10	.379	87	26.812	52	−.036	107	26.833	105	1.722
87	26.805	11	.453	87	26.819	53	1.219	107	26.830	106	.105
87	26.796	12	−1.373	87	26.810	54	−.513	107	26.822	107	−2.427
87	26.798	13	−.749	87	26.814	55	.181	107	26.823	108	−1.632
87	26.792	14	−1.621	87	26.805	56	−1.491	107	26.813	109	−3.298
87	26.797	15	−.415	87	26.819	57	1.056	107	26.820	110	−1.101
87	26.801	16	.322	87	26.816	58	.402	112	26.815	111	—
87	26.796	17	−.677	87	26.808	59	−1.107	112	26.816	112	—
87	26.800	18	.156	87	26.814	60	−.012	112	26.813	113	—
87	26.811	20	1.994	87	26.808	61	−1.143	112	26.826	114	1.476
87	26.810	21	1.253	87	26.808	62	−1.117	112	26.821	115	−.413
87	26.805	22	.072	87	26.806	63	−1.446	112	26.827	116	.304
87	26.813	23	1.356	87	26.800	64	−2.415	112	26.829	117	.091
87	26.805	24	−.373	87	26.811	65	−.381	112	26.828	118	−.648
87	26.811	25	.650	87	26.821	66	1.321	112	26.826	119	−1.269
87	26.815	26	1.159	87	26.821	67	1.197	112	26.826	120	−1.156
87	26.821	27	1.884	87	26.817	68	.400	112	26.833	121	.348
87	26.805	28	−1.268	87	26.814	69	−.182	112	26.835	122	.334
87	26.803	29	−1.519	87	26.816	70	.132	112	26.826	123	−2.061
87	26.806	30	−.911	87	26.823	71	1.302	112	26.827	124	−1.433
87	26.802	31	−1.535	87	26.823	72	1.181	112	26.825	125	−1.600
87	26.804	32	−1.089	87	26.816	73	−.147	112	26.823	126	−1.658
87	26.821	33	1.679	87	26.828	74	1.895	72	26.822	303	—
87	26.808	34	−.664	87	26.826	75	1.383	72	26.791	304	—
87	26.803	35	−1.454	87	26.825	76	1.087	72	26.739	305	—
87	26.801	36	−1.648	87	26.814	77	−.897	72	26.827	306	1.758
87	26.805	37	−.913	87	26.831	78	1.983	72	26.816	307	.342
87	26.808	38	−.428	107	26.816	90	—	72	26.804	308	−.034
87	26.804	39	−1.066	107	26.821	91	—	72	26.822	309	.282
87	26.809	40	−.247	107	26.813	92	—	72	26.817	310	−.016
87	26.805	41	−.911	107	26.817	93	.268	72	26.832	311	.277
87	26.808	42	−.411	107	26.821	94	.717	72	26.831	312	.041

TABLE 13.4   Test Statistics and Autocorrelation Estimates for Example 13.1

Lag, k	Compensator setting				$S_n^{(k)}$	$Var(S_n^{(k)})$	NU(k)	$\hat{\rho}_k$
	87	107	112	72				
1	20.563	10.651	8.447	.582	40.333	107	3.90	.38
2	16.121	7.172	4.498	.115	27.906	103	2.75	.27
3	9.765	−2.670	4.028	.492	11.615	99	1.17	.12
4	11.877	−5.794	2.193	.065	8.341	95	.86	.09
5	7.470	−0.516	3.167	.501	10.622	91	1.11	.12
6	5.771	1.281	2.940	.072	10.064	87	1.08	.12

The $S_n^{(k)}$ values given in column 6 are the sums across runs given in columns 2–5, the variances given in column 7 are actually the total number of products summed to obtain $S_n^{(k)}$. The standardized NU(k) statistics are given in column 8. The lag 1 statistic is NU(1) = 3.90 with a p-value of 0.00005 as a test for positive autocorrelation. The estimate of ρ_1 is $\hat{\rho}_1 = 0.38$. The lag 2 value is NU(2) = 2.75 with a p-value of 0.003. The values of NU(k) for k = 3, 4, 5, and 6 are not significant at the usual levels of, say, $\alpha = 0.10$ or smaller. We feel that these tests and estimated autocorrelations are consistent with an autoregressive model of order 1, that is, AR(1), for the regression errors. This time series model will be discussed in some detail in section 13.2.1. ∎

13.1.2 Constant Mean and Variance Processes, Individual Measurements, or Subgrouped Data

The approach formulated in this section for testing for autocorrelation considered testing for autocorrelation of the error terms from linear regression models. Of course, the constant mean model is a special case that obtains when only the intercept term is present in the regression model, so the approach given here is readily implemented for constant means models. This is apparent by writing a sequence (X_i) in the form of (13.1.8).

$$X_i = \mu + \epsilon_i \qquad (13.1.8)$$

Note, particularly, that this approach permits us to test for autocorrelation with subgrouped data for which there does not exist a test in the literature, to our knowledge.

Suppose that samples are periodically taken from a process, and that sample i consists of n_i measurements made on consecutively made units of production. Then we can compute Q-statistics from the ith sample using one of the formulas for individual measurements given in formulas (7.4.1)–(7.4.4). From the samples that are large enough to give at least $k + 1$ Q statistics, we can compute the NU(k) test statistic, and an estimate of autocorrelation. For example, if we use either (7.4.3) or (7.4.4) to compute the Q-statistics from each sample, then a sample of size n_i gives $(n_i - 2)$ Q-statistics. If all samples are of the same size $n_i = 4$, say, then we get just two Q-statistics from the ith sample, say Q_{i1} and Q_{i2}. Then if there are J samples available, we would have the statistics

$$S^{(1)}_{(2,2,\cdots,2)} = \sum_{i=1}^{J} Q_{i1}Q_{i2}, \quad NU(1) = \frac{S^{(1)}_{(2,2,\cdots,2)}}{\sqrt{J}} \qquad (13.1.8)$$

for testing for lag 1 autocorrelation. With samples of size four, we can only test for lag one autocorrelation. With samples of size five, or larger, we can test for lag 2 autocorrelation, etc.

13.1.3 Robustness

Some results were also given in M-Q91 that indicate that the tests are pretty robust to the normality assumption. That is, even if the error distribution is not normal, the tests will have sizes approximately correct under the independence null hypothesis, and reasonable power to detect nonzero autocorrelation.

13.1.4 Testing for Autocorrelation in Q-Statistics Sequences

The tests for autocorrelation considered in this section were interpreted in terms of inferences about autocorrelations of the error terms of a linear regression model, including a constant mean normal model as a special case. However, recall that we have given formulas for computing sequences of Q-statistics in many different model settings that are nominally either exactly or approximately i.i.d. standard normal statistics for stable processes. Thus we can compute the NU(k) statistics given above from any of these sequences, in order to test if these sequences of Q-statistics indeed are independent. Of course, if these sequences that are nominally i.i.d. for stable processes are autocorrelated, we shall have to try to explain the basis for this result. There is potential in this for detecting inadequacies in our charting program.

13.1.5   Spurious Autocorrelations Resulting from Model Misspecification

A common problem in testing autocorrelation of regression errors is the appearance of spurious autocorrelation due to misspecification of the regression model itself. For example, if the "true" regression function has a deterministic trend, such as for an exponential or quadratic regression function and Q-statistics from a simple linear regression model are computed, then the Q-statistics will tend to track one another. This will result in significant tests for autocorrelation that are actually due to using an incorrect model. An approach for determining if significant tests for autocorrelation are due to using an incorrect regression model given in M-Q91 involves splitting the data as illustrated in Example 13.2, which is Example 2 in M-Q91.

Example 13.2: The 20 y-values in Table 13.5 were generated from the quadratic model.

$$y_i = 1 + 0.05x^2 + \epsilon_i$$

TABLE 13.5   Data and Q-Residuals for Example 13.2

x	y	Q	Q'
1	4.10585	—	—
2	1.84976	—	—
3	2.27203	—	—
4	3.63638	.83766	.83766
5	6.88702	1.33556	1.33556
6	6.72663	.26211	.26211
7	6.28006	−.38554	−.38554
8	6.31325	−.57817	−.57817
9	6.07366	−.82606	−.82606
10	8.66134	.58678	.58678
11	8.02143	−.32480	—
12	11.98955	1.77307	—
13	13.32778	1.50438	—
14	13.71418	.86521	−.84304
15	13.99398	.36368	−.90446
16	14.79788	.26601	−.67361
17	18.82935	1.98346	1.06124
18	18.94198	1.04947	−.06025
19	19.95746	.87303	−.25784
20	23.36098	1.94325	1.15477

where the ϵ_i's are i.i.d. $N(0, \sigma^2)$. The Q residuals in Table 13.5 were computed assuming the linear model

$$y = \beta_0 + \beta_1 x + \epsilon$$

The data set was then partitioned into two sequences consisting of the first ten and second ten values, and the Q' residuals given in Table 13.5 were computed from these two sequences. The lag 1 test statistic computed from the 17 Q values computed from the full set before partitioning was

$$NU(1) = 2.60485 \text{ with } pv = 0.0046$$

which is highly significant.

The data from the two partitioned sequences of seven Q' values each gave a lag 1 test statistic

$$NU'(1) = 0.54683 \text{ with } pv = 0.29.$$

Since the test for the split data is not significant while the test for the full set of data is significant, we conclude that the result for the full set is due to forcing the data to an inadequate model. ∎

13.2 SPC FOR STATIONARY PROCESSES BASED ON AUTOREGRESSIVE MODELS

Manufacturing processes generally have many elements that influence somewhat a quality variable, and due to inertia in the process this may result in measurements taken on parts made near each other in time being more alike than those made farther apart. The result is that the autocorrelation ρ_k is expected to be positive and to be a monotone decreasing function of the lag k. Such inertial processes can sometimes be adequately modeled by first-order autoregressive processes, that is, by what is often called an AR(1) process in time series analysis (see Box and Jenkins 1976).

The reader will recall that the SPC methods considered earlier in this book were based on the assumption of a sequence of random variable's $(X_t)_{t \geq 1}$, say, that are identically and independently distributed. Indeed, the two functions of classical SPC are to determine the adequacy of this model and to detect deviations from it arising from some special causes that influence the process. However, for inertial processes, among others, the assumption of independent observations may not be tenable. In the following section we will consider modeling a process with a first-order autoregressive model for the values of the quality variable. In section 13.2.2 we will consider modeling the values of a quality variable with a linear regression model with autocorrelated errors when these errors can be modeled by a first order autoregressive model.

13.2.1   SPC Using the AR(1) Model

Consider a sequence of values of a quality variable

$$X_1, X_2, \cdots, X_t, \cdots$$

The AR(1) model for this sequence is given in (13.2.1).

$$X_t - \mu = \rho(X_{t-1} - \mu) + a_t$$

or $\quad X_t = \xi + \rho X_{t-1} + a_t$

(13.2.1)

for $\xi = (1 - \rho)\mu$, $-1 < \rho < 1$, and $(a_t)_{t \ge 1}$ a sequence of i.i.d. $N(0, \sigma_a^2)$ random variables.

Then the results in display (13.2.2) can be obtained.

For $t = 1, 2, \cdots$

$$E(X_t) = \mu = \frac{\xi}{1 - \rho}$$

$$\mathrm{Var}(X_t) = \sigma^2 = \frac{\sigma_a^2}{1 - \rho^2}$$

(13.2.2)

$\rho_k = \mathrm{Corr}(X_t, X_{t+k}) = \rho^k$ for $k = 1, 2, \cdots$

When ρ is positive ($0 < \rho < 1$), as we expect for inertial systems, the sequence of autocorrelations $(\rho^k)_{k \ge 1}$ is a decreasing geometric series of positive functions. We assume that there is available a realization $x_1, x_2, \cdots, x_n$ of observations of the quality variables in time order. Then we estimate the parameters μ, ρ, and ξ by $\hat{\mu}$, $\hat{\rho}$, and $\hat{\xi}$ as follows.

$$\hat{\mu} = \bar{x} = \frac{1}{n} \sum_{t=1}^{n} x_t$$

$$\hat{\rho} = \frac{\sum_{t=1}^{n-1} (x_t - \bar{x})(x_{t+1} - \bar{x})}{\sum_{t=1}^{n} (x_t - \bar{x})^2}$$

(13.2.3)

$$\hat{\xi} = \hat{\mu}(1 - \hat{\rho})$$

When the observation X_{t-1} is observed, suppose we wish to forecast or predict the value of the next observation, that is, of X_t. Denote this predicted value by $\hat{X}_t$, and we will use the following predicted value, based on the estimates $\hat{\xi}$ and $\hat{\rho}$ from the prior data set.

$$\hat{X}_t = \hat{\xi} + \hat{\rho}X_{t-1}, \quad t = 2, 3, \cdots \qquad (13.2.4)$$

Then the residuals e_t from the fitted model are given in (13.2.5).

$$e_t = X_t - \hat{X}_t, \quad t = 2, 3, \cdots \qquad (13.2.5)$$

If the model in (13.2.1) is adequate to model the process, then the sequence $(e_t)_{t\geq 2}$ are approximately i.i.d. $N(0, \sigma_a^2)$ statistics. Thus we can study this sequence to decide if (13.2.1) is an adequate model for the process, and to try to recognize special events that cause upsets from this model.

We will make an SPC chart of this sequence $(e_t)_{t\geq 1}$ of fitted residuals by transforming them to a sequence of Q-statistics using the transformations for individual observations given in section 7.4. In many cases the IMUU transformation of (7.4.4) is the appropriate choice; however, if the model parameters are well estimated, one of the other cases given in (7.4.1), (7.4.2), or (7.4.3) can be used.

Example 13.3: In order to illustrate the charting techniques discussed in this section with data of known structure, we have simulated 100 observations from an AR(1) model with $\mu = 50$, $\sigma_a = 1$, and $\rho = 0.7$. We will analyze these data by acting as though the model and parameters are not known. We initially plot a runs chart of these data in Fig. 13.1a, and compute the following summary statistics and estimates.

$$\overline{X} = 50.55$$

$$NU(1) = 6.13$$

$$\hat{\rho} = 0.62$$

$$PV - MSSD = 1.3E - 10$$

$$MSSD = 0.82$$

By inspecting the runs chart, we note that there appears to be a trend for small groups of consecutive points to be nearly equal. This tendency is not strongly apparent. However, both the NU(1) test and the MSSD test are highly significant. The significance of the MSSD test implies that if we are to make individual measurements charts, then either MSSD or the moving range must be used to estimate the standard deviation.

Next, we use the estimates $\overline{X} = 50.55$ and MSSD = 0.82 to plot retrospective IMKK Q-charts for the variance and the mean. The chart for sigma is given in Fig. 13.1b, and it appears to be in control. However, the mean chart is given in Fig. 13.1c and gives strong out-of-control signals.

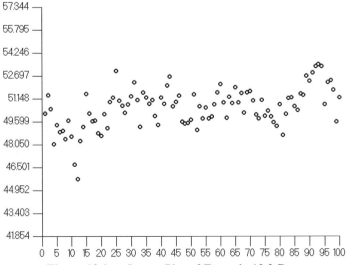

Figure 13.1a Scatter Plot of Example 13.3 Data

Shewhart Q-Chart for SIGMA : IMKK

XBAR = 50.55146, SD = 1.343177, RMSSD = .8218238, PV-MSSD = 1.310039E-10

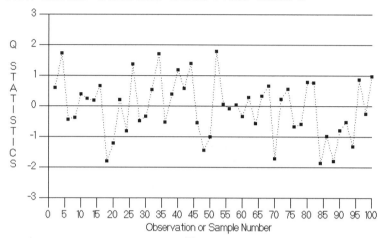

Figure 13.1b   Sigma Chart Using $\overline{X}$ = 50.55 for μ, and $\hat{\sigma}$ = 0.82 for σ

Shewhart Q-Chart for MEAN : IMKK

XBAR = 50.55146, SD = 1.343177, RMSSD = .8218238, PV-MSSD = 1.310039E-10

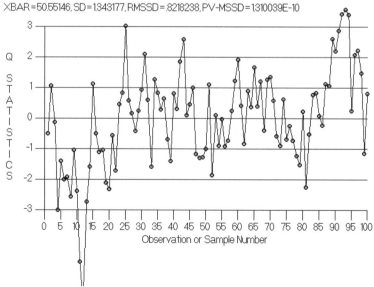

Figure 13.1c   Mean Chart Using $\overline{X}$ = 50.55 for μ, and $\hat{\sigma}$ = 0.82 for σ

The sigma chart made using the IMUU transformations is very similar to the chart in Fig. 13.1b and is therefore omitted to save space. However, the IMUU chart for the mean is given in Fig. 13.1d and, we feel, reveals the autocorrelation patterns very clearly.

Finally, we have computed the IMUU Q-statistics from the sequence of residuals from (13.2.5). The e_t residuals we computed using, of course, the estimated values of the parameters as in (13.2.4). The Shewhart chart of these values is shown in Fig. 13.1e which indicates, we fell, that the AR(1) model describes the data well.

13.2.2 SPC for the Multiple Linear Regression Model with AR(1) Error Structure

In sections 11.1 and 11.3 we considered SPC for data that can be modeled by a simple linear regression model or a multiple linear regression model with independent errors in both cases. Now, there are many applications of regression models where the assumption of independent errors is suspect. For example, we think that the errors of most regression models for toolwear are positively autocorrelated. The approach that we give here to treating these problems assumes that there is available a set of data that can be used to study the autocorrelation structure as discussed in section 13.1.1. Suppose that analysis of this data set indicates that a regression model with AR(1) autocor-

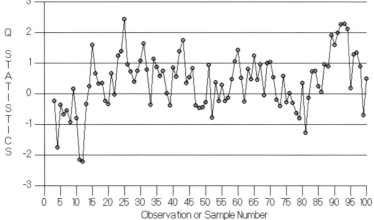

Figure 13.1d   Mean Chart for Unknown μ and σ, that is, Case IMUU

Shewhart Q-Chart for MEAN : AR1

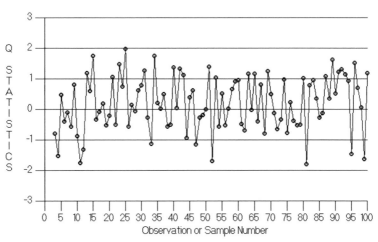

Figure 13.1e   Mean Chart Based on Residuals from the AR(1) Model

related errors is a reasonable model to entertain, and moreover, let $\hat{\rho}$ denote the estimate of the lag 1 autocorrelation from this analysis.

With this background we are interested in performing on-line charting in real time. Suppose that the sequence of data observed is denoted

$$(\overset{*}{\mathbf{x}}_1', \overset{*}{y}_1'), \ (\overset{*}{\mathbf{x}}_2', \overset{*}{y}_2'), \ \cdots \tag{13.2.6}$$

where the regression model is written in terms of this "star" notation as

$$\overset{*}{\mathbf{y}} = \overset{*}{\mathbf{X}}\beta + \overset{*}{\epsilon} \tag{13.2.7}$$

for $\overset{*}{\mathbf{x}}_i' = (\overset{*}{x}_{i1}, \cdots, \overset{*}{x}_{ip})$ the ith row of $\overset{*}{\mathbf{X}}$, and $\overset{*}{\mathbf{y}}_1 = (\overset{*}{y}_1, \cdots, \overset{*}{y}_n)'$.

We use the estimate $\hat{\rho}$ to transform star values as follows (See Morrison 1983, p. 237). Put

$$\mathbf{y}' = (\sqrt{1 - \hat{\rho}^2} \ \overset{*}{y}_1, \ \overset{*}{y}_2 - \hat{\rho}\overset{*}{y}_1, \cdots, \ \overset{*}{y}_n - \hat{\rho}\overset{*}{y}_{n-1}) \tag{13.2.8}$$

and the jth column of $\overset{*}{\mathbf{X}}$ is transformed to the jth column of a matrix $\mathbf{X}$, which is

$$(\sqrt{1 - \hat{\rho}^2}\, \overset{*}{x}_{1j},\; \overset{*}{x}_{2j} - \hat{\rho}\overset{*}{x}_{1j},\; \cdots,\; \overset{*}{x}_{nj} - \hat{\rho}\overset{*}{x}_{n-1,j})' \qquad (13.2.9)$$

If the model in (13.2.7) is valid with AR(1) autocorrelated errors $\overset{*}{\epsilon}$, then the following model written using the transformed values will have independent errors ϵ.

$$\mathbf{y} = \mathbf{X}\beta + \epsilon \qquad (13.2.10)$$

Then we can use this transformed data, $\mathbf{y}$ and $\mathbf{X}$, to make SPC charts from the results given in section 11.3.

Example 13.4: To illustrate the charts and analysis presented in this subsection, we have simulated 100 observations from a simple linear regression model:

$$y_i = 4.2 - 0.001i + \epsilon_i$$

$$\text{for } \epsilon_i = 0.8\epsilon_{i-1} + a_i$$

and the a_i are i.i.d. $N(0, 0.02^2)$ random variables. The value of $\sigma_a = 0.02$ corresponds to $\sigma = \text{SD}(\epsilon_i) = \dfrac{\sigma_a}{\sqrt{1 - \rho^2}} = \dfrac{0.02}{\sqrt{1 - .8^2}} = 0.033$. A scatter plot of the data is given in Fig. 3.2a. The linear trend is apparent in this plot and careful examination suggests positive autocorrelation.

The regression Q-chart of Chapter 11 is given in Fig. 13.2b, and in this chart the autocorrelation is obvious. The parameter estimates and lag 1 test statistic are

$$\hat{\beta}_0 = 4.2, \quad \hat{\beta}_1 = -0.00099, \quad \hat{\sigma} = 0.0327,$$

$$\hat{\rho} = 0.77, \quad \text{and} \quad \text{NU}(1) = 11.45$$

The parameter values are all near the values used to simulate the observations, and the test statistic is highly significant. Recall that NU(1) is approximately a standard normal statistic under the null hypothesis of zero lag 1 autocorrelation, and this value means a highly significant positive autocorrelation. This chart that ignores the autocorrelation of the errors shows that the regression model with independent errors is inadequate for this data.

The control chart made from these data using the transformation scheme above for autocorrelated error structure is given in Fig. 13.2c.

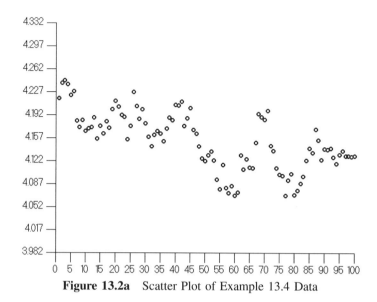

Figure 13.2a Scatter Plot of Example 13.4 Data

That is, using the estimated value $\hat{\rho}$ of the lag 1 autocorrelation from a simple linear regression model the values were transformed using (13.2.8) and (13.2.9). From these transformed values a simple linear regression Q-chart was made in the manner given in Chapter 11. We feel that the chart in Fig. 13.2c indicates that the regression model with

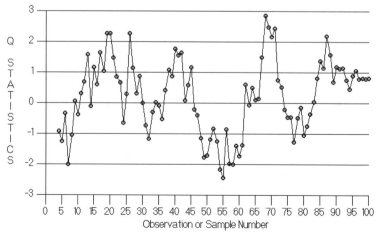

Figure 13.2b Regression Q-Chart of Example 13.4 Data

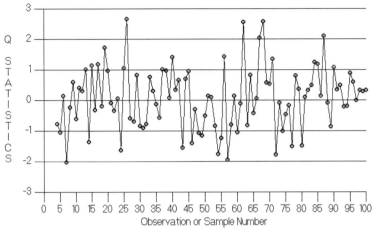

Shewhart Q-Chart for MEAN : MLAR
b0 = 4.201674, b1 = -9.701247E-04, SIGMAHAT = 1.941306E-02, NU(1) = .3676565, QRho= 2.986333E-02

Figure 13.2c *Q*-Chart for Simple Linear Regression Data with AR(1) Errors of Example 13.4

autocorrelated errors is a major improvement over the model with in-dependent errors which gives the chart in Fig. 13.2b.

13.2.3   An EWMA-Based *Q*-Chart for Nonstationary Autocorrelated Processes

The EWMA chart for detecting monotone shifts of the mean for a classical stable process was presented in section 6.2. In sections 13.2.1 and 13.2.2 we considered using first-order autoregressive processes to model and chart data from processes with either a constant mean or a mean that varies in a deterministic fashion and can be modeled by a regression model. However, the EWMA can be used effectively to fore-cast or predict future values for many processes with positively auto-correlated observations. It can be shown to be the ideal way to predict a future value in a time series

$$X_1, \cdots, X_t, \cdots$$

that is described by a difference equation model of the following form.

$$X_t = X_{t-1} + a_t - \theta a_{t-1} \qquad (13.2.11)$$

Where $-1 < \theta < 1$, the λ in equation (6.2.1) is given by $\lambda = 1 - \theta$, and the sequence $(a_t)_{t \geq 0}$ are i.i.d. $N(0, \sigma_a^2)$. In time series analysis this is called an integrated-moving-average model of order one, [IMA(1, 1)]. Then the optimal forecast or predicted value at time t; given $X_1, \cdots, X_{t-1}$; is given by (6.2.2) as the EWMA at time $t - 1$, namely:

$$\hat{X}_t = \lambda \sum_{i=0}^{t-2} (1 - \lambda)^i X_{t-1-i} + (1 - \lambda)^{t-1} X_0$$

where X_0 is a starting value and $\lambda = 1 - \theta$. This can be immediately rewritten in the following form:

$$\hat{X}_t = \lambda X_{t-1} + (1 - \lambda)\hat{X}_{t-1} \qquad (13.2.12)$$

which is more convenient for computing.

The one step ahead prediction error at time t is given by

$$e_t = X_t - \hat{X}_t \qquad (13.2.13)$$

If $\hat{X}_t$ is a good predictor of X_t, these prediction errors should be an approximately uncorrelated sequence. From this sequence of prediction errors, we can compute a sequence of Q-statistics by using the individual measurements formulas of section 7.4. These Q-statistics can be plotted on charts (Shewhart, EWMA, CUSUM) to study the stability of the process. Note that when λ has been selected in advance, this procedure can be carried out point-by-point as the data points (observations) are taken in real time by using the IMUU transformations.

We must choose a value of the smoothing constant λ, however, the methods described in section 6.2 are not appropriate because they were based on assuming the classical stable model, which assumes independence of observations. To choose a value of λ, we assume that a calibration data set $X_1, X_2, \cdots, X_n$ is available from the process. To estimate λ, we use the value that minimizes the sum of squares of the prediction errors computed from these calibration data. That is, for

$$SS(\lambda) = \sum_{t=2}^{n} e_t^2 = \sum_{t=2}^{n} (X_t - \hat{X}_t)^2$$

we choose λ that minimizes this quantity. Montgomery (1991, p. 349) states that he has found this to work reasonably well in a wide variety of practical situations.

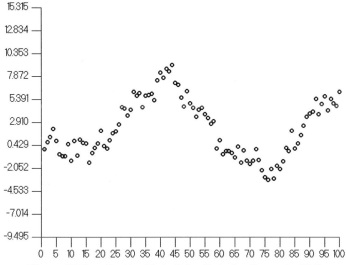

Figure 13.3a   Scatter Plot of the Data for Example 13.5

Example 13.5: To illustrate the technique given in this section, we have generated 100 observations from the IMA(1, 1) model with $\theta = 0.25$ and $\sigma_a^2 = 1$. A scatter plot of these data is given in Fig. 13.3a. An individual measurement (IMUU) Q-chart of these data is given in Fig. 13.3b, and it shows that the "process" generating the data is badly

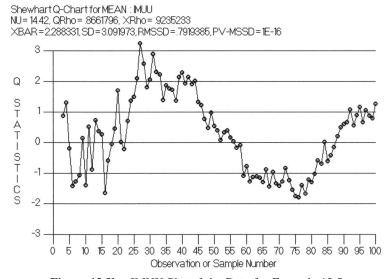

Figure 13.3b   IMUU Plot of the Data for Example 13.5

out of control with respect to the classical stable model. The pattern on this Q-chart is essentially the same as that on the scatter plot of Fig. 13.3a.

The EWMA prediction error residuals Shewhart Q-chart is given in Fig. 13.3c. Although in this case we know $\lambda = 1 - \theta = .75$, this plot was made using the estimated value of λ of 0.74, which was the estimated value obtained by minimizing $SS(\lambda)$ above. The reader should recall that by Shewhart's definition a process is stable or in-control with respect to a quality variable if values of the quality variable are predictable. The chart in Fig. 13.3c clearly indicates that the process generating these data is stable, provided an EWMA (with $\lambda = 0.74$) is used to predict future values.

13.3 SUMMARY

In earlier chapters we have considered SPC charting methods for models that assume either observations themselves or residuals from regression models are i.i.d. random variables. In this chapter we have given some methods for testing the independence assumption and for charting some processes that do not permit this assumption.

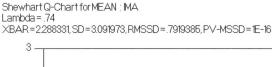

Shewhart Q-Chart for MEAN : IMA
Lambda = .74
XBAR = 2.288331, SD = 3.091973, RMSSD = .7919385, PV-MSSD = 1E-16

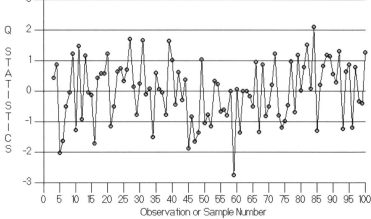

Figure 13.3c   IMUU Q-Chart for the EWMA Residuals for Example 13.5

TABLE P13.1

i	x	i	x	i	x	i	x
1	3.99	11	4.05	21	4.06	31	4.06
2	4.02	12	4.05	22	4.02	32	4.07
3	4.08	13	4.04	23	3.98	33	4.05
4	4.09	14	4.03	24	4.00	34	3.99
5	4.14	15	4.06	25	4.04	35	3.97
6	4.12	16	4.05	26	4.04	36	4.03
7	4.13	17	4.04	27	3.98	37	3.97
8	4.13	18	4.07	28	4.07	38	4.04
9	4.05	19	4.09	29	4.06	39	4.04
10	4.02	20	4.04	30	4.07	40	4.07

PROBLEMS

13.1 Study the data in Table P13.1 by
  (a) Plotting IMUU Shewhart charts for sigma and μ. Note the values of the supplementary statistics: $\bar{x}$, S, NU, XRHO, PV-MSSD. Discuss the chart and these values.
  (b) By using the values of $\bar{x}$ and XRHO from part (a), make an AR(1) Q-chart for this data.
  (c) Discuss your results.

13.2 Study the data in Table P13.2 by
  (a) Plotting IMUU Shewhart charts for sigma and μ. Note the values of the supplementary statistics: $\bar{x}$, S, NU, XRHO, PV-MSSD. Discuss the chart and these values.

TABLE P13.2

i	x	i	x	i	x	i	x
1	4.00	11	3.87	21	3.85	31	4.05
2	4.01	12	3.83	22	3.85	32	4.40
3	4.08	13	3.83	23	3.91	33	4.12
4	4.01	14	3.87	24	3.92	34	4.10
5	4.07	15	3.90	35	3.97	35	4.12
6	4.06	16	3.85	26	4.05	36	4.10
7	4.01	17	3.88	27	4.07	37	4.10
8	4.03	18	3.81	28	3.99	38	4.05
9	3.96	19	3.81	29	4.01	39	4.06
10	3.94	20	3.86	30	4.05	40	4.06

(b) By using the values of $\bar{x}$ and XRHO from part (a), make an AR(1) Q-chart for this data.

(c) Discuss your results.

CHAPTER 14

Q-Charts for Two or More Quality Variables

In the preceding chapters we have considered statistical process control methods using observed values on a single variable. There are often two or more variables that can be measured or counted which give relevant information on the process. Dimensional measurements may be made on lengths and widths, inner and outer diameters, true position coordinates may be made in two or three dimensions, several electrical or chemical variables may be evaluated on each unit of product, and so on. Some variables may be continuous and some may be discrete. Sometimes the variable of primary interest may not be observable and control can only be maintained by utilizing other related variables. Concern here is largely with using two or more measurements taken simultaneously and studying the stabilitiy of the joint distribution of the variables. This is accomplished by studying the stability of parameters.

The methods presented in this chapter are based on the multivariate normal distribution and the multinomial distribution. A particularly readable introduction to multivariate statistical analysis based on the multivariate normal distribution is given by Morrison (1983).

14.1 THE MULTINORMAL DISTRIBUTION

Suppose that we are to measure and study values on p ($p \geq 2$) quality variables that we denote by the column vector

$$\mathbf{x} = (x_1, x_2, \cdots, x_p)' \qquad (14.1.1)$$

This vector is said to have a *multivariate normal* or *multinormal* distribution if the joint density function of its p elements is

$$f(\mathbf{x}) = \frac{1}{(2\pi)^{p/2}|\mathbf{\Sigma}|^{1/2}} \exp\left\{-\tfrac{1}{2}(\mathbf{x} - \boldsymbol{\mu})'\mathbf{\Sigma}^{-1}(\mathbf{x} - \boldsymbol{\mu})\right\} \quad (14.1.2)$$

The *mean vector* of this multinormal distribution is given by

$$E(\mathbf{x}) = \boldsymbol{\mu} = (\mu_1, \mu_2, \cdots, \mu_p)'$$

where $E(x_i) = \mu_i$ for $i = 1, \cdots, p$. The *covariance matrix* is given in
(14.1.3), where $\text{Cov}(x_i, x_j) = \sigma_{ij} = \sigma_{ji}$, and $\text{Var}(x_i) = \sigma_{ii}$. For the function in (14.1.2) to be a probability density, $\mathbf{\Sigma}$ must be a symmetric
positive definite matrix.

$$\text{Cov}(\mathbf{x}, \mathbf{x}') = \mathbf{\Sigma} = \begin{bmatrix} \sigma_{11} & \sigma_{12} & \cdots & \sigma_{1p} \\ \sigma_{12} & \sigma_{22} & \cdots & \sigma_{2p} \\ \vdots & \vdots & \ddots & \vdots \\ \sigma_{1p} & \sigma_{2p} & \cdots & \sigma_{pp} \end{bmatrix} \quad (14.1.3)$$

14.2   PARAMETER ESTIMATION FOR THE MULTINORMAL DISTRIBUTION

A sample of size n from a p-variate multinormal distribution is an $n \times p$ matrix that we denote as follows.

$$\mathbf{X}_n = \begin{bmatrix} x_{11} & x_{12} & \cdots & x_{1p} \\ x_{21} & x_{22} & \cdots & x_{2p} \\ \vdots & \vdots & \ddots & \vdots \\ x_{n1} & x_{n2} & \cdots & x_{np} \end{bmatrix} = \begin{bmatrix} \mathbf{x}_1' \\ \mathbf{x}_2' \\ \vdots \\ \mathbf{x}_n' \end{bmatrix} \quad (14.2.1)$$

Denote by $\bar{\mathbf{x}}$ and $\mathbf{S}$ the vector of sample means and the sample
covariance matrix. That is

$$\bar{\mathbf{x}} = \begin{bmatrix} \bar{x}_1 \\ \bar{x}_2 \\ \vdots \\ \bar{x}_p \end{bmatrix}, \quad \text{and} \quad \mathbf{S} = \begin{bmatrix} s_{11} & s_{12} & \cdots & s_{1p} \\ s_{12} & s_{22} & \cdots & s_{2p} \\ \vdots & \vdots & \ddots & \vdots \\ s_{1p} & s_{2p} & \cdots & s_{pp} \end{bmatrix} \quad (14.2.2)$$

where

$$\bar{x}_j = \frac{1}{n} \sum_{k=1}^{n} x_{kj}, \; S_{ij} = \frac{1}{n-1} \sum_{k=1}^{n} (x_{ki} - \bar{x}_i)(x_{kj} - \bar{x}_j) \quad (14.2.3)$$

for $i = 1, \cdots, p$ and $j = 1, \cdots, p$.

Next, suppose m samples are available to estimate the process parameters μ and Σ, with n_r vector observations in the rth sample for $r = 1, \cdots, m$. Let $\bar{x}_r$ and S_r denote the sample mean vector and covariance matrix from the rth sample, as in (14.2.2) and (14.2.3). Then put

$$\bar{\bar{x}} = \frac{1}{N} \sum_{r=1}^{m} n_r \bar{x}_r, \quad N = \sum_{r=1}^{m} n_r \quad (14.2.4)$$

and

$$S_{\text{pooled}} = \frac{1}{N-m} \sum_{r=1}^{m} (n_r - 1) S_r \quad (14.2.5)$$

Then $\bar{x}_r$ and S_r are unbiased estimates of μ and Σ, so $\bar{\bar{x}}$ and S_{pooled} are also unbiased estimates of μ and Σ.

14.3 MULTIVARIATE MEAN Q-CHARTS FOR INDIVIDUAL MEASUREMENTS

Let $x_1, x_2, \cdots$ denote a sequence of p-variate observations. Most often these measurements are taken in time order. We present methods here for plotting charts sequentially in time order as these sets of measurements are made. When the rth set of measurements, that is, vector, is taken, we will use it to plot a point. In the notation introduced in the last section, this observation is denoted

$$x_r = (x_{r1}, x_{r2}, \cdots, x_{rp})' \quad (14.3.1)$$

Let $\bar{x}_r$ and S_r denote the sample mean vector and sample covariance matrix, respectively, computed from the first r observations. Note that these are sequential statistics. These statistics can be conveniently computed using the following updating formulas.

$$\bar{x}_r = \frac{1}{r} [(r-1)\bar{x}_{r-1} + x_r] \quad (14.3.2)$$

$$S_r = \left(\frac{r-2}{r-1}\right) S_{r-1} + \frac{1}{r}\,(\mathbf{x}_r - \bar{\mathbf{x}}_{r-1})(\mathbf{x}_r - \bar{\mathbf{x}}_{r-1})' \qquad (14.3.3)$$

There are well-known analogues of the univariate formulas of (3.4.5).

We will consider the same cases as those considered for univariate observations in section 7.4. If the population mean vector $\boldsymbol{\mu}$ is known and the population covariance matrix $\boldsymbol{\Sigma}$ is also known, we call this Case KK, and so on, as in section 7.4. We transform the rth observation vector $\mathbf{x}_r$ to standardized normal Q-statistics as follows. These formulas are analogues of those given in Chapter 7 for univariate observations.

Case KK: $\boldsymbol{\mu} = \boldsymbol{\mu}_0$ known and $\boldsymbol{\Sigma} = \boldsymbol{\Sigma}_0$ known

$$Q_r(\mathbf{x}_r) = \Phi^{-1}\{G_p(A_r)\} \quad r = 1, 2, \cdots \qquad (14.3.4)$$

for

$$A_r = (\mathbf{x}_r - \boldsymbol{\mu}_0)'\boldsymbol{\Sigma}_0^{-1}(\mathbf{x}_r - \boldsymbol{\mu}_0)$$

Case UK: $\boldsymbol{\mu}$ unknown and $\boldsymbol{\Sigma} = \boldsymbol{\Sigma}_0$ known

$$Q_r(\mathbf{x}_r) = \Phi^{-1}\{G_p(A_r)\} \quad r = 2, 3, \cdots \qquad (14.3.5)$$

for

$$A_r = \left(\frac{r-1}{r}\right) (\mathbf{x}_r - \bar{\mathbf{x}}_{r-1})'\boldsymbol{\Sigma}_0^{-1}(\mathbf{x}_r - \bar{\mathbf{x}}_{r-1})$$

Case KU: $\boldsymbol{\mu} = \boldsymbol{\mu}_0$ known and $\boldsymbol{\Sigma}$ unknown

$$Q_r(\mathbf{x}_r) = \Phi^{-1}\{F_{p,r-1-p}(A_r)\} \quad r = p + 2, p + 3, \cdots \qquad (14.3.6)$$

for

$$A_r = \left(\frac{r-1-p}{p(r-2)}\right) (\mathbf{x}_r - \boldsymbol{\mu}_0)'\mathbf{S}_{r-1}^{-1}(\mathbf{x}_r - \boldsymbol{\mu}_0)$$

Case UU: $\boldsymbol{\mu}$ unknown and $\boldsymbol{\Sigma}$ unknown

$$Q_r(\mathbf{x}_r) = \Phi^{-1}\{F_{p,r-1-p}(A_r)\} \quad r = p + 2, p + 3, \cdots \quad (14.3.7)$$

for

$$A_r = \left(\frac{(r - 1)(r - 1 - p)}{rp(r - 2)}\right) (\mathbf{x}_r - \bar{\mathbf{x}}_{r-1})' \mathbf{S}_{r-1}^{-1}(\mathbf{x}_r - \bar{\mathbf{x}}_{r-1})$$

Note particularly that for case UK we can obtain Q-statistics only for $r \geq 2$, and for cases KU and UU only for $r \geq p + 2$. For case UK we must have one prior observation in order to compute $\bar{\mathbf{x}}_{r-1}$. For the last two cases we must have $r = p + 2$ observations to compute $\mathbf{S}_{r-1}^{-1}$.

When the process is stable with a p-variate multinormal distribution the Q-statistics for cases KK, UK, and UU are independently distributed $N(0, 1)$ statistics. Those for case KU are $N(0, 1)$ and approximately independent. That the statistics are $N(0, 1)$ distributed is obvious from well-known distribution theory and the probability integral transformation. Independence can be shown using arguments similar to those for univariate cases in Appendix 7B. Tang (1995a) gave the transformation in (14.3.7) and referred to a proof of independence for this case in Tang (1995b).

14.4 MULTIVARIATE MEAN Q-CHARTS FOR SUBGROUPED MEASUREMENTS

As with univariate data, it will often be desirable to take observations in subgroups. Multivariate charts from subgrouped data will, as for univariate charts, be more sensitive to detect mean shifts, and the assumption of normality is not as important due to the central limit theorem.

Suppose that vector observations are taken in subgroups and that the subgroups are taken in time order. We assume that the ith subgroup or sample contains n_i vector observations. We wish to compute a statistic Q_r when the rth subgroup becomes available. Denote the jth observation vector from the ith subgroup by $\mathbf{x}_{ij}$ for $i = 1, \cdots, r$ and $j = 1, \cdots, n_i$. Then define the statistics of (14.4.1).

Subgroup Statistics:

$$\overline{\mathbf{x}}_i = \frac{1}{n_i} \sum_{j=1}^{n_i} \mathbf{x}_{ij},$$

$$\mathbf{S}_i = \frac{1}{n_i - 1} \sum_{j=1}^{n_i} (\mathbf{x}_{ij} - \overline{\mathbf{x}}_i)(\mathbf{x}_{ij} - \overline{\mathbf{x}}_i)'$$

Sequential Statistics:

For $N_r = n_1 + \cdots + n_r$ put

$$\overline{\overline{\mathbf{x}}}_r = \frac{1}{N_r} \sum_{i=1}^{r} n_i \overline{\mathbf{x}}_i = \frac{1}{N_r} [N_{r-1}\overline{\overline{\mathbf{x}}}_{r-1} + n_r\overline{\mathbf{x}}_r]$$

$$\mathbf{S}_{pooled,r} = \frac{1}{N_r - r} \sum_{i=1}^{r} (n_i - 1)\mathbf{S}_i$$

$$= \frac{1}{N_r - r}[(N_{r-1} - r + 1)\mathbf{S}_{pooled,r-1} + (n_r - 1)\mathbf{S}_r]$$

$$\mathbf{S}_{pooled,0} = \mathbf{0}$$

(14.4.1)

Using these sequential statistics we define the Q-statistics for the four cases. As for the individual measurements formulas, these are the vector analogues of the corresponding formulas for subgrouped univariate observations.

Case KK: $\boldsymbol{\mu} = \boldsymbol{\mu}_0$ known and $\boldsymbol{\Sigma} = \boldsymbol{\Sigma}_0$ known

$$Q_r = \Phi^{-1}\{G_p(A_r)\} \quad r = 1, 2, \cdots \tag{14.4.2}$$

for

$$A_r = n_r(\overline{\mathbf{x}}_r - \boldsymbol{\mu}_0)'\boldsymbol{\Sigma}_0^{-1}(\overline{\mathbf{x}}_r - \boldsymbol{\mu}_0)$$

Case UK: $\boldsymbol{\mu}$ unknown, $\boldsymbol{\Sigma} = \boldsymbol{\Sigma}_0$ known

$$Q_r = \Phi^{-1}\{G_p(A_r)\} \quad r = 2, 3, \cdots \tag{14.4.3}$$

for

$$A_r = \frac{n_r N_{r-1}}{N_r} (\overline{\mathbf{x}}_r - \overline{\overline{\mathbf{x}}}_{r-1})'\boldsymbol{\Sigma}_0^{-1}(\overline{\mathbf{x}}_r - \overline{\overline{\mathbf{x}}}_{r-1})$$

Case KU: $\mu = \mu_0$ known, Σ unknown

$$Q_r = \Phi^{-1}\{F_{p,N_r-r-p+1}(A_r)\} \quad r = 1, 2, \cdots \quad (14.4.4)$$

for

$$A_r = n_r \left(\frac{N_r - r + 1 - p}{p(N_r - r)}\right) (\bar{\mathbf{x}}_r - \mu_0)' \mathbf{S}_{\text{pooled},r}^{-1} (\bar{\mathbf{x}}_r - \mu_0)$$

Case UU: $\mu = \mu_0$ unknown, Σ unknown

$$Q_r = \Phi^{-1}\{F_{p,N_r-r-p+1}(A_r)\} \quad r = 2, 3, \cdots \quad (14.4.5)$$

for

$$A_r = \left(\frac{n_r N_{r-1}(N_r - r + 1 - p)}{N_r p(N_r - r)}\right) (\bar{\mathbf{x}}_r - \bar{\bar{\mathbf{x}}}_{r-1})' \mathbf{S}_{\text{pooled},r}^{-1} (\bar{\mathbf{x}}_r - \bar{\bar{\mathbf{x}}}_{r-1})$$

When the vector observations are from a stable process with a multinormal distribution, the Q-statistics for cases KK, UK, and UU are independent $N(0, 1)$ random variables. That they are $N(0, 1)$ is immediate, and a proof of independence for Case UU can be made along the lines of that for the univariate case given for (7.3.4) in Appendix 7B. Tang (1995a) gave the transformation in (14.4.5) for the special case when all subgroups are equal. He also gave some simulation results that demonstrated that the charts for the cases of unknown parameters give patterns very similar to those for the case with known parameters. He did not give the independence result, however.

14.5 DISCUSSION OF MULTIVARIATE MEAN CHARTS

Suppose we denote by μ_0 and Σ_0 the nominal values of the mean vector and covariance matrix. For a stable process, μ and Σ are equal to μ_0 and Σ_0 for all observations. Now, if μ should change from $\mu = \mu_0$ to $\mu = \mu_1 \neq \mu_0$, then it can be shown that the distributions of the Q-statistic given in sections 14.3 and 14.4 depend on the mean and covariance matrix only as a function of the *Mahalanobis distance* δ^2 given by

$$\delta^2 = (\boldsymbol{\mu}_1 - \boldsymbol{\mu}_0)'\boldsymbol{\Sigma}^{-1}(\boldsymbol{\mu}_1 - \boldsymbol{\mu}_0)$$

This δ^2 is a nonnegative quantity that measures distance between the two points $\boldsymbol{\mu}_0$ and $\boldsymbol{\mu}_1$ in p-space. It generally will increase in value as $\boldsymbol{\mu}$ moves away from $\boldsymbol{\mu}_0$, for $\boldsymbol{\Sigma} = \boldsymbol{\Sigma}_0$ constant. It is important to note that these Q-charts control only δ^2, and signals on these charts will be difficult, or impossible, to interpret in terms of the individual variables. Indeed, irregular patterns on these charts could possibly be due to changes in any of the p means or $p(p + 1)/2$ elements in the covariance matrix; or even due to inadequacy of the multinormal distribution to model the data. Thus, these multivariate charts are omnibus charts that generally can warn us of process problems, and we will usually then follow up signals on these charts by plotting univariate mean and variance charts to study the individual components.

Much of the discussion given in earlier chapters for univariate charts obtains also for these multivariate charts. For example, if some parameters shift to new values during operations (say $\boldsymbol{\mu}$ shifts from $\boldsymbol{\mu} = \boldsymbol{\mu}_0$ to $\boldsymbol{\mu} = \boldsymbol{\mu}_1$) and does not change again, then the charts that use in-line data to estimate $\boldsymbol{\mu}$ (cases UK and UU) will eventually drift back to indicate a stable process. This is, of course, what we should expect and desire of the charting process. The process *is stable* after the shift.

Note particularly that not only do changes in the values in the mean vector $\boldsymbol{\mu}$ influence δ^2, but also changes in the elements of $\boldsymbol{\Sigma}$ may be reflected in values of δ^2. However, it will generally be difficult to predict the patterns that might result from changes in the elements of $\boldsymbol{\Sigma}$.

Changes in $\boldsymbol{\mu}$ when $\boldsymbol{\Sigma}$ remains constant will generally result in a pattern of larger values of the plotted statistics. Thus signals by the 1-of-1 and 4-of-5 tests on the positive side of the Q-charts plot are of primary interest. Signals of a decreasing mean of the plotted points are more difficult to interpret. Such negative signals might be due to changes in $\boldsymbol{\Sigma}$. In applications such negative signals might mean that the data are being fudged, i.e., are not honest.

14.6   SOME EXAMPLES WITH GENERATED DATA

When the measurements used to make charts using any of the formulas of sections 14.3 and 14.5 are from a stable multinormal process, the charts will show patterns of independent $N(0, 1)$ statistics, just as for the many univariate charts presented in earlier chapters. To illustrate these charts we have generated some data sets of known model structure.

Example 14.1: For this example we generated 100 observations from a $p = 3$ variable multinormal distribution with μ and Σ as follows.

$$\mu_0 = (5.8,\ 4.8,\ 3.7)'$$

$$\Sigma_0 = \begin{bmatrix} .033 & .003 & .037 \\ .003 & .084 & .030 \\ .037 & .030 & .060 \end{bmatrix}$$

The Shewhart chart for these 100 observations, using the case UU formulas, is given in Fig. 14.1. Although point 29 is below -3, the chart shows a stable overall pattern, as, of course, it should.

Next, we generated another set of 50 observations. The first 25 observations had the same mean and covariance matrix given above. However, the last 25 has the same covariance matrix but a sightly different mean vector as follows.

$$\mu_1 = (5.85,\ 5.0,\ 3.7)'$$

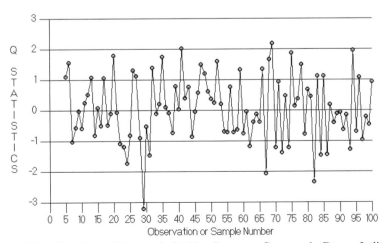

Shewhart Q-Chart for MEAN : MIMUU

Figure 14.1 Shewhart Chart of Stable Process Generated Data, Individual Measurements

This gives a Mohalanobis distance parameter of $\delta^2 = 0.0035$, or $\delta = 0.059$.

The Q-statistics for this data were computed from the case UU formulas also, and the Shewhart chart is given in Fig. 14.2. Note that there is a 4-of-5 signal immediately after the mean shift (actually 5-of-5), and the chart drifts back to a stable pattern. ∎

Example 14.2: For this example we generated 30 subgroups of size $n = 6$ each from the multinormal distribution with mean vector $\boldsymbol{\mu}_0$ and covariance matrix $\boldsymbol{\Sigma}_0$ given in Example 14.1. A Shewhart Q-chart of these subgrouped data is given in Fig. 14.3, where the case UU transformations were used. The process, of course, shows a stable pattern. ∎

14.7 CONTROL CHARTS FOR CORRELATION

The mean control charts studied in the earlier sections of this chapter actually "control" the Mahalanobis distance parameter δ^2, so that signals indicate this parameter has changed. When a chart implies that δ^2 has changed, we know that this could be because some of the means, variances or correlations have changed. We can study the stability of the individual means and variances by plotting univariate Q-charts

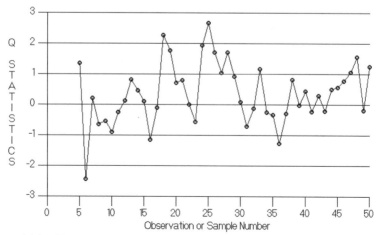

Figure 14.2 Shewhart Chart for Generated Data with Mean Shift After Point 25

Shewhart Q-Chart for MEAN : MSGUU

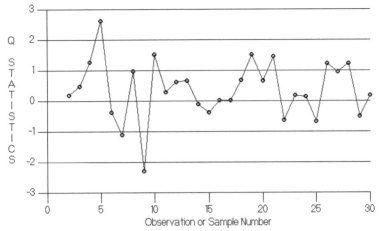

Figure 14.3 Shewhart Q-Chart of Generated Multinormal Subgrouped Data

(Shewhart, EWMA, CUSUM) for them. Other parameters of interest are the pairwise covariances—or correlations. We consider here charts to monitor a nominal value of the correlation coefficient between two quality variables.

One place where a correlation control chart can be useful is to study the correlation between a quality variable and another system or environmental variable. This approach was first suggested by Shewhart as a way to study the system of assignable (special) causes of variation. If another quantitative variable is correlated with a quality variable, then this information may be useful in removing assignable causes or in removing common causes in continuous improvement programs.

In this section we assume that a pair of random variables, say (X, Y), are distributed in a bivariate normal distribution, that is, a multinormal distribution with $p = 2$. We consider a sequence of subgroups of observations. Let (x_{ij}, y_{ij}) denote the jth bivariate observation in the ith subgroup.

Then for

$$\rho = \text{Corr}(X, Y) = \frac{\text{Cov}(X, Y)}{\sqrt{\text{Var}(X)\ \text{Var}(Y)}}$$

we wish to make charts to monitor ρ. Suppose that ρ has a nominal value $\rho = \rho_0$, and we make charts to detect a shift of ρ away from this value. We consider the case when $\rho_0 = 0$ and when $\rho_0 \neq 0$ separately.

If $\rho_0 = 0$, then put

$$T = r_i \sqrt{\frac{n_i - 1}{1 - r_i^2}} \tag{14.7.1}$$

where r_i is the sample correlation coefficient and n_i is the number of observations in the ith subgroup of observations. If (X, Y) has a bivariate normal distribution, then T is a student-t statistic with $n_i - 2$ degrees of freedom. So for this case we can define a sequence of Q-statistics as in (14.7.2).

$$Q_i = \Phi^{-1} \left[H_{n_i-2} \left(r_i \sqrt{\frac{n_i - 1}{1 - r_i^2}} \right) \right] \quad i = 1, 2, \cdots \tag{14.7.2}$$

For the case when $\rho_0 \neq 0$, we use a transformation due to Fisher (1931). Put

$$Q_i = \frac{\sqrt{n_i - 3}}{2} \left[ln \left(\frac{1 + r_i}{1 - r_i} \right) - ln \left(\frac{1 + \rho_0}{1 - \rho_0} \right) \right] \tag{14.7.3}$$

and when n_i is large this Q is approximately a $N(0, 1)$ statistic and can be plotted on a standard Q-chart. Since the function

$$\frac{1}{2} ln \left(\frac{1 + r}{1 - r} \right) = \tanh^{-1} r$$

is a monotone increasing function of r, points above the UCL$(Q) = 3$ signal an increase in ρ above ρ_0, and conversely for points below LCL$(Q) = -3$.

14.8   THE X^2 CONTROL CHART, GENERAL FORMULATION OF X^2 CHARTS

In the preceding sections of this chaper methods based upon the assumption of a joint multivariate normal distribution of measurements were considered. In this section techniques are considered based on samples from multinominal distributions. The general setting for the multinomial distribution may be described as follows. Suppose that points are observed in an outcome space that is partitioned into subsets $A_1, A_2, \ldots, A_k$ which are mutually exclusive and exhaustive. That is, $A_i \cap A_j = \emptyset$, the empty set, when $i \neq j$, and $A_1 \cup \ldots \cup A_k$ is the outcome space. Then let $p_i = P(A_i)$ for $i = 1, \ldots, k$.

Suppose that n independent outcomes are observed in this outcome space and let n_i denote the number of these outcomes that are in event A_i for $i = 1, \ldots, k$. Then the values $(n_1, n_2, \ldots, n_k)$ constitute an observed value on an multinomial random variable with probability function

$$p(n_1, n_2, \ldots, n_k) = \frac{n!}{n_1! n_2! \cdots n_k!} p_1^{n_1} p_2^{n_2} \cdots p_k^{n_k} \quad (14.8.1)$$

where $n_1 + \ldots + n_k = n$ and $p_1 + \ldots + p_k = 1$. The quantity n_i has a binomial marginal distribution, so that if n is large the standardized variable

$$\frac{n_i - np_i}{\sqrt{np_i(1 - p_i)}}$$

is approximately a $N(0, 1)$ random variable. Thus, if the n_i's were independent, we would expect that the sum of squares of these standardized binomial random variables would be approximately a χ_k^2 random variable. However, since these binomial random variables satisfy the linear constraint $n_1 + \cdots + n_k = n$, they are not independent. It can, however, be shown that a related result given in the following holds.

$$X^2 = \sum_{i=1}^{k} \frac{(n_i - n\,p_i)^2}{n\,p_i} \text{ is approximately a } \chi_{k-1}^2 \text{ random variable} \quad (14.8.2)$$

In applications it is necessary to decide when the approximation in (14.8.2) is adequate for practical purposes. Much as been written in the literature about this point and a common recommendation is that the approximation is adequate if the smallest value of np_i is at least 4 or 5.

For the special case when $k = 2$ we have $n_1 + n_2 = n$ and $p_1 + p_2 = 1$, and can write

$$X^2 = \frac{(n_1 - np_1)^2}{np_1} + \frac{(n_2 - np_2)^2}{np_2}$$

$$= \frac{(n_1 - np_1)^2}{np_1} + \frac{(n_1 - np_1)^2}{n(1 - p_1)} = \frac{(n_1 - np_1)^2}{np_1(1 - p_1)}$$

which is approximately a $\chi^2(1)$ random variable.

Observe that $E(n_i) = np_i$ since n_i has a binomial marginal distribution. The n_i are often called the *observed cell frequencies* and the values np_i are called the *expected cell frequencies*. The formula for X^2 is often written using notation suggestive of this terminology as follows.

$$X^2 = \sum_{i=1}^{k} \frac{(O_i - e_i)^2}{e_i}, \quad \text{where}$$

O_i = observed cell frequency

e_i = expected cell frequency

(14.8.3)

The statistic X^2 is itself a discrete random variable and is a general distance measure between the vector of observed cell frequencies $O' = (O_1, O_2, \cdots, O_k)$ and the vector of expected cell frequencies $e' = (e_1, e_2, \cdots, e_k)$. In particular, if $O_i = e_i$ for all $i \in \{1, \ldots, k\}$ then $X^2 = 0$. Thus, if the expected cell frequencies vector e has a particular value e_0 which is assigned under a null hypothesis in a hypothesis testing problem, or a nominal value under a model for a production process, then we should reject the null hypothesis in the testing problem, or signal an out-of-control condition in a process control application when X^2 is too large.

In many problems the cell probabilities p_i will depend upon a number of parameters, say $\theta = (\theta_1, \cdots, \theta_c)'$, and then, of course, the expected cell frequencies e will also depend upon these parameters. These parameters must be known as nominal operating values for the process by estimation from preliminary calibration samples.

We can compute values of X^2 for samples from the multinomial distribution and plot these values on a chart with an α probability upper control limit given in (14.8.4) to monitor the process parameters θ to detect changes in these parameters as signals of an unstable process.

$$UCL\ (X^2) = \chi^2_{\alpha,k-1}$$
$$CL(X^2) = \chi^2_{.5,k-1}$$

(14.8.4)

The plotting can also be carried out by transforming to an $Q(X^2)$-chart as follows.

$$\text{Put } u = G_{k-1}(X^2)$$
$$Q(X^2) = \Phi^{-1}(u)$$

(14.8.5)

The values Q_t are plotted with control limit $UCL = q_\alpha$ and $CL = 0$.

14.9   THE X^2 CHART TO CONTROL A SET OF PERCENTAGES

In this section we consider using an X^2 chart to study the stability of a set of of percentages. A generic situation where an X^2 chart for percentages might be useful is one where the products of a process are grouped into more than two categories. The p-chart studied in Chapter 5 is often used when products are classified as either defectives or nondefectives. Sometimes, however, it may be desirable or necessary to classify products into three or more categories, possibly including nondefectives as a category. A particular example of classifying products into several groups is provided by the piston cylinders drilled into motor blocks. These cylinders are gauged and classified into several groups that will later determine the ring size to be fitted into each. It would be important to detect shifts from the nominal percentages falling into the different groups because this could signal deterioration in the quality of the drilling process. This also creates problems in providing the required percentages of rings of various sizes at the point of assembly.

As a particular example, suppose that 100 units of product from a process during a specific time period are screened into four categories, and the percentages are $e_j = 100\ p_j$ for $j = 1, 2, 3, 4$. In particular, let these percentages be $e_1 = 20$, $e_2 = 16$, $e_3 = 42$, and $e_4 = 22$. Table 14.1 shows data from 8 samples of 100 units each and Table 14.2 shows the details of the computations for samples 1, 2, 7, and 8. A record of the computations for the individual cells, such as that given for selected

TABLE 14.1   Data for X^2 Chart

j	0_1	0_2	0_3	0_4	X^2	$u = G_3(X^2)$	$Q(X^2)$
1	22	14	36	28	2.95	.601	.26
2	19	17	40	24	0.38	.056	−1.59
3	17	13	53	17	5.03	.834	.97
4	18	19	45	18	1.70	.363	−.35
5	24	12	35	29	5.19	.842	1.00
6	22	20	46	12	6.13	.895	1.25
7	15	12	57	16	9.25	.974	1.94
8	13	10	62	15	16.45	.999	3.09

TABLE 14.2   Data and Computations for an X^2 Control Chart

Sample	Cell	(a) e_i	(b) O_i	(c) $O_i - e_i$	(d) $\dfrac{(O_i - e_i)^2}{e_i}$
1	1	20	22	2	0.20
1	2	16	14	−2	0.25
1	3	42	36	−6	0.86
1	4	22	28	6	1.64
					$X_1^2 = \overline{2.95}$
2	1	20	19	−1	0.05
2	2	16	17	1	0.06
2	3	42	40	−2	0.09
2	4	22	24	2	0.18
					$X_2^2 = \overline{0.38}$
7	1	20	15	−5	1.25
7	2	16	12	−4	1.00
7	3	42	57	15	5.36
7	4	22	16	−6	1.64
					$X_7^2 = \overline{9.25}$
8	1	20	13	−7	2.45
8	2	16	10	−6	2.25
8	3	42	62	20	9.52
8	4	22	15	−7	2.23
					$X_8^2 = \overline{16.45}$

cells in Table 14.2, will aid in interpreting any out-of-control signals on the X^2 chart. A $Q(X^2)$ 3-sigma chart for the data of Table 14.1 is shown in Fig. 14.4.

This X^2 chart shows clearly a move away from the expected cell frequencies in the last three samples. Column (c) in Table 14.2 shows that large values of X^2 for samples 7 and 8 are due mainly to large values of observed cell frequencies in cell 3. The cell 3 frequency is increasing while the other cell frequencies decrease. Observe that $(O_1 - e_1) + \cdots + (O_k - e_k) = 0$, so that the sum of the values in column (c) of Table 14.2 for each sample must sum to 0.

In the foregoing, we have assumed that the sample size n is constant. This assumption is not necessary and will not be satisfied for many potential applications. With varying sample sizes, we shall have different expected cell frequencies for different samples, and the condition that expected cell frequencies be large enough, at least four or five, must be applied for every sample. This will amount to specifying a minimally adequate sample size. The computations for the unequal samples case are made as in Table 14.2, except that the expected cell frequencies will now vary between samples. The purpose of the chart is still to detect changes in the cell proportions p_1, p_2, $\cdots$, p_k. The lower control limit for this X^2 control chart for percentages or proportions is usually taken to be zero. Large values of X^2 indicate that the cell proportions are changed from the nominal values; however, very

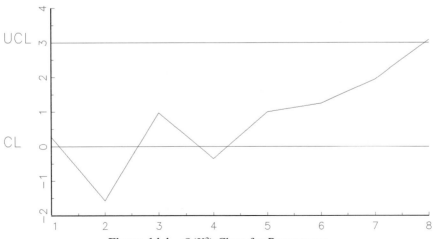

Figure 14.4 $Q(X^2)$ Chart for Percentages

small values indicate that the cell proportions are too close to the nominal values. Thus, very small vaues of X^2 mean that the observed values are more like the expected values than they should be with random sampling. Such small values may mean that there has been an error in the calculations or that the sampling procedure is no longer random.

14.9.1   Relation to *p*-Charts

It may have occurred to the reader that a set of k proportions p_1, p_2, $\cdots$, p_k could be controlled by keepng a binomial *p*-chart for each observed sample proportion $\hat{p}_i = 0_i/n$. If a set of k such charts are maintained with 3-sigma limits, then it can be shown that the control achieved is approximately the same as that for the X^2 chart when the *UCL* is taken to be $\chi^2_{.0027,k-1}$ (see Duncan 1950).

The advantage in using the X^2 chart is that most of the information from the k individual charts is summarized on one chart. The individual *p*-charts have the advantage of showing immediately which cell expectations have changed, and the direction of change.

14.9.2   Setting Up an *X*² Chart

A Stage I application of an X^2 chart is similar to a Stage I application of other charts such as, say, $\bar{x}$ or *p*-charts. In this stage we use the chart to attempt to achieve control of the process by identifying and eliminating special causes of variation; by establishing nominal values for the proportions $p_1, \ldots, p_k$, and establishing minimal sample sizes.

To establish control and to estimate the expected cell frequencies, suppose that 30 samples of 100 units each are taken from the process. From the grand sample of 3000 we make preliminary estimates of the proportions in each of the $k = 4$, say, classes. Using these estimates we compute preliminary control limits and then plot the 30 values of X^2, or $Q(X^2)$, on a chart. If this chart shows out-of-control conditions, the special or assignable related causes should be investigated and eliminated.

14.10   SUMMARY

It is often the case that more than one variable can be observed on each unit of product, and these multivariate observations will carry more information about the process than univariate observations. In this chapter we have given some methods for plotting multivariate data from the multinormal and multinomial distributions. The Q-charts given for the multinormal distribution permit charting with or without prior data, and thus permit charting short runs of multinormal data.

PROBLEMS

14.1 The data in Table P14.1 are true-position coordinates made by a coordinate measuring machine (in cm). They are from parts randomly selected from production from 30 consecutive work days. Make a multivariate mean chart(s) of these data to decide if true-position has slipped during this period of 30 days. Make any supplementary univariate or bivariate charts you feel may be useful. Discuss your results.

14.2 Each day 1000 units of product from a large plant are chosen randomly, inspected, and classified into five categories. The process percentages in the categories have nominal values of $e_1 = .5$, $e_2 = 1.1$, $e_3 = 2.2$, $e_4 = 3$, and $e_5 = 93.2$. Table P14.2 gives the data obtained over a two-week period. Make a $Q(X^2)$ chart to study the stability of the process.

TABLE P14.1

i	x_1	x_2	x_3	i	x_1	x_2	x_3
1	3.53	2.00	3.01	16	3.53	2.01	2.98
2	3.55	2.01	3.02	17	3.52	2.01	2.98
3	3.54	2.02	3.02	18	3.50	2.00	2.95
4	3.54	2.02	2.99	19	3.53	2.01	2.97
5	3.49	1.97	2.93	20	3.53	2.03	3.00
6	3.54	2.01	3.04	21	3.51	1.97	2.95
7	3.52	2.01	2.99	22	3.49	2.00	2.95
8	3.55	2.01	3.00	23	3.57	2.00	2.99
9	3.56	2.03	3.00	24	3.54	2.04	2.97
10	3.55	2.00	3.00	25	3.47	2.01	2.92
11	3.51	2.00	3.01	26	3.53	2.00	3.00
12	3.56	2.03	3.02	27	3.54	2.02	3.02
13	3.51	2.00	2.95	28	3.52	2.01	3.03
14	3.55	2.04	3.07	29	3.52	2.00	3.02
15	3.55	2.01	3.01	30	3.51	1.99	2.96

TABLE P14.2

Day	O_1	O_2	O_3	O_4	O_5
1	8	13	25	28	926
2	7	5	20	34	934
3	4	13	24	32	927
4	3	11	17	22	947
5	3	8	21	22	946
6	3	15	29	35	918
7	4	14	30	34	918
8	14	22	26	40	898
9	8	10	24	33	925
10	8	12	14	44	922

Appendix

TABLE A.1   Standard Normal Distribution Function

$$Pr\{Z \le z\} = \Phi(z) = \int_{-\infty}^{z} \frac{1}{\sqrt{2\pi}}\, e^{-x^2/2}\, dx$$

z	$-.00$	$-.01$	$-.02$	$-.03$	$-.04$	$-.05$	$-.06$	$-.07$	$-.08$	$-.09$
-3.9	.00005	.00005	.00004	.00004	.00004	.00004	.00004	.00004	.00003	.00003
-3.8	.00007	.00007	.00007	.00006	.00006	.00006	.00006	.00005	.00005	.00005
-3.7	.00011	.00010	.00010	.00010	.00009	.00009	.00008	.00008	.00008	.00008
-3.6	.00016	.00015	.00015	.00014	.00014	.00013	.00013	.00012	.00012	.00011
-3.5	.00023	.00022	.00022	.00021	.00020	.00019	.00019	.00018	.00017	.00017
-3.4	.00034	.00032	.00031	.00030	.00029	.00028	.00027	.00026	.00025	.00024
-3.3	.00048	.00047	.00045	.00043	.00042	.00040	.00039	.00038	.00036	.00035
-3.2	.00069	.00066	.00064	.00062	.00060	.00058	.00056	.00054	.00052	.00050
-3.1	.00097	.00094	.00090	.00087	.00084	.00082	.00079	.00076	.00074	.00071
-3.0	.00135	.00131	.00126	.00122	.00118	.00114	.00111	.00107	.00104	.00100
-2.9	.00187	.00181	.00175	.00169	.00164	.00159	.00154	.00149	.00144	.00139
-2.8	.00256	.00248	.00240	.00233	.00226	.00219	.00212	.00205	.00199	.00193
-2.7	.00347	.00336	.00326	.00317	.00307	.00298	.00289	.00280	.00272	.00264
-2.6	.00466	.00453	.00440	.00427	.00415	.00402	.00391	.00379	.00368	.00357
-2.5	.00621	.00604	.00587	.00570	.00554	.00539	.00523	.00508	.00494	.00480
-2.4	.00820	.00798	.00776	.00755	.00734	.00714	.00695	.00676	.00657	.00639
-2.3	.01072	.01044	.01017	.00990	.00964	.00939	.00914	.00889	.00866	.00842
-2.2	.01390	.01355	.01321	.01287	.01255	.01222	.01191	.01160	.01130	.01101
-2.1	.01786	.01743	.01700	.01659	.01618	.01578	.01539	.01500	.01463	.01426
-2.0	.02275	.02222	.02169	.02118	.02068	.02018	.01970	.01923	.01876	.01831
-1.9	.02872	.02807	.02743	.02680	.02619	.02559	.02500	.02442	.02385	.02330
-1.8	.03593	.03515	.02438	.03362	.03288	.03216	.03144	.03074	.03005	.02938
-1.7	.04457	.04383	.04272	.04182	.04093	.04006	.03920	.03836	.03754	.03673
-1.6	.05480	.05370	.05262	.05155	.05050	.04947	.04846	.04746	.04648	.04551
-1.5	.06681	.06552	.06426	.06301	.06178	.06057	.05938	.05821	.05705	.05592
-1.4	.08076	.07927	.07780	.07636	.07493	.07353	.07215	.07078	.06944	.06811
-1.3	.09680	.09510	.09342	.09176	.09012	.08851	.08691	.08534	.08379	.08226
-1.2	.11507	.11314	.11123	.10935	.10749	.10565	.10383	.10204	.10027	.09853
-1.1	.13567	.13350	.13136	.12924	.12714	.12507	.12302	.12100	.11900	.11702
-1.0	.15866	.15625	.15386	.15151	.14917	.14686	.14457	.14231	.14007	.13786
$-.9$	.18406	.18141	.17879	.17619	.17361	.17106	.16853	.16602	.16354	.16109
$-.8$	.21186	.20897	.20611	.20327	.20045	.19766	.19489	.19215	.18943	.18673
$-.7$	.24196	.23885	.23576	.23270	.22965	.22663	.22363	.22065	.21770	.21476
$-.6$	.27425	.27093	.26763	.26435	.26109	.25785	.25463	.25143	.24825	.24510
$-.5$	.30854	.30503	.30153	.29806	.29460	.29116	.28774	.28434	.28096	.27760
$-.4$	.34458	.34090	.33724	.33360	.32997	.32636	.32276	.31918	.31561	.31207
$-.3$	.38309	.37838	.37448	.37070	.36693	.36317	.35942	.35569	.35197	.34827
$-.2$	.42074	.41683	.41294	.40905	.40517	.40129	.39743	.39358	.38974	.38591
$-.1$	.46017	.45620	.45224	.44828	.44433	.44038	.43644	.43251	.42858	.42465
$.0$	.50000	.49601	.49202	.48803	.48405	.48006	.47608	.47210	.46812	.46414

TABLE A.1 (Continued)

z	.00	.01	.02	.03	.04	.05	.06	.07	.08	.09
0	.50000	.50399	.50798	.51197	.51595	.51994	.52392	.52790	.53188	.53586
.1	.53983	.54380	.54776	.55172	.55567	.55962	.56356	.56749	.57152	.57535
.2	.57926	.58317	.58706	.59095	.59483	.59871	.60257	.60642	.61026	.61409
.3	.61791	.62172	.62552	.62930	.63307	.63683	.64058	.64431	.64803	.65173
.4	.65542	.65910	.66276	.66640	.67003	.67364	.67724	.68082	.68439	.68793
.5	.69146	.69497	.69847	.70194	.70540	.70884	.71226	.71566	.71904	.72240
.6	.72575	.72907	.73237	.73565	.73891	.74215	.74537	.74857	.75175	.75490
.7	.75804	.76115	.76242	.76730	.77035	.77337	.77637	.77935	.78230	.78524
.8	.78814	.79103	.79389	.79673	.79955	.80234	.80511	.80785	.81057	.81327
.9	.81594	.81859	.82121	.82381	.82639	.82894	.83147	.83398	.83646	.83891
1.0	.84134	.84375	.84614	.84849	.85083	.85314	.85543	.85769	.85993	.86214
1.1	.86433	.86650	.86864	.87076	.87286	.87493	.87698	.87900	.88100	.88298
1.2	.88493	.88686	.88877	.89065	.89251	.89435	.89617	.89796	.89973	.90147
1.3	.90320	.90490	.90658	.90824	.90988	.91149	.91309	.91466	.91621	.91774
1.4	.91934	.92073	.92220	.92364	.92507	.92647	.92785	.92922	.93056	.93189
1.5	.93319	.93448	.93574	.93699	.93822	.93943	.94062	.94179	.94295	.94408
1.6	.94520	.94630	.94738	.94845	.94950	.95053	.95154	.95254	.95352	.95449
1.7	.95543	.95637	.95728	.95818	.95907	.95994	.96080	.96164	.96246	.96327
1.8	.96407	.96485	.96562	.96638	.96712	.96784	.96856	.96926	.96995	.97062
1.9	.97128	.97193	.97257	.97320	.97381	.97441	.97500	.97558	.97615	.97670
2.0	.97725	.97778	.97831	.97882	.97932	.97982	.98030	.98077	.98124	.98169
2.1	.98214	.98257	.98300	.98341	.98382	.98422	.98461	.98500	.98537	.97574
2.2	.98610	.98645	.98679	.98713	.98745	.98778	.98809	.98840	.98870	.98899
2.3	.98928	.98956	.98983	.99010	.99036	.99061	.99086	.99111	.99134	.99158
2.4	.99180	.99202	.99224	.99245	.99266	.99286	.99305	.99324	.99343	.99361
2.5	.99379	.99396	.99413	.99430	.99446	.99461	.99477	.99492	.99506	.99520
2.6	.99534	.99547	.99560	.99573	.99585	.99598	.99609	.99621	.99632	.99643
2.7	.99653	.99664	.99674	.99683	.99693	.99702	.99711	.99720	.99278	.99736
2.8	.99744	.99752	.99760	.99767	.99774	.99781	.99788	.99795	.99801	.99807
2.9	.99813	.99819	.99825	.99831	.99836	.99841	.99846	.99851	.99856	.99861
3.0	.99865	.99869	.99874	.99878	.99882	.99886	.99889	.99893	.99896	.99900
3.1	.99903	.99906	.99910	.99913	.99916	.99918	.99921	.99924	.99926	.99929
3.2	.99931	.99934	.99936	.99938	.99940	.99942	.99944	.99946	.99948	.99950
3.3	.99952	.99953	.99955	.99957	.99958	.99960	.99961	.99962	.99964	.99965
3.4	.99966	.99968	.99969	.99970	.99971	.99972	.99973	.99974	.99975	.99976
3.5	.99977	.99978	.99978	.99979	.99980	.99981	.99981	.99982	.99983	.99983
3.6	.99984	.99985	.99985	.99986	.99986	.99987	.99987	.99988	.99988	.99989
3.7	.99989	.99990	.99990	.99990	.99991	.99991	.99992	.99992	.99992	.99992
3.8	.99993	.99993	.99993	.99994	.99994	.99994	.99994	.99995	.99995	.99995
3.9	.99995	.99995	.99996	.99996	.99996	.99996	.99996	.99996	.99997	.99997

TABLE A.2 **Upper Percentage Points of the Chi-Squared Distribution, $\chi^2_{\alpha,\nu}$**

				α		
ν	.99865	.995	.99	.975	.95	.90
1	$.0^5 29$	$.0^4 393$	$.0^3 157$	$.0^3 982$	$.0^2 393$	.0158
2	$.0^2 270$	.0100	.0201	.0506	.103	.211
3	.0297	.0717	.115	.216	.352	.585
4	.106	.207	.297	.484	.711	1.064
5	.238	.412	.554	.831	1.145	1.610
6	.423	.676	.872	1.237	1.635	2.204
7	.656	.989	1.239	1.690	2.167	2.833
8	.931	1.344	1.646	2.180	2.733	3.490
9	1.241	1.735	2.088	2.700	3.325	4.168
10	1.584	2.156	2.558	3.247	3.940	4.865
11	1.954	2.603	3.053	3.816	4.575	5.578
12	2.350	3.074	3.571	4.404	5.226	6.304
13	2.768	3.565	4.107	5.009	5.892	7.042
14	3.206	4.075	4.660	5.629	6.571	7.790
15	3.662	4.601	5.229	6.262	7.261	8.547
16	4.135	5.142	5.812	6.908	7.962	9.312
17	4.624	5.697	6.408	7.564	8.672	10.085
18	5.126	6.265	7.015	8.231	9.390	10.865
19	5.641	6.844	7.633	8.907	10.117	11.651
20	6.169	7.434	8.260	9.591	10.851	12.443
21	6.707	8.034	8.897	10.283	11.591	13.240
22	7.256	8.643	9.542	10.982	12.338	14.041
23	7.814	9.260	10.196	11.689	13.091	14.848
24	8.382	9.886	10.856	12.401	13.848	15.659
25	8.959	10.520	11.524	13.120	14.611	16.473
26	9.543	11.160	12.198	13.844	15.379	17.292
27	10.135	11.808	12.879	14.573	16.151	18.114
28	10.735	12.461	13.565	15.308	16.928	18.939
29	11.341	13.121	14.256	16.047	17.708	19.768
30	11.954	13.787	14.953	16.791	18.493	20.599
35	15.107	17.192	18.509	20.569	22.465	24.797
40	18.385	20.707	22.164	24.433	26.509	29.051
45	21.767	24.311	25.901	28.366	30.612	33.350
50	25.235	27.991	29.707	32.357	34.764	37.689
55	28.777	31.735	33.570	36.398	38.958	42.060
60	32.383	35.534	37.485	40.482	43.188	46.459
70	39.758	43.275	45.442	48.758	51.739	55.329
80	47.314	51.172	53.540	57.153	60.391	64.278
90	55.017	59.196	61.754	65.647	69.126	73.291
100	62.844	67.328	70.065	74.222	77.929	82.358

TABLE A.2 (Continued)

ν	α						
	.5	.10	.05	.025	.01	.005	.00135
1	.455	2.706	3.841	5.024	6.635	7.879	10.273
2	1.386	4.605	5.991	7.378	9.210	10.597	13.215
3	2.366	6.251	7.815	9.348	11.345	12.838	15.630
4	3.357	7.779	9.488	11.143	13.277	14.860	17.800
5	4.351	9.236	11.070	12.833	15.086	16.750	19.821
6	5.348	10.645	12.592	14.449	16.812	18.548	21.739
7	6.346	12.017	14.067	16.013	18.475	20.278	23.580
8	7.344	13.362	15.507	17.535	20.090	21.955	25.361
9	8.343	14.684	16.919	19.023	21.666	23.589	27.093
10	9.342	15.987	18.307	20.483	23.209	25.188	28.785
11	10.341	17.275	19.675	21.920	24.725	26.757	30.442
12	11.340	18.549	21.026	23.337	26.217	28.300	32.070
13	12.340	19.812	22.362	24.736	27.688	29.819	33.671
14	13.339	21.064	23.685	26.119	29.141	31.319	35.250
15	14.339	22.307	24.996	27.488	30.578	32.801	36.808
16	15.338	23.542	26.296	28.845	32.000	34.267	38.347
17	16.338	24.769	27.587	30.191	33.409	35.718	39.870
18	17.338	25.989	28.869	31.526	34.805	37.156	41.377
19	18.338	27.204	30.144	32.852	36.191	38.582	42.871
20	19.337	28.412	31.410	34.170	37.566	39.997	44.352
21	20.337	29.615	32.671	35.479	38.932	41.401	45.82
22	21.337	30.813	33.924	36.781	40.289	42.796	47.278
23	22.337	32.007	35.172	38.076	41.638	44.181	48.725
24	23.337	33.196	36.415	39.364	42.980	45.559	50.163
25	24.337	34.382	37.652	40.646	44.314	46.928	51.591
26	25.336	35.563	38.885	41.923	45.642	48.290	53.011
27	26.336	36.741	40.113	43.195	46.963	49.645	54.423
28	27.336	37.916	41.337	44.461	48.278	50.993	55.828
29	28.336	39.087	42.557	45.722	49.588	52.336	57.225
30	29.336	40.256	43.773	46.979	50.892	53.672	58.615
35	34.336	46.059	49.802	53.203	57.342	60.275	65.477
40	39.335	51.805	55.758	59.342	63.691	66.766	72.209
45	44.335	57.505	61.656	65.410	69.957	73.166	78.835
50	49.335	63.167	67.505	71.420	76.154	79.490	85.374
55	54.335	68.796	73.311	77.380	82.282	85.749	91.837
60	59.335	74.397	79.082	83.298	88.379	91.952	98.236
70	69.334	85.527	90.531	95.023	100.425	104.215	110.867
80	79.334	96.578	101.879	106.629	112.329	116.321	123.317
90	89.334	107.565	113.145	118.136	124.116	128.299	135.617
100	99.334	118.498	124.342	129.561	135.807	140.169	147.793

TABLE A.3 Upper Percentage Points for the Student-t Distribution, $t_{\alpha,\nu}$

					α					
ν	.4	.25	.1	.05	.025	.01	.005	.0025	.00135	.0005
1	.325	1.000	3.078	6.314	12.706	31.821	63.657	127.321	235.784	636.619
2	.289	.815	1.886	2.920	4.303	6.965	9.925	14.089	19.206	31.599
3	.277	.765	1.638	2.353	3.182	4.541	5.841	7.453	9.219	12.924
4	.271	.741	1.533	2.132	2.776	3.747	4.604	5.598	6.620	8.610
5	.267	.727	1.476	2.015	2.571	3.365	4.032	4.773	5.507	6.869
6	.265	.718	1.440	1.943	2.447	3.143	3.707	4.317	4.904	5.959
7	.263	.711	1.415	1.895	2.365	2.998	3.499	4.029	4.530	5.408
8	.262	.706	1.397	1.860	2.306	2.896	3.355	3.833	4.277	5.041
9	.261	.703	1.383	1.833	2.262	2.821	3.250	3.690	4.094	4.781
10	.260	.700	1.372	1.812	2.228	2.764	3.169	3.581	3.957	4.587
11	.260	.697	1.363	1.796	2.201	2.718	3.106	3.497	3.850	4.437
12	.259	.695	1.356	1.782	2.179	2.681	3.055	3.428	3.764	4.318
13	.259	.694	1.350	1.771	2.160	2.650	3.012	3.372	3.694	4.221
14	.258	.692	1.345	1.761	2.145	2.624	2.977	3.326	3.636	4.140
15	.258	.691	1.341	1.753	2.131	2.602	2.947	3.286	3.586	4.073
16	.258	.690	1.337	1.746	2.120	2.583	2.921	3.252	3.544	4.015
17	.257	.689	1.333	1.740	2.110	2.567	2.898	3.222	3.507	3.965
18	.257	.688	1.330	1.734	2.101	2.552	2.878	3.197	3.475	3.922
19	.257	.688	1.328	1.729	2.093	2.539	2.861	3.174	3.447	3.883
20	.257	.687	1.325	1.725	2.086	2.528	2.845	3.153	3.422	3.849
21	.257	.686	1.323	1.721	2.080	2.518	2.831	3.135	3.400	3.819
22	.256	.686	1.321	1.717	2.074	2.508	2.819	3.119	3.380	3.792
23	.256	.685	1.319	1.714	2.069	2.500	2.807	3.104	3.361	3.768
24	.256	.685	1.318	1.711	2.064	2.492	2.797	3.091	3.345	3.745
25	.256	.684	1.316	1.708	2.060	2.485	2.787	3.078	3.330	3.725
26	.256	.684	1.315	1.706	2.056	2.479	2.779	3.067	3.316	3.707
27	.256	.684	1.314	1.703	2.052	2.473	2.771	3.057	3.303	3.690
28	.256	.683	1.313	1.701	2.048	2.467	2.763	3.047	3.291	3.674
29	.256	.683	1.311	1.699	2.045	2.462	2.756	3.038	3.280	3.659
30	.256	.683	1.310	1.697	2.042	2.457	2.750	3.030	3.270	3.646
35	.255	.682	1.306	1.690	2.030	2.438	2.724	2.996	3.229	3.591
40	.255	.681	1.303	1.684	2.021	2.423	2.704	2.971	3.199	3.551
45	.255	.680	1.301	1.679	2.014	2.412	2.690	2.952	3.175	3.520
50	.255	.679	1.299	1.676	2.009	2.403	2.678	2.937	3.157	3.496
55	.255	.679	1.297	1.673	2.004	2.396	2.668	2.925	3.142	3.476
60	.254	.679	1.296	1.671	2.000	2.390	2.660	2.915	3.130	3.460
70	.254	.678	1.294	1.667	1.994	2.381	2.648	2.899	3.111	3.435
80	.254	.678	1.292	1.664	1.990	2.374	2.639	2.887	3.096	3.416
100	.254	.677	1.290	1.660	1.984	2.364	2.626	2.871	3.077	3.390
125	.254	.676	1.288	1.657	1.979	2.357	2.616	2.858	3.061	3.370
∞	.253	.674	1.288	1.645	1.960	2.326	2.576	2.807	3.000	3.291

TABLE A.4 Percentage Points of the F Distribution, $F_{0.10; \nu_1, \nu_2}$

					ν_1					
ν_2	1	2	3	4	5	6	7	8	9	10
1	39.86	49.50	53.59	55.83	57.24	58.20	58.91	59.44	59.86	60.19
2	8.53	9.00	9.16	9.24	9.29	9.33	9.35	9.37	9.38	9.39
3	5.54	5.46	5.39	5.34	5.31	5.29	5.27	5.25	5.24	5.23
4	4.55	4.33	4.19	4.11	4.05	4.01	3.98	3.96	3.94	3.92
5	4.06	3.78	3.62	3.52	3.45	3.41	3.37	3.34	3.32	3.30
6	3.78	3.46	3.29	3.18	3.11	3.06	3.01	2.98	2.96	2.94
7	3.59	3.26	3.07	2.96	2.88	2.83	2.79	2.75	2.73	2.70
8	3.46	3.11	2.92	2.81	2.73	2.67	2.62	2.59	2.56	2.54
9	3.36	3.01	2.81	2.69	2.61	2.55	2.51	2.47	2.44	2.42
10	3.29	2.92	2.73	2.61	2.52	2.46	2.41	2.38	2.35	2.32
11	3.23	2.86	2.66	2.54	2.45	2.39	2.34	2.30	2.27	2.25
12	3.18	2.81	2.61	2.48	2.39	2.33	2.28	2.25	2.21	2.19
13	3.14	2.76	2.56	2.43	2.35	2.28	2.23	2.19	2.16	2.14
14	3.10	2.73	2.52	2.40	2.31	2.24	2.19	2.15	2.12	2.10
15	3.07	2.70	2.49	2.36	2.27	2.21	2.16	2.12	2.09	2.06
16	3.05	2.67	2.46	2.33	2.24	2.18	2.13	2.09	2.06	2.03
17	3.03	2.65	2.44	2.31	2.22	2.15	2.10	2.06	2.03	2.00
18	3.01	2.62	2.42	2.29	2.20	2.13	2.08	2.04	2.01	1.98
19	2.99	2.61	2.40	2.27	2.18	2.11	2.06	2.02	1.98	1.96
20	2.98	2.59	2.38	2.25	2.16	2.09	2.04	2.00	1.97	1.94
21	2.96	2.58	2.37	2.23	2.14	2.08	2.02	1.98	1.95	1.92
22	2.95	2.56	2.35	2.22	2.13	2.06	2.01	1.97	1.93	1.90
23	2.94	2.55	2.34	2.21	2.12	2.05	2.00	1.95	1.92	1.89
24	2.93	2.54	2.33	2.19	2.10	2.04	1.98	1.94	1.91	1.88
25	2.92	2.53	2.32	2.18	2.09	2.02	1.97	1.93	1.90	1.87
26	2.91	2.52	2.31	2.17	2.08	2.01	1.96	1.92	1.88	1.85
27	2.90	2.51	2.30	2.17	2.07	2.01	1.95	1.91	1.87	1.84
28	2.89	2.50	2.29	2.16	2.06	2.00	1.94	1.90	1.87	1.84
29	2.89	2.50	2.28	2.15	2.06	1.99	1.94	1.89	1.86	1.83
30	2.88	2.49	2.28	2.14	2.05	1.98	1.93	1.88	1.85	1.82
40	2.84	2.44	2.23	2.09	2.00	1.93	1.87	1.83	1.79	1.76
60	2.79	2.39	2.18	2.04	1.95	1.88	1.82	1.78	1.74	1.71
125	2.75	2.35	2.13	1.99	1.89	1.82	1.77	1.72	1.68	1.65
∞	2.71	2.30	2.08	1.95	1.85	1.78	1.72	1.67	1.63	1.60

TABLE A.4 (Continued)

ν_2	ν_1									
	12	14	16	20	24	30	40	60	125	∞
1	60.71	61.07	61.35	61.74	62.00	62.27	62.53	62.79	63.07	63.32
2	9.41	9.42	9.43	9.44	9.45	9.46	9.47	9.48	9.48	9.49
3	5.22	5.21	5.20	5.18	5.18	5.17	5.16	5.15	5.14	5.13
4	3.90	3.88	3.86	3.84	3.83	3.82	3.80	3.79	3.78	3.76
5	3.27	3.25	3.23	3.21	3.19	3.17	3.16	3.14	3.12	3.10
6	2.91	2.88	2.86	2.84	2.82	2.80	2.78	2.76	2.74	2.72
7	2.67	2.64	2.62	2.60	2.58	2.56	2.54	2.51	2.49	2.47
8	2.50	2.48	2.46	2.42	2.40	2.38	2.36	2.34	2.32	2.29
9	2.38	2.35	2.33	2.30	2.28	2.26	2.23	2.21	2.18	2.16
10	2.28	2.26	2.23	2.20	2.18	2.15	2.13	2.11	2.08	2.06
11	2.21	2.18	2.16	2.12	2.10	2.08	2.05	2.03	2.00	1.97
12	2.15	2.12	2.09	2.06	2.04	2.01	1.99	1.96	1.93	1.90
13	2.10	2.07	2.04	2.01	1.98	1.96	1.93	1.90	1.88	1.85
14	2.05	2.02	2.00	1.96	1.94	1.91	1.89	1.86	1.83	1.80
15	2.02	1.99	1.96	1.92	1.90	1.87	1.85	1.82	1.79	1.75
16	1.99	1.95	1.93	1.89	1.87	1.84	1.81	1.78	1.75	1.72
17	1.96	1.93	1.90	1.86	1.84	1.81	1.78	1.75	1.72	1.69
18	1.93	1.90	1.88	1.84	1.81	1.78	1.75	1.72	1.69	1.66
19	1.91	1.88	1.85	1.81	1.79	1.76	1.73	1.70	1.67	1.63
20	1.89	1.86	1.83	1.79	1.77	1.74	1.71	1.68	1.64	1.61
21	1.88	1.84	1.82	1.78	1.75	1.72	1.69	1.66	1.62	1.59
22	1.86	1.83	1.80	1.76	1.73	1.70	1.67	1.64	1.60	1.57
23	1.85	1.81	1.78	1.74	1.72	1.69	1.66	1.62	1.59	1.55
24	1.83	1.80	1.77	1.73	1.70	1.67	1.64	1.61	1.57	1.53
25	1.82	1.79	1.76	1.72	1.69	1.66	1.63	1.59	1.56	1.52
26	1.81	1.77	1.75	1.71	1.68	1.65	1.62	1.58	1.54	1.50
27	1.80	1.76	1.74	1.70	1.67	1.64	1.60	1.57	1.53	1.49
28	1.79	1.75	1.73	1.69	1.66	1.63	1.59	1.56	1.52	1.48
29	1.78	1.75	1.72	1.68	1.65	1.62	1.58	1.55	1.51	1.47
30	1.77	1.74	1.71	1.67	1.64	1.61	1.57	1.54	1.50	1.46
40	1.72	1.68	1.65	1.61	1.57	1.54	1.51	1.47	1.42	1.38
60	1.66	1.62	1.59	1.54	1.51	1.48	1.44	1.40	1.35	1.29
125	1.60	1.56	1.53	1.48	1.45	1.41	1.37	1.32	1.26	1.19
∞	1.55	1.51	1.47	1.42	1.38	1.34	1.30	1.24	1.17	1.00

TABLE A.4 (Continued)

ν_2	ν_1									
	1	2	3	4	5	6	7	8	9	10
1	161.45	199.50	215.71	224.58	230.16	233.99	236.77	238.88	240.54	241.88
2	18.51	19.00	19.16	19.25	19.30	19.33	19.35	19.37	19.39	19.40
3	10.13	9.55	9.28	9.12	9.01	8.94	8.89	8.85	8.81	8.79
4	7.71	6.94	6.59	6.39	6.26	6.16	6.09	6.04	6.00	5.96
5	6.61	5.79	5.41	5.19	5.05	4.95	4.88	4.82	4.77	4.74
6	5.99	5.14	4.76	4.53	4.39	4.28	4.21	4.15	4.10	4.06
7	5.59	4.74	4.35	4.12	3.97	3.87	3.79	3.73	3.68	3.64
8	5.32	4.46	4.07	3.84	3.69	3.58	3.50	3.44	3.39	3.35
9	5.12	4.26	3.86	3.63	3.48	3.37	3.29	3.23	3.18	3.14
10	4.97	4.10	3.71	3.48	3.33	3.22	3.14	3.07	3.02	2.98
11	4.84	3.98	3.59	3.36	3.20	3.10	3.01	2.95	2.90	2.85
12	4.75	3.89	3.49	3.26	3.11	3.00	2.91	2.85	2.80	2.75
13	4.67	3.81	3.41	3.18	3.03	2.92	2.83	2.77	2.71	2.67
14	4.60	3.74	3.34	3.11	2.96	2.85	2.76	2.70	2.65	2.60
15	4.54	3.68	3.29	3.06	2.90	2.79	2.71	2.64	2.59	2.54
16	4.49	3.63	3.24	3.01	2.85	2.74	2.66	2.59	2.54	2.49
17	4.45	3.59	3.20	2.97	2.81	2.70	2.61	2.55	2.49	2.45
18	4.41	3.56	3.16	2.93	2.77	2.66	2.58	2.51	2.46	2.41
19	4.38	3.52	3.13	2.90	2.74	2.63	2.54	2.48	2.42	2.38
20	4.35	3.49	3.10	2.87	2.71	2.60	2.51	2.45	2.39	2.35
21	4.33	3.47	3.07	2.84	2.69	2.57	2.49	2.42	2.37	2.32
22	4.30	3.44	3.05	2.82	2.66	2.55	2.46	2.40	2.34	2.30
23	4.28	3.42	3.03	2.80	2.64	2.53	2.44	2.38	2.32	2.27
24	4.26	3.40	3.01	2.78	2.62	2.51	2.42	2.36	2.30	2.25
25	4.24	3.39	2.99	2.76	2.60	2.49	2.40	2.34	2.28	2.24
26	4.22	3.37	2.98	2.74	2.59	2.47	2.39	2.32	2.27	2.22
27	4.21	3.35	2.96	2.73	2.57	2.46	2.37	2.31	2.25	2.20
28	4.20	3.34	2.95	2.71	2.56	2.44	2.36	2.29	2.24	2.19
29	4.18	3.33	2.93	2.70	2.55	2.43	2.35	2.28	2.22	2.18
30	4.17	3.32	2.92	2.69	2.53	2.42	2.33	2.27	2.21	2.16
40	4.09	3.23	2.84	2.61	2.45	2.34	2.25	2.18	2.12	2.08
60	4.00	3.15	2.76	2.53	2.37	2.25	2.17	2.10	2.04	1.99
125	3.92	3.07	2.68	2.44	2.29	2.17	2.08	2.01	1.96	1.91
∞	3.84	3.00	2.61	2.37	2.22	2.10	2.01	1.94	1.88	1.83

TABLE A.4 (Continued)

ν_2 \ ν_1	12	14	16	20	24	30	40	60	125	∞
1	243.91	245.36	246.46	248.01	249.05	250.10	251.14	252.20	253.30	254.30
2	19.41	19.42	19.43	19.45	19.45	19.46	19.47	19.48	19.49	19.50
3	8.74	8.72	8.69	8.66	8.64	8.62	8.59	8.57	8.55	8.53
4	5.91	5.87	5.84	5.80	5.77	5.75	5.72	5.69	5.66	5.63
5	4.68	4.64	4.60	4.56	4.53	4.50	4.46	4.43	4.40	4.36
6	4.00	3.96	3.92	3.87	3.84	3.81	3.77	3.74	3.70	3.67
7	3.58	3.53	3.49	3.45	3.41	3.38	3.34	3.30	3.27	3.23
8	3.28	3.24	3.20	3.15	3.12	3.08	3.04	3.01	2.97	2.93
9	3.07	3.03	2.99	2.94	2.90	2.86	2.83	2.79	2.75	2.71
10	2.91	2.87	2.83	2.77	2.74	2.70	2.66	2.62	2.58	2.54
11	2.79	2.74	2.70	2.65	2.61	2.57	2.53	2.49	2.45	2.40
12	2.69	2.64	2.60	2.54	2.51	2.47	2.43	2.38	2.34	2.30
13	2.60	2.55	2.52	2.46	2.42	2.38	2.34	2.30	2.25	2.21
14	2.53	2.48	2.44	2.39	2.35	2.31	2.27	2.22	2.18	2.13
15	2.48	2.42	2.38	2.33	2.29	2.25	2.20	2.16	2.11	2.07
16	2.42	2.37	2.33	2.28	2.24	2.19	2.15	2.11	2.06	2.01
17	2.38	2.33	2.29	2.23	2.19	2.15	2.10	2.06	2.01	1.96
18	2.34	2.29	2.25	2.19	2.15	2.11	2.06	2.02	1.97	1.92
19	2.31	2.26	2.22	2.15	2.11	2.07	2.03	1.98	1.93	1.88
20	2.28	2.23	2.18	2.12	2.08	2.04	1.99	1.95	1.89	1.84
21	2.25	2.20	2.16	2.10	2.05	2.01	1.97	1.92	1.86	1.81
22	2.23	2.17	2.13	2.07	2.03	1.98	1.94	1.89	1.84	1.78
23	2.20	2.15	2.11	2.05	2.01	1.96	1.91	1.87	1.81	1.76
24	2.18	2.13	2.09	2.03	1.98	1.94	1.89	1.84	1.79	1.73
25	2.17	2.11	2.07	2.01	1.96	1.92	1.87	1.82	1.77	1.71
26	2.15	2.09	2.05	1.99	1.95	1.90	1.85	1.80	1.75	1.69
27	2.13	2.08	2.04	1.97	1.93	1.88	1.84	1.79	1.73	1.67
28	2.12	2.06	2.02	1.96	1.92	1.87	1.82	1.77	1.71	1.66
29	2.10	2.05	2.01	1.95	1.90	1.85	1.81	1.75	1.70	1.64
30	2.09	2.04	2.00	1.93	1.89	1.84	1.79	1.74	1.68	1.62
40	2.00	1.95	1.90	1.84	1.79	1.74	1.69	1.64	1.57	1.51
60	1.92	1.86	1.82	1.75	1.70	1.65	1.59	1.53	1.46	1.39
125	1.83	1.77	1.73	1.66	1.61	1.55	1.49	1.43	1.34	1.25
∞	1.75	1.69	1.65	1.57	1.52	1.46	1.40	1.32	1.22	1.00

TABLE A.4 (Continued)

ν_2	ν_1									
	1	2	3	4	5	6	7	8	9	10
1	647.79	799.50	864.16	899.58	921.85	937.11	948.22	956.66	963.29	968.63
2	38.51	39.00	39.17	39.25	39.30	39.33	39.35	39.37	39.39	39.40
3	17.44	16.04	15.44	15.10	14.89	14.74	14.62	14.54	14.47	14.42
4	12.22	10.65	9.98	9.61	9.36	9.20	9.07	8.98	8.90	8.84
5	10.01	8.43	7.76	7.39	7.15	6.98	6.85	6.76	6.68	6.62
6	8.81	7.26	6.60	6.23	5.99	5.82	5.70	5.60	5.52	5.46
7	8.07	6.54	5.89	5.52	5.29	5.12	5.00	4.90	4.82	4.76
8	7.57	6.06	5.42	5.05	4.82	4.65	4.53	4.43	4.36	4.29
9	7.21	5.72	5.08	4.72	4.48	4.32	4.20	4.10	4.03	3.96
10	6.94	5.46	4.83	4.47	4.24	4.07	3.95	3.86	3.78	3.72
11	6.72	5.26	4.63	4.28	4.04	3.88	3.76	3.66	3.59	3.53
12	6.55	5.10	4.47	4.12	3.89	3.73	3.61	3.51	3.44	3.37
13	6.41	4.97	4.35	4.00	3.77	3.60	3.48	3.39	3.31	3.25
14	6.30	4.86	4.24	3.89	3.66	3.50	3.38	3.29	3.21	3.15
15	6.20	4.76	4.15	3.80	3.58	3.42	3.29	3.20	3.12	3.06
16	6.12	4.69	4.08	3.73	3.50	3.34	3.22	3.13	3.05	2.99
17	6.04	4.62	4.01	3.67	3.44	3.28	3.16	3.06	2.99	2.92
18	5.98	4.56	3.95	3.61	3.38	3.22	3.10	3.01	2.93	2.87
19	5.92	4.51	3.90	3.56	3.33	3.17	3.05	2.96	2.88	2.82
20	5.87	4.46	3.86	3.52	3.29	3.13	3.01	2.91	2.84	2.77
21	5.83	4.42	3.82	3.48	3.25	3.09	2.97	2.87	2.80	2.73
22	5.79	4.38	3.78	3.44	3.22	3.06	2.93	2.84	2.76	2.70
23	5.75	4.35	3.75	3.41	3.18	3.02	2.90	2.81	2.73	2.67
24	5.72	4.32	3.72	3.38	3.16	3.00	2.87	2.78	2.70	2.64
25	5.69	4.29	3.69	3.35	3.13	2.97	2.85	2.75	2.68	2.61
26	5.66	4.26	3.67	3.33	3.11	2.95	2.82	2.73	2.65	2.59
27	5.63	4.24	3.65	3.31	3.08	2.92	2.80	2.71	2.63	2.57
28	5.61	4.22	3.63	3.29	3.06	2.90	2.78	2.69	2.61	2.55
29	5.59	4.20	3.61	3.27	3.04	2.88	2.76	2.67	2.59	2.53
30	5.57	4.18	3.59	3.25	3.03	2.87	2.75	2.65	2.58	2.51
40	5.42	4.05	3.46	3.13	2.90	2.74	2.62	2.53	2.45	2.39
60	5.29	3.93	3.34	3.01	2.79	2.63	2.51	2.41	2.33	2.27
125	5.15	3.80	3.22	2.89	2.67	2.51	2.39	2.30	2.22	2.15
∞	5.03	3.69	3.12	2.79	2.57	2.41	2.29	2.19	2.12	2.05

TABLE A.4   (Continued)

	ν_1									
ν_2	12	14	16	20	24	30	40	60	125	∞
1	976.71	982.53	986.92	993.10	997.25	1001.41	1005.60	1009.80	1014.19	1018.21
2	39.42	39.43	39.44	39.45	39.46	39.47	39.47	39.48	39.49	39.50
3	14.34	14.28	14.23	14.17	14.12	14.08	14.04	13.99	13.95	13.90
4	8.75	8.68	8.63	8.56	8.51	8.46	8.41	8.36	8.31	8.26
5	6.53	6.46	6.40	6.33	6.28	6.23	6.18	6.12	6.07	6.02
6	5.37	5.30	5.24	5.17	5.12	5.07	5.01	4.96	4.90	4.85
7	4.67	4.60	4.54	4.47	4.42	4.36	4.31	4.25	4.20	4.14
8	4.20	4.13	4.08	4.00	3.95	3.89	3.84	3.78	3.73	3.67
9	3.87	3.80	3.74	3.67	3.61	3.56	3.51	3.45	3.39	3.33
10	3.62	3.55	3.50	3.42	3.37	3.31	3.26	3.20	3.14	3.08
11	3.43	3.36	3.30	3.23	3.17	3.12	3.06	3.00	2.94	2.88
12	3.28	3.21	3.15	3.07	3.02	2.96	2.91	2.85	2.79	2.73
13	3.15	3.08	3.03	2.95	2.89	2.84	2.78	2.72	2.66	2.60
14	3.05	2.98	2.92	2.84	2.79	2.73	2.67	2.61	2.55	2.49
15	2.96	2.89	2.84	2.76	2.70	2.64	2.59	2.52	2.46	2.40
16	2.89	2.82	2.76	2.68	2.63	2.57	2.51	2.45	2.38	2.32
17	2.83	2.75	2.70	2.62	2.56	2.50	2.44	2.38	2.31	2.25
18	2.77	2.70	2.64	2.56	2.50	2.44	2.38	2.32	2.25	2.19
19	2.72	2.65	2.59	2.51	2.45	2.39	2.33	2.27	2.20	2.13
20	2.68	2.60	2.55	2.46	2.41	2.35	2.29	2.22	2.15	2.09
21	2.64	2.56	2.51	2.42	2.37	2.31	2.25	2.18	2.11	2.04
22	2.60	2.53	2.47	2.39	2.33	2.27	2.21	2.15	2.07	2.00
23	2.57	2.50	2.44	2.36	2.30	2.24	2.18	2.11	2.04	1.97
24	2.54	2.47	2.41	2.33	2.27	2.21	2.15	2.08	2.01	1.94
25	2.52	2.44	2.38	2.30	2.24	2.18	2.12	2.05	1.98	1.91
26	2.49	2.42	2.36	2.28	2.22	2.16	2.09	2.03	1.95	1.88
27	2.47	2.40	2.34	2.25	2.19	2.13	2.07	2.00	1.93	1.85
28	2.45	2.37	2.32	2.23	2.17	2.11	2.05	1.98	1.90	1.83
29	2.43	2.36	2.30	2.21	2.15	2.09	2.03	1.96	1.88	1.81
30	2.41	2.34	2.28	2.19	2.14	2.07	2.01	1.94	1.86	1.79
40	2.29	2.21	2.15	2.07	2.01	1.94	1.88	1.80	1.72	1.64
60	2.17	2.09	2.03	1.94	1.88	1.82	1.74	1.67	1.58	1.48
125	2.05	1.97	1.91	1.82	1.76	1.69	1.61	1.52	1.42	1.31
∞	1.95	1.87	1.80	1.71	1.64	1.57	1.49	1.39	1.26	1.00

TABLE A.4 (Continued)

ν_2	ν_1 1	2	3	4	5	6	7	8	9	10
1	16210.72	19999.50	21614.74	22499.58	23055.80	23437.11	23714.57	23925.41	24091.00	24224.49
2	198.50	199.00	199.17	199.25	199.30	199.33	199.36	199.38	199.39	199.40
3	55.55	49.80	47.47	46.20	45.39	44.84	44.43	44.13	43.88	43.69
4	31.33	26.28	24.26	23.16	22.46	21.98	21.62	21.35	21.14	20.97
5	22.79	18.31	16.53	15.56	14.94	14.51	14.20	13.96	13.77	13.62
6	18.64	14.54	12.92	12.03	11.46	11.07	10.79	10.57	10.39	10.25
7	16.24	12.40	10.88	10.05	9.52	9.15	8.89	8.68	8.51	8.38
8	14.69	11.04	9.60	8.81	8.30	7.95	7.69	7.50	7.34	7.21
9	13.61	10.11	8.72	7.96	7.47	7.13	6.89	6.69	6.54	6.42
10	12.83	9.43	8.08	7.34	6.87	6.55	6.30	6.12	5.97	5.85
11	12.23	8.91	7.60	6.88	6.42	6.10	5.87	5.68	5.54	5.42
12	11.75	8.51	7.23	6.52	6.07	5.76	5.53	5.35	5.20	5.08
13	11.37	8.19	6.93	6.23	5.79	5.48	5.25	5.08	4.93	4.82
14	11.06	7.92	6.68	6.00	5.56	5.26	5.03	4.86	4.72	4.60
15	10.80	7.70	6.48	5.80	5.37	5.07	4.85	4.67	4.54	4.42
16	10.58	7.51	6.30	5.64	5.21	4.91	4.69	4.52	4.38	4.27
17	10.38	7.35	6.16	5.50	5.08	4.78	4.56	4.39	4.25	4.14
18	10.22	7.22	6.03	5.38	4.96	4.66	4.45	4.28	4.14	4.03
19	10.07	7.09	5.92	5.27	4.85	4.56	4.35	4.18	4.04	3.93
20	9.94	6.99	5.82	5.17	4.76	4.47	4.26	4.09	3.96	3.85
21	9.83	6.89	5.73	5.09	4.68	4.39	4.18	4.01	3.88	3.77
22	9.73	6.81	5.65	5.02	4.61	4.32	4.11	3.94	3.81	3.70
23	9.64	6.73	5.58	4.95	4.54	4.26	4.05	3.88	3.75	3.64
24	9.55	6.66	5.52	4.89	4.49	4.20	3.99	3.83	3.70	3.59
25	9.48	6.60	5.46	4.84	4.43	4.15	3.94	3.78	3.65	3.54
26	9.41	6.54	5.41	4.79	4.38	4.10	3.89	3.73	3.60	3.49
27	9.34	6.49	5.36	4.74	4.34	4.06	3.85	3.69	3.56	3.45
28	9.28	6.44	5.32	4.70	4.30	4.02	3.81	3.65	3.52	3.41
29	9.23	6.40	5.28	4.66	4.26	3.98	3.78	3.61	3.48	3.38
30	9.18	6.36	5.24	4.62	4.23	3.95	3.74	3.58	3.45	3.34
40	8.83	6.07	4.98	4.37	3.99	3.71	3.51	3.35	3.22	3.12
60	8.49	5.80	4.73	4.14	3.76	3.49	3.29	3.13	3.01	2.90
125	8.17	5.53	4.49	3.91	3.54	3.28	3.08	2.93	2.80	2.70
∞	7.88	5.30	4.28	3.72	3.35	3.09	2.90	2.75	2.62	2.52

TABLE A.4 (Continued)

ν_2	ν_1									
	12	14	16	20	24	30	40	60	125	∞
1	24426.40	24571.80	24681.50	24836.00	24939.60	25043.60	25148.20	25253.10	25362.80	25463.20
2	199.42	199.43	199.44	199.45	199.46	199.47	199.48	199.48	199.49	199.50
3	43.39	43.17	43.01	42.78	42.62	42.47	42.31	42.15	41.98	41.83
4	20.71	20.52	20.37	20.17	20.03	19.89	19.75	19.61	19.46	19.33
5	13.38	13.22	13.09	12.90	12.78	12.66	12.53	12.40	12.27	12.14
6	10.03	9.88	9.76	9.59	9.47	9.36	9.24	9.12	9.00	8.88
7	8.18	8.03	7.92	7.75	7.65	7.53	7.42	7.31	7.19	7.08
8	7.02	6.87	6.76	6.61	6.50	6.40	6.29	6.18	6.06	5.95
9	6.23	6.09	5.98	5.83	5.73	5.63	5.52	5.41	5.30	5.19
10	5.66	5.53	5.42	5.27	5.17	5.07	4.97	4.86	4.75	4.64
11	5.24	5.10	5.00	4.86	4.76	4.65	4.55	4.45	4.33	4.23
12	4.91	4.78	4.67	4.53	4.43	4.33	4.23	4.12	4.01	3.90
13	4.64	4.51	4.41	4.27	4.17	4.07	3.97	3.87	3.75	3.65
14	4.43	4.30	4.20	4.06	3.96	3.86	3.76	3.66	3.54	3.44
15	4.25	4.12	4.02	3.88	3.79	3.69	3.59	3.48	3.37	3.26
16	4.10	3.97	3.88	3.73	3.64	3.54	3.44	3.33	3.22	3.11
17	3.97	3.84	3.75	3.61	3.51	3.41	3.31	3.21	3.09	2.98
18	3.86	3.73	3.64	3.50	3.40	3.30	3.20	3.10	2.98	2.87
19	3.76	3.64	3.54	3.40	3.31	3.21	3.11	3.00	2.89	2.78
20	3.68	3.55	3.46	3.32	3.22	3.12	3.02	2.92	2.80	2.69
21	3.60	3.48	3.38	3.24	3.15	3.05	2.95	2.84	2.73	2.62
22	3.54	3.41	3.32	3.18	3.08	2.98	2.88	2.77	2.66	2.55
23	3.48	3.35	3.26	3.12	3.02	2.92	2.82	2.71	2.60	2.48
24	3.42	3.30	3.20	3.06	2.97	2.87	2.77	2.66	2.54	2.43
25	3.37	3.25	3.15	3.01	2.92	2.82	2.72	2.61	2.49	2.38
26	3.33	3.20	3.11	2.97	2.87	2.77	2.67	2.56	2.44	2.33
27	3.28	3.16	3.07	2.93	2.83	2.73	2.63	2.52	2.40	2.29
28	3.25	3.12	3.03	2.89	2.79	2.70	2.59	2.48	2.36	2.25
29	3.21	3.09	2.99	2.86	2.76	2.66	2.56	2.45	2.33	2.21
30	3.18	3.06	2.96	2.82	2.73	2.63	2.52	2.42	2.30	2.18
40	2.95	2.83	2.74	2.60	2.50	2.40	2.30	2.18	2.06	1.93
60	2.74	2.62	2.53	2.39	2.29	2.19	2.08	1.96	1.83	1.69
125	2.54	2.42	2.32	2.18	2.08	1.98	1.86	1.74	1.59	1.42
∞	2.36	2.24	2.14	2.00	1.90	1.79	1.67	1.54	1.36	1.00

TABLE A.5 Constants for Classical 3-Sigma Normal Distribution Control Charts

| | $\overline{X}$-Charts | | | S-Charts | | | | | | | R-Charts | | | | |
n	A	A_2	A_3	c_4	B_3	B_4	B_5	B_6	d_2	d_3	D_1	D_2	D_3	D_4
2	2.121	1.880	2.659	0.7979	0	3.267	0	2.606	1.128	0.853	0	3.686	0	3.267
3	1.732	1.023	1.954	0.8862	0	2.568	0	2.276	1.693	0.888	0	4.358	0	2.574
4	1.500	0.729	1.628	0.9213	0	2.266	0	2.088	2.059	0.880	0	4.698	0	2.282
5	1.342	0.577	1.427	0.9400	0	2.089	0	1.964	2.326	0.864	0	4.918	0	2.114
6	1.225	0.482	1.287	0.9515	0.030	1.970	0.029	1.874	2.534	0.848	0	5.078	0	2.004
7	1.134	0.419	1.182	0.9594	0.118	1.882	0.113	1.806	2.704	0.833	0.204	5.204	0.076	1.924
8	1.061	0.373	1.099	0.9650	0.185	1.815	0.179	1.751	2.847	0.820	0.388	5.306	0.136	1.864
9	1.000	0.337	1.032	0.9693	0.239	1.761	0.232	1.707	2.970	0.808	0.547	5.393	0.184	1.816
10	0.949	0.308	0.975	0.9727	0.284	1.716	0.276	1.669	3.078	0.797	0.687	5.469	0.223	1.777
11	0.905	0.285	0.927	0.9754	0.321	1.679	0.313	1.637	3.173	0.787	0.811	5.535	0.256	1.744
12	0.866	0.266	0.886	0.9776	0.354	1.646	0.346	1.610	3.258	0.778	0.922	5.594	0.283	1.717
13	0.832	0.249	0.850	0.9794	0.382	1.618	0.374	1.585	3.336	0.770	1.025	5.647	0.307	1.693
14	0.802	0.235	0.817	0.9810	0.406	1.594	0.399	1.563	3.407	0.763	1.118	5.696	0.328	1.672
15	0.775	0.223	0.789	0.9823	0.428	1.572	0.421	1.544	3.472	0.756	1.203	5.741	0.347	1.653
16	0.750	0.212	0.763	0.9835	0.448	1.552	0.440	1.526	3.532	0.750	1.282	5.782	0.363	1.637
17	0.728	0.203	0.739	0.9845	0.466	1.534	0.458	1.511	3.588	0.744	1.356	5.820	0.378	1.622
18	0.707	0.194	0.718	0.9854	0.482	1.518	0.475	1.496	3.640	0.739	1.424	5.856	0.391	1.608
19	0.688	0.187	0.698	0.9862	0.497	1.503	0.490	1.483	3.689	0.734	1.487	5.891	0.403	1.597
20	0.671	0.180	0.680	0.9869	0.510	1.490	0.504	1.470	3.735	0.729	1.549	5.921	0.415	1.585
21	0.655	0.173	0.663	0.9876	0.523	1.477	0.516	1.459	3.778	0.724	1.605	5.951	0.425	1.575
22	0.640	0.167	0.647	0.9882	0.534	1.466	0.528	1.448	3.819	0.720	1.659	5.979	0.434	1.566
23	0.626	0.162	0.633	0.9887	0.545	1.455	0.539	1.438	3.858	0.716	1.710	6.006	0.443	1.557
24	0.612	0.157	0.619	0.9892	0.555	1.445	0.549	1.429	3.895	0.712	1.759	6.031	0.451	1.548
25	0.600	0.153	0.606	0.9896	0.565	1.435	0.559	1.420	3.931	0.708	1.806	6.056	0.459	1.541

n = Sample Size

For $n \geq 25$

$$A = \frac{3}{\sqrt{n}}, \quad A_3 = \frac{3}{c_4\sqrt{n}}, \quad c_4 = \frac{\Gamma\left(\dfrac{n}{2}\right)}{\Gamma\left(\dfrac{n-1}{2}\right)}\sqrt{\frac{2}{n-1}} \cong \sqrt{1 - \frac{4(n-1)}{4n-3}}$$

$$B_3 = 1 - (3/c_4)\sqrt{1 - c_4^2}, \quad B_4 = 1 + (3/c_4)\sqrt{1 - c_4^2}$$

$$B_5 = c_4 - 3\sqrt{1 - c_4^2}, \quad B_6 = c_4 + 3\sqrt{1 - c_4^2}$$

REFERENCES

American Society for Quality Control, Automotive Division. 1986. *Statistical Process Control Manual.* ASQC, Milwaukee, Wisconsin.

Anderson, T. W. 1958. *An Introduction to Multivariate Statistical Analysis.* John Wiley & Sons, New York.

Banks, J. 1989. *Principles of Quality Control.* John Wiley & Sons, New York.

Barnard, G. A. 1959. Control Charts and Stochastic Processes. *Journal of the Royal Statistical Society, Ser. B.,* 21, p. 239.

Basu, D. 1955. On Statistics Independent of a Complete Sufficient Statistic. *Sankhya,* 15, pp. 377–380.

Benneyan, J. C. 1995. Design of Statistical *g* Control Charts for Nosocomial Infection: Number of Days Between Infections *g* Charts and Other Alternatives. *1st International Applied Statistics in Medicine Conference Proceedings,* Dallas.

Benneyan, J. C., and Kaminsky, F. C. 1995. Modeling Discrete Data in SPC: The *g* and *h* Charts. *48th Annual Quality Congress Proceedings,* pp. 32–42.

Bourke, P. D. 1991. Detecting a Shift in Fraction Nonconforming Using Run-Length Control Charts With 100% Inspection. *Journal of Quality Technology,* 23(3), pp. 225–238.

Box, G.E.P., and Cox, D. R. 1964. An Analysis of Transformations. *Journal of the Royal Statistical Society, Series B,* pp. 211–243.

Box, G.E.P., and Jenkins, G. M. 1976. *Time Series Analysis Forecasting and Control,* 2nd ed., Holden-Day, Oakland, CA.

Burr, I. W. 1954. Short Runs. *Industrial Quality Control,* 11(2), pp. 16–22.

Calvin, T. W. 1984. Quality Control Techniques for "Zero Defects," *IEEE Transactions on Components, Hybrids, and Manufacturing Technology,* 6, pp. 323–328.

Cameron, J. M. 1977. *Measurement Assurance.* Office of Measurement Standards, Institute of Basic Standards, National Bureau of Standards.

Champ, C. W., and Woodall, W. H. 1987. Exact Results for Shewhart Control Charts With Supplementary Runs Rules. *Technometrics,* 29(4), pp. 393–399.

Chan, L. K., Cheng, S. W., and Spiring, S. A. 1988. A New Measure of Process Capability: C_{pm}. *Journal of Quality Technology,* 20(3), pp. 162–175.

Chan, T. F., Golub, G. H., and Le Veque, R. J. 1983. Algorithms for Computing the Sample Variance: Analysis and Recommendations. *The American Statistician* 37, pp. 242–247.

Chou, Y.-M., Owen, D. B., and Borrego, S. A. 1990. Lower Confidence Limits on Process Capability Indices. *Journal of Quality Technology,* 22(3), pp. 223–229.

Crowder, S. V. 1987a. Average Run Lengths of Exponentially Weighted Moving Average Control Charts. *Journal of Quality Technology,* 19(3), pp. 161–164.

———. 1987b. A Simple Method for Studying Run Length Distributions of Exponentially Weighted Moving Average Charts. *Technometrics,* 29(4), pp. 401–407.

———. 1989. Design of Exponentially Weighted Moving Average Schemes. *Journal of Quality Technology,* 21(3), pp. 155–162.

Deming, W. E. 1986. *Out of the Crisis.* Massachusetts Institute of Technology, Center for Advanced Engineering Study.

Duncan, A. J. 1950. A Chi-Square Chart for Controlling a Set of Percentages. *Industrial Quality Control,* 6, pp. 11–15.

———. 1974. *Quality Control and Industrial Statistics.* Richard D. Irwin, Inc., Homewood, IL.

Eisenhart, Churchill. 1963. Realistic Evaluation of the Precision and Accuracy of Instrument Calibration Systems. *Journal of Research of the National Bureau of Standards—C. Engineering and Instrumentation.* Vol. 67C, No. 2.

Elshennawy, A. K., Ham, I., and Cohen, P. H. 1988. *Quality Progress,* January, pp. 59–65.

Ferguson, W. K., and Bruun, G. 1952. *A Survey of European Civilization.* Houghton Mifflin Company, New York.

Farnum, N. R. 1994. *Modern Statistical Quality Control and Improvement.* Duxbury Press, Belmont, CA.

Finison, L. J., Spencer, M., and Finison, K. S. 1993. Total Quality Management in Health Care: Using Individuals Charts in Infection Control. *47th Annual ASQC Quality Congress Transactions,* pp. 349–359.

Fisher, R. A. 1922. On the interpretation of χ^2 from contingency tables and the calculation of P. *Journal of the Royal Statistical Society, Series A,* 85, 87–94.

———. 1931. *Statistical Methods for Research Workers.* 4th ed., Oliver and Boyd, Ltd., New York.

General Motors Supplier Development: General Procedure. (The GP-3 manual) 1989.

Goh, T. N. 1987. A Control Chart for Very High Yield Processes. *Quality Assurance* 13, No. 1, pp. 18–22.

Guenther, W. C. 1977. *Sampling Inspection in Statistical Quality Control.* MacMillan Publishing Co., New York.

Hald, A. 1952. *Statistical Theory with Engineering Applications.* John Wiley and Sons, New York.

Haldane, J.B.S. 1945. On a Method of Estimating Frequencies. *Biometrika* 33, pp. 222–225.

Hawkins, D. W. 1981. A CUSUM for a Scale Parameter. *Journal of Quality Technology,* 13(4), pp. 228–231.

———. 1987. Self Starting CUSUMS for Location and Scale. *The Statistician,* 36, pp. 299–315.

———. 1993. Robustification of Cumulative Sum Charts by Winsorization. *Journal of Quality Technology,* 25(4), pp. 248–261.

Hillier, F. S. 1964. $\overline{X}$ Chart Control Limits Based on a Small Number of Subgroups. *Industrial Quality Control* 20(8), pp. 24–29.

———. 1969. $\overline{X}$- and R-Chart Control Limits Based on a Small Number of Subgroups. *Journal of Quality Technology,* 1(1), pp. 17–26.

Hunter, W. G., and Kartha, C. P. 1977. Determining the Most Profitable Target Value for a Production Process. *Journal of Quality Technology* 9, pp. 176–181.

Imai, M. 1986. *Kaizen: The Key to Japan's Competitive Success.* McGraw-Hill, New York.

Ishikawa, K. 1982. *Guide to Quality Control,* Asian Productivity Organization, Tokyo.

———. 1985. *What Is Total Quality Control? The Japanese Way.* Prentice-Hall, Englewood Cliffs, N.J.

———. 1990. *Introduction to Quality Control,* 3A Corporation, Tokyo.

Jackson, J. E. 1972. All Count Distributions Are Not Alike. *Journal of Quality Technology,* 4(1), pp. 86–92.

Johnson, N. L., and Kotz, S. 1969. *Distributions in Statistics: Discrete Distributions.* Houghton Mifflin Company, Boston, MA.

Juran, J. M. 1994. The Upcoming Century of Quality. *Quality Progress,* August, pp. 29–37.

Kaminsky, F. C., Benneyan, J. C., Davis, R. D., and Burke, R. J. 1992. Statistical Control Charts Based on a Geometric Distribution. *Journal of Quality Technology,* 24(2), pp. 63–69.

Kane, Victor E. 1986. Process Capability Indices. *Journal of Quality Technology,* 18(1), pp. 41–52.

———. 1989. *Defect Prevention: Use of Simple Statistical Tools.* Marcel Dekker, New York.

Kemp, K. W. 1962. The Use of Cumulative Sums for Sampling Inspection Schemes. *Applied Statistics,* 11, pp. 16–31.

Kendall, M. G., and Stuart, A. S. 1958. *The Advanced Theory of Statistics, Volume 1: Distribution Theory.* Hafner Publishing, New York.

———. 1961. *The Advanced Theory of Statistics, Volume 2: Inference and Relationship.* Hafner Publishing, New York.

Koons, G. F., and Luner, J. J. 1991. SPC in Low-Volume Manufacturing: A Case Study. *Journal of Quality Technology,* 23(4), pp. 287–295.

Lehmann, E. L. 1959. *Testing Statistical Hypotheses.* John Wiley & Sons, New York.

———. 1983. *Theory of Point Estimation.* John Wiley & Sons, New York.

Lucas, J. M., and Saccucci, M. S. 1990. Exponentially Weighted Moving Average Control Schemes: Properties and Enhancements. *Technometrics,* 32(1), pp. 1–12.

Mace, A. E. 1964. *Sample-Size Determination.* Reinhold Publishing, New York.

Mandel, B. J. 1969. The Regression Control Chart. *Journal of Quality Technology,* 1(1), pp. 1–9.

Marr, R. L., and Quesenberry, C. P. 1991. A NU Test for Serial Correlation of Residuals From One or More Regression Regimes. *Technometrics,* 33(4), pp. 441–457.

Manuele, J. 1945. Control Chart for Determining Tool Wear. *Industrial Quality Control,* 1, pp. 7–10.

Miller, F. L., Jr., and Quesenberry, C. P. 1979. Power Studies of Tests for Uniformity, II. *Communications in Statistics—Simulation and Computation* B8(3), pp. 271–290.

Mizuno, Shigeru. 1988. *Company-Wide Total Quality Control.* Asian Productivity Organization.

Montgomery, D. C. 1985, 1991. *Introduction to Statistical Quality Control.* John Wiley & Sons, New York.

Morrison, D. F. 1976. *Multivariate Statistical Methods.* McGraw-Hill, New York.

———. 1983. *Applied Linear Statistical Methods.* Prentice-Hall, New Jersey.

Nelson, L. S. 1978. Best Target Value for a Production Process. *Journal of Quality Technology* 10.

———. 1982. Control Charts for Individual Measurements. *Journal of Quality Technology* 14, pp. 172–173.

———. 1983. The Deceptiveness of Moving Averages. *Journal of Quality Technology* 15(2), pp. 99–100.

———. 1984. The Shewhart Control Chart—Tests for Special Causes. *Journal of Quality Technology* 16(4), pp. 237–239.

———. 1989. Standardization of Shewhart Control Charts. *Journal of Quality Technology* 21(4), pp. 287–289.

Neyman, Jerzy. 1937. "Smooth" Test for Goodness of Fit. *Skandinavisk Aktuarietidskrift* 20, pp. 149–199.

Olmstead, P. S. 1967. Our Debt to Walter Shewhart. *Industrial Quality Control,* 24(2), pp. 72–73.

O'Reilly, F. J., and Quesenberry, C. P. 1972. Uniform Strong Consistency of Rao-Blackwell Distribution Function Estimators. *Annals of Mathematical Statistics* 43, pp. 1678–1679.

————. 1973. The Conditional Probability Integral Transformation and Applications to Obtain Composite Chi-Square Goodness-of-Fit Tests. *Annals of Statistics* 1, pp. 74–83.

Ott, E. R., and Schilling, E. G. 1990. *Process Quality Control: Troubleshooting and Analysis of Data.* McGraw-Hill, New York.

Palm, A. C. 1992. Some Aspects of Sampling for Control Charts. *Statistics Division Newsletter: ASQC* 12(4), pp. 20–23.

Patil, G. P. 1963. Minimum Variance Unbiased Estimation and Certain Problems of Additive Number Theory. *Annals of Mathematical Statistics,* 34, pp. 1050–1056.

Pettitt, A. N. 1977. Testing the Normality of Several Independent Samples Using the Anderson-Darling Statistic. *Journal of the Royal Statistical Society C* 26, pp. 156–161.

Proschan, F., and Savage, I. R. 1960. Starting a Control Chart. *Industrial Quality Control* 16, pp. 12–13.

Quesenberry, C. P. 1986. Screening Outliers in Normal Process Control Data with Uniform Residuals. *Journal of Quality Technology* 18(4), pp. 226–233.

————. 1988. An SPC Approach to Compensating a Tool–Wear Process. *Journal of Quality Technology* 20(4), pp. 220–229.

————. 1990a. Screening Outliers in Process Control Regression Data with Uniform Residuals, II. *Journal of Quality Technology* 22(2), pp. 87–94.

————. 1990b. SPC Binomial Q-Charts for Short or Long Runs. *Institute of Statistics Mimeo Series, No. 1982, Raleigh, North Carolina: North Carolina State University,* September.

————. 1991a. SPC Q-Charts for Start-Up Processes and Short or Long Runs. *Journal of Quality Technology* 23(3), pp. 213–224.

————. 1991b. SPC Q-Charts for a Binomial Parameter p: Short or Long Runs. *Journal of Quality Technology* 23(3), pp. 239–246.

————. 1991c. SPC Q-Charts for a Poisson Parameter λ: Short or Long Runs. *Journal of Quality Technology* 23(4), pp. 296–303.

————. 1993. The Effect of Sample Size on Estimated Limits for $\overline{X}$ and X Control Charts. *Journal of Quality Technology* 25(4), pp. 237–247.

————. 1995a. On Properties of Q-Charts for Variables. *Journal of Quality Technology* 27(3), pp. 184–203.

————. 1995b. On Properties of Binomial Q-Charts for Attributes. *Journal of Quality Technology* 27(3), pp. 204–213.

————. 1995c. On Properties of Poisson Q-Charts for Attributes. *Journal of Quality Technology* 27(4), pp. 293–303.

————. 1995d. Geometric Q-Charts for High Quality Processes. *Journal of Quality Technology* 27(4), pp. 304–315.

————. 1995e. Response to Discussants of the Q-Statistics Papers. *Journal of Quality Technology* 27(3), pp. 333–343.

————. 1995f. On Optimality of Q-Charts for Outliers in SPC. *Statistical Theory and Applications, Papers in Honor of Herbert A. David,* Springer-Verlag, New York.

Quesenberry, C. P., and Quesenberry, C., Jr. 1982. On the Distribution of Residuals from Fitted Parametric Models. *Journal of Statistical Computation and Simulation* 15, pp. 129–140.

Quesenberry, C. P., Giesbrecht, F. G., and Burns, J. C. 1983. Some Methods for Studying the Validity of Normal Model Assumptions for Multiple Samples. *Biometrics* 39, pp. 735–739.

Quesenberry, C. P., and Starbuck, R. R. 1976. On Optimal Tests for Separate Hypotheses and Conditional Probability Integral Transformations. *Communications in Statistics—Theory and Methods,* A5(6), pp. 507–524.

Quesenberry, C. P., Whitaker, T. B., and Dickens, J. W. 1976. On Testing Normality Using Several Samples: An Analysis of Peanut Aflatoxin Data. *Biometrics,* 32, pp. 753–759.

Roberts, S. W. 1959. Control Chart Tests Based on Geometric Moving Averages. *Technometrics* 1, pp. 239–250.

————. 1966. A Comparison of Some Control Chart Procedures. *Technometrics* 1, pp. 239–250.

Robinson, Jeffrey A. 1984. Analysis of Variance in Single-Gage Repeatability and Reproducibility Studies. *General Motors Research Report:* GMR 248C.

Robinson, P. B., and Ho, T. Y. 1978. Average Run Lengths of Geometric Moving Average Charts by Numerical Methods. *Technometrics* 20, pp. 85–93.

Roes, K.C.B., Does, R.J.M.M., and Schurink, Y. 1993. Shewhart—Type Control Charts for Individual Observations. *Technometrics,* 25, pp. 188–198.

Ryan, T. P. 1989. *Statistical Methods for Quality Improvement.* John Wiley & Sons, New York.

Sankaran, M. 1959. On the Non-central χ^2 Distribution. *Biometrika* 46, pp. 235–237.

Seber, G.A.F. 1977. *Linear Regression Analysis.* John Wiley & Sons, New York.

Seheult, A. H., and Quesenberry, C. P. 1971. On Unbiased Estimation of Density Functions. *Annals of Mathematical Statistics,* 42, pp. 1434–1438.

Sheaffer, R. L., and Leavenworth, R. S. 1976. The Negative Binomial Model for Counts for Units of Varying Size. *Journal of Quality Technology,* 8(2), pp. 158–163.

Shewhart, W. A. 1931. *Economic Control of Quality of Manufactured Product,* D. van Nostrand Co., New York.

Stephens, M. A. 1986. Tests Based on EDF Statistics, Chapter 6 in *Goodness-of-Fit Techniques,* edited by R. B. D'Agostino and M. A. Stephens. Marcel-Dekker, New York.

Suzaki, Kiyoshi. 1987. *The New Manufacturing Challenge,* The Free Press, New York.

Taguchi, Genichi. 1981. *On-line Quality Control During Production.* Japanese Standards Association, Tokyo, Japan.

Tang, P. K. 1995a. Mean Control of Multivariate Processes with Specific Reference to Short Runs. *Proceedings: International Conference on Statistical Methods and Statistical Computing for Quality and Productivity Improvement,* Vol. II, Contributed Papers, August 17–19, 1995, Seoul, Korea.

————. 1995b. Mean Control for Multivariate Normal Processes, 54 EQRM 15, Dept. of Computer and Mathematical Sciences Technical Report, Victoria University of Technology.

Tukey, John W. 1977. *Exploratory Data Analysis.* Addison-Wesley Publishing, Reading, MA.

Tukey, J. W., and Moore, P. G. 1954. Answer to query 112, *Biometrics,* 10, 562–568.

Vance, L. C. 1986. Average Run Lengths of Cumulative Sum Control Charts for Controlling Normal Means. *Journal of Quality Technology* 18(3), pp. 189–193.

Wadsworth, H. M., Jr., Stephens, K. S., and Godfrey, A. B. 1986. *Modern Methods for Quality Control and Improvement.* John Wiley & Sons, New York.

Weiler, H. 1952. On the Most Economical Sample Size for Controlling the Mean of a Population. *Annals of Mathematical Statistics* 23, pp. 247–254.

Western Electric Company. 1956. *Statistical Quality Control Handbook.*

Wheeler, D. J. 1989. *Evaluating the Measurement Process,* 2nd ed. SPC Press, Knoxville, TN.

Youngs, E. A., and Cramer, E. M. 1971. Some Results Relevant to Choice of Sum and Sum-of-Product Algorithms. *Technometrics* 13, pp. 657–665.

A software program, prepared by the author, called Q-Charts, plots most of the Q-charts and makes many of the other computations required in implementing the methods presented in this book. It is available commercially from the following:

QUE Technologies, Inc.
224 Northbrook Drive
Raleigh, NC 27609-5614
Phone: 919-787-7918

Please write or call for information on this program.